T0328924

Routledge Handbook of Climate Justice

The term "climate justice" began to gain traction in the late 1990s following a wide range of activities by social and environmental justice movements that emerged in response to the operations of the fossil fuel industry and, later, to what their members saw as the failed global climate governance model that became so transparent at COP15 in Copenhagen. The term continues to gain momentum in discussions around sustainable development, climate change, mitigation and adaptation, and has been slowly making its way into the world of international and national policy. However, the connections between these remain unestablished.

Addressing the need for a comprehensive and integrated reference compendium, the *Routledge Handbook of Climate Justice* provides students, academics and professionals with a valuable insight into this fast-growing field. Drawing together a multidisciplinary range of authors from the Global North and South, this Handbook addresses some of the most salient topics in current climate justice research, including just transition, urban climate justice and public engagement, in addition to the field's more traditional focus on gender, international governance and climate ethics. With an emphasis on facilitating learning based on cutting-edge specialised climate justice research and application, each chapter draws from the most recent sources, real-world best practices and tutored reflections on the strategic dimensions of climate justice and its related disciplines.

The *Routledge Handbook of Climate Justice* will be essential reading for students and scholars, as well as being a vital reference tool for those practically engaged in the field.

Tahseen Jafry is a Professor at Glasgow Caledonian University (GCU), Scotland, UK and the Director of GCU's Centre for Climate Justice.

"Climate justice names the central problem – and solution – for this century and beyond. In this collection, you will learn why this is and, in these still-early stages of thinking and CJ movement-building, which debates are raging."

Patrick Bond, *Distinguished Professor of Political Economy,*
University of the Witwatersrand, Johannesburg

"This Handbook is a timely and significant contribution to the growing body of academic literature on climate justice. It comes at a critical turning point in UNFCCC climate negotiations with the imminent review of the Paris Agreement. It is an excellent knowledge resource bound to be of particular interest to academics, practitioners and students engaged in the field of climate change and climate justice."

Mary Robinson, *President, Mary Robinson Foundation – Climate Justice*

Routledge Handbook of Climate Justice

Edited by Tahseen Jafry

ASSISTANT EDITORS

MICHAEL MIKULEWICZ
AND
KARIN HELWIG

LONDON AND NEW YORK

First published 2019 by Routledge

2 Park Square, Milton Park, Abingdon, Oxon, OX14 4RN
605 Third Avenue, New York, NY 10017

Routledge is an imprint of the Taylor & Francis Group, an informa business

First issued in paperback 2020

British Library Cataloguing-in-Publication Data
A catalogue record for this book is available from the British Library

Library of Congress Cataloging-in-Publication Data
A catalog record has been requested for this book

ISBN: 978-1-138-68935-0 (hbk)
ISBN: 978-0-367-73259-2 (pbk)

Typeset in Bembo
by Apex CoVantage, LLC

Contents

Contents

Figures

Tables

Contributors

Ritwika Basu is a Senior Research Associate in the Practice team at the Indian Institution for Human Settlements (IIHS). She is a Geography graduate from TERI School of Advanced Studies, Delhi. She primarily studies human dimensions of the changing environment-development nexus at various scales. At IIHS, she is part of the ongoing climate change adaptation project called ASSAR. Her primary focus is on the role of social differentiators in exacerbating risks, including climatic risks for vulnerable communities is select semi-arid regions of Karnataka. Additionally, questions of differential vulnerability and the multiple ways in which people cope, accumulate or adapt form the core of her work. She also co-teaches courses on climate change and development and climate policy framework as part of IIHS teaching and capacity-building initiatives.

Amir Bazaz is Lead-Practice at Indian Institution for Human Settlements (IIHS). He holds a PhD in Management from the Indian Institute of Management Ahmedabad, with a specialisation in Public Systems. He works on issues at the intersection of economics, climate change mitigation and adaptation and sustainable development. He has substantial experience working with various integrated assessment frameworks and modelling arrangements. At IIHS, Amir is the Regional Research Lead for a multi-partner, multi-year climate adaptation research project – Adaptation at Scale in Semi-Arid Regions (ASSAR). He has been a regular team member for many "Disaster and Climate Resilience" projects at IIHS and teaches regularly in the Urban Fellows and the Urban Practitioners Program.

Idil Boran is Associate Professor in the Department of Philosophy, York University, Toronto, Canada, specialising in social and political philosophy. Her work covers a range of issues from diversity and cultural inclusiveness to global political theory. In recent years, her focus has been on global climate governance. Boran's publications appeared in *American Philosophical Quarterly*; *Public Affairs Quarterly*; *Philosophy and Public Philosophy Quarterly*; *Ethics, Policy, and Environment*; and *Science and Engineering Ethics*. She is the lead co-author of the entry on "Climate Change Justice" for *Routledge Encyclopaedia of Philosophy Online*.

Kim Bouwer is a Lecturer at the University of Strathclyde. Her research interests lie in energy and climate change law, the governance of natural resources and private law. Kim contributes to the ERC-funded BeneLex project, where her work explores benefit-sharing concepts in the context of the international climate change regime. She also researches litigation in the context of climate change, and the regulation and governance of energy efficiency and low-carbon technologies. Kim teaches climate change and energy law, environmental law and private law. In her current role she is acting programme director of the LLM in Global Environmental Law and Governance. Before her doctorate, Kim worked as a lawyer.

David Brown is a climate justice researcher with interests in REDD+ and "avoided deforestation." He is fascinated by how justice-based concerns are constructed in multiscalar climate governance, particularly the ways in which climate justice norms underpin and justify policy discourse. He has recently completed a PhD at Coventry University that empirically examined the REDD+ policy regime through a climate justice lens. In his thesis, he conducted a multiscalar and climate justice–led examination of the REDD+ partnership between Norway and Ethiopia. He is continuing to work on issues of climate justice as part of a research role that is investigating the linkages among climate change, environmental degradation and labour exploitation.

Jason Byrne is Professor of Human Geography and Planning at the University of Tasmania, Hobart, Australia. His research focuses on urban political ecologies of greenspace and climate change adaptation, addressing environmental injustices stemming from urban planning and management. Recent projects include thermal inequities arising from urban greening policies. He is an editorial board member of *Local Environment* and the *Journal of Political Ecology*.

Edward Cameron is both a practitioner and academic specialising in climate change and human rights. He currently serves as Senior Advisor to Business for Social Responsibility (BSR), The Red Cross Red Crescent Movement, the Asia Foundation and the World Business Council on Sustainability (WBCSD). His work focuses on engaging the private sector to reduce climate risk and strengthen resilience. Edward holds a PhD in Social Sciences, Business and Economics from Åbo Akademi University; an MA in European Studies from Katholieke Universiteit Leuven; and a BA in Political Science and History from University College Dublin.

J. Mijin Cha is an Assistant Professor in the Urban and Environmental Policy Department at Occidental College. Prior to Occidental College, Dr. Cha spent over a decade working with think tanks and policy advocacy organisations on local, state and national policy campaigns. Her research interests lie at the intersection of inequality and climate change, with particular focus on environmental and climate justice, just transition, green economy and bridging the labour movement and environmental movement. Dr. Cha is a graduate of Cornell University, holds a JD from the University of California, Hastings College of the Law, and LLM and PhD degrees from the University of London, SOAS. She is a member of the California Bar Association and a Fellow at Cornell University's Worker Institute.

Jayajit Chakraborty is a Professor of Geography in the Department of Sociology and Anthropology and the Director of the Socio-Environmental and Geospatial Analysis Lab at the University of Texas at El Paso. His research interests are located at the intersection of hazards geography, health geography and urban geography, and encompass a wide range of environmental and social justice concerns. He has authored or co-authored more than 70 peer-reviewed publications, and his research has been supported by multiple grants from the U.S. National Science Foundation (NSF), Environmental Protection Agency (EPA), Association of American Geographers (AAG), Florida Department of Transportation and several other agencies.

Beth Christie is a Lecturer in Outdoor, Environmental and Sustainability Education at the University of Edinburgh. She is Programme Director for the MSc Learning for Sustainability and Associate Editor of the *Journal of Adventure Education and Outdoor Learning*. Her research interests span themes such as teaching and learning in outdoor environments, the practice and policy of learning for sustainability within Scottish education and the relationships between and within nature, gender and outdoor education.

Eric Chu is a Lecturer in Planning and Human Geography in the School of Geography, Earth and Environmental Sciences at the University of Birmingham (UK). His research is on climate change governance in cities, with particular emphasis on the globally comparative perspectives of socio-spatial change, development planning and environmental justice. He has written extensively on issues of inclusion, equity and justice in the context of climate change adaptation in cities.

Roa Petra Crease is a human geographer from the University of Auckland. Her research focuses on the gendered impacts of climate change in the Philippines and explores climate injustices through a gendered lens. She is involved in ongoing projects that seek to examine how sustainable development goals can align with scientific research projects, and the role of women in climate justice movements.

Jim Crowther is senior lecturer in adult and community education at the University of Edinburgh. He was a co-founder of the International Popular Education Network (PEN) in 1990 and its coordinator until 2016. He was also editor of *Studies in the Education of Adults* between 2010 and 2015. He has written extensively on adult education and democracy, the politics of policy, critical literacy and learning in social movements.

Brandon Derman is assistant professor of environmental studies at the University of Illinois at Springfield, where he teaches courses in environmental policy and law, and interdisciplinary perspectives on climate change. A geographer and socio-legal scholar, Brandon's research has appeared in the *Annual Review of Law and Social Science, Climate Policy, South African Journal on Human Rights, Transactions in GIS, Transportation Research Review* and edited volumes. His is currently developing a book manuscript, with the working title *Making Climate Justice*.

Maria DiGiano is a Scientist at the Earth Innovation Institute (EII), a San Francisco-based organisation committed to advancing the transition to low-emissions rural development. Maria received her MS and PhD degrees from the School of Natural Resources and Environment at the University of Florida, with concentrations in Anthropology and Tropical Conservation and Development. She also holds a BA in History from the University of North Carolina. Maria's research interests and expertise include community-based natural resource management, land tenure and land use governance and political ecology.

Karen Toni Fisher is a human geographer from the University of Auckland. Her research examines the intersections of development, gender and natural resource management in the Global North and Global South. She employs feminist and postcolonial theorising to explore the intersections between environmental and social injustices for people living in poverty both in the Global North and Global South.

Sara Fuller is Senior Lecturer in the Department of Geography and Planning, Macquarie University, Australia. Her research explores concepts and practices of justice in the context of global environmental change, with an empirical focus on grassroots, community and activist responses to climate change. She previously held postdoctoral positions at Durham University, UK and City University of Hong Kong and conducted research on low-carbon transitions and climate governance; NGO discourses of energy justice; low-carbon communities and social justice; and energy vulnerability in communities. Her current research investigates the politics and governance of urban climate justice across the Asia-Pacific region.

Anna Fünfgeld is a researcher and PhD candidate at the University of Freiburg's Department of International Politics, as well as at the GIGA German Institute of Global and Area Studies in Hamburg. Her academic background is in political science, human geography and social and cultural anthropology. Anna's research centres on natural resource governance and energy and climate politics, particularly in Indonesia/Southeast Asia. She has recently worked as an academic advisor for the Rosa Luxemburg Foundation (RLS) and published two papers with RLS on (in) justices in the Indonesian energy sector, where she elaborates on the importance of a social justice perspective for understanding energy-related struggles in Indonesia.

Alexandre Gajevic Sayegh is a Senior Research Fellow at the MacMillan Center for International and Area Studies and a Lecturer at the Department of Political Science at Yale University. He is currently lecturing on "The Ethics of Climate Change," among other courses. He also collaborates with environment politics initiatives at Yale. He is particularly interested in climate ethics and its relation to climate policy. His articles on climate justice have appeared in *Ethics, Policy & Environment*, the *Journal of Global Ethics* and the *Critical Review of International Social and Political Philosophy*. He has a forthcoming book titled *Justice in a Non-Ideal World*. One of its central case studies is climate justice.

Kristian Gareau recently completed a Master's degree at Concordia University in Montreal/ Tiohtià:ke. His thesis examined the social and political conflicts against tar sands pipelines in Canada, blending multiple theoretical approaches from political ecology, cultural politics, environmental sociology, geography and indigenous studies. He has been active in climate justice movements since the UN Climate Change COP 11 International Youth Declaration in 2005.

Devleena Ghosh is an Associate Professor in the Social and Political Sciences at the Faculty of Arts and Social Sciences, University of Technology Sydney (UTS). She is Chief Investigator for the climate-related research projects, "The Coal Rush and Beyond: Coal reliance, climate change and contested futures in Australia, India and Germany," 2014–2018 and "Decarbonising Electricity: a Comparison in Socio-ecological Relations," 2018–2022. She is also Stream Leader in the UTS Research Centre for Climate Justice. Her research interests lie in the fields of colonial, postcolonial, environmental and global studies, specifically in the Indian Ocean region. Devleena has been on numerous advisory panels for the Australian Federal and New South Wales state governments, dealing specifically on issues relating to the Indian community.

Jen Gobby is a PhD candidate at McGill University and is part of the Economics for the Anthropocene partnership (https://e4a-net.org/). She has been an activist for over 15 years and is actively engaged in the climate justice, anti-pipeline and Indigenous land defence movements across Canada. As an activist-scholar using participatory methods for collaborative theorising, Jen is "thinking with" activists about how large-scale systems change happens and endeavouring to do movement-relevant research that can contribute to strengthening movements' ability to bring about radical systems transformation towards decolonising and decarbonising Canada.

James Goodman conducts research into socio-political change and climate justice. He is lead Chief Investigator for climate-related research projects, "The Coal Rush and Beyond: Coal reliance, climate change and contested futures in Australia, India and Germany," 2014–2018 and "Decarbonising Electricity: a Comparison in Socio-ecological Relations," 2018–2022. In 2017, with six other academics, he initiated a new Climate Justice Research Centre at UTS. He is an

Associate Professor in Social and Political Sciences at the Faculty of Arts and Social Sciences at UTS, where he has been based since 1996. He is author or co-author of 12 books.

Sonia Graham is a postdoctoral researcher at the Institute of Environmental Sciences and Technology (ICTA) at the Autonomous University of Barcelona. During her postdoctoral research at the University of Melbourne, she developed a typology of "lived values" that enables decision-makers to identify which social values are affected by climate change impacts, such as sea-level rise, and the importance of incorporating such values into policies to ensure fairer outcomes. The typology also enables local communities to articulate which values are important to them, and thus influence the policy-making process.

Marco Grasso is an Associate Professor in Political Geography in the Department of Sociology and Social Research, University of Milan-Bicocca. His research interests include climate justice, international climate change governance, adaptation and social vulnerability to climate change, and human security.

Jason Gray is an environmental attorney, climate professional, author and conservationist. He is currently Chief of the Climate Change Program Evaluation Branch, which oversees and implements the Cap-and-Trade Program at the California Air Resources Board (CARB). He has also worked on environmental education, biodiversity conservation, local capacity building and sustainable development projects with the U.S. Peace Corps and World Wildlife Fund in the Central African country of Gabon. Jason received a Bachelor's degree in Biology and French from Gonzaga University and a Juris Doctor and Certificate in Environmental and Natural Resources Law from Lewis & Clark Law School.

Karin Helwig is a lecturer at Glasgow Caledonian University, Scotland, UK. She gained an MA in Policy and Gender Issues from VUA, the Netherlands. After some time working in nature conservation management, she obtained an MSc in Energy and Environmental Management and a PhD in Environmental Risk Assessment at GCU. She has worked on national and international research projects on pharmaceutical pollution, farm emission abatement, aquatic monitoring, phosphorus recovery and private water supplies, increasingly focusing on governance and stakeholder engagement within these contexts. Since 2017, she has been involved in GCU's Centre for Climate Justice, where her main interests are water governance and gender issues.

Jean Hillier is Emeritus Professor of Sustainability and Urban Planning at RMIT University, Melbourne, Australia. Her research interests include post-structural planning theory and methodology for strategic practice in conditions of uncertainty. Recent books include *Connections: exploring contemporary planning theory and practice* with Patsy Healey (2015), edited with Jonathan Metzger; *Deleuze and Guattari for Planners* (InPlanning e-book, 2013); and *Complexity and the Planning of the Built Environment* (2012), edited with Gert de Roo and Joris Van Wezemael.

Donna Houston is a Senior Lecturer in the Department of Geography and Planning at Macquarie University, Sydney, Australia. Her current research explores the political ecologies of urban nature, critical and creative geographies of activism and place-making and urban planning and environmental/climate justice in multispecies worlds.

Tahseen Jafry is a Professor at Glasgow Caledonian University (GCU), Scotland, UK and the Director of GCU's Centre for Climate Justice. She has developed a sound academic base for climate justice research and education. Tahseen is qualified as both an engineer and a social scientist and has accumulated extensive research and development experience over 20 years. Her work has spanned 14 countries in the Global South covering Sub-Saharan Africa, South Asia and the Small Island States. She is an experienced lecturer at both the postgraduate and undergraduate levels on environmental management, sustainability and climate justice, and supervises theses to doctorate level. Tahseen's current research interests include the justice and equity aspects of climate change, gender and poverty targeting, the management of natural resources, the geopolitical nature of climate justice and the psycho-social impacts of climate change.

Alan Jarandilla Nuñez is the Executive Director of Change The System, a non-profit organisation that works towards sustainable development from a systemic change perspective. Alan is a vocal activist for climate justice, indigenous peoples' rights and sustainable development.

Javier Kinney is a Yurok Tribal citizen and serves as the Director of the Office of Self-Governance for the Yurok Tribe. He has attained BA Degrees in History and Native American Studies from the University of California, Davis, an MA degree in Law and Diplomacy, specialising in Development Economics and International Law from Tufts University-Fletcher School of Law and Diplomacy and a JD from Suffolk Law School. Mr. Kinney has extensive experience advising Tribal governments with expertise in areas of strategic actions, climate change, natural resource management, mediation, negotiations, public policy, economic development, youth empowerment, land acquisition, tribal governance, philanthropic partnerships, protection of tribal cultural resources and water policy.

Sonja Klinsky is an Assistant Professor at the School of Sustainability at Arizona State University. Her work has continually centred around the justice dilemmas presented by climate change and climate change policy design and has often featured transdisciplinary collaboration. These collaborations have sought to generate theoretically sound and politically relevant proposals for constructively addressing debates about justice and fairness embedded in climate policy decision-making at all scales. In addition to this policy-oriented work, she has also done research on public perceptions of climate justice dilemmas and policy options, and has extensively engaged in supporting broader public engagement on climate justice issues.

Katharine Knox is currently a freelance consultant, and was formerly Policy and Research Manager at the Joseph Rowntree Foundation (JRF), where she initiated and led JRF's programme of research and policy and practice development on climate change and social justice and community resilience to climate change in the UK. Katharine has a background in social and public policy research and has written a range of articles on how climate change may affect poverty and disadvantage in the UK, including recent contributions for *Energy Justice in a Changing Climate* (Zed Books, 2015) and *Zero Carbon Britain: Making it happen* (Centre for Alternative Technology, 2017).

Dunja Krause is a Research Officer at the United Nations Research Institute for Social Development (UNRISD) in Geneva, Switzerland, where she leads the work on social justice implications of environmental and climate policies. A geographer by training, she has specialised in development geography, risk and vulnerability research and climate change adaptation. She is the author of the chapter "Sustainable Development in Times of Climate Change" in the 2016 UNRISD Flagship Report *Policy Innovations for Transformative Change*.

Anne Maree Kreller is a PhD scholar at the University of New South Wales, Australia. She is an activist researcher who has spent 20 years facilitating a community housing cooperative that supports low- to middle-income adults to build a sustainable space in Sydney. Her empirical research seeks to understand how sea-level rise adaptation policies can simultaneously encourage collective action and deliver justice.

So-Young Lee is a Senior Researcher at the Institute for Global Environmental Strategies (IGES), where she manages research on sustainability governance and climate social co-benefits for the underprivileged. She specialises in Environmental Sociology and lectures on climate justice at Waseda University (Japan), Beijing Normal University (China) and Korea University (ROK). Dr. Lee is author and co-author of 11 books and multiple articles on environment and society.

Diana MacCallum is a Senior Lecturer in the Department of Planning and Geography at Curtin University, Perth, Western Australia. Her research interests include the practices and discourses of planning governance, community involvement in urban and regional development, and social innovation.

Jane Maher is finalising her PhD in the Geography Department, School of Natural Science in Trinity College Dublin. Her PhD research focuses on the effect of gender mainstreaming in climate change adaptation for vulnerable communities in developing countries. Prior to commencing her PhD, Jane completed an MSc in Environment and Development in Trinity College Dublin (graduating 2012), with a research focus on women in agriculture, and has published in this area. Jane has worked as a researcher for various organisations and projects such as Concern Worldwide to examine women's usage of climate-smart agricultural techniques such as Conservation Agriculture in Concern projects.

Sennan Mattar is a PhD candidate at Glasgow Caledonian University and has expertise in environmental science, energy management and sustainable development, having worked as an environmental consultant and in the renewable energy section of the UK regulator, Ofgem. As part of GCU's Centre for Climate Justice, his doctoral thesis focuses on the consequences of climatic change in rural and urban areas on informal settlements in Lusaka from a climate justice perspective.

Enyinnaya Mbakwem is a PhD candidate at Glasgow Caledonian University and an environmental consultant with expertise in sustainable development, renewable energy and carbon footprint management. He holds an MSc in Renewable Energy and Environmental Management. Also, as part of the Centre for Climate Justice, his doctoral thesis focuses on the plight of forced climate migrants in the Niger Delta region of Nigeria from a climate justice perspective, with a view to inform socially inclusive climate policies and practices in Nigeria.

Callum McGregor is Lecturer in Education at the University of Edinburgh and currently directs the MSc Social Justice and Community Action. He has published on climate change activism as public pedagogy and community-based responses to climate change. His broader teaching and research interests span critical pedagogy, social movement learning and community education, with a particular focus on climate change.

Magaly Medeiros is a Biologist with a Masters in Development and Environment and a specialty in Ecology and Natural Resource Management. Magaly has served as the Director of Studies and Research for the Environmental Secretariat of Acre, Brazil, through which she coordinated the Integrated Environmental Management Project (PGAI), under the Political Program for Tropical

Forests (PPG7). She currently serves as the President of Acre's Institute for Climate Change and Regulation of Environmental Services.

Kavya Michael is an Associate Fellow in the Centre for Global Environmental Research (Earth Science and Climate Change Division) at The Energy and Resources Institute (India). She has a background in human ecology, political economy of the environment as well as environmental inequalities. Her research examines the multiple intersections of climate change/environmental hazards, urban inequality and development in Indian cities. Her work is oriented strongly within the urban climate justice paradigm and has emphasised the need to bring a climate justice lens to cities.

Michael Mikulewicz is a postdoctoral researcher at the Centre for Climate Justice at Glasgow Caledonian University, Scotland, UK. He uses human responses to climate change as the basis to study issues of inequality, exclusion and exploitation, with his research firmly embedded within critical social theory. Michael obtained his PhD in Human Geography from the University of Manchester, UK, with his thesis investigating the post-politics of adaptation to climate change in sub-Saharan Africa. Before that, he received an MA in Politics and International Relations from the University of Aberdeen, Scotland and an MSc in Environmental Studies from California State University, Fullerton.

Bruce C. Mitchell is Senior Analyst at the National Community Reinvestment Coalition. He holds a PhD from the University of South Florida in Geography and Environmental Science and Policy. As an urban geographer, he specialises in the application of quantitative methods, including conventional and spatial statistics, remote sensing and GIScience. Dr. Mitchell's research interests include urban geography and economics, public policy and housing, social vulnerability, climate justice and neighbourhood resiliency. He has authored and co-authored publications for the U.S. Department of the Treasury, the W.R. Kellogg Foundation and the National Community Reinvestment Coaltion (NCRC).

Tom Morton is Associate Professor of Journalism and Stream Leader in the Research Centre for Climate Justice at the University of Technology Sydney. He is a Chief Investigator on the international interdisciplinary research project "The Coal Rush and Beyond: Coal reliance, climate change and contested futures in Australia, India and Germany," and reporter/producer of the award-winning radio documentary series *Beyond the Coal Rush*. He is currently Chief Investigator for "Decarbonising Electricity: a Comparison in Socio-ecological Relations," 2018–2022. His research focuses on environmental journalism, climate communication and the socio-ecological relations of renewable energy. Prior to joining UTS in 2010, he was a journalist and radio documentary producer with the Australian Broadcasting Corporation (ABC) for more than 20 years, and has a PhD in German Language and Literature.

Susan P. Murphy is the coordinator of the MSc in Development Practice at Trinity College Dublin. Susan's research interests are in international political theory, human rights and climate change, gender and social inclusion. She has published widely on matters related to ethics and global development, including one book with Springer Studies titled *Global Justice – Responsibility in an Interconnected World*. Susan lectures on gender, climate justice and development research and practice. She is the Director of Trinity International Development Initiative (TIDI) and Chair of the Board of Trustees, Oxfam Ireland.

Francisca Oliveira de Lima Costa (Yakashawãdawa), also known as Francisca Arará is an Indigenous leader of the Arará People. Francisca is a professor with a graduate degree from the

Federal University of Acre. She teaches theoretical and practical classes in elementary education at the Arará Indigenous School in the Arará Indigenous Land of Igarapé Humaitá, and also leads a training course for Indigenous teachers. Currently, Francisca is an Indigenous Advisor in the Organization of Indigenous Teachers of Acre (OPIAC) and the Acre Agroforestry Agents Movement Association (AMAAIAC), working on project management, elaboration of didactic material and political representation with grassroots governmental and non-governmental institutions locally, regionally and internationally.

Meg Parsons is a human geographer from the University of Auckland. Her research is transdisciplinary, encompassing human geography, indigenous studies and environmental history, and focuses on indigenous peoples' experiences of and responses to climate change. She is involved in collaborative research projects with indigenous communities in Australia, New Zealand and Samoa, which examine what constitutes fair, just and sustainable adaptation actions in response to changing environmental conditions.

Patricia E. (Ellie) Perkins is a Professor in the Faculty of Environmental Studies, York University, Toronto, where she teaches ecological economics, community economic development, climate justice and critical interdisciplinary research design. Her research focuses on feminist ecological economics, climate justice and participatory governance. She directed international research projects on community-based watershed organising in Brazil and Canada and on climate justice and equity in watershed management with partners in Mozambique, South Africa and Kenya. She has authored many articles, book chapters and other publications. She is an editor of the journal *Ecological Economics*. She holds a PhD in Economics from the University of Toronto.

Emeline Pluchon is an Environmental Law Specialist with the United Nations Environment Programme (UN Environment)'s Regional Office for Asia and the Pacific. Prior to joining UN Environment, Emeline worked as an in-house lawyer in an energy company in Paris, where she was responsible for providing legal advice on environmental matters related to offshore projects. Emeline holds an LLM in International Energy and Environmental Law from the University of Oslo and a Masters in Comparative Law from the University of Paris Panthéon Sorbonne.

Emilie Prattico is currently Director of Development at We Mean Business, where she leads work aimed at scaling the impact of the coalition of business-facing climate NGOs. She has worked with the transportation, manufacturing, apparel, extractives and agriculture sectors on supply chain sustainability and climate impacts. Emilie teaches as a university lecturer in philosophy, sociology and design thinking. She speaks French, English, German and Italian. Emilie holds a PhD in Philosophy from Northwestern University, an MS in Management and Sustainability from HEC (Paris) and a BA in Philosophy and Theology from the University of Oxford.

Michael Reder studied philosophy, theology and economics in Munich, Tubingen and Fribourg (Sw.) and wrote his doctoral thesis on global governance. He is Professor of Practical Philosophy at the Munich School of Philosophy and head of the Institute for Ethics and Social Philosophy. He is also one of the heads of the centre for environmental ethics at the Munich School of Philosophy. He has conducted various research projects on the philosophical foundation of theories of globalisation, climate change and justice and the ecological impacts on the global common good. Currently, he is the principal investigator of a project on the representation of future generations as challenge for theories of democracy and one of the co-investigators on transnational practices of solidarity.

Annalisa Savaresi is Lecturer in Environmental Law at Stirling University, where she co-directs an interdisciplinary Master's programme in Environmental Policy and Governance. Her research focuses on climate change response measures, environmental liability and the interplay between environmental and human rights law. Her work has been published in numerous peer-reviewed outlets and has been widely cited. She has served as a consultant for prestigious think tanks and organisations, and advised governments and governmental bodies. She is a member of the IUCN World Commission on Environmental Law and associate editor of the *Review of European, Comparative and International Law*.

Eurig Scandrett is a Senior Lecturer in Public Sociology at Queen Margaret University, Edinburgh. He worked as an environmental scientist before moving into community education, and was Head of Community Action at Friends of the Earth Scotland. He has published on environmental justice in Scotland, India and Palestine.

Colleen Scanlan Lyons is a cultural anthropologist specialising in strategic planning for forest conservation, international network building and social inclusion in sustainable development. She currently serves as the Project Director for the Governors' Climate and Forests Task Force (GCF) and is the co-Director of the LEEP Innovation Lab. She is also a Research Associate with the Environment and Society Group in the University of Colorado's Institute of Behavioral Science and an Adjunct Professor in the Anthropology Department. Her expertise includes project development and management and she focuses on the social aspects of climate resilience and forest conservation as well as community participation, mobilisation and empowerment.

Tessa Sheridan completed a Master's degree in Energy and Environmental Management at Glasgow Caledonian University in 2017, achieving a distinction. During her time at GCU, she became particularly interested in the subject of climate justice, and therefore chose to focus her research project in this area. The subject of her research was investigating the role of climate justice in United Nations Framework Convention on Climate Change (UNFCCC) climate finance and providing recommendations on how to better achieve climate justice in the UNFCCC climate finance landscape, using conceptual frameworks. She is interested in pursuing further research on the issues surrounding climate finance, particularly in how climate finance can be used to help achieve climate justice.

Tom Sparks is a Senior Research Fellow at the Max Planck Institute for Comparative Public Law and International Law, where he works on statehood, self-determination, international environmental law and international legal theory. Tom is also a member of the Board of Directors of Amnesty International UK, and is Project Lead of the Interdisciplinary Climate Governance Project, a collaboration among international lawyers, political economists and climate scientists to imagine innovative politico-legal solutions to the challenges facing climate governance. Opinions expressed in his academic work do not necessarily represent the views of the organisations with which he is affiliated.

Wendy Steele is an Associate Professor with the Centre for Urban Research and the School of Global, Urban and Social Studies at RMIT University, Melbourne, Australia. Her research focuses on the governance and planning of wild cities in a climate of change. Specific projects include an emphasis on the climate-just city and re-thinking critical urban infrastructure. She is an international editorial member of the journal *Urban Policy and Research*.

Nejma Tamoudi studied political science, philosophy and religious studies in Munich and Paris. She wrote her Master's thesis on Charles Taylor's moral ontology and is currently a PhD student at the Munich School of Philosophy working on Paul Ricœur's concept of the "Social Imaginary" from a socio-philosophical perspective. She is a research assistant in the project "Future Generations as Blind Spot of Democracy." Together with Michael Reder and Simon Faets, she wrote the upcoming article (2018), "Fresh Perspectives on Intergenerational Justice: Comments on Social Criticism, Temporality, and Future Narratives," for the *Yearbook Practical Philosophy in a Global Perspective*.

Brian Tokar has been writing on climate justice for more than ten years, including his book *Toward Climate Justice: Perspectives on the Climate Crisis and Social Change* (Revised edition, New Compass Press, 2014) and several contributions to the *Routledge Handbook of the Climate Change Movement* (2014). He has written and edited five other books, including *Agriculture and Food in Crisis* (co-edited with Fred Magdoff, Monthly Review Press, 2010), is a Lecturer in Environmental Studies at the University of Vermont and a board member of the Institute for Social Ecology as well as 350Vermont, an affiliate of the global 350.org network.

Jörg Tremmel is a Permanent Lecturer at Eberhard Karls University of Tübingen. Tremmel holds two PhDs, one in philosophy and one in social sciences. From 2009 to 2010, he was a research fellow at the London School of Economics and Political Science, both at its Centre for Philosophy of Natural and Social Science and also (part-time) at the Grantham Institute for Climate Change Research. From 2010 to 2016, Tremmel was the incumbent of a Junior Professorship for Intergenerationally Just Policies at the Institute for Political Science of Tübingen University. His research interests lie mainly in political theory and political philosophy.

Eric Zusman is a Research Leader at the Institute for Global Environmental Strategies (IGES) in Japan. In his current position, he is working on the governance for the implementation of the Sustainable Development Goals. Dr. Zusman has also worked on environmental issues in Asia, including publishing articles and book chapters on water scarcity, air pollution regulation, environmental law and state capacity in greater China.

Acknowledgements

The Editorial Team – Tahseen, Michael and Karin – would like to express their sincere gratitude to all chapter contributors not only for their submissions but also for their patience and understanding during the editorial and production process. The submissions culminated in this Handbook exemplify the breadth, depth and nature of climate justice. We hope that the contents and messages from the chapters will inspire, motivate and be a driver for achieving a climate-just world.

Tahseen would also like to acknowledge and thank Assistant Editors, Michael and Karin, for their continued support, dedication and commitment to the completion of this truly mammoth task.

Thanks are also due to the 154 Primary 6 pupils from Camstradden, Elmvale, Haghill Park, St Bartholomew's and St Monica's primary schools in Glasgow, who contributed to the creation of the climate justice tree of hope, as seen on the front cover of this Handbook. We are very grateful to Ken Rice from Glasgow Caledonian University for taking the time to photograph the tree for us.

Every effort has been made to contact the copyright holders. If any have been inadvertently overlooked, the publishers will be pleased to make the necessary arrangements at the first opportunity.

1

Introduction

Justice in the era of climate change

Tahseen Jafry, Michael Mikulewicz and Karin Helwig

On April 17, 2017, the Mauna Loa Observatory in Hawaii recorded its first-ever carbon dioxide (CO_2) reading that exceeded 410 parts per million (ppm), a concentration of the greenhouse gas (GHG) not seen in the Earth's atmosphere for at least 3 million years (Lindsey, 2017). Moreover, climatologists predict that, if unaddressed, humanity's reliance on fossil fuels is likely to further increase CO_2 concentration to levels from the early Eocene – or over 50 million years ago (Foster et al., 2017). It is thus no surprise that temperature data from NASA shows rapid warming in the past few decades, with 2016 being the warmest on record (Cook et al., 2016). Meanwhile, the World Meteorological Organization (WMO) highlights that the rapidly increasing atmospheric levels of CO_2 and other greenhouse gases have the potential to initiate unprecedented changes in climate systems, leading to "severe ecological and economic disruptions" (WMO, 2017, p. 1).

This evidence unequivocally points to the anthropogenic nature of climate change and therefore to the need to address what by many is seen as humanity's greatest challenge in the 21st century. Indeed, climate change has already started to impact all aspects of social life – food production, the built environment, biodiversity, health, human security and the economy, to name but a few. Owing not just to the ever-more-detailed climate data but more importantly to the observed and lived experiences of those affected by climate impacts, it is becoming increasingly evident that a fundamental change in how our societies operate is urgently needed (Jafry and Platje, 2016). Climate change brings with it shifts in material and power balances, and a "business-as-usual" scenario will entrench or further deepen inequalities and exacerbate environmental damage. It is not unreasonable to expect that those who are materially and politically disadvantaged will bear the brunt of climate impacts, while those at the top of the socio-political ladder steer their lives towards a more climate-proof future (Mikulewicz, 2018). Issues ranging from water access and food security, to health-related impacts of chronic and acute climate events, to the political exclusion from making decisions on how to address climate change impacts and from sharing the benefits of these decisions are only some of the problems that may be in store for many countries, cities, communities and individuals over the next few decades. These challenges further complicate the prospects for attaining the Sustainable Development Goals (SDGs), which among other human development priorities explicitly seek to reduce global inequalities and promote climate action.

That said, there has been some optimism in the international area of climate governance as of late. The painstakingly made progress in the run-up to COP21 culminated with the widely applauded Paris Agreement. The accord, which has been signed by 195 countries and ratified by 176 as of May 2018 (United Nations, 2018), builds upon the United Nations Framework Convention on Climate Change (UNFCCC) and aims to strengthen the global response to planetary warming by limiting the rise of global temperature to below 2 degrees Celsius and striving not to exceed 1.5 degrees Celsius. However, for the first time in history, and unlike the Kyoto Protocol, the accord brings all nations into a common effort to combat climate change and to adapt to its effects, with enhanced support to assist developing countries in doing so. As such, it charts a new course in global climate governance, aiming to secure appropriate financial flows and new technology and capacity-building frameworks to support action by the most vulnerable countries in line with their own national objectives. For instance, the COP23 in Bonn that took place in November 2017 saw policy developments around phasing out existing coal power plants by more than 20 countries, including Canada, Finland, France, Mexico and the United Kingdom; targets for scaling up biofuel use in Brazil, China, Egypt, France, India, Morocco and Mozambique; and the announcement of the "InsuResilience" global initiative, which looks to provide insurance to hundreds of millions of vulnerable people by 2020.

At the same time, however, there have been calls for scrutinising just how equitable the mitigation and adaptation mechanisms proposed by the Paris Agreement as well as by other international, national and local frameworks for addressing climate change are. Similarly, it is clear that climate change has not been caused by all the parties to the Convention equally and, conversely, that its impacts will not be felt across the planet uniformly. Historically, industrialised countries have developed by implementing an economic model which has disproportionately exploited the Earth's resources and exacerbated socio-economic inequality across scales (Harvey, 2003). Meanwhile, evidence indicates that the less-industrialised countries feel more severely the detrimental effects of this development model and the impacts of climate change that it has produced (Mikulewicz, 2018; Niang et al., 2014; Shrestha, 2013; Thomas and Twyman, 2005). The face of this climate injustice have often been those who are in the frontline of climate-related impacts – the poorest and most marginalised in both the Global North and the Global South, who frequently lack access to the economic, social and political structures necessary to ensure that their views are recognised, their interests represented and their needs addressed (Tagg and Jafry, 2018). With climate change signifying a large-scale redistribution of both power and resources (Marino and Ribot, 2012), the potential for growing inequality resulting from climate change *and* from the ways in which we respond to it has become an important strand of critical climate change research. These complex and intractable questions of equity and fairness have given rise to the highly diverse – and by many seen as controversial – field of climate justice, which explicitly recognises that these "climate inequalities" exist and need to be confronted (Goodman, 2009; Meikle et al., 2016; Thorp, 2014). But this has also led to questions about what climate justice actually means given its diverse nature, and how it can be achieved, if at all.

Definitions and "images" of climate justice

The term "climate justice" began to gain traction in the late 1990s following a wide range of activities by social and environmental justice movements that emerged in response to the operations of the fossil fuel industry and, later, to what their members saw as the failed global climate governance model that became so transparent in 2009 at COP15 in Copenhagen (Bruno et al., 1999; Schlosberg and Collins, 2014). But the prominence of climate justice has also been fuelled by the growing consensus among critical observers that technological innovation alone has proved insufficient to address the stratifying nature of climate-related challenges, including limited and increasingly unequal access to food, water and energy. These issues call for new approaches and methods to address the inequitable nature of climate change and its impacts. And while perspectives on what climate justice actually means and how it can be achieved vary greatly even within this volume, its editors and authors agree that climate justice, through its inherent concern for fairness and equity in the context of climate change, provides a robust lens through which to chart this uneven climate change terrain.

Over the last decade, however, the field has seen rapid growth into a wide range of disciplines, a trend we sought to reflect in this Handbook. Climate justice means different things to different people and, to complicate matters further, different things to the same people depending on a particular time and space (Thorp, 2014). The term is articulated differently by social movements, NGOs, academics and policymakers (Schlosberg and Collins, 2014). Recognising this conceptual and contextual diversity, Glasgow Caledonian University's Centre for Climate Justice conducted a thorough review of climate justice definitions (Meikle et al., 2016). Through this exploratory process, a range of current approaches to climate justice were identified and reflected on. These centre on:

- A vision to dissolve and alleviate the unequal burdens created by climate change.
- A commitment to address the disproportionate burden of the climate crisis on the poor and marginalised.
- The recognition that the most vulnerable are the most deserving.
- Triple inequality – responsibility, vulnerability and mitigation.
- Dismantling the fossil fuel corporate power structure.
- A commitment to reparations and fair distribution of the world's wealth.
- A way to encapsulate the equity aspects of climate change.
- An effort to redress global warming by reducing disparities in development and power structures that drive climate change and continued injustice.
- A human rights-based approach to climate justice safeguarding the rights of the most vulnerable affected by climate change.
- Looking at environmental and human impacts of climate change through the lens of social justice, human rights and concern for indigenous peoples.

Reflecting on the multitude of existing approaches, the Centre has concluded that, in its various forms, climate justice "recognises humanity's responsibility for the impacts of greenhouse gas emissions on the poorest and most vulnerable people in society by critically addressing inequality and promoting transformative approaches to address the root causes of climate change" (Meikle et al., 2016, p. 497). Thus, despite the heterogeneity of climate justice perspectives, these have (at least) one thing in common: the focus on the equity and justice aspects inherent to both the causes and the effects of climate change. The "root causes" mentioned previously refer to greenhouse gas emissions caused by the traditional economic growth model, with a concomitant understanding that poverty and power imbalances act as "multipliers" for the negative impacts of climate change (Meikle et al., 2016).

The term continues to gain momentum in discussions around sustainable development, climate change, mitigation and adaptation, and has been slowly making its way into the world of international and national policy. However, progress in this arena could be much faster. Indeed, a critique often lodged against climate justice centres on its anti-establishment roots (Heffron and McCauley, 2018). The politically disruptive nature of the discourse often employed by climate activists has the (perhaps unintended) consequence of being perceived as divisive by those in power. Indeed, the framing of climate change as a rights or (in)justice issue affecting people and their environments (often personified by Mother Nature), and the emphasis on the uneven nature of the global economic, social and political system seem to have little traction among decision-makers. Similarly, the focus on historical responsibility and how the resource footprint, overconsumption and fossil fuel dependence of the Global North has caused the people living in the Global South to become recipients of externalised environmental costs as "social sinks" (Pettit, 2004, p. 102) seem to evoke a scant policy response. At the level of international negotiations, as demonstrated by one of the chapters in this Handbook for instance, repayment of the "climate debt" by the wealthy nations of the North for the damage done in the South is seen as a non-starter among most high-level climate negotiators.

Given these issues, there are voices asking if leading developed and developing countries to wrangle in this way undermines international solidarity, on which, after all, the Paris Agreement is arguably predicated. Yet at the same time, climate justice has become a focal point for organisation for indigenous peoples and marginalised communities around the world, as some of the chapters in this volume will demonstrate. Seen from this perspective, it can be argued that climate justice unites and empowers rather than divides.

And there are many more contentious questions for the field. For example, in moving towards a world beyond fossil fuels, can we also transition to a world beyond the injustices that have accompanied the fossil fuel economy? Can or should we see this as an opportunity to redefine the direction of "development" whereby human rights and the environment take precedence over economic growth? Indeed, one of the key questions that emerged during the compilation of this Handbook is the extent to which climate justice can be achieved within the current economic system and its governance structures. For instance, do we need global corporations, with all the power they yield, to be on board to ensure a swift and efficient transfer of finance, capacity and support, or is it necessary to reject those very structures and systems? Or, will compensation for the removal of historical responsibility rebalance inequalities? And can we ensure that it does not reward elites but actually reaches those who need it the most?

Thus, given these issues of definition, "images," and practical applications of climate justice, what lies ahead for the field? Should it abandon its undisputedly anti-establishment heritage to become more broadly acceptable in the world of politics and policy? In other words, should the concept head in the direction of praxis by being strategically translated into climate policies and governance procedures? Indeed, can climate justice even be operationalised, and if so, how? Or, should the term remain circumscribed to the world of social activism and academia as a rallying call for social mobilisation and research, leaving the sphere of climate policy and development practice to more "apolitical" concepts such as resilience or risk management? This Handbook does not attempt to directly answer these difficult questions, but illustrates arguments on both sides, highlighting the contentious nature of climate justice.

Rationale and contents of the handbook

Since the 1990s, a number of authors have written about various aspects of climate justice. However, the connections between these remain unestablished – a conceptual diversity that is often used to critique the term (see Heffron and McCauley, 2018; Jenkins, 2018). The application of climate justice to topics such as finance, business, just transition, development policy, urban environments, gender or natural resource management remains ambiguous. Moreover, over the years, the field has seen an interesting migration across scales. Despite having emerged from within environmental justice movements at the local level, the bulk of climate justice research and activism has historically been concerned with the international level of climate governance (Fisher, 2015). However, this has been changing over the last ten or so years, and this Handbook mirrors this change. A significant number of the chapters presented here are about local places and local people – cities, neighbourhoods and communities – and as such they address scales at which tangible climate injustice is actually felt. In a similar vein, this volume includes chapters focusing on both developed and developing countries, as it should not be forgotten that while the North-South division seems perhaps the most striking when looking at the global scale, there also exist significant social, economic and political inequalities *within* both camps that can be further exacerbated by climate change impacts.

With this fluidity and diversity that characterises climate justice in mind, a more comprehensive and integrated reference compendium in the subject area was needed for students, academics, professionals and practitioners to explain in more detail what the concept offers and what its various applications may be. This Handbook equips readers with information necessary to develop their understanding, skills and frames of reference in this area of critical inquiry. The emphasis throughout the Handbook is on facilitating learning based on cutting-edge specialised climate justice research and application. This knowledge is delivered in chapters that draw from the most recent sources, real-world best practices, research projects, tutored reflections on the strategic dimensions of climate justice and its related disciplines, with contributions from a multidisciplinary range of academics, activists and practitioners from the Global North and South alike. The Handbook aims to provide insights into a core range of themes to suit the academic and professional development needs of those engaged in the field of climate change and justice. In addition to the more traditional focus on gender, international governance and climate ethics, the chapters in this Handbook also address some of the most salient topics in current climate justice research, including just transition, urban climate justice and public engagement.

Contents of the handbook

The Handbook is divided into **eight** parts.

Part one of the handbook concerns the theories and origins of climate justice

It presents a collection of chapters which provide both a theoretical and historical context for the field. Chapter 2 by Brian Tokar highlights several essential aspects of climate justice and its continuing contribution to the global movement for climate action. In Chapter 3, Idil Boran reflects on normative inquiry into climate justice and discusses the principles of distributive justice, compensatory justice, justice as basic rights, egalitarian distribution of atmospheric shares and global and intergenerational justice. Climate-reliable ethical theories are explored in Chapter 4 by Jörg Tremmel, who uses a thought experiment rooted in climate ethics to discuss the issue of negotiating GHG emission reduction targets from an intergenerational perspective. Nejma Tamoudi and Michael Reder provide a narrative account of temporality in climate justice in Chapter 5, in which they emphasise the historically shaped socio-environmental relationality that conceptions of climate justice inevitably entail.

Part two of the handbook focuses on governance, policy and litigation in the context of climate justice

Chapter 6 by Susan Murphy explores geopolitical processes through the lens of financing, and questions how matters related to allocation of duties and responsibilities can be tackled through the new structures and frameworks of the Nationally Determined Contributions (NDCs). In

Chapter 7, Tom Sparks evaluates the dominant theory of statehood in a time of rising seas and sinking islands, and discusses how increasingly damaging climate change will be to the coherence of the idea of the State and to the rights of the most adversely affected individuals. In Chapter 8, Ritwika Basu and Amir Bazaz explore the idea of re-imagining "justice" as well as the imperatives of improving procedural and distributive justice. They use the city of Siliguri in India as a case study to unpack the local practices of justice-making by examining the role of non-state actors as key mediators of just outcomes. In Chapter 9, Katharine Knox examines the concept of climate justice in a developed country context, drawing on the interdisciplinary research programme of the Joseph Rowntree Foundation, which examined the social impacts and social justice implications of climate change in the UK from 2008–17. Annalisa Savaresi and Kim Bouwer explore the use of benefit-sharing to support the achievement of equity and justice in climate change governance in Chapter 10. The authors consider how benefit-sharing has been used thus far at the international, national and subnational levels and how it may be more systematically used to carve out a space to better embed equity and justice considerations into climate change law and policy. In Chapter 11, Emeline Pluchon highlights the growing role of the judiciary in advancing climate justice and demonstrates how judges in South Asia have been at the forefront of this trend. She outlines some of the challenges faced in this context, discusses how judges are coming together to share experiences and advance climate justice, and reflects on how judicial leadership in South Asia could be a model for peers around the world.

Part three of the handbook focuses on the links between climate justice, finance and business

In Chapter 12, Alexandre Gajevic Sayegh offers an account of the principles of climate justice that should regulate climate finance and discusses what some of the central practical implications of these principles are. Tessa Sheridan and Tahseen Jafry further explore the concept of climate finance for climate justice in Chapter 13. They offer a critique of the current UNFCCC governance structure as a suitable channel for delivering climate finance and argue for a more decentralised system that is more effective and conducive to justice. A set of design elements for carbon pricing informed by climate justice is discussed in Chapter 14 by Edward Cameron, with the goal of ensuring effective, efficient and equitable GHG emission reductions in a Paris-compliant world. The chapter highlights that carbon prices and supporting policies should be developed in a participatory, transparent and accountable manner, with full respect for human rights. Sharing the burden of climate change via climate finance and business models is the topic discussed in Chapter 15 by Emilie Prattico.

Part four of the handbook concerns just transition

In Chapter 16, J. Milin Cha uses the case study of the coal-dominant region of Ruhr, Germany to present the negative economic and social consequences of decarbonisation on communities and workers dependent on fossil fuel extraction as a fundamental concern of climate justice, which needs to be addressed while transitioning to a low-carbon economy. This is followed by Chapter 17, where Anna Fünfgeld draws on two local case studies from Indonesia to explore the dimensions of (in)justice related to the nation's coal sector. She identifies what social justice theory in general and climate and energy justice frameworks in particular can add to our understanding of energy production and distribution and the related decision-making structures. Chapter 18 by James Goodman, Devleena Ghosh and Tom Morton compares energy transitions in India, Germany and Australia, demonstrating how climate action is embedded in justice concerns. It focuses especially on the socio-political drivers and barriers to energy transitions in the three contexts in order to better understand the links between decarbonisation and climate justice. In Chapter 19, Marco Grasso articulates the responsibilities Big Oil has in relation to climate change and assigns a duty of financial rectification of the harm done based on these responsibilities. In Chapter 20, David Brown presents a multiscalar, climate justice-based analysis of the emerging Reducing Emissions from Deforestation and Forest Degradation (REDD+) policy regime. Based on empirical research, the conceptions of climate justice which underpin and justify the discourse and practices of actors in the Norwegian-Ethiopian REDD+ partnership are critically assessed and examined.

Part five of the handbook focuses on urban climate justice

Chapter 21 by Wendy Steele, Jean Hillier, Donna Houston, Jason Byrne and Diana MacCallum outlines the framework of the climate-just city as a conceptual and analytical lens for taking the urban equity agenda forward within the context of climate change. In Chapter 22, Sara Fuller critically discusses the ways in which carbon footprinting reconfigures responsibility for climate action in the city and often obscures important questions about the roles and responsibilities of other actors, based on empirical data from a low-income neighbourhood in Hong Kong. Chapter 23 by Eric Chu and Kavya Michael presents the cases of Bangalore and Surat in India to examine how the reorganisation of labour, together with its associated economic networks and spatial infrastructure, is emblematic of the shifting interconnections between uncertain climate change risks and experiences of local economic transformations. Anne Maree Kreller and Sonia Graham investigate in Chapter 24 how local residents and decision-makers perceive the fairness of sea-level rise adaptation policies in Botany Bay, the most vulnerable coastal region of Sydney, Australia. In Chapter 25, Bruce Mitchell and Jayajit Chakraborty discuss the concept of "thermal inequity" in the city and, through quantitative spatial analysis conducted in multiple U.S. urban areas, explore its relationship with socio-economic disadvantage.

Part six of the handbook discusses the relationship between climate justice and gender

In Chapter 26, Patricia Perkins discusses climate justice, gender and intersectionality, and explores how environmental and climate injustice experiences are gendered in both rich and poor countries. Roa Petra Crease, Meg Parsons and Karen Fisher draw in Chapter 27 on feminist political ecology and intersectionality approaches to examine efforts to address climate and gender injustices in the Philippines. In Chapter 28, Jane Maher presents a multiscalar analysis assessing the evolution of gender mainstreaming in climate change adaptation policies from international to national and subnational levels in Malawi. She also explores the differentiated vulnerabilities and coping mechanisms of social groups in the Lower Shire Valley. Chapter 29 by So-Young Lee and Eric Zusman draws upon a series of applied case studies from Southeast Asia to demonstrate that women frequently have untapped potential to mitigate climate change. The authors argue that one of the keys to unlocking that potential is to take advantage of the recent trends in international climate negotiations to make climate governance more participatory.

Part seven of the handbook concerns climate justice movements and struggles

In Chapter 30, Brandon Derman argues for the need to "ground" climate justice by making climate injustices more legible and resonant by relating them to other kinds of social, economic and political oppression. As a case study for his qualitative analysis, he uses the advocacy apparatus of the National Association for the Advancement of Colored People (NAACP) and its Environmental and Climate Justice Program (ECJP). This is followed directly by Alan Jarandilla Nuñez in Chapter 31, who examines the cosmocentric conception of climate justice as understood by many indigenous people in the Andean region, and juxtaposes it with the anthropocentric understanding of the term that currently dominates academic and public debates. In Chapter 32, Colleen Scanlan Lyons, Maria DiGiano, Jason Gray, Javier Kinney, Magaly Medeiros and Francisca Oliveira de Lima Costa demonstrate how indigenous peoples and tribal authorities are collaborating with state and provincial government actors to mitigate climate change, address structural and procedural inequalities, and promote climate justice. Jen Gobby and Kristian Gareau explore in Chapter 33 the conversations with members of the anti-pipeline movements in Canada, arguing that they offer valuable insights into the underlying drivers for the country's climate and racial inequality crises and hint at more transformative approaches for addressing them.

Part eight of the handbook discusses the emerging areas in climate justice

In Chapter 34, Sonja Klinsky discusses the challenges for public engagement beyond academia in the context of climate justice, which she identifies in the breadth and multidimensionality of the climate problem, the complexity of solidarity in this multifaceted and multiscalar context, and the moral weight of climate injustice. Sennan Mattar and Enyinnaya Mbakwem explore in Chapter 35 the increasingly critical issue of climate-induced migration and displacement, and discuss how it affects the human right to a decent quality of life. In Chapter 36, Callum McGregor, Eurig Scandrett, Beth Christie and Jim Crowther discuss the issue of climate justice education in Scotland, and challenge the "neoliberal public pedagogy" that equates the particular interests of the transnational capitalist class and the "national interest." They argue that educators require strategies for exploring the ways in which diverse emotional responses to climate change are ideologically inflected. Finally, transformative approaches rooted in inclusive political processes to tackle climate change and to achieve climate justice are the subject of Chapter 37 by Dunja Krause.

Beyond a doubt, much has been written about the topics touched upon in this volume. Library shelves are crowded with books on natural resource management, climate finance, urban planning or international development in the context of climate change. But it is not just the fact of talking about these issues that matters. How we talk about them, how we frame them and how we discuss them is of equal, if not higher, importance. There are plenty of non-political ways to explain or address the causes and impacts of climate change. Discourses of ecological modernisation, climate-resilient growth, capacity building, risk assessment and management, among others, seem to dominate climate governance and, in fact, research (see Bassett and Fogelman, 2013). This volume offers a more unique, human-centred perspective that foregrounds the ethical dimensions of the climate issue, as we believe that the need for envisioning and pursuing climate justice in the rapidly warming and stratifying world now seems more important than ever.

Finally, it is our view as editors that the sheer diversity of approaches to climate justice – rather than being the field's weakness – is in fact its strength. It would indeed be somewhat contradictory to expect rigid conceptual compliance to a term rooted in equity, fairness and political emancipation. Thus, all the following chapters testify to the enormous flexibility of climate justice in studying the different facets of inequality and injustice inherent to climate change. Clearly, climate justice is a highly normative field, in the sense that it prioritises certain values and ideals over others when analysing social and political issues. Pursuing climate justice reflects a vision of, and a desire to work towards, a more equitable and socially just society in, and perhaps despite, the era of climate change. It is our hope that this volume will offer a modest contribution to this formidable effort.

References

Bassett, T. J., Fogelman, C., 2013. Déjà vu or something new? The adaptation concept in the climate change literature. *Geoforum* 48, 42–53. https://doi.org/10.1016/j.geoforum.2013.04.010

Bruno, K., Karliner, J., Brotsky, C., 1999. *Greenhouse Gangsters vs. Climate Justice*. Transnational Resource and Action Center, San Francisco, CA.

Cook, J., Oreskes, N., Doran, P.T., Anderegg, W.R.L., Verheggen, B., Maibach, E.W., Carlton, J.S., Lewandowsky, S., Skuce, A.G., Green, S.A., Nuccitelli, D., Jacobs, P., Richardson, M., Winkler, B., Painting, R., Rice, K., 2016. Consensus on consensus: A synthesis of consensus estimates on human-caused global warming. *Environmental Research Letters* 11, 048002. https://doi.org/10.1088/1748-9326/11/4/048002

Fisher, S., 2015. The emerging geographies of climate justice: The emerging geographies of climate justice. *The Geographical Journal* 181, 73–82. https://doi.org/10.1111/geoj.12078

Foster, G.L., Royer, D.L., Lunt, D.J., 2017. Future climate forcing potentially without precedent in the last 420 million years. *Nature Communications* 8, 14845.

Goodman, J., 2009. From global justice to climate justice? Justice ecologism in an era of global warming. *New Political Science* 31, 499–514. https://doi.org/10.1080/07393140903322570

Harvey, D., 2003. *The new imperialism*. Oxford University Press, Oxford; New York.

Heffron, R.J., McCauley, D., 2018. What is the 'just transition'? *Geoforum* 88, 74–77. https://doi.org/10.1016/j.geoforum.2017.11.016

Jafry, T., Platje, J. (Joost), 2016. Editorial. *International Journal of Climate Change Strategies and Management* 8, 474–476. https://doi.org/10.1108/IJCCSM-05-2016-0068

Jenkins, K., 2018. Setting energy justice apart from the crowd: Lessons from environmental and climate justice. *Energy Research & Social Science* 39, 117–121. https://doi.org/10.1016/j.erss.2017.11.015

Lindsey, R., 2017. Climate Change: Atmospheric Carbon Dioxide [WWW Document]. https://climate.gov/news-features/understanding-climate/climate-change-atmospheric-carbon-dioxide

Marino, E., Ribot, J., 2012. Special issue introduction: Adding insult to injury: Climate change and the inequities of climate intervention. *Global Environmental Change* 22, 323–328. https://doi.org/10.1016/j.gloenvcha.2012.03.001

Meikle, M., Wilson, J., Jafry, T., 2016. Climate justice: Between mammon and mother earth. *International Journal of Climate Change Strategies and Management* 8, 488–504. https://doi.org/10.1108/IJCCSM-06-2015-0089

Mikulewicz, M., 2018. Politicizing vulnerability and adaptation: On the need to democratize local responses to climate impacts in developing countries. *Climate and Development* 10, 18–34. https://doi.org/10.1080/17565529.2017.1304887

Niang, I., Ruppel, O., Abdrabo, M., Essel, A., Lennard, C., Padgham, J., Urquhart, P., 2014. Africa, in: Barros, V.R., Field, C.B., Dokken, D.J., Mastrandrea, M.D., Mach, K.J., Bilir, T.E., Chatterjee, M., Ebi, K.L., Estrada., Y.O., Genova, R.C., Girma, B., Kissel, E.S., Levy, A.N., MacCracken, S., Mastrandrea, P.R., White, L.L. (Eds.), *Climate Change 2014: Impacts, Adaptation, and Vulnerability. Part B: Regional Aspects. Contribution of Working Group II to the Fifth Assessment Report of the Intergovernmental Panel on Climate Change*. Cambridge University Press, Cambridge, UK; New York, NY, pp. 1199–1265.

Pettit, J., 2004. Climate justice: A new social movement for atmospheric rights. *IDS Bulletin* 35, 102–106. https://doi.org/10.1111/j.1759-5436.2004.tb00142.x

Schlosberg, D., Collins, L.B., 2014. From environmental to climate justice: Climate change and the discourse of environmental justice. *Wiley Interdisciplinary Reviews: Climate Change* 5, 359–374. https://doi.org/10.1002/wcc.275

Shrestha, M.K., 2013. Internal versus external social capital and the success of community initiatives: A case of self-organizing collaborative governance in Nepal. *Public Administration Review* 73, 154–164.

Tagg, N., Jafry, T., 2018. Engaging young children with climate change and climate justice. *Research for All* 2, 34–42. https://doi.org/10.18546/RFA.02.1.04

Thomas, D.S.G., Twyman, C., 2005. Equity and justice in climate change adaptation amongst natural-resource-dependent societies. *Global Environmental Change* 15, 115–124. https://doi.org/10.1016/j.gloenvcha.2004.10.001

Thorp, T.M., 2014. *Climate Justice*. Palgrave Macmillan, London, UK. https://doi.org/10.1057/9781137394644

United Nations, 2018. Chapter XXVII: Environment. 7. d Paris Agreement [WWW Document]. https://treaties.un.org/pages/ViewDetails.aspx?src=TREATY&mtdsg_no=XXVII-7-d&chapter=27&clang=_en (accessed 5.15.18).

WMO, 2017. The state of greenhouse gases in the atmosphere based on global observations through 2016. *Greenhouse Gas Bulletin* 13.

Part I
Theories of climate justice

2

On the evolution and continuing development of the climate justice movement

Brian Tokar

From its origins nearly two decades ago, the concept of climate justice has come to prominence as a research agenda, an ethical and legal framework, and perhaps most significantly as the basis for an engaged grassroots response to the unfolding global climate crisis. Climate justice highlights the disproportionate impacts of climate changes on the most vulnerable and marginalised human populations, as well as the limitations of conventional political responses to rising climate instability and the compelling need for systemic solutions. Representatives of the most impacted "frontline" communities around the world have come forward as among the most articulate and inspired voices at many international forums, and their lived experiences and cultural wisdom have come to shape the political understanding and strategies of social movement actors. Advocates for climate justice have emerged as a unique critical voice in climate diplomacy, raised a comprehensive challenge to various technological and market-oriented approaches to the climate crisis that are viewed as "false solutions," and challenged political interests linked to the fossil fuel industry in many countries (Tokar 2014).

This chapter will address the growing body of evidence supporting a climate justice outlook, the evolution of climate justice as a social movement perspective and the critiques offered by climate justice advocates of the prevailing currents in climate diplomacy. We will consider some of the contributions this perspective offers to the wider global movement for climate action and assess the challenges going forward as climate impacts continue to mount and fossil fuel interests are politically resurgent in key countries. As climate scientists project an increasingly short time horizon to transform energy and transportation systems, among other economic sectors, a justice-centred perspective is sometimes believed to conflict with climate pragmatism. We will review some of the problems and potentialities that arise as policymakers and social movement actors continue to navigate the contested terrain of effective climate action.

Climate justice science and human impacts

As of 2017, the five hottest years in the history of systematic weather reporting had all occurred since 2010, according to the U.S. National Oceanic and Atmospheric Administration (Schmidt and Arndt 2017). Individual countries and regions frequently report record-setting high temperatures, increasingly erratic rainfall and severe regional impacts, including the rapid disappearance of late summer Arctic ice. Extreme weather events increasingly dominate world and national headlines, from the 2003 heatwave that reportedly killed over 50,000 people in Western Europe (Battisti and Naylor 2009, 242) to catastrophic storms that have battered the eastern and southern United States and recent waves of unprecedented wildfires across the American West. For several decades, however, the impacts on tropical and subtropical regions have been most severe. Years of persistent drought have brought acute hunger to over 8 million people in the Horn of Africa (Oxfam 2017) and many more in parts of southern Africa and the war-torn Middle East. Major population centres across South Asia have flooded during the past decade, and two of the most severe typhoons to ever reach landfall have devastated communities in the Philippines and Fiji Islands (Samenow 2016). Still, public attention has often focused on severe climate impacts in U.S. states such as Texas and Florida, even as some of the same storm systems and patterns have had far greater impacts on Caribbean islands and the river deltas of South Asia.

While it remains challenging for scientists to measure the precise climate contributions to particular weather events, three central aspects are clear: (1) the pace of weather-related disasters is increasing rapidly, upsetting even the authoritative projections of the global insurance industry (Munich Re 2015); (2) these trends are fully consistent with the predictions of climate models for the behaviour of a warmer, more turbulent atmosphere (Hansen et al. 2014); and (3) when the climate contributions to particular weather events can be calculated, the signal of global warming often emerges as a central contributing factor (Min et al. 2011; Coumou and Rahmstorf 2012; Fischer and Knutti 2015). A few years ago, Oxfam International (2009) reported that of 250 million people impacted annually by various natural disasters, 98% face climate-related hazards. The UN Office of the High Commissioner for Human Rights (OHCHR) has cited a more modest, but still disturbing figure of 262 million people affected during the five-year period between 2000 and 2004 (Atapattu 2016, 76). A decade ago, the UN Development Program (Watkins 2007, 16) revealed that one out of every 19 people in the so-called developing world was affected by a climate-related disaster between 2000 and 2004, compared to one out of every 1,500 people in the OECD countries. Columbia University's International Earth Science Information Network has predicted that by 2050 the world could see as many as 700 million climate refugees (Parenti 2011, 7).

IPCC findings and human rights

The disproportionate impacts highlighted by climate justice advocates are also echoed in the last two reports of the Intergovernmental Panel on Climate Change (IPCC). In 2007, the IPCC concluded (17) that populations with "high exposure, high sensitivity and/or low adaptive capacity" would bear the greatest burdens from climate impacts, including "increases in malnutrition and consequent disorders . . .; increased deaths, disease and injury due to heat waves, floods, storms, fires and droughts; the increased burden of diarrheal disease; the increased frequency of cardio-respiratory diseases . . .; and, the altered spatial distribution of some infectious disease vectors," including malaria (12). The IPCC's Fifth Assessment Report in 2014 (2014a, 12) included a much more thorough review of climate justice concerns among its enumeration of key climate risks identified with high confidence in current scientific assessments. These include:

- Risk of death, injury, ill-health, or disrupted livelihoods in low-lying coastal zones and small island developing states and other small islands, due to storm surges, coastal flooding and sea-level rise.

- Risk of severe ill-health and disrupted livelihoods for large urban populations due to inland flooding in some regions. . . .
- Risk of mortality and morbidity during periods of extreme heat, particularly for vulnerable urban populations and those working outdoors in urban or rural areas.
- Risk of food insecurity and the breakdown of food systems linked to warming, drought, flooding and precipitation variability and extremes, particularly for poorer populations in urban and rural settings.
- Risk of loss of rural livelihoods and income due to insufficient access to drinking and irrigation water and reduced agricultural productivity, particularly for farmers and pastoralists with minimal capital in semi-arid regions.

The panel further determined, also with high confidence, that "[c]limate-related hazards constitute an additional burden to people living in poverty, acting as a threat multiplier often with negative outcomes for livelihoods" (IPCC 2014b, 11). Further, "[c]limate-related hazards affect poor people's lives directly through impacts on livelihoods, such as reductions in crop yields or destruction of homes, and indirectly through increased food prices and food insecurity" (ibid.).

Researchers at McGill University in Canada and the University of Maine in the U.S. examined climate-related shifts in population density to develop an index of climate vulnerability for various regions, and their findings affirm the veracity of a climate justice outlook. "[T]he regions of greatest vulnerability are generally distant from the high-latitude regions where the magnitude of climate change will be greatest," they reported, highlighting the especially heightened vulnerability of people in arid regions of the tropics and subtropics. "Furthermore," they continued, "populations contributing the most to greenhouse gas emissions on a per capita basis are unlikely to experience the worst impacts of climate change" (Samson et al. 2011, 532).

Legal scholar and international human rights attorney Sumudu Atapattu (2016) has identified some of the most trenchant obstacles to achieving climate justice within traditional legal frameworks, especially the difficulty of establishing causal links between climate changes and particular impactful events, along with the multiplicity of factors that contribute to climate-related catastrophes. Further, current law appears ill-suited to address the underlying causes of human rights violations in order to prevent future harms (71). While the UN Human Rights Council has cited the special vulnerability of small island nations, coastal arid and semi-arid regions, and "developing countries with fragile mountainous ecosystems" (69), those who are forced to relocate from such regions currently "have no legal status under international refugee law" (71). Climate change threatens numerous widely acknowledged human rights, including the right to life, health, housing, livelihood, food, water, self-determination, freedom of movement, culture and property (76–86). To fully address these impacts, however, requires us to consider the underlying causes of climate change in "the current development paradigm with its roots in capitalism" (96). Without addressing root causes, Atapattu argues, "it is impossible to design an effective legal regime" (96). The persistent inadequacy of legal, diplomatic and political efforts to address the climate crisis and uphold core principles of justice and human rights has fuelled the evolution of climate justice as an international social movement framework.

Origins of climate justice

The first generally acknowledged reference to climate justice appeared in a 1999 report titled *Greenhouse Gangsters vs. Climate Justice* by the San Francisco-based Corporate Watch group (Bruno et al. 1999). The report focused on the petroleum industry and its hegemonic political influence, but it also described an initial approach to climate justice, including (in summary):

- Addressing the root causes of global warming by holding corporations accountable;
- Opposing the destructive impacts of oil development, and supporting communities most affected by weather-related disasters;
- Looking to environmental justice communities (see later discussion) and organised labour for strategies to encourage a just transition away from fossil fuels;
- Challenging corporate-led globalisation and the disproportionate influence of international financial institutions.

The CorpWatch authors were active supporters of the U.S. movement for environmental justice, which emerged in the 1980s and remains a focus for urban, indigenous and poor rural populations confronting the disproportionate exposure of African American, Latino/a, Native American and Asian American communities to environmental hazards. The movement was galvanised by successful local campaigns against toxic hazards, as well as a 1987 church-sponsored report, *Toxic Wastes and Race*, which revealed that the racial composition of communities is by far the largest factor in the siting of hazardous waste facilities in the U.S. (Commission for Racial Justice 1987).

In 1991, a National People of Colour Environmental Leadership Summit issued a broadly comprehensive public statement against environmental racism and for environmental justice. By the mid-1990s, leaders such as Tom Goldtooth of the Indigenous Environmental Network (IEN) were articulating the need to bring the deepening climate crisis into this framework, and the movement's second Leadership Summit in 2002 issued a document titled "10 Principles for Just Climate Change Policies in the U.S." (Anonymous 2002).

Also throughout the 1990s, international NGOs such as the World Rainforest Movement, Friends of the Earth International and the Third World Network drew public attention to local struggles of indigenous and other land-based peoples in the Global South against the rising levels of resource extraction that accompanied neoliberal economic policies. They joined with Corp-Watch, IEN and others at a meeting on the island of Bali in 2002 to develop the Bali Principles of Climate Justice, a comprehensive, 27-point program aimed to "begin to build an international movement of all peoples for Climate Justice" (CorpWatch US et al. 2002). Two years later, international activists concerned about the inequities inherent in the 1997 Kyoto Protocol's market-based emissions trading provisions gathered in Durban, South Africa and drafted the Durban Declaration on Carbon Trading, which eventually received nearly 300 endorsements worldwide (Carbon Trade Watch et al. 2004).

When the UN's annual climate conference (COP) was held on Bali in 2007, representatives of communities disproportionately affected by global inaction on climate presented a strong and unified showing both inside and outside the official proceedings, and a more formal worldwide network emerged under the slogan "Climate Justice Now!" At a series of side events, press conferences and protests throughout the Bali conference, representatives of affected communities, indigenous peoples, women, peasant farmers and their allies articulated their call for "genuine solutions that include:

- leaving fossil fuels in the ground and investing instead in appropriate energy- efficiency and safe, clean and community-led renewable energy;
- radically reducing wasteful consumption, first and foremost in the North, but also by Southern elites;

- huge financial transfers from North to South, based on the repayment of climate debts and subject to democratic control . . .;
- rights-based resource conservation that enforces Indigenous land rights and promotes peoples' sovereignty over energy, forests, land and water;
- sustainable family farming and peoples' food sovereignty."

(Climate Justice Now 2007, 2008)

A more detailed statement of principles for Climate Justice Now (CJN), developed the following year, begins in part:

> From the perspective of climate justice, it is imperative that responsibility for reducing emissions and financing systemic transformation is taken by those who have benefited most from the past 250 years of economic development. Furthermore, any solutions to climate change must protect the most vulnerable, compensate those who are displaced, guarantee individual and collective rights, and respect peoples' right to participate in decisions that impact on their lives.

(Climate Justice Now 2008)

By 2010, the CJN network included some 750 international organisations, including grassroots groups throughout the Global South, and had become a reliable communications hub for those seeking to further these goals (Climate Justice Now 2010).

Climate justice as a social movement

Over the past decade, climate justice has come to encompass several distinct but complementary currents from various parts of the world. In the Global South, demands for climate justice unite an impressive diversity of indigenous and other land-based people's movements. They include rainforest dwellers opposing new mega-dams and palm oil plantations, African and Latin American communities resisting land appropriations for industrial agriculture and agrofuel production, Pacific Islanders facing the loss of their homes due to rising seas, and peasant farmers fighting for food sovereignty and basic land rights, among many others. A statement to the 2009 UN Copenhagen climate conference from the worldwide confederation of peasant movements, La Vía Campesina, stated in part:

> Climate change is already seriously impacting us. It brings floods, droughts and the outbreak of pests that are all causing harvest failures. I must point out that these harvest failures are something that the farmers did not create. Instead, it is the polluters who caused the emissions who destroy the natural cycles. . . . [W]e will not pay for their mistakes.

(Saragih 2009)

In North America, environmental justice activists continue to be among the leading voices for climate justice, especially representatives from communities of colour that have been resisting daily exposure to chemical toxins and other environmental hazards for more than 30 years. Many view the climate justice movement as a continuation of the U.S. civil rights legacy, and of their communities' continuing "quest for fairness, equity and justice," as described by the environmental justice pioneer Robert Bullard at a landmark 2009 gathering in New York City. The Grassroots Global Justice Alliance (GGJ) continues to bring delegations of U.S. environmental justice activists to the annual UN climate conferences, while the Labor Network for Sustainability and allied groups work to raise support for climate justice among the ranks of organised labour in the U.S. (ggjalliance.org, labor4sustainability.org).

As European and U.S. activists prepared for the 2009 UN climate conference in Copenhagen, a third complementary approach to climate justice emerged, which represents a continuing evolution of the global justice or "alter-globalisation" movement that arose in opposition to the World Trade Organization and annual global economic summits during the late 1990s and early 2000s. A March 2010 discussion paper from the European Climate Justice Action network (CJA) explained that "Climate Justice means linking all struggles together that reject neoliberal markets and working towards a world that puts autonomous decision making power in the hands of communities." The paper concluded: "Fundamentally, we believe that we cannot prevent further global warming without addressing the way our societies are organized – the fight for climate justice and the fight for social justice are one and the same" (Anonymous 2010a). Although CJA proved to be short-lived, this approach continues to be expressed through ongoing networks such as Rising Tide – which has had chapters in the UK, U.S., Mexico, Ecuador and Australia – as well as offshoots of the historic UK Climate Camp movement, which organised high-profile actions between 2006 and 2010 at major power plant sites, Heathrow Airport and various financial institutions tied to the fossil fuel industry (Rising Tide North America n.d.).

In recent years, larger international NGOs and activist networks such as 350.org have increasingly embraced a climate justice perspective, arousing some controversy among groups that assert a founding stake in the integrity of the concept. Climate justice and indigenous rights were central themes of the massive People's Climate March in New York City in 2014; however, this raised criticism of global networks such as Avaaz that were perceived as diluting the message of the event (Foran 2015). Following the failure of the Paris climate conference in 2015 to agree upon legally binding and enforceable mitigation measures, 350.org allied with groups around the world to initiate a series of protest actions, focused on global centres of fossil fuel production and transport, with a unified message to "Break Free from Fossil Fuels" (breakfree2016.org). These events were noteworthy for their international scope, simultaneously militant and celebratory character, and collaborations between the international network and organised efforts of frontline communities in many countries.

Meanwhile, various newer networks emerged, expressing a more uncompromising climate justice message, particularly in North America. Several organisations led by communities of colour in the U.S. established a Climate Justice Alliance in 2012, promising a nationwide campaign for a just transition away from fossil fuel dependence. They have focused primarily on supporting ongoing community efforts in three locations: the economically depressed former automobile manufacturing centre of Detroit; the oil refinery town of Richmond, California; and the territory of the Navajo nation in the U.S. Southwest, with its long history of resistance to intensive resource extraction (www.ourpowercampaign.org). Following the 2014 People's Climate March in New York, the Alliance held a two-day People's Climate Justice Summit, featuring testimony from frontline community delegations. In 2015, the Alliance joined with GGJ and IEN to bring a delegation of frontline activists to join the civil society protests around the Paris climate summit (Browne and Goldtooth 2016).

During the same period, various anti-capitalist and ecosocialist groups in the U.S. and Canada launched a System Change Not Climate Change network. This network also organised events in New York in 2014, just prior to the People's Climate March, and has organised online seminars and other educational events. Rising Tide North America, along with its counterparts in the UK and Australia, organises extended direct action campaigns against fossil fuel expansion in various locales, while highlighting perceived "false solutions" to global warming and articulating its own counter-systemic political message (risingtidenorthamerica.org). While challenging political dynamics have complicated efforts to forge a fully unified climate justice movement in North America, many activists on the ground remain committed to broader alliance building. One detailed strategy paper by a prominent African American organiser acknowledged underlying tensions, but also encouraged long-term working relationships based on mutual concerns, open sharing of resources and maintaining a stance of "solidarity, not charity," resolutely focused upon the "[e]mpowerment of traditionally disenfranchised groups" (Patterson 2013).

Climate justice and climate diplomacy

In 2009, the UN climate conference in Copenhagen (COP 15) ended in a near-deadlock, with several countries objecting to the side-lining of the Kyoto Protocol's enforceable emissions limits and the substitution of a plan for voluntary national "contributions" to climate mitigation (Tokar 2014, 49–64). Ever since Copenhagen, the annual Conferences of the Parties to the UN Climate Convention (UNFCCC) have featured systematic interventions from civil society groups and some Global South delegations, seeking a justice-centred approach to the ongoing climate negotiations. Between Copenhagen and Paris, delegates from the North and South clashed repeatedly over an array of issues, including the future of Kyoto's emissions limits, mitigation goals and greenhouse gas reduction targets, financing and technology transfers for an energy transition in the Global South, reporting and monitoring requirements, and the nature of the negotiation process itself (Khor 2010). As Northern delegates pushed to retain the carbon markets and other "flexible mechanisms" of the Kyoto Protocol while abandoning mandatory emissions targets, many Southern delegates and civil society representatives took precisely the opposite position.

In April of 2010, Bolivian president Evo Morales sponsored a climate justice-centred "World People's Conference on Climate Change and the Rights of Mother Earth" in the city of Cochabamba. Some 30,000 civil society representatives, social movement actors and public officials from around the world met to draft a comprehensive set of principles, rooted in indigenous views of social and environmental harmony and anti-colonialism. The delegates proposed a Universal Declaration on the Rights of Mother Earth, condemned the use of carbon markets, as well as the commodification of forests for carbon offsets under the UNFCCC's REDD (Reducing Emissions from Deforestation and Degradation of Forests) program, and called for an International Climate and Environmental Justice Tribunal to judge and penalise activities that promote climate change and contaminate the earth (Anonymous 2010b).

At subsequent UN COPs, delegates attempted to bring the substance of the Cochabamba agreements to the table, but were repeatedly blocked by delegates from wealthy countries. As North-South polarisation grew during these years, and most Northern countries outside of Western Europe officially withdrew from the Kyoto Protocol, Global South representatives protested both inside and outside the proceedings, denouncing the suggested 2-degree global warming limit as a "death sentence for Africa, small island states, and the poor and vulnerable worldwide" (quoting Friends of the Earth International chair Nnimmo Bassey, in Petermann and Langelle 2012, 29). In Warsaw in 2013, African delegates walked out of the conference *en masse* to protest their continuing marginalisation in the official proceedings. Concerted efforts to raise the problem of already experienced losses and damages from extreme weather events were dismissed by the Obama administration's lead U.S. climate negotiator Todd Stern (2013) as merely an "ideological narrative of fault and blame," as he simultaneously disparaged the longstanding principle of national responsibility for historic emissions.

The agreement that was eventually reached in 2015 in Paris offered a rhetorical nod to many climate justice concerns, but its substance fell far short of satisfying the substantive concerns of climate justice advocates. The agreement's Preamble referred to the "principle of equity," the reality that some people are "particularly vulnerable" to climate impacts, the rights of indigenous peoples, migrants and children, as well as principles of "gender equality," "intergenerational equity" and the "imperatives of a just transition of the workforce." The Preamble further highlighted the imperative of biodiversity protection, "recognized by some cultures as Mother Earth," and even "the importance for some of the concept of 'climate justice'" (UNFCCC 2015, 21). In contrast, Article 15 of the operational part of the agreement proposed a "mechanism to facilitate implementation and promote compliance," but only in the form of an international "expert-based" committee that is to be "transparent, non-adversarial and non-punitive" (ibid., 29). The revised emissions reduction proposals that signatory countries have pledged to bring to the table in subsequent rounds of negotiation would remain wholly voluntary. The document offered a nod to Global South concerns to address current climate-related losses and damage, but the text explicitly denied "a basis for any liability or compensation" (ibid., 8).

While 188 countries brought proposals for their "Intended Nationally Determined Contributions" to climate mitigation to the table in Paris, independent assessments of the various "contributions" affirmed that the Paris outcome fell far short of what officials had promised. While the text of the agreement confirmed the Copenhagen goal of limiting average global warming to 2 degrees Celsius, and the Preamble pledged to "pursue efforts to limit the temperature increase to 1.5°C above pre-industrial levels" (ibid., 22), two independent research collaboratives projected a global temperature rise between 2.2 and 3.5 degrees Celsius by 2100 if all current pledges were to be fully implemented (www.climateactiontracker.org, www.climateinteractive.org). It is important to note here that a 2-degree diplomatic baseline is by no means a "safe" level of warming, but rather the point at which the likelihood of catastrophic, uncontrollable climate disruptions would reach about 50% (Rogelj et al. 2012; Peters et al. 2013).

Contributions of climate justice

With this celebrated but substantively uncertain diplomatic outcome, combined with the current U.S. administration pledging to withdraw from even its modest commitments under the Paris agreement, climate justice advocates have redoubled their efforts. Bold direct action campaigns have helped halt the construction of coal-fired power plants, major oil and gas pipelines, and the expansion of hydrofracturing ("fracking") technology for fossil fuel extraction in many regions. Innovative cross-sectoral alliances, most notably between climate campaigners and organised labour, have helped raise political support for a more rapid and just transformation of the world's energy and transportation systems (labor4sustainability.org, leapmanifesto.org). Let us now review several of the outstanding contributions that climate justice advocates continue to bring to the wider global movement for climate action.

First and foremost, climate justice campaigners continue to highlight the disproportionate impacts of climate disruptions on the lives and livelihoods of the most vulnerable and politically marginalised populations, from indigenous nations and peasant communities in the South to impoverished urban centres in the Global North. The leadership, priorities and strategic insights of frontline activists are at the centre of effective climate justice organising and lend a far greater urgency to climate action in all its diverse forms.

Second, climate justice advocates bring an understanding that the institutions and economic policies responsible for climate destabilisation are also underlying causes of poverty and economic inequality. For many activists, the built-in growth imperative and increasing concentrations of wealth that are central to modern capitalism are at the roots of both social and environmental problems, and a transition to a more inclusive and democratic economic system is necessary to meaningfully address the climate crisis. Climate justice advocates also remain highly sceptical of efforts to implement climate policies through market mechanisms such as the trading of pollution permits and the creation of carbon offsets, citing the substantive inadequacies of existing carbon trading programs, as well as the long-range consequences of further commodifying the atmosphere (Böhm and Dabbhi 2009).

Third, climate justice brings a broadly intersectional outlook into the climate movement. The concept of "intersectionality" was first proposed by the feminist legal scholar Kimberle Crenshaw (n.d., 2) in an effort to "conceptualize the way the law responded to issues where both race and gender discrimination were involved," and has been embraced by climate justice activists as a means to address the many common threads that link environmental abuses to patterns of discrimination by race, class, gender, sexual orientation and other social factors. This awareness is further reinforced by organisational and interpersonal practices aimed at challenging manifestations of oppression and social hierarchy both within the climate movement and in society at large.

Additionally, many climate justice campaigns strive to link efforts to challenge climate-damaging practices to an alternative vision of a future without fossil fuels. The resistance is symbolised by the term "blockadia," popularised by Naomi Klein (2014, 293–336), and first coined by the nonviolent campaigners of the Texas-based Tar Sands Blockade. Their creative direct actions aimed to block the construction of the controversial Keystone XL pipeline, which would transport oil from the Canadian tar sands in central Alberta to refineries and shipping terminals on the U.S. Gulf Coast. Blockadia is envisioned as a distinct new geographic and political space, replicated throughout the world, where people committed to direct action live and work in a cooperative and liberated fashion. The reconstructive dimensions of the movement are symbolised by the French Basque term "alternatiba," which was adopted as the theme of a bicycle tour that encircled France during the summer of 2015 to highlight scores of local alternative projects in various economic sectors (Combes 2014; alternatiba.eu/en). Many movement actors view the convergence of oppositional and reconstructive strands of activity as a crucial step toward catalysing fundamental changes.

Further, climate justice advocates believe that policy changes need to be substantively driven by the priorities and agendas that emerge from grassroots campaigns. Elite-oriented policymaking, where corporate interests often shape political agendas behind the scenes, has not served the needs of people or the planet, and a new approach, driven from below, is proposed. A related concept, framed mainly by circles of international labour activists, is energy democracy, an agenda for community-based public sector ownership of renewable energy projects and energy distribution utilities. In an era of widespread privatisation of formerly public services, energy democracy represents a distinct counter-narrative. "Renewable energy technologies," according to labour activist and scholar Sean Sweeney (2014, 4), "have the potential to completely transform the global energy system by 2030 and also change the political and class relations around energy production and consumption. But the transition must be planned and coordinated in a democratic manner."

Energy democracy also has the potential to help address the concerns of local opponents of renewable energy installations, who often object to the increasingly massive scale and distant ownership of many wind and solar developments (Phadke 2011; Agnew 2017). While earlier wind power projects in both Europe and the U.S. were often built and owned by local, cooperative entities, today's larger-scaled projects are more likely to be developed by remote corporate owners (Maegard 2010; Shaffer 2016). Larger turbines and installations can be justified by their increased power output and efficiency, but local opposition to larger-scale projects often impedes overall progress toward a renewable future. This reinforces the need for a more genuinely transformative approach.

Future challenges

It is clear that numerous longer-range questions and challenges remain for those committed to a climate justice perspective. How can a movement mainly rooted in local initiatives help catalyse a social and economic transformation capable of addressing the vast magnitude of global climate threats? How can a thoroughgoing energy transition be sustained in a period where the political influence of fossil fuel interests is on the rise in key countries, along with interests that are fundamentally hostile to the public sector of the economy? Can we envision an improved quality of life for most people in the world in a future freed from fossil fuel dependence? And what manner of transitions are feasible in the Global South, where the daily effects of climate disruptions are most apparent, yet the imperatives of poverty-reduction are perennially co-opted by elites who remain focused on economic growth (Bidwai 2012)?

Important differences remain as to what manner of energy transition is most compatible with a climate justice outlook. Could a rapidly accelerated wave of renewable energy development serve to foster job creation and relieve global poverty as promoted by "green growth" advocates (Pollin 2015), or is this incompatible with the worldwide economic contraction projected as necessary by some climate scientists and promoted by European degrowth advocates (Demaria et al. 2013)? Are current strategies to expand the use of renewable energy sources compatible with demands for a just transition, supporting the needs of workers and sustaining models of democratic community control? If the necessary energy and economic transitions prove incompatible with the imperatives of capitalist growth, can more thoroughgoing economic changes occur rapidly enough to prevent climate catastrophe?

Challenging questions raised by climate justice advocates are already impacting current policy debates in the U.S. and beyond. For example, many climate activists agree that measures are necessary to compel polluting industries to pay the costs of their greenhouse gas emissions, but serious differences in approach are impacting political outcomes. A recent ballot initiative for a carbon tax in Washington state in the Pacific Northwest was voted down in 2016, after advocates of a "revenue neutral" proposal – substituting a carbon fee for a portion of existing taxes – were the first to get their initiative onto the state-wide ballot (Roberts 2016). Environmental justice groups, concerned about the disproportionate impacts of energy taxes on low-income households, objected to the lack of dedicated funding to facilitate energy transitions for those individuals and families. Ultimately, those concerns divided mainstream from justice-centred environmentalists, and the proposal was voted down.

In California in 2017, the state legislature approved a long-term renewal of the state's climate policies, centred upon a cap-and-trade system for carbon dioxide emissions permits. Not only did the proposal fail to address the particular needs of people living near centres of concentrated pollution, but the plan further constrained the ability of local and regional pollution control agencies within the state to enact appropriate emissions standards (Murphy 2017). Nationally in the U.S., a carbon tax proposal that has gained the support of prominent Republican Party elders would substantially overturn all other regulation of greenhouse gases by federal agencies (Feldstein et al. 2017). Clearly, such a proposal would grant an unprecedented primacy to market-oriented mechanisms for pollution control and implies an exceptional confidence in the rationality and integrity of capitalist markets. If such policies represent a future standard for "climate pragmatism," those seeking to simultaneously advance the goals of climate action and social justice will face a very long road ahead. However, if climate mitigation can be effectively aligned with the pressing needs of marginalised communities worldwide, it could portend a uniquely comprehensive and effective solution to a considerable array of social and environmental ills.

This chapter has highlighted several essential aspects of climate justice and its continuing contributions to the global movement for climate action, in particular:

- A consistent focus on the disproportionate impacts of climate disruptions on the world's most vulnerable peoples, those who generally contribute the least to excessive emissions of greenhouse gases;
- Various distinct contributions to climate movement strategies, rooted in the outlooks of frontline communities and highlighting the systemic implications of a justice-centred perspective, links to other kindred justice movements and a synthesis of critical and reconstructive approaches to climate action;
- Several challenging political questions that are raised by this perspective, including the problem of economic growth in the emerging energy transition and the implications of policy proposals in the Global North that may tend to sideline justice-centred concerns.

It is hoped that this discussion will help illuminate the continuing relevance of climate justice in today's world and advance more just and equitable approaches to climate policy in Northern and Southern countries alike.

References

Agnew, O. 2017. Vermont and the Meaning of Green. *Nexus Media*. Downloaded 14 July 2017 from https://nexusmedianews.com/vermont-and-the-meaning-of-green-aa5c0b5f7003.

Anonymous. 2002. *10 Principles for Just Climate Change Policies in the US*. Downloaded 14 June 2012 from www.ejnet.org/ej/climatejustice.pdf.

———. 2010a. *What Does Climate Justice Mean in Europe? A Discussion Paper*. Via Climate Justice Action email list, 26 March.

———. 2010b. *People's Agreement*. Cochabamba: World People's Conference on Climate Change and the Rights of Mother Earth. Downloaded 27 June 2012 from http://pwccc.wordpress.com/2010/04/24/peoples-agreement/.

Atapattu, S. 2016. *Human Rights Approaches to Climate Change: Challenges and Opportunities*. London: Routledge.

Battisti, D.S. and R.L. Naylor. 2009. Historical Warnings of Future Food Insecurity With Unprecedented Seasonal Heat. *Science 323*, 240–244.

Bidwai, P. 2012. Climate change, equity and development: India's dilemmas. In N. Hällström, ed., *What Next?: Climate, Development and Equity*. Uppsala: Dag Hammarskjöld Foundation.

Böhm, S. and S. Dabbhi, eds. 2009. *Upsetting the Offset: The Political Economy of Carbon Markets*. London: Mayfly Books.

Browne, J. and T. Goldtooth. 2016. *We Are Mother Earth's Red Line: Frontline Communities Lead the Climate Justice Fight Beyond the Paris Agreement*. Grassroots Global Justice Alliance, Indigenous Environmental Network and Climate Justice Alliance. Via email.

Bruno, K. et al. 1999. *Greenhouse Gangsters vs. Climate Justice*. San Francisco: Transnational Resource & Action Center.

Bullard, R. 2009. *Comments at "Advancing Climate Justice: Transforming the Economy, Public Health and Our Environment" Conference*. New York: Fordham University. 30 January. Personal communication.

Carbon Trade Watch et al. 2004. *Climate Justice Now! The Durban Declaration on Carbon Trading*. Downloaded 11 August 2010 from www.durbanclimatejustice.org/durban-declaration/english.html.

Climate Justice Now. 2007. *What's Missing from the Climate Talks? Justice! Press Release*. Via Durban Group for Climate Justice email list 14 December 2007.

Climate Justice Now. 2008. *Principles of Unity*. Via Climate Justice Now email list 12 May 2008.

Climate Justice Now. 2010. *CJN! Network Members*. Downloaded 10 September 2012 from climate-justice-now.org/category/climate-justice-movement/cjn-members.

Combes, M. 2014. *Towards Paris 2015: Challenges and Perspectives*. Paris: Attac France. 18 November, via email.

Commission for Racial Justice. 1987. *Toxic Wastes and Race in the United States*. New York: United Church of Christ.

CorpWatch US et al. 2002. *Bali Principles of Climate Justice, 29 August 2002*. Downloaded 14 June 2012 from www.ejnet.org/ej/bali.pdf.

Coumou, D. and S. Rahmstorf. 2012. A Decade of Weather Extremes. *Nature Climate Change 2*. 491–496.

Crenshaw, K. n.d. Intersectionality: The Double Bind of Race and Gender. *Perspectives*. Downloaded 9 June 2014. Reprinted in Lindgren, J. R., et al. 2011. *The Law of Sex Discrimination*, Boston: Wadsworth/ Cengage, 455-56.

Demaria, F. 2013. What Is Degrowth? From an Activist Slogan to a Social Movement. *Environmental Values 22*. 191–215.

Feldstein et al. 2017. A Conservative Case for Climate Action. *New York Times*. 8 February.

Fischer, M. and R. Knutti. 2015. Anthropogenic Contribution to Global Occurrence of Heavy-Precipitation and High-Temperature Extremes. *Nature Climate Change 5*. 560–564.

Foran, J. 2015. *Thoughts on the Road to Paris* (Compilation). Downloaded 8 August 2015 from parisclimatejustice. org.

Hansen, J. et al. 2014. *Global Temperature Update Through 2013*. Downloaded 21 January 2014 from columbia.edu.

IPCC. 2007. *Contribution of Working Group II to the Fourth Assessment Report of the Intergovernmental Panel on Climate Change*. Summary for Policymakers. Geneva: Intergovernmental Panel on Climate Change. Downloaded 1 October 2007 from ipcc.ch.

IPCC. 2014a. *Climate Change 2014: Impacts, Adaptation and Vulnerability*. Summary for Policymakers. Geneva: Intergovernmental Panel on Climate Change. Downloaded 30 March 2014 from ipcc.ch.

IPCC. 2014b. *Climate Change 2014: Impacts, Adaptation and Vulnerability*. Technical Summary. Geneva: Inter-governmental Panel on Climate Change. Downloaded 30 March 2014 from ipcc.ch.

Khor, M. 2010. Complex Implications of the Cancun Climate Conference. *Economic and Political Weekly* (Mumbai) *45:52*. 10–15.

Klein, N. 2014. *This Changes Everything: Capitalism vs. the Climate*. New York: Simon & Schuster.

Maegard, P. 2010. Denmark: Politically-Induced Paralysis in Wind Power's Homeland and Industrial Hub. In K. Abramsky, ed., *Sparking A Worldwide Energy Revolution*. San Francisco: AK Press, 489–494.

Min, S.-K. et al. 2011. Human Contribution to More-Intense Precipitation Extremes. *Nature 470*. 378–381.

Munich Re. 2015. *Natural Catastrophes 2014: Analyses, Assessments, Positions*. Munich: Münchener Rück-versicherungs-Gesellschaft/Geo Risks Research Group. Downloaded 8 June 2016 from munichre.com.

Murphy, K. 2017. Debate Rages Over California Cap-and-Trade Deal, Concessions to Big Oil. *San Jose Mercury News*. 11 July. Downloaded 13 August 2017 from mercurynews.com.

Oxfam. 2009. *The Right to Survive: The Humanitarian Challenge for the Twenty-First Century*. London: Oxfam International.

Oxfam. 2017. *A Climate in Crisis: How Climate Change Is Making Drought and Humanitarian Disaster Worse in the Horn of Africa*. 27 April.

Patterson, J. 2013. *And the People Shall Lead: Centralizing Frontline Community Leadership in the Movement Towards a Sustainable Planet*. Washington: NAACP Environmental and Climate Justice Program. Via email.

Parenti, C. 2011. *Tropic of Chaos: Climate Change and the New Geography of Violence*. New York: Nation Books.

Petermann, A. and O. Langelle. 2012. UN Climate Conference. *Z Magazine*. February. 29–33.

Peters, G.P. et al. 2013. The Challenge to Keep Global Warming Below 2 °C. *Nature Climate Change 3*. 4–6.

Phadke, R. 2011. Resisting and Reconciling Big Wind: Middle Landscape Politics in the New American West. *Antipode 43:3*.

Pollin, R. 2015. The New Green Economy, *The Nation*. 16 November. 13–18.

Rising Tide North America, n.d. *Our History*. Downloaded 18 June 2012 from www.risingtidenorthamerica. org/about-rising-tide-north-america/our-history.

Roberts, D. 2016. *The Left vs. a Carbon Tax: The Odd, Agonizing Political Battle Playing Out in Washington State*. Downloaded 18 October 2016 from vox.com/2016/10/18/13012394/i-732-carbon-tax-washington.

Rogelj, J. et al. 2012. Global Warming Under Old and New Scenarios Using IPCC Climate Sensitivity Range Estimates. *Nature Climate Change 2*. 248–253.

Samenow, J. 2016. Fiji Reeling After Devastating Cyclone Winston, Among the Strongest Ever to Strike Land. *Washington Post*. 22 February.

Samson, J. et al. 2011. Geographic Disparities and Moral Hazards in the Predicted Impacts of Climate Change on Human Populations. *Global Ecology and Biogeography 20*. 532–544.

Saragih, H. 2009. *Why We Left Our Farms to Come to Copenhagen*. Downloaded 8 December 2009 from commondreams.org.

Schmidt, G. and D. Arndt. 2017. *Global Temperature Time Series: NOAA GlobalTemp*. NOAA/NASA Annual Global Analysis for 2016. 17 January. Downloaded 21 July 2017 from nasa.gov.

Shaffer, D. 2016. Wind Power Industry Surges, and Expects Steady Growth. *Minneapolis Star Tribune*. 28 January.

Stern, T.D. 2013. *The Shape of a New International Climate Agreement*. Downloaded 10 January 2014 from www.state.gov/e/oes/rls/remarks/2013/215720.htm.

Sweeney, S. 2014. Working Toward Energy Democracy. In Worldwatch Institute, ed., *State of the World 2014: Governing for Sustainability*. Washington: Island Press.

Tokar, B. 2014. *Toward Climate Justice: Perspectives on the Climate Crisis and Social Change*. Porsgrunn, Norway: New Compass.

UNFCCC. 2015. *Adoption of the Paris Agreement, Paris: United Nations Framework Convention on Climate Change*. 12 December. Downloaded 13 December 2015 from unfccc.int.

Watkins, K. 2007. *Human Development Report 2007/2008: Fighting Climate Change: Human Solidarity in a Divided World*. Downloaded 29 November 2007 from undp.org.

3

On inquiry into climate justice

Idil Boran

Introduction

Over a quarter century of multilateral negotiations on climate change reveals why global climate change is, as is often underlined, one of the toughest challenges of our times. On the one hand, accumulated scientific knowledge about the effects of systemic human activity on the atmosphere calls for comprehensive and globally coordinated action. On the other hand, the efforts at the international level are unceasingly confronted by an enormous complexity of the process of collectively transitioning to low-carbon and climate-resilient economies. This complexity is inseparably interwoven with questions of justice (Shue, 1992, 1995, 1999, 2014; Roser & Seidel, 2016; Moellendorf, 2012, 2014; Vogler, 2016, Chapter 5). Global climate change is the result of human activity. Moreover, both the patterns that contribute to climate change and the levels and kinds of vulnerability in the face of its effects are significantly imbalanced across the world. Put differently, anthropogenic global climate change serves as a magnifying mirror reflecting the global imbalances and inequalities. But what proves to be particularly challenging is not so much recognising that climate change raises questions of justice; rather, it is reaching an understanding about how justice is to be envisioned in an age of climate change. Positions begin to bifurcate, leading to a multiplicity of contending visions of justice in the effort to tackle global climate change.

This chapter steps back and displays an overview of the landscape of these bifurcations. It provides neither a full survey of what has been written about climate justice nor a simple catalogue of the arguments and their technicalities.[1] Rather, this chapter is a reflective exploration of the *diversity* of visions of justice. It begins by acknowledging a distinction between two modes of involvement in the pursuit of climate justice: as social movement on one side and as formal inquiry on the other The subsequent section outlines an understanding of climate justice as formal inquiry and explains its theoretical orientation and framework. Equipped with this insight, an exploration of the normative perspectives into climate justice follows. The purpose is to see if the principles and arguments that seemingly differ from one another nevertheless cluster around a theoretical centre, giving this field of inquiry its distinctive but contingent characteristics. The concluding section provides a brief account of new directions for inquiry into climate justice.

Two modes in the pursuit of climate justice: social movement vs. normative inquiry

If one is hard put to find a unified conception of climate justice, it's because there isn't one. The climate justice discourse, broadly understood, is characterised more by its heterogeneity than by a single unifying characteristic. This makes the task of providing a working definition of "climate justice" particularly challenging. Instead of looking for a definition, one may be in a better position to start out by simply recognising climate justice as a complex activity, one that has its basis both in theory and in practice, with varying degrees of emphasis put on one or the other. A predominant feature of this activity is its subjecting the social, political and economic fabric to critical scrutiny against the backdrop of global climate change. The scope of this critical outlook can be domestic, transnational, or global. But most importantly, as an activity, climate justice is not limited to providing a critique of the current state of the world. It is also dedicated to developing as a response a vision of social and political fabric, with its laws and institutions. These observations do not amount to a definition, but they do hint at the ramifications of the critical outlooks that ensue from this vantage point, and a vast array of visions of what might be called a "climate just" world.

In this vast landscape, two different attitudes can be identified. They are distinguishable from one another in that they represent, at bottom, distinct modes of involvement in the pursuit of justice. One could even go further and say that they reflect two different convictions about the sort of activity climate justice is, each with its own assumptions about the political space providing the conduit for its pursuit and about its actors. On one side, there is the pursuit of climate justice as being primarily an endeavour of social practice, a driver of change. Its main preoccupation is with social change. Its site is predominantly that of civil society and activism. This general attitude can be referred to as *climate justice as social movement*, its operative term being "movement." On the other side, there is a body of sustained work whose focus is on climate justice as an object of formal inquiry. This endeavour prioritises the consistency with which conceptions of justice are formulated in light of norms and principles. A principled investigation above all, it is carried out against the backdrop of accumulated knowledge about climate instability due to human activities as well as existing inequalities across the globe that climate change threatens to exacerbate. As cognitive activity, it places a premium on the rigour with which competing formulations are adjudicated, and aims to develop well-rounded conceptions of justice that can withstand the test of rational scrutiny. Its site is that of academic discourses and, as a specialised form of inquiry, it has given rise to a growing body of work in the field of moral and political philosophy. To distinguish this mode from the former, one may refer to it as *climate justice as normative inquiry*, its operative term being "inquiry."

The theory and practice of putting the social fabric under criticism

Inquiry into justice has a long pedigree. Throughout its rich history, a wide array of visions of justice, differing from one another both in form and in essence, have been developed.[2] While a review of conceptions of justice is not within the purview of this chapter, it is worth highlighting some of its key characteristics. Firstly and foremost, the pursuit of justice, as a major theme of political philosophy, stems from a concern with how to best arrange collective life (Miller, 1998). Inquiry consists of examining the social, political and economic fabric in light of standards and ideals to aspire to and of values to live by. Secondly, the pursuit of justice is almost always a response to conflict in the social and political make-up that constitutes the domain of the public. Collective life means a clash of purposes. To think about justice is to engage in a systematic reflection on how to carve out a public realm where conflicting claims can be settled on a footing of mutual respect and guided by principles acceptable to all. Thirdly, and relatedly, to engage in systematic reflection on justice is to put the existing social order, the fabric of law and institutions, under criticism. These are not immutable or exhaustive features. In highlighting them, my goal is to underscore some of the distinguishable features of the pursuit of justice. But this pursuit cannot be complete if it is limited to merely diagnosing the sources of injustice. It must also develop a vision specially designed to eliminate the injustices it has identified. It must begin to lay the foundations of a positive conception of justice. Few put this as clearly as John Rawls, when he writes that among political philosophy's objectives is that of identifying principles capable of giving a sense of orientation in the shaping of public life (Rawls, 2001, p. 3; 2007, p. 10).

What follows is an overview of the debates on climate justice as a formal inquiry that captures these features.[3] This overview is not intended to be a full investigation about all underlying assumptions in the debates and their roots. Instead, I distinguish in outline some of the main points of contention in the contemporary debate on climate justice among normative theorists. The intent is not to cover all that has been written on the subject. As will become clear, the debates over principles of justice have been carried out at a high level of abstraction. In highlighting some of the salient lines of the discussions, one may be able to see a theoretical centre around which principles and arguments that seemingly differ from one another may be so assembled as to bring to light their underlying commonalities.

Intersecting threads of normative inquiry into climate justice

Normative inquiry into climate justice is a very young debate. Earlier work highlighting the moral implications of global warming goes back to the 1990s (e.g., Jamieson, 1992, 1996; Shue, 1992, 1994, 1999; Grubb, 1995; Beckerman & Pasek, 1995). But the turn from sparse scholarly interest to an upsurge of writings forming a distinctive literature in moral and political theory occurred when a global response to climate change proved to be a far slower and more arduous process than many had hoped. A body of work, standardly described broadly as the *climate ethics* literature, began to take shape.[4]

A central tenet of *climate ethics* is the claim that climate change presents, above all, a moral challenge. In a review article published in 2004, Stephen Gardiner makes this point (Gardiner, 2004a), setting the tone for subsequent work (e.g., Brown, 2013; Gardiner & Weisbach, 2016; see also Hayward, 2012; Moellendorf, 2014).[5] But in laying stress on the moral challenge of climate change, theorists do not merely say that climate change is a moral problem. They also imply, directly or indirectly, that in most policy discussions the moral challenge of climate change is not sufficiently recognised. In other words, they register their discontent with the public debates and insist that climate change is treated all too frequently merely as a technical problem. It is either approached as a problem of public administration, to be addressed by policymakers, or as a matter of designing economic policy, to be guided by economists. To look at it from these perspectives is to look at the issue from the wrong angle. The real problem, moral theorists exhort, is that climate change raises a moral problem for the world. Arguments informed by moral principles, not by economic or administrative expediency, should shape policy (Gardiner, 2004a, 2011, 2016; Brown, 2013).[6] Two distinct attitudes arise from these considerations. Some discuss the various ways in which ethics and moral responsibility matter in designing climate policy (e.g., Cafaro, 2011; Moellendorf, 2014). Others embark upon a diagnostic search to elucidate why ethical considerations have not sufficiently informed policy debates (e.g., Brown, 2013). Among those who seek diagnostic arguments, a subset maintains that traditional theories of ethics and political theory are simply not well-equipped to deal with the complexity of climate change. These theorists contend that the major ethical theories such as utilitarianism, deontology, as well as major schools of thought in political theory, such as liberal political theory, lack the resources to deal with the problem of climate change (e.g., Jamieson 2014; Jamieson and Di Paola, 2016).

Inquiry into climate justice stems from this broader discourse on climate ethics. It is intimately interwoven with arguments pertaining to climate ethics as delineated earlier. In fact, the terms "climate ethics" and "climate justice" are frequently used interchangeably as a distinctive feature of this field of inquiry. The central concern of theorists has been with rational justification of moral duties in the face of climate change. Steve Vanderheiden states that climate justice is a query into moral responsibilities (Vanderheiden, 2008a, Chapter 5). For Stephen Gardiner, disregarding climate justice amounts to a violation of ethical norms. Concepts of ethics, such as respect and fairness, he stipulates, are "strongly related to the more general notion of justice" (Gardiner 2016, p. 99). These are not unusual examples, but are representative of the tone and content of the work on climate justice. In short, although the details vary, contemporary theorists tend to regard climate justice as a particular application of climate ethics.[7] Climate ethics forms a broader category, and climate justice a subset that is concerned with proposals for a fair allocation of duties in the response to climate change.[8] As Moellendorf acknowledges, climate justice has come to be equated with inquiry into *how to assign responsibilities* through an international treaty (Moellendorf, 2012, p. 133).[9]

This way of framing the query on climate justice did not simply appear as a revelation. The focus on justification of moral duties can be traced to prior work. In a review article, Darrel Moellendorf elaborates on the influence of the broader global justice debate on the way climate justice is conceptualised (Moellendorf, 2012; see also, Caney, 2005; Moore, 2008; Hayward, 2007, 2009).[10] A review of the global justice debate is not within the scope of this chapter, but it is worth noting that normative inquiry into climate justice inherits from global justice its focus on the justification of moral responsibilities. Broadly, the philosophical debate on global justice is concerned with the scope of moral obligations. A major front in this debate separates two major camps: moral cosmopolitanism on one side and statism on the other. Moral cosmopolitans uphold the principle of moral equality of all. If everyone is a moral equal, then moral obligations extend globally. While statism does not deny moral equality, its adherents accept that limiting obligations of mutual support and cooperation within state borders is justified. This divide has given rise to a heated debate over responsibilities against the backdrop of global inequalities. Cosmopolitans support fair distribution of responsibilities across borders. Against their statist counterparts, they argue that inequalities of income and wealth across the globe ground a responsibility to remedy these inequalities. Because earlier theorists of climate justice were immersed in the debate over moral cosmopolitanism, they saw the distribution of responsibilities about climate change as an extension of the broader global justice debates (e.g., Caney, 2005, 2012; Moore, 2008; Jamieson, 2001; Hayward, 2007, 2009; Vanderheiden, 2008a, Chapter 3, 2009, pp. 269–270). This is not the only source of influence, however. The focus on allocation of responsibilities was also influenced by the multilateral negotiations under the United Nations Framework Convention on Climate Change (UNFCCC) with its focus on equitable burden allocation before and after the signing of the Kyoto Protocol (see, for example, Grubb, 1990, 1995; Grubb, Vrolijk, & Brack, 1999; Paterson & Grubb, 1996; Baer, Fieldman, Athanasiou, & Kartha, 2008; Baer et al., 2000; Baer, 2013a & b Friman, 2016; Vanderheiden, 2008a; see also Boran & Katz, 2017). These two sources of influence – from the global justice literature and from the international negotiations during the Kyoto Protocol era – have built on one another, solidifying an allocation-centrist approach to climate justice.[11]

This theoretical framework left an imprint in the literature. The contending arguments share in common an underlying assumption that the object of climate justice is that of establishing fair allocation of responsibilities regarding the burdens of climate change. This view is so common that Simon Caney simply states that the question of justice is about specifying "who should take responsibility," "who should perform and how much" (Caney, 2016, p. 24). In navigating the terrain, a helpful heuristic is to organise the debates into three pairs of contestations. This is not the only way of organising the competing perspectives on justice, but it is helpful in that it displays how some of the frequently invoked arguments stand in relation to one another. Of these three, the first is the contestation between distributive vs. corrective justice perspectives and, the second, between egalitarianism vs. basic rights. The third represents a more general contestation over whether climate justice should be an instantiation of global justice or of intergenerational justice.

Distributive justice vs. corrective justice

In normative inquiry into climate justice, arguments that appeal to distributive ideal support allocating responsibilities in a way that is sensitive to wealth or income inequalities across the globe. These arguments support a system of cooperation where those who are wealthier are to accept an obligation of justice toward those who are less affluent. By contrast, arguments that appeal to ideals of corrective justice support allocating responsibilities to correct or remedy a wrong, past or present.[12] Distributive and corrective perspectives are not mutually exclusive. In fact, as it will be seen later, they end up supporting strikingly similar conclusions.[13] Theorists tend to agree that a just allocation of duties would hold developed countries responsible and accountable in an international burden-sharing scheme. What distinguishes the two perspectives is the structure of the justificatory argument in support of differentiated burden allocation, holding developed countries morally responsible to take on a heavier burden in the global response to climate change.

Defenders of distributive justice invoke a principle of *ability to pay*. To invoke *ability to pay* is to support an allocation of duties in proportion to economic capacity. It would be unfair, its supporters argue, to expect those who have less resources to pay as much as those who are richer in addressing a shared problem (Shue, 2014, Chapter 9). As a conception of climate justice, ability to pay encapsulates a non-historical and patterned conception of distributive justice. Informed by an idea of distributive justice, it envisions a system of cooperation whereby those who are better off support the less well off. One can see a special affinity with the debate over global justice. Theories of global justice focus on global inequalities around the world and support various distributive proposals to respond to these inequalities (e.g., Moellendorf, 2012; Roberts & Parks, 2007; Shue, 1999, 2014; Caney, 2005, 2010c).

A well-known variant of the corrective justice approach appeals to a *historical responsibility principle*. Its defenders argue that a fair allocation of burdens cannot be indifferent to past practices.[14] Here, historical trends of greenhouse gas emissions, not the level of affluence, serve as the criterion for the allocation of duties. The argument unfolds as follows. Climate change is the outcome of aggregate human activity since industrialisation. The societal make-up of developed countries have their roots in industrialisation, intertwined with a colonial history. Countries and regions that are disproportionately vulnerable to climate risks have neither contributed to this historical trajectory nor fully benefited from it. In the face of climate change, they stand not just vulnerable against its effects but unfairly vulnerable. Developed countries must take on the burden of reducing emissions not so much because they have the means to do so, but because they bear a moral duty to rectify the adverse effects of climate change as beneficiaries of past practices (Neumayer, 2000; Farber, 2007; Miller, 2008; Meyer, 2013).[15]

Both the distributive and corrective justice perspectives have been met with criticism. Against ability to pay, critics point to an ambiguity over whether the duty is to be assigned to states or to individuals (Moellendorf, 2012, p. 136). Given that global cooperation on climate change is to be the result of treaty negotiations, one might assume that states should be the bearers of responsibility, but this implies that responsibility will be devolved to the individual members of states. This opens the way to an argumentative tangle. For, assigning responsibilities to states as such is not sensitive to economic inequalities *within* states. Moreover, one may wonder whether the state system is not in the first place subject to criticism for perpetuating those inequalities that are objectionable from a global justice point of view. Some critics (e.g., Posner & Weisbach, 2010, Chapter 4) argue that global distributive justice is to be discussed on its own ground and should not be annexed into a reflection on climate change policy. Others find this separation unpersuasive, and they insist, as Baer (2013b) does, that questions of climate justice and global inequalities are inescapably intertwined.

Arguments from historical responsibility have been fraught with epistemic difficulties. This is because in order to hold some people morally responsible for an outcome, one must establish a direct causal link between the actions of those people and this outcome. Global climate change is a complex phenomenon resulting in an incremental rise in greenhouse gases (GHGs) in the atmosphere over time. Intuitive at first, one cannot pinpoint to wrongdoers so they can be held accountable for the wrongdoing (Adler, 2007; Caney, 2010b, pp. 125–127; Posner & Weisbach, 2010, Chapter 5). As Steve Vogel explains, the challenge is really a social problem, resulting not from specific actions but from a series of human decisions and practices (Vogel, 2015, p. 202). To try to determine who has caused the wrongdoing, for Vogel, will result in answers that are never satisfactory. Proponents of historical responsibility tend to retort that the point is not about identifying the individuals who might be causally responsible, but rather about assigning moral liability to states, based on their collective historical trends. A recurrent objection to historical responsibility has been to argue that past generations did not know about the effects of industrialisation on the atmosphere, opening a discussion about whether this makes past emissions morally excusable (Bell, 2011b). Others provide a more nuanced criticism and argue that holding states responsible means that the responsibility will be devolved to their current citizens, and it is unclear whether the citizens of a given state deemed to bear a historical responsibility are all responsible in the same way. Some of these may have been actively working on reducing emissions more than others. It seems unfair, critics argue, to hold that these people are not meeting their historical responsibilities even if their governments do not (Posner & Weisbach, 2010, p. 104).

In sum, diverging in many ways, both distributive and corrective approaches seem to converge on one vision. Climate justice is about an equitable allocation of burdens. Allocation has to be differentiated. Developed countries have to assume a heavier burden in a global response to climate change. The disagreements are over the argumentative routes taken to reach this conclusion (Shue, 1999, p. 531).

Egalitarianism vs. basic rights

Egalitarian perspectives support a system of atmospheric equal shares. In contrast, those in the basic rights camp seek to ground moral duties to protect the fundamental interests of those vulnerable to the effects of climate change. This debate differs from the previous one on an important point. In the distinction between distributive justice and corrective justice, both sides start out from a premise that a fair allocation of burdens must be *differentiated*. In the distinction between egalitarianism and basic rights, both sides start out from a premise of equality as a non-differentiated universal moral axiom. Broadly, supporters of equal shares appeal to an equal claim to the atmosphere and defenders of basic rights lend credence to an equal claim to vital interests in health and subsistence.

The egalitarian position on climate justice – also termed *equal atmospheric shares* – starts out from a principle of moral equality. If everyone is a moral equal as a matter of universal principle, then each has an equal moral claim to the Earth's resources. If the absorptive capacity of the atmosphere is a resource that belongs to everyone, and everyone has an equal claim to it, it follows that emission rights should be distributed equally across the world. This idea finds expression in Vanderheiden's work, where he describes the atmosphere as "a shared good to which multiple parties have competing claims, demanding adjudication under the terms of justice" (2008a, p. 104). Of all the approaches to climate change justice, few positions propose a fully fledged system of equal distribution of atmospheric shares as does the equal shares approach. The logic by which the equal shares approach proceeds is fundamentally distributive. It consists of dividing a shared resource into basic units and ensuring that everyone has its fair share. But it is motivated by a specific ideal of fair distribution, one that is founded on thoroughgoing egalitarianism: an *equal division* and allotment of the atmosphere. As with the principle of historical responsibility, the idea of an equal right to access the atmosphere can be traced to the earliest discussions in the international climate negotiations pertaining to the fairness of an international treaty on climate change (Grubb et al., 1992, p. 312; Grubb 1995, p. 485; see also Beckerman & Pasek, 2001, p. 182). Its most committed defenders are Grubb (1995), Vanderheiden (2008a & b) and Singer (2002, 2010); see also Moellendorf (2011), Gosseries (2005) and Baer et al. (2000).

There is an internal debate among supporters of equal shares over whether equal distribution of atmospheric shares should follow a forward-looking or a retrospective logic.[16] Supporters of the forward-looking logic propose to calculate what remains of the atmosphere's absorptive capacity *from now onward* (e.g., Vanderheiden, 2008a). They then propose an equal division of the remaining stock across the current population worldwide. Supporters of the retrospective logic are not satisfied with this suggestion. They argue that an equal distribution must take into account countries' past emissions in the calculation of equal shares (e.g., Grubb, 1995; Neumayer, 2000; Singer, 2002). Simply dividing the atmospheric pie at the present time would not amount to a genuinely egalitarian distribution. After all, developed countries have emitted far in excess of their "historic" equal per capita share, leaving current members of low-emitting states with less. Those with sympathies with this reasoning insist that a system of equal atmospheric shares imposes a moral duty on members of developed countries to accept reduced rights to emit today (e.g., Neumayer, 2000, p. 188).

These conceptions of equal atmospheric rights are countered by proposals for a system of fundamental rights. Defenders of fundamental rights also start out from a universal premise. Their starting moral axiom, however, is not grounded on thoroughgoing egalitarianism but rather on a principle of *human rights*.[17] Its central tenet is that climate change threatens the lives and bodily integrity, health and subsistence of members of communities most vulnerable to its adverse effects. These interests are so fundamental that their protection is matter of human rights. For Caney, for example, a human rights approach identifies *moral thresholds* below which no human being should be allowed to fall. Anthropogenic climate change threatens to breach these moral thresholds (Caney, 2010a; see also, Bell, 2011a; Shue, 2011).

There have been fraught confrontations between defenders of the equal atmospheric shares perspectives on one side and supporters of human rights approaches on the other. Noted in Beckerman and Pasek (2001, p. 180), this tension can be seen clearly in the works of Caney (2010a, 2012), Bell (2011a) and Hayward (2007). Each side insists that their proposed allocation formula is the superior one from a moral point of view. And yet one is led to wonder whether these disputes may not be over small differences.

For example, some defenders of a human rights approach, such as Caney, concede that their position amounts to being a particular allocation of allowances to emit GHGs. They argue that fulfilling fundamental interests (such as meeting the basic needs for subsistence) require emitting GHGs. The most vital interests in subsistence, they argue, entail a right to emit as a matter of human rights (Caney, 2012, pp. 286–287, note 70). Other defenders of a human rights approach prefer separating human rights from emission rights. For example, Hayward (2007) asserts that human rights are not to emissions. It is "the ends of subsistence that are significant for human rights" (p. 441). And perhaps these disputes reveal just how rarefied the debates over the allocation of rights and responsibilities have become. After all, both sides reach the conclusion that developed countries have a moral responsibility toward those who are most vulnerable to climate change, and that this responsibility entails accepting a heavier burden in the response to climate change.[18]

The equal shares approaches have been fraught with numerous difficulties. Some of the disenchantment arises because it makes state-level entitlements depend on population size (Grubb, 1995, p. 485). Countries with a large population, regardless of their level of development or affluence, would receive large entitlements to pollute. Posner and Weisbach raise this issue and point out that states with a larger population will be able to claim more allowances to emit (2010, p. 131). A staunch defender of equal atmospheric shares would rebut this objection by claiming that countries' entitlements depending on their population size is fundamental to the spirit of per capita equal distribution. Nevertheless, this seems unsettling to many defenders of climate change justice. There seems to be a tacit agreement across the spectrum that the developed countries should accept heavier burdens as a matter of climate justice, and allocating responsibilities by any other criterion is potentially a complicating rather than simplifying factor. This is why Vanderheiden, for example, goes no small distance explaining how his defence of equal atmospheric shares is compatible with the tenets of historical responsibility.

Furthermore, the retrospective variant of the equal shares approach is met with the same objections that are typically levelled against the historical responsibility perspective. Its defenders find themselves having to provide an airtight justification of who exactly is causally responsible for the diminished stock of atmospheric shares. But mostly, the equal shares approach gets embroiled in a vortex of difficulties when put under scrutiny. One may wonder, for example, whether seeing the atmosphere as an object to be divided up for balancing rights and entitlements is not itself a problematic proposition. Doing so seems to turn the atmosphere into a heavily commodified entity divisible into portions, very much like a pie. Then, it treats these portions as objects of rights and obligations. Some theorists advance, as Hayward does, that human interactions with the non-human world "occur within a single biophysical reality" (2007, p. 445), and argues that reallocating fair shares is a way of paying off an ecological debt. But this seems to introduce a curiously metaphysical take on the atmosphere. The reasoning appeals to concepts, such as a unified biophysical reality or ecological debt, that seem compelling not because they are demonstrable but because they are unquestionable.[19] And finally, seeing the atmosphere as an object for a reckoning of rights and obligations not only reinforces a commodification of the atmosphere but also reinforces a zero-sum logic where one's gain is the other's loss.

Against the basic rights perspective, objections arise along similar lines to those encountered by the historical responsibility arguments. If the claim is that global climate change causes violation of human rights holding some agents morally responsible for these violations, then critics will want to see a basis for this causal claim. But there is a further challenge. If climate justice is about protecting basic rights, then it concedes to the most minimal forms of protection. But few would disagree that what is needed is much more than attending to the most basic needs. If the goal is comprehensive transformations toward low-carbon and climate-resilient societies, keeping the focus on meeting basic needs sets the sights low, and remains silent on the positive steps needed toward these transformations. The basic rights approach therefore risks committing to a view of justice that is stringent but very limited in scope.

Global justice vs. future generations

So far, we have seen that most of the considerations of climate justice have an affinity with conceptions of global justice. Differing in many ways when it comes to argumentative procedure, they agree in one respect: they all support an allocation of the burdens of climate change as instantiations of global responsibilities. Nevertheless, some theorists are of the view that climate justice cannot be merely about assigning responsibility against the backdrop of global inequalities, but should also be about responsibilities toward future generations.

This proposition opens up into an intricate interplay between global justice and intergenerational justice perspectives. Some work on climate justice puts emphasis on an intergenerational outlook (e.g., Gardiner, 2004a&b, 2011), while others aim to incorporate both global and intergenerational outlooks (e.g., Vanderheiden, 2008a; Gosseries, 2005). Gardiner presents climate change as being not only a global challenge raising questions of international fairness but also an intergenerational one (Gardiner, 2011). Vanderheiden is concerned with a global system of equal atmospheric shares, but also incorporates sustained discussions on taking into account intergenerational cooperation, and discusses the analytic challenges it poses (Vanderheiden, 2008a, Chapter 4). And yet, in their attempts to present a picture of climate justice that is sensitive to both global inequalities and to the projected interests of future generations, these authors also reveal a tension between the global and intergenerational outlooks. When Gardiner suggests that climate change presents an intergenerational challenge, for example, he also implies that looking at climate change as a matter of intra-generational equity misses the point. This is another way of saying that the intergenerational problem is the more pressing one of the two. Indeed, in an earlier essay, Gardiner states that the intergenerational challenge is the *real* challenge (Gardiner, 2001). Allocation of moral responsibility should be guided, instead or as much, he insists, by a sense of obligation toward future generations.

The question of obligations to future generations is a broader question that predates the debate over climate justice.[20] On climate change, the debate over intergenerational justice and responsibilities toward future generations developed into two parallel and rarely intersecting branches.

One branch has its origins in an earlier debate over the economics of climate policy. It is about whether the costs of combating climate change should be discounted. A highly technical question, discounting is primarily about rational justification of time-gaining strategies. It asks whether, and how much, action should be taken today for benefits to be gained in the future. With the publication of the Stern Report (Stern, 2007), who argued against postponing action on climate change, discounting became a central question. Stern's arguments were countered by Nordhaus, who responded with arguments for more modest expenditures today (Nordhaus, 2007, 2008).[21] The response of moral theorists has been to question any time-gaining strategy on the basis that it disvalues the interests of future generations (Davidson, 2015; Caney, 2008; see also, Posner & Weisbach, 2010, Chapter 7).

Another branch focuses on responsibilities toward future generations more broadly. The concern is whether responsibilities can be meaningfully grounded toward people who do not exist today. This question becomes thorny because most conceptions of justice require tangible holders, or claimants, or rights. Since future generations do not yet exist, it seems unclear how they can claim or hold rights. This leads some to focus on a clash of interests between generations. On the one hand, it seems to be in the interest of *future* generations if the current generation assumed intergenerational duties toward them and reduced greenhouse emissions accordingly.

On the other hand, it seems to be in the interest of the *current* generation to delay climate action. Rather than analysing this question as a matter of economic cost balancing, moral theorists regard it as a clash of moral interests and responsibilities, as exemplified in Gardiner's concept of an intergenerational tragedy of the commons (Gardiner, 2001, 2011). Intricate disputes arise about whether there is a moral basis at all for a system of rights and responsibilities across generations (see, Beckerman & Pasek, 2001; Page, 2006, 2008; McKinnon, 2012).[22]

Arguments in favour of responsibilities toward future generations are also fraught with difficulties. Above all, there is a real danger in entertaining visualisations of future people as moral interlocutors. Since the picture is necessarily that of an imagined future, the projections and visualisations almost always end up reflecting what the theorist wanted to see all along. Once again, claims about what kind of life future generations will live become undeniable, not because they are demonstrable, but because they are unquestionable. To any undertaking that has the pursuit of rigour as its hallmark, this is a serious concern. Projected considerations about the lives of future generations risk creating parallel worlds to try out various abstracted arguments. But this is also when theories of climate justice risk detracting attention from the concrete work that needs to be done before the world runs out of the carbon budget.

The future of normative inquiry on climate justice

Normative inquiry into climate justice has not prioritised empirical examinations assessing the workability of its propositions. The debates are rich in arguments but poor in case studies. The proposals put forth are assessed on the basis of the power of their normative premises, the argumentative strength of the justifications backing their conclusions, and how well they respond to objections levelled against them. This does not mean that there are no concrete lessons to learn, however. Perhaps the most telling laboratory case in the last decade is the re-orientation that has taken place in the UN-led international climate negotiations process. In Copenhagen in 2009, the first round of negotiations for a replacement to the Kyoto Protocol catapulted into a near-death experience. This was a wakeup call. After this point, it became exceedingly clear that continuing on the same path, following the same logic, which consists of looking for an international agreement on negotiated economy-wide targets, will simply not put the world on track. The difficulties experienced could not be explained just as a matter of feasibility. To think so would be to assume that feasibility is a fixed point independent of collective imagination and resolve. Exploring a new logic, one that moves away from a hierarchical architecture to a facilitative one, where all put in their best contribution, was a feat of political and diplomatic imagination. This is why the Paris Agreement, adopted in 2015 after several years of intense work, is seen by many as opening a new path. The UN Sustainable Development Goals adopted the same year broaden the scope of actions through intertwining threads of climate and sustainability pathways. In this process, a lesson learned is the structure of the normative debate on climate justice – with its proposals to allocate responsibilities between developing countries, on one side, and wealthy countries, on the other – bears the unmistakable marks of a distinctive period in the history of the international effort on climate change. The facilitative spirit of the intergovernmental process reflects a marked effort to move beyond this binary frame and respond to the wide diversity of circumstances, needs and priorities across borders and regions, as well as changing emission patterns. Whether and how it succeeds is to be seen, and much depends on the actions of both state and non-state actors.

Against this dynamic backdrop, normative inquiry into climate justice will also need to rethink its parameters. Some may be tempted to think that justice and equity are no longer central, and that the Paris Agreement's architecture is all about implementation. It is a mistake to think this way. As Klinsky et al. (2017) aptly remark, justice will always remain central to the climate effort. It will move in new directions and explore new questions that the allocation-centric approaches left unexplored. Indeed, recent work began to propose to reorient the focus away from allocation to embedding norms of justice in the processes of political dialogue (e.g., Breakey, 2015; Boran, 2017). Others are reflecting on questions of justice as the process moves toward a multi-actor climate engagement (e.g., Kuyper, Linnér, & Schroeder, 2018). And yet others are exploring a concept of just transition focused on social justice concerns (e.g., Patterson et al., 2018). None of these new directions are mutually exclusive. More importantly, these newer perspectives are still coarse and preliminary, but they show that inquiry into climate justice is not inert. New perspectives need to be tried out and new domains of climate justice explored.

Acknowledgements

Parts of this chapter rely on the *Routledge Encyclopaedia of Philosophy* entry on "Climate Change Justice," co-written with Corey Katz (Boran & Katz, 2017). While these parts have been largely re-written, Corey Katz's contribution to this background work is duly acknowledged. This chapter was written during a research visit at the *German Development Institute/Deutsches Institut für Entwicklungspolitik*, Bonn. I am grateful for the warm hospitality with which I was received. In particular, I am indebted to Sander Chan for the many conversations and collaborations. Special thanks are due to Dawn Bazely at York University for accrediting me to the UN Climate Change meetings as an observer for consecutive years. I wish to acknowledge Dan McArthur and anonymous reviewers for their questions and suggestions on an earlier draft.

Notes

1 For an encyclopaedic review, see Boran and Katz (2017); a book-length introduction of normative inquiry into climate justice is Roser and Seidel (2016); a comprehensive defence is provided by Shue (2014); Moellendorf (2012) reviews the issues in relation to global justice; for a review of climate justice from a human rights perspective, see Bell (2013); a treatment from an international theory perspective is Vogler (2016, Chapter 5); for critical approaches, see Posner and Weisbach (2010). See also Grubb (1995) for an earlier account of key issues of equity and justice arising from climate change.

2 For historical overviews, see Wolin (2004); Dunn (1996); Rawls (2007). For an account of recent debates, see Kymlicka (2002).

3 This outline is based on the *Routledge Encyclopedia of Philosophy* entry titled "Climate Change Justice," co-authored with Corey Katz (Boran & Katz, 2017). Corey Katz's contributions to this background work are duly acknowledged.

4 Volumes compiling papers providing normative discussions of climate justice from various perspectives include Vanderheiden (2008b); Gardiner et al. (2010); Arnold (2011). Some prominent monographs that set the tone for the normative debate over climate justice include Gardiner (2011); Vanderheiden (2008a); Moellendorf (2014). For a discussion of climate ethics and the connection drawn between ethics and climate justice, see Gardiner (2004a); Brown (2013); Singer (2002).

5 Gardiner and Weisbach (2016) is a book in debate format containing stand-alone writings by two authors in opposite camps. Arguments in defence of climate ethics find expression in Part I. Part II levels criticisms against climate ethics by driving home feasibility concerns arising in the context of international politics.

6 Moellendorf (2014) outlines a more moderate version of this claim. For Moellendorf, moral perspectives on climate policy can be articulated without claiming exclusivity. Gardiner (2004a&b, 2011, 2016) and Brown (2013), however, hold a stronger disjunctive view, one that requires a choice between either a moral outlook or an outlook from other specialised disciplines, economics, public administration, etc. They insist that the economic or public administration lens brings in disciplinary biases, distorts the problems and proposes false solutions. Critics point out in return, as Beckerman and Pasek do, that "claiming to be moralists is no guarantee that one's particular views are, in fact justified, or even 'moral' by most people's standards." Human history is only too full of horrific suffering, they aver, "inflicted by some human beings

on some other human beings acting out of what they thought were the highest moral considerations, such as saving the victims' souls" (Beckerman & Pasek, 2001, p. 7). What exactly is the moral dimension of climate change is one of the unresolved questions at the heart of the climate justice debates.

7 In political philosophy, this assumption is contested. For a critical discussion, see Ripstein (2009).

8 Here, use of the term "response to climate change" is deliberately vague. In the earlier years of the international treaty negotiations, it was common to focus almost exclusively on mitigation efforts to prevent climate change. Multilateral negotiations under the UNFCCC leading up to the first climate agreement – the Kyoto Protocol – were predominantly focused on mitigation, as emission reduction pathways. As time went on, it became increasingly accepted that a response to climate change cannot be limited to mitigation efforts, but must also include adaptation, finance, as well as a mechanism for loss and damage. The Paris Agreement adopted in 2015 and ratified in 2016, reflect this diversification. Additionally, interconnections between the response to climate change and sustainable development are increasingly being recognised after the adoption of the Sustainable Development Goals in 2015.

9 Equating climate justice with fairness in the allocation of responsibilities pertaining to the costs or burdens of climate change is a paradigmatic assumption in the climate change ethics literature. This tendency is so common that Caney simply uses the term "climatic responsibilities" as the primary question of climate justice (Caney, 2012, pp. 257–258). The emphasis is sometimes put on rights as much as on responsibilities. Caney, as with other theorists, alternates between rights and responsibilities. Indeed, the two concepts mirror one another. The justification of rights generates an obligation for others to respect these rights. Conversely, moral responsibilities can be justified by appeal to rights. Whether focused on rights or on responsibilities, the key question is over how to distribute or allocate them. See, for example, Beckerman and Pasek (1995, 2001, Chapter 10), Caney (2005, 2010c, 2012), Shue (1999, 2014), McKinnon (2015), Miller (2008), Moore (2008), Vanderheiden (2008a, 2009), Hayward (2007), Page (2008), Baer et al. (2000).

10 A review of the global justice literature is not within the scope of this chapter. For an overview, see Brooks (2008). For an accessible critical overview, see Scheffler (2014).

11 This is not to suggest that theorists agree with the outcomes of the multilateral negotiations. Many are fiercely critical of the UNFCCC process (e.g., Gardiner, 2004b). It is to suggest that the debate over what climate justice requires, and how equity and fairness is to be conceptualised in an international agreement, did not arise within a theoretical vacuum. The debate has been considerably influenced by the particular way in which demands for equity were voiced in the international climate negotiations surrounding the Kyoto Protocol. Historical responsibility, for example, was invoked in early negotiations and slowly gained "recognition during the late 1990s as an important node for negotiating differentiation" (Friman, 2016, p. 286). Also referred to as the Brazilian Proposal, historical responsibility has been voiced as a way of operationalising the principle of common but differentiated responsibilities. For a catalogue of allocation models invoked in the UNFCCC, see Bodansky (2004). For earlier considerations of allocation models predating the formal treaty negotiations, see Epstein and Gupta (1990).

12 This approach can also be termed "remedial justice." The idea of remedial justice finds expression in Miller (2008). In the climate justice literature, however, "corrective justice" is more commonly used. See, for example, Posner and Weisbach (2010, Chapter 5); Adler (2007).

13 See, for example, Shue (1999). Some theorists discuss both ideals. See, for example, Meyer and Roser (2006), Meyer (2013).

14 It is not uncommon for arguments for historical responsibility to appeal to the polluter pays principle. See, for example, Caney (2010c), Neumayer (2000, p. 187). However, the polluter pays principle can also ground allocating responsibilities in a non-retrospective manner. A forward-looking formulation in light of a polluter pays principle finds expression in the works of Henry Shue. See, for example, Shue (1999, p. 534).

15 Note that Neumayer (2000) provides an argument for historical responsibility that overlaps with equal atmospheric shares. His arguments illustrate how the different perspectives on allocative formulae are not mutually exclusive. For a review of the historical responsibility arguments both in the literature and in climate negotiations in the Kyoto era, see also, Friman (2016).

16 Grubb refers to this dichotomy as "contemporary and historical per capita allocations," respectively (1995, p. 485).

17 It should be noted that there are two lines of inquiry into human rights (Forst, 2016, p. 22). One consists of outlining legal duties based in international human rights. In this vein, the human rights approach consists of "locating the idea of human rights in international political and legal practice" (Forst, 2016, p. 22). The other is to examine the moral basis of human rights and develop arguments that ground a

duty to protect basic and urgent interests. In the climate justice literature, the latter attracts defenders. See, for example, Caney (2010a); Bell (2011a).

18 The exception is a position called *grandfathering*. This is the view that special allowances should be given to developed countries. The reasoning is that high-emitting countries have a carbon dependence, and that abrupt emission reduction policies can be disruptive if detrimental. Grandfathering proposes a particular reading of a system of atmospheric shares, where developed countries would be provided extra allowances. Support for grandfathering is rare on grounds of justice. See Bovens (2011) for one such defence. For a critical take, see Hayward (2007, p. 449).

19 For a critique of the use of metaphysical concepts in environmental philosophy, see Vogel (2015, Chapter 1).

20 For earlier work, see Hubin (1976); Schwartz (1978). For general introductions and analyses, see Gosseries and Meyer (2009); Thompson (2009). Note that the term *intergenerational* includes both future and past generations, and some scholars include, as Janna Thompson does, questions of historical responsibilities in their studies of intergenerational justice (Thompson, 2009). These questions are usually taken up as broader questions, which may include, but are not limited to, responsibilities regarding climate change.

21 The technical details of this debate are not within the scope of this chapter. For an accessible critical discussion, see Posner and Weisbach (2010, pp. 146–149).

22 For a critical response, see Heath (2013).

References

Adler, M. D. (2007). Corrective justice and liability for global warming. *University of Pennsylvania Law Review, 155*, 1859–1867.

Arnold, D. G. (2011). *The ethics of global climate change*. Cambridge: Cambridge University Press.

Baer, P. (2013a). The greenhouse development rights framework for global burden sharing: Reflection on principles and prospects. *Wiley Interdisciplinary Reviews: Climate Change, 4*(1), 61–71.

Baer, P. (2013b). Who should pay for climate change? "Not me." *Chicago Journal of International Law, 13*, 507–525.

Baer, P., Fieldman, G., Athanasiou, T., & Kartha, S. (2008). Greenhouse development rights: Towards an equitable framework for global climate policy. *Cambridge Review of International Affairs, 21*(4), 649–669.

Baer, P., Harte, J., Haya, B., Herzog, V. A., Holdren, J., Hultman, N. E., . . . Raymond, L. (2000). Equity and greenhouse gas responsibility. *Science, 289*(5488), 2287–2287.

Beckerman, W., & Pasek, J. (1995). The equitable international allocation of tradable carbon emission permits. *Global Environmental Change, 5*(5), 405–413.

Beckerman, W., & Pasek, J. (2001). *Justice, posterity, and the environment*. Oxford: Oxford University Press.

Bell, D. (2011a). Does anthropogenic climate change violate human rights? *Critical Review of International Social and Political Philosophy, 14*, 99–124.

Bell, D. (2011b). Global climate justice, historic emissions, and excusable ignorance. *The Monist, 94*, 391–411.

Bell, D. (2013). Climate change and human rights. *Wiley Interdisciplinary Reviews: Climate Change, 4*(3), 159–170.

Bodansky, D. (2004). International climate efforts beyond 2012: A survey of approaches. *Pew Center on Global Climate Change*. Retrieved 4 September 2017, from www.c2es.org/publications/international-climate-efforts-beyond-2012-survey-approaches.

Boran, I. (2017). Principles of public reason in the UNFCCC: Rethinking the equity framework. *Science and Engineering Ethics, 23*(5), 1253–1271.

Boran, I., & Katz, C. (2017). Climate change justice. In *The Routledge encyclopedia of philosophy*. Taylor and Francis. Retrieved 28 August 2017, from www.rep.routledge.com/articles/thematic/climate-change-justice/v-1.

Bovens, L. (2011). A Lockean defense of grandfathering emission rights. In D. G. Arnold (Ed.), *The ethics of global climate change* (pp. 124–144). Cambridge: Cambridge University Press.

Breakey, H. (2015). COP20's ethical fallout: The perils of principles without dialogue. *Ethics, Policy & Environment, 18*(2), 155–168.

Brooks, T. (Ed.). (2008). *The global justice reader*. London: Wiley Blackwell.

Brown, D. (2013). *Climate change ethics: Navigating the perfect moral storm*. Abington, Oxon.: Routledge.

Cafaro, P. (2011). Beyond business as usual: Alternative wedges to avoid catastrophic climate change and create sustainable societies. In D. G. Arnold (Ed.), *The ethics of global climate change* (pp. 192–215). Cambridge: Cambridge University Press.

Caney, S. (2005). Cosmopolitan justice, responsibility, and global climate change. *Journal of International Law*, *18*, 747–775.

Caney, S. (2008). Human rights, climate change, and discounting. *Environmental Politics*, *17*(4), 536–555.

Caney, S. (2010a). Climate change, human rights, and moral thresholds. In S. Gardiner, S. Caney, D. Jamieson, & H. Shue (Eds.), *Climate ethics: Essential readings* (pp. 163–177). Oxford: Oxford University Press.

Caney, S. (2010b). Cosmopolitan justice, responsibility, and global climate change. In S. Gardiner, S. Caney, D. Jamieson, & H. Shue (Eds.), *Climate ethics: Essential readings* (pp. 122–145). Oxford: Oxford University Press.

Caney, S. (2010c). Climate change and the duties of the advantaged. *Critical Review of International Social and Political Philosophy*, *13*(1), 203–228.

Caney, S. (2012). Just emissions. *Philosophy & Public Affairs*, *40*(4), 255–300.

Caney, S. (2016). Climate change and non-ideal theory. In C. Heyward & D. Roser (Eds.), *Climate Justice in a Non-Ideal World* (pp. 21–42). Oxford: Oxford University Press.

Davidson, M. D. (2015). Climate change and the ethics of discounting: Climate change and the ethics of discounting. *Wiley Interdisciplinary Reviews: Climate Change*, *6*(4), 401–412.

Dunn, J. (1996). *The history of political theory and other essays*. Cambridge: Cambridge University Press.

Epstein, J. M., & Gupta, R. (1990). *Controlling the greenhouse effect: Five global regimes compared*. Washington, DC: Brookings Institution.

Farber, D. A. (2007). Basic compensation for victims of climate change. *University of Pennsylvania Law Review*, *155*(6), 1605.

Forst, R. (2016). The point and ground of human rights. In D. Held & P. Maffettone (Eds.), *Global political theory* (pp. 22–39). Malden, MA: Polity.

Friman, M. (2016). Consensus rationales in negotiating historical responsibility for climate change. *International Environmental Agreements*, *16*, 285–305.

Gardiner, S. (2001). The real tragedy of the commons. *Philosophy & Public Affairs*, *30*(4), 387–416.

Gardiner, S. (2004a). Ethics and global climate change. *Ethics*, *114*(3), 555–600.

Gardiner, S. (2004b). The global warming tragedy and the dangerous illusion of the Kyoto protocol. *Ethics & International Affairs*, *18*(1), 23–39.

Gardiner, S. (2011). *A perfect moral storm: The ethical tragedy of climate change*. New York, NY: Oxford University Press.

Gardiner, S. M. (2016). In defence of climate ethics. In S. M. Gardiner & D. A. Weisbach (Eds.), *Debating climate ethics* (pp. 2–130). New York: Oxford University Press.

Gardiner, S., Caney, S., Jamieson, D., & Shue, H. (Eds.) (2010). *Climate ethics: Essential readings*. Oxford: Oxford University Press.

Gardiner, S., & Weisbach, D. (2016). *Debating climate ethics*. New York, NY: Oxford University Press.

Gosseries, A. (2005). Cosmopolitan luck egalitarianism and the greenhouse effect. *Canadian Journal of Philosophy*, *35*(suppl.1), 279–309.

Gosseries, A., & Meyer, L. H. (2009). *Intergenerational justice*. Oxford: Oxford University Press.

Grubb, M. (1990). *Energy policies and the greenhouse effect* (Volumes 1 & 2). London, UK; Aldershot, Hants, UK; Brookfield, VT: Royal Institute of International Affairs.

Grubb, M., Sebenius, J., Magalhaes, A., & Subak, S. (1992). Sharing the burden. In I. M. Mintzer (Ed.), *Confronting climate change: Risks, implications, and responses* (pp. 305–322). Cambridge: Cambridge University Press.

Grubb, M. (1995). Seeking fair weather: Ethics and the international debate on climate change. *International Affairs*, *71*(3), 463–496.

Grubb, M., Vrolijk, C., & Brack, D. (1999). *The Kyoto protocol: A guide and assessment*. London; Washington, DC: Royal Institute of International Affairs, Energy and Environmental Programme; Distributed in North America by the Brookings Institution.

Hayward, T. (2007). Human rights versus emissions rights: Climate justice and the equitable distribution of ecological space. *Ethics & International Affairs*, *21*(4), 431–450.

Hayward, T. (2009). International political theory and the global environment: Some critical questions for liberal cosmopolitans. *Journal of Social Philosophy*, *40*(2), 276–295.

Hayward, T. (2012). Climate change and ethics. *Nature Climate Change*, *2*(12), 843–848.

Heath, J. (2013). The structure of intergenerational cooperation. *Philosophy & Public Affairs*, *41*(1), 31–66.

Hubin, D. C. (1976). Justice and future generations. *Philosophy & Public Affairs*, *6*(1), 70–83.

Jamieson, D. (1992). Ethics, public policy, and global warming. *Science, Technology & Human Values*, *17*(2), 139–153.

Jamieson, D. (1996). Ethics and intentional climate change. *Climatic Change, 33*, 323–336.

Jamieson, D. (2001). Climate change and global environmental justice. In C. A. Miller & P. N. Edwards (Eds.), *Changing the atmosphere: Expert knowledge and environmental governance*. Cambridge, MA: MIT Press.

Jamieson, D. (2014). *Reason in a dark time: Why the struggle against climate change failed – and what it means for our future*. Oxford: Oxford University Press.

Jamieson, D., & Di Paola, M. (2016). Political theory for the anthropocene. In D. Held & P. Maffettone (Eds.), *Global political theory* (pp. 254–280). Malden, MA: Polity.

Klinsky, S., Roberts, T., Huq, S., Okereke, C., Newell, P., Dauvergne, P., . . . Bauer, S. (2017). Why equity is fundamental in climate change policy research. *Global Environmental Change, 44*, 170–173.

Kuyper, J. W., Linnér, B.-O., & Schroeder, H. (2018). Non-state actors in hybrid global climate governance: Justice, legitimacy, and effectiveness in a post-Paris era. *Wiley Interdisciplinary Reviews: Climate Change, 9*(1), e497.

Kymlicka, W. (2002). *Contemporary political philosophy: An introduction* (2nd ed.). Oxford: Oxford University Press.

McKinnon, C. (2012). *Climate change and future justice: Precaution, compensation, and triage*. Abingdon, Oxon: Routledge.

McKinnon, C. (2015). Climate justice in a carbon budget. *Climatic Change, 133*(3), 375–384.

Meyer, L. H. (2013). Why historical emissions should count *Chicago Journal of International Law, 13*(2), 597–614.

Meyer, L. H., & Roser, D. (2006). Distributive justice and climate change. The allocation of emission rights. *Analyse & Kritik, 28*(2), 223–249.

Miller, D. (1998). Political philosophy. In *The Routledge encyclopedia of philosophy*. Taylor and Francis. Retrieved 4 September 2017, from www-rep-routledge-com.ezproxy.library.yorku.ca/articles/overview/political-philosophy/v-1.

Miller, D. (2008). Global justice and climate change: How should responsibilities be distributed. *The Tanner Lectures on Human Values*. Retrieved 21 August 2018, from https://tannerlectures.utah.edu/_documents/a-to-z/m/Miller_08.pdf

Moellendorf, D. (2011). Common atmospheric ownership and equal emissions entitlements. In D. G. Arnold (Ed.), *The ethics of global climate change* (pp. 104–123). Cambridge: Cambridge University Press.

Moellendorf, D. (2012). Climate change and global justice. *WIREs Climate Change, 3*, 131–143.

Moellendorf, D. (2014). *The moral challenge of dangerous climate change: Values, poverty, and policy*. Cambridge: Cambridge University Press.

Moore, M. (2008). Global justice, climate change and Miller's theory of responsibility. *Critical Review of International Social and Political Philosophy, 11*, 501–517.

Neumayer, E. (2000). In defence of historical accountability for greenhouse gas emissions. *Ecological Economics, 33*(2), 185–192.

Nordhaus, W. D. (2007). A review of the Stern review on the economics of climate change. *Journal of Economic Literature, 45*(3), 686–702.

Nordhaus, W. D. (2008). *A question of balance: Weighing the options on global warming policies*. New Haven, CT: Yale University Press.

Page, E. A. (2006). *Climate change, justice and future generations*. Cheltenham, UK; Northampton, MA: Edward Elgar.

Page, E. A. (2008). Distributing the burdens of climate change. *Environmental Politics, 17*(4), 556–575.

Paterson, M., & Grubb, M. (Eds.). (1996). *Sharing the effort: Options for differentiating commitments on climate change; Report of a workshop held at the Royal Institute of International Affairs, London June 1996*. London: Royal Institute of International Affairs.

Patterson, J. J., Thaler, T., Hoffmann, M., Hughes, S., Oels, A., Chu, E., . . . Jordan, A. (2018). Political feasibility of 1.5°C societal transformations: The role of social justice. *Current Opinion in Environmental Sustainability, 31*, 1–9.

Posner, E., & Weisbach, D. (2010). *Climate change justice*. Princeton, NJ: Princeton University Press.

Rawls, J. (2001). *Justice as fairness: A restatement* (E. Kelly, Ed.). Cambridge, MA: Harvard University Press.

Rawls, J. (2007). *Lectures on the history of political philosophy* (S. Freeman, Ed.). Cambridge, MA: Belknap Press of Harvard University Press.

Ripstein, A. (2009). *Force and freedom: Kant's legal and political philosophy*. Cambridge, MA: Harvard University Press.

Roberts, J. T., & Parks, B. C. (2007). *A climate of injustice: Global inequality, North-South politics, and climate policy*. Cambridge, MA: MIT Press.

Roser, D., & Seidel, C. (2016). *Climate justice: An introduction.* Abingdon, Oxon: Routledge.

Scheffler, S. (2014). The idea of global justice: A progress report. *Harvard Review of Philosophy, 20,* 17–35.

Schwartz, T. (1978). Obligations to posterity. In R. I. Sikora & B. Barry (Eds.), *Obligations to future generations* (pp. 3–13). Philadelphia, PA: Temple University Press.

Shue, H. (1992). The unavoidability of justice. In A. Hurrell & B. Kingsbury (Eds.), *The international politics of the environment: Actors, interests, and institutions* (pp. 373–393). Oxford: Oxford University Press.

Shue, H. (1994). After you: May action by the rich be contingent upon action by the poor? *Indiana Journal of Global Legal Studies, 1,* 325–353.

Shue, H. (1995). Ethics, the environment and the changing international order. *International Affairs, 71,* 453–461.

Shue, H. (1999). Global environment and international inequality. *International Affairs, 75,* 531–545.

Shue, H. (2011). Human rights, climate change, and the trillionth ton. In D. G. Arnold (Ed.), *The ethics of global climate change* (pp. 292–314). Cambridge: Cambridge University Press.

Shue, H. (2014). *Climate justice: Vulnerability and protection.* Oxford: Oxford University Press.

Singer, P. (2002). *One world: The ethics of globalization.* New Haven, CT: Yale University Press.

Singer, P. (2010). One atmosphere. In S. Gardiner, S. Caney, D. Jamieson, & H. Shue (Eds.), *Climate ethics: Essential readings* (pp. 181–199). Oxford: Oxford University Press.

Stern, N. H. (Ed.). (2007). *The economics of climate change: The Stern review.* Cambridge: Cambridge University Press.

Thompson, J. (2009). *Intergenerational justice: Rights and responsibilities in an intergenerational polity.* New York, NY: Routledge.

Vanderheiden, S. (2008a). *Atmospheric justice: A political theory of climate change.* Oxford, UK: Oxford University Press.

Vanderheiden, S. (2008b). Climate change, environmental rights, and emissions shares. In S. Vanderheiden (Ed.), *Political theory and global climate change* (pp. 3–66). Cambridge, MA: MIT Press.

Vanderheiden, S. (2009). Allocating ecological space. *Journal of Social Philosophy, 40*(2), 257–275.

Vogel, S. (2015). *Thinking like a mall: Environmental philosophy after the end of nature.* Cambridge, MA: MIT Press.

Vogler, J. (2016). *Climate change in world politics.* Energy, Climate and the Environment. Basingstoke, Hampshire, UK; New York, NY: Palgrave Macmillan.

Wolin, S. (2004). *Politics and vision: Continuity and innovation in western political thought.* Princeton, NJ: Princeton University Press.

4

Fact-insensitive thought experiments in climate ethics

Exemplified by Parfit's non-identity problem

Jörg Tremmel

Introduction

A thought experiment is a deviation or abstraction from reality, much as a "model" is a simplification. The latter is never a completely true representation of the real system, which is far too complex to replicate in its entirety. It is for this reason that Box and Draper (1987) wrote, "essentially, all models are wrong, but some are useful."[1] This sentence applies to thought experiments, too.

This article is devoted to the methodological status of the non-identity problem in the context of climate ethics (as a shorthand, the term "climate non-identity problem," C-NIP, is used).[2] The next section contemplates thought experiments in general. The subsequent section zeros in on the NIP and distinguishes between the C-NIP in the formulations of Derek Parfit and the NIP in other areas. The task of that section is to argue that there is a cogent counterargument against the C-NIP that has so far been widely overlooked by the proponents of the Parfitian account of the C-NIP. In the concluding section, the threat that the C-NIP may mislead climate policy decision-makers – if it is treated as a "real-world problem" instead of a thought experiment – is discussed.

Fact-sensitive vs. fact-insensitive thought experiments

Thought experiments play a crucial role in all philosophical subdisciplines, including climate ethics. What are their defining features? All thought experiments are, in one way or another, counterfactual (or, depending on how these words are defined, unrealistic, hypothetical, imaginary, etc.). Thought experiments may be descriptions of situations that are *possible* logically and terminologically even if they are not *possible in our real world* – that is, earth with its laws of nature and its people as they are. I will call this type "fact-insensitive thought experiments". They may also be descriptions of situations that have not happened, but in fact could have happened, as they are congruent with all real-world circumstances ("fact-sensitive thought experiments").[3] Apart from containing elements of counterfactuality, there is no consensus about the nature and the function of thought experiments in ethics. To be sure, calling every fictional story, novel or movie that has not really happened as told a "thought experiment" would stretch the concept too far.

Thought experiments differ from fiction in several ways. First, they do not come out of the blue. There is a context. This context can be a puzzle that has not been solved for some time, and the newly devised thought experiment is a contribution aimed to help solve the puzzle. It is also possible that the thought experiment generates new open questions. To put it differently: a fictional scenario published as a stand-alone piece is not a thought experiment but a piece of literature. Second, as a result of this, thought experiments are (or at least should be) extremely cognizant of details. Each parameter of the imagined thought experiment is important, as the omission or addition of parameters will change the engendered intuitions. Third, one more difference between a thought experiment and any other form of fiction, such as a novel or a movie, is the briefness of the former. The written description of a thought experiment is seldom more than a few paragraphs.

Parfit's "non-identity problem" in the context of climate change

The non-identity problem was first formulated by Schwartz (1978), Adams (1979) and Bayles (1980), then described in greater detail by Kavka (1978, 1982), and developed most effectively by Parfit (1984), in his book *Reasons and Persons*.

In the renowned *Stanford Encyclopedia of Philosophy*, the entry about the NIP has been contributed by Melinda A. Roberts, and it starts as follows:

> The non-identity problem focuses on the obligations we think we have in respect of people who, by our own acts, are caused both to exist and to have existences that are, though worth having, unavoidably flawed – existences, that is, that are flawed if those people are ever to have them at all.[4]

It is indisputable that the NIP applies to procreative decisions. Take, for instance, the case of a woman who is raped by a stranger and becomes pregnant as a result. If an abortion is ruled out, this act will induce the existence of a particular child with a unique genetic endowment. The child that comes into existence owes its traits (e.g., colour of skin) to the genes of both the mother and the father. It is clear that if this child had not been created from the particular genetic material from which it was in fact created, then this person would never have existed.[5] According to the "person-affecting" intuition, an act can be wrong only if that act makes things worse for a particular person.[6] But assuming that the procreated child in this example has a life worth living, the act that created it was not bad for that child, as it owes its very existence to this act. Accordingly, the rapist has inflicted harm upon the mother, but not upon the child itself. Hence, the child has no grounds to complain, as a life worth living arguably is in any case better than not being born at all. Thus, we cannot say that this child (or any particular child) has been wronged, or made worse off, by any act that is the deciding factor for its existence.

In this article, the validity of the NIP in "close-to-the-birth clinic" procreative contexts is not disputed at all. But there is a danger of overestimating the ambit of the NIP. Axel Gosseries, for instance, ponders:

> Yet, it appears that the scope of the non-identity problem extends far beyond these biomedical cases. Hence, the non-identity challenge should be taken very seriously. While not affecting all our decisions, be they of a bioethical nature or not . . ., it certainly affects *many* of our policy choices as well as the meaningfulness of ascribing rights to future people in such cases.[7]

And Schwartz claims: "whatever we may owe ourselves or our near posterity, we have no obligation extending indefinitely or even terribly far into the future to provide any widespread, continuing benefit to our descendants."[8]

In the context of climate ethics, the following of Parfit's classic examples is the most relevant:

> Depletion: Suppose that, as a community, we must choose whether to deplete or conserve certain kinds of resources. If we choose Depletion, the quality of life over the next two centuries would be slightly higher than it would have been if we had chosen Conservation, but it may later be much lower. Life at this much lower level would, however, still be well worth living.[9]

Parfit goes on to say:

> If we choose Depletion rather than Conservation, this will lower the quality of life more than two centuries from now. But the particular people who will then be living would never have existed if instead we had chosen Conservation. So our choice of Depletion is not worse for any of these people.[10]

It does not really matter if a resource or a sink (such as the atmosphere with its capacity to absorb greenhouse gases) is used in this example: to transfer Parfit's "depletion problem" in the context of climate ethics, replace "depletion" by "high emissions" and "conservation" by "low emissions." In 2010, Parfit did this himself when he adapted his "depletion problem" in "Energy policy and the further future," a chapter of *Climate Ethics: Essential Readings* (ed. by S. Gardiner, S. Caney, D. Jamieson and H. Shue). He states:

> The Risky Policy: Suppose that, as a community, we have a choice between two energy policies. Both would be completely safe for at least two centuries, but one would have certain risks for the further future. If we choose the Risky Policy, the standard of living would be somewhat higher over the next two centuries. We do choose this policy. As a result there is a similar catastrophe two centuries later, which kills and injures thousands of people.[11]

Parfit's parallel cases of the "depletion problem" and the similar "climate policy problem" is to this day the point of reference for many climate ethicists (and other ethicists).[12] Clark Wolf, for instance, formulates the C-NIP as follows:

> The US President faces a decision that will determine the future of energy policy and will influence the availability of energy alternatives for many generations in the future. Policy A will create dramatic but relatively short-term benefits for the next two or three generations, but is expected to lead to environmental disaster in the long run. Policy B will yield slightly lower benefits in the proximate future, but these benefits will be sustainable for the foreseeable future.[13]

Edward Page has a similar description of the C-NIP; he just calls the two policy options "Kyoto Lite" (this being the high emissions policy) and "Contraction and Convergence" (the low emissions policy).[14] The implications are the same: "since harm-based, or identity-dependent, reasoning is deeply ingrained in the ethics, law and common sense morality of most countries, the non-identity problem suggests that our duties to posterity may be weaker, and less extensive, than is often supposed."[15]

Or see the C-NIP in the formulation of Steve Vanderheiden:

> Given our choice between policies that Parfit calls "Conservation" and "Depletion" – options that can be taken to represent effective and ineffective climate policy – and the different levels of material prosperity that are likely to result from either option, the identities of future persons turn on our present decisions. . . . As a result of choosing a high-growth, high-consumption, and high-pollution path, the planet's future capacity to fulfil human wants and needs will likely be significantly diminished by environmental degradation and climatic instability, worsening conditions for those inhabiting the future world. While we can reliably predict these adverse consequences for those who *would* live in a polluted and depleted future world, Parfit argues that we cannot validly say that our present policy choice actually harms any future person.[16]

Gosseries illustrates the problem by describing the situation of a father who drives to work every day with his car, thus emitting greenhouse gases.[17] If his daughter were to someday reproach him for this, he could respond that the point in time of his return home to his wife from work in the evening also affected the point in time of their coitus. If he had instead used his bicycle, he might have caused less harm to the environment, but then his daughter, the one who is now reproaching him, would never have been born. A different sperm would have fertilised a different ovum, so that instead of individual X, individual Y would have been born.

Note, however, that there is an important difference between the setting in which a generation A collectively brings generation C, instead of generation B, into existence (as the formulations of the C-NIP of Parfit, Wolf, Vanderheiden and Page suggest) and Gosseries' setting in which an individual father A brings child C, instead of B, into existence. In Gosseries' "car-loving father" example, the case is made for a different point in time of conception by the same two people, the parents. In contrast, Parfit, Wolf and Page argue that a certain climate *policy* will lead to the effect that different people (prospective parents) will meet, mate and make children.[18]

The rejoinder against the C-NIP that is laid out in the following will disarm both versions: the collective and the individual C-NIP. In short, with regard to climate policy, the NIP overlooks the difference between probability and determinacy. It treats each event as if it would be deterministically responsible for the birth of particular children, thereby ignoring the potpourri of antecedent events.

This may be illustrated as follows: imagine that a proponent of the C-NIP claims: "If we emit a lot of greenhouses gases in the next 200 years, this might be bad for future generations, but it will also impact who will be meeting, mating and making children with whom. As a result, a different set of people will come into existence compared with any alternative policy." His listener might answer: "Okay, your claim sounds 100% correct."

But then a bystander steps in and argues: "But this is not the only factor that will have an impact on who will be meeting, mating and making children with whom. I have heard that the government will extend the opening times in bars from 11 pm to 3 am. This will also have an impact on who will be meeting, mating and making children with whom, won't it?"

Her counterpart nods and replies: "Well, this is also correct. But then the first factor, the high emissions policy, might account for 50% of the stated effect, and the change in opening times will account for the other 50%."

But then another bystander steps in and interjects: "According to reliable forecasts, the number of female students at universities will double within the next ten years. This will definitely have an impact on who will be meeting, mating and making children with whom." The other two contend: "Then all three factors that have been mentioned may account for 33% each."

Another bystander steps in and adds: "Don't forget the new dating app for smartphones! It will also have an impact on who will be meeting, mating and making children with whom." And then the group catches sight of a huge crowd of people who are queuing up to add still more factors that have a bearing on who will be meeting, mating and making children with whom.

The takeaway from this story is that a myriad of factors affect who comes into existence and who does not. The impact of the high emissions policy, as one single factor, is miniscule. It is therefore misleading to say that the high emissions policy will be *causal* in determining who comes into existence.

Let us once again look at Gosseries' example, which suggests that the father might justify his environmentally harmful driving habits to his daughter by using the non-identity argument. But must the daughter now really fall silent? She could answer as follows:

> Are you really trying to tell me that this behaviour of yours, which is harmful to succeeding generations, is responsible for the fact that I was conceived on 14 March 1996 at 8:11:43 pm? It's true that you are always driving a car and that this habit may have been the reason that you were at home half an hour earlier than you would have been if you'd taken your bike. But on the day of my conception, if you were not caught in a traffic jam on the way home, and if you hadn't petted the cat on the way in, you would also have come through the door a few minutes earlier. And if you hadn't gone to the refrigerator just before having sex with my mother, the point in time of my conception would also have been different. And anyway, the only reason you had had to work so long since the beginning of 1996 was that the government had just passed a law lifting the restrictions on overtime work, which they had to do to meet the challenge of Chinese competition. All of these factors – and a billion other ones – are more responsible than you driving your car for the fact that I was conceived at exactly 8:11:43 pm. So your car journey is not *the* reason and thus no excuse for the fact that you're polluting the atmosphere.[19]

The logic that underlies the C-NIP, both the collective and the individual action version, implies that good or bad results are literally *caused* by certain policies or acts. Parfit uses the following picture: "As we have seen, children conceived at different times would in fact be different children. So the proportion of those later born who would owe their existence to our choice would, like ripples in a pool, steadily grow."[20] The ripple analogy is very instructive, but not in the sense of how Parfit used it in his climate ethics article. We must rather think of a pool or pond into which, at the same moment, a great number of stones are thrown. Think of the ripples that will be generated by this action. They will superimpose each other and create a picture that looks very non-linear, or chaotic, to the observer. Now refine this analogy and imagine that the stones are of different sizes, from small pebbles to rocks. A great number of these are thrown simultaneously into the water. Now think of the picture of the ripples this will cause. The stone that symbolised the high emissions policy will make a ripple, but all the other stones will also make ripples, sometimes much bigger ripples. Therefore, the claim that all or almost all climate-related actions of members of the currently living generation *determine* not only what the conditions of life of future people will be but also which people will exist in the first place is misleading.

Note that I do not say that the so-called snowball effect of each ripple in the previous example is minimal. The snowball effect relates the accumulative effects of each policy over time. Indisputably, the overlap between the members of generation A who actually will come into existence as a result of a high emissions policy and members of generation B who would come into being if a low emissions policy were implemented would initially be very high, and over the course of time become smaller. Assume for the sake of the argument that as a result of the initial and accumulated effects due to a high emissions policy, one-quarter of the population changes their procreation pattern. In a population with 80 million people, after 180 years the population would consist entirely of different individuals (assuming generations of 30 years). This can be calculated mathematically as follows:

> Given a population of 80 million, 60 million are initially unaffected. In the first round of marriages, each of those unaffected has a chance of 6/8 to meet a partner who is likewise unaffected. After the first generation, there will therefore be 6/8 x 60 million unaffected people. Of the entire population V, the initial number of unaffected people (the 0th generation) is B0; then, after one generation, the number of still unaffected people will be $B_1 = (B_0/V) \times B_0 = (B_0)^2/V$. Since the second round of marriages will involve the same conditions, after two generations, the number of remaining unaffected people will be $B_2 = (B_1/V) \times B_1 = (B_0)^4/V^3$. After the n-th generation, it will be $B_n = (B_0)^{(2n)} / [V^{(2n-1)}]$. Solving that for a (the number of generations) yields $n = \ln [\ln(B_n/V) / \ln(B_0/V)] / \ln 2$. In this example:

> $n = \ln [\ln(1/80000000) / \ln(60000000/80000000)] / \ln 2$; this yields $n = 5.983124$.
> Since one generation corresponds to 30 years, there would, after 5.983124×30 years (i.e., 179.49 years) be only one remaining unaffected person.

The point is that there is a snowball effect *for each policy*, not for just one of them. So we have to come back to the *relative* weight of each factor in explaining a certain outcome. The concept of (in)significance, as it is routinely applied in statistics, is instructive here. In inferential statistics, one calls factors statistically "insignificant" if they are considered not having enough explanatory power. Statistical insignificance does not mean, however, that the effect being tested for does not exist. What is an appropriate insignificance level, is the subject of a convention. Quite often, a probability of 1 in 20 ($\alpha = 0.05$) is chosen, although, depending on context, this is by no means the only appropriate value.[21] Note, however, that levels of (in)significance of the C-NIP are so low that they are virtually zero in the real-world context. To illustrate this, let us have a closer look at the sequence of events and acts that may have happened before the conception of child A in time t_0, and let's assume the existence of child A would have been thrown "off track" if only one of these slightest changes in this sequence had happened. All antecedent events that were decisive for the birth of child A are the "population" in the parlance of statisticians.

Here you go: Three months before the conception, the parents of A had married. Two years before, they had met in a disco for the first time. Before entering this disco that very night, each of the prospective parents considered him/herself to be single, but wanted to enter into a relationship. In the club were 175 men and 243 women who were potential partners for each of the (later) parents of child A. Twenty-five years before, the U.S. president had announced that he would leave the Paris climate agreement, which led to a high emissions policy in the U.S. during the following years. On the same day, all the other heads of state and government and all the heads of major corporations made climate-relevant decisions, too.

Some 2000 years before, a Roman legionary who had the best chances to become emperor was killed by a falling roof tile when he marched through the streets of Rome. One day before, a bird had picked this particular roof tile loose. For the sake of argument, we assume that all these acts and events are "causal" for the conception of child A. The takeaway from this story: If the number of factors that influence who will be meeting, mating and making children with whom converges towards infinity, the influence of each particular factor converges towards zero. The more indirect the acts and events are related to the actual act of birth, the weaker the potency of the NIP.

It seems to be helpful to distinguish at least two different types of non-identity cases that have distinct logical features:

1   Cases in which the genetic identity of the parents is *not* open to the course of events that are antecedent to the conception (and as a result of this limitation the genetic identity of the conceived child). The genetic identity of the child must be the result of the shuffle of the gametes of these two persons. For instance, Parfit's classical "14-year-old girl"[22] falls into this category; likewise, all reproductive services that gynaecologists or obstetricians provide for a couple which wishes to have a child and needs assistance.
2   Cases in which the genetic identity of the parents is open to the course of events that are antecedent to the conception. Parfit's "risky climate policy" case falls into this category, likewise all cases of redress for historical injustice-cases.

The second class encompasses the C-NIP and the "insignificant-causal-factors" argument has even more bite here. The thicker the potpourri of antecedent events, the more problematic it is to call one single factor the "deciding factor." At any rate, the significance level of a *single* antecedent event, say the car ride in Gosseries' example, is extremely low in any of the examples. Even in cases in which the genetic identity is not open to variations, in the real world there is still a very high number of possible combinations of egg and sperm cells because every second, a man's genetic endowment, consisting of some 200 million gametes, is constituted anew.

Recall that Roberts's definition of the NIP (see earlier discussion) speaks of duties "in respect of people who, by our own acts, are *caused* [my emphasis] both to exist and to have existences that are, though worth having, unavoidably flawed." Proponents of the C-NIP construct a *mono-causal* relationship, thereby ignoring the multi-causal context. This is misleading. When we think about what *caused* something, we might hold variable A responsible for 50% of the effect, variable B for 30% and variable C for 19%. We know in the back of our mind that there are an indefinable number of additional variables that aggregate up to the last 1%, but we normally don't understand causality in that way. When a judge lists the causes of a car accident in his summing up, he will say that a slight drunkenness was 80% responsible, and a dispute in the car with the co-driver was to blame for the rest. He will not say: "Another cause is that the road was constructed in this area." But this statement would be logically correct, for if a road-building company had not built this road, say, just before the accident has happened, the accident would not have happened on this specific road. But not every causal factor is a significant causal factor. An inadequate concept of causality is implied if the C-NIP is couched in terms like "caused," "because of" or "due to."

Understanding the C-NIP as a thought experiment

But is the C-NIP a thought experiment, after all? Let's see if it fulfils the aforementioned criteria:

1   Counterfactuality? Yes, ignoring statistical insignificance and treating a probabilistic relationship as a deterministic one is fact-insensitive.
2   From a context? This surely is the case. The broader context of the C-NIP is future ethics, which deal with questions such as "Do we have obligations to posterity?" This is a standard (and crucial) question for all full-fledged theories of intergenerational justice.

3   Cognizant of details? Yes, for instance, Parfit is cognizant in speaking of a policy (instead of individual behaviour) to make the non-identity argument as strong as possible. Roberts acknowledges: "The 'depletion example' is a thicket of details."[23]

4   Briefness? Yes, the C-NIP in the aforementioned formulations (e.g., Derek Parfit's or Clark Wolf's) is succinct.

As a thought experiment, the C-NIP could be formulated as follows:

> "Imagine that a certain climate policy *would* determine who will be born in the future." (forward-looking version)

and

> "Imagine that a certain climate policy in the past *would* have determined who is currently in existence." (backward-looking version)[24]

Lest it be misunderstood: This is a fascinating, thrilling, compelling and riveting thought experiment,[25] but to call it a thought experiment gives it a completely different methodological status than a hypothesis or theory (which could be true, after all). Recalling Box's and Draper's famous sentence about models, cited earlier, does Parfit state somewhere that the NIP is, in fact, an abstraction from reality and thus not a counterargument against a low emissions policy? Quite the opposite: Parfit's statements make clear that he has absolutely no doubts regarding the validity of the non-identity problem in the context of emission policies: "We may remember a time when we were concerned about effects on future generations, but had overlooked my point about personal identity. We may have thought that a policy like Depletion would be against the interest of future people."[26]

The belief that the C-NIP (and non-identity problems of the same structure) are serious threats for theories of intergenerational justice and our moral obligations towards posterity formulated by them is still mainstream in contemporary philosophy. Mulgan noted in 2002 that the non-identity challenge is to this day "plaguing present Western theories of generational justice."[27] By the same token, Wolf (2009) states: "The non-identity problem calls into question whether distant future persons might claim rights against members of the present generation. . . . For this reason, some theorists have more or less abandoned the idea of intergenerational justice altogether."[28] In 2016, Gheaus still calls the NIP "the most difficult obstacle for theories of intergenerational justice."[29] And in his influential entry on "Intergenerational Justice" in the *Stanford Encyclopedia of Philosophy*, Lukas Meyer (2015) summarises: "Derek Parfit's work has defined the problems of how we can and should relate to future people."[30] Nowadays, one seeks in vain in survey articles and philosophical reference works for statements that qualify the C-NIP, which could take for instance the form: "Plausibly, the availability of contraceptives has a much greater impact on who will be born in the future than climate policies." Or: "Possibly, climate policies have hardly any impact on who will be born in the future." Instead of outlining arguments about insignificance, Meyer's encyclopaedia entry gives the following account of reactions to the NIP:

> We can distinguish four main responses to the "Non-Identity-Problem" so understood (compare Boonin 2008, 134 ff; Page 2008; Heyd 2009; Roberts 2015; Wrigley 2012, 178): First, some philosophers hold the view that future people whose existence depends upon currently living people's actions cannot have rights vis-à-vis the latter people's actions (see

Schwartz 1978; cf. Adams 1979; Kavka 1982; Parfit 1984, part iv; Boonin 2008; Roberts 2009). Second, others argue that currently living people can violate the rights of future people even if the former cannot harm the latter (see Kumar 2003). If so, future people cannot have welfare rights vis-à-vis currently living people insofar as violating welfare rights implies setting back or harming the interests of the right holders. Third, we can attempt to limit the practical significance of the non-identity-problem by limiting the relevant actions to those that are not only likely but indeed necessary conditions of the existence of the concerned person.[31] Finally, some have sought to circumvent the non-identity problem by suggesting an alternative notion of harm that is unaffected by the non-identity-problem, the so-called "Threshold Conception of Harm" (Hanser 1990; 2009; McMahan 1998; Shiffrin 1999; Meyer 2003; 2009; Harman 2004; 2009; Rivera-López 2009).[32]

Roberts lists in her encyclopaedia entry on the non-identity problem (which refers to all types of the NIP, not just the C-NIP) five proposed solutions to the non-identity problem: (1) a seemingly wrong act is not in fact wrong; (2) an act is wrong by virtue of impersonal effects; (3) an act is *bad* for a future person without making that person *worse off*; (4) the non-identity problem is seen as a non-identity fallacy; and (5) an act is wrong in virtue of the agent's reasons, attitudes and intentions.

The fourth approach is her own that she spelled out in *The Non-identity Fallacy: Harm, Probability and Another Look at Parfit's Depletion Example* (2007). In fact, in this article her line of reasoning seems to resemble mine (even if she couches her argument in different). Roberts acknowledges that "the non-identity problem is really a collection of problems that have different logical features."[33] She distinguishes between three types: "won't-do-better problems", "can't-do-better problems" and "can't expect-better" problems.

And Roberts concludes her article as follows:

"The can't-expect-better problem is thus best understood as a probability problem, and indeed as a fallacy. As such, it raises no serious questions about how it is that we can harm people whom we by the same act cause to exist. If my analysis is correct, then the can't-expect-better problem can take its place as another in a long line of riveting probability problems that we can in the end mercifully set aside – a result that would in no way diminish its significance in helping us understand the structure of moral theory but that may leave us free to retain the person-based intuition as a basic part of that structure."[34]

The counterargument against the NIP, as Roberts repeats 2015,

is limited to the large class of non-identity cases that reason from (a) had the act under scrutiny not been performed, the person who exists and suffers as an effect of that act *very probably* would never have existed at all and (b) that existence is worth having to the conclusion (c) that act does not make things worse for, or harm, that person. But that large class of cases also happens to be a very significant class of cases. It includes Kavka's slave child and pleasure pill cases, Parfit's depletion and risky policy cases, Broome's climate change case and cases involving historical injustices.[35]

It would be beyond the scope of this article to introduce to the reader this quite diverse bunch of "can't-expect-better" problems (as Roberts calls them) and discuss if they are really similar in structure and if my "insignificant-causal-factors" rejoinder argument applies to all of them, but I second Roberts when she focuses (like Kavka before her)[36] on the "precariousness" of any person coming into existence and on the importance of considerations about (im)probability. It is surprising that she does not repeat her worries more prominently in her free-of-charge encyclopaedia entry (which is presumably more often read than her fee-based article). At any rate, the mainstream and those scholars that specifically address the NIP in the context of climate change (e.g., Parfit, Broome or Meyer, maybe save Roberts) depict it as a serious problem that might be more or less successfully skirted but is definitively "more" than just a thought experiment. Page takes great effort with counterstrategies against the "non-identity theorists,"[37] as he calls them. He first describes the problem:

> This line of reasoning, which has been called the *non-identity problem*, calls into question many, though by no means *all*, of our duties to future generations. It leaves intact, for example, duties to those descendants whose identities are beyond our influence, as well as those whose lives will not be worth living as a result of our behaviour. . . . It also leaves intact objections to Kyoto Lite [the high emissions climate policy] grounded in identity-independent goals such as utility maximisation or the perfection of the human species. Finally, it leaves intact "deontological" objections that explain the wrong-doing in such cases to the intentions and state of mind of the policy-choosers, not the outcomes of the various policy choices.[38]

But also Page believes that, despite such limitations, the non-identity argument presents a profound challenge for anyone who theorises that ravaging the climate is ethically wrong: "The non-identity problem, however, shows us that very few future persons will be harmed by the adoption of Kyoto Lite since, if a different approach to climate change had been taken, a different set of persons would have come into existence."[39] As possible solutions, Page cites the notions of specific interests (Woodward),[40] subjunctive harm (Meyer)[41] and collective interests (Page's own approach).[42]

But if the C-NIP had indeed the methodological status of a thought experiment, there would be no need to circumvent or to "solve" (cf. the title of Boonin's 2008 paper) it. Thought experiments do not have to be "solved."

It is important that the community of philosophical scholars is clear about the status of the C-NIP. First, it should be recognised within the philosophical community that the C-NIP is a thought experiment. The way the C-NIP is currently presented in key philosophical texts (such as the entries of the *Stanford Encyclopedia of Philosophy*) may mislead climate policy decision-makers. This is the point I will now turn to.

Communicating the non-identity problem to climate policy-makers

More than some other fields of ethics, climate ethics is related to pressing real-world problems. It is no exaggeration to state that overcoming dangerous climate change may even be crucial for humankind's long-term wellbeing.[43] With regard to the question of "who owes what to whom" in climate ethics, politicians and decision-makers are in need of reliable ethical theories when negotiating climate targets and compensation payments. Climate ethicists have, to a certain degree, a responsibility to deliver theories that are beneficial for real-world scenarios.[44] At least they have a clear responsibility to be precise about the methodological status of the problems that they discuss. This is even more the case given that philosophers play an increasingly important role in the Intergovernmental Panel on Climate Change (IPCC). The IPCC was set up at the request of member governments of the main international treaty on climate change, the United Nations Framework Convention on Climate Change (UNFCCC), which was drawn up in 1992 at the Earth Summit in Rio. According to its principles,

> the role of the IPCC is to assess on a comprehensive, objective, open and transparent basis the scientific, technical and socio-economic information relevant to understanding the scientific basis of risk of human-induced climate change, its potential impacts and options for adaptation and mitigation.[45]

The IPCC reports are a major source of information for the UNFCCC signatory nations. For a long time, scholars from normative disciplines (such as moral and political philosophers and theorists) were not part of the IPCC. This has changed recently when the philosophers Lukas Meyer, John Broome and Marc Fleurbaey became members.

Is the C-NIP a helpful tool for policy-makers when they strive for conclusions? Parfit expresses some doubts about this when he writes:

> I shall therefore end with a practical question. When we are discussing social policies, should we ignore the point about personal identity? Should we allow ourselves to say that a choice like that of the Risky Policy or of Depletion might be against the interests of people in the further future? This is not true. Should we pretend that it is? Should we let other people go on thinking that it is? If you share my intuitions, this seems permissible. We can then use such claims as a convenient form of shorthand. Though the claims are false, we believe that this makes no moral difference. So the claims are not seriously misleading.[46]

But falsehood is falsehood, and if the claim that a risky climate policy is not harmful for (distant) future people were really true (I have argued here that this claim is, in fact, false), then this would indeed present a problem for all theories that postulate that we have climate-related duties towards (distant) future people. Imagine if politicians and practitioners had taken Parfit's claim seriously in the global climate negotiations[47] of the recent past, or imagine if they took it seriously in the years to come. If climate policy decision-makers really believed that a high emissions policy will not harm the people who live in the future, they might be less inclined to agree on curbing emissions – to the detriment of future generations. If they take the NIP "for real," then they will be hindered in their judgement of what is the fairest and most reasonable distribution of emissions among all parties affected, especially between present and future people.[48]

Conclusion

It was argued that the climate non-identity problem, in contrast to how it is depicted in prominent philosophical texts, has the status of a thought experiment. By treating it as a "real world problem", it is given more potency and maybe more attention than it deserves. "So what? What's wrong with that?" one might ask. "Let philosophers dwell on this fascinating problem in their ivory towers." But philosophers have already left their ivory towers. It is thus high time for the philosophical community to get a new understanding of the Parfitian claim that a risky climate policy is not harmful for (distant) future people. If the protagonists of the C-NIP spread the message that we might intuitively think that we have climate-related obligations to future generations, but upon philosophical scrutiny, this should be ignored because of the non-identity problem, then policy-makers (governmental and other) would be seriously mislead.

Acknowledgments

I authored a piece about the NIP in 2014 ("The Non-Identity Problem: An Irrefutable Argument Against Representation of Future Generations?" In: *Theories of Sustainable Development*, edited by J. Enders and M. Remig, London: Routledge, pp. 126–144). At that time, I lacked the methodological background to link the NIP to thought experiments. In retrospect, I find my earlier text to be preliminary and hope that the answers given in this present work are more convincing, or at least less preliminary. I am indebted to a great number of students and colleagues for insightful comments or suggestions over the last four years. I am also very grateful to Antony Mason who reviewed and smoothed my English. Lastly, my many thanks to the editor of this article at Routledge for their close attention to detail, which I much appreciate.

Notes

1 Box and Draper (1987, 424).
2 "Non-identity problem/nonidentity problem" is spelt in the literature in two ways. I have followed Parfit (using the hyphen).
3 Page (2007, 18) argues the case for hypothetical, but not imaginary, thought experiments in his book *Climate Change, Justice and Future Generations*:

> While a coherent approach to issues of intergenerational ethics requires extensive appeal to hypothetical examples (which, for example, attempt to tease out our convictions about the merits of climate change policies which will have differential impacts on the quality of life of future populations), it is my view that appeals to imaginary examples should be avoided wherever possible. Imaginary examples are those which "involve logical possibilities that could occur only in a world very different from ours."

And he continues in a footnote, citing Jamieson (1993, 484): "Hypothetical examples, by contrast, 'involve instances of situations or events that have occurred, or could occur without requiring us to rewrite physics or change our basic conception of how the world works'."

4 Roberts (2015); Roberts has written several books and articles about the NIP before, among them Roberts (1998).
5 Mulgan (2002, 6).
6 Roberts (2015).
7 Gosseries (2008, 460).
8 Schwartz (1978, 3) Likewise Heyd (1992, 80).
9 Parfit (2010, 114).
10 Parfit (2010, 114–115).
11 Parfit (2010, 112).
12 E.g., Gosseries (2002; 2008), Vanderheiden (2006; 2008), Page (2007; 2008), Roberts and Wassermann (2009), Mazor (2010), Broome (1992; 2004, 125–130), Wolf (2009).
13 Wolf (2009, 95).
14 Page (2007, 133).
15 Page (2007, 134).
16 Vanderheiden (2008, 122).
17 Gosseries (2008, 460).
18 Heyd (1992, 193–203) pointed out (in different words than mine) that in examples such as the "car-loving father," the habit of driving may be responsible for the creation of the particular child of this father (the nonidentity problem may apply), but the air pollution that comes with this habit is also lowering the level of wellbeing for all other children in the neighbourhood (the nonidentity does not apply to them). Tremmel (2009, 39) calls this the "your neighbour's children" argument which he illustrates graphically. This argument against the NIP can be ruled out if it is assumed, changing Gosseries' example, that all fathers in one community simultaneously engage in the same habit. Thus, Parfit's Risky Policy example is cognizant of the detail that a *policy* example (assuming that all agents do collectively the same thing) builds a stronger case for the proponents in the C-NIP than *individual behaviour* examples.
19 Tremmel (2015, 137).

20 Parfit (2010, 113).
21 Wasserstein and Lazar (2016).
22 Parfit (1987, 358).
23 Roberts (1998, 299).
24 Page frames this in terms of global climate change as follows (2007, 137):

> For, if it is nonsensical to compensate present persons for ancient wrongs committed to their ances-tors, it is likewise nonsensical to insist that countries that contributed the vast majority of greenhouse emissions prior to 1990, have more than a modest harm-based duty to pay for the costly measures needed to reduce emissions. This because the greenhouse emissions that contributed to the climate problem originated in acts and policies that also modified the size and composition of subsequent generations of all countries. If we find this implausible, it is worth asking whether a world without carbon industries would have supported a rise in the world population from 2.5 billion in 1950 to over 6.4 billion people in 2005.

25 I can tell from my own experience that it is riveting as I planned to spend much less time studying the NIP than I in fact ended up investing in it.
26 See Parfit (2010, 115). Or, with almost the same wording, Parfit (1987, 367).
27 Mulgan (2002, 8).
28 Wolf (2009, 96).
29 Gheaus (2016, 491).
30 Meyer (2015).
31 [Here, Meyer refers to Roberts (1998) in an endnote.]
32 The fourth response, a new understanding of the term 'harm', is Meyers own attempt to circumvent the NIP.
33 Roberts (2007, 271).
34 Roberts (2007, 311).
35 Roberts (2015).
36 Kavka (1982, 93).
37 Page (2008, 10).
38 Page (2007, 134).
39 Page (2007, 135).
40 Woodward (1986).
41 Meyer (2004).
42 Page (2007, 153–158; 2008).
43 For estimations of the physical ills that will come with human-induced climate change, see, e.g., World Bank (2013).
44 Cf. Roberts (2007, 271):

> If we do end up with theories that are too complex, vague, nuanced and indefinite to be assessed or applied, or are so narrow that our acceptance of them must be tentative pending an understanding of how they fit into a broader theory, there will be practical implications. For example, we would surely need to suspend hope that moral theory might have some advice to offer courts as they struggle to decide hard "future person" cases in the law.

45 IPCC (2013).
46 Parfit (2010, 118).
47 United Nations Framework Convention on Climate Change, Conference of the Parties, in short "COP". In the COP 21 in Paris 2015, a global accord was agreed.
48 See Tremmel (2013), Tremmel and Robinson (2014) (with further references) for a synthesis of climate ethics theories.

References

Adams, R. M. 1979. 'Existence, self-interest, and the problem of evil'. *Nous*, 13(1): 53–65.
Bayles, M. D. 1980: *Morality and population policy*. University, Ala.: University of Alabama Press.
Boonin, D. 2008. 'How to solve the non–identity problem'. *Public Affairs Quarterly*, 22: 129–159.

Box, G. E. P. and N. R. Draper. 1987. *Empirical Model-Building and Response Surfaces*. Hoboken: John Wiley & Sons.

Broome, J. 1992. *Counting the Cost of Global Warming*. Cambridge: The White Horse Press.

Broome, J. 2004. *Weighing Lives*. Oxford: Oxford University Press.

Gheaus, A. 2016. 'The right to parent and duties concerning future generations'. *The Journal of Political Philosophy*, 24(4): 487–508.

Gosseries, A. 2002. 'Intergenerational justice'. In H. LaFollette (Ed.), *The Oxford Handbook of Practical Ethics* (pp. 459–484). Oxford: Oxford University Press.

Gosseries, A. 2008. 'On future generations' future rights'. *Journal for Political Philosophy*, 16(4): 446–474.

Hanser, M. 1990. 'Harming future people'. *Philosophy & Public Affairs*, 19: 47–70.

Harman, E. 2004. 'Can we harm and benefit in creating?'. *Philosophical Perspectives*, 18(1): 89–113.

Hanser, M. 2009. 'Harming and Procreating'. In M. A. Roberts and D. T. Wassermann (Eds.), *Harming Future Persons: Ethics, Genetics and the Non-Identity Problem* (pp. 179–199). Berlin and Heidelberg: Springer.

Harman, E. 2009. 'Harming as causing harm'. In M. A. Roberts and D. T. Wasserman (Eds.), *Harming Future Persons: Ethics, Genetics and the Nonidentity Problem* (pp. 137–154). Dordrecht: Springer.

Heyd, D. 1992. *Genethics: Moral Issues in the Creation of People*. Berkeley: University of California Press.

Heyd, D. 2009. 'The intractability of the nonidentity problem'. In M. A. Roberts and D. T. Wasserman (Eds.), *Harming Future Persons* (pp. 3–25). Dordrecht: Springer.

IPCC. 2013. Principles Governing IPCC Work (PDF). Approved 1–3 October 1998, last amended 14–18 October 2013. www.ipcc.ch/pdf/ipcc-principles/ipcc-principles.pdf (accessed 6 February 2015).

Jamieson, D. 1993. 'Method and moral theory'. In P. Singer (Ed.), *A Companion to Ethics* (pp. 476–487). Oxford: Blackwell.

Kavka, G. S. 1978. 'The futurity problem'. In R. Sikora and B. Barry (Eds.), *Obligations to Future Generations* (pp. 186–203). Philadelphia: Temple University Press.

Kavka, G. S. 1982. 'The paradox of future individuals'. *Philosophy & Public Affairs*, 11: 93–112.

Kumar, R. 2003. 'Who can be wronged?'. *Public Affairs*, 31(2): 99–118.

McMahan, J. 1998. 'Wrongful Life: Paradoxes in the Morality of Causing People to Exist'. In J. Coleman (Ed.), *Rational Commitment and Social Justice: Essays for Gregory Kavka* (pp. 208–247). Cambridge: Cambridge University Press.

Mazor, J. 2010. 'Liberal justice, future people, and natural resource conservation'. *Philosophy and Public Affairs*, 38: 380–408.

Meyer, L. H. 2003. 'Past and future. The case for a threshold conception of harm'. In L. H. Meyer, S. L. Paulson and T. W. Pogge (Eds.), *Rights, Culture, and the Law: Themes From the Legal and Political Philosophy of Joseph Raz* (pp. 143–159). Oxford: Oxford University Press.

Meyer, L. H. 2004. 'Compensating wrongless historical emissions of greenhouse gases'. *Ethical Perspectives*, 11(1): 20–35.

Meyer, L. H. 2009. 'Intergenerationelle Suffizienzgerechtigkeit'. In N. Goldschmidt (Ed.), *Generationengerechtigkeit. Ordnungsökonomische Konzepte* (pp. 281–322). Tübingen: Mohr Siebeck.

Meyer, L. H. 2015. 'Intergenerational justice'. In E. N. Zalta (Ed.), *The Stanford Encyclopedia of Philosophy*. First published April 3, 2003; substantive revision August 10, 2015. https://plato.stanford.edu/entries/justice-intergenerational/

Mulgan, T. 2002. 'Neutrality, rebirth and intergenerational justice'. *Journal of Applied Philosophy*, 19(1): 3–15.

Page, E. 2007. *Climate Change, Justice, and Future Generations*. Cheltenham: Edward Elgar.

Page, E. 2008. 'Three problems of intergenerational justice'. *Intergenerational Justice Review*, Issue 3: 9–12.

Parfit, D. 1987. *Reasons and Persons* (3rd rev. ed.). Oxford: Oxford University Press. Original edition published 1984.

Parfit, D. 2010. 'Energy policy and the further future. The identity problem'. In S. M. Gardiner, et al. (Eds.), *Climate Ethics: Essential Readings* (pp. 112–121). Oxford: Oxford University Press.

Rivera-López, E. 2009. 'Individual procreative responsibility and the non-identity problem'. *Pacific Philosophical Quarterly*, 90: 336–363.

Roberts, M. A. 1998. *Child Versus Childmaker: Future Persons and Present Duties in Ethics and the Law*. Lanham: Rowman & Littlefield.

Roberts, M. A. 2007. 'The Nonidentity Fallacy: Harm, Probability and Another Look at Parfit's Depletion Example'. *Utilitas*, 9: 267–311.

Roberts, M. A. 2009. 'What is the wrong of wrongful disability? From chance to choice to harms to persons'. *Law and Philosophy*, 28: 1–57.

Roberts, M. A. 2015. 'The nonidentity problem'. In E. N. Zalta (Ed.), *The Stanford Encyclopedia of Philosophy*. First published July 21, 2009; substantive revision September 25, 2015. https://plato.stanford.edu/entries/nonidentity-problem/

Roberts, M. A. and D. T. Wassermann (Eds.). 2009. *Harming Future Persons: Ethics, Genethics and the Nonidentity Problem*. Berlin and Heidelberg: Springer.

Schwartz, T. 1978. 'Obligations to posterity'. In R. Sikora and B. Barry (Eds.), *Obligations to Future Generations* (pp. 3–13). Philadelphia: Temple University Press.

Shiffrin, S. V. 1999. 'Wrongful life, procreative responsibility, and the significance of harm'. *Legal Theory*, 5(2): 117–148.

Tremmel, J. 2009. *A Theory of Intergenerational Justice*. London: Earthscan.

Tremmel, J. 2013. 'Climate change and political philosophy: Who owes what to whom?'. *Environmental Values*, 22(6): 725–749.

Tremmel, J. 2015. 'The Non-Identity Problem: An Irrefutable Argument Against Representation of Future Generations?' In J. Enders and M. Remig (Eds.): *Theories of Sustainable Development* (pp. 126–144). London: Routledge.

Tremmel, J. and K. Robinson. 2014. *Climate Ethics: The Climate Change Conundrum*. London: Palgrave Macmillan and I.B. Tauris.

Vanderheiden, S. 2006. 'Conservation, foresight, and the future generations problem'. *Inquiry*, 49: 337–352.

Vanderheiden, S. 2008. *Atmospheric Justice: A Political Theory of Climate Change*. Oxford: Oxford University Press.

Wasserstein, R. L. and N. A. Lazar. 2016. 'The ASA's statement on p-values: Context, process, and purpose'. *The American Statistician*, 70(2): 129–133.

Wolf, C. 2009. 'Do future persons presently have alternate possible identities?'. In M. A. Roberts and D. T. Wassermann (Eds.), *Harming Future Persons: Ethics, Genetics and the Non-Identity Problem* (pp. 93–114). Berlin and Heidelberg: Springer.

Woodward, J. 1986. 'The non-identity problem'. *Ethics*, 96(4): 804–831.

World Bank. 2013. *Turn Down the Heat: Climate Extremes, Regional Impacts, and the Case for Resilience*. Washington, DC: The World Bank.

Wrigley, A. 2012. 'Harm to future persons: Non-identity problems and counterpart solutions'. *Ethical Theory and Moral Practice*, 15: 175–190.

5

A narrative account of temporality in climate justice

Nejma Tamoudi and Michael Reder

Tension between reason and implementation in the climate ethics and policy debate

Climate change is one of the most urgent challenges today. While human-caused global warming will fundamentally change the ecosystem of planet earth in the long run, its side effects (i.e., weather extremes like floods and droughts) are already having immense negative impacts on the living conditions of today's people, especially in the Global South. Hence, climate change not only refers to a spatial, but also temporal dimension of moral reasoning and thereby poses a pressing problem for global (Edenhofer et al. 2012) as well as intergenerational justice (Gardiner 2011; Shue 2014). At the same time, the various summits on climate change that have taken place during the last decades represent a way of politically responding to these climate impacts. Since the Rio Conference in 1992, for example, much research has been done, especially focusing on various forms of mitigation and adaptation pathways. As a result, a variety of research networks within and outside the IPCC emerged that tried to improve knowledge about climate impacts and its possible developments in order to empirically support sustainability-oriented climate policies. The Copenhagen Summit 2009, however, marked a daunting turning point. Back then, many scientists and political activists resigned given the fact that negotiations had failed despite conclusive facts about the urgent need to react and significantly limit global warming.

Undoubtedly, the political situation has changed after the Paris Agreement 2015. But the experience of Copenhagen still resonates: Although climate policies seem to be *reasonable* given the facts, their implementation in social, economic and political processes repeatedly appears to be stretched to its limits. Besides various political reasons (e.g., setbacks in global governance, influence of the economic system, or inherent limits of the political will), there is also an impediment deriving from the fact that the discourse on climate justice tends to ignore the specific characteristics of social life and its fundamental temporal structure.

Thus, we argue that the moral debate in part aggravates the practical realisation of its climate principles by relying on a conception of normativity which is based on a rationalistic tradition of knowledge and a corresponding liberal political tradition. Beside all theoretical advantages (e.g., the rejection of alternative facts on climate change or the reasoning for a justice-oriented basic structure of the global socio-political), both traditions nevertheless also imply some problems. Mainly, they draw on a separation of contextual human engagement in epistemic, moral and socio-political practices, eventually detaching us from directly perceiving demands of climate justice on a theoretical as well as practical level. This not only states a problem for global justice and its challenge of respectfully considering the variety of normative differences and life-worlds across the globe, but it also affects the intergenerational side of climate ethics insofar as the aforementioned detachment is accompanied by a disregard of the temporal dimension of human life, in general, and climate ethics in particular. Even though climate justice is fundamentally related to considerations about future impacts, temporality constitutes no inherent part of its moral reasoning.

Hence, it is our objective to highlight the hitherto unconsidered entanglement of climate justice claims, practical embeddedness and temporality. We argue that temporality occupies a special role within this triad as its dynamic contains a decisive, integrative as well as critical thrust. Eventually, temporality supports the constitution of a "(global) social imaginary" (i.e., a cluster of ethical values, moral norms, symbolic representations and institutionalised practices unfolding and integrating the different dimensions of the social). Such an imaginary eventually provides an ontological, normative and conceptual precondition for any critical evaluation and practical implementation of climate justice principles and policies. We further suggest that temporality is best conceived by narrative figurations constituting a socio-historical concept of time, which mediates the different intersubjective as well as environmental relations human beings experience throughout their lives. Additionally, emphasising the close nexus between temporality and narrativity provides the basis for justifying deliberative processes of collective narrative imagination as an essential part of any future ethical account. Finally, the corresponding time-sensitive position of moral reasoning can empower new forms of intergenerational coexistence and transtemporal solidarity, which help motivating, criticising and transforming socio-political realities in light of climate justice claims. This would help academics and activists in situations like after the Copenhagen Summit not to resign, but to explore new (political) narratives on climate justice.

Limitations of the discourse on climate justice

The current debate on climate justice often starts by describing structural forms of injustice facing present as well as future climate impacts. One basic assumption is that industrialised and newly industrialised countries are mainly responsible for climate change, whereas poor populations in developing countries are mostly affected by its dangerous impacts due to their geographical position and the fact that their means of adapting to changing climate conditions are distinctly lower. Therefore, the following separation of main polluters and main victims poses a problem of injustice that can only be solved adequately if justice is expanded on the spatial as well as on the temporal scale. Furthermore, the tight correlation between climate impacts and poverty suggests that solutions to the problem should not be restricted to the distribution of emission rights alone, but should also include a global distribution of wealth in a wider sense, concerning natural, human and social capital (Edenhofer et al. 2012). Hence, reflections on climate justice indicate the need of re-modelling our understanding of global inter-societal and -generational relations.

Against this background, many concepts of climate justice within the current debate are rooted in a rationalistic tradition focusing on equal global and intergenerational rights securing scientifically defined standards of living. Mostly, their argumentation is based on an abstract moral reasoning, according to which different parties (i.e., "the polluting North," "the suffering South," or "future generations") are singled out as individual actors and subsequently addressed from a timeless and external, therefore allegedly neutral standpoint of moral reasoning. In this perspective, Simon Caney identifies two major types of climate justice employed in the current discourse, namely a burden-sharing and a harm-avoiding approach:

> One starts by focusing on how the burden of combating the problem should be shared fairly among the duty-bearers. An agent's responsibility, then, is to do her fair share. . . . The second perspective . . . works back from this to deduce who should do what. . . . This perspective is concerned with the potential victims . . . and it ascribes responsibilities to others to uphold these entitlements.
>
> *(Caney 2015, 125f)*

Therefore, on a theoretical level, accounts of climate justice initially ask how much we owe each other as reciprocal recipients of moral reasons and rights without any concrete specification of the where and when. Their basic assumptions seem to imply both contextually isolated actors and normative claims based on a time-transcending universal theory of moral obligations.

In this regard, theories of climate justice also often ask how burdens have to be shared or responsibilities have to be distributed in order to reach a specific threshold of living standards for people who are or will be affected by climate impacts. Lukas Meyer, for example, develops a threshold conception of harm arguing that current political practices could only become harmful to "individual members" of current or future generations if they cause living standards to drop below a minimum threshold. Consequently, political practices are morally problematic if they weaken the right of (future) people to live a life above such minimum standards (Meyer 2003).

In addition, many theories of climate justice argue for (global) political institutions or human rights regimes to ensure the practical operationalisation of their respective universal moral claims. Insofar as human rights are often interpreted as a moral ideal, which is able to implement universal moral claims for climate justice in a nonetheless diversified political sphere, they constitute one of the key instruments within the debate (Reder and Köhler 2016).

Although the discussion about non-ideal theory in the context of climate justice is increasing, most of the approaches still endorse such an idealised concept of normativity, which is mostly embedded in the concept of human rights (Heyward and Roser 2016). Caney, for example, states "that a human rights perspective has important insights and any account of the impacts of climate change which ignores its implications for people's enjoyment of human rights is fundamentally incomplete and inadequate" (Caney 2010, 89).

Unsurprisingly, climate justice often implies a concept of moral universality that not only promotes context neutrality, but also misses the integration of reflections on temporality as an inherent part of future-oriented ethics. Although climate ethics does entail a prominent temporal dimension when focusing on possible impacts, its corresponding moral principles originate from the aforementioned universal and therefore timeless reflection with no footing in concrete experiences of temporality (Lindemann 2006; Wallack 2006). Hence, moral reasoning and temporality appear to be independent of each other, reducing the latter to the logic of natural causality (i.e., to a chronological sequence of equal units).

Such a Newtonian-inspired physical and linear conception of time is infinitely expandable towards the past and future and falls into line with the overall rationalistic character of climate ethics (Faets et al. 2018). Just like space, time is conceptualised as an a priori cognitive category that rationality is relying on. Hence, it is situated at the epistemological roots of certainty, and thereby, fundamentally lies beyond our reach. Such a development can be traced back to the modern ideal of disengagement, which deprives rationality from its natural embeddedness in different socio-cultural as well as psycho-physiological references. Resulting in a concept of objectivity which resists all possible alienating influences provided by nature, such a rationalistic approach leads to a fundamental separation of a controllable and principally atemporal nature from human rationality and its capacity of dominating the former in our interests (Latour 1991; Plumwood 1991; Taylor 1995). Eventually, temporality only enters moral judgements under the lead of a cognitive dimension exemplified by scientific contributions which are supposed to provide climate justice claims with knowledge about environmental processes and possible future developments.

Compared to moral theory in general, the pivotal role science plays in climate ethics results from the "slow violence" (Nixon 2011) that climate change implies and its multidimensional influences eventually constituting it as a "hyper object" distributed in time and space (Morton 2013). Ultimately, the concomitant difficulties in predicting climate effects directly point towards science and its temporal grid as the central domain of future prognoses and measurements. Thus, albeit the latter playing an important role in defining principles of climate justice, the corresponding debate seems to occur in a timeless place (Meyer 2008). Temporality only constitutes an external informatory part of moral reasoning. Such a time-transcending standpoint eventually has to be understood as a theoretical construction which disregards the fact that people are always already living in time and, therefore, cannot escape the basic temporal characteristic of social reality. Of course, ethical positions have to abstract from current contexts, factors, interests etc. in order to justify universal moral claims. However, if the specifications of social reality and its temporal dimension are left out, climate ethics tends to ignore that values are only accepted within social practices. These practices not only motivate people to become active in the first place, but they also help to implement long-ranging political strategies in concrete social life (Joas 2000). If ethical arguments intend to be reasonable, they have to be formulated within contexts that are concurrently embedded in temporality itself.

Temporality and the (global) social imaginary

Climate change is fundamentally characterised by the complexity of slow and mostly invisible environmental processes and our attempts to calculate them as a function of a given scientific time grid. Thus, the resulting prognosis of possible impacts constitutes a human transformation reducing climate developments to a single domain of certainty. Following Barbara Adam, the exclusive assignment of temporality to a quantifiable fact further promotes the establishment of "clock time" (Adam 1995, 1998) — i.e., a time of economic exchange, technological machinery and definite calculability. Such a concept of time, however, needs to be conceived as historically developed and therefore to a certain extent as contingent. In that regard, time functions as an extended representation of our dynamic socio-environmental interconnectedness with the world.

Against the backdrop of neutrality and calculability, the contemporary prevalence of clock time consequently leads to an alienation of people from the different socio-cultural as well as environmental time rhythms of their individual *Lebenswelt*. As Hartmut Rosa or Robert Hassan argue, such an alienation eventually corresponds with various forms of acceleration, which try to unify and bend the detached temporal diversity of socio-environmental practices into the dominance of one single concept of time (Rosa 2010), leading to a questionable "speed society" (Hassan 2009).

Such studies on time, acceleration and speed are emphasising the fact that concepts of time are always built at the various intersections of cosmic and environmental rhythms with the complexity of intergenerational life spans. The resulting "human time" (Ricœur 1985) (e.g., seasonal change, calendric regularity, or atomic timing) consequently entails a complexity of temporal processes synchronised in a socio-cultural transformation or mimesis of the way we originally relate to each other and the (in-)animated world surrounding us (Latour 1991; Adam 1998).

Thus, time constitutes a collectively shaped socio-cultural fact, which is based on our lived experience and is constantly reproduced through material as well as social practices.

These various socio-environmental practices imply a heterogeneous set of constitutive rules, normative ideals and symbolic structures of meaning constituting the social world. Hence, they are part of a social imaginary and its practical as well as representational mediation of the individual and the collective (Castoriadis 1987; Taylor 2007; Steger and James 2013). In times of pressing environmental crises, such a mediation often evolves around specific socio-environmental imaginaries (Levy and Spicer 2013; Jasanoff and Kim 2015; Milkoreit 2017a). Along with its ontological, normative and conceptual mode of social integration, the social imaginary further possesses an inevitable diachronic structure emerging at the intersection of our socio-environmental relationalities and their corresponding dialectic of temporal change and persistence. By connecting past experiences and future expectations, temporality, therefore, constitutes the integrative baseline according to which the normative structure of the social imaginary is articulated and enacted (Ricœur 1986). Conceiving temporality in such close connection with relationality eventually ascribes a normative texture to time and thereby reveals it as a constitutive part of socio-environmental recognition processes. Hence, temporality and normativity are strongly interrelated phenomena of our daily acting, and planning is fundamentally relied on.

The challenge of moral discounting in future ethics has emphasised how the significance of moral claims decreases, the further away relevant objects of concern seem to be. Instead of simply reducing moral discounting to a psychological phenomenon, we should first acknowledge the fact that climate justice principles incorporated in demands to curb global warming, reduce greenhouse gases, or secure biodiversity will eventually stay meaningless as long as their universal intention is not practically embedded and temporally indexicalised. Thus, the ability to criticise their presentism requires at first to consider the close connection between the definition of moral goals and notions of temporal urgency. Ultimately, every diachronic division into past, present and future times involves a separation of the reasonably expectable from mere speculations fundamentally supporting the formation of political short- and long-term calculations. This is also true for scientific data and calculations as "no climate scenario is ever neutral or unambiguously true" (Mehnert 2016, 5). This is of course no reason to ignore the important insights of climate research, but instead to better understand the social and cultural background of future scenarios (Reder 2017) and to explore new forms of (political) deliberating about scenarios by integrating stakeholders rooted in different practices (Kowarsch and Edenhofer 2016).

At the same time, climate ethics shows that although we are operating within the same human rights-based pattern of argumentation, different experiences of temporality can induce varying conceptions of temporal proximity and moral priority. On the one hand, the northern hemisphere, for example, is socio-economically better suited to adapt to occurring environmental disasters and thus is able to save time to further reflect on possibilities of an endangered planetary future. On the other hand, the Global South is extremely challenged in coping with life-threatening impacts in a vulnerable present. Despite the prevalence of clock time as a globally accepted temporal grid, our interactions are still scarred by varying temporal experiences leading to morally contesting claims. One of the most prominent current example of heterogeneous temporalities within global simultaneity are the Sustainable Development Goals (SDGs). On the one hand, their diversity enables us to display that climate challenges might differ in urgency according to their spatial occurrence. As a global paradigm, however, they oblige us to a shared concept of prosperity. These considerations further indicate an expansion of the social imaginary towards the global level (Steger and Patomäki 2010). Despite regional differences, paradigms like the SDGs refer to a global temporal mediation of actual threats and possible impacts, eventually leading to transregionally shared conceptions of sustainability, equality or equity.

Consequently, reflecting on temporality can help raise awareness for spatio-temporal differences influencing the reasonability of climate justice claims (May and Thrift 2001). Hence, it breaks open the unilateral reduction of temporal heterogeneity to one system of counting and thereby pluralises our normative capacities. It is important to notice that a time-transcending as well as context-transcending universal approach towards climate ethics can easily lead to an unrecognised precedence of specific and contemporary ways of argumentation over future impacts. Such presentism would entail a continuous transmission of inequalities supporting the initially mentioned division into climate change victims and main polluters. Instead, we have to find new forms of deliberatively integrating different social and cultural practices with their embedded concepts of time and underlying experiences of temporality into the discourse both on climate impacts and climate justice (Reder 2017).

However, beside all positive functions a (global) social imaginary also implies an excluding mechanism integrating communities by separating them from other societies or nature (Anderson 1991). In that regard, its integrative capacity is posing an obstacle limiting chances of globally meeting climate change. Its inherent temporal dimension also distinguishes them in an intergenerational manner. When future ethics ask if (and how much) we owe to people who will live *after* the current generation, they presuppose such an excluding distinction between people living today and those living in the future. It is on this basis that future generations are identified as individuals who have a normative status and, thus, also rights and duties (Gosseries and Meyer 2009).

Although both assumptions are not wrong from a philosophical perspective, they nevertheless imply problems which are, again, connected to the conceptualisation of social life. According to that, different generations can never be separated distinctly because "different generations" always already live together at the same time as part of social reality. Even present generations are not a closed homogeneous unit, but consist of different plural and dynamic parts that overlap and modify each other. This synchrony of generations within the "current generation" is often not considered enough, supporting the aforementioned unacknowledged presentism of climate moral reasoning (Faets et al. 2018).

These comments lead to the fundamental question of how we should conceptualise human reality on the whole. The synchrony of different generations already shows that human reality always has a relational structure. Individuals could not be isolated from each other, although some theories tend to do so on a theoretical level. Human reality is mainly characterised by people's indissoluble social interconnectedness. It is above all social relations (e.g., as practices or discourses) through which people develop into who they are. This relational concept of human beings also implies a diachronic dimension: people are always related both to the past and the future. Thus, one important (and sometimes neglected) challenge for the discourse on climate justice is how this diachronic relationality should be conceptualised in a convincing way. One set of theories, which is rooted in such a relational concept of human being, are narrative approaches.

A narrative account of climate justice and its temporal implications

The reflection on the function and also importance of the social imaginary in reference to the synergy of moral claims, practical embeddedness and temporality has already shown that the discourse on climate justice should not be reduced to rationalistic frameworks, but should be extended to alternative approaches. In this context, the adoption of a narrative account is helpful because it explicitly elaborates on the social and diachronic relationality of human beings. Following Paul Ricœur, narrativity can be conceptualised as a process of symbolic representation based on a time-sensitive productive social imagination (Ricœur 1986). Regarding the basic assumption that our pre-reflexive reference to the world is never based on neutral conjunctions of retentionally memorised and protentionally envisioned perceptions, narrative accounts conceive our primordial embeddedness as always already symbolically shaped (Ricœur 1985; Carr 1991). Hence, they directly follow the already mentioned integration of our socio-environmental as well as diachronic relationality into an encompassing social imaginary and its shared beliefs, symbols and institutions.

In that regard, narrativity can be linked to the cognitive as well as social aspects of individual and collective imagination. Such processes are located at the intersection of theoretical knowledge formation with social practices of interaction (Milkoreit 2017a, 2017b). Hence, imagination relies on practical as well as material structures of coherence referring to historically sedimented conceptual, linguistic and normative contexts of meaning (Ricœur 1986). Consequently, imagination constitutes a socially framed practice of adapting to the world. At the same time, its creative dimension emphasises our ability of transcending the latter towards alternatively envisioned states.

Narrativity, then, provides us with a way of figuratively representing the diachronic aspect such as an imagination involves by turning the fundamental temporal unfolding of our being in the world and its multidimensionality of material as well as socio-cultural references into a goal-directed plot structure. In doing so, narrative approaches are based on a continuum between fictionality and reality pointing towards the fact that all representations of past, present and future events necessarily imply aspects of varying possibilities (Carr 1991; Ricœur 1985). Every change (e.g., of narrator and/or reader position, plot structure, character specification, or semantic choice) eventually leads to a different appropriation of the world. Hence, narrative approaches can imaginatively renounce themselves from the here and now, thereby taking alternative ways of temporal representation into account. Apart from simply drawing on scientifically defined time grids and their fixed sequential order, they enable us to modify them (e.g., stretch, reverse, or arrange in parallel) referring to the aforementioned "plurivectoral" (Mertens and Craps 2018, 139) dimension of temporal experience.

By demarcating distant futures as imaginative horizons of expectation, narrativity implies a meta-ethical dimension ordering present as well as past actions and events in light of possible alternatives. In this context, a narrative is a kind of story, with which we "construct disparate facts in our own worlds and weave them together cognitively in order to make sense of our reality" (Patterson and Monroe 1998, 315). Hence, narrativity contributes a new ordering of events which leads to a critical re-evaluation of habituated validity claims as well as power structures. By providing the base for future plans and actions, such evaluations, ultimately, induce a readjustment of contemporary images of socio-environmental relationality and its diachronic evolvement, leading to a practical reshaping of reality (Daley 2016). Doing so, narrative approaches necessarily imply a pluralisation of temporal experiences and normative positions entering our moral deliberations. Instead of deducing principles from a disengaged transtemporal position, they critically question their validity by making hitherto-unheard positions (e.g., future generations or nature) perceptible (Young 2000; Dobson 2014).

Eventually, this further provides the opportunity of overcoming the rationalistic dualism between nature and culture by explicitly taking considerations of deep and social ecology into account. Resting upon the literary entanglement of different perspectives throughout a story (e.g., author, reader, narrator and character) (Newton 1995), narratively enhanced moral reasoning, thus, explicitly points towards a phenomenologically inspired mediation of the other as potential victim of my actions, thereby integrating various experiential, epistemic and normative communities, i.e., highlighting their reciprocal vulnerability and dependencies (Ricœur 1990; Carr 1991). Therefore, narratively accompanied approaches to climate justice are not limited to abstract moral reasoning and disengaged individual right-bearers, but refer to concrete socio-environmental life-worlds and their diverse visions of a just and sustainable linking of past, present and future times. Ultimately, this raises a transregional awareness for engaging with "the challenges of time, place and human agency that climate change poses" (Mehnert 2016, 43). At the same time, narratives influence the self-understanding of social and political actors and constitute both individual and collective identities and policies (Koschorke 2012).

Finally, narrative accounts are not reducible to one specific "literary genre," but constitute a world-displaying, reality-making and meaning-generating variation of temporal experiences (Daley 2016). Climate change narratives, thus, are not limited to representing reality as it seems to be. Insofar as they refer to creatively outlined *possible* impacts and their quasi-retrospective consequences for contemporary moral reasoning, they are able to overcome the representational challenge of climate justice approaches to rely on the unthinkable and unforeseeable of distant futures. Confronted with unlimited threats and challenges, they help humans to nevertheless structure respectively, "come to know, understand, and make sense of the social world" (Somers 1994, 606). Although many scientific scenarios as well as climate models inside and outside the IPCC are already relying on such a narrative outlining of the future, a consequent integration as internal, rather than external aspect of moral reasoning is still missing.

Besides supporting climate scenario modelling, imagination-based narrativity also constitutes a variety of other cultural practices which could be helpful to root the discourse on climate justice in the social life and to start a broad debate about how people want to live. One of those is climate fiction, which explicitly draws on the affective dimension of story-telling (e.g., in novels, films, or theatre productions), transcending the average human life span by an increased level of fictionality. Hypothetical scales like the "Anthropocene" (Clark 2015), for example, hereby receive a kind of creative configuration. Evaluating the contribution of climate fiction in light of the debate about climate justice eventually is due to the domain of ecocriticism, which refers to a combination of scientific research and cultural studies with literature critique (Garrard 2014; Wapner and Elver 2016). Moreover, ecocriticism is calling attention to the fact that today we are dealing with an "altered culture of time in which access to the past and especially to the future appears more limited than before in cultural self-awareness. If the teleological form of the nineteenth-century novel mediated the relationship between past and future in an era in which the future had become unpredictable on the basis of past social patterns, then the postmodernist novel confronts the more radically contingent future of Western societies in the late 20th century by projecting the temporal mode of the future into the narrative present and past" (Heise 1997, 67). Besides referring to the close entanglement of temporality and narrativity, ecocriticism, hence, adds an important meta-critique of possible narrative forms.

As another cultural practice, religions also supply (culturally embedded) narratives of climate justice all around the world. Although especially in western societies religions seemed destined to lose their importance with progressive modernisation and individualisation, they still play an important role both in western societies and worldwide (Martin 2005; Casanova 2010). Thus, the discourse on the social role of religions in post-modern societies recommenced about 20 years ago, and it is still going on (Habermas 2008). One important argument is that religions supply moral and political resources facing different challenges like climate change. Especially, religious narratives contribute to attaching climate justice to a basic understanding of nature and its temporal dimension. For instance, nearly all religions offer a narrative understanding of creation, emphasising the protection of nature and environment as fundamental of religious practice (Bloomquist and Machila 2009). As Gardner pointed out, in almost all religions the idea of "sacred ground" plays an important role (Gardner 2006). Within such a narrative of creation the social dimension of human beings – or "created man" as religiously phrased – is pronounced

(Reder 2012). Moreover, these narratives also always imply a temporal dimension which shows that human beings are related to the past and future at the same time.

Narratives about climate justices (like they are embedded in fiction or religions) could help to root the normative and political discourse in socio-cultural practices. They show that climate justice claims could (and should) not be formulated in only one reasonable paradigm but be linked to different narratives. This would help both to reflect about temporality as an inherent part of the discourse on climate change and to find other ways to support these claims in the political field. These arguments lead us to some concluding remarks on the political importance of a narrative account to climate justice.

Outlook on a political perspective

As we have shown, narrative approaches help to reformulate the concept of normativity embedded in the current discourse on climate justice. They provide access to the synergy of moral claims, practical embeddedness and temporality. First, reflections on narratives emphasise that ethical standards like sustainability and justice claims never exist in pure abstraction, but within specific socio-environmental contexts articulated by the relevant narrator. Second, narratives draw on our temporal existence and productive imagination, which ethical claims gain their integrative and critical potential from. Third, such references are synthesised in a (global) social imaginary that has profound consequences, both for people's everyday life and politics. As stated in the beginning, our individual and collective engagement in climate justice and corresponding human rights is at risk as long as this complexity of influences is not considered.

Fourth, the underlying imagination processes on which narrative approaches are based also motivate people to promote climate justice more than an abstract reference to a neutral and universal reason can. By compensating the lack of immediacy as well as uncertainty climate change entails and by tying their story or scenario back to concrete social imaginaries, narrative approaches can change the detachments of climate policies and mitigation strategies back to people's daily lives and concerns. Contrary to a concept of climate politics which reduces the political to technical solutions for climate impacts on the fundament of expert knowledge, such approaches want to stimulate narratives (and the public participatory debate about them) without which a fundamental political change won't happen (Milkoreit 2017b).

Hanna Arendt (1968) already pointed out the importance of such narratives to overcome injustice and to open a debate about future visions in general and political pathways in particular (Morgenstern 2014). And Markus Llanque (2014) argues that such narratives are necessary to complete rational arguments in the political field and to reflect and discuss who should be considered a part of the political. Climate impacts especially ask for such a reflection, both in a global and diachronic perspective. This is the reason why the discourse on climate justice should also focus on narratives as cultural practices and their political role.

Finally, narratives can shift focus from a passive adaptation to climate change's injustice and unavoidability towards an active figuration and shaping of the future. Although iconic symbols illustrating dramatic urgencies are an essential part of climate fiction (Nixon 2011; Mertens and Craps 2018), recent research has shown that apocalyptic scenarios (Skrimshire 2010) only activate people insofar as they entail a utopian aspect (Moylan and Baccolini 2007) of still being able to change the future. By relying on individual and collective imagination, narrativity can illustrate such collective envisioning. Thereby, narrativity entails a political dimension that cannot simply be reduced to the social imaginary as an already existing set of institutions and socio-political norms. Instead, it calls for a deliberation of political time itself (Saward 2017; Cohen 2018), which ultimately transcends given reality towards a collectively imagined future state. Such a collective deliberation about time can enhance the ability of political systems to transnationally raise awareness and a willingness to criticise and change our socio-environmental relationalities and their negative impacts. This might be an important step toward promoting climate justice in the political sphere.

References

Adam, B. (1995) *Timewatch: The Social Analysis of Time*. Polity Press, Cambridge

Adam, B. (1998) *Timescapes of Modernity: The Environment and Invisible Hazards*. Routledge, London

Anderson, B. R. (1991) *Imagined Communities: Reflections on the Origin and Spread of Nationalism*. Verso, London

Arendt, H. (1968) *Men in Dark Times*. Harcourt, Brace and World, New York

Bloomquist, K. L. and Machila, R. (2009) *God, Creation & Climate Change: A Resource for Reflection & Discussion*. Lutheran World Federation, Geneva

Caney, S. (2010) 'Climate Change, Human Rights and Moral Thresholds', in S. Humphreys (ed), *Human Rights and Climate Change*. Cambridge University Press, Cambridge

Caney, S. (2015) 'Two Kinds of Climate Justice', *Political Theory Without Borders*, vol 22, no 2, pp 18–45

Carr, D. (1991) *Time, Narrative, and History*. Indiana University Press, Bloomington and Indianapolis

Casanova, J. (2010) 'Religion in Modernity as Global Challenge', in M. Reder and M. Rugel (eds), *Religion und die umstrittene Moderne*. Kohlhammer, Stuttgart

Castoriadis, C. (1987) *The Imaginary Institution of Society*. Polity Press, Cambridge

Clark, T. (2015) *Ecocriticism on the Edge: The Anthropocene as a Threshold Concept*. Bloomsbury, London and New York

Cohen, E. F. (2018) *Political Value of Time: Citizenship, Duration, and Democratic Justice*. Cambridge University Press, Cambridge

Daley, L. (2016) 'Alexis Wright's Fiction as World-Making', *Contemporary Women's Writing*, vol 10, no 1, pp 8–23

Dobson, A. (2014) *Listening for Democracy: Recognition, Representation, Reconciliation*. Oxford University Press, Oxford

Edenhofer, O. et al. (eds) (2012) *Climate Change, Justice and Sustainability: Linking Climate and Development Policy*. Springer, New York and London

Faets, S. et al. (2018) 'Fresh Perspectives on Intergenerational Justice: Comments on Social Criticism, Temporality, and Future Narratives', *Yearbook Practical Philosophy in a Global Perspective*, no 2, pp 279–304

Gardiner, S. M. (2011) 'Climate Justice', in J. S. Dryzek, R. B. Norgaard, and D. Schlosberg (eds), *The Oxford Handbook of Climate Change and Society*. Oxford University Press, Oxford

Gardner, G. T. (2006) *Inspiring Progress: Religions' Contributions to Sustainable Development*. World Watch Institute, Washington, DC.

Garrard, G. (ed) (2014) *The Oxford Handbook of Ecocriticism*. Oxford University Press, Oxford

Gosseries, A. and Meyer, L. (eds) (2009) *Intergenerational Justice*. Oxford University Press, Oxford

Habermas, J. (2008) *Between Naturalism and Religion*. Polity Press, Cambridge

Hassan, R. (2009) *Empires of Speed: Time and the Acceleration of Politics and Society*. Brill, Leiden

Heise, U. K. (1997) *Chronoschisms: Time, Narrative, and Postmodernism*. Cambridge University Press, Cambridge

Heyward, C. and Roser, D. (eds) (2016) *Climate Justice in a Non-Ideal World*. Oxford University Press, Oxford

Jasanoff, S. and Kim, S.-H. (eds) (2015) *Dreamscapes of Modernity: Sociotechnical Imaginaries and the Fabrication of Power*. University of Chicago Press, Chicago

Joas, H. (2000) *The Genesis of Values*. University of Chicago Press, Chicago

Koschorke, A. (2012) *Wahrheit und Erfindung. Grundzüge einer Allgemeinen Erzähltheorie*. Fischer, Frankfurt/M

Kowarsch, M. and Edenhofer, O. (2016) 'Principles or Pathways? Improving the Contribution of Philosophical Ethics to Climate Policy', in C. Heyward and D. Roser (eds), *Climate Justice in a Non-Ideal World*. Oxford University Press, Oxford

Latour, B. (1991) *Nous n'avons jamais été modernes: Essais d'anthropologie symétrique*. La Découverte, Paris

Levy, D. L. and Spicer, A. (2013) 'Contested Imaginaries and the Cultural Political Economy of Climate Change', *Organization*, vol 20, no 5, pp 659–678

Lindemann, H. (2006) 'Wrinkels in Time: Narrative Approaches to Ethics', in G. Pfleiderer and C. Rehmann-Sutter (eds), *Zeithorizonte des Ethischen. Zur Bedeutung der Temporalität in der Fundamental- und Bioethik*. Kohlhammer, Stuttgart

Llanque, M. (2014) 'Metaphern, Metanarrative und Verbindlichkeitsnarrationen. Narrative in der Politischen Theorie', in W. Hofmann, J. Renner and K. Teich (eds), *Narrative Formen der Politik*. Springer, Berlin

Martin, D. (2005) *On Secularization: Towards a Revised General Theory*. Ashgate, Aldershot

May, J. and Thrift, N. (2001) *Timespace: Geographies of Temporality*. Routledge, London and New York.

Mehnert, A. (2016) *Climate Change Fictions: Representations of Global Warming in American Literature*. Palgrave Mcmillan, New York.

Mertens, M. and Craps, S. (2018) 'Contemporary Fiction vs. the Challenge of Imagining the Timescale of Climate Change', *Studies in the Novel*, vol 50, no 1, pp 134–153

Meyer, L. (2003) 'Past and Future. The Case for a Threshold Conception of Harm', in L. Meyer et al. (eds), *Rights, Culture, and the Law: Themes From the Legal and Political Philosophy of Joseph Raz*. Oxford University Press, Oxford

Meyer, L. (2008) 'Intergenerational Justice', http://plato.stanford.edu/entries/justice-intergenerational/ accessed 15. March 2018

Milkoreit, M. (2017a) 'Imaginary Politics: Climate Change and Making the Future', *Elementa. Science of the Anthropocene*, vol 5, no 62, np

Milkoreit, M. (2017b) *Mindmade Politics: The Cognitive Roots of International Climate Governance*. MIT Press, Cambridge, MA

Morgenstern, K. (2014) '"All Sorrows Can Be Borne If You Put them in a Story". Funktionen der Narrativität für das politische Denken bei Hannah Arendt', in W. Hofmann, J. Renner and K. Teich (eds), *Narrative Formen der Politik*. Springer, Berlin

Morton, T. (2013) *Hyperobjects: Philosophy and Ecology After the End of the World*. University of Minnesota Press, Minneapolis and London

Moylan, T. and Baccolini, R. (2007) *Utopia, Method, Vision: The Use Value of Social Dreaming*. Lang, Oxford

Newton, A. Z. (1995) *Narrative Ethics*. Harvard University Press, Cambridge, MA

Nixon, R. (2011) *Slow Violence and the Environmentalism of the Poor*. Harvard University Press, Cambridge and London

Patterson, M. and Monroe, K. R. (1998) 'Narrative in Political Science', *Annual Review of Political Science*, vol 1, pp 315–331

Plumwood, V. (1991) 'Nature, Self, and Gender: Feminism, Environmental Philosophy, and the Critique of Rationalism', *Hypathia*, vol 6, no 1, pp 3–27

Reder, M. (2012) 'Religion in the Public Sphere: The Social Function of Religion in the Context of Climate and Development Policy', in D. Gerten and S. Bergmann (eds), *Religion in Environmental and Climate Change: Suffering, Values, Lifestyles*. Bloomsbury, New York

Reder, M. (2017) 'Narrating the Future: Between Scientific Scenarios and Political Deliberation – A Pragmatist Comment', in N. Dahlhaus and D. Weißkopf (eds), *Future Scenarios of Global Cooperation – Practices and Challenges*. Käte Hamburger Kolleg, Duisburg.

Reder, M. and Köhler, L. (2016) 'Human Rights as a Normative Guideline for Climate Policy', in M. Düwel and G. Bos (eds), *Human Rights and Sustainability – Moral Responsibilities for the Future*. Routledge, Oxford

Ricœur, P. (1985) *Temps et Récit. Tome 3*. Seuil, Paris

Ricœur, P. (1986) *Du Texte à l'Action. Essais d'Herméneutique II*. Seuil, Paris

Ricœur, P. (1990) *Soi-même comme un Autre*. Seuil, Paris

Rosa, H. (2010) *Alienation and Acceleration: Towards a Critical Theory of Late-Modern Temporality*. NSU Press, Malmö and Arhus

Saward, M. (2017) 'Agency, Design and "Slow Democracy"', *Time and Society*, vol 26, no 3, pp 362–383

Shue, H. (2014) *Climate Justice: Vulnerability and Protection*. Oxford University Press, Oxford

Skrimshire, S. (ed) (2010) *Future Ethics: Climate Change and Apocalyptic Imagination*. Continuum, London

Somers, M. R. (1994) 'The Narrative Constitution of Identity: A Relational and Network Approach', *Theory and Society*, vol 23, no 5, pp 605–649

Steger, M. B. and James, P. (2013) 'Levels of Subjective Globalization: Ideologies, Imaginaries, Ontologies', *Perspectives on Global Development and Technology*, vol 12, no 1–2, pp 17–40

Steger, M. B. and Patomäki, H. (2010) 'Social Imaginaries and Big History: Toward a New Planetary Consciousness?', *Futures*, vol 42, no 10, pp 1056–1063

Taylor, C. (1995) 'Overcoming Epistemology', in C. Taylor (ed), *Philosophical Arguments*. Harvard University Press, Cambridge, MA

Taylor, C. (2007) *Modern Social Imaginaries*, Duke University Press, Durham

Wallack, M. (2006) 'Justice Between Generations: The Limits of Procedural Justice', in J. Tremmel (ed), *Handbook of Intergenerational Justice*. Edward Elgar, Cheltenham and Northampton

Wapner, P. and Elver, H. (eds) (2016) *Reimagine Climate Change*. Routledge, Abingdon and New York

Young, I. M. (2000) *Inclusion and Democracy*. Oxford University Press, Oxford

Part II

Climate justice governance, policy and litigation

Global political processes and the Paris Agreement

A case of advancement or retreat of climate justice?

Susan P. Murphy

Introduction

National pathways to the The Paris Agreement (UNFCCC 2015) on Climate Change, and the years of international negotiation leading up to this, are marked by patterns of acceptance and resistance, almost in equal measure. The scientific consensus regarding the anthropogenic impacts on the natural environment and the practical implications of this in the form of changing climates, disappearing ecosystems and species, and wide-scale human and non-human impacts to the planet (IPCC 2014) seem to have largely been accepted by the majority of leaders in political, industry and business, religious, and governance communities. However, what this implies for citizens of distinct states, industry and businesses, political and religious leaders is the subject of deep dispute, conflict and resistance on multiple scales. Indeed, overarching normative questions related to the allocation of responsibilities for the outcomes of collective actions, and who ought to do what for whom have been central to the negotiations within the international climate change regime, and rest at the heart of some of the tensions of the new framework for managing climate action outlined in the Paris Agreement.

Although these questions remain unresolved – and indeed the Agreement has come under direct attack from political leaders in one of the largest emitting nations[1] – the Paris COP21 negotiation process and outcomes marks a distinct shift within the climate change governance regime. It has moved from a formal intergovernmental legally binding agreement (Kyoto Protocol) with prescribed targets for emissions reductions, rights and responsibilities allocations across states, with the most highly industrialised developed states carrying the responsibility to drive mitigation and adaptation actions – including financial, technical and capacity-building support to developing states – to what has been called a "bottom-up" innovative approach based on a system where all states (Parties) will voluntarily develop and oversee their individual nationally determined contributions (NDCs).

This shift moves away from justice-based principles to guide in the distribution of responsibilities towards principles of voluntariness and what might be termed "disbursed responsibility." Such an adaptation brings fresh opportunities. It offers the potential to mitigate deeply entrenched blockages to climate action concerning political and funding constraints, asymmetric ex-ante knowledge and preference requirements of top-down, narrow government-funded approaches. However, it also generates a range of new risks for current and future generations and the non-human environment in the distinctly non-ideal circumstances of the global climate change governance regime. Responsibility for action has been disbursed across a much wider range of actors, but it remains unclear how the rights and interests of all those affected by changing climates can be respected and protected in this new landscape of voluntariness.

The non-ideal circumstances of climate justice

That climate change gives rise to considerations of justice is, as Henry Shue (2014) has said, "unavoidable." Hume's circumstances of justice (1978, 1975), which include conditions of moderate scarcity of resources (see, for example, Rockstrom et al. 2009), limited altruism and mutual disinterestedness, can be found to underpin the climate change negotiations. From the signing of the Kyoto Protocol in 1997 to the emergence of the Paris Agreement in December 2015, the most powerful and highest emitting state members of the United Nations Framework Convention for Climate Change (UNFCCC) Conference of Parties (COP) had systematically failed to collectively demonstrate the required level of impartiality, magnanimity and vision necessary to ensure that human and non-human development and wellbeing can be protected and respected in an age of climate change. The unrelenting use and abuse of the biological, physical and chemical components of the earth's environment by human beings without sufficient regard for the reach and consequences of such actions has left us with some of the most pressing problems ever faced by the human species (IPCC 2013). Further, there is a disconnect between those who are at greatest risk of harm and those benefiting from this activity. Thus, justice – a distinctly relational and human concept and practice – is necessary to navigate and arbitrate among conflicting interests. In addition to altering emissions-dependent development paths and unsustainable production and consumption patterns, principles of justice, as scholars have argued for decades (see, for example, Caney 2014; Shue 2014; Gardiner 2011; Jamieson 2008), are required to guide in the institutional arrangements to manage the distribution of the benefits and burdens, rights and responsibilities, fairly and equitably. Justice, very broadly speaking, refers to each person getting what s/he needs, deserves or is entitled to. Fairness, again broadly speaking, refers to judgements and evaluations based on some explicit and agreed-upon criteria of impartiality (Murphy 2011).

However, as decades of rigorous scholarship across disciplines from philosophy to the humanities and the sciences can attest, conceptualisations of justice and fairness, and the most appropriate principles of justice to guide action in this space, are highly contested (Gardiner, Caney, Jamieson and Shue 2010; Okereke and Coventry 2016; Holland 2017). The realm of climate change is marked by distinctly non-ideal circumstances, and thus, or so I will argue, lends itself most appropriately to a non-idealised theorising about justice. The circumstances are described as non-ideal in the sense that all parties will not and do not take responsibility for their actions and fulfil their duties (privatising their gains and socialising the externalities); there is a distinct lack of formal coercive institutions in place to enforce principles of justice at the international scale; the circumstances of climate change are marked by practical and scientific uncertainty regarding the temporal and spatial effects of climate change and the causal connections between particular emissions and particular events (IPCC 2013); the outcomes of adaptation interventions aimed at local scale and sectoral-level resilience building can be uncertain (Arndt and Tarp 2017; Paavola and Adger 2006); and the negotiations are marked by a plurality of reasonable (and sometimes unreasonable) values, justifications and motivations that are possibly irreconcilable and incompatible. This then points to the need for alternative, non-idealised approaches if progress is to be achieved.

Non-ideal theorising about climate justice

By non-ideal theorising about justice, the following draws upon and expands the idea of justice articulated by Amartya Sen (2009). Sen has developed what he describes as a comparative method which he claims allows for social comparisons between "more" and "less" just conditions within and between actual societies, giving adequate consideration to actual circumstances. His task is "to investigate realisation-based comparisons that focus on the advancement or retreat of justice" (Sen 2009: 8). This, he describes broadly, is the method of "consequential evaluation" (Sen 2000). Sen argues that "judgements about justice have to take on board the task of accommodating different kinds of reasons and evaluative concerns" (Sen 2009: 395). Thus, the outcomes do not aim towards ideal ends of full and complete justice, but to more modest ends that are more just, rather than less just. Such an approach, I suggest, offers a promising pathway to evaluating the processes employed at COP21, which culminated in the Paris Agreement, which, at the time of writing, has been ratified by 179 parties out of 197 Parties to the Convention (UNFCCC 2018), and also the outcome from this process.

Chapter overview

This chapter addresses the following question: does the process and outcome of the Paris Agreement lead to an advancement of or a retreat from climate justice concerns? Scholarly contributions from the disciplines of political philosophy and social science have focused heavily, according to Simon Caney (2014), on the distributive – or burden-sharing – elements of climate justice over the last three decades. This is also evident in the practice-based advocacy space of climate justice, where organisations such as the Mary Robinson Foundation-Climate Justice have actively advocated for the equitable distribution of the benefits and burdens of climate change globally (2011). However, other important dimensions of justice are relevant to explore in addressing this question, and indeed that have emerged through the process of negotiating a new climate agreement. Firstly, the processes of negotiation and agreement at the Paris COP21 marked a distinct shift away from traditional climate change regime treaty negotiations from the top-down, command-control model evident in the Kyoto Protocol to a bottom-up approach whereby states determine their commitments for themselves and commit to reporting these back into the international climate governance architecture to be shared with all others. This prompts normative questions relating to procedural justice and principles that now guide the climate change governance regime. How is fairness secured, protected and progressed? Secondly, regarding the outcomes of COP21, there are normative questions related to the status and possibility of remedy and rectificatory justice in light of the recognition of Loss and Damage within the Paris Agreement. Thirdly, in relation to the distribution of responsibility for mitigation and adaptation measures, does the voluntary NDC framework of the Paris Agreement point to more or less just outcomes? Overall, with the introduction of new elements and instruments, what are the implications of the Paris Agreement for harm-avoidance (or forward-looking) justice and burden-sharing (or backward-looking/historical claims) justice, both of which, according to Simon Caney (2014), are essential elements of a theory of justice in an age of climate change?

The following will begin with an overview of the Paris Agreement and how this represents a distinctive shift in content and approach. It will then examine the global political processes that informed COP21 and the Paris Agreement and ethically evaluate the process of negotiation and the outcomes of COP 21 and the Paris Agreement from a climate justice perspective with a particular focus on procedural justice. More specifically, it examines both the process and institutional structures that supported the attainment of the Agreement and the framework that has emerged to guide action. It will utilise a blend of methods including content analysis and analytical methods of testing for clarity, coherence, consistency and logic drawn from the discipline of normative political theory to enable a comparative consequential evaluation of both the processes and outcomes.

Pathway to the Paris Agreement

Political processes and activities that culminated in the Paris Agreement at COP21, in December 2015, were ongoing for many years before this event (Lyster 2017). Following what many regarded as the failure to reach agreement on a legally binding protocol and instrument to replace the Kyoto Protocol at COP15 (UNFCCC 2009), it seemed clear to those involved, as well as observers, that a new approach would be required to facilitate the development of an international agreement. At COP17 (UNFCCC 2011) in Durban, South Africa, the Ad Hoc Working Group on the Durban Platform for Enhanced Action (ADP) was established with a mandate to develop:

> A protocol, another legal instrument or an agreed outcome with legal force under the Convention applicable to all Parties, which is to be completed no later than 2015 in order for it to be adopted at the twenty-first session of the Conference of the Parties (COP) and for it to come into effect and be implemented from 2020.
>
> *(UNFCCC 2011 decision 1/CP.17)*

ADP invited submissions from all Parties and delivered a series of draft negotiating texts throughout 2015. Efforts were made to ensure that the process of negotiation was open, transparent and inclusive. The draft documents were made publically available through the UNFCCC open access website, and a wide range of groups – state and non-state – were invited to provide input, review, comment, advise and engage with the early drafts of the key negotiating texts.

Removing blockages and barriers to agreement

From differentiated to disbursed responsibility

Entering into 2015 there was a strong division of positions between the negotiating parties. As Santos notes, there were "normative deadlocks over responsibilities to be undertaken, the definition of the efforts to be made, the sharing of the massive costs to address the problem, the distribution of rights to emit, and types of agents that should bear the burdens" (Santos 2017: 1). A key area of conflict concerned the underlying equity principle of "Common but differentiated responsibilities" (CBDR) as outlined in the Convention (UNFCCC 1992) and activated through the Kyoto Protocol. Negotiating teams divided mainly along traditional lines with developed states, representing highly industrialised high-income states, emphasising the "common responsibility" aspect of this principle and sought for all states to share in the division of responsibilities. Developing states, on the other hand, entered the negotiations with a strong focus on the "differentiated responsibility" aspect of the principle and sought exemption from obligations that might interfere with their economic development pathways, and further sought bolder leadership and greater action from developed states in the form of emissions-reduction activity, financial supports for adaptation and mitigation, and increased delivery of technical and capacity-building supports (Okereke and Coventry 2016: 837; Dimitrov 2016; Santos 2017). The issue of historical responsibility is widely reported to have been one of the key sticking points leading to the failure to secure a Global Agreement at earlier Conference of Party summits. Thus, before the conference, a shift was already evident whereby the language of negotiation moved from the principle of "Common but differentiated responsibility" to the language of "Common but differentiated responsibility and respective capabilities in the light of different national circumstances." This linguistic elaboration effectively disbursed and displaced responsibility from those historically responsible for emitting the highest amounts of greenhouse gases, to all Parties (Okereke and Coventry 2016). It also solidified future state-based justifications for inaction and behavioural change avoidance. However, it can be argued that this turn dissolved a key political blockage in the negotiations and enabled Parties to move forward to seek new grounds for consensus and agreement.

From principles of justice to principles of virtue

The Agreement enshrines the principle of voluntary action (indeed, the term "voluntary" appears five times in the core text (Articles 6 and 9)) in relation to the content and ownership of the NDC approach, and financing – thus, applying to the core areas of mitigation, adaptation and financing the transition. This marks a substantial move away from ideals of perfect justice that aim towards enforcement of prescribed action based on an understanding of what is right, correct and lawful towards imperfect ideals of what is good and appropriate, opening the space for an indeterminate range of actions that states could undertake. It can be argued that this shift removes the blockages evident over the previous decades linked to political constraints, lack of public funds and political will, information asymmetries and epistemic gaps concerning the solutions and right actions to take to drive climate change. In practice, top-down, precisely prescribed approaches are extremely unlikely to yield the types of innovations and transformations required to drive the transition to emissions reductions and sustainable development.

COP21 and the negotiation process

The transparent approach adapted by UNFCCC by sharing the drafts of the negotiating text through multiple iterations using its online open access forum provided unique insights into the arduous and delicate process of negotiation and consensus-building in conditions marked by asymmetrical power relationships and dense political dynamics. In early February 2015, the ADP released the Geneva negotiating text, which included over 54,494 words and contained 103 points of consideration, including numerous options. Over the course of the following ten months, this was reduced to a final text containing 29 Articles expressed in 7,380 words (December 2015). According to commentators and observers, the most substantive changes emerged in the final days and hours of the negotiating process in the Paris Conference (Dimitrov 2016; Weisser and Muller-Mahn 2017).

It is important to note that the Agreement should be read in conjunction with the accompanying Decision 1/CP.21, as there is additional critical information contained in this document that sheds important light on the implications and practical intent of the Agreement. For example, Article 8 of the Agreement addresses the matter of loss and damage, outlining how Parties will engage to deepen understandings, support and action on losses and damages arising as a consequence of climate change that have not been and will not – or indeed cannot – be addressed through adaptation measures. Recognition of such harms is a critical element to enable compensation and remedy. However, Paragraph 51 of the Decisions document clearly states that the Conference "agrees that Article 8 of the Agreement does not involve or provide a basis for any liability or compensation" (1/CP.21: 8). Thus, although the Agreement itself appears to represent an advancement of justice, it can be argued that the Decision document equally appears to counter and neutralise this advancement.

Evaluating the outcomes

For some the negotiating process was evidence of advanced skills of diplomacy – "a political success in climate negotiations and traditional state diplomacy" (Dimitrov 2016: 1). For others it represented a "post-democratic turn" where reasoning and evaluation was privatised and hidden with public declarations of progress stage-managed to mask the lack of democratic deliberation in the emerging agreement (Weisser and Muller-Mahn 2017: 802). Indeed, according to Okereke and Coventry (2016: 838), "the emerging regime that saw a new global agreement reached in Paris in 2015 remains dogged by a widely acknowledged lack of fair and effective participation by developing countries and non-state actors." But how do we navigate and evaluate between these opposing accounts? How might we examine the justness of the institutional processes and procedures through which decisions were made?

In addressing this question it may be helpful to distinguish between the horizontal and vertical features of the institutional processes and procedures, as well as the agent-based and structural features of the process. This requires consideration of a range of matters including transparency and openness, fairness and public legitimacy,[2] inclusive participation and recognition[3] and epistemic justice,[4] as important dimensions of procedurally just processes.[5]

Transparency and openness

Both advocates and critics of the Paris Agreement and the COP21 negotiation process agree that, firstly, the UNFCCC is often praised for its transparent and inclusive approach. Indeed, the work of the ADP over the years since its inception in 2011 points to a commitment to transparent and inclusive engagement. However, secondly, both also agree that the two weeks of the Paris Summit represented the space and site where the most critical and contentious negotiations took place. Indeed, final decisions emerged behind closed doors with select parties included and all others excluded from the decision-making process and reasoning. In their damning critique of the Paris Process, Weisser and Muller-Mahn (2017) argue that,

> [I]f the stages are the places where the international political economy of climate change is publically legitimised and defended, the backrooms constitute the spaces in which it is subject to heavy dispute. These disputes are often not solved by the better argument but by strategies and tactics that push vested interests. These interests are kept in the shadows on purpose as they would delegitimate a whole range of states and their agendas in environmental governance.
>
> *(2017: 811)*

For advocates of the summit and outcomes, these points are not disputed. The political strategy of intentionally privatising decision-making and reducing the space for public deliberation and democratic participation has been lauded by some as a master class in diplomacy (Dimitrov 2016). Access for state and non-state actors was managed and restricted. In the second week, governments were issued with a limited number of passes for entry into negotiating spaces, and civil society actors were excluded fully from these critical decision-making sites, with selected sessions being televised over the course of the summit. The final days of the summit were completely given over to private consultation, with no official negotiation or public deliberations taking place. Radoslav Dimitrov, a government representative in the process, argues that "the Paris outcome was made possible by the heavy use of secrecy. . . . Secrecy is common in diplomacy, but the French finessed it to a new level" (2016: 6).

Thus, the final negotiation and decision-making stages were clearly not transparent or open. Some will argue that this was a necessary political strategy to enable agreement to emerge; others will argue that this marks a post-democratic turn that put politics and public deliberation aside in favour of private interest and technocratic management. From a normative perspective it would seem that the exclusive and exclusionary nature of the process, whereby those affected by the decisions and outcomes were not granted access to the deliberation process and debates, would thus not meet the minimal requirements of a procedurally just process. Opportunities to engage in public reasoning and debate were intentionally closed and silenced; the interests of the negotiating partners were not made explicit – indeed, the process itself seems to represent an example of the complete opposite of ideal conditions to reach a fair and legitimate Agreement;[6] it is unclear if those affected by the decisions were included or excluded from the negotiating chambers, and if and how their positions and interests were considered. Rather than attempting to seek some level of impartiality and distance from vested interests, it appears as though self-interest (states' interests and corporate interests) were central to the process.

However, the infrastructure and procedures established to oversee the development, delivery and sharing of the NDCs does at least provide some indication that the framework now in place to guide climate action and decision making can facilitate greater transparency and openness. The majority of Parties submitted intentional nationally determined contributions before the event and continued to submit these after the conference. The Agreement requires Parties to commit to review NDCs on a recurring basis and to seek to "progress" their ambition over time. Thus, each Party has an opportunity to view what others are (or are not) doing and achieving over the coming years. The data that should emerge from this process, assuming this is sufficiently robust, can thus be utilised to inform future negotiations and actions.

Fairness and public legitimacy

In spite of the findings of opaqueness and exclusion in the process of negotiation outlined here, it is also important to reflect on whether the content of the Agreement has produced an institutional approach that can advance justice and lead to improved outcomes for all concerned.

It seems clear that the Paris Agreement reflects and reinforces national sovereignty and the state as the locus of all action and decision making within the climate change governance regime. Rather than moving towards a more globalised institutional architecture to enforce legally binding actions and arbitrate among competing national interests, the Nationally Determined Contributions framework on the basis of voluntary cooperation repositions the role of the state and unilateral action as the most appropriate framework for decision making and action.

From the perspective of public legitimacy, it seems reasonable to assume that states are then expected to justify their plans to their local population and manage the implementation of projects and programmes at the local level. Rather than a post-democratic turn, it could be argued that the new approach creates the conditions for significantly more, rather than less, democratic deliberation and input from a wider range of actors and agents within each state. Further, it can be argued that this approach recognises the problem-solving capacities of states and supports states in navigating their situated contexts to make the most appropriate decisions on a range of national issues. Depending on how state sovereignty is defined (Ronzoni 2012) and actualised, this may not necessary lead to less just outcomes. Thus, it can be argued that although the initial process was exclusive and non-democratic, the outcome Agreement creates the conditions for states to take a wider, more expansive, inclusionary approach to resolve problems with and for its populations. Rather than operating towards a set of externally prescribed rules, goals and targets, a bottom-up and voluntary approach allows flexibility to respond to problems as they arise. It can create the possibilities of setting more ambitious and far-reaching targets, and include a whole-of-society approach to planning and development. It can be argued that this is the most appropriate approach in non-ideal complex circumstances marked by a high degree of uncertainty and unwillingness to act on the part of some member states.

However, for many, this shift to reinforcing national sovereignty and state-centred deliberation will be a cause of concern. In the absence of mechanisms for enforcement, it is not clear that this approach can protect fairness and promote just outcomes either within individual states or between states. The retreat to voluntariness implies that states cannot be sanctioned for failing to deliver on their commitments. States cannot be forced (rather, they will be encouraged) to increase their commitments to reflect their responsibilities for the outcomes of their action. They cannot be held accountable for the effects of their actions over temporal and spatial distances. States cannot be coerced into a rights-based approach to their development planning and practices (De Shutter 2011), thus leaving hidden the multiscalar dimensions of climate justice and injustices that already evident in relation to land rights and indigenous communities, for example (Fairhead, Leach and Scoones 2012; Leach, Fairhead and Fraser 2012). These are real-world practical concerns for already vulnerable and historically marginalised communities and populations.

Finally, this framework does not reflect or include the range of relevant semi-state, non-state and trans-state actors. From a normative perspective, it is not clear that appropriate and sufficiently just institutions are currently in place to respect, protect and fulfil the rights of all, not to oversee the fair distribution of benefits and burdens across populations and borders. Indeed, given contemporary levels of inequality not only between states but within states (both developed and developing), it seems unlikely that this new approach will lead to "more just" rather than "less just" outcomes. The Agreement does nothing to address the unequal starting positions of the Parties, and there is no commit to take actions to level the international playing field, or address the structural features that produce and sustain the contemporary global political economy. Further, given the absence of clear justice and/or equity indicators in the monitoring mechanisms (see, for example, Articles 6 and 15) proposed, there is no certainty that some vulnerable and marginalised communities will not be worse off under the new arrangements.

Inclusive participation: recognition, epistemic and remedial justice

In the opening paragraphs of the Agreement (2015), it is stated that all Parties acknowledge the following:

> [C]limate change is a common concern of humankind, Parties **should**, when taking action to address climate change, respect, promote and consider their respective obligations on human rights, the right to health, the rights of indigenous peoples, local communities, migrants, children, persons with disabilities and people in vulnerable situations and the right to development, as well as gender equality, empowerment of women and intergenerational equity.
>
> *[emphasis added by the author]*

Thus, the acknowledgement that climate change is a common concern of all humankind would then suggest a whole-of-society approach to participation in climate action planning, for mitigation and adaptation is instrumentally necessary to secure successful outcomes and intrinsically essential in democratic and consent-based contexts. However, as the term "should" rather than "shall" is used in this acknowledgement, it is not clear if States are obliged to extend consideration to all in their actions, or are merely encouraged to do so. Further, a cursory glance at the specific Articles entailed in the Agreement does not point to encouraging signs of inclusive participation. For example, the term *gender* is mentioned only twice (Article 7, in relation to adaptation, and Article 11, in relation to capacity building); indigenous populations are only mentioned once (Article 7); and human rights and justice do not feature in any of the substantive articles of the text. Indeed, reference to "Climate Justice" is noted as an important concept "for some" when taking action on climate change. Earlier drafts of the negotiating texts included substantially stronger commitments to justice, rights and the protection and promotion of the interests of marginalised populations (see, for example, the options included in the Geneva Negotiating Text, February 2015). The intentional removal of such text from the substantive articles and the apparent decreasing commitment to these elements does not point to advancement for justice in this regard.

Further, during the process of negotiating the text, it would seem fair to suggest that the interests of all those affected by climate change should feature in considerations on climate action and planning. Although all states were represented and had a vote on the final Agreement, counting the number of those with voting rights is not a sufficient indicator of participation. Rather, recognition of all agents as agents in equal standing – evidence that voices have not only been raised but actually listened to and heard – is also a necessary element of procedural justice, in particular in non-ideal circumstances that lack a clear framework and enforcement mechanisms for addressing conflict and non-or-mal performance. Further, the voices of non-state and transnational actors were distinctly missing from the negotiations and are absent in the Agreement.

One step forward?

The evolution of the Article on "Loss and Damage," which can be examined through an analysis of the draft documents from February 2015 through to the final agreement in December 2015, provides an interesting example of voices being raised but not being heard. On entering into negotiations, there seemed to be consensus within developed states that they would not accept any basis for liability and compensation for historical responsibilities (Lyster 2017; Okereke and Coventry 2016). Numerous options were examined through the negotiating stages, including an option not to reference loss and damage at all. However, developing countries and the most vulnerable states, including low-income least developed and small island developing states, insisted that "loss and damage" must be recognised within the agreement. Thus, Article 8 emerged as part of the final Agreement. However, as mentioned earlier, the accompanying Decisions document (1.CP/17) removed the possibility of using this as a basis for remedial justice, the attribution of liability or the possibility of compensation. This indicates that the voices of the most vulnerable populations were raised, but it is not at all clear that they were understood, accepted or listened to in any substantive sense.

A similar argument can be made in the case of the Scientific Community. In spite of rigorous research, multiple scenario testing and rich sets of recommendations, the final Agreement does not contain mandatory targets to restrict global average temperature increases. Article 2 specifies an aspiration to hold "the increase in the global average temperature to well below 2°C above pre-industrial levels and pursue efforts to limit the temperature increase to 1.5°C above pre-industrial." It seems to be clear that the scientific findings and key recommendations acknowledge, but binding mandatory action has not followed.

However, in both of these cases it is still important to note that the inclusion of a "loss and damage" clause, and the inclusion of the commitment to take action to hold the increase in temperatures to below 2 degrees Celsius (albeit through voluntary NDCs), are both important advancements in the battle to contain and address harms that will arise (indeed, are already evident) as a consequence of climate change. As such, their inclusion in this Agreement is to be welcomed, and indeed, albeit imperfectly, they mark an advancement in climate justice. Both of these clauses, if given serious attention and action, could lead to more just outcomes for affected populations.

Conclusion

Overall, this evaluation finds that the Agreement represents some advancement in a number of critical areas of climate justice. These include firstly, the inclusion of a "Loss and Damage" article which gives recognition to the remedial dimensions of climate justice; secondly, the commitment to take bold action to reduce emissions, transition economies towards sustainable pathways, and to hold increases in global temperatures to below 2 degrees Celsius, which highlights the collective responsibilities of all parties; and thirdly, in broadening the basis of participation and engagement with the possibility for a whole-of-society bottom-up engagement, thus recognising the agency and autonomy of all those affected by changing climates. However, as noted earlier, in the absence of mechanisms to allocate responsibility and liability, the "Loss and Damage" article remain under-specified. In the absence of enforcement mechanisms and a strong institutional framework, mitigation commitments remain in the realm of voluntariness. Principles of public reasoning, democratic deliberation and procedural fairness required to give rise to a whole-of-society approach to climate change will continue to vary, temporally and spatially.

Thus, the agreement that emerged represents both advances in some areas but a significant retreat in other areas that, on balance, indicate a long path ahead for seeking institutions and principles of distributive and remedial justice. Further, without principles to guide in public practical reasoning, deliberation and evaluation, the framework that has emerged from Paris risks introducing new forms of injustice in the form of epistemic exclusion of those who are most exposed to the harmful effects of climate change – internationally and intergenerationally. In spite of these concerns, the chapter argues that the Paris Agreement represents a small step towards more just rather than less just outcomes, albeit imperfect and incomplete. This is to be welcomed and protected in the contemporary non-ideal circumstances of the global climate change regime.

Notes

1 I refer here to the U.S. President Trump's decision to withdraw the U.S. from the Paris Agreement, 2017. (www.theguardian.com/us-news/video/2017/jun/01/donald-trump-us-will-withdraw-from-paris-agreement-video)

2 See Sen (2009) and O'Neill (2000, 2001), on public and practical reasoning and methods of evaluation and justification.

3 See Irish Marion Young's work on recognition, justice and difference.

4 See Miranda Fricker (2007) on the demands of epistemic justice.

5 See contributions on different accounts of procedural justice in the climate change space in Holland (2017); Paavola and Adger (2006); Schlosberg, Collins and Niemeyer (2017).

6 See, for example, Rawls's Original Position and the use of the Veil of Ignorance; or Habermas's Ideal Speech Situation.

References

Arndt, C. and F. Tarp, 2017. "Aid, Environment and Climate Change." *Review of Development Economics* 21(2): 285–303.

Caney, S., 2014. "Two Kinds of Climate Justice: Avoiding Harm and Sharing Burdens." *The Journal of Political Philosophy* 22(2): 125–149.

Dimitrov, R. S., 2016. "The Paris Agreement on Climate Change: Behind Closed Doors." *Global Environmental Politics* 16(3): 1–11.

Fairhead, J., M. Leach, and I. Scoones, 2012. "Green Grabbing: A New Appropriation of Nature?" *The Journal of Peasant Studies* 39(2): 237–261.

Fricker, M., 2007. *Epistemic Injustice: Power and the Ethics of Knowing.* Oxford University Press, New York.

Gardiner, S., 2011. *A Perfect Moral Storm: The Ethical Tragedy of Climate Change.* Oxford University Press, New York.

Gardiner, S., S. Caney, D. Jamieson, and H. Shue, 2010. *Climate Ethics: Essential Reading.* Oxford University Press, New York.

Holland, B., 2017. "Procedural Justice in Local Climate Adaption: Political Capabilities and Transformational Change." *Environmental Politics* 26(3): 391–412.

Hume, D., 1975. *An Enquiry Concerning the Principles of Morals in Enquiries Concerning Human Understanding and Concerning the Principles of Morals,* edited by L. A. Selby-Bigge, revised by P. H. Nidditch. Clarendon Press, Oxford.

Hume, D., 1978. *A Treatise of Human Nature,* edited by L. A. Selby-Bigge, revised by P. H. Nidditch. Clarendon Press, Oxford.

IPCC, 2013. *Climate Change 2013: Synthesis Report.* Contribution of Working Groups I, II and III to the Fifth Assessment Report of the Intergovernmental Panel on Climate Change [Core Writing Team, R.K. Pachauri and L.A. Meyer (eds.)]. IPCC, Geneva, Switzerland.

IPCC, 2014: *Climate Change 2014: Synthesis Report.* Contribution of Working Groups I, II and III to the Fifth Assessment Report of the Intergovernmental Panel on Climate Change [Core Writing Team, R.K. Pachauri and L.A. Meyer (eds.)]. IPCC, Geneva, Switzerland.

Jamieson, D., 2008. *Ethics and the Environment: An Introduction.* Cambridge University Press, New York.

Leach, M., J. Fairhead, and J. Fraser, 2012. "Green Grabs and Biochar: Revaluing African Soils and Farming in the New Carbon Economy." *The Journal of Peasant Studies* 39(2): 285–307.

Lyster, R., 2017. "Climate Justice, adaptation and the Paris Agreement: A Recipe for Disasters?" *Environmental Politics* 26(3): 438–458.

Mary Robinson Foundation-Climate Justice, 2011. *Principles of Climate Justice.* Available at www.mrfcj.org/principles-of-climate-justice/

Murphy, S., 2011. "Fairness." In *Encyclopaedia of Global Justice.* Switzerland: Springer Publications doi: https://doi.org/10.1007/978-1-4020-9160-5_257.

Okereke, C. and P. Coventry, 2016. "Climate Justice and the International Regime: Before, During and After Paris." *WIREs Climate Change* 7: 834–851.

O'Neill, O., 2000. *Bounds of Justice.* Cambridge University Press, Cambridge.

O'Neill, O., 2001. "Practical Principles and Practical Judgement." *The Hastings Centre Report* 31(4): 15–23.

Paavola, J. and W. N. Adger, 2006. *Fairness in Adaptation to Climate Change.* MIT Press, Cambridge, MA.

Rockström, J., W. Steffen, K. Noone, Å. Persson, F. S. Chapin, III, E. Lambin, T. M. Lenton, M. Scheffer, C. Folke, H. Schellnhuber, B. Nykvist, C. A. De Wit, T. Hughes, S. van der Leeuw, H. Rodhe, S. Sörlin, P. K. Snyder, R. Costanza, U. Svedin, M. Falkenmark, L. Karlberg, R. W. Corell, V. J. Fabry, J. Hansen, B. Walker, D. Liverman, K. Richardson, P. Crutzen, and J. Foley., 2009. "Planetary Boundaries: Exploring the Safe Operating Space for Humanity." *Ecology and Society* 14(2): 32 [online]. www.ecologyandsociety.org/vol14/iss2/art32/

Ronzoni, M., 2012. "Two Conceptions of State Sovereignty and Their Implications for Global Institutional Design." *Critical Review of International Social and Political Philosophy* 15(5): 573–591.

Santos, M., 2017. "Global Justice and Environmental Governance: An Analysis of the Paris Agreement." *Revista Brasileria de Politica Internacional* 60(1).

Schlosberg, D., L. Collins, and S. Niemeyer, 2017. "Adaptation Policy and Community Discourse: Risk, Vulnerability and Just Transformation." *Environmental Politics* 26(3): 413–437.

Sen, A., 2000. "Consequential Evaluation and Practical Reason." *The Journal of Philosophy* 97(9): 477–502.

Sen, A., 2009. *The Idea of Justice.* Allen Lane Published by the Penguin Group, London.

Shue, H., 2014. *Climate Justice: Vulnerability and Protection.* Oxford University Press, Oxford.

UNFCCC 1992 United Nations Famrework Convention on Climate Change. Available at https://unfccc.int/resource/docs/convkp/conveng.pdf

UNFCCC 2009 The Copenhagen Accord. Available at https://unfccc.int/resource/docs/2009/cop15/eng/l07.pdf

UNFCCC 2011 Establishment of the Ad Hoc Working Group on the Durban Platform for Enhanced Action (ADP). Available at https://unfccc.int/resource/docs/2011/cop17/eng/09a01.pdf#page=2

UNFCCC 2015 The Paris Agreement. Available at http://unfccc.int/paris_agreement/items/9485.php

UNFCCC 2018 Ratification status. Available at https://unfccc.int/process/the-paris-agreement/status-of-ratification

Weisser, F. and D. Muller-Mahn, 2017. "No Place for the Political: Micro-Geographies of the Paris Climate Conference 2015." *Antipode* 49(3): 802–820.

Young, I. M., 1990. *Justice and Politics of Difference.* Princeton University Press, Princeton.

7

Statehood in an era of sinking islands

*Tom Sparks**

Introduction

Few now dispute the brute fact of climate change, or the role of humans in bringing it about. Although there remain disagreements among scientists about the likely consequences of global temperature rises for low-lying and small-island States (compare, for example MacLean and Kench 2015; Albert et al. 2016; Duvat et al. 2017), as sea levels rise and storm events become more severe and more frequent, we are forced to confront the possibility that the entire territories of some States may be rendered uninhabitable or may disappear completely. International law is well accustomed to changes in its membership through the formation and demise of States, and d'Aspremont even uses the colourful vocabulary of the "birth" and "death" of States to explain the phenomenon (d'Aspremont 2014; see also Fazal 2007), but the looming reality of anthropogenic climatic change forces us to face another possibility, and one the current toolkit of international law is ill-equipped to tackle. As a result of climate change, certain low-lying and island States may not merely lose personality to be replaced by another, but may "die" in a sense that is much more profound: that they cease to exist without another international person taking their place. As will be argued, that prospect presents very serious challenges to the viability of the current paradigm of statehood, in light of the risk to individuals in times of unprecedented internal and external displacement and migration (Rigaud et al. 2018).

This chapter examines the problem of statehood in an era of sinking islands, and concludes that an *anthropic shift* in international law's understanding of statehood is necessary. The present, territory-focused, paradigm cannot adequately protect communities and individuals in the face of these extreme events, and the development of an anthropocentric model of the State is therefore indicated. The next section examines what is called here the "Jellinekian paradigm," finding its focus on territory problematic in the context of climate change, while the following section examines what the implications are for the rights of individuals of the loss of personality of the submerged State. The section "Statehood for the Anthropocene – the anthropic state" then considers the potential of the concept of *Anthropocene-consciousness* as an ideational lens through which statehood could be reappraised and repurposed to meet the changed circumstances of a warming world.

Sinking islands and the Jellinekian paradigm

In 1933 the International Conference of American States adopted the Montevideo Convention on the Rights and Duties of States (Montevideo Convention). Article 1 of that convention provides a definition of a State that has subsequently been treated as highly authoritative (Crawford 2006, 45 et *seq*). There it is declared that:

> The state as a person of international law should possess the following qualifications:
>
> a   a permanent population;
> b   a defined territory;
> c   government; and
> d   capacity to enter into relations with other states.
>
> *(Montevideo Convention 1933, Article 1)*

That formula, defining the State as a territorial entity within which there is a population and a government, long predates the conclusion of the accord in 1933. The territorial basis of the State (or its close cognates of "the nation," "the commonwealth," "the Kingdom") can be traced through international law thought from at least the writings of Jean Bodin in the 16th century (Bodin 1576, this edn. 1967), and Hugo Grotius and Samuel Pufendorf in the 17th (Grotius 1625; Pufendorf 1672), to the emergence at the turn of the 20th century of the Jellinekian *Drei-Elementen-Lehre* (Jellinek 1914) that was formalised at Montevideo.

Though the Anglophone tradition of international law tends to treat the Montevideo convention as its starting point in discussions of statehood (see, for example, Brownlie 2003, 70; Craven 2014, 220; Shaw 2017, 157), other schools – notably the German tradition – draw directly on Jellinek's trinity, without the need for the fourth criterion of capacity to enter into relations with other States that is included in Montevideo. Despite these differences, there is little disagreement over Jellinek's core criteria, and it is therefore common to almost all modern accounts of statehood that the State is a territory in which there is a population subject to political authority. That is to say, the State's structures, laws and institutions apply to the persons and objects within a given physical space, and the rights of the State over that space exclude the influence of any other State. Although numerous international law scholars have found fault with these formulations – Grant, for example, calls Montevideo "over-inclusive, under-inclusive, and outdated" (Grant 1998–1999, 453; see further Sterio 2010–2011; Sparks forthcoming) – they remain ubiquitous. Recent advances in thought surrounding statehood – such as in the formulations given by Grant (1998–1999), Sterio (2010–2011, 2013), and perhaps most influentially by Crawford (2006) – add depth and complexity to the sparse territory-population-government account, but do not fundamentally depart from what is here termed in shorthand the *Jellinekian paradigm*: the view that the State consists of a political community that is organised territorially.

The question of whether a State could survive the loss of its territory has generally been answered negatively by classical international law. In its decision in the *Deutsche Continental Gas-Gesellschaft* arbitration, for example, the arbitral tribunal declared that a State "does not exist unless it fulfills [*sic*] the conditions of possessing a territory, a people inhabiting that territory, and a public power that is exercised over the people and the territory" (*Deutsche Continental Gas-Gesellschaft*, 1929). Marek states the proposition yet more baldly, even using the example of a sinking island:

> With regard to the material elements of a State, the argument is so obvious as to be unnecessary. That a State would cease to exist if for instance the whole of its population were

to perish or to emigrate, or if its territory were to disappear (e.g., an island which became submerged) can be taken for granted.

(Marek 1954)

The logic of this absolute dependence on territory is simple and, viewed from within the Jellinekian system, virtually inescapable. According to the (dominant) positivist tradition of international law, the single most important hallmark of a State is its sovereignty. In this context, sovereignty's most significant aspect is exclusivity: a freedom from any control save that of international law, and there only to the extent that the State has accepted the obligations to which it is subject.[1] Smith gives the classic formulation:

The society must be a sovereign independent state, that is to say, its internal control of all persons and things within its territory must be complete and exclusive, and its external relations must be independent of the control of any other society.

(Smith 1911, 27; see also Oppenheim 1912, 109)

Modern authorities understand sovereignty in a similar way:

[S]overeignty itself, with its retinue of legal rights and duties, is founded upon the fact of territory. Without territory a person cannot be a state. [. . . F]undamental legal concepts [such] as sovereignty and jurisdiction can only be comprehended in relation to territory.

(Shaw 2017, 361, references omitted)

Crawford objects to the use of the term *sovereignty* in this context – he argues that sovereignty is a legal consequence of statehood, rather than an attribute of a State (Crawford 2006, 32–33, 89) – but substitutes the idea of independence. While noting several caveats and exceptions (pp. 67–89), he cites Judge Huber's declaration in the *Island of Palmas* arbitration that "[i]ndependence in regard to a portion of the globe is the right to exercise therein, to the exclusion of any other State, the functions of a State" (*Island of Palmas*, 1928, 838; discussed in Crawford 2006, 62–66).

In short: an entity can only be a State if it is independent (or "sovereign"), meaning that within a defined area it performs the functions of a State to the exclusion of all others. It is possible neither for an entity which is under the control of another to achieve statehood, nor for two States to exercise plenary authority over the same territory. This strong territorial focus has displaced earlier forms of political organisation that privileged personal allegiance over spatially defined authority – such as condominium, suzerainty (or vassalage) and the authority of the Pope – which it has relegated to being primarily of historical interest.[2] In other words, the territorially delineated entitlements of what has here been called the Jellinekian paradigm cannot adequately accommodate the notion of the displaced State. Short of a cession of territory and the reestablishment of the old State in a new location, the powerful territorial logic of the system demands that only one power be acknowledged over any given point on the earth's surface. That is not to say, however, that States displaced by climate change will instantly cease to be. As Wallace-Bruce notes, in another context:

[I]nternational law does not contemplate the "demise" of a state. Because the international legal system was designed to operate on a permanent basis and states were expected to be in existence forever, no provision has been made for a state which collapses to the point of being totally defunct.

(Wallace-Bruce 2000, 67)

It may be a consequence of this that there is, as Crawford and others have noted, a strong presumption in favour of a State's continued existence even when there is a defect in its fulfilment of one or more of the statehood criteria (Crawford 2006, 701; Wong 2013, 362–364; von Paepcke 2014, 202). The effect of this uncertainty in demise is that, as Wong has it, "extinction will not occur as soon as the first wave covers the last rock" (Wong 2013, 390). Indeed, international law has long tolerated the continued formal existence of "States" that lacked governments, governmental authority and defined borders (see, for example, Crawford's discussion of Somalia and the Democratic Republic of Congo in 2006, 91–92 et *seq*, and general remarks at 700–701 et *seq*), and it may therefore be presumed that it will seek pragmatic solutions to the plight of sunken island nations. Nevertheless, the Jellinekian paradigm's insistence on territorial sovereignty means that it cannot comfortably accommodate the continuity of a State lacking a (habitable) territory.

The (as yet hypothetical) case of a State displaced by the submersion of an island or the inundation of a low-lying coastline demonstrates the concern. Even on the assumption that the body politic of the State remains sufficiently coherent for the requirements of population, government and international capacity to remain intact, the State has to exist *somewhere*. Its population and its officials are phenomenal entities which cannot exist in abstraction, but rather will necessarily be physically present in a particular location. But with the exception of the high seas, Antarctica and a few contested zones, every part of the earth's surface is acknowledged to be the sovereign territory of a State. The displaced State could seek to acquire territory over which to exercise sovereignty, but failing that possibility (and the practical obstacles are indeed significant – see Rayfuse 2009, 8; McAdam 2010, 123; Wong 2013, 383), it is likely to find itself within the territory of another acknowledged State. But that is a non-sequitur: two entities cannot, according either to the doctrine of sovereignty or independence, exercise to the exclusion of all others the functions of a State over the same area. One entity's claim to the space must ultimately supersede the other, and it is only the *triumphator* that will be acknowledged as "State" within that zone. This leaves island States in a highly uncertain position. Absent a more permanent solution to the problem of a sunken island State, it is likely that the ineluctable logic of territoriality will gradually reassert itself, reducing the State displaced by climate change to a pressure group or a fiction.

Questioning territoriality

The previous section has examined the conceptual barriers the Jellinekian paradigm of statehood poses to the continuation of personality of States, the territories of which have been submerged or rendered uninhabitable as a result of a warming climate. Section 3 will look beyond the Jellinekian paradigm and ask what a coherent model of statehood would look like in the Anthropocene, but the next section will first consider why the loss of the State's personality should be a cause for concern.

The sunken State – why does statehood matter?

Statehood is, of course, a highly emotive issue. But as the centrality of the State to the world governmental system attests, it is and remains of great practical significance. A people shorn of the protection of a State is disadvantaged in numerous ways, from the lack of an entity with standing to engage with international institutions and other States on terms of equality, to the lack of a locus around which the identity of a group can coalesce for the purposes of collective self-determination. Lack of space prevents a fuller exploration of these – and many other – concerns associated with the loss of statehood of sinking islands, but it is worth expanding briefly on what is, in the present author's opinion, the most alarming prospect: the loss of the State's ability to protect its displaced population.

Worldwide, 2017 saw the highest levels of displacement and migration ever recorded. Conflicts in Syria, Yemen, the Central African Republic and South Sudan, the campaign of ethnic cleansing against the Rohingya people in Myanmar, and an estimated one person every second displaced by environmental or weather-related events created a global population of 65.6 million displaced people, of whom 22.5 million qualify as refugees or asylum seekers under the United Nations Refugee Convention (United Nations High Commissioner for Refugees 2018). In the face of these unprecedented levels of forced migration, UN and other relief agencies have reported serious shortfalls in funding and capacity to support the needs and rights of displaced persons (United Nations Development Programme 2016, 145; see also Nebehay 2017; H. Grant 2015).

Yet these levels of migration pale into insignificance compared to the estimates of climate-related displacement. A recent World Bank report estimates that without urgent action, in sub-Saharan Africa, South Asia and Latin America alone more than 143 million people are likely to be internally displaced by 2050 (Rigaud et al. 2018, xix et seq). The United Nations Development Programme's report on climate change puts the figure even higher. A 3–4 degrees Celsius rise in global temperature, it estimated, could displace 330 million people through flooding alone, and it noted that even at present more than one billion people worldwide live in slum conditions on fragile hillslopes and riverbanks that are at a high risk of flooding and subsidence as a result of a changing climate and associated weather events (United Nations Development Programme 2007, 9 et seq).

These risks are of course not unique to small island States or countries with a low average elevation, but here the problems are particularly acute. Four archipelagic States have an average elevation of less than two metres above sea level – Kiribati, Maldives, Marshall Islands and Tuvalu, and two – Maldives and Tuvalu – each have a high point only five metres above sea level (Central Intelligence Agency 2018). In a world already struggling equitably to cope with the challenges posed by mass displacement, the impending necessity of evacuating these States entirely – together with countless others from the low-elevation coastal zone (LECZ), areas at risk of desertification and beyond – threatens human suffering on a vast scale (see further Mattar and Mbakwem, in this volume).

As McAdam has convincingly demonstrated in her excellent book, *Climate Change, Forced Migration, and International Law*, this is a challenge the international legal architecture currently in place is ill-equipped to cope with (2012, see also 2007, 2010, 2014). Whether one seeks to employ the frameworks of international refugee law, complementary protection, statelessness or human rights, the prospect of significant numbers of climate migrants being left without a State (and therefore without recourse to the State-to-State frameworks of diplomatic protection) threatens further to disadvantage a group that is already acutely vulnerable (McAdam 2012, see generally, esp. 39–54, 90, 142; McAdam 2007, 198–202; Peters 2016, 388–407; Ragheboom 2017, 293–340, esp. 337). This difficulty in reconciling the Jellinekian paradigm with the reality of the sinking island thus exacerbates the existing gaps in the international protection regime. Although the statehood of sinking islands remains an under-studied topic in international law, a number of important scholarly contributions have been made in the area which discuss solutions within the territorial paradigm to the sinking islands problem. These can broadly be grouped into three types: (1) relocation, or the transposition of a State's population and institutions to a territory ceded by another State; (2) maintenance of maritime entitlements, under which the boundaries of the State's maritime zones are frozen at their current extent and do not diminish when territory shrinks or is lost in order that (in the soft version) a displaced State may continue to benefit from the sea's natural resources or (in the strong version) the State may continue to exist on the basis of its sovereignty over *maritime* territory; and (3) the State in exile, or the continuance of the State as a legal person despite that it lacks a territory, and its population may be scattered. The discussion of these possibilities will not be repeated here. It is sufficient to note that none provides more than a partial solution, nor a reliable means to secure the rights of island States and their inhabitants.[3] Each is fighting against the Jellinekian logic, and as those discussions show, it seems likely that that logic will ultimately reassert itself. Rather, in order to secure the continued existence of the sunken island and thus provide a measure of protection to its displaced population, it is necessary to step outside of the Jellinekian paradigm of the territorially defined State.

Beyond territoriality – mobilising the Anthropocene

Though the discussion thus far has demonstrated a need to look beyond territoriality and to explore new ways of understanding the concept of statehood,[4] in practice it is far from simple to break free of the territorial State paradigm. As the author has argued elsewhere, to alter the idea of statehood is not a simple matter of changing a legal rule. Rather, the statehood paradigm needs to be understood as a social structure created and maintained, as Giddens has explained, through recursive social activity (Giddens 1984, 2, 17–18 et *seq*; Sparks forthcoming). To break free of a particular *social construction of reality*, as is statehood, is not a matter of *choosing* to change the rule, but rather of social agents in general *acting on the belief that a different rule pertains*. As Giddens explains:

> Human social activities, like some self-reproducing items in nature, are recursive. That is to say, they are not brought into being by social actors but continually recreated by them via the very means whereby they express themselves as actors. In and through their activities agents reproduce the conditions that make these activities possible.
>
> *(Giddens 1984, 2)*

States – institutionalised social facts – thus bear the qualities both of Searle's *observer dependent features* and of a Durkheimian "thing": though they are created by the beliefs and attitudes of social agents, they are nevertheless not "plastic to the will" (Searle 2003; Giddens 1978, 35). Changes to their nature occur as a result of social agents *acting in accordance with their new nature*. That is what is meant by recursive creation: the structure dictates the action, which determines the structure, and so on.

Although changes of this kind usually occur gradually over time in ways that are almost unnoticeable, moments of rupture are also possible. If social attitudes change suddenly – perhaps as a result of changing conditions which highlight the deficiencies in the existing arrangements – observed realities will change concomitantly (Kuhn 2009). The following section will argue that the fact of anthropogenic climate change has the potential to provoke just such a moment of rupture, and that the consciousness of the Anthropocene – of the vast changes human activity is wreaking on the world system – offers a conceptual focus through which a reconceptualisation of the State may occur.

In the almost unimaginable reaches of geological time, the Earth has passed through a number of different eras, periods, epochs and stages. These different periodisations are defined by changes – of different magnitudes, though all substantial – in the atmosphere, climate, biology or geology of the planet. The present epoch as currently recognised, for example, is known as the *Holocene* and is usually taken to date from the end of the last ice age, approximately 11,700 years BP (before present) (Cohen et al. 2013). Other events marking the boundaries between epochs include asteroid impacts, periods of massive seismic or volcanic activity, significant changes in atmospheric chemistry and mass extinction events. However, an increasing number of scientists now argue that the influences of human civilisation on the earth system have had or are having an impact equivalent to one of these global geological events, and that we should now be understood to have entered a new epoch: the *Anthropocene*.

The term "Anthropocene" was originally coined by Crutzen and Stoermer (Crutzen and Stoermer 2000), building upon work previously done by Lyell in 1833, Stoppani in 1873 and Vernadsky and others in the 1920s (Crutzen and Stoermer 2000; Crutzen 2002). Crutzen and Stoermer argued that:

> Considering [the] major and still growing impacts of human activities on earth and atmosphere, and at all, including global, scales, it seems to us more than appropriate to emphasize the central role of mankind in geology and ecology by proposing to use the term "anthropocene" for the current geological epoch.
>
> *(Crutzen and Stoermer 2000, 17)*

Crutzen later expanded on this line of argument, declaring that because of "anthropogenic emissions of carbon dioxide, [the] global climate may depart significantly from natural behaviour for many millennia to come," and that "[u]nless there is a global catastrophe – a meteorite impact, a world war or a pandemic – mankind will remain a major environmental force" over that timescale (Crutzen 2002, 23). For that reason, he argued that it would be appropriate to designate a new global epoch, in which the influence of humans superseded natural effects on the geo-atmospheric system.

Although Svante Arrhenius had argued that carbon dioxide emissions (both natural and anthropogenic) had the potential to alter the climate as early as 1897 (Arrhenius 1897), the topic received little attention until the 1950s, and the emerging scientific consensus did not break through into the politico-public consciousness until the 1980s. The year 1988 is when the then-Director of the NASA Goddard Institute for Space Studies, James Hansen, gave testimony before a U.S. Senate committee and declared the existence of a "cause and effect relationship with the greenhouse effect" (Hansen 1988), as well as when the World Meteorological Organization's (WMO's) World Conference on the Changing Atmosphere concluded that human pollution is causing climatic warming, and in which the WMO formed the Intergovernmental Panel on Climate Change. At that point, it seems reasonable to conclude, the existence of a set of geo-atmospheric changes of sufficient magnitude to be defined as a geological epoch coincided with an awareness of (the magnitude of) those changes in the public consciousness, such that *it became possible for the mere fact of living in a new geological epoch to produce social effects*. Almost 400 years after becoming a or the major driver of global environmental change, we became *Anthropocene-conscious*.

The International Geological Congress, the International Commission on Stratigraphy and other relevant bodies have yet to formally endorse the Anthropocene epoch, and it therefore remains officially correct to refer to the current epoch as the Holocene. Even absent formal recognition, however, the concept is beginning to influence debates in politics and law, including international environmental law, where it is incorporated in particular into the writings of Kotzé (see 2016, and further 2015, 2017), with important contributions made also by Robinson (2014), Vidas et al. (2015), Vordermayer (2015) and Torres Camprubí (2016). The present author agrees that having regard to the magnitude of the influence humans are having on the geo-atmospheric system is valuable across a number of areas of law and politics, including – as will be argued below – the law of statehood.

Statehood for the Anthropocene – the anthropic State

Anthropocene-consciousness is a useful concept, too, in the context of statehood. As has been argued already, the realities of the Anthropocene – of rising sea levels as a result of human-induced climate change – present a very significant challenge to the Jellinekian paradigm of statehood. These acute problems combine with many longstanding critiques of the approach (see e.g., Grant 1998–1999, 453; Sterio 2010–2011), and may suffice to provoke a moment of rupture of the kind Kuhn describes in his *Structure of Scientific Revolutions*. There he notes that a new paradigm can only supplant the old "after a pronounced failure in the normal problem-solving activity" of science: "The novel theory seems a direct response to crisis" (Kuhn 2009, 74–75). If the point of failure has not already been reached, the realities of climate change seem likely to precipitate a crisis.

However, Kuhn also notes that:

> [A] scientific theory is declared invalid only if an alternate candidate is available to take its place. [. . .] The decision to reject one paradigm is always simultaneously the decision to accept another, and the judgment leading to that decision involves the comparison of both paradigms with nature *and* with each other.
>
> *(Kuhn 2009, 77)*

In other words, the failures of the Jellinekian account will not lead to its decline; rather, it is necessary for that paradigm to be supplanted with a new theory of statehood, which has greater explanatory potential. The question is therefore posed of what a theory of statehood for the Anthropocene would look like (Torres Camprubí 2016, 277–278), and it is suggested that the question begs an answer. In parallel to the shift to Anthropocene-consciousness, it is necessary to make another conceptual leap. In place of the territorial State, the Anthropocene demands an anthropocentric account of statehood.

Functional territory

In order to imagine the anthropic State, it is instructive to consider the role territory plays in enabling the concept of State to perform the functions ascribed to it in international law as these are currently conceived. There are three main functions which the concept of State performs: (1) personification, or the rationalisation of the mass of individuals in a State into a single person-ality for the purpose of law; (2) delineation, or the ascription to one person rather than another primary competence to make and enforce rules; and (3) identification, or the ability to differenti-ate between acts of individuals which either do or do not also have the character of acts of the State (this argument is set out in detail in Sparks, forthcoming). Of these functions, territory is primarily relevant to the question of delineation. Under this heading, the concept of State serves as a means of ascribing authority over particular individuals and events to one or another author-ity-centres within the constellation of international persons. In other words, it provides a means whereby it is possible to say that in one instance a rule instituted by A should apply, whereas another instance should be governed by the equivalent rule governing community B. The con-cept of territory aids in the performance of this task by delineating authority spatially: it divides the land surface of the earth into geographical parcels which pertain to the communities and governance systems which inhabit them. These then form the basis for understanding relative claims to control over space for the purpose of the exercise of internal sovereignty, governance, and the choice each political community makes as to the forms and structures of socio-political organisation that pertain to it. Some means of delimiting authority is a necessary function of any multi-polar world order. In a non-hierarchical system of States, international law must have the capacity to exclude as illegitimate the exercise of control by States over areas beyond their ambits, in order that communities have the opportunity to determine for themselves how their political and social life should be organised.

Put another way, the necessity of delineation comes into being as a result of the principle of international life that socio-political communities are entitled to self-determination. That principle – now firmly entrenched in the positive law of international society through the UN Charter (1948, Articles 1(2), 2(4)), the common first Article of the human rights covenants (ICCPR/ICESCR, 1966, Article 1) and numerous declarations of the UN General Assembly (UNGA Res 545(IV); 637(VII); 1514(XV); 2526(XXX)); and recognised in the judgements and opinions of the International Court of Justice (ICJ)[5] – stands for the principle that socio-political communities, understood for these purposes as the populations of entire States, have the right to decide by which structures and principles their shared life should be organised and governed without the interferences of those beyond the community. The principle has its theoretical roots in individual self-determination.

Individual self-determination may in turn be defined as the contention that all individual human agents should have the opportunity (that is to say, the actualised right) to decide upon and to pursue their individual conception of the good (Nozick 1974, ix; Dworkin 1977, this edn. 2005, 272–273; Raz 1979, 220). In other words, because human beings are "capable of forming and acting on intelligent conceptions of how their lives should be lived," they should have the opportunity to live whatever form of life seems best to them (Dworkin 2005, 272–273). That contention is inherently social, and is so for two reasons. It is, first, a concept which has application only in a social setting: a lone individual has no right to self-determination. Indeed, their self-determination is a meaningless concept, given that their capacity of action is both free from the constraint of any other will and that it is vastly limited by the necessities of survival. This second is implicated, too, in the second social aspect of self-determination: that many of the goods which provide the individual the security of person and the freedom from need necessary to enable self-determination are best achieved socially, whether it be protection from the actions of others, or the pursuit of higher living standards though collective endeavour (Durkheim 1972, 232; Leakey 1981, 211). Social and political communities, therefore, whether formed incidentally to these needs or in pursuit of them, are themselves vehicles for the expression of individual self-determination.

The presence of the individual in a social setting gives meaning to the idea of self-determination, but it also presents challenges. Hobbes's famous warning that absent the regulation of violence, human life would be "solitary, poor, nasty, brutish, and short" presents a very bleak picture of humans, but one that is sadly credible (Hobbes 1651, §62). Although the idea of consistency – derived by neo-Kantians from Kant's *categorical imperative* (Kant 1785, this edn. 2002, 217; Korsgaard 1996, 136 et *seq*; Gewirth 1978–9) – requires that each individual be accorded the same standard of treatment, it would be both naïve and contrary to historical experience to expect this principle of internal consistency alone to provide an adequate degree of assurance of the rights of individuals. Some form of social regulation and ordering – perhaps in the form of law, law-making and law-enforcing institutions – may be posited, therefore, and that in turn implies a concept of *jurisdiction*. In other words, the idea of social regulation implies and requires that it be possible to determine *to whom* the obligations of the system apply, and *how* and *where* an individual is entitled to claim the protection of them. Kelsen refers to this idea in his description of law as a social technique: law applies to a particular society, and therefore requires an understanding of *membership* of a society – of who is, and who is not, a part of it (Kelsen 1945, this edn. 1999, 19).

Taken together, these observations demand the conclusion that the State's ambit, and thus the necessity of delineation, flows from the existence of a coherent socio-political community, and not the other way around. Territory is a consequence; it is the community that is primary. In turn, that observation leads to the intriguing conclusion that geographical boundedness is only one possible method of delimitation, rather than a necessary or transcendental aspect of an inter-community legal order. Even viewed in this way, as *anthropocentric*, the idea of the State resists reconceptualisation, however. In a world structured along geographical lines, speculation about non-territorial organisations of political authority seems appropriate only to the realm of science fiction,[6] or to hark back to a pre-Westphalian barbarism (see text to note 2). Yet this, too, is a hallmark of a paradigm. As Kuhn remarks, when operating within a paradigm the scientist does not "see something *as* something else; instead they simply see it." Priestly, to give Kuhn's example, did not see "oxygen as dephlogisticated air"; what he saw *was* dephlogisticated air (Kuhn 2009, 85). In parallel, "in most instances the existence of a system of more or less distinct territorial units as the foundation of human governance is not even questioned" (Murphy 1996, 81). It is difficult or impossible to see territory *as* delineation: territory *is* delineation.

This prompts Kuhn to describe the structure of paradigm change as a scientific revolution. The observation goes further than a change of vision, it implies a change of reality: "though the world does not change with a change of paradigm, the scientist afterwards works in a different world" (Kuhn 2009, 121). Kuhn seems uncomfortable with – though remains committed to – this observation, saying that "I am convinced that we must learn to make sense of statements that at least resemble these," but in the world of the social rather than the natural sciences, this thesis needs no special effort to integrate. Rather, it accords entirely with the view of social reality developed by Giddens that was discussed earlier: social reality is a concatenation of agency and structure, in which those forces recursively create and sustain each other (Giddens 1984, see generally, esp. 24–25). When social perceptions of reality change, they do so in response to changes in structures; when social structures change, they do so in response to changes in actualised perception. To paraphrase Balibar's observation in a connected context, the question then becomes "under what conditions would [non-territorial statehood] become thinkable? And if it has become necessary as an object of thought, under what conditions would [it] also become possible as an institution?" (Balibar 2014).

Articulating the anthropic State

The answer may be that it has not been sufficiently articulated. The territorial State is a failing paradigm. If the theory is not yet in crisis, then a crisis seems to be near at hand. Yet it has not been displaced, and cannot yet be finally rejected: it retains sufficient power to render the imagination of its successor difficult or impossible. It *enables and constrains* the discourses of the system as it presently exists, and thus defines the limits of reality (Giddens 1984, 25). But it may be speculated that the shift from the territorial State to the anthropic State both will and will not involve a fundamental restructuring of the international world order. It will in the sense that international lawyers will afterwards work in a different world. The conceptual lens will have shifted, and – to use the somewhat inadequate metaphor of perception – our interpretation of social reality will have changed concomitantly. There may as a result be significant changes: different outcomes will be enabled and different possibilities constrained by the shift from territorialism to anthropocentricism. Yet the world will remain fundamentally the same in the sense that many or most of the changes that occur will be noumenal, in the way in which we as social agents interact with the world. And where changes project beyond the internal viewpoint into the phenomenal world, these will follow logically from the paradigm, and will be neither unexpected nor revolutionary. They may, however, be at once subtle and profound. The anthropic State does not necessarily mean that entities will regularly overlap territorially, merely that territory will lose its central place in the understanding of what States are and how they function. New principles of organisation will emerge to replace it, and it remains difficult to formulate what those might or will be.[7] That is an ongoing project, but on the basis of the argument thus far, it is possible to make certain preliminary observations.

It has been argued that territory, despite the emphasis placed upon it by the current criteria of statehood, is not central to the idea of the State. Rather, it is a consequence which, like other aspects of the institution, flows from the coming together of different socio-political communities under the framework of a non-hierarchical legal order. Territory serves the function of delineating authority-spaces for the purpose of recognising and preserving the separate character of these communities: it is directly derived from the necessity of ascertaining to which people and which events different communities pertain for the purposes of political self-determination and intra-societal governance. In other words, the existence of the self-determining community, and not the geographical line in the sand, is conceptually prior.

The idea of anthropic statehood refocuses the statehood concept away from the all-consuming focus on territory, towards the existence of a self-determining community. Through the self- and co-identification of the individuals involved as members of a social and political group, the community constitutes itself as such, and thereby makes a normative claim concerning its political authority over itself. It is inherent in its self-determination that decisions concerning the community should be made by individuals who are a part of it, rather than those who are outside it. It follows that both the legitimacy of an individual's influence over the community and the legitimacy of the community's authority over the individual hinge on a proper identification of which individuals are and which are not a part of the community. Thus the self-determination of the community requires some form of delineation.

Through this and the other functions of the statehood concept – personification and identification – international law gives effect to the self-determination of socio-political communities. The claim that it is necessary to move away from the territorial model of statehood is therefore less radical than might at first be supposed. First, when it is stripped back to its conceptual core it is clear that the concept of the State has no necessary connection to territory; rather, territory is instrumentalised in order to fulfil the functions of the statehood concept for the purposes of international law. Second, to move away from a territorial model of statehood does not necessitate jettisoning the idea of territory entirely: many States will continue, at least at some level, to be territorial entities. Instead of the Jellinekian/Montevidean checklist of territory, population and government, the anthropic State is premised on an interaction between the latter two: a self-determining socio-political community. Many or most such communities will continue to be primarily territorially organised, in the sense of being geographically coherent. People in community with each other tend to live in proximity. But the shift from territory to anthropocentricism also has two consequences which are of great significance in the sinking islands context. First, if the State is defined primarily in relation to a political community, then its displacement (and even the loss of the territory where it was located) ceases artificially to be an existential threat to it. Of course, such a displacement could disrupt the life of the community to such an extent that it ceases to function as such, but where a community persists, its legal existence will continue. Second, unlinking territory and statehood removes the need for exclusive territorial control. A displaced community could therefore exist – certainly temporarily, and perhaps also in the long term – alongside another community without the personality of either necessarily being threatened.[8]

Such an argument is only the first step in conceptualising the anthropic State. There remain a host of practical and theoretical questions to be answered – such as the inter-relationship between anthropic statehood and jurisdiction, nationality and citizenship; the application of fundamental doctrines such as the use of force and sovereignty over natural resources; maritime entitlements; and the ambit of human rights conventions, investment treaties and even environmental regulations. It is necessary also to consider the relationship with and effects on the internal understanding of what States are of any changes to the conception at the international level. Those questions are beyond the scope of this chapter, but they form a forward research agenda that will need to be addressed in order to render the non-territorial State "thinkable," and both to understand and realise its potential to provide a more coherent basis for statehood in the Anthropocene.

Conclusion

As this chapter has argued, the dominant Jellinekian paradigm of statehood is unable, on a number of grounds, to meet the challenges of the Anthropocene. Not only does the insistence on territory in itself demand the conclusion that a State that has lost its territory will ultimately (even if not instantly) cease to be, but the logic is sufficiently inflexible that it cannot easily accommodate even the partial solutions – relocation, maritime entitlements and the State in exile – which seek to reconcile it with the urgent need of the sinking islands scenario. Moreover, the inadequacies of the international protection regime place those displaced from sinking islands and similar environmental disasters in a position of great vulnerability. Lacking the protection of a State able to exercise its diplomatic good offices and avail itself of the machinery of international law in order to defend their rights, that vulnerability becomes acute. There is, therefore, a compelling case for the maintenance of the statehood of sinking islands.

Therefore, this chapter has argued that one should now look beyond the Jellinekian paradigm. It mobilised the concept of Anthropocene-consciousness, and argued that a parallel anthropic shift is necessary in the understanding of statehood. Such a model would place the existence of a self-determining community at the heart of statehood, in distinction to the dominant theory of the State which privileges territory. Indeed, it was suggested that such a shift would not be a radical change in the underlying theory of the State, nor a leap into a historical unknown – previous epochs of international law have understood political allegiance primarily in personal terms (see note 2 and accompanying text). Rather, it would be better analogised to a change of perception. Even under the current paradigm, the function served by territory – that of delineating authority-spaces – is directly derived from the necessity of ascertaining to which people and events different communities pertain for the purposes of political self-determination. The existence of the community, rather than the geographical line in the sand, is primary.

Nevertheless, it remains difficult to envisage a multi-polar world order that does not divide authority on the basis of territory. It was argued with Kuhn that this is one of the hallmarks of a paradigm: it assimilates the function and the object. We cannot see territory *as* delimitation: within the paradigm territory *is* delimitation. And yet the paradigm will not, if Kuhn's observations in the sciences hold true in this context, be displaced until and unless it is supplanted by a new conception of the State; by a new paradigm. As this chapter has argued, the Jellinekian paradigm is increasingly unable to meet the needs of international society, and that situation is likely to worsen as a result of threats to States from climate change. There is a need for a new understanding of statehood – statehood for the Anthropocene – and further work is therefore warranted to articulate the anthropic State. Now is the time to focus on these questions, in order that something remains standing as rising seas wash away the territorial State.

Notes

* The author would like to thank Professor Anne Peters, Dr Gleider Hernández and Mr Jakob Lehners for their helpful comments and suggestions, which have substantially improved the chapter. The remaining errors, infelicities and omissions are my responsibility alone.
1 The focus on State consent requires certain caveats in the modern international legal system, most notably in relation to the concepts of general principles of law – which emerge as a result of a broad usage rather than out of consent *per se* – and norms *ius cogens*. Both categories of obligation remain difficult to define, and are hotly debated. See, for example, important contributions by Bin (1953), Herczegh (1969), Bassiouni (1990), Pellet (2006, 764–773), Thirlway (2013, I:232–246), Yotova (2017), and Shaw (2017, 72–78) on general principles of law; and Verdross (1937), Hannikainen (1988), Bassiouni (1996), Orakhelashvili (2006), Linderfalk (2011, 2012, 2013), and Weatherall (2015) on *ius cogens*. Simma and Alston discuss both in the context of human rights law (1988–1989).
2 See Verzjil (II: 1969, 339 et *seq*); Bartelson (1995, 88 et *seq*); Crawford (2006, 284 et *seq*, 321–323); Samuels (2008); Cassese (2012, 53). Looking further back, the highly complex interplay of the concepts of territoriality (*Urbem/Provincia*) and citizenship in the law and practice of Rome offer a fascinating contrast with their modern descendants. Note, for example, Ando's observation that the Antonine Constitution enacted by the Emperor Caracalla granted citizenship in some cases to "persons living on land deemed foreign" (Ando 2016, 23), even while Taylor observes that for many decades not all those born free in Rome itself were full citizens, and even among these there were distinctions in rights to property, access to justice and other matters (Taylor 2016). See also Williamson (2005, 191–201, et *seq*).
3 McAdam has been, and continues to be, the most important voice (see 2010, 2012), and valuable contributions have also been made by Markovich and Annandale (2000), Rayfuse (2009; 2010), Rayfuse and Crawford (2012), Wong (2013), von Paepcke (2014), Yamamoto and Esteban (2014) and Torres Camprubí (2016).
4 A notable attempt to imagine a post-territorial world order was the globalisation-inspired debate of the late 20th century, which sought to imagine, from cosmopolitan, socialist and other standpoints, a world without sovereign States. These conceptions ranged from the minimal (permeability of borders and alignment of certain areas of policy-making – see, e.g. Habermas (2000)) to visions of a global "State" (see, e.g. Falk 1975; Kiang 1984), with a great many points ranged along the spectrum in between (see, e.g. Bateson 1990; Camilleri 1990; Held 1995; Linklater 1998a, 1998b; Bellamy 2003). Although not directly relevant to the question of territoriality – it primarily concerned the appropriateness of the concept of *sovereignty* for the future development of world society/ies – the debate foreshadowed certain of the ideas discussed here. In particular, its focus on permeability of national boundaries – common to most strands – overlaps to some extent with the discussion here on territoriality.
5 See *Case Concerning East Timor (Portugal v Australia)*, Merits, Judgment (1995) ICJ Reports 90; *Legal Consequences of the Construction of a Wall in the Occupied Palestinian Territory*, Advisory Opinion (2004) ICJ Reports 136.
6 A particularly intriguing, if somewhat dystopian, vision of overlapping sovereignties can be found in China Miéville's novel, *The City & the City* (Miéville, China 2009).
7 Here, too, it is instructive to consider the idea of non-sovereign States (this term is intended to capture the various conceptions of pre-, post-, and redistributed sovereignty that were produced by this rich and wide-ranging debate) discussed in note 4. As noted there, though non-identical, that debate also called into question the territorial conception of statehood, and perhaps presaged to that extent the anthropic concept of statehood discussed here.
8 Although superficially similar, this idea would have relatively little overlap with the existing idea of a government in exile. The latter is a political estate motivated by a belief on the part of the host (and perhaps other governments and international bodies) that a change of government in a State was unlawful – perhaps as a result of events such as a coup against a democratically elected government, or occupation by another State – and depends on recognition. It also carries with it few legal rights or effects. See Talmon (1998); Crawford (2006, 34).

Bibliography

Albert, S., J. X. Leon, A. R. Grinham, J. A. Church, B. R. Gibbes, and C. D. Woodroffe. 2016. 'Interactions Between Sea-Level Rise and Wave Exposure on Reef Island Dynamics in the Solomon Islands'. *Environmental Research Letters* 11(5): 054011. doi:10.1088/1748-9326/11/5/054011.

Ando, C. 2016. 'Sovereignty, Territoriality and Universalism in the Aftermath of Caracalla'. In *Citizenship and Empire in Europe 200–1900: The Antonine Constitution After 1800 Years*, edited by Ando, C. Stuttgart: Franz Steiner Verlag.

Arrhenius, S. 1897. 'On the Influence of Carbonic Acid in the Air Upon the Temperature of the Earth'. *Publications of the Astronomical Society of the Pacific* 9: 14.

Balibar, E. 2014. *Equaliberty*. Translated by Ingram, J. Durham: Duke University Press.

Bartelson, J. 1995. *A Genealogy of Sovereignty*. Cambridge: Cambridge University Press.

Bassiouni, M. C. 1990. 'A Functional Approach to General Principles of International Law'. *Michigan Journal of International Law* 11: 768.

Bassiouni, M. C. 1996. 'International Crimes: Jus Cogens and Obligatio Erga Omnes'. *Law and Contemporary Problems* 59: 63.

Bateson, M. C. 1990. 'Beyond Sovereignty: An Emerging Global Civilization'. In *Contending Sovereignties: Redefining Political Community*, edited by Walker R. B. J., and Mendlovitz, S. H. Boulder: Lynne Rienner Publishing.

Bellamy, R. 2003. 'Sovereignty, Post-Sovereignty and Pre-Sovereignty: Three Models of the State, Democracy and Rights within the EU'. In *Sovereignty in Transition*, edited by Walker, N. Oxford: Hart Publishing.

Bin, C. 1953. *General Principles of Law as Applied By International Courts and Tribunals*. London: Stevens & Sons Ltd.

Bodin, J. 1967. *Six Books of the Commonwealth*. Translated by Tooley, M. J. Oxford: Basil Blackwell. First Published 1576.

Brownlie, I. 2003. *Brownlie's Principles of Public International Law*. 6th ed. Oxford: Oxford University Press.

Camilleri, J. A. 1990. 'Rethinking Sovereignty in a Shrinking, Fragmented World'. In *Contending Sovereignties: Redefining Political Community*, edited by Walker, R. B. J., and Mendlovitz, S. H. Boulder: Lynne Rienner Publishing.

Cassese, A. 2012. 'States: Rise and Decline of the Primary Subjects of the International Community'. In *The Oxford Handbook of the History of International Law*, edited by Fassbender, B., and Peters, A. Oxford: Oxford University Press.

Central Intelligence Agency. 2018. *World Factbook*. Accessed 23 March 2018. www.cia.gov/library/publications/the-world-factbook.

Cohen, K. M., S. C. Finney, P. L. Gibbard, and J.-X. Fan. 2013. 'The ICS International Chronostratigraphic Chart'. *Episodes* 36: 199–204. Accessed 30 March 2018. www.stratigraphy.org/ICSchart/ChronostratChart2017-02.pdf.

Craven, M. 2014. 'Statehood, Self-Determination and Recognition'. In *International Law*, edited by Evans, M. D. 4th ed. Oxford: Oxford University Press.

Crawford, J. 2006. *The Creation of States in International Law*. 2nd ed. Oxford: Clarendon Press.

Crutzen, P. J. 2002. 'Geology of Mankind'. *Nature* 415: 23.

Crutzen, P. J., and E. F. Stoermer. 2000. 'The "Anthropocene"'. *Global Change Newsletter* 41: 17.

d'Aspremont, J. 2014. 'The International Law of Statehood: Craftsmanship for the Elucidation and Regulation of Births and Deaths in the International Society'. *Connecticut Journal of International Law* 29: 201.

Durkheim, E. 1972. 'Religion and Ritual'. In *Emile Durkheim: Selected Writings*, edited by Giddens, A. Cambridge: Cambridge University Press.

Duvat, V. K. E., A. K. Magnan, R. M. Wise, J. E. Hay, I. Fazey, J. Hinkel, T. Stojanovic, H. Yamano, and V. Ballu. 2017. 'Trajectories of Exposure and Vulnerability of Small Islands to Climate Change'. *WIREs Climate Change* 8(6): 478. doi:10.1002/wcc.478.

Dworkin, R. 2005. *Taking Rights Seriously*. London: Gerald Duckworth & Co. Ltd. First Published 1977.

Falk, R. 1975. *A Study of Future Worlds*. New York: The Free Press.

Fazal, T. M. 2007. *State Death: The Politics and Geography of Conquest, Occupation, and Annexation*. Princeton: Princeton University Press.

Gewirth, A. 1978–1979. 'The Basis and Content of Human Rights'. *Georgia Law Review* 13: 1143.

Giddens, A. 1978. *Durkheim*. London: Fontana Press.

Giddens, A. 1984. *The Constitution of Society: Outline of the Theory of Structuration*. Cambridge: Polity Press.

Grant, H. 2015. 'UN Agencies "Broke and Failing" in Face of Ever-Growing Refugee Crisis'. *The Guardian*, 6 September. Accessed 23 March 2018. www.theguardian.com/world/2015/sep/06/refugee-crisis-un-agencies-broke-failing.

Grant, T. D. 1998–1999. 'Defining Statehood: The Montevideo Convention and Its Discontents'. *Colombia Journal of Transnational Law* 37: 403.

Grotius, H. 1625. *De Jure Belli Ac Pacis, Libri Tres*. Paris: Nicolaum Buon.

Habermas, J. 2000. 'Beyond the Nation-State? On Some Consequences of Economic Globalisation'. In *Democracy in the European Union: Integration Through Deliberation*? edited by Eriksen, E. O., and Fossum, J. E. Oxford: Routledge.

Hannikainen, L. 1988. *Peremptory Norms (Jus Cogens) in International Law: Historical Development, Criteria, Present Status*. Helsinki: Finnish Lawyers Publishing Company.

Hansen, J. 1988. 'Statement of Dr James Hansen, Director, NASA Goddard Institute for Space Studies'. Presented at *the Energy and Natural Resources Committee*, United States Senate, 24 June. United States Senate.

Held, D. 1995. *Democracy and the Global Order: From the Modern State to Cosmopolitan Governance*. Stanford: Stanford University Press.

Herczegh, G. 1969. *General Principles of Law and the International Legal Order*. Budapest: Akadémiai Kiadó.

Hobbes, T. 1651. *Leviathan: Or the Matter, Forme and Power of a Common Wealth Ecclesiasticall and Civil*. London: Andrew Crooke.

Jellinek, G. 1914. *Allgemeine Staatslehre*. 3rd ed. Berlin: Julius Springer.

Kant, I. 2002. *Groundwork for the Metaphysics of Morals*. Edited by Hill Jr., T. E., and Zweig, A. Translated by Zweig, A. Oxford: Oxford University Press. First Published 1785.

Kelsen, H. 1999. *General Theory of Law and the State*. Translated by Wedberg, A. Clark: Lawbook Exchange. First Published 1945.

Kiang, J. 1984. *One World: The Approach to Permanent Peace on Earth and the General Happiness of Mankind*. Notre Dame: One World Publishing Co.

Korsgaard, C. M. 1996. *The Sources of Normativity*. Edited by O'Neill, O. Cambridge: Cambridge University Press.

Kotzé, L. J. 2015. 'The Anthropocene's Global Environmental Constitutional Moment'. *Yearbook of International Environmental Law* 25: 24.

Kotzé, L. J. 2016. *Global Environmental Constitutionalism in the Anthropocene*. Oxford: Hart Publishing.

Kotzé, L. J., ed. 2017. *Environmental Law and Governance for the Anthropocene*. Oxford: Hart Publishing.

Kuhn, T. S. 2009. *The Structure of Scientific Revolutions*. 3rd ed. Chicago: University of Chicago Press.

Leakey, R. E. 1981. *The Making of Mankind*. London: Book Club Associates.

Linderfalk, U. 2011. 'The Creation of Jus Cogens – Making Sense of Article 53 of the Vienna Convention'. *Zeitschrift Für Ausländisches Öffenliches Recht Und Völkerrecht* 71: 359.

Linderfalk, U. 2012. 'What Is So Special About Jus Cogens? – On the Difference Between the Ordinary and the Peremptory International Law'. *International Community Law Review* 14: 3.

Linderfalk, U. 2013. 'The Source of Jus Cogens Obligations – How Legal Positivism Copes With Peremptory International Law'. *Nordic Journal of International Law* 82: 369.

Linklater, A. 1998a. *The Transformation of Political Community: Ethical Foundations of the Post-Westphalian Era*. Cambridge: Polity Press.

Linklater, A. 1998b. 'The Idea of Citizenship and the Development of the Modern State'. In *European Citizenship, Multiculturalism, and the State*, edited by Preuss, U. K., and Requejo, F. Baden-Baden: Nomos Verlagsgesellschaft.

MacLean, R., and P. Kench. 2015. 'Destruction or Persistence of Coral Atoll Islands in the Face of 20th and 21st Century Sea-Level Rise?'. *WIREs Climate Change* 6(5): 445.

Marek, K. 1954. *Identity and Continuity of States in Public International Law*. Geneva: Librairie E. Droz.

Markovich, V., and D. Annandale. 2000. 'Sinking Without a Life Jacket: Sea Level Rise and the Position of Small Island States in International Law'. *Asia Pacific Journal of Environmental Law* 5(2): 135.

McAdam, J. 2007. *Complementary Protection in International Refugee Law*. Oxford: Oxford University Press.

McAdam, J. 2010. '"Disappearing States", Statelessness and the Boundaries of International Law'. In *Climate Change and Displacement: Multidisciplinary Perspectives*, edited by McAdam, J., 105. Oxford: Hart Publishing.

McAdam, J. 2012. *Climate Change, Forced Migration and International Law*. Oxford: Oxford University Press.

McAdam, J. 2014. 'Human Rights and Forced Migration'. In *The Oxford Handbook of Refugee and Forced Migration Studies*, edited by Fiddian-Qasmiyeh, E., Loescher, G., Long, K., and Sigona, N. Oxford: Oxford University Press.

Miéville, China. 2009. *The City & the City*. London: Macmillan.

Montevideo Convention on the Rights and Duties of States, adopted 26 December 1933, in force 26 December 1934, 165 League of Nations Treaty Series 19.

Murphy, A. B. 1996. 'The Sovereign State System as Political-Territorial Ideal: Historical and Contemporary Considerations'. In *State Sovereignty as Social Construct*, edited by Biersteker, T. J., and Weber, C. Cambridge: Cambridge University Press.

Nebehay, S. 2017. 'U.N. Warns of New Syrian Refugee Wave to Europe If Aid Dries Up'. *Reuters*, 12 December. Accessed 23 March 2018. www.reuters.com/article/us-mideast-crisis-syria-un-refugees/u-n-warns-of-new-syrian-refugee-wave-to-europe-if-aid-dries-up-idUSKBN1E629V?il=0.

Nozick, R. 1974. *Anarchy, State and Utopia*. Oxford: Basil Blackwell.

Oppenheim, L. F. L. 1912. *International Law: A Treatise – Volume 1: Peace*. 2nd ed. London: Longmans, Green and Co.

Orakhelashvili, A. 2006. *Peremptory Norms in International Law*. Oxford: Oxford University Press.

Paepcke, F. von. 2014. *Statehood in Times of Climate Change: Impacts of Sea Level Rise on the Concept of States*. Frankfurt am Main: PL Academic Research.

Pellet, A. 2006. 'Article 38'. In *The Statute of the International Court of Justice: A Commentary*, edited by Zimmermann, A., Tomuschat, C., and Oellers-Frahm, K. Oxford: Oxford University Press.

Peters, A. 2016. *Beyond Human Rights: The Legal Status of the Individual in International Law*. Translated by Huston, J. Cambridge: Cambridge University Press.

Pufendorf, S. 1672. *De Jure Naturæ et Gentium Libri Octo*. Londini Scanorum [Lund]: Vitus Haberegger in association with Adami Junghans.

Ragheboom, H. 2017. *The International Legal Status and Protection of Environmentally-Displaced Persons: A European Perspective*. Leiden: Brill/Nijhoff.

Rayfuse, R. 2009. 'W(h)ither Tuvalu? International Law and Disappearing States'. *UNSW Law Research Paper*, No. 2009-9. https://ssrn.com/abstract=1412028.

Rayfuse, R. 2010. 'International Law and Disappearing States: Utilising Maritime Entitlements to Overcome the Statehood Dilemma'. *UNSW Law Research Paper*, No. 2010-52. https://ssrn.com/abstract=1704835.

Rayfuse, R., and E. Crawford. 2012. 'Climate Change, Sovereignty and Statehood'. In *International Law in an Era of Climate Change*, edited by Rayfuse, R. and Scott, S. Cheltenham: Edward Elgar Publishing.

Raz, J. 1979. 'The Rule of Law and Its Virtue'. In *The Authority of Law: Essays on Law and Morality*, edited by Raz, J., 210. Oxford: Clarendon Press.

Rigaud, K. K., A. de Sherbinin, B. Jones, J. Bergmann, V. Clement, K. Ober, J. Schewe, et al. 2018. *Groundswell: Preparing for Internal Climate Migration*. Washington, DC: World Bank.

Robinson, N. A. 2014. 'Fundamental Principles of Law for the Anthropocene?'. *Environmental Law and Policy* 44(1/2): 13.

Samuels, J. 2008. 'Condominium Arrangements in International Practice: Reviving an Abandoned Concept of Boundary Dispute Resolution'. *Michigan Journal of International Law* 29(4): 727.

Searle, J. 2003. 'Social Ontology and Political Power'. In *Socializing Metaphysics: The Nature of Social Reality*, edited by Schmitt, F. F. Lanham: Rowman & Littlefield Publishers Inc.

Shaw, M. 2017. *International Law*. 8th ed. Cambridge: Cambridge University Press.

Simma, B., and P. Alston. 1988–1989. 'The Sources of Human Rights Law: Custom, Jus Cogens, and General Principles'. *Australian Yearbook of International Law* 12: 82.

Smith, F. E. 1911. *International Law*. 4th ed. London: J. M. Dent & Sons Ltd.

Sparks, T. forthcoming. 'The State'. In *Concepts for International Law: Contributions to Disciplinary Thought*, edited by d'Aspremont, J., and Singh, S. Cheltenham: Edward Elgar Publishing.

Sterio, M. 2010–2011. 'A Grotian Moment: Changes in the Legal Theory of Statehood'. *Denver Journal of International Law and Policy* 39: 209.

Sterio, M. 2013. *The Right to Self-Determination Under International Law: 'Selfistans,' Secession, and the Rule of the Great Powers*. London: Routledge.

Talmon, S. 1998. *Recognition of Governments in International Law: With Particular Reference to Governments in Exile*. Oxford: Clarendon Press.

Taylor, T. S. 2016. 'Social Status, Legal Status and Legal Privilege'. In *The Oxford Handbook of Roman Law and Society*, edited by du Plessis, P., Ando, C., and Tuori, K. Oxford: Oxford University Press.

Thirlway, H. 2013. *The Law and Procedure of the International Court of Justice: Fifty Years of Jurisprudence*. Vol. I. Oxford: Oxford University Press.

Torres Camprubí, A. 2016. *Statehood Under Water: Challenges of Sea-Level Rise to the Continuity of Pacific Island States*. Leiden: Brill/Nijhoff.

United Nations Development Programme. 2007. *Human Development Report 2007/2008 – Fighting Climate Change: Human Solidarity in a Divided World*. http://hdr.undp.org/sites/default/files/reports/268/hdr_20072008_en_complete.pdf.

United Nations Development Programme. 2016. *Human Development Report 2016*. http://hdr.undp.org/sites/default/files/2016_human_development_report.pdf.

United Nations High Commissioner for Refugees. 2018. *Global Trends*. Accessed 28 March 2018. www.unhcr.org/globaltrends2016/.

Verdross, A. 1937. 'Forbidden Treaties in International Law'. *American Journal of International Law* 31(4): 571.

Verzjil, J. H. W. 1969. *International Law in Historical Perspective*. Volume II. International Persons. Leiden: A. W. Sijthoff-Leiden.

Vidas, D., J. Zalasiewicz, and M. Williams. 2015. 'What Is the Anthropocene – And Why Is It Relevant for International Law?'. *Yearbook of International Environmental Law* 25: 3.

Vordermayer, M. 2015. '"Gardening the Great Transformation": The Anthropocene Concept's Impact on International Environmental Law Doctrine'. *Yearbook of International Environmental Law* 25: 79.

Wallace-Bruce, N. L. 2000. 'Of Collapsed, Dysfunctional and Disoriented States: Challenges to International Law'. *Netherlands International Law Review* 47(1): 53.

Weatherall, T. 2015. *Jus Cogens: International Law and the Social Contract*. Cambridge: Cambridge University Press.

Williamson, C. 2005. *The Laws of the Roman People: Public Law in the Expansion and Decline of the Roman Republic*. Ann Arbor: University of Michigan Press.

Wong, D. 2013. 'Sovereignty Sunk – The Position of Sinking States at International Law'. *Melbourne Journal of International Law* 14: 346.

Yamamoto, L., and M. Esteban. 2014. *Atoll Island States and International Law: Climate Change Displacement and Sovereignty*. Heidelberg: Springer.

Yotova, R. 2017. 'Challenges in the Identification of the "General Principles of Law Recognized by Civilized Nations": The Approach of the International Court'. *Canadian Journal of Comparative and Contemporary Law* 3: 269.

8

Reimagining development practice

Mainstreaming justice into planning frameworks

Ritwika Basu and Amir Bazaz

Introduction

Manifestations of climate change and responses thereof operate in a multi-scale and multi-actor context, where uncertainties intersect with capacity (to become resilient), stakes and outcomes in myriad ways (Ostrom, 2010). There is no doubt that the impacts of climate change are far-reaching and its manifestations are often non-linear, complex and difficult to attribute and trace. In spite of the steady advancements in the vast body of knowledge generated to solve the "wicked" problem of climate change, its problematisation and consequently conception of promising solutions remain obscure (Wise et al., 2014). Among other reasons, attribution by way of distinction between development-induced setbacks and specifically the role of climate in it remains a serious concern (Conway and Mustelin, 2014). The ensuing debate, however, affirms this as a non-issue (Dessai et al., 2009; Steffen et al., 2015). Efforts to mainstream climate responses must not be thus hindered by procedural impediments (ibid), especially given the mounting evidence pointing to its undeniable contribution to deepening development setbacks (Field and and Barros, 2014).

Planned development practice draws on the concerted efforts of institutions: robust intent (successfully) shaping processes, and planned resource flows to serve the overarching objectives of "good development" and equitable growth. These require clear articulation of responsibility, accountability measures and incentive structures. It thus forefronts concern of justice; not because the end goals are equitable development and growth, but primarily because the realisation of such growth demands additional hidden costs when faced with additional stressors such as climate change. This renders climate justice highly politicised (Fisher, 2015), scale and resource sensitive (Schlosberg and Collins 2014; Shi et al., 2016).

The mainstream justice debate is prominently pitched at the international scale, to prompt nation-states to contest rights and responsibilities and mobilise collective responses to the unforgiving impacts of climate change (Baylis et al., 2017). The translation of justice in the realm of climate change at scales below (subnational and further down), however, exhibits plurality in connotations, framing and approaches to making "justice." To that effect, individual nation-states, although sovereign entities and uniquely dispositioned to frame and tackle their own development challenges and aspirations, in principle are all bound by (universal) demands of smooth delivery of services and sustained development regardless of their international commitments. The question of justice at the local scale therefore assumes a different texture. In that, justice often mirrors discursive traits in the context of social welfare and human development. This is further discussed in the subsequent sections using the case of Siliguri. The attempt is to deconstruct the two primary strands of the justice debate – procedural and distributive in the context of our case – and thereby ascertain its positionality in the landscape of climate change-development space.

Cities as crucibles for re-imagining and realising justice

Crucial development frameworks reflect consensus around the transformative potential of cities in mitigating some of the burgeoning challenges associated with climate change, development and globalisation. The unprecedented rate of urbanisation[1] drives collective thinking around cities as seats of solutions rather than as hotbeds of problems. In that, opportunities lie in the concentration of economic activities, human potential and networks, although environmental and humanitarian concerns associated with housing, basic services, health, education and employment present grave sustainability challenges. In either case, opportunity or challenge, cities warrant urgent attention in the context of paradigm shifts for sustenance of the planet and humans alike. Thus, sustainable yet differentiated (countries as non-homogenous entities with unique opportunities and challenges) pathways of realising full potential of growth, prosperity and wellbeing conceived democratically form the core of many of these emerging agendas.

Justice in global development frameworks

Global frameworks such as the Sustainable Development Goals (SDGs) or the New Urban Agenda (NUA) are time-bound blueprints for countries to tackle some of the most critical concerns, including extreme poverty, global inequality and sustainable urbanisation (United Nations Conference on Housing and Sustainable Urban Development 2016). The ubiquitous nature of some of these problems has transpired into incisive discourse and solutions across scales. However, in practice justice is highly contextual: tied to local institutions, a local notion of agency and, as Sen (1992: p. 43) argues, assemblage of "capabilities to translate goods into fulfilling functionalities." In his assessment of justice through capabilities, Sen and others have underscored the relevance of "individual freedoms" to not only access "primary goods," but to have the ability and the "freedom to choose between different ways of living." Therefore, the justice-making process is scale-centric but also guided by subjectivity and individual notions of desirability and wellbeing (Sen, 1992).

And we know from exemplary works of some of the greatest scholars of all times debating the individual versus collective rationality (for collective wellbeing) vis-à-vis the inherent tendency of humans to maximise individual gains. Rawls in promulgating the ground-breaking "Theory of Justice" (1972) thus argued that tenets of utility as a means to distribute goods and wellbeing is deeply flawed; it is "inconsistent with the idea of reciprocity: p. 13" which is at the heart of the idea of a well-ordered society. Following this, many have questioned the efficacy of the pragmatic notion of sacrifice by some for the greater good of humankind, or as Raul puts it: "good in the aggregate: p. 13." This is still at the epicentre of global discourse on justice pertaining to humanitarian and development crisis of concerning magnitude, including climate change.

Going back to the global frameworks, we find a strong semblance of justice (or fairness) in varying degrees and articulation – and in redistribution of endowments (material capabilities) towards that. In that, we examine how constituents of justice are articulated in the core objectives. Take, for example, the SDGs, which are a universal set of goals, targets and indicators which were ratified by all member states at the 2015 United Nations General Assembly and are relevant for countries worldwide.

Drawing from the Handbook for localising SDGs for local government and practitioners, we observe that out of the 17 goals, eight aim to achieve universal access (for all) in the context of specific goals. Thus, equity is central to all eight. For example, Goal 8 promotes "sustained, inclusive and sustainable economic growth for all" (Cities SDG Guide: p. 19). The targets and indicators are tuned to the growth priorities of different regions across the world and so are realistically achievable. Likewise, an equal number of goals explicitly aim to reduce inequality and are thus indicative of distributive justice. In the case of the latter, while all goals in principle mirror universality, some goals nest universality within specific target groups, such as women and girls (Goal 5), or a specific economic class, as in the case of Goal 8.

This is to correct the historic trajectories of injustice, and thereby transform the structural drivers that make the experience and outcomes of injustice highly uneven and layered. Additionally, there are separate goals calling for "reduction in inequality" and for "peace, justice and strong institutions." As often is the case, procedural aspects of justice are more challenging to conceive in measurable goals, and the detailed process visions/documents at every local context would yield how far participation, agency and representation are internalised. Additionally, to achieve the qualitative aspects of "inclusivity," per capita measures of growth are often inadequate in catering to its many nuances. Therefore, local imaginations of development vision by sector, demography and other socio-cultural and political determinants of regional disparities are crucial.

The NUA acknowledges the progress made since the two conferences of United Nations on Human Settlements (1976 and 1996), and subsequent adoption of the Millennium Development Goals (2000) in improving the lives of millions of urban dwellers, including large sections of urban poor living in slums and informal settlements. It also takes into account the recent milestones achieved since 2015, particularly the 2030 Agenda for Sustainable Development and the Addis Ababa Agenda on Development Finance. However, the challenges mentioned previously persist, especially growing inequality, which are identified as irrefutable obstacles to sustainable development. The NUA thus presents a set of urban-centric standards and principles for planning, construction, development, management and improvement of cities.

Like SDGs, the NUA provides a roadmap for governments and non-government actors such as civil society organisations (CSOs) and private sector across scales; it consists of five main dimensions of implementation: (1) national urban policies, (2) urban legislation and regulations, (3) urban planning and design, (4) local economy and municipal finance and (5) local implementation. The NUA underscores linkages between livelihood resilience, improving quality of life and "good urbanisation" through reinvigorated urban policies, drawing from Goal 11 on Sustainable cities and communities (SDSN, 2016). It further emphasises culture and cultural diversity as important contributors to the vision of inclusive, sustainable development by way of heralding new ways of living that promote conscious and sustainable choices in consumption and production. Thus, justice is at the heart of the NUA, a development framework agreed upon by nation-states.

Siliguri context

Siliguri is situated in a narrow strip bounded by three international borders: Bhutan to the northeast, Bangladesh to the south and Nepal to the west and in close proximity to China. It is popularly known as the gateway to the northeastern states of India owing to its strategic location at the foothills of the Eastern Himalayas, access to which has significantly improved in terms of road and rail connectivity over the years. Siliguri is also characterised by its location on the banks of the *Mahananda River* and is inundated by two smaller rivulets called the *Jorapani* and *Phuleswari*. These rivers

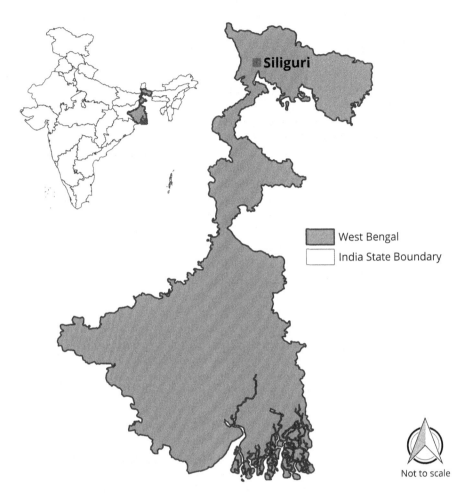

Figure 8.1 **Map of Siliguri.**

Sources: Survey of India (1999), IIHS Analysis (2018).

have played a pivotal role in the city settlement growth. The rivers prominently shape the city's disaster and health profile. Land use, river bed encroachment and protection, and the fact that these hazard-prone areas (such as river beds) are also poverty hotspots of the city remains a grave concern.

Administratively, it is divided between two districts of Darjeeling and Jalpaiguri in North Bengal. Siliguri has witnessed rapid growth in the past decades owing to a number of economic, political and social factors. It has witnessed a population growth rate (decadal growth rate) of 8.7% in the last decade (between 2001 and 2011 census years) and is further projected to grow at a decadal growth rate of almost four times this by 2021 (government statistics; Census of India, 2011). Among non-economic drivers, the partition of India and Pakistan in 1947 followed by the creation of Bangladesh in 1971 and wars with China and Pakistan (1962 and 1965) have been landmark events triggering mass influxes of people (Pramanik and Mukherjee, 2013). Apart from that, ethnic and political violence and uprisings have also shaped people's movements in and out of this region. Other contributing factors relevant to this day are linked to its commercial profile, relevance for trade in natural resources (timber, tea and other forest-based industries), tourism and in recent years for education and health prospects for a large section of people who are either financially deprived, locationally disadvantaged or both (ibid). Numerous small-scale industries such as flour mills, steel, furniture manufacturing units and state-promoted or self-initiated home-based industries have sprung up in the last few decades.

These have been instrumental in attracting people for employment, especially from rural areas and small towns from adjoining districts and states (Debnath and Ray, 2017). This is true of most Indian cities, where growth is largely attributed to internal migration shaped by structural regional development dynamics (Srivastava, 2012; Bhagat, 2016). The nature of employment in the city is suspected to be largely informal (Government of India, 2015).

In a territorial context, large-scale regional environmental changes and the associated unviability of agrarian-based livelihood systems has driven migration to the nearby towns and cities as a significant risk management and livelihood diversification strategy. This migration potentially adds further pressure on city resources. Cities that are plagued with weak financial and institutional regimes find it difficult to manage civic situations that arise due to in-migration. As a result, the experience of urban life for migrants is largely unpleasant, with severe resource constraints and a poor quality of life. In many cases, empirical evidence suggests that migrants residing in vulnerable and hazardous hotspots are more exposed to risks, which worsen their already poor coping capacities.

At present, Siliguri is the third largest urban area in the state of West Bengal (Government of India, 2015). Going by its current urbanising trajectory, alongside the regional economic and political dynamics,[2] Siliguri's development concerns may further escalate to unforeseen levels. The carrying capacity of the city is already stretched; complex manifestations of current growth are visible in multiple crucial dimensions of human wellbeing such as clean drinking water, safe housing, land shortage, public sanitation and health, traffic congestion and related health ailments, and overall welfare provision, especially to the growing urban poor.

In terms of climate resilience, although city governments across India including Siliguri are increasingly cognizant of climate risks multiplying development challenges and retarding progress at all levels, active interventions or planning that mainstream climate concerns at the onset are still lagging. The Government of India (2015) identifies solid waste management and associated concerns such as localised flooding and disease outbreaks as one of the foremost concerns in this regard. Additionally, in terms of preparedness to disasters such as floods and occasional flash floods, the absence of city-scale contingency plans and an active Disaster Management Cell is a concern. Furthermore, the Urban Local Bodies (ULBs) in times of urban floods, which is a fairly common feature of Siliguri, primarily depend on external support. Lack of resources and planning has resulted in reactionary responses or inaction rather than anticipatory responses or measures for proactive preparedness. The report also identifies economic deprivation of a large section of the population, employment-related concerns and poverty as key areas that erode people's overall capacity to cope with risks, climatic and otherwise.

Urban poverty and services: governance dimensions

As per the 74th Constitutional Amendment Act, the ULBs are entrusted with specific poverty-reduction and empowerment goals. These are achieved through the three-tiered system of decentralised governance, wherein resources often flow from the central to the state government, and state government further channels a portion of it to various cities and towns as part of specific schemes and interventions. The CDP thus also illustrates the institutional architecture pertaining to all aspects of city governance, including the governance of service provision to the most marginal, eradication of poverty and livelihood empowerment, which are key to our study.

There are several schemes targeting poverty alleviation, housing for the poor (IHSDP),[3] access to basic services (e.g., Public Distribution System and public taps), credit mobilisation for women (through Self-Help Groups), sanitation in slums (ILCS) and others for specific backward and disadvantaged groups (such as VAMBAY)[4] being implemented in the city. As the name suggests, the Urban Poverty Eradication (UPE) housed under the Public Works Department of the Siliguri Municipal Corporation (SMC) is the nodal agency for most schemes. However, the modalities of financial flows, beneficiaries and access, exclusion are often under-reported and perhaps under-studied as well due to politicisation of monitoring and evaluation processes, and other generic gaps in stock-taking processes for heightened effectiveness. The implementation of the interventions of the UPE, including their largest – slum development and upgradation program – are facilitated by the ward-level civic institutions called the Community Development Societies (CDS). The proximity of CDS to people enables uptake of schemes, notwithstanding issues of distributive justice: exclusion, selective participation and further relegation of some (often migrants) shaped by politics of information access. The CDP articulates these issues but also identifies overcrowding, constant inflow of people and limited resources compounding challenges of governing for and of the poor in the city (Valmiki Ambedkar Awas Yojana 2018).

Recapitulating the context of the Cities in India, it is widely recognised that considerable gaps still exist in smaller and rapidly growing Indian cities between the "city building" development agenda and vulnerability reduction for those who are most at risk. The imperative of delivering adequate services (water, sanitation, solid waste, drainage and power) and equitable access to land and housing to the bulk of city residents is still a matter of debate. Indian cities or, in general, cities in the Global South, have a critical goal to ensure the vulnerability reduction and build resilience into growth and development processes through employment generation and poverty reduction. Managing and building key infrastructure and housing transitions are additional imperatives. Breaking through this institutional gap will be central to an emerging city-centric developmental agenda in India. It needs support and a range of new forms of community–public–private partnerships and other innovative forms of developmental engagement and innovations in governance.

Thus, factors that hinder well-intentioned government programs to enable sustained efforts at inclusive development and urban poverty reduction (a proxy for understanding dimensions of justice) legitimise the need for "other" actors, usually non-state ones, in this space. This is largely a systematic circumvention of constitutionally mandated institutional architecture, deliberately created to manage the politics of inclusion and development.

Approach

In our analysis, we focus on a development initiative called CapaCities, a capacity-building initiative that is being funded by the Swiss Agency for Development and Cooperation in India. Our methods and material are focused on the CapaCities project, with primary data sources being written project material and interviews with key stakeholders, including local political administration.

We argue that actionable strategies and the deliberative phase are both foregrounded by an "Agenda" setting phase, wherein non-state actors create windows of opportunities that could circumvent institutional inertia and create innovative opportunities. Thus, non-state actors emerge as critical nodes that offer innovative institutional space, which is at a distance from local and regional political economy considerations. Figure 8.1 illustrates the typology of actors and mediators that are instrumental in the formulation and implementation of development plans. At the centre of the diagram is the crux of the case, i.e., how local development processes at the city scale perceive and respond to the issue of, for example, growing in-migration. The arrows highlight the interactions between different entities and processes that shape this discourse and actions thereof.

Methodology

We use the case of Siliguri to examine how non-state actors navigate the political economy land-scape and work towards defining an agenda that is aimed at vulnerability reduction and poverty alleviation. The key phases of the agenda setting that have been analysed here are actionable strategies and the deliberative space (imagining migration into the city), recognising that both climate resilience and developmental progress are essential for the city development agenda and progress. For example, we use the case of examining "migration into the city" as an exploratory framework but largely commenting on the various stages of how migration and climate resilience are thought through within the political and administrative spaces (refer to Figure 8.1).

We distinguish between "operational" and "framing" methodology. While the operating methodology relied on specific material to draw insights from, it was the "framing" methodology that is important in our study. The underlying argument is that framing is a discursive process and therefore demands iterations; the stages are captured in Figure 8.2. Framing is an action embedded within the research process. Methodologically, it is thus a discursive space that allows for political manoeuvring and thereby incorporates elements of justice.

A combination of key informant interviews with city-level government officials across hierar-chies of practice, secondary policy reviews and focussed group discussions with men, women and mixed groups (undertaken separately) was carried out to chart out the planned and lived experi-ences of the same. Furthermore, community-based groups, such as SHGs and elected members constituting the institutionalised CDS, were interviewed to understand the operational aspects of inclusion, participation and distributive practices pertaining to state-led development interven-tions. These were key in highlighting opportunities for addressing equity considerations, but also in identifying some of the bottlenecks characterising socially heterogeneous context, fractured power relations between the "state" and "subject," and changing definitions and subjectivity, linked with the notion of "subject" in a migrant city such as Siliguri.

Discussion

While the government at various levels recognises multiple urban challenges, the commitment is largely to improve the experience of urban life through various programs and missions. Initial find-ings, however, indicate that the experience of (inclusive) program delivery has been essentially weak with large pockets of extant vulnerability. These arise from a lack of heterogeneous needs assessment and the consequent need for locating appropriate solutions. Inadequate (inclusive) processes and mechanisms, political economy and culturally entrenched parochial tendencies such as patriarchy are the primary reasons. The grand hope is that generic improvements in service provisioning would benefit (even in some measure) the urban poor, and therefore there is an implicit reliance on autono-mous responses and action by the urban poor. We argue that this is a flawed public goods argument, and provisioning should be motivated by the group that is the most vulnerable. For example, India's city infrastructure upgradation program, as one of its elements, encourages local government to plan for large-scale source augmentation of water supply. While the plan might be reasonable, it is not in line with the most pressing requirements. Many within the city landscape do not have piped-water connections and, therefore, we argue that the "justice" criteria in the way of water provisioning should be given primacy over supply augmentation. Although equity considerations are inbuilt into the programmatic system by design, constraints arising from realities of political economy obstruct equity in implementation. Non-state actors could act as a bridge in this context.

In the subsequent section, using the case of Siliguri and specific examples of actionable strat-egies and discursive agenda setting, we demonstrate how the top-down processes of program

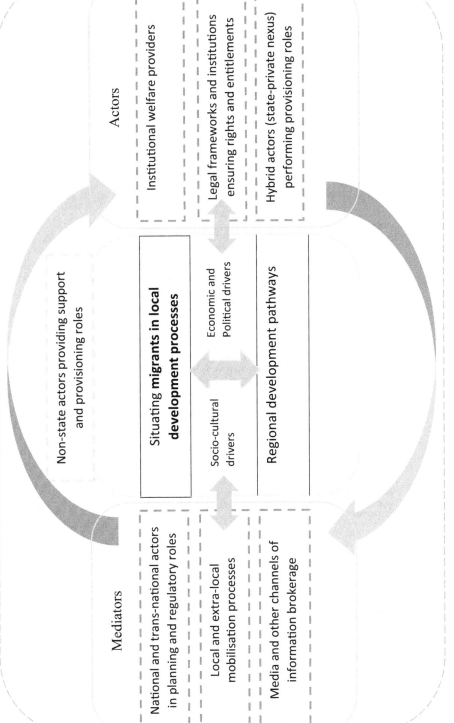

Figure 8.2 Framework to situate processes shaping development outcomes in the city context.

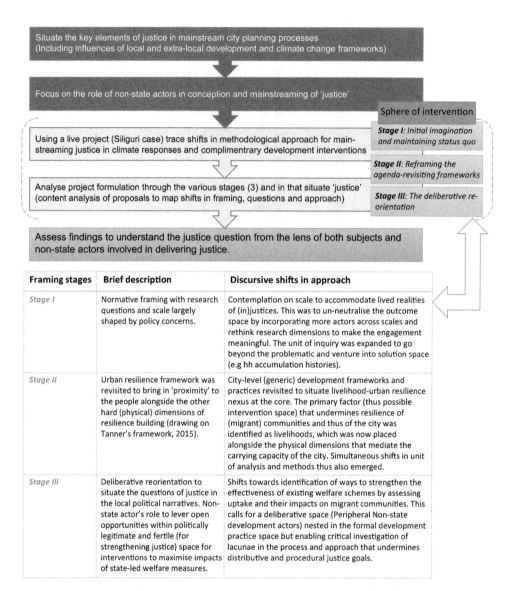

Figure 8.3 Delineation of the methodological approach followed and the discursive shifts in approach to mainstream justice in research framework and outcomes.

delivery are located in bottom-up spaces, and are guided by intensive processes of needs assessment or local ideas of development. This, we argue, is because of the institutional space of developmental intervention that is available.

A common phase – agenda setting

The Swiss Agency for Development and Cooperation decided to support city authorities in addressing challenges due to climate change though a project called CapaCities. The aim was to strengthen select cities' capacities for planning and implementing measures for coping with the effects of a changing climate in an informed and integrated manner. This intervention is in line with the Government of India's National Mission on Sustainable Habitat (NMSH), which strives to address climate change by integrating both adaptation and mitigation actions into urban planning, as well as with a new programme on Urban Infrastructure called Atal Mission for Rejuvenation and Urban Transformation (AMRUT). Thus, a non-state actor (SDC) recognised capacity gaps in the planning and implementation apparatus of city governments and set an agenda aimed at improving developmental outcomes and building adaptive capacities. In essence, the agenda articulated the creation of a middle-space to harness various kinds of innovation while navigating the political economy landscape.

The finer elements of this phase recognised that interventions need to enhance the resilience and adaptive capacity of people, institutions and ecosystems so as to respond to the impacts of climate variability and change. The programme thus defined the imperatives of mainstreaming climate change adaptation into development planning at multiple levels of governance (central, state and municipalities). The strategic orientation of the terms of reference envisioned development of plans drawing on participatory approaches. Additionally, monitoring and evaluation frameworks were to be set up; for instance, setting up of the interdepartmental team (in the form of a City Development Committee). The basic strategy was to mobilise appropriate expertise, provide capacity building of city authorities and other private and public stakeholders in each sector, and support the development and implementation of specific action plans to achieve quick-win measures (accelerating delivery of just outcomes).

Actionable strategies

The CapaCities project in Siliguri is an example of non-state actors (in this case, ICLEI South Asia and Partners) implementing strategies based on priorities and needs identified by the SMC (ULBs). While the consortium (CapaCities team) provides expertise, both the space and agency for piloting interventions is facilitated by the city government and para-government bodies through the State machinery, such as ward-level committees, CDS and local leaders' influence. The activities undertaken are guided by the broad objectives of transition towards lower greenhouse gas (GHG) emissions and enhanced resilience through planned mitigation and adaptation activities. For instance, at present, a pilot installation of water auditing systems and simultaneous training of a "team of caretakers" is underway to enable detection of leakage and restoration to minimise water loss in the formal water supply chain. The other two interventions are towards an integrated ward-level solid waste management system, and installation of air quality monitoring systems. Both are to reduce pressure on Siliguri's resources and people (e.g., pulmonary diseases are on the rise) associated with solid waste and air pollutants. While the former is in line with the National Swacch Bharat Mission and claims to replicate the goals at a minuscule scale of ward (Swacch Wards), the latter is to generate knowledge regarding air quality status for the city government to take necessary actions (Swacch Bharat Mission, 2018). The results of air quality monitoring are further displayed on a live digital board outside of the SMC building, thus making the information public.

The fact that both solid waste and air quality issues incrementally erode adaptive capacities of city dwellers, especially the urban poor, and thereby prevents them from participating in the urban economy to the best of their abilities, further entrenches their vulnerability. This is thus an illustrative example of how justice criteria can be mainstreamed into not only the developmental and climate resilience narrative but also practice. We argue that these processes could gradually contribute to a growing body of evidence base on which adaptation and mitigation measures can be planned and implemented.

The deliberative space

We use the example of the examination of the migration framing narrative as an entry point to discuss the processes and design of how justice criteria was given prominence and how it emerged as a central enquiry. We argue that the process emerges discursively, wherein political spaces are tactfully navigated, but concerns due to the presence of a non-state actor is positioned as people- and welfare-centric rather than as policy.

Stage I: initial imagination and maintaining the status quo

While the terms of reference were broadly identified (as indicated earlier), a non-state actor was approached to examine migration-climate resilience questions. The starting point of the framing narrative was largely driven by policy concerns, albeit maintaining neutrality in discourse, and assumption of large-scale homogeneity at the backdrop. We observe that the way the framing narrative was defined would (most likely) lead to normative outcomes and, therefore, normative policy orientations and would largely replicate itself on predictable lines, that only reinforce top-down interventions. For example, the non-state actors began by focusing on migration questions that were largely policy-focused and policy-oriented and were not located in the day-to-day experience of migrant lives. While this is acceptable as a research agenda, it is largely expected that normative positions would get replicated.

The level of inquiry was planned at multiple scales: (1) within the household; (2) at the city scale; and (3) at a multi-level governance scale, and argued for a multi-level policy discourse for its management. Agreeably, household-level enquiry normatively reflects concerns of justice. However, the overall research frame may have resulted in advocating for an implementation agenda that prioritises city-level strategies but may lose sight of the underlying equity (household-level) considerations. Hence, a discursive approach was thought desirable; it must locate the framing in lived challenges but does not attempt to over-generalise and play political proxy. This led the framing scaffolding to re-examine the evolving narrative frameworks and understand the need for constructing migration challenge as a justice enquiry.

Stage II: reframing the agenda – going back to frameworks

It was, therefore, important to go back to foundational frameworks of resilience – the broad objective of the CapaCities project. Resilience is increasingly being used as a conceptual lens to inform climate change, disaster management and development policies (Bahadur and Tanner, 2014; Meerow and Newell, 2016; Chelleri et al., 2015) because it provides a useful framework to analyse adaptation processes and identify appropriate policy responses (Nelson et al., 2007). Thus, for examining climate action in the urban area, a resilience lens helps by (1) examining the system as a whole, and (2) forefronts the dynamic and multiscalar nature of risks and responses.

However, more recently, urban resilience frameworks have moved towards emphasising the criticality of "people, politics and power" in resilience building (Bahadur and Tanner, 2014), noting that it is "inevitably a contested process in which diverse stakeholders are involved and their motivations, power dynamics, and trade-offs play out across spatial and temporal scales" (Meerow and Newell, 2016: 46).

Based on these theoretical advances, it is recognised that examination of urban risk and resilience needs to follow a particular orientation, which is by design wedded to the idea of justice and equity. While the migration framing in the CapaCities project narrative evolved, exploration of the most recent frameworks of enquiry enabled locating migration as a livelihood problem and, thus, emphasising the need for the problem definition to be people oriented. The framing narrative, therefore, focused on the following broad elements:

- Building on Tanner et al. (2015) to think about solutions with migrant lives/experiences as central to problem space but also possible solutions. In essence, the frame started sought solutions that focus on constraints and opportunities facing migrants in sustaining livelihoods. The role of various actors, including city government, was identified for in-depth exploration at the backdrop of this broad template.
- Further, to rethink the nexus of migrant-city accumulation strategies. Households accumulate various kinds of capital (human, social, physical), while the role of the state is to create an enabling environment for such accumulation strategies. These strategies rely on people as the source of solutions but allow us to explore the intervention landscape from the state perspective.

These framing innovations were critical in terms of recognising justice to be mainstreamed into the developmental agenda of the city.

Stage III: the deliberative re-orientation – acknowledging opportunities while acknowledging the importance of politics

The next big challenge with regards to the framing narrative is to unpack the guiding elements into specific questions; questions that are politically navigable subscribe to the local political economy and have a "justice" orientation. It is vital to understand that political legitimacy is crucial to examine developmental questions, and therefore framing enquiry questions that are politically relevant is important. Political acceptance might come in many ways, but most prominently is tightly linked to local welfare policies that are locally constructed, implemented and managed.

For example, through interactions with the Mayor (political head), we realised that migration in the context of Siliguri is perceived more or less positively. Similar views were expressed by the ward councillors. The Mayor and the councillors were unanimously in support of enhancing the overall wellbeing (justice) of the slum dwellers. Despite severe funding challenges from the state government, they strive to implement many pro-poor initiatives through their core funds. From these interactions we felt that the local government would benefit from an analysis of the effectiveness of the different development initiatives undertaken in different Wards. Particularly, livelihood strengthening schemes such as skill development can (and must) be leveraged to build resilience of the migrant slum dwellers through income generation and assimilation into the city's economy.

The overall objective of the migration study then shifted towards identification of ways to strengthen the effectiveness of existing pro-poor schemes by assessing their uptake and impacts amongst the migrant community in select wards. We argue that this shift in the framing agenda – from an opportunity created by a non-state actor (SDC) to re-assess the location of the framing agenda in local, drawing from the lived realities of migrants, and finally, gaining political legitimacy and support through examining migration through the livelihood and welfare lens – is a perfect shift towards mainstreaming justice into the development agenda. It is vital, therefore, to design a deliberative space that creates local political legitimacy but restrains from super-imposing normative frameworks and co-develops an agenda that is locally tenable and politically acceptable.

Conclusion

While institutionalised participation is instrumental, especially in shaping need-based policy derivatives, beneficiary participation is often undermined due to underlying paternalistic tendencies in State-led welfare provisioning. The non-state actors can potentially alter this space. They can strengthen a culture of dialogue and empower recipients of such welfare to actively find a voice and role in shaping the processes and outcomes of social policies and welfare. However, in reality often supranational non-state actors functioning in a neoliberal development paradigm further pose a risk of weakening representation, autonomy and legitimacy of other non-state actors such as traditional committees, religious groups and so on. This is due to their policy steering actions that need to navigate and function within the narrow institutional space offered by the state agencies. Nevertheless, fostering an ecosystem of democratic non-state actors offers many opportunities that can be leveraged for equitable and just development processes and outcomes. Policy spaces can be levered open for emergence of multiple interpretations of needs and solutions in such a varied landscape. It is important to note, however, that the existence and influence of many non-state actors, as in this case, are influenced by the socio-political context and are heavily contingent on relations within and outside of the organisational structure. This generates interesting questions on the viability of redefining justice and the deliberate shifting of development contours in a co-dependent landscape such as this one.

Despite the challenges, increasing momentum for democratisation of local social development, alongside the global mandates such as international agreements and commitments, impart non-state actors (external as well as local) with competitive benefits of being at a vantage point. This allows them to get an impartial overview of complex processes and to selectively intervene in development processes; they can be at the periphery and make inroads to influence the core of social policy-making. However, further deliberation on institutionalisation of non-state actors' capacity, agency and role in the process is required to overcome some of the challenges such as vague accountability, co-optation and perpetuation of social exclusion, while maximising their strengths in mediating right-based processes.

Notes

1 By 2050, the world's urban population is expected to nearly double.
2 In the late 1980s, a violent movement for a separate state of Gorkhaland was initiated by the the the Gorkha National Liberation Front (GNLF) and the people of Darjeeling. The agitation led to formation of a semi-autonomous body in 1988 called the Darjeeling Gorkha Hill Council (DGHC) and a new party called the Gorkha Janmukti Morcha (GJM) to mobilise the demand for a separate state. From time to time, violent outbursts still take place. In June last year, the GJM called for an indefinite shutdown, principally targeting public offices.
3 Integrated Housing and Slum Development Program. Find more information here: http://ud-hp.in/pdf/IHSDP-Guidelines.pdf
4 Valmiki Ambedkar Awas Yojana is a centrally sponsored scheme for the benefit of slum dwellers below the poverty line. Find more information here: https://www.jdajammu.in/vambay.php

References

Bahadur, A. and Tanner, T. (2014) 'Transformational resilience thinking: Putting people, power and politics at the heart of urban climate resilience', *Environment and Urbanization*, 26(1), pp. 200–214.
Baylis, J., Smith, S. and Owens, P. eds. (2017) *The globalization of world politics: An introduction to international relations.* Oxford: Oxford University Press.
Bhagat, R.B. (2016) 'Internal migration in India: Are the underclass more mobile?', In *India Migrations Reader* (pp. 132–150). New Delhi: Routledge.

Census of India (2011) *Government of India*, accessed 30 April, 2018, http://censusindia.gov.in/2011-Common/CensusData2011.html

Chelleri, L., Waters, J.J., Olazabal, M. and Minucci, G. (2015) 'Resilience trade-offs: Addressing multiple scales and temporal aspects of urban resilience', *Environment and Urbanization*, 27(1), pp. 181–198.

Conway, D. and Mustelin, J. (2014) 'Strategies for improving adaptation practice in developing countries', *Nature Climate Change*, 4(5), p. 339.

Debnath, M. and Ray, S. (2017) 'Migration and rapid urban growth: A study on Siliguri city', *Asian Journal of Research in Business Economics and Management*, 7(6), pp. 117–126.

Dessai, S., Hulme, M., Lempert, R. and Pielke, R. (2009) 'Do we need better predictions to adapt to a changing climate?', *Transactions American Geophysical Union*, 90(13), pp. 111–112.

Field, C.B. and Barros, V.R. eds. (2014) *Climate change 2014: Impacts, adaptation, and vulnerability* (Vol. 1). Cambridge and New York: Cambridge University Press.

Fisher, S. (2015) 'The emerging geographies of climate justice', *The Geographical Journal*, 181(1), pp. 73–82.

Government of India (2015) *City Development Plan, Ministry of Urban Development, Siliguri*, accessed 30 April 2018, http://siligurismc.in/userfiles/file/siliguri-CDP-final-report-29April15.pdf

India, U.N., 2015. *India and the MDGs. Towards a Sustainable Future for All.* United Nations Country Team–India.

Integrated Housing and Slum Development Policy, Department of Municipal Affairs, Government of West Bengal, accessed 9 April 2018, www.wbdma.gov.in/HTM/MUNI_IHSDP.htm

International Council for Local Environmental Initiatives (2016) *CapaCities, Swiss agency for development and cooperation*, accessed 9 April 2018, http://capacitiesindia.org/at-a-glance/

Meerow, S. and Newell, J.P., 2016. Urban resilience for whom, what, when, where, and why? *Urban Geography*, pp. 1–21.

Nelson, D.R., Adger, W.N. and Brown, K. (2007) 'Adaptation to environmental change: Contributions of a resilience framework', *Annual Review of Environment and Resources*, 32.

Ostrom, E. (2010) 'A multi-scale approach to coping with climate change and other collective action problems', *Solutions*, 1(2), pp. 27–36.

Pramanik, A. and Mukherjee, S.R. (2013) 'Urbanisation, migration and expenditure pattern of the urban poor: A study of inner & Peripheral City squatter settlements in Siliguri Municipal Corporation Area (SMCA) of West Bengal in India', *The Macrotheme Review*, 2(6), pp. 116–136.

Rawls, J. (1972) *A theory of justice*. Oxford: Oxford University Press.

Schlosberg, D. and Collins, L.B. (2014) 'From environmental to climate justice: Climate change and the discourse of environmental justice', *Wiley Interdisciplinary Reviews: Climate Change*, 5(3), pp. 359–374.

Sen, A. (1992) *Inequality reexamined*. New York: Clarendon Press.

Shi, L., Chu, E., Anguelovski, I., Aylett, A., Debats, J., Goh, K., Schenk, T., Seto, K.C., Dodman, D., Roberts, D. and Roberts, J.T. (2016) 'Roadmap towards justice in urban climate adaptation research', *Nature Climate Change*, 6(2), p. 131.

Srivastava, R., 2012. 'Changing employment conditions of the Indian workforce and implications for decent work'. *Global Labour Journal*, 3(1), pp. 63–90.

Steffen, W., Richardson, K., Rockström, J., Cornell, S.E., Fetzer, I., Bennett, E.M., Biggs, R., Carpenter, S.R., De Vries, W., de Wit, C.A. and Folke, C. (2015) 'Planetary boundaries: Guiding human development on a changing planet', *Science*, 347(6223), p. 1259855.

Sustainable Development Solutions Network (2016) *Getting Started with the SDGs in Cities.* [online] New York: UNSDSN. Available at: http://unsdsn.org/wp-content/uploads/2016/07/9.1.8.-Cities-SDG-Guide.pdf [Accessed 24 Sep. 2018].

Swacch Bharat Mission, Ministry of Housing and Urban Affairs, Government of India, accessed 11 April 2018. www.swachhbharaturban.in/sbm/home/#/SBM

Tanner, T., Lewis, D., Wrathall, D., Bronen, R., Cradock-Henry, N., Huq, S., Lawless, C., Nawrotzki, R., Prasad, V., Rahman, M.A. and Alaniz, R. (2015). 'Livelihood resilience in the face of climate change'. *Nature Climate Change*, 5(1), p. 23.

United Nations Conference on Housing and Sustainable Urban Development (2016) *New Urban Agenda*, accessed 9 April 2018, http://habitat3.org/the-new-urban-agenda/

Vamiki Ambedkar Awas Yojana, Ministry of Urban Development, Government of India, accessed 9 April 2018, www.wbdma.gov.in/HTM/MUNI_VAMBAY_More.htm

Wise, R.M., Fazey, I., Smith, M.S., Park, S.E., Eakin, H.C., Van Garderen, E.A. and Campbell, B. (2014) 'Reconceptualising adaptation to climate change as part of pathways of change and response', *Global Environmental Change*, 28, pp. 325–336.

9

Climate justice in the UK

Reconciling climate change and equity issues in policy and practice in a developed country context

Katharine Knox

Introduction

This chapter examines the concept of climate justice and its application in the UK, drawing on the interdisciplinary research programme of the Joseph Rowntree Foundation (JRF), which funded research on the social justice implications of climate change in the UK over the period 2009–17. It argues that while climate justice is often seen as an international and developing world issue, it is also an agenda that is critical to address in developed countries, including the UK, but is as yet only a nascent consideration for policymakers and practitioners. The chapter explores what climate justice means in a UK context, with reference to the United Nations (UN) climate change and sustainable development agreements to which the UK Government is party. It focuses primarily on issues of distributional injustice in the causes and consequences of climate change for society and illustrates how climate change may create injustice in a developed country, considering both the direct and indirect impacts of climate change and related responses. It introduces and explores the concept of "climate disadvantage" as a product of underlying issues of social vulnerability interacting with exposure to hazards, such as flooding or extreme heat, to amplify the social risks of climate impacts, particularly for those who already face social disadvantage. The chapter also explores the evidence base on social justice in emerging policy and practice responses in the UK, and the extent to which these are addressing social vulnerability and equity issues, considering both mitigation and adaptation agendas. Finally, it briefly turns to consider matters of procedural justice and climate change. It highlights the ongoing challenges climate change poses for issues of poverty and disadvantage in the UK and the importance of multifaceted policy responses to affect change. The evidence highlights how climate justice needs to be considered not just as an issue for developing countries, but also as a domestic agenda, if we are to avoid climate change exacerbating existing inequalities or creating new forms of disadvantage as its effects hit home, whether in the form of increasing floods and heatwaves or changes in the cost of living due to the indirect effects of climate change.

Climate justice in a UK context

"Climate justice" is often thought of as a concern primarily in the context of the developing world, and is interconnected with questions of economic and social development and human rights (Knox, 2016). It is a term which encompasses many issues and defies simple definition. In essence, it concerns the equity of outcomes for different people and places associated with the consequences of climate change and the fairness of related responses both internationally and within nations. There are many aspects which underpin this, linked to political, social, economic and environmental conditions. Climate justice has been defined as:

> Ensuring that collectively and individually we have the ability to prepare for, respond to and recover from climate change impacts – and the policies to mitigate or adapt to them – by considering existing vulnerabilities, resources and capabilities.
>
> *(Banks et al., 2014)*

> By "just" we mean: some chance of a safe climate for future generations; an equal distribution of the remaining global carbon budget between countries; and a transition in the UK in which the costs are distributed progressively, and where everyone's essential needs for housing, transport and energy use are met.
>
> *(Childs, 2011)*

These definitions are not uncontested. The first definition perhaps underplays the urgent need to reduce greenhouse gas emissions. And the proposed equal distribution of the carbon budget across countries in the second definition does not address questions about the "common but differentiated responsibility" of nations across the developed and developing world for emissions reduction, considering responsibility for both historic and future emissions (UN, 1992).

Questions of social justice have often stymied international negotiations on climate change responses, raising as they do questions about different nations' economic growth trajectories, fair distribution of the benefits and burdens of emissions reduction and the unequal consequences of climate change (Elliot and Cook, 2016). Even if nations deliver on their pledges for emission reduction agreed upon at Paris, there is a high chance that global temperature increases will exceed the 1.5-degree threshold States have committed to work towards, posing major threats to the future of some nations and societies, including small island states. A global average temperature increase of 2 degrees is only just still considered to be a viable goal (Anderson, 2012, 2015). Equally, the questions of loss and damage and fair financing to support climate change adaptation have been a sticking point internationally. Developed nations have been criticised for failing to deliver promised resources to less-developed nations to alleviate the potentially disastrous consequences of climate change, including threats to life and livelihoods. Major social justice issues, for example, concerning the protection and human rights of migrants moving in response to climate change impacts, remain as yet unaddressed under international law.

The recently agreed-upon United Nations Sustainable Development Goals, established in 2015 as successors to the Millennium Development Goals, set out an ambitious international agenda for action by 2030. Goal 1 seeks to end poverty in all its forms everywhere, and goal 13 is to take urgent action to combat climate change and its impacts. This is a global plan for action within a generation, agreed to by 193 countries, seeking to balance human wellbeing and prosperity with protecting the planet through sustainable development that takes account of the needs of future generations (UN, 2016).

Despite the UK's responses being led by the Department for International Development, it is clear that to achieve this ambition requires substantial action within the UK itself, and, in both the international and UK context, aspirations to end poverty and address climate change are in fact interlinked, although their manifestations may vary. While the pressures of climate change are undoubtedly frequently more acute in developing countries, the Intergovernmental Panel on Climate Change highlights that:

> Risks are unevenly distributed and are generally greater for disadvantaged people and communities in countries at **all** levels of development.
>
> *(IPCC, 2014)*

Climate change compounds poverty and poverty increases vulnerability to climate change (JRF, 2016). Notwithstanding the substantial international equity issues arising in relation to climate change, this chapter argues that climate justice is not just an issue for developing nations, but is also an issue for the developed world. The distributional and procedural justice implications of climate change do not just apply internationally across time and space, affecting relations among nations, but also apply within nations, with implications for relationships between different parts of society and associated national and local responses.

This chapter highlights the interconnections between poverty, social vulnerability and climate change, and examines how these links play out within the UK to create climate injustice. It identifies four main manifestations of climate injustice and examines associated evidence and its implications for related policy responses:

- Inequities in responsibility for carbon emissions (causes);
- Inequities in the social impacts of climate change (consequences);
- Inequities in how the costs and benefits of responses are shared (responses); and
- Procedural injustice (governance).

Inequities in responsibility for carbon emissions

When considering underlying responsibilities for the problem of climate change, it is clear that questions about associated greenhouse gas emissions are not just a matter of unequal distribution of wealth among nations, but also of inequalities within nations. In the UK context, research shows a clear correlation between levels of income and carbon emissions at the household level: wealthier households are responsible for a much greater proportion of emissions. The Centre for Sustainable Energy (CSE) highlights a substantial disparity across the income spectrum. UK households in the highest income decile are responsible for 16% of the nation's household energy and personal transport emissions, while the poorest 10% are responsible for just 5% of these emissions (Preston *et al.*, 2013). The effect of income on emissions is greater for transport than for household energy use: the wealthiest households are responsible for seven to eight times as many emissions for private travel for leisure and commuting to work and ten times as many for air travel, but only twice as much for energy use in the home (Preston *et al.*, 2013). Other forms of consumption (for example, in relation to leisure activities) also highlight how greater wealth drives greater emissions, with other factors, such as tenure, household composition and urban/rural location, also having important effects (Druckman and Jackson, 2009, 2010).

The challenge of how individual behaviours and practices interact with emissions outcomes is a substantial field of research, but one which shows that attitudes and behaviours are not always aligned. In fact, quite the contrary; individuals espousing pro-environmental attitudes may be among the biggest emitters and are not necessarily living lifestyles in keeping with their values (Quilgars *et al.*, 2016). More typically, those on lower incomes, for whom climate change may appear to be a distant and far from pressing concern, are usually contributing far less to the problem, and often already ration their energy use to manage limited household finances. Households in acute poverty can be forced to choose between eating and heating, or to limit both, due to the pressure on their incomes (Lambie-Mumford and Snell, 2015).

This analysis on emissions clearly raises questions about the equity issues associated with how different parts of society contribute to the climate change problem and to what extent this should inform responses. At the national level, the UK *Climate Change Act 2008*, one of the first pieces of climate change legislation in the world, creates a statutory framework for action. It requires the UK Government to establish national carbon budgets, in recognition that the carbon carrying capacity of the atmosphere is finite, and that this resource, like others, needs to be managed. Establishing carbon budgets for five-year periods has been a marker of policy and a principle guiding attempts to reduce emissions, considering the contribution of different sectors and opportunities for action. This rightly focuses on the major emitting sectors, including industry and agriculture, and opportunities for upstream emissions reduction, including alternatives to fossil fuels in energy supply. In industry, the Government has recognised that the "polluter pays" principle should play some part in how carbon emissions are reduced. Market mechanisms have generally been favoured over regulatory constraints, with Government remaining supportive of the EU emissions trading scheme, for example, though the benefits for mitigation are not always clear, while attempts to use building regulations to enforce delivery of zero-carbon homes were abandoned in 2015.

The role of households in reducing carbon budgets and "behaviour change" initiatives have been part of the policy agenda, but the distributional aspects of this, and how differential contributions to the problem at a household level should, or could, inform or affect responsibilities or approaches to sharing the costs of remedial action, have been less of a focus. While some policies have sought to alleviate fuel poverty at the same time as improving home energy efficiency, less consideration has been given to the question of underlying emissions contributions across the income spectrum, or whether carbon budgeting should be considered locally at the household level, in the same way as it is nationally, to achieve more sustainable consumption.

The notion of personal or household carbon budgets may not be politically popular and may perhaps seem more of an esoteric preoccupation of academia than a focus for policymakers, but a strand of research on this topic in the late 2000s may become more pertinent if concerns about what is a fair share of the diminishing carbon budget are applied to households at some point in future. If the issue does become politically salient, we can anticipate research about personal carbon allowances and personal carbon trading being revisited and questions opened up on how to take account of social heterogeneity in associated budgets. Alongside income, work by the Centre for Sustainable Energy suggests a number of challenges would need to be considered in establishing personal carbon allowances, including household size, how children are treated, rurality, the size and type of property people live in and heating fuel (White *et al.*, 2013).

Constraining household carbon use may not be a vote winner, and personal carbon budgets may be too prescriptive and impractical to implement, not least for equity reasons, but Horton and Doran's work on sustainable consumption (2011) indicates that people are willing to countenance limits on their consumption if they perceive there to be a finite resource under threat that needs to be conserved, as long as such constraints do not allow free riders to ignore the system. Their work suggests that regulation may have a place in future approaches to household-level carbon reduction to address public concerns and support "fair shares" in the allocation of resources (Horton and Doran, 2011). Nonetheless, there is a need to understand what people consider to be acceptable constraints on their choices. Research by Druckman *et al.* (2011) explored public attitudes to what might constitute a *sustainable* minimum living standard, finding that people were more willing to countenance reducing their fuel consumption in the home than altering their food consumption patterns, which was seen as eroding choice. People were also reluctant to travel by more sustainable means without action to address their concerns over safety, convenience and costs. Clearly, any efforts to reduce public consumption as part of the drive to reduce carbon emissions faces barriers in public acceptability, and Druckman's research suggests there are more barriers to reducing people's carbon footprints for food and travel than for domestic energy use. These findings are also borne out in practice; in a new housing scheme in York, where people's carbon footprints are being monitored over time, reducing transport emissions has proven a more intractable issue than reducing energy use in the home (Quilgars *et al.*, 2016).

The difference in emissions profiles across the income spectrum also raises other implications for policy responses. In general, it has been argued that policies which target high transport use may be less regressive than those targeting high household energy use. This is because people on higher incomes tend to travel further and more frequently than those on lower incomes, while household energy use is already often rationed by households struggling to get by, with prevailing housing conditions affecting people's ability to reduce demand (Preston *et al.*, 2013). However, due to the fact that low-income households spend a greater proportion of their incomes on fuel duty and vehicle excise duty than higher-income households, policies targeted here can still be regressive (Banks *et al.*, 2014). However, Dresner *et al.* (2013) found that carbon taxes can be designed in such a way that low-income households can be protected – but this generally requires compensation for these households through the benefits system, making policies revenue-neutral overall – which does not create particular policy incentives to introduce them. Investment in public transport, which benefits low-income households, conversely, could have a more redistributive effect. Clearly, social policies that alleviate poverty while also addressing carbon reduction goals are to be welcomed, but, at the household level, there may also be a need to think more about incentivising higher-income households to reduce emissions and curtail unsustainable consumption patterns. The failure of the Green Deal, discussed later, shows there is some way to go on this issue.

It is clear that placing responsibility upon households for reducing emissions has limitations when the use of fossil fuels remains programmed into our national and local infrastructure and continues to underpin our day-to-day activities at home, work and in our travel patterns (Druckman and Jackson, 2010). It is only through wider systemic changes, which reduce reliance on fossil fuels, address energy supply and demand, support sustainable choices and, arguably, challenge the prevailing economic orthodoxies to establish a more circular economy, that we are likely to make progress, notwithstanding the contribution that households, especially those on higher incomes, can play through their consumption practices and lifestyle changes.

Inequities in the social impacts of climate change

Underlying issues of poverty and disadvantage not only affect the emissions patterns that drive climate change, but they are also significant in the distributional impacts of climate change. Climate change will have a whole range of direct and indirect consequences for society. The latest UK Climate Change Risk Assessment documents the major national risks as: flooding and coastal change risks to communities, business and infrastructure; risks to health, wellbeing and productivity from high temperatures; risks of shortages in the public water supply; risks to domestic and international food production and trade; risks to natural capital, including ecosystems, soils and biodiversity; and new and emerging pests and diseases (Committee on Climate Change, 2016).

These consequences of climate change will not be felt equally either spatially or socially. Different parts of the UK are more at risk of flooding, drought, coastal erosion and heat stress. The Southeast of England, for example, is infamously drier than parts of the Middle East, and London and the South of England are also likely to bear the brunt of higher temperatures (Benzie *et al.*, 2011). Some areas will suffer multiple stressors – coastal areas, for example, may be at risk of a combination of coastal and river flooding, coastal erosion, sea-level rise and storm surges. Research on climate and coastal change in 2010 found five areas of particular concern along the UK coast: South Wales, Northwest Scotland, Yorkshire and Lincolnshire, East Anglia and the Thames Estuary. In these areas, future sea-level rise is expected to be particularly rapid or to have greater impact because it will be combined with an increase in storminess and increased coastal erosion (Fernandez Bilbao *et al.*, 2011). The high prevalence of social deprivation, older populations and reliance on low-income, seasonal jobs and on maritime economies, combined with poor transport connections and physical isolation, will also reinforce disadvantage along particular parts of the UK coast.

Just as climate change will have varied spatial impacts, so too, will it have differential social impacts. People have different capabilities and capacities to respond to the challenges created by extreme weather, so that climate hazards will lead to unequal impacts on people's wellbeing (Lindley *et al.*, 2011). Factors creating vulnerability in the context of different hazards vary, but personal, social and environmental factors are all important. Older people, babies and those in poor health may be particularly vulnerable to heatwaves, in part due to greater sensitivity to increased temperatures. These vulnerabilities can be compounded by the wider social context. Evidence from the Chicago heatwave in 1995 shows, for example, how social isolation and fear of crime were major factors in determining uneven patterns of harm. Old people died alone, sometimes in rooms with windows and doors locked, due to fear of crime. Neighbourhood decline was also found to have led to a loss of public spaces with air conditioning in which vulnerable people could gather to keep cool (Klinenberg, 2002). Similarly, in the European heatwave of 2003, older people in nursing homes saw the greatest increase in deaths. While their health situation was a factor, other issues were also important, including the institutional context, heating system controls and general management and operation of the homes (Lindley *et al.*, 2011). A culture which sees old people as cold, and hence a tendency to focus on keeping people warm, combined with fixed routines which are not adjusted for the weather, with heating systems sometimes on throughout the year, and controls managed offsite, can all add to the risks posed by heatwaves in care settings (Gupta *et al.*, 2016).

Flooding will similarly have differential impacts depending on people's social context. Income matters, as people on low incomes may not be able to afford property-level flood resilience measures and are also less likely than those on higher incomes to have home contents insurance (Sayers *et al.*, 2017). Other social factors are also important – tenure affects the extent to which residents can adapt their homes, with those in private and social rented homes likely to be reliant on their landlord for building insurance as well as any major modifications to improve flood resilience. Other factors in the built and natural environment are also important. For example, green spaces can help to offset flood risk, whereas areas lacking sustainable drainage face amplified risks. Living in a ground floor or basement flat may be more problematic in a flood, whereas in a heatwave, being in a high-rise flat may exacerbate the negative effects of high temperatures.

Pre-existing social vulnerabilities and disadvantage will interact with climate change impacts, including more frequent or severe flooding and higher temperatures, to create "climate disadvantage" (Lindley *et al.*, 2011). Research by Lindley *et al.* on flooding and heat (2011) and subsequently by Sayers *et al.* on flooding under a range of climate change scenarios (2017) highlights the spatial implications of extreme weather by providing maps illustrating how indicators of social vulnerability coincide with hazard exposure to create disadvantage across the UK (see the Climate Just website at www.climatejust.org.uk). Lindley *et al.* find a North-South divide in flood disadvantage, with this being greatest in the Yorkshire and Humber region (Lindley *et al.*, 2011). Sayers *et al.* (2017) find both geographic and systemic disadvantage for vulnerable communities, with over half of the 1.5 million people living in socially vulnerable neighbourhoods exposed to flooding residing in just ten local authorities. Cities in relative economic decline, coastal areas and dispersed rural communities experience levels of flood disadvantage above the UK average, suggesting that flood risk could undermine economic growth in areas that need it most (Sayers *et al.*, 2017).

Climate change will also affect the costs of living in various ways (Watkiss *et al.*, 2016). Firstly, climate change will have a direct bearing on household expenditure and demand for energy for heating and cooling the home, with some positive impacts, for example, higher temperatures are likely to reduce demand for household heating. Secondly, household costs will also be affected indirectly, for example, as floods increase, so overall household insurance premiums are likely to go up, due to increased pay-outs for flood damage. Impacts of climate change overseas will also affect UK households, for example, if there are food price spikes following crop failures and poor harvests that affect international commodity markets. Thirdly, the costs of policy responses to climate change will affect household budgets, for example, due to carbon reduction costs being added to home energy bills. While these examples will hit people's pockets, the costs of climate change will not always be felt financially, but may be borne in other ways, including through health and social impacts, for example, where temperatures rise and households cannot afford to take remedial steps to keep cool.

Lower-income households are likely to feel the effects of climate change on their finances more than those on higher incomes, for several reasons. First, lower-income households tend to spend a greater proportion of their household income on basic household items, including energy and food. When prices rise, they will either need to pay more to maintain their household consumption patterns or cut back if this becomes unaffordable, as already often happens for those on the lowest incomes when adverse circumstances restrict spending choices. On the other hand, if there is less need for household heating, low-income households may benefit disproportionately compared to those on higher incomes for the same reason. Second, low-income households are likely to see a reduction in their quality of life if they cannot take steps to reduce the consequences of climate change. As temperatures rise, despite the associated problems for climate change mitigation, there will be an increasing demand for cooling systems in the home. But those on the lowest incomes are less likely to be able to afford this provision, or may live in tenanted properties which they cannot physically alter, and so are more likely to suffer negative consequences to their health instead (Watkiss *et al.*, 2016). Third, as noted previously, there are differential patterns of risk, meaning that low-income households in some cases face disproportionate risks, for example, in relation to coastal flooding, creating systemic disadvantage (Sayers *et al.*, 2017).

Watkiss *et al.* calculate the potential cost of climate change impacts across a basket of household expenditure items and assess the implications for a typical couple household living on what is considered to be a minimum acceptable income (Watkiss *et al.*, 2016). They find that the impact on average across all households in the near term may be modest, compared to the incomes households need to meet their basic needs, reaching up to £750 per household per year (up to 5% of an annual household budget), though with great margins of uncertainty. Longer term, the costs are expected to become more certain and more substantial. For those directly affected, the costs are clearly more significant than any average proposition; for example, where people's homes are flooded, insurance claims have recently averaged £50,000 (Watkiss *et al.*, 2016). Lower-income households, however, are also far less likely to have the safety net of household insurance or any savings or assets to deal with material losses when a crisis occurs.

Clearly, poverty creates vulnerability in the context of climate change, and people living on a low income are likely to see a greater impact on their wellbeing from increases in the costs of living for basic household items than those with more resources at their disposal. The relationship between aspects of poverty and social vulnerability is also likely to interact with climate risks to create further disadvantage. Housing markets are likely to be affected in the longer term if the insurance industry moves to fully risk-reflective market pricing (O'Neill and O'Neill, 2012). Recent work on resilience identifies managing household budgets and community capacity as critical pinchpoints in any local systemic attempts to build resilience in the context of climate change (Fazey *et al.*, 2017).

Inequities in how the costs and benefits of climate change responses are shared

Climate change will impact directly on the costs of basic household items as illustrated above, but it will also create additional costs through the application of policy responses. For example, carbon taxes applied through energy bills will impact on the costs of living, with particularly regressive impacts for low-income households (Watkiss *et al.*, 2016). The Centre for Sustainable Energy has found compelling evidence of a triple injustice, whereby households on the lowest incomes, who are least responsible for creating carbon emissions, also face a disproportionate burden from the costs of policy responses linked to carbon reduction, while benefiting less than wealthier households from measures introduced (Preston *et al.*, 2013). More recent research has also raised questions about the fairness of adaptation policies, including national flood investment programmes, and whether these are taking sufficient account of distributional issues (England and Knox, 2015, Sayers *et al.*, 2017).

The CSE's analysis of carbon reduction policies and their costs in 2013 showed that low-income households did not benefit to the same extent as higher-income households from Government policies to reduce household emissions and improve energy efficiency. Overall, they found the combined impact of policies on household energy bills in England would generate an estimated average 8% savings by 2020, resulting in a bill of £1,180. However, the wealthiest households were expected to see an average 12% reduction on their bills compared to only 7% for those on the lowest incomes. The total energy bill already represents a far higher proportion of income for poorer households, equating to over 10% of income for the poorest households compared to just over 1% for the wealthiest households (Preston *et al.*, 2013). The CSE's analysis also highlighted that projected savings were highly contingent upon assumptions about the savings certain policies might generate, particularly policies to improve the energy efficiency of products and appliances. Without these measures, projected savings on bills disappeared for those on the lowest incomes, who instead could see a 9% increase in their bills, while the wealthiest households would still see a slight (2%) decrease in their bills. As poorer households are less likely than wealthier households to be able to afford to replace old appliances with more energy-efficient models, and may, in fact, prefer cheaper second-hand goods, these policy assumptions appear problematic and may overstate the benefits of policy to low-income households (Preston *et al.*, 2013).

The CSE's work also exposed injustices in who benefits from other policy measures. They found that over half of all households would not benefit directly from any measures by 2020, although policies could still add £50 to their bills. While the Warm Homes Discount benefits lower-income households, as it enables energy suppliers to provide discounts on bills to particular priority groups, other policies, such as the Feed in Tariff, are more regressive. The Feed in Tariff helped households installing renewable energy to benefit from guaranteed payment from electricity suppliers for energy generated and used and surplus exported to the grid. However, the initial capital outlay required put this plan out of reach of most low-income households. The

CSE's analysis showed that the 12% of households expected to benefit from this policy by 2020 would save a substantial £360 a year on their bills, but the remaining 88% of households would see no benefit, while still paying £10 towards the costs. The aborted Green Deal, which might have incentivised higher-income households to take out loans for energy efficiency works in the expectation of future savings, was also poorly pitched in its financial terms. While the related Energy Company Obligation has assisted lower-income households, including those facing fuel poverty, to benefit from energy efficiency measures, the Government has been criticised for failing to retain a national publicly funded fuel poverty programme in England. By contrast, the devolved nations have preferred to retain such programmes (Preston et al., 2013).

Considered as a whole, these policies do not offer a particularly equitable approach, and critics have called for a clearer focus on improving the energy efficiency of homes and reducing the energy bills of those in fuel poverty, with targeted programmes for vulnerable low-income households (Ekins and Lockwood, 2011; Stockton and Campbell, 2011) and greater use of taxation to fund carbon reduction measures, to support a more progressive approach (Preston et al., 2013).

Turning to climate change adaptation policies, there has been less engagement with how the costs and benefits of policies have been borne across the income distribution or the justice issues arising (Banks et al., 2014). Local authorities have not tended to prioritise social justice in adaptation (Welstead et al., 2012), although practice is evolving, with some examples of positive local action (Banks et al., 2014). There has also been some national engagement with questions of equity, for example, in the use of social tariffs in water pricing and considerations of vulnerability in heatwave planning (Benzie et al., 2011). However, such approaches are still at an early stage and are not applied systematically.

A policy area where social justice has been considered more explicitly is flood risk management. Recent research, however, also highlights limitations in approaches here; although there has been policy engagement with social justice principles, there is an apparent mismatch in relation to how flood investment is targeted in the context of deprivation. An analysis of national expenditure on flood risk management found that only 13% of planned expenditure was targeted at the 20% most deprived areas (England and Knox, 2015). Subsequent analysis also suggests that socially vulnerable areas face systemic disadvantage through experiencing disproportionate risk compared to other areas and, for some types of flood risk, vulnerable areas face disproportionately higher levels of continuing floodplain development. Of just under 300,000 homes built in the most socially vulnerable neighbourhoods from 2008 to 2014, nearly 14% were in areas prone to fluvial or coastal flooding. New developments in areas prone to more frequent coastal and surface water flooding have disproportionately taken place in the most vulnerable neighbourhoods. For example, in coastal floodplains, 31% of all developments, or 22,241 properties, were built in the 20% most vulnerable neighbourhoods, while in areas prone to surface water flooding, 24% of recent developments, or 22,456 properties, were built in the 20% most vulnerable neighbourhoods. If all things were equal, only 20% would be found in these areas. By the 2080s, all of these new residential developments are expected to see an increase in flood risk, but the increase in risk is disproportionately higher in the most vulnerable neighbourhoods, particularly at the coast (Sayers et al., 2017). By then, the safety net provided by cross subsidy in insurance premiums through the Flood Re scheme will also have disappeared, meaning that flood insurance will become increasingly unaffordable just when climate change makes flood impacts likely to become more acute (O'Neill and O'Neill, 2012).

These findings point to the need for flood risk management policy to more proactively target areas of flood disadvantage. Significantly, under the Environment Agency's Long-Term Investment Scenarios, which assess cost-beneficial approaches to investment, Sayers et al., (2017) find that there is an economic as well as a moral case for investment in more vulnerable areas. While policies on flood investment are key, there is also a need for more holistic responses, with the planning system, building regulations, insurance arrangements, economic development and social policies all working together to mitigate risk. To inform this, there needs to be greater recognition of the multiple benefits of holistic interventions, which both facilitate risk reduction and wider health and social benefits, providing opportunities to meet multiple policy goals, for example, acknowledging the role of green infrastructure in providing amenity and recreational value and supporting people's health and wellbeing, as well as alleviating flood risk.

As Sayers *et al.* (2017) highlight, policy responses to address climate disadvantage need to take account not only of the physical characteristics of neighbourhoods but also their social fabric. A whole range of actions are needed, including support for the development of community and social networks, a shake-up of the habitual practices of institutions to prepare for future risks and consideration of the distribution of income. These are all factors affecting the extent to which climate events are likely to translate into welfare losses, and all are associated with different potential policy responses (Lindley *et al.*, 2011).

Procedural injustice

While this evidence has highlighted many of the distributional inequities raised by climate change, this final section considers procedural justice and questions about how decisions are governed to respond to the challenges raised. While the overall societal changes necessary to effectively withhold global temperature increases and to avoid dangerous climate change are not beyond reach, they require public engagement and consensus to create political legitimacy for action, and arguably, this has not yet been achieved to the degree needed for the major transformations climate change implies. There are also important questions of intergenerational justice, whereby decisions made now – or inertia and apathy today – will impact on future generations, potentially creating a world that is uninhabitable (*New York Magazine*, 2017).

Procedural justice requires consideration of issues of participation and governance to understand how different sectors of society inform decisions and the rules of the game for engagement. Bell and Rowe (2012) suggest a number of important principles should be applied in decision-making around climate change to promote greater fairness, including the principle of proportionality, enabling those with the greatest stake to have a greater say in decisions. They suggest that since the least well-off will often be most affected, these groups should have the most power in making climate policies and decisions (Bell and Rowe, 2012). Disadvantaged communities, however, suffer from a lack of recognition, creating obstacles to participation (Bulkeley and Fuller, 2012), and, in practice, such aspirations are often sidelined in current political processes. While new policies require an impact assessment, there is no formal or set assessment of the distributional consequences (Walker, 2010), and, while consultations are usually public and open to all, they typically gain responses only from experts in the field, rather than engaging communities most affected by, and central to, the process (Banks *et al.*, 2014). Environmental governance needs to recognise the voice of affected communities, the impacts of different choices and support consideration of alternatives to negotiate and agree on pathways forward (Walker, 2010).

In addition to concerns over a democratic deficit in decision-making, one of the major challenges for governance is considering the appropriate spatial scale for decisions and where responsibilities and levers for change apply. Since the regional planning tier was removed in England, addressing issues of flood disadvantage across a whole river catchment area that crosses local authority boundaries, or creating subregional responses to challenges such as those facing the east coast of England, are harder to address, relying on a duty to cooperate among local authorities. At the same time, the introduction of neighbourhood planning is intended to bring opportunities for greater engagement closer to home, within geographies that are more meaningful to local communities. However, neighbourhood planning is at an early stage, and the extent of its engagement with climate change concerns is not yet established. Recent research suggests that the local planning system more generally is currently failing to deliver on its potential in regulating in the public interest to reduce carbon emissions and prepare for the impacts of climate change (TCPA, 2016). Arguably, supporting communities to get a greater share in the financial benefits of new infrastructure, including for renewable energy, could facilitate their development, but caution is needed; while recognising the negative impacts that developments can have, communities cannot be bribed to accept a scheme (Cowell et al., 2012). Even if incentives are provided to improve public acceptance of new infrastructure, this will not defray the challenges or preclude the apparent tug-of-war between national and local tiers of governance in relation to development. While Government policies on onshore wind have been described as creating an effective moratorium on new onshore wind farms (TCPA, 2016), recent local planning decisions to refuse fracking have been overturned at the national level to ensure that schemes proceed, showing that local democratic decision-making is always prey to political priorities at higher levels of governance, and the voice of communities can be ignored.

Building community resilience in the context of climate change is one vital part of the response needed, and there have been increasing policy drivers to support community resilience building in recent years as part of localism policies. However, the Government agenda has largely been framed in terms of civil contingencies, with a focus on addressing short-term shocks in the context of emergency planning, rather than the longer-term, more systemic stresses climate change implies. While the UK benefits from an active civil society, current evidence suggests that community action on issues with mitigation benefits, including energy efficiency, renewables generation and food-growing activities, is much more common than action supporting adaptation, with limited community action in relation to heat or water scarcity (although local flood risk groups are more prevalent). This may reflect people's experience, with adaptation concerns still a newer agenda, while flooding has evidently galvanised civic action. It may also reflect the fact that action on energy and food growing more clearly speaks to a wider range of public interests and concerns at this point in time, not simply a climate change agenda (Twigger-Ross et al., 2015). However, recent action research in London on responding to urban heat (Burchell et al., 2017) and in Scotland on building community resilience in the context of climate change (Fazey et al., 2017) both point to a willingness of local voluntary and community groups, residents and other actors to directly engage with climate change questions when these are made salient. While local community participation can provide an important local mandate and focal point for action, responses also need to continue to recognise the critical role that statutory institutions and the private sector have to play. Encouraging communities to take a lead on resilience has not been accompanied by resources to support action at the local level, and the resilience agenda has been critiqued as a thinly veiled attempt to reduce the role of the state and devolve responsibilities for action to communities (Twigger-Ross et al., 2015). While many communities are playing important roles in leading action, there is a danger that, if existing capabilities and vulnerabilities are ignored, in shifting responsibility onto civil society for building resilience to climate change, the Government may reinforce rather than reduce existing vulnerability, fuelling further social inequalities as climate change consequences bite.

Conclusions

This chapter has shown the relevance of questions about climate justice in a developed nation like the UK. As yet, there is limited evidence that the equity issues highlighted here are significantly affecting national or local policy and practice responses, although some elements have begun to enter policy consciousness, including through the latest UK Climate Change Risk Assessment evidence report, approaches to flood risk management policy and, to a lesser extent, the dawn of recognition of the risks of overheating in the care sector (CCC, 2016). While local social vulnerability and climate change hazard exposure maps and wider evidence are now available on the Climate Just website, which had 20,000 viewers in its first 18 months of operation, and over 200 (mainly public sector) practitioners have been engaged in related training, there are insufficient drivers or incentives to ensure consideration of climate disadvantage is mainstreamed. The pressures of austerity, welfare reform, public sector spending cuts and consequent staffing reductions in local government are all conspiring to diminish local capacity to respond to climate change at all. At the same time, national statutory drivers and levers for action are limited and, in some cases, have been eroded in recent years. This is despite the Paris Agreement of 2015 and scientists' warnings about the diminishing window for action to reduce emissions and avoid global temperatures increasing by more than 1.5 degrees Celsius.

The role of communities in building resilience is part of the picture, but capacities to act vary, and achieving systemic change calls for a more coordinated, coherent and holistic response, integrated from a national to local level, which squarely addresses issues of vulnerability and poverty. The risk is that otherwise climate change will simply exacerbate existing inequalities, compounding poverty and place-based disadvantage where the worst effects are felt, and bringing disadvantage to other groups too, which may be experienced, for example, through housing market impacts from flooding and health impacts of heat as well as threats to livelihoods in particular areas or industries. This makes the imperative to bring questions of equity and justice and climate change responses into alignment more pressing. There is an urgent need for leadership at all levels. At a recent workshop reviewing the impacts of the JRF programme on climate justice, experts in the field commented on the need to go back to basics to build public consensus on the need for action on climate change and the importance of creating the political legitimacy and democratic mandate for action (Climate Outreach, 2017). Arguably, people are more likely to support climate change mitigation and adaptation policies if they reflect a fair balance of responsibility, capability and need. Policy responses also provide an opportunity to address other social needs and create a fairer society. Equitable processes that widen participation and address justice can help to manage conflict and to build consensus in responses, as well as mobilising assets and generating wider benefits from actions than a narrow economic approach allows (Banks *et al.*, 2014). It is critical that in the UK, as elsewhere, social justice and climate change agendas come together, each informing and informed by the other, to build a safe, fair and sustainable future.

References

Anderson, K., 2012. *Climate change going beyond dangerous: Brutal numbers and tenuous hope.* What Next, 111: Climate Development and Equity. Uppsala, Sweden: What Next Forum.

Anderson, K., 2015. World view: Talks in the city of light generate more heat. *Nature*, 528: 437.

Banks, N., Preston, I. Hargreaves, K. Kazmierczak, A. Lucas, K. Mayne, R. Downing, C., and Street, R., 2014. *Climate change and social justice: An evidence review.* York: Joseph Rowntree Foundation.

Bell, D. and Rowe, F., 2012. *Are climate policies fairly made?* York: Joseph Rowntree Foundation.

Benzie, M., Harvey, A., Burningham, K., Hodgson, N., and Siddiqi, A., 2011. *Vulnerability to heatwaves and drought: Case studies of adaptation to climate change in south-west England.* York: Joseph Rowntree Foundation.

Bulkeley, H. and Fuller, S., 2012. *Low carbon communities and social justice.* York: Joseph Rowntree Foundation.

Burchell, K. Fagan-Watson, B., King, M. and Watson, T. with Cooper, C. Holland, D. Jennings, H. Palmer, S. Thorne, D., and Whitehead, C., 2017. *Developing the role of community groups in local climate resilience: Final report of the Urban Heat Project.* London: Policy Studies Institute.

Childs, M., 2011. *Just transition: Is a just transition to a low-carbon economy possible within safe global carbon limits?* London: Friends of the Earth.

Climate Outreach, 2017. *Climate justice: Developing the future UK agenda for action*. Oxford: Climate Outreach.

Committee on Climate Change (CCC), 2016. *UK climate change risk assessment 2017 synthesis report: Priorities for the next five years*. London: Committee on Climate Change.

Cowell, R., Bristow, G., and Munday, M., 2012. *Wind energy and justice for disadvantaged communities*. York: Joseph Rowntree Foundation.

Dresner, S., Preston, I., White, V., Browne, J., Ekins, P., and Hamilton, I., 2013. *Designing carbon taxation to protect low income households*. York: Joseph Rowntree Foundation.

Druckman, A., Hartfree, Y., Hirsch, D., and K. Perren, 2011. *Sustainable income standards: Towards a greener minimum?* York: Joseph Rowntree Foundation.

Druckman, A. and Jackson, T., 2009. The carbon footprint of UK households 1990–2004: A socio-economically disaggregated, quasi multiregional input-output model. *Ecological Economics* 68(7): 2066–2077.

Druckman, A. and Jackson, T., 2010. *An exploration into the carbon footprint of UK households*. RESOLVE working paper 02-10. Guildford: University of Surrey, Research Group on Lifestyles, Values and the Environment.

Ekins, P. and Lockwood, M., 2011. *Tackling fuel poverty during the transition to a low carbon economy*. York: Joseph Rowntree Foundation.

Elliott, D. and Fielder Cook, L., 2016. *Climate justice and the use of human rights law in reducing greenhouse gas emissions*. Geneva: Quaker United Nations Office.

England, K., and Knox, K., 2015. *Targeting flood investment and policy to minimize flood disadvantage*. York: Joseph Rowntree Foundation.

Fazey, I, Carmen, E., Rao–Williams, J., Hodgson, A., Fraser, J., Cox, L., Scott, D., Tabor, P., Robeson, D., Searle, B.A., Lyon, C., Kenter, J., and Murray, B., 2017. *Community resilience to climate change: Outcomes of the Scottish Borders Climate Resilient Communities Project*. Dundee: University of Dundee, Centre for Environmental Change and Human Resilience.

Fernandez-Bilbao, A., Zsamboky, M., Smith, D., Knight, J., and Allan, J., 2011. *Impacts of climate change on disadvantaged coastal communities*. York: Joseph Rowntree Foundation.

Gupta, R., Walker, G., Lewis, A., Barnfield, L., Gregg, M., and Neven, L., 2016. *Care provision fit for a future climate*. York: Joseph Rowntree Foundation.

Horton, T. and Doran, N., 2011. *Climate change and sustainable consumption: What do the public think is fair?* York: Joseph Rowntree Foundation.

Intergovernmental Panel on Climate Change (IPCC), 2014. *Climate change 2014 synthesis report*. IPCC.

Joseph Rowntree Foundation, 2016. *UK poverty: Causes, costs and solutions*. York: Joseph Rowntree Foundation.

Klinenberg, E., 2002. *Heatwave: A social autopsy of disaster in Chicago*. Chicago, IL: University of Chicago Press.

Knox, J., 2016. *Report of the Special Rapporteur on the issue of human rights obligations relating to the enjoyment of a safe, clean, healthy and sustainable environment*. Report to the 31st session of the UN Human Rights Council. (A/HRC/31/52).

Lambie-Mumford, H. and Snell, C., 2015. *Heat or eat: Food and austerity in rural England: Final report*. Working Papers of the Communities and Culture Network, 6.

Lindley, S., O'Neill, J. Kandeh, J. Lawson, N. Christian, R., and O'Neill, M., 2011. *Climate change, justice and vulnerability*. York: Joseph Rowntree Foundation.

New York Magazine, 2017. The Uninhabitable Earth. *New York Magazine*. 10 July.

O'Neill, J. and O'Neill, M., 2012. *Social justice and the future of flood insurance*. York: Joseph Rowntree Foundation.

Preston, I. White, V. Thumim, J., Bridgeman, T., and Brand, C., 2013. *Distribution of carbon emissions in the UK: Implications for domestic energy policy*. York: Joseph Rowntree Foundation.

Quilgars, D., Dyke, A., Tunstall, R., and West, S., 2016. *A sustainable community: Life at Derwenthorpe 2012–15*. York: Joseph Rowntree Foundation.

Sayers, P.B., Horritt, M., Penning Rowsell, E., and Fieth, J., 2017. *Present and future flood vulnerability, risk and disadvantage: A UK assessment*. A report for the Joseph Rowntree Foundation. Oxford: Sayers and Partners LLP.

Stockton, H. and Campbell, R., 2011. *Time to reconsider UK energy and fuel poverty policies?* York: Joseph Rowntree Foundation.

Town and Country Planning Association (TCPA), 2016. *Planning for the climate challenge? Understanding the performance of English local plans*. London: TCPA.

Twigger-Ross, C., Brooks, K., Papadopoulou, L., Orr, P., Sadauskis, R., Coke, A., Simcock, N., Stirling, A., and Walker, G., 2015. *Community resilience to climate change: An evidence review*. York: Joseph Rowntree Foundation.

United Nations, 1992. *UN Framework Convention on Climate Change (UNFCCC)*. New York: United Nations.

United Nations, 2016. *The sustainable development goals report*. New York: United Nations.

Walker, G., 2010. Environmental justice, impact assessment and the politics of knowledge: The implications of assessing the social distribution of environmental outcomes. *Environmental Impact Assessment Review*, 30(5): 312–318.

Watkiss, P., Cimato, F., Hunt, A., and Morley, B., 2016. *Climate change impacts on the future cost of living*. London: Paul Watkiss Associates.

Welstead, J., Brisley, R., Hindle, R., and Paavola, J., 2012. *Socially just adaptation to climate change*. York: Joseph Rowntree Foundation.

White, V., Thumim, J., and Preston, I., 2013. *Personal carbon allowances: Distributional implications associated with personal travel and opportunities to reduce household emissions*. Project Paper no. 3. Bristol: Centre for Sustainable Energy. www.climatejust.org.uk [accessed 2/10/2017].

10

Equity and justice in climate change law and policy

A role for benefit-sharing

Annalisa Savaresi and Kim Bouwer

Introduction

The term *climate justice* is commonly used to refer to corrective and distributive justice considerations associated both with the impacts of climate change and of climate change response measures.[1] At the international level, climate change law inherently seeks to address the distribution of resources for climate change mitigation and adaptation, and the allocation of shares in a global carbon budget. Solving the climate problem demands solutions to global distributive justice questions – most notably, those concerning the transfer of capacity, finance and technologies to tackle climate change – that are acceptable to all concerned. The debate on climate justice is thus intrinsically linked with (although not limited to) that on inter-state equity, and ultimately revolves around how to share the burdens associated with a global transition towards low-carbon societies, as well as of coping with a changing climate.

There is, however, another, less explored equity dimension inherent to climate change governance, which has to do with how the advantages and disadvantages of specific climate change response measures are allocated. When climate change response measures, such as incentives for forest carbon conservation, are adopted in a given state or region, there will inevitably be winners and losers. For example, those previously enjoying unfettered access to forest products may be excluded, whereas others may receive payments to preserve forest ecosystems, including seeking optimisation of their carbon storage potential.

The notion of benefit-sharing has been increasingly deployed in contexts such as these to allocate advantages derived from the adoption and implementation of climate change response measures. This use is far from unique to climate change governance. Indeed, the concept of benefit-sharing is widely deployed in the context of law and policy on use and conservation of natural resources and related traditional knowledge at the international, transnational, national and subnational levels.[2] While benefit-sharing is not explicitly mentioned in climate change treaties, benefit-sharing requirements have increasingly been used as a means to compensate, reward and involve various sets of stakeholders in climate change adaptation and mitigation activities at the national and subnational levels.[3]

In this chapter, we consider how the concept of benefit-sharing is or might be used to achieve equity and fairness in climate change governance. After a short introduction on the concept of benefit-sharing, we explore its potential contribution to the achievement of climate justice. We therefore look at how benefit-sharing has been used in climate change governance thus far, distinguishing between inter- and intra-state relationships. The chapter concludes with suggestions on how the concept of benefit-sharing may be more systematically used to carve out a space to better embed equity and justice considerations into climate change law and policy, both at the inter- and at the intra-state level.

The concept of benefit-sharing

Benefit-sharing arrangements are widespread practice in the context of various natural resource management and extractive activities, both to mitigate the negative impacts of and reduce opposition to and increase the social acceptance of projects.[4] The contours of benefit-sharing obligations are context-specific and depend on the applicable legal frameworks, as well as on industry practices. So in a given context benefit-sharing arrangements may be the result of requirements embedded in national or international law, voluntary guidelines adopted by national and subnational governments, or corporate social responsibility practices. One exception to this rather fragmented picture concerns indigenous peoples, whose right to mutually acceptable benefit-sharing arrangements for extractive activities and developments taking place on their lands is recognised in international law.[5] In relation to other groups, instead, the matter is not as clear-cut and largely depends on the type of activity and the relevant legal frameworks.

A growing number of law and policy instruments refer to benefit sharing with regard to the use of natural resources (e.g., in relation to mining, forestry and the use of marine resources), environmental protection (biodiversity conservation) and the use of traditional knowledge.[6] The concept of benefit-sharing has been significantly developed in biodiversity law, especially in connection with non-human genetic resources.[7]

The practice shows that the notion of "benefit" encompasses both monetary and non-monetary advantages, and may extend beyond the formal remit of a given project (e.g., concerning the conservation and sustainable use of a natural resource, such as a watercourse or a forest), extending to subjects that are not actively involved in project-related activities.[8] Recent academic work has sought to add normative depth to the concept of benefit-sharing, emphasising the importance of who decides on the nature of benefits, as well as the need for a dialogic, participatory conception of sharing, whereby the determination of benefits should reflect the values and priorities of those participating.[9] This literature suggests that the expression "fair and equitable" benefit-sharing draws attention to the necessity to protect the rights and interests of vulnerable subjects, as well as the need for inclusion of both procedural and substantive safeguards in relationships regulated by law and that are characterised by power imbalances.[10]

The notion of benefit-sharing may also be viewed as a bridge between states' obligations under climate change and human rights law.[11] In human rights law, benefit-sharing is a means to ensure that indigenous peoples and traditional communities fairly and equitably share the benefits arising from activities in relation to their lands, territories or resources, including their traditional knowledge.[12] State obligations in this area revolve around consultation procedures to establish the benefits that the affected indigenous peoples and traditional communities are to receive; as well as effective remedies for violations of their rights, and just and fair redress for harm resulting from activities affecting their lands, territories or resources.[13]

The relationship between climate change and human rights law has been at the centre of much focus in recent years.[14] Over the last decade the Human Rights Council has increasingly drawn attention to the potential of human rights obligations, standards and principles to "inform and strengthen" climate change law- and policy-making, by "promoting policy coherence, legitimacy and sustainable outcomes."[15] The Council has issued resolutions calling upon states to "integrate, as appropriate, human rights in their climate actions at all levels."[16] This nexus is particularly important, as the implementation of climate response measures has amply demonstrated that they risk creating perverse incentives to violate human rights.[17] In order to tackle this concern, the Preamble to the Paris Agreement acknowledges that, whenever parties take action to address climate change, they should "respect, protect and consider their respective obligations on human rights."[18] The Paris Agreement's reference to parties' human rights obligations encompasses obligations in treaties they have ratified already or may ratify in future. By forging an explicit link with human rights instruments, the Paris Agreement's preamble reaffirms states' duty to respect, promote and take into consideration their existing human rights when they adopt measures to tackle climate change and its impacts.[19] This duty encompasses benefit-sharing arrangements, at least in as far as indigenous peoples and traditional communities are concerned.

While the debate on burden sharing in multilateral climate governance continues in negotiations on the rulebook of the Paris Agreement, fertile ground already exists to ensure that climate change response measures are consistent with justice and do not reinforce existing inequalities. This chapter therefore considers how benefit-sharing has been used so far, commenting on its potential to be systematically used to carve out a space to better address equity and justice considerations in climate change law and policy.

Benefit-sharing in the climate regime: the story thus far

This section looks at how benefit-sharing arrangements have been used thus far in climate change law and policy to tackle equity and justice questions arising at the intra- and inter-state levels. These are discussed in that order.

Intra-state benefit-sharing

Law and policy at the national and subnational level increasingly use benefit-sharing arrangements to mitigate the negative impacts of, reduce opposition to and increase the social acceptance of climate change response measures.[20] Law and policy on forest uses and renewable energy generation are cases in point and are considered here in further detail.

Forest uses

In the last decade, international climate change law has played an important role in coordinating "bottom-up" efforts[21] to reduce forest loss and enhance forest cover in developing countries, in the context of so-called REDD+ policies. As with any other climate change response measures, the adoption of measures to stimulate greater forest carbon sequestration is laden with complex equity questions, associated with the changes to extant forest governance arrangements.[22] While forest conservation is doubtlessly a desirable outcome, the livelihood of many poor people in developing countries greatly depends on the extraction of forest resources.

To seek the protection of both vital ecosystems and vulnerable people, guidance adopted by parties to the United Nations Framework Convention on Climate Change (UNFCCC)[23] – and subsequently referenced in the Paris Agreement[24] – includes specific social and environmental safeguards.[25] These safeguards request that REDD+ activities promote and support the participation of relevant stakeholders; respect the knowledge and rights of indigenous peoples and local communities; and, more generally, enhance "social benefits."[26] The interpretation of these safe-guards depends on domestic law, as well as on states' international obligations.[27]

While REDD+ safeguards do not explicitly require benefit-sharing arrangements, these are in practice routinely used as a means to designate who gets rewarded for REDD+ activities.[28] Evidence from practice suggests that the negotiation of benefit-sharing arrangements has at times facilitated "unprecedented" opportunities of dialogue with stakeholders on the ground.[29] However, so far benefit-sharing arrangements have predominantly focused on revenue-sharing arrangements, rather than on genuine participation in decision-making. Decision-making on benefit-sharing reportedly tends to be dominated by governmental agencies and donors, with limited participation from traditional forest stewards, such as indigenous peoples.[30] The inclusion of the poor and most vulnerable remains a great challenge, together with the mitigation of the negative impacts that they may suffer as a result of REDD+ activities.[31] The adoption of a more inclusive approach to benefit-sharing has been described not only as "a good thing to do," but also as "essential for achieving optimal outcomes ."[32]

Renewable energy

Very similar considerations apply to renewable energy generation, where benefit-sharing prac-tices often build upon those developed in the extractive and mining sectors, with local communi-ties living in the vicinity of a project receiving various economic and non-economic advantages from project developers. The widespread practice of "benefit-packages" typically entails mon-etary payments per capacity installed,[33] but developers may also provide other benefits, such as electricity at discounted prices or grants to support energy efficiency.[34] The practice of offering shares in projects developed by commercial operators may in and of itself be viewed as a means to share economic benefits with local communities and to involve them in local energy gover-nance.[35] Project developers may furthermore offer local communities non-monetary benefits, such as the development of common facilities for recreation or education.[36] Such "benefits" raise the question of the extent to which community benefits may become a means for the provision of public services, which should reach communities regardless of the development of renewable energy capacity.[37]

In recent years, renewable energy generation policies have progressively shifted away from treating communities as passive recipients of benefits and towards promoting "ongoing social contract(s) with society"[38] and "genuine two-way street and a fair exchange(s) rather than a token payment representing a small portion of profit."[39] Local residents may thus be involved in the determination of what benefits they receive, to various degrees. The practice of so-called community protocols has emerged as a means to empower communities in the context of their relations with developers, as well as authorities.[40] Intermediaries reportedly play an important role in the design of model templates for community protocols and, more generally, in engendering community capacity to negotiate benefits.[41] Some law-makers have developed guidelines on community benefits.[42] There is, however, a great deal of variation in practice amongst states, and even within the same state.[43]

This evolution in the approach to benefit-sharing in climate change response measures aligns with developments observed in other areas of environmental law and policy. Yet, benefit-sharing arrangements still tend to be perceived as a bribe to secure project approval and/or minimise public resistance from local communities.[44] And while some literature points to opportunities associated with greater institutionalisation of benefits – for example, by means of systematic stan-dardised payments, decided by independent authorities[45] – as well as with their framing in more positive terms in policy parlance,[46] evidence emerging from early movers does not necessarily corroborate this proposition.[47]

Inter-state benefit-sharing

Benefit-sharing arrangements in the global governance of climate change feature both on an inter-state basis but also with respect to the interactions between agencies at the transnational level.[48] The actualisation of benefit-sharing is underdeveloped at an inter-state level, and there is value in reflecting on its role. Clear international norms of fair and equitable benefit-sharing could provide a useful conceptual lens through which to examine flows of finance and other public goods. In addition, international law obligations could ensure that benefit-sharing arrangements at lower levels of governance are informed by concepts of fairness and equity, subject of course to what is permitted by local law and patterns of practice.[49]

The distribution of climate finance and transfer of climate technologies under the climate regime are areas where such enquiries could be relevant. These mechanisms are of heightened importance in supporting developing countries to achieve the ambition outlined in their nationally determined contributions.[50] Clear norms at the international level in this area would ensure that, when introduced, benefit-sharing arrangements complied with established principles. While this is not the place for an in-depth discussion of what this might entail, in the following the idea of "sharing" is emphasised, as an ongoing, process-based activity, in contrast to a one-directional delivery, where one party might have full control.

Climate finance

The adoption of the Paris Agreement has stimulated discussion in response to new urgency in the distribution and readiness to receive climate finance. Much of the focus in climate finance relates to "sufficiency, sources, and supply," how to scale up climate finance,[51] or the processes and relationships surrounding the distribution and use of climate finance by state parties and intermediaries established under the climate regime,[52] such as the Global Environmental Facility (GEF) and the Green Climate Fund (GCF).

While the core focus remains on mobilisation, this renewed attention has created fresh opportunities to examine how tools and mechanisms in climate finance support or undermine the achievement of justice and fairness. As discussed earlier, benefit-sharing could play a significant role by ensuring that actions taken to implement the Paris Agreement are consistent with equity and justice. Taking this approach has the potential to ensure that climate actions might help alleviate, rather than reinforce, existing injustices.

Some intermediary bodies make direct provision for benefit-sharing within the recipient state. For instance, the Adaptation Fund expressly requires that activities supported by the Fund "shall" provide fair and equitable access to the benefits of those activities, in a way that enhances their sustainable development potential and does not worsen existing inequities.[53] The provision of substantive and procedural safeguards should go some way to ensuring that projects implemented through the climate funds achieve equitable outcomes.[54]

Things being as they are, there has been little review or evaluation as to how these obligations are implemented at either a state or fund level.[55] Most bodies empowered to mobilise and supply climate finance have been subject to questions of their distribution of finance; the reasons for this are varied, but they include an absence of equitable reasons for the decisions made in relation to the allocation of finance.[56] Flows of funding are conceptualised as a unidirectional process, and the states in receipt of finance are subject to weak review and reporting mechanisms.[57]

A clear set of principles, agreed upon at the inter-state level, could provide a valuable framework through which parties could establish and assess benefit-sharing arrangements in relation to climate finance. Clear norms could support a strongly equitable approach to benefit-sharing. For instance, adhering to norms and requirements for ongoing dialogue as part of a "sharing" approach could go some way to ensuring that climate finance was used in a way that supported ongoing equitable outcomes.

Climate change technology transfer

The Paris Agreement makes provision for the transfer of technology and capacity building.[58] Technology transfer is important as "means of implementation" or support for all states fully to achieve their mitigation and adaptation goals. Contrasted with climate finance, no explicit provision is made for benefit-sharing arrangements to be implemented in connection with the transfer of climate change technologies. However, it may be argued that the use of benefit-sharing concepts can support and inform just and equitable processes in relation to technology transfer.

Substantial work has been done concerning the merits of a partnership-based approach in international climate change technology transfer.[59] A partnership-based or co-development approach requires an ongoing dialogue between involved parties, and the introduction of formal benefit-sharing obligations could support the development of benefit-sharing within these technology arrangements. Under such arrangements, benefit-sharing could provide both a protective safeguard and a system of active engagement, supporting less powerful parties and ensuring continuing engagement on the uses and development of climate change technologies. Some scholars conceptualise this as a participatory process that requires fully informed engagement of both parties, while acknowledging that substantive participation may not be achieved in practice.[60] This of course raises other questions about the scope and potential of international norms fully to inform local-level practice.

Existing cooperation initiatives – such as collaborative centres for climate change research and development that aim to foster innovation and the building of capacity[61] – reflect this broader thinking, but could benefit from formalised benefit-sharing arrangements. The inclusion of benefit-sharing arrangements in this cooperation could reflect a commitment to protect the rights and interests of all participants, with particular attention to more vulnerable ones. The framing of benefit-sharing as "fair and equitable" reflects the need for inclusion of both procedural and substantive dimensions of justice in what might otherwise be a very unequal relationship where power and control is entirely vested in one party.[62]

Benefit-sharing and the future of the climate regime

The concept of benefit-sharing bears significant potential as a tool, providing both protective procedural safeguards and normative substance to relationships and activities within climate change governance. The use of benefit-sharing arrangements potentially stands to avoid the entrenchment of existing inequalities and to bring about just and equitable outcomes.

In this chapter, we have discussed the deployment of and potential for the deployment of benefit-sharing in climate change law and policy. In so doing, we have drawn on theoretical approaches to benefit-sharing in human rights and biodiversity law. Far from being only an expedient term of reference, international legal obligations under human rights and biodiversity law provide a template for a more normatively developed approach to benefit-sharing. This notion encompasses multiple streams of diverse benefits and requires a common understanding of what the benefits at stake are and how they ought to be shared. In this connection, benefit-sharing is better understood as a process, rather than a one-off exercise, of good-faith engagement among different actors, laying the foundations for a long-term "partnership."[63] This understanding goes beyond existing practice, and there is ample scope for further work to be undertaken to develop concepts of benefit-sharing in relation to climate change law and policy. This raises questions about the potential for mutually supportive interpretation between the climate change regime and human rights and biodiversity law.

The practice of benefit-sharing at the intra-state level shows that much remains to be done in order to ensure that climate change response measures do not perpetuate or deepen existing injustice. Benefit-sharing practice from biodiversity and human rights law suggests the need for culturally appropriate, good-faith, consensus-building processes, with a view to agreeing on modalities of decision-making, rather than simply giving them a share in profits.[64] As opposed to mere compensation to make up for lost control over resources and income-generation opportunities, benefit-sharing could provide new opportunities for income generation and continued, and possibly enhanced, control over the use of the lands and resources.[65]

Similarly, we have briefly explored how both explicit benefit-sharing arrangements, and the broader concepts of benefit-sharing, could support fair and equitable outcomes at the inter-state and transnational level. These approaches have the potential to ensure just and equitable outcomes, if properly deployed. Establishing clear principles of benefit-sharing at the international level can provide a useful framework both to support the development of and to establish whether climate change support mechanisms are actualised in a just and equitable manner. As discussed, there is considerable scope for increased attention on developing concepts of benefit-sharing where this is already included as an obligation but significantly underutilised. In addition, the potential exists for benefit-sharing approaches to support equitable practices and outcomes in existing partnership arrangements.

Notes

This article is prepared under and in service to *The Benelex Project: Benefit-sharing for an equitable transition to the green economy* at the Strathclyde Centre for Environmental Law and Governance, University of Strathclyde. The project is generously funded by a grant from the European Research Council. The authors thank the tireless project team and advisors, and the reviewers for their helpful comments on earlier versions of this article.

1 See, e.g., (Caney, 2009; International Bar Association, 2014; Lyster, 2016; Soltau, 2009; Thorpe, 2014).
2 (Morgera, 2016a).
3 (Savaresi, 2014).
4 See, for example, the analysis in (Dupuy, 2014; Fisher, 2007).
5 International Labour Organization's (ILO) Convention no. 169 Concerning Indigenous and Tribal Peoples in Independent Countries 1989, 28 ILM 1382. See also *UN Special Rapporteur on the situation of human rights and fundamental freedoms of indigenous peoples*, Report U.N. Doc. E/CN.4/2003/90, 66; and *2012 Expert Mechanism: Follow-up report on indigenous peoples and the right to participate in decision-making with a focus on extractive industries* (A/HRC/21/52) (A/HRC/21/55) 39. For an analysis, see (Morgera, 2016b).
6 (Morgera, 2016a).
7 Ibid.
8 See e.g. (Armeni, 2016; Luttrell et al., 2013).
9 (Morgera, 2016a) and (Parks & Morgera, 2015).
10 (Morgera, 2016a) and (Savaresi, 2013).
11 (Savaresi, 2014).
12 Framework Principles on Human Rights and the Environment, "Report of the Special Rapporteur on the issue of human rights obligations relating to the enjoyment of a safe, clean, healthy and sustainable environment," UN Doc A/HRC/37/59, 24 January 2018, Annex, Framework Principle 15.

13 Ibid.
14 The intersection is explored at length in (Savaresi, 2018).
15 See the preambles to Human Rights Council, Resolution 10/4, A/HRC/RES/10/4, 25 March 2009; Resolution 18/22, A/HRC/RES/18/22, 17 October 2011; and Resolution 26/27, A/HRC/RES/26/27, 15 July 2014.
16 Human Rights Council, Resolution 32/33, A/HRC/RES/32/33, 18 July 2016; and Resolution 35/20, A/HRC/RES/35/20, 7 July 2017.
17 As noted, e.g., in Ole W. Pedersen, "The Janus-head of human rights and climate change: Adaptation and mitigation" (2011) 80 *Nordic Journal of International Law* 403.
18 Paris Agreement, preamble.
19 (Savaresi, 2018).
20 (Savaresi, 2014).
21 On the bottom-up nature of REDD+, see (Savaresi, 2016a).
22 As suggested in (Savaresi, 2012).
23 This guidance is included in a set of decisions adopted by the conference of the parties to the UNFCCC between 2007 and 2015. These decisions are collected in (UNFCCC Secretariat, 2016).
24 Paris Agreement, Article 5.2.
25 Decision 1/CP.16, Cancún Agreements, UN Doc FCCC/CP/2010/7/Add.1, Appendix I, para. 2.
26 Ibid.
27 (Savaresi, 2016b).
28 As evidenced, for example, in (Pham et al., n.d.; Wong Grace Yee et al., 2017).
29 (Lee & Pistorius, 2015, p. 16).
30 (Pham et al., n.d., p. 21).
31 (Luttrell et al., 2013, p. 51).
32 (Forest Dialogue Secretariat, 2014)
33 See, for example, Scottish Parliament Brief, "Renewable energy: Community benefit and ownership," 2012, 13.
34 See, for example, "Vattenfall, wind energy: Exploring the benefits to your community," available at: <https://corporate.vattenfall.co.uk/globalassets/uk/projects/nocton-fen/community_investment_packages.pdf>
35 (McHarg, 2016, pp. 301–302).
36 (Barrera-Hernandez, Barton, Godden, Lucas, & Rønne, 2016, p. 8).
37 As suggested, for example, in (Wynberg & Hauck, 2014).
38 As reported in ClientEarth, "Community power report" (ClientEarth 2016), available at: <www.clientearth.org/reports/community-power-report-250614.pdf> accessed 5 June 2017, 123.
39 See, for example, Scottish Parliament's Economy, Energy and Tourism Committee, "Report on the achievability of the Scottish Government's renewable energy targets," SP Paper 220, 2012, 243.
40 See (Parks, 2016).
41 As noted, for example, in (Bristow, Cowell, & Munday, 2012, p. 1115).
42 As noted, for example, in (Cowell, Bristow, & Munday, 2011).
43 See the review of practice in (Savaresi, 2017).
44 See, e.g., (Walker, Russel, & Kurz, 2017).
45 Ibid.
46 See, for example, (Rudolph, Haggett, & Aitken, 2017, p. 10).
47 (Jørgensen, 2017).
48 (Savaresi, 2014).
49 (Parks, 2016).
50 See, e.g., (de Coninck & Sagar, 2017) and (Zahar, 2016).
51 (Buchner, Oliver, Wang, Carswell, Meattle, & Mazza, n.d.).
52 For an overview (Thompson, 2016), see Table 7.1.
53 Adaptation Fund Environmental and Social Policy (2013) 2. As highlighted above, some activities under the Adaptation Fund may take place at a local or national level.
54 Further examples include: The Green Environment Fund environmental policy requires full respect for the rights of Indigenous peoples, which includes the right to "culturally appropriate economic and social benefits" (GEF Policy on Agency Minimum Standards on Environmental and Social Safeguards (2013 ed.) Criterion 4 – also Minimum requirements 4.8). The GEF policy also acknowledges that benefits received under it can extend beyond receipt of funds (see Minimum Requirement 4.6). The GCF recognises the need

for benefit sharing amongst Indigenous peoples (Green Climate Fund, "Guiding framework and procedures for accrediting national, regional and international implementing entities and intermediaries, including the fund's fiduciary principles and standards and environmental and social safeguards," 2014, para 39).

55 If these are indeed obligations – see Savaresi (n. 28).

56 Discussed in (Yamineva & Kulovesi, 2013).

57 (Zahar, 2016).

58 Articles 10 and 11 respectively; (Rajamani, 2016).

59 See (Bouwer, 2018) for a discussion of how the technology needs assessment (TNA) process under the climate regime can go some way towards supporting needs-based achievement of climate technology transfer. The Technology Executive Committee (which conducts the TNAs) does not make any reference to benefit-sharing, but we argue that the approach taken is compatible with the concept of benefit-sharing as an element of the right to science. Also see (Ockwell, Sagar, & Coninck, 2015) and (Sagar, Bremner, & Grubb, 2009).

60 (Armeni, 2016, p. 415) and (Parks & Morgera, 2015, p. 356).

61 (Ockwell & Byrne, 2016).

62 (Morgera, 2016a).

63 (Parks & Morgera, 2015).

64 Ibid.

65 Ibid.

Bibliography

Armeni, C. (2016). Participation in environmental decision-making: Reflecting on planning and community benefits for major wind farms. *Journal of Environmental Law, 28*(3), 415–441. https://doi.org/10.1093/jel/eqw021

Barrera-Hernandez, L., Barton, B., Godden, L., Lucas, A., & Rønne, A. (Eds.). (2016). Introduction. In *Sharing the costs and benefits of energy and resource activity: Legal change and impact on communities* (pp. 1–22). Oxford, UK: Oxford University Press.

Bouwer, K. (2018). Insights for climate technology transfer from international environmental and human rights law. *Journal of Intellectual Property Rights*, forthcoming.

Bristow, G., Cowell, R., & Munday, M. (2012). Windfalls for whom? The evolving notion of 'community' in community benefit provisions from wind farms. *Geoforum, 43*(6), 1108–1120. https://doi.org/10.1016/j.geoforum.2012.06.015

Buchner, B., Oliver, P., Wang, X., Carswell, C., Meattle, C., & Mazza, F. (n.d.). *Global landscape of climate finance 2017: Climate investment analysis*. Retrieved from https://climatepolicyinitiative.org/publication/global-landscape-of-climate-finance-2017/

Caney, S. (2009). Climate change, human rights and moral thresholds. In S. Humphreys (Ed.), *Human rights and climate change* (pp. 69–90). Cambridge, UK: Cambridge University Press.

Cowell, R., Bristow, G., & Munday, M. (2011). Acceptance, acceptability and environmental justice: The role of community benefits in wind energy development. *Journal of Environmental Planning and Management, 54*(4), 539–557. https://doi.org/10.1080/09640568.2010.521047

de Coninck, H., & Sagar, A. (2017). Technology development and transfer (Article 10). In D. Klein, M. P. Carazo, M. Doelle, J. Bulmer, & A. Higham (Eds.), *The Paris Agreement on climate change: Analysis and commentary*. Oxford, UK: Oxford University Press.

Dupuy, K. E. (2014). Community development requirements in mining laws. *The Extractive Industries and Society, 1*(2), 200–215. https://doi.org/10.1016/j.exis.2014.04.007

Fisher, C. (2007). *International experience with benefit-sharing instruments for extractive resources*. Washington, DC: Resources for the Future. Retrieved from www.rff.org/research/publications/international-experience-benefit-sharing-instruments-extractive-resources

Forest Dialogue Secretariat. (2014). *Country options for REDD+ benefit sharing*. Forest Dialogue. Retrieved from http://theforestsdialogue.org/sites/default/files/tfdreview_countryoptionsforreddplusbenefitssharing_en.pdf

International Bar Association. (2014). *Achieving justice and human rights in an era of climate disruption*. London. Retrieved from www.ibanet.org/PresidentialTaskForceClimateChangeJustice2014Report.aspx

Jørgensen, M. L. (2017). *Functioning of compensation mechanisms regarding local acceptance of wind energy projects*. Presented at the European Environmental Law Forum Annual Conference, Copenhagen, Denmark.

Lee, D., & Pistorius, T. (2015). *The impacts of international REDD+ finance.* Climate and Land Use Alliance. Retrieved from www.climateandlandusealliance.org/wp-content/uploads/2015/09/Impacts_of_International_REDD_Finance_Report_FINAL.pdf

Luttrell, C., Loft, L., Fernanda Gebara, M., Kweka, D., Brockhaus, M., Angelsen, A., & Sunderlin, W. D. (2013). Who should benefit from REDD+? Rationales and realities. *Ecology and Society, 18*(4), 52–70.

Lyster, R. (2016). *Climate justice and disaster law.* Cambridge, UK: Cambridge University Press.

McHarg, A. (2016). Community benefit through community ownership of renewable generation in Scotland: Power to the people? In L. Barrera-Hernandez, B. Barton, L. Godden, A. Lucas, & A. Rønne (Eds.), *Sharing the costs and benefits of energy and resource activity* (pp. 297–315). Oxford, UK: Oxford University Press.

Morgera, E. (2016a). The need for an international legal concept of fair and equitable benefit sharing. *European Journal of International Law, 27*(2), 353–383.

Morgera, E. (2016b, December 20). *Under the radar: Fair and equitable benefit-sharing and the human rights of indigenous peoples and local communities related to natural resources.* Rochester, NY: SSRN Scholarly Paper. Retrieved from https://papers.ssrn.com/abstract=2887803

Ockwell, D., & Byrne, R. (2016). Improving technology transfer through national systems of innovation: Climate relevant innovation-system builders (CRIBs). *Climate Policy, 16*(7), 836–854.

Ockwell, D., Sagar, A., & Coninck, H. de. (2015). Collaborative research and development (R&D) for climate technology transfer and uptake in developing countries: Towards a needs driven approach. *Climatic Change, 131*(3), 401–415. https://doi.org/10.1007/s10584-014-1123-2

Parks, L. (2016). *Challenging power asymmetries from the bottom up? Community protocols and the convention on biological diversity at the global/local crossroads.* Rochester, NY: Social Science Research Network, SSRN Scholarly Paper No. ID 2884965. Retrieved from https://papers.ssrn.com/abstract=2884965

Parks, L., & Morgera, E. (2015). The need for an interdisciplinary approach to norm diffusion: The case of fair and equitable benefit-sharing. *Review of European, Comparative & International Environmental Law, 24*(3), 353–367.

Pham, T. T., Brockhaus, M., Wong, G., Dung, L. G., Tjajadi, J. S., Loft, L., . . . Mvondo, A. C. (n.d.). *Approaches to benefit sharing: A preliminary comparative analysis of 13 REDD+ countries.* Retrieved October 10, 2014, from www.cifor.org/library/4102/approaches-to-benefit-sharing-a-preliminary-comparative-analysis-of-13-redd-countries/

Rajamani, L. (2016). The 2015 Paris Agreement: Interplay between hard, soft and non-obligations. *Journal of Environmental Law, 28,* 337–358.

Rudolph, D., Haggett, C., & Aitken, M. (2017). Community benefits from offshore renewables: The relationship between different understandings of impact, community, and benefit. *Environment and Planning C: Politics and Space.* https://doi.org/10.1177/2399654417699206

Sagar, A., Bremner, C., & Grubb, M. (2009). Climate innovation centres: A partnership approach to meeting energy and climate challenges. *Natural Resources Forum, 33,* 274–284.

Savaresi, A. (2012). The human rights dimension of REDD. *Review of European Comparative & International Environmental Law, 21,* 102–113.

Savaresi, A. (2013). The international human rights law implications of the Nagoya Protocol. In E. Morgera, M. Buck, & E. Tsioumani (Eds.), *The 2010 Nagoya Protocol on access and benefit-sharing in perspective* (pp. 53–81). Leiden: Martinus Nijhoff.

Savaresi, A. (2014). *The emergence of benefit-sharing under the climate regime. A preliminary exploration and research agenda.* SSRN Scholarly Paper, Edinburgh Law School. Retrieved from http://papers.ssrn.com/sol3/papers.cfm?abstract_id=2524335

Savaresi, A. (2016a). A glimpse into the future of the climate regime: Lessons from the REDD+ architecture. *Review of European, Comparative & International Environmental Law, 25*(2), 186–196. https://doi.org/10.1111/reel.12164

Savaresi, A. (2016b). The legal status and role of safeguards. In C. Voigt (Ed.), *Research handbook on REDD+ and international law* (pp. 126–156). Cheltenham, UK: Edward Elgar Publishing.

Savaresi, A. (2017). *The rise of community energy from grassroots to mainstream: The role of law and policy.* Rochester, NY: Social Science Research Network, SSRN Scholarly Paper No. ID 3027695. Retrieved from https://papers.ssrn.com/abstract=3027695

Savaresi, A. (2018). Climate change and human rights: Fragmentation, interplay and institutional linkages. In S. Duyck, S. Jodoin, & A. Johl (Eds.), *Routledge handbook of human rights and climate governance* (pp. 31–43). New York: Routledge, Taylor & Francis Group.

Soltau, F. (2009). *Fairness in international climate change law and policy.* Cambridge, UK: Cambridge University Press.

Thompson, A. (2016). The global regime for climate finance: Political and legal challenges. In K. R. Gray, C. P. Carlarne, & R. Tarasofsky (Eds.), *The Oxford handbook of international climate change law*. Oxford, UK: Oxford University Press.

Thorpe, T. M. (2014). *Climate justice: A voice for the future*. Houndmills, UK and New York, NY: Palgrave Macmillan.

UNFCCC Secretariat. (2016). *Key decisions relevant for reducing emissions from deforestation and forest degradation in developing countries (REDD+)*. Bonn. Retrieved from http://unfccc.int/files/land_use_and_climate_change/redd/application/pdf/compilation_redd_decision_booklet_v1.2.pdf

Walker, B. J. A., Russel, D., & Kurz, T. (2017). Community benefits or community bribes? An experimental analysis of strategies for managing community perceptions of bribery surrounding the siting of renewable energy projects. *Environment and Behavior, 49*(1), 59–83. https://doi.org/10.1177/0013916515605562

Wong, G. Y., Loft, L., Brockhaus, M., Yang, A. L., Pham, T. T., Assembe-Mvondo, S., & Luttrell, C. (2017). An assessment framework for benefit sharing mechanisms to reduce emissions from deforestation and forest degradation within a forest policy mix. *Environmental Policy and Governance, 27*(5), 436–452. https://doi.org/10.1002/eet.1771

Wynberg, R., & Hauck, M. (2014). Sharing the benefits from the coast. In R. Wynberg & M. Hauck (Eds.), *Sharing benefits from the coast: Rights, resources and livelihoods*. Claremont, South Africa: University of Cape Town Press.

Yamineva, Y., & Kulovesi, K. (2013). The new framework for climate finance under the United Nations Framework Convention on Climate Change: A breakthrough or an empty promise? In E. J. Hollo, K. Kulovesi, & M. Mehling (Eds.), *Climate change and the law* (pp. 191–223). Netherlands: Springer. https://doi.org/10.1007/978-94-007-5440-9_9

Zahar, A. (2016). The Paris Agreement and the gradual development of a law on climate finance. *Climate Law, 6*(1–2), 75–90. https://doi.org/10.1163/18786561-00601005

11

Leading from the bench

The role of judges in advancing climate justice and lessons from South Asia

Emeline Pluchon

Introduction

Judges are increasingly emerging in South Asia, and some other jurisdictions around the world, as important actors in the fight against climate change. A series of landmark decisions have been handed down over the last ten or so years, pushing Governments and industry to act to address climate change and to safeguard environmental rights of citizens. In many of these cases the courts have found creative solutions to the issues before them, leading to tensions in certain jurisdictions and accusations of possible judicial overreach. Judges in South Asia have responded courageously, clear-eyed in the view they can and must play a crucial role in advancing environmental rights and climate justice.

This chapter explores the contribution of the judiciary in advancing climate justice. It outlines how they have played a crucial role on this matter and how they have been at the frontline of the struggle against environmental degradation and climate change. The first part will examine various emerging trends in South Asia and, more broadly, such as the development of environmental constitutionalism, expanding access to justice in courts in South Asia, and the unique and innovative approach taken by the judges to advance climate justice. The second part will then review some of the main challenges faced by the judiciaries. Finally, the chapter will provide observations on how judges are interacting and collaborating to share experiences and advance climate justice, and how networking is a significant opportunity for the judiciaries around the world to be inspired by the engagement of judges in South Asia.

Key developments and trends in climate litigation in South Asia

Environmental constitutionalism in South Asia

Courts around the world are adjudicating an increasing number of disputes regarding climate change. As of March 2017, approximately 1,120 climate change cases had been filed in 24 countries (Sabin Center for Climate Change Law, 2018). While the large majority of these are in the USA, some of the landmark cases come from South Asia, and increasingly so. One key trend in South Asia – and globally – has been on using national constitutional frameworks that express environmental rights, also named environmental constitutionalism. As explained by James R. May and Erin Daly (2018, p. 5):

> environmental constitutionalism is a relatively recent phenomenon at the confluence of constitutional law, international law, human rights, and environmental law. It embodies the recognition that the environment is a proper subject for protection in constitutional texts and for vindication by constitutional courts worldwide.

All over the world, countries' constitutions are thus increasingly recognising explicitly or implicitly environmental rights. Environmental constitutionalism takes different forms, some constitutions include substantive rights,[1] others procedural rights,[2] or duties on the individual or the state to protect the environment.[3] Some constitutions contain specific provisions, such as the Uruguayan constitution that recognises the right to water[4] or the Ecuadorian constitution that affirms the right of nature.[5]

The judiciary has largely contributed to environmental constitutionalism, in both situations where constitutions either explicitly protect or not the environment. In South Asia, in some countries where the constitutions do not recognise environmental rights (e.g., Pakistan), the judges have played an important role to constitutionalise these types of rights by looking at the fundamental rights in the constitution, such as the right to life, dignity, equality or free expression, through a green lens.

One of the landmark cases in this regard comes from Pakistan. In the case *Ashgar Leghari v. Federation of Pakistan* (2015), a farmer brought a claim about the National Climate Change Policy and the Framework for Implementation of Climate Change Policy (the Framework). The plaintiff claimed that inaction on behalf of the government to implement the Framework breached his fundamental rights to life and to human dignity, under articles 9 and 14 of the Constitution.

The Lahore High Court, after underlining that the claim was "a clarion call for the protection of fundamental rights of the citizens of Pakistan, in particular, the vulnerable and weak segments of the society who are unable to approach this Court," affirmed that "the delay and lethargy of the State in implementing the Framework offends the fundamental rights of the citizens which need to be safeguarded" (*Ashgar Leghari v. Federation of Pakistan*, 2015, para. 6 and 8).

Some pending cases might also have significant consequences. In the Philippines, a group of non-governmental organisations and citizens filed a petition in 2015, requesting the Commission on Human Rights of the Philippines to investigate the responsibility of oil, gas, coal and cement companies for human rights violations or threats resulting from the impacts of climate change (*Greenpeace Southeast Asia and Others*, 2015). In India, a petitioner recently brought an action against the government arguing that India's existing environmental law and climate change policies, as well as the Paris Agreement, compel the national government to take greater action to mitigate climate change (*Pandey v. India*, 2017). The petitioner cited national legal provisions, the precautionary and sustainable development principles, as well as other judicial decisions such as *Urgenda Foundation v. Kingdom of the Netherlands* (2015). In this latter case, the court, on the basis of the Dutch Constitution, had ruled that the federal government had a duty to reduce greenhouse gas emissions and take mitigation measures.

The link between human rights and environmental issues in South Asia has been highlighted by the UN Special Rapporteur on Human Rights and the Environment, John H. Knox, in his report on the issue of human rights obligations in relation to the enjoyment of a safe, clean, healthy and sustainable environment (UN Human Rights Council, 2017). Lalanath De Silva explained this trend, by the fact that "environmental activism in South Asia is almost always about survival. In this context, issues such as involuntary displacement and re-settlement, provision of basic human needs of water and sanitation, become central to environmental law" (De Silva, 1999, p. 249).

By vindicating environmental rights through the spectrum of constitutionalism, judges' actions can have a large impact. Even if the courts' decisions cannot change the whole environmental policy of a State, they can play an important role by influencing the legal and executive branches to adopt regulations in the same directions. They are also an important indicator of the growing awareness of environmental constitutionalism, of the influence that courts' decisions could have on other countries (Daly et al., 2017), as well as of their significant potential.

Expanding access to justice through courts in South Asia

The path to courts is strewn with hurdles that make it difficult for citizens to defend their rights. People encounter difficulties to prove an infringement, damage and the causation link between the breach of the duty to act or to care and the harm that occurred. For instance, in the Bangladesh case *Dr. Mohiuddin Farooque v. Bangladesh* (1997), in which the claimant challenged the legality of a flood action plan, the court initially rejected the claim on the grounds that the petitioner had no standing. At the global level all citizens encounter the same difficulty. The U.S. case, *Comer v. Murphy Oil USA, Inc.* (2012) illustrates this issue. In this lawsuit, the plaintiffs claimed that global warming contributed to Hurricane Katrina and asserted that a group of oil companies should be recognised as responsible for the damage caused by the violent windstorm. The court decided that the claimants lacked standing because "their alleged injuries [were] not fairly traceable to the defendant's conduct."

Bearing these difficulties in mind, judges have tried to expand access to justice on environmental matters to advance climate justice through various mechanisms; these include the introduction of the concept of public interest litigation for environmental and climate change issues, the recognition of standing to sue for future generations, and for natural resources. By doing so, they also enhanced the power that the citizens have over public authorities.

Public interest litigation

In South Asia, courts have seen a considerable rise of public litigation cases linked to human rights and environmental issues. Public interest litigation is a legal proceeding in which reparation is sought with regard to injury to the public in general. As public interest litigation allows a citizen to bring a suit as a matter of public interest, or a concerned person to support the cause of another poor or underprivileged one, it has become an increasingly used mechanism.

In India, the judiciary have developed a broad jurisprudence of public interest litigation on environmental issues since the mid-1980s (Mate, 2013). *Narmada Bachao Andolan v. Union of India* (2000) and *M.C. Mehta v. Union of India* (1998) are some of the major public litigation cases in this area. The Indian Supreme Court's public interest guidelines indicate even explicitly that "Petitions pertaining to environmental pollution, disturbance of ecological balance, . . . forest and wild life" will be ordinarily entertained as public interest litigation (Supreme Court of India, 2003, p. 2). Nevertheless, this instrument does not mention climate change.

In Pakistan, the judges have followed the same trend. One of the first public interest litigation cases in the environmental sector was *Roedad Khan v. Federation of Pakistan and 41 Others* (1990), where the petitioner brought a claim against quarrying activities carried out by a cement company and stone-crushing activities in the Margallah Hills National Park that posed a serious environmental and health hazard to the inhabitants of Islamabad. The court did not take any specific order in this case, but, thanks to the publicity created by the claim, the Government took remedial action. In *General Secretary, West Pakistan Salt Miners Labour Union (CBA) Khewral, Jhelum v. The Director, Industries and Mineral Development* (1994), the Lahore High Court, aware of the potential impact of public interest litigation cases on environmental matters, affirmed its position to be flexible regarding procedural constraints.

In Asia, other countries such as Sri Lanka and Bangladesh have also observed the emergence of public interest cases where development, human rights and environment were at stake, such as the *Bulankulama and Others v. Secretary, Ministry of Industrial Development and others* (2000). China has also seen rapid growth in environmental public interest litigation since 2015 following amendments to relevant environmental legislation, and the number of policy documents published by the Chinese government (de Boer and Whitehead, 2016)

Others part of the world have demonstrated that public interest litigation could be an important tool for facilitating access to justice for environmental and climate change issues. In the USA, Alaskans brought a claim against oil and power companies over the impact of climate change on their village (*Native Village Kivalina v. ExxonMobil Corp.*, 2012). In Belgium, over 10,000 citizens argued that the government must take greater measures to reduce greenhouse gas emissions in order to comply with Belgian law (*VZW Klimaatzaak v. Kingdom of Belgium & Others*, 2015).

Ability to represent future generations

Some courts have gone even further to expand access to justice, by pushing the right to bring a claim to the court for the future generations. In Southeast Asia, the Philippines Supreme Court, in the case *Juan Antonio, Anna Rosario and Jose Alfonso Oposa & Others v. The Honourable Fulgencio S. Factoran Jr*. (1993), ruled that petitioners' children could file a class action for their generation as well as for the succeeding generations. The court said that "their personality to sue in behalf of the succeeding generations can only be based on the concept of intergenerational responsibility insofar as the right to a balanced and a healthful ecology is concerned." It was globally the first time that a court recognised the right to future generations to bring a claim.

The need to protect youth and the future generations has also been highlighted by a recent petition in Pakistan. The petitioner, in *Ali v. Federation of Pakistan*, is a seven-year-old girl who lives in Karachi. In the petition, it is claimed that she and other Pakistani children are extremely affected by the rise of greenhouse gases in the atmosphere, which not only harms and threatens their mental and physical health, quality of life and wellbeing, but also violates their right to life and the fundamental rights of the Petitioner and future generations of Pakistan. In the *Pandey v. India* (2017) case, presented earlier, the petitioner is a nine-year-old child from the Uttarakhand region and the claim is also based on the concept of intergenerational equity.

The American continent has also seen these kinds of cases before its courts; in *Juliana v. United States*, originally filed in 2015, 21 plaintiffs aged from 10 to 21 brought a suit against the government, claiming that it has contributed to climate change in violation of the plaintiffs' constitutional rights. They affirmed that the government had known for years that carbon dioxide emissions from the burning of fossils fuels destabilise the climate. The government tried on many occasions, without success, to have this case dismissed. In 2015, the government filed a motion to dismiss the case, and in 2017 a petition for a writ of mandamus. Recently, the federal district court for the District of Oregon decided that the trial will take place on October 29, 2018 (*Juliana v. United States*).

The effectiveness of this standing could be debated, but it has the advantage to address the situations of long-term environmental damage, when the damage is more harmful for the future generations than the present one (May and Daly, 2018). If the pending Indian and Pakistani cases are successful, it could be a defining step for the region.

Recognition of natural resources as legal entities

Judges in South Asia have taken another step, by recognising that natural resources have standing to sue for their own protection. In *Mohd. Salim v. State of Uttarakhand and others* (2017) case, the High Court of Uttarakhand in India held that the Rivers Ganges and Yamuna were legal persons with all corresponding rights. Later, the same court extended legal personality to the Gangotri and Yamunotri glaciers in the case *Miglani v. State of Uttarakhand & others* (2017). These developments are mirrored in New Zealand, where members of the indigenous Maori tribes have disputed with the Crown the status of the Whanganui River in the framework of the Treaty of Waitangi for many years. In 2014, they finally signed a settlement that granted the river its own legal identity, with the rights and duties of a legal person.

In consequence, by opening the doors of the courts to people to fight environmental degradation and climate change, the judiciaries have expanded the possibility for citizens to hold government responsible. They thus encourage the legislative and executive branches to act in such a way to respect their obligations. As in India, Pakistan and their neighbouring countries, the practice to relax the standing rules for environmental issues is well-established, and given the future impacts of climate change, it is likely that these judiciaries will continue on the same vein in climate change cases.

Innovative judicial remedies in South Asia to advance climate justice

To ensure that issues of environmental protection and climate change are dealt with in a robust and active manner, judges in South Asia have taken a lead in ordering innovative judicial remedies.

For example, some courts in South Asia have developed an innovative approach to deal with environmental cases, by appointing commissions to investigate the issues at stake, make recommendations and even facilitate the implementation of courts' decisions. In Pakistan, the commissions that were initially appointed for environmental issues are now used in climate change lawsuits. Empowered of various competencies, such as studying the technical dimensions of a case and reporting on these issues (*Ms. Shehla Zia and others v. WAPDA*, 1994), or examining the suitability of an infrastructure and giving advice on the optimal environmentally appropriate manner to build it (*City District Government v. Muhammad Yousaf*, 2003) or to facilitate the implementation of a court decision (*Syed Mansoor Ali Shah v. Government of Punjab*, 2007), these commissions have helped the judges to equip themselves with science-based expertise and the possibility to provide technical and suitable solutions to environmental issues (Hassan, 2006). The judiciary has demonstrated the effectiveness and utility of appointing commissions with a climate change case (*Ashgar Leghari v. Federation of Pakistan*, 2015).

The Supreme Court in Bangladesh, following its Indian counterpart on environmental matters, has recently started to appoint commissions to follow the implementation of their decisions, such as in *Bangladesh Environmental Lawyers Association v. Bangladesh* case (Karim et al., 2012).

Other approaches to safeguard the environment and the citizens have seen the courts develop remedies ordering environmental impact assessments of public projects, ordering changes to current practice and orders to request the government to create new policies. In *Karnataka Industrial Areas Development Board v. Sri C. Kenchappa & Ors* (2006), farmers, who owned lands for cattle, were affected by the acquisition of lands by the government and brought a claim for restraining the government from converting the lands for industrial purpose. The Indian Supreme Court mentioned the importance of climate change and ordered the public authorities to carry out a study to properly consider the adverse environmental impact of development on the environment. In *Gaurav Kumar Bansal v. Union of India and Ors* (2017), where the petitioner claimed that adverse impact of the flood and landslide disaster that occurred in Uttarakhand in 2013 could have been mitigated with an effective implementation of the Disaster Management Act 2005, the tribunal went even further by directing each state to formulate a state plan for disaster management to comply with this Act.

Recently, the National Green Tribunal in India also sought to address climate change. As indicated by Jacob et al. (2018), the Tribunal, wanting to mitigate the emission levels, sought to force the thermal power plants to use coal with only a certain level of ash content (Jacob et al., 2018), citing the case *Rantandeep Randari v. State of Maharashtra* (2015). In *Court on its own motion v. State of Himachal Pradesh and others* (2014), concerning the degradation of the environment in Rohtang pass, in Himachal Pradesh, the Tribunal ordered specific measures to the state government. After highlighting the impact of the emissions of black carbon on glaciers and drawing a link between global warming and melting glaciers, it requested that the state government, amongst others measures, ban the use of any kind of plastic bags, restrict the number of vehicles that can cross the area, and impose a pollution tax on tourists.

In *Indian Council for Enviro-legal Action (ICELA) v. Ministry of Environment, Forest and Climate Change and Ors* (2015), the plaintiff brought a claim to stop some industries from emitting HFC-23, a gas categorised as a greenhouse gas under the Kyoto Protocol. The Tribunal affirmed that "it is undisputable that the greenhouse gases have impact on global warming and global warming has affect on several facets on human life i.e., air, ecology agriculture and the whole socio economic life in every part of the globe" (para. 19) and decided that since the HFC-23 issue "is a part of policy of Government of India at the global level . . . it may not be advisable for [the court] to provide bridging gaps in policy particularly at this stage" (para. 27). Nevertheless, even though it took the decision not to intervene, it requested that the state determines appropriate measures under the existing law.

Finally, the judiciary has shown boldness and creativity in awarding damages. For instance, in *Vellore Citizens Welfare Forum v. Union of India & Ors* (1996), the court decided that no industry causing serious water pollution should be permitted within one kilometer from the embankment of the water sources. It ordered the government to appoint a body to deal with the situation created by the tanneries and other polluting industries in the state of Tamil Nadu, and decreed that this authority should implement the precautionary principle and the polluter pays principle and determine the compensation to be recovered. It then clearly indicated how this compensation should be calculated: "The authority shall compute the compensation under two heads namely, for reversing the ecology and for payment to individuals." The court, by clearly defining how the government should act, and by precisely indicating how the compensation should be allocated, did its utmost to address the environmental harm and to give reparation to the environment, as well as to the affected population.

Two aspects emerge from these cases. First, it is the willingness of the judges to tackle administrative lethargy and to force private and public entities to address environmental degradation and climate change. In most of the cases the State is the defendant or co-defendant, and a large number of cases focus on government inaction to address global warming. The duty to mitigate climate impacts and to implement adaptation measures to help communities cope with climate change is thus viewed as the responsibility of the State. The keenness to address administrative passivity is more specifically illustrated by the creative, detailed and specific measures ordered by the courts, therefore leaving no room for improvisation and interpretation of the verdict by the parties.

The second aspect is the judicial notice of the climate change. The judges have recognised that "Climate Change is a defining challenge of our time and has led to dramatic alterations in our planet's climate system" (*Ashgar Leghari*, 2015, para. 6) and that "Global warming has a direct impact on environment and ecology of any zone" (*Court on its own motion v. State of Himachal Pradesh and others*, 2014, para. 31). These cases show no debate on the existence of global warming. The scientific consensus that greenhouses gases resulting from human activities cause climate change is admitted by the courts. This feature can be recognised as a significant element for the success of the future climate cases.

Challenges for courts in advancing climate justice

Judges' engagement is not without challenges. The rule of the separation of powers is one of them. Judges don't have any power to change the law or enforce their own decision, but many have chosen to engage, because they know that they can play a crucial role in advancing environmental rights, by collaborating and influencing the private and public sectors, the government and the legislative branch. The judiciary often go further than interpreting legal documents, such as constitutions or regulations. They decide to act where they perceive the government or the parliamentarians have failed to fulfil their duty.

For instance, in *M.C. Mehta v. Union of India* (1998), the court ordered the bus fleet operator to replace its vehicle fuel source from petrol and diesel to compressed natural gas by 31 March 2001. In some cases, the Court even developed and managed a new policy on its own. Thus, in the case *T.N. Godavarman Thirumulpad v. Union of India* (1995), the Indian Supreme Court ordered all non-forestry activities which had not received explicit approval to stop, but also set up a new forest policy and ordered investigations into various complaints of illegal mining operations. With this decision, the Supreme Court has been criticised as overstepping its authority and supplanting both the legislative power and the executive power.

Even though the judges can be criticised for things such as making policies that do not follow the policy-planning objectives of the State and can create inconsistency and incoherence (Puvimanasinghe, 2009), their significant role in the fight against climate change for the protection of the environment needs to be acknowledged.

In addition, the judiciary often encounters difficulties to enforce orders. Remedial orders in constitutional environmental cases are specifically considered to be amongst the most difficult to enforce (Daly and May, 2018). Judges experience difficulties for different reasons. First, orders have frequently many sides, as they often call for the involvement of a multitude of people and bodies to collaborate and take action. Second, environmental policies may be perceived to be at the detriment of industrialisation, economic growth or urbanisation, which generally represent society goals (Daly and May, 2018). The defendants, public or private entities, are thus reluctant to comply with court orders.

Taking these challenges into account, some courts have developed mechanisms to avoid or reduce these problems. In *Farooque v. Government of Bangladesh* (2001), the Court even mentioned that the petitioner had the possibility to approach the court to ask directions as and when necessary so that the objective of the Act could be achieved effectively (*Farooque v. Government of Bangladesh*, 2001, para. 47).

Increasing regional judicial cooperation to advance climate justice

As further warming is expected in the coming decades, the number of climate change cases can be expected to increase in South Asia and around the world. How best to prepare the judiciary to achieve climate justice is the primary question. In the light of the latest climate change litigation, some aspects, such as a thorough understanding of international and national environmental and climate change law, as well as scientific questions, appear crucial to adjudicate these issues. As both are fast-evolving areas, training and support are essential.

Aware of the importance to interact, collaborate and share challenges and experiences on climate change issues, judges from the region called for the creation of a specific network. In 2010, the Asian Judges Network on Environment (AJNE) was created, with the support of the Asian Development Bank and partners. The objective of this network, which assembles senior judges of the Association of Southeast Asian Nations (ASEAN) and the South Asian Association for Regional Cooperation (SAARC), is to facilitate capacity-building and to promote closer ties among members over shared questions. At the global level, the Global Judicial Institute for the Environment (GJIE) is an important forum to strengthen the capacity of judges in applying and enforcing environmental and climate change laws. The GJIE has been supported by the United Nations Environment Programme (UN Environment).

With this support, judges from the AJNE network and other jurisdictions met in Pakistan, in February 2018. A colloquium, called the "Asia Pacific Judicial Colloquium on Climate Change: using constitutions to advance environmental rights and achieve climate justice," was hosted by the Lahore High Court. The colloquium assembled around 250 participants from the region and globally, including judges and other legal stakeholders (e.g., barristers, prosecutors, civil society and academics).

The aim of this meeting was to build the capacity of judges in the Asia Pacific region in applying environmental constitutionalism to achieve climate justice and advance environmental rights. During this event the judiciary and legal stakeholders in the region acknowledged the environmental challenges faced by South Asia and the world, and recognised the need for members of the judiciary and other legal stakeholders to increase awareness on environmental issues amongst them and the public, as well as to strengthen their capabilities to understand and apply environmental national and international laws.

Through training and networking, the judiciary has a chance to turn to extra-territorial approaches to adjudicate its national cases. It is a considerable opportunity for judges from all over the world to be inspired by the innovation and the creativity of South Asian judges to advance climate justice. By increasing access to courts and recognising the need and value of technical experts, South Asian judiciaries, and mainly the Indian and Pakistani courts, have shown a leading role to play in Asia and worldwide. There are numerous opportunities for the judges at the global level to use South Asian techniques. For instance, due to the similarities between the constitutional legal instruments, the judges could rely on cases based on constitutional rights to advance climate justice. In addition, as global warming continues to worsen and its impacts on human society to intensify, this kind of claim could be increasingly used before courts.

Conclusion

"Protection of environment is our collective responsibility," said the former Chief Justice of the Lahore High Court Mansoor Ali Shah, recently appointed as judge of the Supreme Court of Pakistan (*The Express Tribune*, 27 August 2017). In the absence of proper solutions to address climate change and to protect the environment and those who live in it, certain courts in South Asia have demonstrated a high level of responsiveness, keenness to act and creativity. Although some of their orders have been criticised for not respecting the concept of the separation of powers, the role of the judges has been defended by others as essential to advance climate justice. They represent a major link between the government and its citizens, giving to both the opportunity to raise their voices in societies where democracy is still in its early stages. Judicial activism is a remarkable tool for advancing climate justice, but it cannot be a substitute for law-making. Climate change cases are not enough to limit global warming and its effects. The need for countries to take real action to protect the environment, the affected populations and the climate is pressing.

Acknowledgements

The author wishes to acknowledge and thank the contribution of Andy Raine, Regional Coordinator for Environmental Law and Governance at UN Environment. The content and views expressed in this article are solely those of the author and do not represent those of UN Environment.

Notes

1 For instance in the Philippines, article II, section 16 of the Constitution: "right to a balanced and healthful ecology in accord to the rhythm and harmony of nature"; in Nepal, article 30 of the Constitution: "each person shall have the right to live in an clean environment"; in Montenegro, article 23 of the Constitution "Everyone shall have the right to a sound environment"; in South Korea, article 35 of the Constitution "All citizens have the right to a healthy and pleasant environment."
2 For instance, article 50 of the Ukrainian Constitution: "Everyone is guaranteed the right of free access to information about the environmental situation."
3 For instance in Bangladesh, article 18A of the Constitution provides "The state shall endeavour to protect and improve the environment and to preserve and safeguard national resources, biodiversity, wetlands, forests and wildlife for the present and future citizens"; in Bhutan, article 5–2 c) of the Constitution states: "The Royal government shall . . . secure ecologically balanced sustainable development while promoting justifiable economic and social development."
4 Article 47 of the Uruguayan Constitution provides "Access to clean water and access to sanitation constitute fundamental human rights."
5 Articles 71 to 74 of the Ecuadorian Constitution.

References

Daly, E., Kotzé, L. and May, J. R. (2017). Introduction to Environmental Constitutionalism, In E. Daly, L. Kotze, J. May & C. Soyap (Eds.), *New Frontiers in Environmental Constitutionalism* (pp. 30–33), Nairobi, United Nations Environment Programme.

de Boer, D. and Whitehead, D. (2016), 'Opinion: The Future of Public Interest Litigation in China', *China Dialogue*, accessed 11 May 2018, <www.chinadialogue.net/article/show/single/en/9356-Opinion-The-future-of-public-interest-litigation-in-China>

De Silva, L. (1999), 'Environmental Law Development in South Asia', *Asia Pacific Journal of Environmental Law*, Vol. 243, pp. 243–249.

Hassan, P. (2006), 'The role of judiciary and judicial commissions on sustainable development issues in Pakistan', Paper presented at the International Judicial Conference organized by the Supreme Court of Pakistan during its Golden Jubilee Celebrations in August 2006, accessed 24 September 2018, <http://www.supremecourt.gov.pk/ijc/Articles/9/7.pdf>

Jacob, V. A., Mishra, B. and Ambashta, R. (2018), 'Climate Change Litigation and Human Rights', accessed 22 August 2018, <www.lawasia.asn.au/sites/default/files/2018-05/Academic-Paper-Climate-Change-Litigation-and-Human-Rights-22Mar2018.pdf>

Karim, Md. S., Benjamin Vincents, O. and Rahim, M. M. (2012), 'Legal Activism for Ensuring Environmental Justice', *Asian Journal of Comparative Law*, Vol. 7 (2012).

Mate, M. (2013) 'Public Interest Litigation and the Transformation of the Supreme Court in India', in *Consequential Court: New Judicial Roles in Comparative Perspective*. Cambridge: Cambridge University Press.

May, J. R. and Daly, E. (2018). *Global Judicial Handbook on Environmental Constitutionalism*. United Nations Environment Programme. <www.ajne.org/sites/default/files/resource/publications/7227/global-judicial-handbook-on-environmental-constitutionalism-2nd-ed.pdf>

Puvimanasinghe, S. F. (2009), 'Towards a Jurisprudence of Sustainable Development in South Asia: Litigation in the Public Interest', *Sustainable Development Law & Policy*, Vol. 10, Issue 1, pp. 41–87, *Fall 2009: Sustainable Development in the Court.*

Sabin Center for Climate Change Law (2018), « Columbia Law School, Climate Change Litigation Database, « accessed 12 April 2018, <http://climatecasechart.com/about/>

Supreme Court of India (2003), "Compilation of Guidelines to be Followed for Entertaining Letters/Petitions Received in this Court as Public Interest Litigation," <http://supremecourtofindia.nic.in/pdf/Guidelines/pilguidelines.pdf>

The Express Tribune (2017), "Free Legal Assistance: Justice Should be Delivered on Poor Man's Doorstep: CJ," <https://tribune.com.pk/story/1492160/free-legal-assistance-justice-delivered-poor-mans-doorstep-cj/>

UN Human Rights Council (2017), "Report of the Special Rapporteur on the Issue of Human Rights Obligations Relating to the Enjoyment of a Safe, Clean, Healthy and Sustainable Environment, A/HRC/34/49," <www.refworld.org/docid/58ad9dd44.html>

Legal cases

Bangladesh

Farooque v. Government of Bangladesh (1997), Writ Petition No. 998 of 1994.

Farooque v. Government of Bangladesh (2001), Writ Petition No. 891 of 1994.

Belgium

VZW Klimaatzaak v. Kingdom of Belgium, et al. (2015) (Court of First Instance, Brussels).

India

Court on its own motion v. State of Himachal Pradesh and others (2014), National Green Tribunal, application No. 237 of 2013.

Gaurav Kumar Bansal v. Union of India and Ors (2017), Writ Petition No. 444 of 2013.

Indian Council for Enviro-legal Action (ICELA) v. Ministry of Environment, Forest and Climate Change and Ors (2015), National Green Tribunal, Original application No. 170 of 2014.

Karnataka Industrial Areas. v. Sri C. Kenchappa & Ors (2006), 6 SCC 371.

M.C. Mehta v. Union of India (1998), INSC 575.

Miglani v. State of Uttarakhand & others (2017), Writ Petition No. 140 of 2015.

Mohd. Salim v. State of Uttarakhand & Others (2017), Writ Petition No. 126 of 2014.

Narmada Bachao Andolan v Union of India (2000), 10 SCC 664.

Pandey v. India (2017), National Green Tribunal, pending case.

Rantandeep Randari v. State of Maharashtra (2015), National Green Tribunal, 15 October 2015.

T.N. Godavarman Thirumulpad v. Union of India (1995), Writ Petition No. 202 of 1995.

Vellore Citizens Welfare Forum v. Union of India & Ors (1996), Writ Petition No. 914 of 1991.

Pakistan

Ali v. Federation of Pakistan (2016), Supreme Court of Pakistan, pending case.

Ashgar Leghari v. Federation of Pakistan (2015), Writ Petition No. 25501/2015, 04/09/2015

Ashgar Leghari v. Federation of Pakistan (2015), Writ Petition No. 25501/2015, 14/09/2015

City District Government v. Muhammad Yousaf (2003), I.C.A. No 798/2002.

General Secretary, West Pakistan Salt Miners Labour Union (CBA) Khewra, Jhelum v. The Director, Industries and Mineral Development (1994), SCMR 2061.

Ms. Shehla Zia and others v. WAPDA (1994), P L D 1994 SC 693.

Roedad Khan v. Federation of Pakistan and 41 Others (1990), WritPetition No. 642/1990.

Syed Mansoor Ali Shah and v. Government of Punjab (2007), C L D 533.

Sri Lanka

Bulankulama and Others v. Secretary, Ministry of Industrial Development and others (2000), LKSC 18.

The Netherlands

Urgenda Foundation v. The State of the Netherlands (2015), HAZA C/09/00456689.

The Philippines

Greenpeace Southeast Asia and Others (2015) No. CHR-NI-2016-0001 pending case.
Juan Antonio, Anna Rosario and Jose Alfonso Oposa & Others v. The Honorable Fulgencio S. Factoran Jr. (1993), G.R. No. 101083.

United States

Comer v. Murphy Oil USA, Inc. (2012), No. 1:11CV220-LG-RHW.
Juliana v. United States (2015), pending case.
Native Village Kivalina v. ExxonMobil Corp. (2012), 696 F.3d 849, 2012 WL 4215921.

Part III

Climate justice, finance and business

12

Climate finance

Moral theory and political practice

Alexandre Gajevic Sayegh

Introduction

Climate finance aims at reducing global greenhouse gas (GHG) emissions, enhancing carbon sinks and reducing the vulnerability of populations and ecosystems to a changing climate. When signing the Paris Agreement in December 2015, advanced economies maintained their pledge to mobilise $100 billion per year by 2020 to address the pressing mitigation and adaptation needs of developing countries. This sum should represent "new and additional" funds to the total climate finance portfolio. Today, not only are present financial commitments far below the mark, but the existing redistributive mechanisms lack a structured method to replenish their resources. Climate finance needs moral theory, effective political practice and insights about how to connect the two.

This chapter presents climate finance as an instrument of climate justice and as a signal for effective climate action. As both an instrument and a signal, it constitutes an applicable response to the development challenge, as it aims at allowing countries to develop economically while reducing their GHG emissions. To do so, this chapter offers an account of what principles of climate justice should regulate climate finance and what are some of the central practical implications of these principles, including what agents should be involved in the distribution (e.g., Multilateral Development Banks, the Green Climate Fund) and what sources of finance should be included (e.g., carbon pricing revenues, but not development aid).

This chapter argues that the principle of historical responsibility and the principle of capacity provide a solid normative foundation for distributing the rights and duties of climate justice finance. It presents the political role of climate finance as one that builds trust and momentum, and alleviates much of the justice-related tensions in global climate negotiations. By promoting low-carbon development in a way that is fair, climate finance would eliminate any comparative advantage to benefit from a carbon-based economy and thus accelerate climate action.

I will first review the political context of climate finance and offer a definition of climate justice finance. I will then present a set of normative guidelines and conditions in order to determine: (a) what agents should contribute to the effort of replenishing the resources of climate justice finance, (b) by how much, (c) what should be counted towards the US$100 billion goal and (d) the function of climate justice finance as a signal to build confidence and momentum.

Climate finance needs a structured mechanism to replenish its resources, which must follow principles of climate justice.

Climate finance from Copenhagen and ten years after

A general definition of climate finance is provided by the UNFCCC:

> [F]inance that aims at reducing emissions, and enhancing sinks of greenhouse gases and aims at reducing vulnerability of, and maintaining and increasing the resilience of, human and ecological systems to negative climate change impacts.
>
> *(UNFCCC, 2014)*

We should distinguish between a broad and a narrow understanding of climate finance. The broad understanding concerns the realm of all investments that target climate change mitigation, adaptation or geoengineering projects. The definition above describes this general practice. The narrow definition concerns justice: it is the portion of all transfers and funds of climate finance, as described, which should be implemented following the interpretation of principles of justice. Call the broad conception *climate finance* and the narrow conception *climate justice finance*.

In the broader conception of climate finance, it could be said that all investments follow moral duties to a certain extent, minimally the obligation to mitigate climate change following the negative duty not-to-harm. To act upon climate change is to fulfil a moral duty. The narrow understanding of the notion of climate finance thus involves not only the duties of a single party to act upon climate change but also the differentiated duties to fund the fight against climate change among a number of parties. Climate justice finance is the site of differentiation of the burdens to fund climate action. It opens the space to an additional duty, one that responds to principles of climate justice finance.

A great number of agents across many sectors (e.g., national governments, private companies, NGOs, courts of justice, individuals) have a duty to fight climate change, but not all agents will pay the same for it. This is in part due to the different amount of GHGs that nations produce and now have an obligation to cut. This is also due in part to a requirement of justice. Climate justice finance, in this sense, aims at determining why some agents have duties to pay for the climate change mitigation and adaptation of others. It applies principles of climate justice to the financing of global mitigation and adaptation in order to observe whether agents have differentiated responsibilities in this matter.

This chapter is concerned with climate justice finance. I will refer to it henceforth with this narrow conception in mind. The chapter will begin by examining the current state of climate justice finance.

The idea of climate justice finance as it has just been defined gained prominence during the Copenhagen summit in 2009. As negotiations were losing strength, the pressure from developing countries to ensure rich countries would rise to the challenge was increasing (Roberts & Weikmans, 2016). To save the day, then Secretary of State Hillary Clinton came up with the idea that rich countries would have to provide US$100 billion a year to help developing nations in their mitigation and adaptation efforts.

The number stuck. In 2015, we read in the Paris Agreement (Paragraph 114) text that the international community

> strongly urges developed country Parties to scale up their level of financial support, with a concrete roadmap to achieve the goal of jointly providing $100 billion annually by 2020

for mitigation and adaptation while significantly increasing adaptation finance from current levels and to further provide appropriate technology and capacity-building support.

(UNFCCC, 2015)

Whether this sum is sufficient for developing nations to accomplish their objectives, and whether it really represents justice, are valid questions. The annual US$100 billion target will not cover all climate-related objectives in developing countries. It does not have this pretention. All these investments would fall on the broad category of climate finance. Countries like India and China alone may invest comparable sums. The ambition of climate justice finance is thus to provide a necessary but not sufficient contribution to the effort of developing countries. For smaller developing countries, even taken as a group, this sum is considerable. This funding is needed for countries to decrease their emissions, develop in a clean way and adapt to climate change.

Consider now that the Green Climate Fund (GCF) is looking for a more structured mechanism to replenish its resources. "Large, global, multilateral funds usually begin with ad hoc contributions from initial contributors, followed by outreach to a broader universe of contributors and, over time, *adopt a more systematic process* to replenish resources" (GCF, 2014). If its objective is then to scale up its distributive capacity, and do so in a way that is fair, it will benefit from a more structured distributive mechanism. This chapter wants to provide guidelines for this replenishing mechanism.

Besides being an instrument of climate justice, climate finance plays a second role: creating the much-needed momentum and sending a signal for global climate action. The sum of US$100 billion annually is certainly sufficient to create this momentum and to signal to the world that developed countries are committed to climate justice. I thus suggest that we should implement climate justice finance, taking as a starting point this figure and its scheduling of annual transfers from 2020. Whether this will be adjusted in the future, as scheduled for 2025, should not concern us here.

In 2016, developed countries produced a document called the "Roadmap to US$100 billion" (Roadmap, 2016). This document gives a good notion about what is currently counted towards the US$100 billion goal and who are the parties involved in the process. In April 2017, developing countries were still urging rich countries to fulfil their pledges made in Copenhagen and Paris. I will show here how the current climate finance context is missing clear ethical guidelines. These guidelines should bring clarity, regularity and structure to: (a) what agents should contribute to the effort of replenishing the resources of climate justice finance, (b) by how much, (c) what should be counted towards the US$100 billion goal, (d) the function of climate justice finance as a signal to build confidence and momentum. Guidelines (a), (b), (c) and (d) are sub-objectives that will allow us to meet the goal of climate finance. I will discuss (a) and (b) first.

Climate finance as an instrument of climate justice

National governments are still today the main agents around climate roundtables. They commit their countries to mitigation and adaptation efforts. Raising US$100 billion annually will indeed require commitment. Yet, we observe since Copenhagen, and especially in the aftermath of the Paris Agreement, that we are in fact in a context of polycentric climate governance and multi-level agency (Dorsch & Flachsland, 2017; Widerberg & Pattberg, 2015). Governments may represent their people in negotiations, but subnational entities such as states, provinces, private companies, NGOs and individuals are increasingly becoming key players in the climate effort (Zelli & Asselt, 2013; Hale, 2016). I will first discuss the responsibility of nations and then include a role for subnational initiatives.

The normative framework I develop here is based on the principles of historical responsibility and of capacity. As opposed to other recent models (Antimiani, Costantini, Markandya, Paglial-unga, & Sforna, 2017; Cui, Zhu, Springmann, & Fan, 2014; Dellink et al., 2009), this chapter aims only to model these two moral principles in practice. I use these principles to determine what countries have a duty to contribute to climate finance and what countries will benefit from it. The "principle of historical responsibility" states that: responsibility should be distributed accord-ing to agents' (moral and causal) historical connection to the problem. Some countries have emitted much more than others in the past. These historically high emitters (i) have caused the present climate crisis where populations around the globe will suffer from the effects of a chang-ing climate and (ii) have denied developing nations the possibility to develop in a way they can afford (Gardiner, 2016). Following the principle of historical responsibility, these nations have a duty to act upon this injustice. In this case, given the harm caused both in terms of impact and in terms of a denied opportunity to develop, this duty extends beyond a duty to mitigate climate change and thus includes a duty to respond for the harms caused. This principle does not take into account countries' capacity to act upon climate change. It includes all countries with con-siderable past emissions.

The second relevant principle in this context is the principle of capacity. The "principle of capacity" states that: "remedial responsibilities ought to be assigned according to the capacity of each agent to discharge them" (Miller, 2001). Not all countries have the same capacity to mitigate and to adapt to climate change. This principle is not based on the notion of harm. It is a principle of fairness. This principle can be coupled with the "principle of benefit," which highlights that the capacity of agents has often been acquired from past GHG emissions. That is, following the principle of capacity supported by the principle of benefit, affluent nations today have a duty to solve the problem of climate change and to help those that cannot do it alone; and this is because they have the capacity to do it, and because this capacity was acquired as a result of past pollution. As for the right-bearers of climate justice, all countries that cannot develop economically in a non-harmful way (i.e. with low GHG emissions) have the right to benefit from climate justice finance.

I have offered elsewhere a practical interpretation of these principles (Gajevic Sayegh, 2017). I will refer here to this reasoning. The principles of historical responsibility and of capacity should be treated as two independent moral variables. Each should be responsible for half of the US$100 billion climate justice finance target (Dellink et al., 2009). Based on the historical emissions of each country, as a percentage of total historical emissions for a given period, we can determine its financial contribution to climate justice finance (I have used 1990–2011 as the period of ref-erence given the best data available, but this can easily be adjusted for different morally relevant reference periods). Using a combination of GDP and GDP per capita, I have determined what countries should be considered capable of contributing to climate justice finance and by how much they should do it (Gajevic Sayegh, 2017). Using jointly what we find from applying the principles of capacity and of historical responsibility, we obtain the final figure per country in terms of their payment to climate justice finance. For example, the annual payment by country for some of the top contributors would be: $29.9 billion for the United States, $7.5 billion for China, $7.3 billion for Japan, $3 billion for Russia and $2.8 billion for Canada. Those of China and Russia are strictly derived from the principle of historical responsibility. Those of European countries such as Germany, the UK and France would be $4.1 billion, $3.1 billion and $2.9 billion respectively from the principle of capacity, to which we need to add the corresponding percentages of the $6 billion that we obtain for the historical responsibly of the European Union during that period.

This reasoning responds to guidelines (a) and (b) – what agents should contribute to the effort of replenishing the resources of climate finance and by how much. But, if we were to include subnational agents, we observe that it provides only a partial answer: it is partial with regards to (a) for the agents' aspect of this question could be clarified further, and partial with regards to (b) because this clarification about agency should also bring further precision about how the funds are generated. I turn now to these points.

Subnational climate finance architecture

As mentioned previously, agents such as cities, states and private companies are necessary to close the emissions reduction gap in climate change mitigation (EBRD & GRI, 2011). If this is indeed the case, two other important implications follow. The normative framework that determines the duty-bearers and the right-bearers of climate finance has to be sensitive to polycentric governance and multi-level agency. Also, the architecture that regulates the replenishing of the resources of climate finance should be one that takes notice of the progress accomplished in climate governance. I will show these three points in turn, starting with the empirical claim that subnational entities are necessary to close the emissions gap.

The empirical claim can be shown via a combination of different observations. Subnational initiatives are necessary for nations to meet their climate change mitigation targets. This can be explained by several factors (Putnam, 1988) (Putnam has suggested this to be the case, but does not review the same factors). The political authority of cities, states and provinces is tailored to target an important portion of national emissions. These subnational entities have statutory authority to move forward in curbing carbon emissions and should use it. Secondly, nations might not always have the political capital to do it: given the political divisions around the climate question, companies, cities and states, along with philanthropists, might be in a better position than a federal government to cut emissions. Thirdly, nations do not always have the knowledge to do it. In a modern economy, given the level of development in the private sector and municipalities, for example, private companies and cities have better knowledge about how to reduce their own emissions. Federal governments should thus implement policy that takes advantage of this knowledge (e.g., market-based instruments to put a price on carbon). Finally, cities, states and companies can also better empower people with the moral sentiment to act upon climate change. This supports the idea that it is time to cast light on a more adequate distribution of the moral duties. I show elsewhere that the new polycentric governance regime requires a more detailed cartography of climate-related duties. In this chapter, I will simply show that these agents should be meaningfully included in the effort to fulfil duties of climate justice finance. These arguments are not meant to diminish the responsibilities of national governments, but rather to distribute duties to other agents in order to accelerate climate action and close the emissions gap.

Now, concerning the architecture of climate finance, I will first discuss one elementary mechanism that could be used to replenish the resources of climate justice finance. In the broader definition of climate finance, companies, states and individuals contribute to financing the fight against climate change by making crucial investments, creating green jobs, developing new technologies and preparing their environment for changes to come. These initiatives are broader in scope than the replenishing of climate justice finance resources in the narrow sense of the term. Also, we must note that companies, states and individuals have contributed and benefited from the cumulative historical emissions of different countries.

This is where carbon pricing comes into play. Carbon pricing already individualises the agents that currently contribute to GHG emissions. It follows a polluters pay principle (Gajevic Sayegh, Forthcoming). Those who presently wish to emit GHGs have to pay for it. Different carbon pricing initiatives – e.g., the Western Climate Initiative (WCI, between

American states and Canadian provinces), the Regional Greenhouse Gas Initiative (RGGI in the Northeastern United States) and the European Union Emissions Trading Scheme (EU ETS) – are already implemented in many parts of the world across different sectors (some may target exclusively industries, energy, transportation, construction, whereas other target a combination of these).

Carbon pricing mechanisms do not map exactly the principles of historical responsibility and capacity. They have the advantage of including more precisely the agents responsible, but they do not do so targeting the historical emissions of these agents and their respective capacity. In order to connect moral theory and political practice in the climate justice debate at this stage, I suggest that we apply the principles of historical responsibility and capacity to national governments and use carbon pricing to seek the contribution of subnational agents. This strategy allows us to apply the moral principles of capacity and historical responsibility while tracking the structure of climate governance already in place. At the global level, governments are the chief agents that negotiate, own explanations to and may place demands upon other nations. Subnational agents can play various roles at the global level (e.g., leadership), but the differentiated burdens of justice will not be modelled on them. Subnational agents can thus contribute to the national effort following the polluters pay principle, while national governments remain the site of application of the two central principles of climate justice. This solution reflects the idea that subnational agents are contributing to the national effort of climate justice finance (and of course to the climate mitigation effort more generally), while allowing the principles of climate justice to be applied at the national level. There is no need to apply the principles twice. The goals of climate finance in the broad sense, of mitigation and of adaptation, also fall on all the relevant agents, national and subnational. For the purposes of climate justice finance, the dual-level normative framework – with the principles of historical responsibility and capacity applied at the global level and carbon pricing mechanisms at the subnational level – seems to offer a good basis to make progress in this debate.

This completes the reasoning about guideline (a). To complete the reasoning about (b), I will show how carbon pricing mechanisms could effectively allow nations to reach their individual climate finance targets. Indeed, by distinguishing between these two levels of analysis, we can more easily see that the goal of climate justice finance is surprisingly attainable. Carbon pricing mechanisms provide more than enough funds for each country to fulfil its duty of global climate justice finance.

From a moral standpoint, putting a price on carbon is a way to connect the polluters with those who suffer from climate change (Gajevic Sayegh, Forthcoming). Pricing carbon to generate revenues and using these revenues to contribute to climate justice finance allows us to link, to a certain extent, the polluters pay principle with compensation for the harm done. This is a subnational level climate ethics reasoning that can thus be linked to the effort of climate justice finance. Now, from a political and economic standpoint, taking a recent estimate for the United States as an example, in 2011, the Congressional Budget Office (CBO) estimated that a cap-and-trade program that would have set a price of $20 per tonne of CO_2 (and increased that price by 5.6% each year thereafter) would raise a total of nearly $1.2 trillion during its first decade (CBO, 2013). This is an average of $115 billion generated each year, which would be more than enough to cover for the $29.9 billion the U.S. would have to transfer in total climate justice finance (this sum might eventually diminish because the GHG emissions cuts could offset the revenues generated by the carbon price increase). That is, even with a low price on carbon emissions, we would generate more than sufficient funds for climate justice finance (this would leave money to, say, compensate low-income households affected by a price increase in carbon-intensive goods or invest in green technologies).

What should count as climate justice finance?

If this reasoning is correct, we have made considerable progress in connecting the moral theory with the political practice of climate finance, notably by tailoring duties of justice to the new context of climate governance, integrating agents in a context of polycentric governance, interpreting principles of climate justice in practice (to further clarify what nations have duties of climate justice and suggest that this could be quantified following these principles) and connecting subnational initiatives with global climate justice finance efforts in order to show that this objective is attainable.

The next question, technical in nature, also has ethical implications – guideline (c): what should count towards the US$100 billion goal? The "Roadmap" document mentioned earlier claims that countries are well underway to meet the US$100 billion goal. This claim does not stand analysis. This is essentially because the US$100 billion goal belongs to the field on climate justice finance and not climate finance in the broad sense. The document's central claim falls short of addressing what should be its primary objective. It does not fill the requirements of climate justice finance.

The World Bank currently provides close to $11 billion in climate finance annually. It has pledged to increase its commitment by one-third. Together, multilateral development banks (MDBs) provide $27.4 billion every year to climate finance in developing countries.

From a normative standpoint, contributions made via the World Bank and other MDBs would fulfil the mission of climate finance under two conditions.

1 They must constitute *new and additional* funds. Investments that were planned before climate justice commitments were maid do not count towards the expected goal of climate justice finance. Similarly, standard development assistance budgets do not respect this condition.
2 They *do not contradict the objective* of climate justice finance (e.g., they do not have to be repaid). Loans cannot be qualified as climate justice finance in the narrow sense. They do not serve the purpose of justice following the basic principles of historical responsibility and capacity, which guide global climate finance.

These two conditions constitute necessary real-world additions to the principles of climate justice finance. For example, export credits or market-based loans should not be counted towards the $100 billion goal. Providing support to corporations from the developed countries to sell their products in developing countries is not what the latter countries – or anyone else – could qualify as a token of climate justice. A report by the Organisation for Economic Co-operation and Development (OECD, 2015) included export credits and market-based loans in its calculations, drawing criticism from developing countries. These criticisms are justified. If the overall target of justice is only being attained by mechanisms that contradict the mission of this target, we cannot reasonably say that the target is being met.

Connectedly, climate justice finance should not be considered as part of development assistance because it is meant to compensate for climate injustices. Condition (1) of new and additional funds would not be met. Other injustices can be compensated by principles of global distributive justice directed towards development. But principles of climate justice are meant to correct climate-related injustices (the portions attributable to the principles of historical responsibility and benefit) and to show fairness in cooperation to solve this crisis (the portion attributed to the principle of capacity, if we were at least abstractly to distinguish between these portions). Climate justice funds cannot be taken away from development assistance. This shows why having strict burden-sharing principles of climate justice is so important and why they have been so ardently debated in the literature (Bell, 2008; Miller, 2009; Posner & Sunstein, 2008; Posner & Weishbach, 2010; Shue, 2014). This chapter argues, however, that there was a missing element in this debate: the identification of the appropriate site of application for burden-sharing principles.

That is, the aggregation of what contributions should be counted towards the objective of climate finance has to be subject to the standards of climate justice. These normative guidelines are still lacking in major documents such as the "Roadmap," OECD and World Bank reports. Following on objective (c) – what should count as a contribution to climate finance – national governments' contributions also have to respect conditions (1) and (2) above. One straightforward way for countries to do so is to step up their commitments to the Green Climate Fund. Many governments have already made pledges to contribute to the GCF.

Note now that the calculation using the principles of historical responsibility and capacity were applied to distribute the burdens of climate justice finance between countries based on the $100 billion total sum. The calculation did not deduce the direct payments from the MDBs (I assume for now that we have these numbers available; I will show later that we do not). If we deduce from the total sum the contributions from MDBs, we could determine following the same methodology the new, and lower, envelope that each country would be responsible for.

To be more precise, we could raise two follow-up questions: whether the internal contributions of MDGs should follow the same methodology based on the principles of historical responsibility and capacity and whether the proportional contribution from each country to the budget of MDBs should be used to calculate its exact total contribution to climate justice finance. Strictly speaking, from an ethics standpoint, if the normative reasoning is correct, we should answer the two questions in the affirmative. This might, however, create a problem of over-determination. Over-determination might affect MDBs at the efficiency and political levels. MBDs can collect and distribute their own funds. Requiring them to follow the principles of historical responsibility and capacity following the same methodology would imply a political loss of side-lining agents that could otherwise be effective, and an efficiency loss in interfering with the decision-making process of these institutions. It is far more important for MDBs to follow criteria (1) and (2), which is applicable to their own decision-making structure, than for them to follow the principles of global climate justice tracking the contributions of each individual country. A position that would disregard the two follow-up questions above would still require all agents, including MDBs, to respect conditions (1) and (2), but allow MBDs to pursue their climate justice finance objectives. In terms of the contributions of each country, the latter position would thus only require us to subtract the total legitimate contributions by MDBs from the total $100 billion target. I believe this less-determined position, which is nonetheless quite demanding from a moral standpoint, to be warranted.

One problem we encounter, however, in climate roundtables, and in documents such as the "Roadmap" and the OECD reports, is that their numbers cannot be trusted. We do not have the total legitimate contributions from MBDs. It has been shown that most projects that were counted towards the objective of climate finance by OECD reports should not have been counted (Roberts & Weikmans, 2016). And it is not clear that all national contributions also have been subject to rigorous analysis.

Following this, I argue that:

1 The contributions by MDBs should follow conditions (1) and (2);
2 The contributions from individual countries should follow conditions (1) and (2), they need to track the principles of climate justice following the methodology given above, and they should be made to the Green Climate Fund;

3 The criteria for receiving funds from the GCF must follow the strictest standards of impact for mitigation, adaptation and green development.
4 Bilateral contributions, such as the ones made by China to other East Asian countries, would count as part of their total contribution provided they follow conditions (1) and (2).

Note that, following the principle of historical responsibility, all countries would have to contribute to climate justice finance (of course, many countries have virtually not contributed to historical emissions, and therefore their payments would be virtually zero). The inclusion of this principle on the one hand might create an incentive for countries to reduce their emissions if they wish to reduce their contributions, but this incentive is likely to be minimal, given that the calculation takes into account cumulative historical emissions. The central role of this principle is rather to demand for all countries that are truly responsible for causing the problem to jointly become part of the solution. This has a function of strengthening the conditions of cooperation. It has for effect to include in the major contributing countries China, India and Indonesia, for instance. Although these countries would not pay based on the principle of capacity, they will pay based on the principle of historical responsibility, as they have contributed to creating the problem. This would be the case, especially if considering emissions from 1990, the date of the first IPCC report. It would be less so if we started counting emissions since 1850 (which would raise nonetheless the question of excusable ignorance), but it would not be negligible given the considerable emissions of GHGs of newly industrialised countries in the past decades. To follow up on this argument, given their historical responsibility in creating the climate crisis, it seems fair to ask these countries to contribute to the global climate justice effort. The primary consequence of this is that a portion of the $100 billion sum would come from high-emitting developing countries. This in turn means that total contribution from developed countries would be slightly lower. This is a bullet that anyone endorsing the climate justice finance proposal defined in this chapter would have to bite.

Of course, these same countries might be beneficiaries of the GCF. Projects from regions in China, India and Indonesia might be approved by the GCF. In a way, these countries might contribute to their own project by funding the GCF, but this would not imply an efficiency loss. If the methodology of approval of the GCF is indeed rigorous, these funds will be well used. Also, given the current levels of climate-related investments in India and China, their climate justice payment will be rather small in comparison and would provide an incentive for rigorous projects funded by the GCF. Moreover, as mentioned and as I will argue, this will show commitment and strengthen the background conditions of cooperation for climate justice finance.

So far, it is unclear that countries will meet the $100 billion goal. The OECD, the UNFCCC Committee on Climate Finance 2016 report and the Roadmap published similar numbers advancing the current state of climate finance investments (UNFCCC, 2016). However, these numbers are based on the claims of developed countries. These claims do not respect the ethical criteria that would allow them to count towards the $100 billion objective of climate justice finance. The UNFCCC (2014) report was already critical of countries providing their own numbers, but it is not clear that the methodology has improved (UNFCCC, 2014). In the current context of Nationally Determined Contributions to climate change mitigation, it seems prima facie reasonable to expect countries to put forward their own contributions to climate finance, but this intuition is mistaken. Climate finance is a tool of climate justice. It aims at responding to the problems of climate justice. The approach that aimed to distribute GHG emissions as a way to implement principles of climate justice has failed. Climate finance offers the most efficient political forum to finally address one of the most contentious questions of climate justice: the distribution of burdens (IPCC, 2014). In comparison to the distribution of GHG emissions reductions (which is now left to countries Nationally Determined Contributions, NDCs), climate justice finance is as morally justified (if not more) and, politically, it is clearly more viable. That said, how much countries will contribute to climate justice finance cannot be left to the discretion of individual countries. It has to be done according to principles of climate justice, and it has to be overseen by the UNFCCC in the current context of climate governance. Otherwise, we would have eclipsed climate distributive justice out of climate change mitigation and of climate finance both. This proposal is a way to prevent this from happening.

A signal: building confidence and momentum

There is a final point to be addressed, point (d): the function of climate finance as a signal to build confidence and momentum. As we have seen so far, developed countries are failing to reassure the world that they will fulfil their climate justice finance pledges, both because the funds have not been mobilised and because the methodology for determining what should count as contributions does not meet the basic requirements of justice. Developed countries are not fulfilling their pledges, and this has to be stated clearly.

It is not currently possible to assess their pledges. Two things could improve this situation: transparency and oversight by the relevant agents. In this sense, including developing countries in the oversight of what counts as climate justice finance is not only required as a matter of just procedure, but would also increase the chances of actually meeting justice standards. Transparency and oversight have to be put in place by the UNFCCC to ensure that bilateral transfers, transfers to the GCF and transfers by MDBs all fulfil climate justice finance conditions. Insisting on a dubious methodology might undermine the basis for global climate finance cooperation. In a gesture of good faith, the overseeing of climate finance should be led by developing nations. Developing nations should not only be consulted, but they should have an active judgement on whether the countries that have duties of climate finance have been fulfilling these duties.

Ultimately, the signalling objective of climate justice finance is for developed countries to tell developing nations that they have the means to develop in a low-carbon way. For instance, it should be clear that projects will be funded to decrease emissions by shutting down existing coal-fired power plants and developing clean energy capacity instead.

The procedure that leads to this signalling needs to be transparent for that signal to be heard and trusted. This will in turn build confidence around the idea that the world is indeed moving towards a post-carbon economy. Climate justice finance can thus build trust and momentum. This is especially so because, by promoting low-carbon development in a way that is fair, climate justice finance would eliminate any comparative advantage to benefit from a carbon-based economy. It would therefore accelerate climate action. It is thus vital that we make sure that by 2020 the annual $100 billion funding is up and running.

Conclusion

Climate justice finance is at a crossroads. It is an effective instrument of climate justice as it could solve the longstanding problem of burden-sharing in global climate negotiations. Achieving the $100 billion goal is feasible in the present context. Also, a fine-grained distribution of moral duties allows us to map globally and domestically who are the agents responsible to fulfil these duties and what should be their contribution in monetary terms. I suggested that the principles of historical responsibility and capacity should be applied to determine the payment of national governments and that carbon pricing should be used to seek the contribution of subnational agents. This strategy allows us to use the moral principles of capacity and historical responsibility while tracking the structure of climate governance already in place, globally and domestically.

As a signal for green development, climate justice finance tells developing countries that development and climate change mitigation are compatible and that are given the means to do it. This signalling will only be effective if developing countries are included in the oversight of what is counted towards climate justice finance.

However, developed countries are failing to fulfil their pledges of climate justice finance. Countries are falling short of their commitments, even when including bilateral transfers, transfers to the GCF and transfers by MDBs. Moreover, the commitments that have been publicised are based on a misleading methodology. Recent reports that have attempted to show progress on their part are most likely undermining the basis of climate justice finance cooperation by basing their arguments on a deceptive methodology.

Climate justice finance is an instrument of climate justice and should be publicised as such. For this to happen, it is imperative that countries scale up their commitments to meet the $100 billion mark, do so following principles of climate justice, and that what counts as climate justice finance contributions follows ethical guidelines. Importantly, these roles accomplished by climate justice finance, by strengthening the background conditions of cooperation, should help to accelerate global climate action.

References

Antimiani, A., Costantini, V., Markandya, A., Paglialunga, E., & Sforna, G. (2017). The Green Climate Fund as an effective compensatory mechanism in global climate negotiations. *Environmental Science & Policy*, 77, 49–68. doi:10.1016/j.envsci.2017.07.015

Bell, D. (2008). Carbon justice? The case against a universal right to equal carbon emissions. In S. Wilks (Ed.), *Seeking environmental justice* (pp. 239–257). Amsterdam: Rodolphi.

CBO. (2013). *Effects of a carbon tax on the economy and the environment.* Congressional Budget Office. Retrieved from https://cbo.gov/publication/44223

Cui, L.-b., Zhu, L., Springmann, M., & Fan, Y. (2014). Design and analysis of the Green Climate Fund. *Journal of Systems Science and Systems Engineering*, 23(3), 266–299. doi:10.1007/s11518-014-5250-0

Dellink, R., Elzen, M. d., Aiking, H., Bergsma, E., Berkhout, F., Dekker, T., & Gupta, J. (2009). Sharing the burden of financing adaptation to climate change. *Global Environmental Change*, 19(4), 411–421. doi:10.1016/j.gloenvcha.2009.07.009

Dorsch, M. J., & Flachsland, C. (2017). A polycentric approach to global climate governance. *Global Environmental Politics*, 17(2), 45–64. doi:10.1162/GLEP_a_00400

EBRD, & GRI. (2011). *The low carbon transition.* Retrieved from https://ebrd.com/news/publications/special-reports/special-report-on-climate-change-the-low-carbon-transition.html.

Gajevic Sayegh, A. (2017). Climate justice after Paris: A normative framework. *Journal of Global Ethics*, 13(3), 344–365. doi:10.1080/17449626.2018.1425217

Gajevic Sayegh, A. (Forthcoming). Pricing carbon for climate justice. *Ethics, Policy & Environment.*

Gardiner, S. (2016). The feasible is political. In S. Gardiner & D. Weishbach (Eds.), *Debating climate ethics.* Oxford, UK: Oxford University Press.

GCF. (2014). *Decisions of the board: Eighth meeting of the board.* Bridgetown, Barbados: Green Climate Fund.

Hale, T. (2016). 'All hands on deck': The Paris Agreement and nonstate climate action. *Global Environmental Politics*, 3(16), 12–22. doi:10.1162/GLEP_a_00362

IPCC. (2014). *Summary for policy makers.* Contributions of Working Group III to the Fifth Assessment Report. Retrieved from https://ipcc.ch/pdf/assessment-report/ar5/wg3/ipcc_wg3_ar5_summary-for-policymakers.pdf.

Miller, D. (2001). Distributing responsibilities. *The Journal of Political Philosophy*, 9, 453–471.

Miller, D. (2009). Global justice and climate change: How should responsibilities be distrbuted? *The Tanner Lectures on Human Values*, 28, 119–156.

OECD. (2015). *Climate finance in 2013–14 and the USD 100 billion goal.* Organisation for Economic Co-operation and Development (OECD) in collaboration with Climate Policy Initiative (CPI).

Posner, E. A., & Sunstein, C. R. (2008). *Justice and climate change.* Harvard Project on International Climate Agreements, Belfer Center for Science and International Affairs, Harvard Kennedy School.

Posner, E. A., & Weishbach, D. (2010). *Climate change justice.* Princeton, NJ: Princeton University Press.

Putnam, R. D. (1988). Diplomacy and domestic politics: The logic of two-level games. *International Organization,* 427–460.

Roadmap. (2016). *Roadmap to US$100 billion.* Australia, Austria, Belgium, Bulgaria, Canada, Croatia, Cyprus, Czech Republic, Denmark, European Commission, Estonia, Finland, France, Germany, Greece, Hungary, Iceland, Ireland, Italy, Japan, Latvia, Liechtenstein, Lithuania, Luxembourg, Malta, Monaco, Netherlands, New Zealand, Norway, Poland, Portugal, Romania, Slovakia, Slovenia, Spain, Sweden, Switzerland, United Kingdom, and United States.

Roberts, T., & Weikmans, R. (2016). *Roadmap to where? Is the '$100 billion by 2020' pledge from Copenhagen still realistic?* Brookings Institution. Retrieved from https://brookings.edu/blog/planetpolicy/2016/10/20/roadmap-to-where-is-the-100-billion-by-2020-pledge-from-copenhagen-still-realistic/.

Shue, H. (2014). *Climate justice.* Oxford, UK: Oxford University Press.

UNFCCC. (2014). *Biennial assessment and overview of climate finance flows report.* Bonn, Germany: United Nations Framework Convention on Climate Change – Standing Committee on Finance.

UNFCCC. (2015). *Adoption of the Paris Agreement.* Paris. Retrieved from https://unfccc.int/sites/default/files/resource/docs/2015/cop21/eng/l09r01.pdf.

UNFCCC. (2016). *Biennial assessment and overview of climate finance flows report.* Bonn, Germany: United Nations Framework Convention on Climate Change – Standing Committee on Finance.

Widerberg, O., & Pattberg, P. (2015). International cooperative initiatives in global climate governance: Raising the ambition level or delegitimizing the UNFCCC? *Global Policy, 6*(1), 45–56. doi:10.1111/1758-5899.12184

Zelli, F., & Asselt, H. v. (2013). Introduction: The institutional fragmentation of global environmental governance: Causes, consequences, and responses. *Global Environmental Politics, 13*(3), 1–13. doi:10.1162/GLEP_a_00180

13

The inter-relationship between climate finance and climate justice in the UNFCCC

Tessa Sheridan and Tahseen Jafry

Introduction

With concern over climate change growing, and climate justice gaining more and more attention, the role of climate finance has become increasingly important – for tackling climate change and righting the injustice it causes. The United Nations Framework Convention on Climate Change (UNFCCC), the official platform for climate negotiations and action, plays an essential role in global climate action and aims to prevent global warming of over 2 degrees Celsius before excessive damage occurs. In achieving this ambitious objective, one of the principles set out by the UNFCCC is that developed countries, known as Annex I countries, should take the lead – as they are the source of the majority of both past and current GHG emissions and thus more responsible (UNFCCC, 2017a). These countries are expected to take mitigation action to make drastic cuts in their GHG emissions from 1990 levels and also provide finance to developing countries to support climate change action, beyond any current financial assistance they provide.

During the UNFCCC's COP15 meeting, developed countries agreed to strive towards the goal of providing $100 billion per year in climate finance to developing countries by 2020 (UNFCCC, 2009). However, research shows that the amount of finance necessary for mitigation and adaptation actions in developing countries far exceeds current climate finance levels – with estimates of mitigation needs approximated at over $600 billion per year (IEA, 2014; WEF, 2013) while adaptation estimates vary from $60 to $100 billion per year in main studies (IPCC, 2014). It does not seem that the $100 billion annual target set by the UNFCCC will be sufficient, and in addition to this, there is doubt over whether this target will even be achieved.

Many of the UNFCCC's funds are struggling – the amount pledged to the Least Developed Countries Fund (LDCF) falls short of what is needed and many projects remain unfunded (UNFCCC, 2016a); the available funds in the Special Climate Change Fund (SCCF) in 2014 only met 30% of the demand for priority projects submitted (SCF, 2014); and the future of the Adaptation Fund (AF) is uncertain due to lack of funding (UNFCCC, 2016b). The Green Climate Fund (GCF), the UNFCCC's newest fund, looks promising – with already $10.3 billion pledged as of March 2017 (GEF, 2017), a number far exceeding pledges made to other funds – however, it is yet to be seen if this will be sufficient to bridge the large finance gap that currently exists. With the financial costs of mitigating and adapting to climate change expected to increase further in the coming decades, it seems likely that the gap between what is needed and what is provided will continue to widen.

In addition to this lack of funding, there are also concerns that the wellbeing and needs of the most vulnerable people are not being represented or considered sufficiently in climate action, and it is unclear how climate justice is represented in UNFCCC climate finance. With climate finance essential for righting the injustices caused and worsened by climate change, it is vital to understand why it is continually falling behind and failing to reach those who need it most.

This conceptual chapter explores the inter-relationship between climate finance and climate justice within the UNFCCC. This is done through the development of a conceptual framework to provide a visual representation of the current UNFCCC climate finance landscape highlighting the constraints and bottlenecks to climate justice, and a refined framework to illustrate the structure of a framework which incorporates justice principles and provides recommendations for integrating justice into UNFCCC climate finance and better protecting the most vulnerable people.

Current UNFCCC climate finance framework

In order to understand how justice fits into the current climate finance landscape within the UNFCCC, a conceptual framework was developed – drawing from literature and UNFCCC documentation – to show the key principles, structure and relationships that shape UNFCCC climate finance (Figure 13.1). This methodology was selected as it allows a more comprehensive approach, providing a deeper understanding of the issues explored than empirical analysis could. A theoretical analysis of the current UNFCC climate finance structure also increases the external validity of this work, drawing on a wide range of existing literature. In addition, as such an approach has not yet been used in literature to analyse climate justice within climate finance, it also provides a novel analysis of the subject matter.

To communicate the conceptual framework clearly, a simple visual representation in the form of flow charts was used. This visual representation of the climate finance landscape helps to provide a better understanding of the finance landscape and how justice fits into it, as it provides greater clarity on the interaction between the mechanisms and principles which define the system.

This framework facilitated the identification of gaps and inefficiencies in the current UNFCCC climate finance structure, in relation to climate justice. For this purpose, the framework was assessed against several main principles of climate justice identified by the Mary Robinson Foundation for Climate Justice (2017), with areas within the framework highlighted for discussion where there appear to be gaps or obstacles to adhering to these principles:

- Respect and protect human rights
- Support the right to development
- Share benefits and burdens equally
- Ensure that decisions on climate change are participatory, transparent and accountable
- Highlight gender equality and equity
- Harness the transformative power of education for climate stewardship
- Use effective partnerships to secure climate justice.

Top-down structure with all responsibility on developed countries

Perhaps the most contentious issue in climate negotiations is the issue of responsibility. This issue has continually created a divide between developed and developing countries, and is particularly heated in the case of climate finance. Due to the historical "responsibility" for climate change of

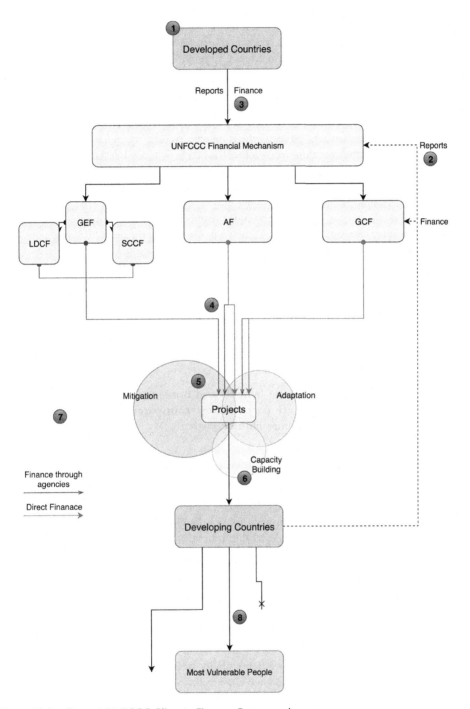

Figure 13.1 Current UNFCCC Climate Finance Framework.

Numbers represent key issues identified, corresponding to the discussion below: 1. Top-down structure with all responsibility on developed countries. 2. Only developed countries required to provide finance and reports 3. Lack of accountability and clarity surrounding finance goals. 4. Indirect and complicated access to finance for developing countries. 5. Lack of adaptation finance. 6. Lack and failure of capacity building. 7. Lack of support for development. 8. Lack of consideration of the most vulnerable people.

developed countries, it is generally viewed that they should therefore be responsible for reducing their own emissions *and* financing climate action in developing countries. However, the disputes over how much developed countries should have to provide and how accountable they should be held for past emissions is both intense and complicated.

The current UNFCCC climate finance framework puts the bulk of responsibility on developed countries, creating a top-down structure which perpetuates these disputes and hinders climate justice. This structure removes control and ownership of climate projects from developing countries, leading to resistance to projects which are perceived as only reflecting the interests of the donor country or implementing entity rather than their own needs (ODI, 2014). It also creates concerns of subordination, with developing countries simply having to accept how finance is being channelled to them while receiving little benefit, and puts too much focus on responsibility, thus detracting from issues such as how finance can be more effective and right current injustices. Although there is some merit in judging responsibility based upon contribution of emissions, in reality this would not offer a feasible solution. Vanderheiden (2015) highlights that following principles of responsibility based on contribution as suggested by some activists would put extremely demanding obligations on some developed countries, which would be entirely unrealistic both politically and economically. According to these observers, it is simply not possible for goals to be achieved unless there is a cohesive global effort.

Without a more equal sharing of responsibility within the UNFCCC, equal participation and a move towards partnership, climate negotiations will continue to be held back by disputes over responsibility, and the agenda of developed countries will continue to be pushed onto developing countries.

> **Justice principles breached: share benefits and burdens equally; ensure that decisions on climate change are participatory, transparent and accountable; use effective partnerships to secure climate justice**

Only developed countries required to provide finance and reports

The separation of countries into developed and developing in the UNFCCC no longer reflects the complex global economic landscape of today (Aglietta et al., 2015). In fact, developing countries continue to play a more dominant role in the global economy, and are increasingly funding climate action both domestically and in other developing countries (Ha et al., 2016). This domestic and "South-South" finance constitutes the majority of climate finance flows (Fankhauser et al., 2016). However, this has been overlooked in UNFCCC climate negotiations, and little effort has been made to record or track these flows (Ha et al., 2016). This is partly due to fear that recognising South-South climate finance in climate negotiations will remove responsibility and pressure from developed countries, and many developing countries still push for a definition of climate finance that limits it to finance provided by developed countries (Ha et al., 2016).

Developing countries also have lesser responsibility in providing reports to the UNFCCC, perpetuating the view of them as helpless and also creating large gaps in information. Although financial and administrative support may need to be provided to aid in the preparation of reports, this information is essential for incorporating justice into finance and creating equality between developed and developing countries.

The current discrepancy between finance and reports from developed and developing countries not only creates gaps in information which make it difficult for climate action to be participatory, transparent and accountable, but also creates unequal burden sharing and perpetuates mistrust between developed and developing countries rather than fostering partnership (Ha et al., 2016).

Justice principles breached: share benefits and burdens equally; ensure that decisions on climate change are participatory, transparent and accountable; use effective partnerships to secure climate justice

Lack of accountability and clarity surrounding finance goals

The voluntary nature and lack of accountability for pledges has meant that climate finance has continually fallen behind what is needed. Also, the lack of clarity surrounding how climate finance should be managed and delivered has led to disputes. While developing countries argue there is a lack of adequate, predictable and long-term finance, and developed countries are evading their responsibilities, developed countries stress the current tough economic conditions and express concern that developing countries are using climate change as an excuse to have their development funded (Okereke and Coventry, 2016). In addition, while developed countries have been supportive of encouraging private finance, developing countries have been insistent that counting it towards the financial obligations of developed countries is allowing them to dodge their responsibilities, and therefore only public finance should be counted (Vanderheiden, 2015; Yamineva, 2016). If agreement is not reached on these issues, and finance continues to lack accountability, the bulk of finance will continue to go towards projects which provide the most financial return and benefit for developed countries, and finance will continue to be held back by disputes.

Justice principles breached: ensure that decisions on climate change are participatory, transparent and accountable

Indirect and complicated access to finance for developing countries

In the UNFCCC, there have been issues of finance being too complicated to access, with the complex bureaucratic processes in place to ensure good performance causing procedures of access to be overly difficult and time consuming (ODI, 2014). Although this is aimed at improving the quality of projects and ensuring integrity, the indirect nature of finance has made it difficult for developing countries to access and make use of finance. Finance channelled through agencies leads to high administrative costs and thus watering down of already too low financial resources. Although direct access is incorporated into some funds, achieving accreditation is too difficult for many developing countries despite the readiness programmes available, and therefore only a small number of countries achieve direct access. Analysis of the GCF and AF, for example, which offer direct access, show that the potential of direct access modalities is not being realised – with only 36.2% of resources committed by the AF and 6.2% of resources committed by the GCF allocated to National Implementing Entities (Colenbrander et al., 2017).

Developing countries have argued that this is "inequitable and burdensome" and call instead for greater generosity (Urpelainen, 2012). This complicated access has meant that developing countries benefit less from climate finance than they otherwise could, thus creating unequal benefit sharing. The accreditation process in its current state makes it too difficult for local-level organisations and subnational governments, which often favour projects more beneficial to the most vulnerable people, to gain access to finance – instead favouring high-level government bodies and large-scale projects which do not address the needs and vulnerabilities of local communities (Colenbrander et al., 2017). The current dominance of indirect finance also means that developing countries have less control over climate finance, and as a result climate action is not truly "participatory" or equitable (Scoville-Simonds, 2016). In addition to this, a structure which limits developing countries' participation in financial decision-making and excludes local-level organisations has led to a dynamic in which donor interests frequently dominate the needs of the recipient, evoking an impression of developed country supremacy rather than equal partnership (Colenbrander et al., 2017).

> **Justice principles breached: share benefits and burdens equally; ensure that decisions on climate change are participatory, transparent and accountable; use effective partnerships to secure climate justice**

Lack of adaptation finance

Adaptation has historically received much less attention than mitigation in global climate negotiations, and there has been a significant disparity in the amount of finance dedicated to adaptation activities compared to mitigation (Okereke and Coventry, 2016; Yamineva, 2016). This is partly due to the framework of the UNFCCC, which gives developed countries the responsibly for finance and therefore the control over where it goes, as mitigation projects are often favoured for their greater benefit to the donor country and greater financial returns.

The GCF is set out to become the major channel for finance pledges to flow through, and aims to solve these issues by creating an equal balance between adaptation and mitigation. As of 2015 the majority of funding, in its first eight projects, has gone towards adaptation activities (Nhamo and Nhamo, 2016). However, this has caused some dispute, with a clear divide between developed and developing countries. Research shows that developed countries would prefer a lower share of funding to go towards adaptation, at an average of 46%, while developing countries would prefer a higher share for adaptation, at 56% on average (Fridahl and Linnér, 2016). The GCF's 50/50 mitigation/adaptation goal has caused discontent amongst developed countries that would prefer a higher share of funding to go towards mitigation. This can be seen in the clear difference in opinion concerning how much of the $100 billion pledge should be channelled through the GCF – with developed countries on average preferring approximately 44%, and developing countries averaging a much higher figure of 71% (Fridahl and Linnér, 2016). This may mean that some developed countries will opt to channel more finance through other funds or mechanisms instead of the GCF, and adaptation will continue to fall behind.

This has caused concern for many developing countries, for which vulnerability to climate change has made adaptation increasingly necessary and urgent, as even if emissions were immediately reduced to zero, inertia means that changes to climate systems would still occur for many years. Without greater support for adaptation, climate finance cannot protect the human rights of the most vulnerable people – as the effects of climate change are becoming increasingly severe and threatening their wellbeing and even survival (UNFCCC, 2010).

> **Justice principles breached: respect and protect human rights**

Lack and failure of capacity building

In implementing climate-related projects, there has often been a failure to fully consider how national policy and regulations and institutional capacity will affect the performance and outcomes of these projects (ODI, 2014). Developing countries differ in their ability to use finance efficiently and capture the economic benefits of climate projects (Román et al., 2016), with various factors such as political instability, lack of infrastructure, lack of knowledge and expertise and lack of advanced technology acting as barriers in many countries.

However, both capacity building and technology transfer continue to lag in UNFCCC climate finance, dominated by mitigation. Although attempts have been made towards funding capacity building, there has been a lack of adequate long-term finance, with donors losing interest and the governments of developing countries thus unable to sustain the momentum (Okereke and Coventry, 2016). Although attempts were made during COP21 to address issues of capacity building, there are still no official goals for capacity-building efforts and no real detail on mechanisms for achieving change (Okereke and Coventry, 2016).

Also, although capacity building, which has traditionally focused on building institutional capacity, education and training, has been the cornerstone of development assistance for many years, it has often failed to successfully achieve its desired objectives (Hope, 2011). This is due to several reasons: capacity building (a) has often concentrated simply on the transfer of knowledge from developed countries, (b) is supply-driven rather than demand-driven (Hope, 2011), (c) often faces conflict between donor and recipient interests, with donor interests frequently dominating (Lopes and Theisohn, 2003), and (d) has shown a lack of engagement at a local level, leading to a failure to consider context and determine the individual capacity deficits and development needs of recipient countries (Hope, 2011). This has led to a lack of ownership of capacity-building projects in developing countries and the perception of foreign imposition (Winkler and Dubash, 2016), subsequently leading to many projects having little success (Hope, 2011).

However, building the capacity of developing countries is essential in the fight against climate change. Without doing so, climate finance will continue to lack efficiency and impact, developing countries will struggle to draw meaningful benefits from projects, development will continually be hindered by climate change and cycles of local vulnerability will be perpetuated.

Justice principles breached: respect and protect human rights; support the right to development; share benefits and burdens equally

Lack of support for development

Despite the urgency of climate change and the need to act, for many developing countries high levels of poverty mean that their top priority is development rather than climate action. However, climate change threatens to worsen poverty and add a further barrier to development (World Bank, 2010), so it is therefore vital that efforts be made towards poverty eradication and climate action simultaneously. This is a difficult task, as development often leads to an increase in emissions, thus creating seemingly conflicting goals which are difficult to balance.

Many developing countries are concerned that the focus on low-carbon development and emissions reductions will be at the expense of other vital objectives such as improving energy access and economic growth. For example, shifting towards low-carbon energy often causes short-term rises in the cost of providing energy access, which is problematic in countries where energy access is already extremely low, and high levels of poverty mean affordability is key (Winkler and Dubash, 2016). This is worsened by the fact that the UNFCCC primarily use GHG metrics to select projects, with development benefits as an unrequired bonus. In the GCF, for example, there is no clear requirement, or preference for, development benefits in mitigation projects, and it is likely GHG metrics will be the main factor of consideration (Winkler and Dubash, 2016).

This shows a lack of integration between climate action and development goals in the UNFCCC. However, for climate action to achieve justice, it must also encourage development.

Developed countries have effectively used up the carbon budget for their own fossil fuel-based development, and have therefore both caused and benefited from climate change. Developing countries have not been able to do so and have also been deprived of the ability to develop in a similar manner without risking severe impacts from climate change. Instead, developing countries will be forced to pursue the untrodden path of low-carbon development. For this reason, advocates of a climate justice perspective observe that it is only just that developed countries use the economic benefits they have gained from fossil fuel development to help developing countries pursue development which is climate-friendly. Climate justice can therefore not be achieved with the current lack of support for development objectives.

Justice principles breached: support the right to development

Lack of consideration of the most vulnerable people

There are several issues which have led to climate finance often not reaching or benefiting those who truly need it.

The distribution of finance, although fairly equitable, does not always prioritise the most vulnerable countries. As the merits of mitigation projects are primarily judged on emission reduction potential based on a baseline scenario, this can lead to complications with countries with very low baseline levels of energy service being overlooked and thus missing out on potential low-carbon development opportunities (Mathy and Blanchard, 2016). The steps the UNFCCC have taken recently in channelling extra climate finance towards least developed countries (LDCs) and small island developing states (SIDS), although a step in the right direction, may also be problematic due to the rigidity of such groupings – as countries which are equally vulnerable but do not belong to these categories may therefore receive inadequate funding (Yamineva, 2016).

While the national distribution of climate finance has gained a lot of focus and been the subject of much scrutiny, subnational distribution has been largely ignored. Research by Barrett (2014) uses adaptation finance in Malawi as a case study to demonstrate the equity issues of finance distribution which occur within developing countries. This research shows that the poorest and most vulnerable communities and districts in Malawi receive the least adaptation finance, with the majority distributed to areas which already have better capacity to use funds, and more established networks – and this is a pattern repeated in other developing countries. In the Maldives, for example, research shows that the majority of adaptation activity has been focused in the main urban areas such as Malé and areas with tourist infrastructure, while smaller residential islands and rural communities have received little attention (Sovacool et al., 2017). There is also evidence of areas being selected due to political reasons in many developing countries, rather than true vulnerability (Barrett, 2014). It cannot be assumed that reaching the most vulnerable countries means that finance will reach the most vulnerable people. In fact, the most vulnerable often receive little benefit from climate action.

In addition to this, issues of equity and justice at a local level have received little attention compared to those at an international level. This poses a problem as climate action and adaptation projects have been shown to often exacerbate existing inequalities in developing countries, creating both "winners and losers" of climate projects (Thomas and Twyman, 2005; Mikulewicz, 2017) – where although some people are better off as the result of a project, others are instead worse off.

Research has also brought to light a variety of instances where climate projects have led to human rights issues and even environmental degradation (Richard, 2016; Okereke and Coventry, 2016; Jakob et al., 2015). Examples include the displacement of communities, the reinforcement of social inequalities, increasing gender inequalities and even creating conflict between government and communities due to changing land values (Okereke and Coventry, 2016; Wong, 2016). One example is the Barro Blanco hydroelectric power plant project carried out in Panama under the Clean Development Mechanism in 2011, where flooding of land caused the displacement of communities, negatively impacted the livelihoods of around 5,000 indigenous farmers and led to the loss of sacred ground and cemeteries. In addition to this, communities were not properly consulted about the project and reported that their concerns were not listened to, and there were reports of violent repression of peaceful protests leaving three dead and more injured (Carbon Market Watch, 2017).

Overall, UNFCCC climate finance shows a pattern of neglecting the needs of the most vulnerable people, leading to projects which often provide them with little or no benefit, and in some cases even exacerbate existing equality issues or cause harm.

Justice principles breached: respect and protect human rights; share benefits and burdens equally

Refined framework

As analysis of the current UNFCCC climate finance framework illustrated that the structure was not conducive to achieving climate justice, so a refined framework (Figure 13.2) which addresses the highlighted obstacles to justice and re-integrates justice principles was developed. This refined framework illustrates clearly the difference in structure between a framework which puts justice principles and achieving climate justice at its core and the current UNFCCC framework, allowing recommendations for moving forward and integrating climate justice into climate finance to be made.

An equal structure with shared responsibility

As shown in the refined framework (Figure 13.2), a more balanced and inclusive structure is suggested for UNFCCC climate finance to move forward – with developed and developing countries positioned horizontally at equal levels, creating a partnership, rather than developed countries at the top with finance flowing down to developing countries, as seen in the current framework (Figure 13.1). Moving away from the current framework within the UNFCCC, which is too heavily focused on responsibility and creates a divide between developed and developing nations, towards a more equal structure, which sees developing countries as active participants in climate finance rather than simply as recipients, is essential to make progress in both climate action and climate justice.

Although it may be that developed countries are responsible for causing climate change, and therefore for solving it, the reality is that developed countries alone cannot tackle such a huge issue, and a global effort is required. Rather than expending valuable time on disputes over responsibility and who should provide what, it is suggested that this debate must be put aside, due to the magnitude of the problems faced. As the developing countries will suffer the most if climate change is not addressed within a reasonable timeframe, it is suggested that it is in their interest to take on more responsibility, and essential to restore climate justice. More equal responsibility may be the boost needed to move past current discord towards more productive climate negotiations and finance, and therefore justice.

More equal responsibility would also give developing countries more control and ownership over climate action, allowing them to benefit more from climate finance and more effectively

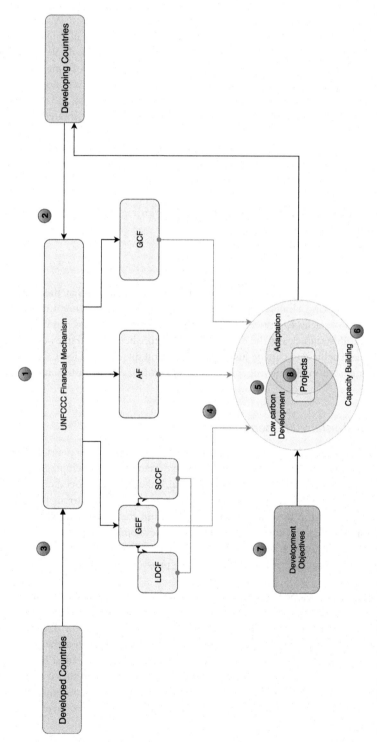

Figure 13.2 Refined UNFCCC Climate Finance Framework.

Numbers shown represent the solutions to the issues identified in the current framework and also correspond to the discussion below: 1. An equal structure with shared responsibility. 2. Developing countries contributing finance and reports. 3. Greater accountability and clarity of finance goals. 4. Direct access to finance for developing countries. 5. More support for adaptation. 6. Greater levels of capacity building. 7. Integration of development objectives. 8. The most vulnerable people at the centre of climate finance.

address their own needs. Although this lack of control of developing countries often stems from concern within the global community about corruption and public fund mismanagement, this concern is often excessive and fails to recognise and take into consideration the individual situations of each country. Creating a more equal power balance is essential for moving forward; however, as corruption and fund mismanagement are still very real issues, they must be taken into consideration when creating this balance.

Creating a dynamic of participation, equal burden and benefit-sharing, partnership within the UNFCCC is essential for climate finance to better address equity issues and achieve climate justice. This can be achieved in part by requiring reporting and financial contributions from developing countries, increasing accountability and clarity of finance goals and ensuring finance is accessible to developing countries – as will be subsequently discussed.

Developing countries contributing finance and reports

Requiring developing countries to also provide reports and contribute to finance would create more productive relations between developed and developing countries, and could stimulate the shift from current dispute-filled negotiations towards a unified global effort – as it creates a more inclusive framework. This would not only lessen the pressure on developed countries, which has caused reluctance and tension, but as previously mentioned would give developing countries more control over finance and projects. It would also help to unlock information and resources, which are vital for both climate action and incorporating justice into climate finance. Climate finance cannot be successful in achieving the goals set out by the UNFCCC without the inclusion of developing countries, and a move away from climate finance as "aid" towards climate finance as a partnership for tackling climate change.

It is important to note, however, that it is not suggested that developing countries should take on completely equal responsibility as developed countries, but simply more than they currently do. In fact, developed countries should continue to provide much larger amounts of finance to the UNFCCC, as this is only fair. However, it should be recognised that developing countries have an important part to play, and their contributions are essential in meeting the UNFCCC's climate and finance goals. As there are already large climate finance flows within and between developing countries (Ha et al., 2016), creating greater equality within the UNFCCC would not require extra financial responsibility from developing countries but simply recognition and reporting of existing finance and integration with the UNFCCC financial mechanism, with assistance to ensure the necessary resources to do so are available. Although developing countries may fear that this will create unrealistic expectations and excessive responsibility, showing leadership and initiative could in fact push developed countries to fulfil their own financial commitments, and help to soothe the strained and contentious global relations undermining climate negotiations by creating more trusting and united relationships between developed and developing countries (Ha et al., 2016).

Greater accountability and clarity of finance goals

A structure which puts more responsibility on developing countries rather than the whole burden on developed countries, as discussed, would create a more balanced power dynamic, which should help to settle disputes over how finance goals are met. It may also encourage developed countries to pledge more. However, in addition to this, measures to increase accountability over meeting pledges would help to unlock finance essential for achieving climate justice. This requires finance goals to be more specific, with greater clarity over how they should be met, in order to reach agreement on recurring disputes and move towards a more unified structure with developed and developing countries working in partnership to solve climate change issues.

Direct access to finance for developing countries

Increasing direct access to finance for developing countries would make financial resources more accessible – cutting administrative costs and increasing control over finance and projects – thus creating a financial structure that increases the agency of developing countries and moves climate finance governance towards equity and justice. Measures should be put in place to either ensure all developing countries have direct access to finance while maintaining integrity and transparency, or ensure that the accreditation process is achievable for all developing countries and sufficient assistance in achieving the necessary capacity to access finance directly is provided. Local-level organisation and government bodies should also be encouraged and assisted in achieving direct access accreditation, to create a more devolved system which supports participation on all levels – with literature suggesting this could help achieve greater levels of justice (Colenbrander et al., 2017).

More support for adaptation

Adaptation is a vital part of achieving climate justice, as it is needed to protect the most vulnerable who are already suffering, and more equality between adaptation and mitigation finance would help to realise climate justice within the UNFCCC climate finance framework. A more balanced framework which gives developing countries more control and involvement in climate finance would likely bring about greater support for adaptation, as it is often a more pressing concern. In addition, more integration between adaptation and mitigation projects could aid this, supporting both needs simultaneously – as well as a move towards framing mitigation projects as low-carbon development, which increases developing countries' capacity to adapt to climate change themselves. Although mitigation is undoubtedly essential for meeting climate change goals, without greater support for adaptation, achieving climate justice is not possible as the most vulnerable people will continue to be at risk. The GCF represents a step in the right direction by balancing its focus on mitigation and adaptation, and this progress should continue.

Greater levels of capacity building

Rather than capacity building being separated from climate action projects, and receiving comparatively low levels of finance, carrying out climate projects through the lens of capacity building would increase the effectiveness of projects and their benefits for recipient countries.

Funding many smaller-scale projects can lead to high transaction costs (Mathy and Blanchard, 2016; Steckel et al., 2017), decreasing the efficiency of climate finance. Also, many small projects will not bring about the transformational change that the UNFCCC seeks, but rather only incremental change – with research into projects funded by the LDCF finding that they were "fragmented" and lacked "integration" and "efficacy" (Sovacool et al., 2017). Instead, funding capacity building to increase the capability of developing countries to carry out climate projects themselves and increase their adaptability to climate change could be more effective in leading to sustained and "transformational" change.

Although, as previously mentioned, capacity building has historically shown low success rates in achieving development objectives, it is essential to effective climate finance, and a more nuanced approach is needed. A more nationalised method of capacity building and development, with developing countries taking responsibility for capacity building while donor countries take on a supportive role, has been suggested (Hope, 2011). This would require a move away from reliance on the external transfer of knowledge from developed countries, towards recognising local capacities and instead building knowledge (Hope, 2008). This approach could reduce the perception of developing countries that developed countries are imposing and exercising control over them, increase ownership of projects and increase the consideration of national needs and priorities – therefore improving the success rates of capacity-building projects (Winkler and Dubash, 2016). This in turn could increase the efficacy and benefits gained from climate projects, and create a better synergy between climate and development.

Integration of development objectives

Climate change and development are inextricably linked, as not only does climate change pose a serious threat to development progress, but advancing development typically increases climate resilience and adaptability to climate change. This relationship is important, as it illustrates that without simultaneously addressing development objectives, the amounts of finance required for climate action will be significantly greater, and the injustices caused by climate change will become progressively more severe. It is also crucial that in dealing with climate change, developing countries are not denied the right to development, and therefore the advantages which come with it that developed countries have benefitted from. However, for climate change goals to be met, this development cannot focus on fossil fuels, forcing developing countries to pursue the untrodden path of low-carbon development – or face the consequences of climate change. Therefore, developing countries' assistance in pursuing low-carbon development must be a crucial part of climate finance for it to be just. However, climate action and development have existed for too long in isolation, meaning that the important relationship between climate and development has been largely ignored in UNFCCC climate finance.

Integrating development goals into climate goals and projects creates a greater focus on development as part of the fight against climate change, and makes use of the synergies which exist between climate finance and development. Without integration of development goals, justice principles are likely to continually fall behind as supporting development takes a back seat to climate action. Also, research shows that climate actions are more likely to be successful in recipient countries if they simultaneously address development objectives (Steckel et al., 2017). This is because greater focus on development goals increases support and ownership of climate projects in developing countries, as there are more benefits for the country itself.

In addition, linking climate finance with national development strategies would ensure that specific and varying regional needs and vulnerabilities are considered and met, and therefore the most vulnerable people are protected. This will require a move away from the GHG metrics favoured by the UNFCCC in allocating funds and selecting projects, towards more holistic metrics which are development and people-centred.

The most vulnerable people at the centre of climate finance

Protecting those who are the most vulnerable to the effects of climate change is a vital part of achieving climate justice, as these people do not have the means or capability to adapt to the effects of climate change and will therefore suffer the most. However, it is evident that the needs of the most vulnerable have not been a key consideration in the decisions made by the UNFCCC regarding climate finance, and the benefits which reach them seem to be few and far between.

For climate finance to achieve protection of the most vulnerable people, they must be put at the heart of climate action, finance and projects. The previously suggested refinements to the UNFCCC climate finance framework (Figure 13.2) should pave the way towards a climate finance landscape which is more considerate and inclusive of the needs of vulnerable people, but further measures are needed to ensure this goal. The requirements and wellbeing of the most vulnerable must be core considerations in the allocation and implementation of projects. This would help to ensure that human rights issues and equity issues at a local level are fully considered in the implementation of projects, encourage more equitable allocation of funds, and increase the likelihood of finance reaching, and directly benefitting, those who need it most.

Discussion

Through the development of the current UNFCCC climate finance framework, it was identified that several justice principles are being neglected and breached, and there are many gaps and obstacles to achieving climate justice (Table 13.1).

Three of the climate justice principles that were found to be breached – sharing benefits and burdens equally; ensuring that decisions on climate change are participatory, transparent and accountable; and using effective partnerships to secure climate justice – can be attributed to the same structural problem within the UNFCCC framework, and were often breached in conjunction. These issues are linked in that they stem from the dynamics between developed and developing countries, in which there is a clear divide stemming from unequal power relations. The principles set out by the UNFCCC, which place developed countries at the top of climate finance, with nearly full responsibility for providing finance to developing countries, have perpetuated this problematic dynamic and allowed the contentious nature of global negotiations to continue. Wen and Xun (2016), for example, state that the financial pressure put on developed countries by developing countries, and the UNFCCC, has led developed countries to often evade their financial responsibilities rather than encouraging them to pledge more. These principles have also caused finance to become exclusionary – not fully recognising existing climate finance flows in developing countries, not requiring reporting to the same level as developed countries and overall not acknowledging that developing countries can play an important part in achieving climate finance goals. This has not only removed control and ownership from developing countries, which only reinforces current power imbalances, but also perpetuates the resentment and mistrust that has festered in climate negotiations between developing and developed nations. With the UNFCCC climate finance framework displaying a clear pattern of uncooperative dynamics, it is not possible for it to achieve climate justice and equity.

These geopolitical disputes have led to other critical issues being overlooked, with the justice principle of supporting development found to be lacking within the structure. It is evident that this is due to the disconnect within the UNFCCC between climate finance and development goals that is shown throughout the framework – as although climate projects are often carried out by development agencies such as the UNDP, these projects often focus solely on climate issues without the integration of broader development goals, and also, inversely, development projects also tend to give little consideration to climate change issues. Issues such as capacity building and development benefits are very much put to the side, seen as bonus benefits or projects rather than an interrelated part of climate action and the bigger picture goal of low-carbon development. These issues are also compounded by the previously discussed dynamics between developed and developing countries, where developed countries hold responsibility and therefore control and power over finances, leading to climate action often failing to take into consideration the

Table 13.1 An overview of the issues discussed in this chapter, along with the way they are addressed by the current and the refined frameworks.

Issue	Current framework	Refined framework
Responsibility and Power Balance	The UNFCCC climate finance structure puts the bulk of responsibility on developed countries and therefore creates a dynamic where developing countries lack control and climate finance often fails to address their needs.	Suggests an equal partnership between developed and developing countries, to increase the participation of developing countries in decision making and allow them to better address their needs.
Contribution to Climate Finance	The UNFCCC climate finance structure puts all responsibility on developed countries to contribute to climate finance goals, ignoring the potential of developing countries, creating contentious relations and causing large gaps in finance and information.	Suggests that the contribution of developing countries to climate finance and reporting of existing climate finance could reduce tension, encourage developed countries to pledge more, unlock vital resources and information and give developing countries more control over finance and projects.
Finance Goals	There is currently a lack of clarity surrounding climate finance goals – how they should be met, used and governed – causing disputes and slow progress. The voluntary nature of pledges also means there is a lack of accountability for achieving goals.	Suggests that making climate finance goals more specific in how they should be met and managed, in addition to creating a more balanced power dynamic between developed and developing countries, would encourage greater accountability and greater progress towards achieving finance goals.
Access to Finance	The current UNFCCC climate finance structure makes it difficult for developing countries to access finance and discourages local-level involvement. Although the GCF and AF have direct access modalities, these are not reaching their potential. This has led to diluted resources and a dominance of large-scale projects with little benefit to recipient countries.	Suggests integrating direct access into all funds and increasing support for accreditation to ensure it is achievable for all developing countries. Also suggests encouraging and assisting accreditation for bodies at different levels – including subnational government and local organisations – to help better address the needs of, and provide greater benefit to, the most vulnerable people.
Adaptation	There is a lack of support for adaptation in the current UNFCCC climate finance landscape, despite the GCF being a step towards this. This is due to a system which gives developed countries more control over finance and projects, leading to more profitable mitigation projects being favoured.	Suggests that creating more equal control and participation between developed and developing countries would encourage greater support for adaptation projects. In addition to this greater integration of mitigation and adaptation projects, and low-carbon development goals, it is suggested to address multiple needs and increase adaptive capacity.

(Continued)

Table 13.1 (Continued)

Issue	Current framework	Refined framework
Capacity Building	A lack of capacity in developing countries has led to climate finance and projects lacking efficacy and hindered developing countries ability to draw benefit from them. Despite this, capacity-building initiatives have been lacking in the UNFCCC, and have also failed due to focusing too heavily on institutional capacity and knowledge transfer.	Suggests that capacity building should be integrated into climate finance and projects as an overarching goal – as it is essential to increase the efficacy of climate finance and increase developing countries' ability to carry out climate projects independently. A more nuanced approach is required, which is more nationalised and focuses on using local capacities while developed countries take on a supporting role, and moves towards building knowledge rather than transferring it.
Development	In many developing countries, high levels of poverty mean that development objectives take priority over climate change measures. At the same time, climate change threatens to hinder development. Despite this important relationship, development objectives have received little recognition in UNFCCC climate finance. Due to climate change, developing countries have been denied the opportunity to develop in the same way as developed countries without risking serious harm. It is therefore essential for justice to be achieved that climate finance aids developing countries in pursuing low-carbon development.	Suggests that assisting developing countries in pursuing low-carbon development is essential to achieve climate justice. Development goals should therefore be integrated into climate finance, aiming to make use of the synergies between climate finance and development and ensure that in tackling climate change, development does not take a back seat. This would have the benefit of strengthening developing countries' ability to deal with the effects of climate change themselves and increasing protection of the most vulnerable people.
Protection of the Most Vulnerable	The UNFCCC climate finance structure shows a lack of consideration of the needs and protection of the most vulnerable people. With a global perspective and heavy focus on mitigation, local-level issues relating to justice have often been overlooked, leading to finance not reaching or benefiting those who need it most.	Suggests that the previously suggested refinements to the UNFCCC climate finance structure should help create a landscape which is more considerate of the needs of the most vulnerable people. In addition, the most vulnerable people must be central to decisions made regarding climate finance, and a more local-level focus is needed.

priorities of the recipient developing countries (ODI, 2014). This is despite research showing that climate finance would be more effective if it were to simultaneously address the development strategies of developing countries (IPCC, 2014). Climate change and development are inextricably linked, and therefore attempting to hold climate finance separately from development goals cannot be effective in reaching the UNFCCC's goal of low-carbon, climate-resilient development, or righting the injustices caused by and worsened by climate change.

The climate justice principle of protecting human rights was also found to be neglected throughout UNFCCC climate finance. These issues stem from a structure which shows a failure to put people, especially those who are most vulnerable, first. Climate justice is a human-centred approach to climate action; however, climate finance within the UNFCCC does not truly integrate human rights. This is clear throughout the literature, with issues of human rights abuses (Jakob et al., 2015; Okereke and Coventry, 2016; Richard, 2016; Wong, 2016), inequitable distribution of funds (Barrett, 2014; Mathy and Blanchard, 2016; Sovacool et al., 2017; Yamineva, 2016) and the deficiency in adaptation funding (Okereke and Coventry, 2016; Yamineva, 2016), supporting the fact that the most vulnerable people are placed at the bottom of the current framework.

The refined framework aims to address these issues by re-integrating justice principles where they were found to be lacking, showing the disparity between a just framework and the current one and suggesting the first steps for moving forward. Despite the significant differences between the current UNFCCC climate finance framework and the refined framework, the relationships between the components and justice principles mean that addressing one will have a domino effect, in that it could precipitate progress in other areas. Addressing the inequitable responsibility and power distribution of climate finance and giving developing countries more responsibility and control will in turn facilitate greater focus on development objectives and countries' individual needs, and this will then help to protect human rights and those who are most vulnerable. Although further measures are necessary to ensure that the benefits of climate finance reach the most vulnerable, and this cannot be guaranteed, changing these dynamics would be a large step forward for achieving climate justice in climate finance.

As these structural issues and problematic dynamics identified within the UNFCCC climate finance framework are far-ranging issues stemming from global relations, bureaucracy and politics, they are relevant in wider climate finance, climate negotiations and action, and addressing them could have far-reaching benefits.

Conclusions and recommendations

The purpose of climate finance in the UNFCCC is to restore the imbalance created by the differing responsibilities and capabilities of developed and developing countries and address climate injustices by providing financial resources for developing countries to carry out climate action (UNFCCC, 2017b). However, it has been shown that climate justice is largely absent within the UNFCCC climate finance framework. A system designed to create justice cannot do so if justice principles are not adhered to. As a result, climate finance under the UNFCCC is insufficient for achieving its goals, not reaching the most vulnerable and has focused too heavily on emission reduction rather than restoring and ensuring justice. However, as the UNFCCC have played a vital role in leading global climate negotiations, understanding the relationship between climate finance and climate justice within the UNFCCC climate finance framework is essential in order to progress towards achieving climate justice.

Through the development of the conceptual frameworks, several key patterns and themes have been identified – namely, the tension and animosity between developing and developed countries, the disconnect between climate action and development, and the neglect of the most vulnerable people. Based on this, three key recommendations are made: (1) climate finance should be a global effort, with both developed and developing countries participating in climate action and climate finance; (2) more integration is needed between climate finance objectives and development objectives; and (3) the needs and protection of the most vulnerable people and communities should be central to climate finance.

These recommendations should provide a starting point for climate finance under the UNFCCC, and perhaps broader climate financing and even climate action, to integrate justice and reach the poorest and most vulnerable people. However, this is not the only way forward, and other alternative solutions may need to be considered. The extent to which justice can ever truly be realised in an international regime such as the UNFCCC, which is dominated by economic and geopolitical interests and slow and bureaucratic processes, is questionable. Perhaps decentralising climate finance in order to make it more reactive, appropriate to national needs and characteristics, and beneficial to countries themselves would be preferential and more conducive to justice. Alternatively, finance for climate action could be channelled through another body or bodies such as National Development Banks. The UNFCCC might be invaluable for creating global agreements for emission reductions and climate action; however, perhaps it is not the most suitable channel for climate-just financing as it stands, and more research is required to explore other potential options for channelling climate finance further.

References

Aglietta, M., et al., 2015. Financing Transition in an Adverse Context: Climate Finance Beyond Carbon Finance. *International Environmental Agreements*, 15, 403–420.

Barrett, S., 2014. Subnational Climate Justice? Adaptation Finance Distribution and Climate Vulnerability. *World Development*, 58, 130–142.

Carbon Market Watch, 2017. *Campaigns: Barro Blanco – Large Hydro Project, Panama*. [online] Available at: http://carbonmarketwatch.org/category/barro-blanco-large-hydro-project-panama/ [Accessed April 10, 2017].

Colenbrander, S., Dodman, D., and Mitlin, D., 2017. Using Climate Finance to Advance Climate Justice: The Politics and Practice of Channelling Resources to the Local Level. *Climate Policy*, 2017, 1–14.

Fankhauser, S., et al., 2016. Where Are the Gaps in Climate Finance? *Climate and Development*, 8(3), 203–206.

Fridahl, M., and Linnér, B.-O., 2016. Perspectives on the Green Climate Fund: Possible Compromises on Capitalization and Balanced Allocation. *Climate and Development*, 8(2), 105–109.

GEF, 2017. *Funding*. [online] Available at: www.thegef.org/about/funding [Accessed February 12, 2017].

Ha, S., Hale, T., and Ogden, P., 2016. Climate Finance in and Between Developing Countries: An Emerging Opportunity to Build On. *Global Policy*, 7(1), 102–108.

Hope, K.R., 2008. *Poverty, Livelihoods, and Governance in Africa: Fulfilling the Development Promise*. New York: Palgrave Macmillan.

Hope, K.R., 2011. Investing in Capacity Development: Towards an Implementation Framework. *Policy Studies*, 32(1), 59–72.

IEA, 2014. *World Energy Investment Outlook*. Paris: International Energy Agency. [online] Available at: www.iea.org/publications/freepublications/publication/WEIO2014.pdf [Accessed February 2, 2017].

IPCC, 2014. *Climate Change 2014: Mitigation of Climate Change*. Contribution of Working Group III to the Fifth Assessment Report of the Intergovernmental Panel on Climate Change. Cambridge: Cambridge University Press.

Jakob, M., Steckel, J.C., Flachsland, C., and Baumstark, L., 2015. Climate Finance for Developing Country Mitigation: Blessing or Curse? *Climate and Development*, 7(1), 1–15.

Lopes, C., and Theisohn, T., 2003. *Ownership, Leadership, and Transformation: Can We Do Better for Capacity Development?* London: Earthscan.

Mathy, S., and Blanchard, O., 2016. Proposal for a Poverty Adaptation-Mitigation Window Within the Green Climate Fund. *Climate Policy*, 16(6), 752–767.

Mikulewicz, M., 2017. Politicizing Vulnerability and Adaptation: On the Need to Democratize Local Responses to Climate Impacts in Developing Countries. *Climate and Development*, 10(1), 18–34.

Mary Robinson Foundation for Climate Justice, 2017. *Principles of Climate Justice*. [online] Available at: www.mrfcj.org/principles-of-climate-justice/ [Accessed February 2, 2017].

Nhamo, G., and Nhamo, S., 2016. Paris (COP21) Agreement: Loss and Damage, Adaptation and Climate Finance Issues. *International Journal of African Renaissance Studies – Multi-, Inter- and Trans disciplinarity*, 11(2), 118–138.

ODI, 2014. *Climate Finance: Is It Making a Difference? A Review of the Effectiveness of Multilateral Climate Funds*. [online] Available at: www.odi.org/publications/8518-climate-finance-making-difference-review-effectiveness-multilateral-climate-funds [Accessed February 15, 2017].

Okereke, C., and Coventry, P., 2016. Climate Justice and the International Regime: Before, During, and After Paris. *WIREs Climate Change*, 7, 834–851.

Richard, V., 2016. Injecting Justice into Climate Finance: Can the Independent Redress Mechanism of the Green Climate Fund Help? *2016 Berlin Conference on Transformative Global Climate Governance "après Paris" Session: A New Institutional Landscape après Paris?*, 24 May 2016.

Román, M.V., Arto, I., and Ansuategi, A., 2016. *What Determines the Magnitude of the Economic Impact of Climate Finance in Recipient Countries? A Structural Decomposition of Value-added Creation Between Countries.* BC3 Working Paper Series 2016-01. Bilbao, Spain: Basque Centre for Climate Change (BC3).

SCF, 2014. *Fifth Review of the Financial Mechanism: Technical Paper.* SCF doc SCF/TP/2014/1. [online] Available at: http://unfccc.int/files/cooperation_and_support/financial_mechanism/standing_committee/application/pdf/technical_paper_fifth_review_of_the_financial_mechanism_18112014__final.pdf [Accessed February 13, 2017].

Scoville-Simonds, M., 2016. The Governance of Climate Change Adaptation Finance: An Overview and Critique. *International Development Policy*, 7.1.

Sovacool, B.K., Linner, B.-O., and Klein, R.J.T., 2017. Climate Change Adaptation and the Least Developed Countries Fund (LDCF): Qualitative Insights From Policy Implementation in the Asia-Pacific. *Climatic Change*, 140, 209–226.

Steckel, J.C., Jakob, M., Flachsland, C., Kornek, U., Lessmann, K., andEdenhofer, O., 2017. From Climate Finance Toward Sustainable Development Finance. *WIRE's Climate Change*, 8(1).

Thomasa, D.S.G., and Twyman, C., 2005. Equity and Justice in Climate Change Adaptation Amongst Natural-Resource-Dependent Societies. *Global Environmental Change*, 15, 115–124.

UNFCCC, 2009. *Decision 2/CP.15: Copenhagen Accord.* UN doc FCCC/CP/2009/11/Add.1. [online] Available at: http://unfccc.int/resource/docs/2009/cop15/eng/11a01.pdf [Accessed February 7, 2017].

UNFCCC, 2010. *Fact Sheet: The Need for Adaptation.* [online] Available at: <http://unfccc.int/files/press/application/pdf/adaptation_fact_sheet.pdf

UNFCCC, 2016a. *Report of the Global Environment Facility to the Conference of the Parties.* UN doc FCCC/CP/2016/6. [online] Available at: www.thegef.org/sites/default/files/documents/UNFCCC_report.pdf [Accessed February 11, 2017].

UNFCCC, 2016b. *Report of the Adaptation Fund Board.* UN doc FCCC/KP/CMP/2016/2. [online] Available at: www.adaptation-fund.org/wp-content/uploads/2016/09/AFB_report_2016.pdf [Accessed February 10 2017].

UNFCCC, 2017a. *First Steps to a Safer Future: Introducing the United Nations Framework Convention on Climate Change.* [online] Available at: http://unfccc.int/essential_background/convention/items/6036.php [Accessed February 9, 2017].

UNFCCC, 2017b. *Understanding Climate Finance.* [online] Available at: http://bigpicture.unfccc.int/content/climate-finance.html [Accessed February 13, 2017].

Urpelainen, J., 2012. Strategic Problems in North–South Climate Finance: Creating Joint Gains for Donors and Recipients. *Environmental Science & Policy*, 21, 14–23.

Vanderheiden, S., 2015. Justice and Climate Finance: Differentiating Responsibility in the Green Climate Fund. *The International Spectator*, 50(1), 31–45.

Wen, Z., and Xun, P., 2016. Study on the Demand of Climate Finance for Developing Countries Based on Submitted INDC. *Advances in Climate Change Research*, 7, 99–104.

Winkler, H., and Dubash, N.K., 2016. Who Determines Transformational Change in Development and Climate Finance? *Climate Policy*, 16(6), 783–791.

Wong, S., 2016. Can Climate Finance Contribute to Gender Equity in Developing Countries? *Journal of International Development*, 28, 428–444.

World Bank, 2010. *World Development Report 2010: Development and Climate Change.* Washington, DC: World Bank.

World Economic Forum, 2013. *The Green Investment Report.* [online] Available at: www3.weforum.org/docs/WEF_GreenInvestment_Report_2013.pdf [Accessed February 2, 2017].

Yamineva, Y., 2016. Climate Finance in the Paris Outcome: Why Do Today What You Can Put Off Till Tomorrow? *RECIEL*, 25(2), 174–185.

14

Carbon pricing and climate justice

Design elements for effective, efficient and equitable greenhouse gas emissions reductions

Edward Cameron

Introduction

The author has worked on climate justice for two decades. He has drafted UN Human Rights Council Resolutions on the issue; designed intergovernmental processes advocating for climate justice; designed training modules on climate justice for development practitioners at multilateral development banks; created philanthropic funds to support climate justice; and has produced a large volume of research for think tanks, non-governmental organisations and academic institutions. Drawing on this legacy of work, this chapter provides a set of design elements for carbon pricing, informed by climate justice, and with the goal of ensuring effective, efficient and equitable greenhouse gas emissions reductions in a Paris-compliant world.

The first section looks at the increasing use of carbon pricing as a means to hold global average temperature to well below 2 degrees Celsius. The case is made for carbon pricing as an effective means to drive down greenhouse emissions and mobilise climate finance; an efficient way to incentivise the changes needed in investment, production and consumption patterns; and an equitable approach to sharing both the burdens and opportunities of the transition to a low-carbon economy. However, this section is also clear in stating the pitfalls of poorly designed carbon pricing mechanisms.

This second section of the chapter presents the intellectual origins and the key principles of climate justice. Among these are the need to avoid the manifest injustice to vulnerable populations by "holding the increase in the global average temperature to well below 2 degrees Celsius above pre-industrial levels and to pursue efforts to limit the temperature increase to 1.5 degrees Celsius above pre-industrial levels" (UNFCCC, 2015, p. 22); the need to respect, protect and fulfil human rights when addressing climate change; the need to prioritise the marginalised and vulnerable when designing climate policy; the importance of overcoming intersecting inequalities when building resilience; the value of participatory, transparent and accountable decision-making processes; and the goal of creating sustainable development pathways for all. The chapter concludes by offering design elements for carbon pricing rooted in the principles of climate justice.

The chapter anticipates two parallel pathways over the coming decades. The first is an increase in exposure to climate-related physical hazards such as extreme weather events, changes in water distribution and threats to biodiversity and ecosystem services (Cameron et al., 2013). Such a pathway would involve substantial consequences for human systems with impacts on poverty alleviation, livelihoods, food security, health, human rights, mobility and mortality. It will be essential to work with frontline communities to anticipate, avoid, absorb and recover from these climate impacts by addressing their underlying vulnerability and building socio-ecological resilience. The second is an acceleration of climate action, and in particular the growth of carbon pricing as a prominent approach to reducing greenhouse gas emissions. Designing and implementing these pricing mechanisms in a manner that avoids the manifest injustice of dangerous climate change; encourages the realisation of human rights for marginalised and vulnerable communities; and shares the benefits of the transition to a low-carbon, climate-resilient economy is the desired outcome of this chapter.

Carbon pricing and climate ambition

A moment for carbon pricing

Carbon pricing is intended to be a financial incentive to invest in clean technology and cut greenhouse gas emissions. A variation of the polluter pays principle, the goal is to correct market failures that currently promote high-carbon production and consumption patterns with substantial costs to socio-ecological systems and instead incentivise investments in low-carbon activities. As Bowen points out, the idea of "internalising" externalities by putting a price on them stretches back to the early 20th century and is often referred to as a Pigovian tax (Bowen, 2011).

The European Union was the first to create an international emissions trading system in 2005. Although it has struggled with poor design and low prices, the system remains the largest in the world to date. China launched pilot emissions trading systems in seven cities and provinces in 2013 and is currently moving towards a national system. At the time of writing, 45 countries and 25 cities, states and provinces use carbon pricing mechanisms. A total of 88 national climate plans include plans or consultations on carbon pricing and/ or market mechanisms (EDF and IETA, 2016). The current total value of these pricing systems is US$82 billion (World Bank and Ecofys, 2018).

In addition, almost 1,400 companies are disclosing plans or current practice of putting a price on carbon emissions through the Carbon Disclosure Project (CDP). This represents an 11% increase from 2016 (CDP, 2017). More recently, the G20's Financial Stability Board's (FSB) Task Force on Climate-related Financial Disclosures (TCFD) explicitly lists internal carbon pricing as a key metric for investors to use when conducting risk assessments and due diligence of companies (CDP, 2017).

Today, 85% of global emissions are currently not priced, and about three-quarters of the emissions that are covered are priced well below the target price of at least US$40–80/t$CO_2$ by 2020 and US$50–100/t$CO_2$ by 2030 identified as being Paris-compliant by the Carbon Pricing Leadership Coalition (High-Level Commission on Carbon Prices, 2017, p. 10). This means there is both evidence of uptake and room for significant expansion of carbon pricing mechanisms over the coming years. It is therefore increasingly important to ensure that the design of these mechanisms is informed by climate justice principles.

Carbon pricing works by increasing the market price of goods and services based on the carbon emissions within their respective supply chains. Products with a high-carbon footprint will be less competitive, either forcing their removal from the market or driving manufacturers to invest in projects to lower the footprint (WBCSD, 2017).

There are numerous ways to price carbon, but the most common approaches are through a tax on GHG emissions, by using a cap-and-trade system and by reducing fossil fuel subsidies:

- A carbon tax directly sets a price on carbon by defining a tax rate on GHG emissions or on the carbon content of fossil fuels. A carbon tax or fee requires economic actors to pay for every tonne of GHGs released into the atmosphere, usually at a fixed price in any given year.
- A cap-and-trade system limits the allowable total volume of emissions in a particular time period from a specified set of sources, and allows those industries with low emissions to sell their extra allowances to larger emitters (High-Level Commission on Carbon Prices, 2017). The system creates a process to balance supply and demand and so establishes a functioning market price for GHG emissions. The cap helps ensure that the required emission reductions will take place to keep the economy in line with a pre-allocated carbon budget.
- Hybrid schemes with elements of both price and quantity controls are also used in various jurisdictions (Hepburn, 2006).
- Reducing fossil fuel subsidies is increasingly viewed as a vital piece of the carbon pricing puzzle. According to research published in the journal *World Development*, estimated subsidies were US$4.9 trillion worldwide in 2013 and US$5.3 trillion in 2015 (6.5% of global GDP in both years). The same research concludes that eliminating this negative emissions price would have reduced global carbon emissions in 2013 by 21%, while raising revenue by 4%, and social welfare by 2.2%, of global GDP. (Coady et al., 2017).

An effective and efficient approach to emissions when properly designed

Well-designed carbon pricing can drive down demand for GHG-intensive activities (Agnolucci, 2009), incentivise low-carbon production and consumption (Adeyemi and Hunt, 2007), encourage investment in clean technology (Huntington, 2006) and raise government revenues (Hallegatte et al., 2015).

Analysis from the U.S. Energy Information Administration's (EIA's) Annual Energy Outlook (AEO) shows that if a $25 per metric tonne carbon price were implemented on CO_2 emissions in the energy sector and progressively increased at a rate of 5% per year, emissions would fall 22% below a reference scenario with no carbon price and 27% below 2005 levels by 2025 (USEIA, 2014). The World Resources Institute has described these findings as conservative, pointing to the experience in British Columbia, where a carbon tax of C$10 per metric tonne was implemented in 2008 and increased by C$5 per year until 2012. Over those five years, CO_2 emissions in British Columbia decreased by 5–15% compared to a no-policy scenario, and the decline in gasoline usage has been over five times larger than expected (Kaufman et al., 2016).

The World Business Council on Sustainable Development (WBCSD) argues that carbon pricing provides the lowest-cost decarbonisation pathway. Direct standards-based regulation can be difficult to deal with, offer limited flexibility for compliance and may be very costly to implement. Carbon pricing offers technology neutrality and compliance flexibility, providing the option to invest immediately in capital investments or buying allowances instead. A cost associated with emissions of carbon dioxide encourages fuel switching in the power sector, initially from coal to natural gas, but then to critical zero-carbon alternatives such as wind, solar and nuclear (WBCSD, 2017).

In addition, carbon pricing raises significant revenue over a sustained period of time, providing options for public sector investment in infrastructure and innovation, pro-growth tax reforms or rebates to low-income households (High-Level Commission on Carbon Prices, 2017). Analysis conducted by the World Bank concluded that a $30/tCO$_2$ domestic carbon tax would raise resources amounting to more than 1.5% of national GDP in half of 87 countries where data are available. And in 60 out of the 87 countries, a $30/tCO$_2$ domestic carbon tax would provide the resources to more than double current levels of social assistance in the country. Even a low-carbon tax at $10/tCO$_2$ would make it possible to significantly scale up social assistance or other investments that benefit poor people, including connections to sanitation and improved drinking water or access to modern energy (Hallegatte et al., 2015).

However, poorly designed carbon prices can have little impact on emissions, distort markets, be difficult to administer, result in political damage for the governments who introduce them and have significant negative impacts on poor, marginalised and vulnerable groups if the social costs of carbon pricing are not properly managed. The evidence suggests that the impact of carbon pricing on real incomes can be regressive, at least in developed countries. As Krechowicz notes, higher carbon prices could lead to a rise in the cost of living in the short term, as the prices of heating and lighting of houses, transport and food all begin to climb (Krechowicz, 2011). Lower-income groups can be disproportionately impacted as they tend to spend a larger proportion of their incomes on energy. As a result, those who are already marginalised and impacted by intersecting inequalities are often asked to carry the additional burden of carbon pricing. Distributional effects can be mitigated by channelling the revenue raised from carbon pricing back to low-income groups in the form of compensatory payments (Bowen, 2011).

The European Emissions Trading Scheme (ETS) is often cited for being a pioneer in carbon pricing mechanisms as well as a cautionary tale on how to avoid the worst and most counter-productive design elements (Cameron and McMahon, 2010). Launched in January 2005, the first phase of the ETS allowed around 13,000 factories and power stations to emit carbon dioxide only if they possess a permit. Companies exceeding individual CO$_2$ emissions targets are able to buy allowances from "greener" ones. Initially the system earned plaudits from around the globe. The price of tradable permits tripled between January 2005 and March 2006. *The Economist* highlights that when the ETS was originally established, the politicians expected the permit price to hover around €10 per tonne. Instead, it rose to a peak of €30 per tonne (*The Economist*, 2006). However, a surplus of 44.2 million metric tonnes in emissions permits caused permit prices to collapse, with carbon credits falling by approximately 60% over a two-week period (Cameron and McMahon, 2010). The surplus was caused by a fundamental design flaw, namely the issuance of too many initial permits by governments eager to please domestic industry. As a result, the first phase of ETS was marked by substantial additional revenue for power-generating companies but little effect on emissions reductions. With carbon rights being allocated at no cost, the subsequent rise in the value of those permits led to large profits. Some power generators have gained by as much as €1 billion per year (*The Economist*, 2006).

As carbon pricing mechanisms expand, the challenge is to enhance the effectiveness of the basic concept while mitigating the negative implications that can occur when systems are poorly designed.

Climate justice and carbon pricing: designing effective, efficient and equitable emissions reductions

An operational theory of climate justice

In his introduction to *The Idea of Justice*, Amartya Sen asks the reader to grapple with a scenario: three children are arguing among themselves about which one of them should have a flute. The first child, Anne, is a trained musician who can make the best use of the flute. The second child,

Bob, is the poorest of the three and owns no other toys or instruments. The third child, Clara, laboured long and hard to make the flute. Each child has a claim that is both legitimate and contestable. The reader is asked who should have the flute (Sen, 2009).

Each child can claim the support of one or more longstanding theory of distributive justice. Anne's claim is rooted in the ideas of utilitarianism, as it is assumed that her ability to use the instrument means she is best placed to derive pleasure from it and in turn to maximise the pleasure in the group, as she is the only one who can produce music that all can enjoy (Rosen, 2003). Bob's claim is backed by egalitarianism, particularly those espoused by John Rawls, as the "Rawlsian justice" principle suggests that the underprivileged should be favoured in dividing costs or benefits, while the "Difference Principle" permits inequalities that work to the advantage of the worst off. Rawls would recognise that all children have a claim on the flute, but the Difference Principle states that social and economic inequalities can be tolerated if "they are to be to the greatest benefit of the least advantaged members of society" (Rawls, 1971). Clara's claim would win the approval of right-libertarians who vigorously defend capitalism self-ownership and property rights. They contend that individuals have a right to be secure in their life, liberty and property – and that these are natural rights independent of government (Boaz, 1998). Clara made the flute, owns the flute and no other claims should override her ownership rights.

A variation on this scenario could be used to describe similarly legitimate and contestable theories of both retributive and restorative justice. The former is concerned with punishment in a manner that is proportionate, serves as a deterrent against future wrongdoing and can provide redress to those harmed (Walen, 2016). The latter creates a process of dialogue to identify who has been harmed, what are their needs, who is responsible and what can be done to repair the harm (Zehr, 2005).

Just as there are many legitimate but contestable theories of justice, there are similarly competing visions of climate justice; and many of these same notions of distributive, retributive and restorative justice are prominent within climate justice. Over the past decade the term has moved from the margins of the climate change discourse into the mainstream; from academic studies and the advocacy of civil society into government and even corporate lexicons. The term climate justice has become so familiar that the casual reader automatically assumes they know what it means and assigns value to it. This masks real debate and division within the climate justice community.

Work on climate justice has also exploded, revealing a concept with tremendous depth and breadth. The Centre for Climate Justice at Glasgow Caledonian University manages a repository of scholarly articles with over 1,000 peer-reviewed academic papers in the field of climate justice.[1] A review of the literature in this repository reveals great diversity. At a conceptual level there are legal, ethical, communications, political science, economic and natural science approaches. The scholarly work prioritises a range of different beneficiaries, including women, youth, indigenous people, the urban poor, island states and populations marginalised by cultural, social, economic and political norms. A large variety of issues are addressed, including mitigation, adaptation, migration, conflict, governance and technology. Different sectors are treated to a climate justice lens, notably those of critical importance to development, including agriculture, infrastructure, water and energy. And finally, there is significant geographical diversity both in terms of the source of the scholarly work and the territories subjected to analysis. Importantly, an analysis of climate justice literature also reveals numerous points of convergence and divergence within the community of practice.

Design elements for carbon pricing aligned with a vision of climate justice

To be effective, climate justice must be capable of influencing real policies. Policy-making consists of the setting of the decision-agenda; the specification of alternatives from which a choice is to be made; an authoritative choice among those specified alternatives; and implementation, review and learning (Kingdon, 2003). Too often, climate justice advocates have concentrated on generic calls to action or have failed to choose among policy alternatives (Cameron, 2016). Climate justice must have something to say about the choices that are actually on offer, be able to adjudicate among policy alternatives and not just speculate on what a "perfectly just" society looks like. As Amartya Sen has written,

> a theory of justice must have something to say about the choices that are actually on offer, and not just keep us engrossed in an imagined and implausible world of unbeatable magnificence. Speculating on what a "perfectly just" society looks like is interesting but does not always advance the cause of justice.
>
> *(Sen, 2009, p. 106)*

The following design elements for carbon pricing represent the author's own composite set of climate justice principles and are offered as guidance for the design and implementation of the growing portfolio of local and national carbon pricing mechanisms across the globe.

1 The primary purpose of climate justice is to avoid "manifest and severe injustices" (Sen, 2009) to the marginalised and vulnerable communities whose homes, health, livelihoods, human rights and lives will be undermined by global mean temperature rises in excess of 2 degrees Celsius.

The original objective of the United Nations Framework Convention on Climate Change is to achieve "stabilization of greenhouse gas concentrations in the atmosphere at a level that would prevent dangerous anthropogenic interference with the climate system" (United Nations, 1992). The Paris Agreement captures this with a tangible temperature goal stating as "holding the increase in the global average temperature to well below 2°C above pre-industrial levels and pursuing efforts to limit the temperature increase to 1.5°C above pre-industrial levels" (UNFCCC, 2015). The aggressive reductions of GHG emissions therefore remain the *sine qua non* of climate justice.

To this end, carbon pricing must drive urgent and ambitious mitigation of GHG emissions consistent with holding global temperatures below 2 degrees Celsius above pre-industrial levels and pursue efforts to limit the temperature increase to 1.5 degrees Celsius above pre-industrial levels in order to be aligned with the core principles of climate justice. The High-Level Commission on Carbon Prices has concluded that the explicit carbon price level consistent with holding temperatures below 2 degrees Celsius is at least US$40–80/ tCO_2 by 2020 and US$50–100/$tCO_2$ by 2030, provided a supportive policy environment is in place (High-Level Commission on Carbon Prices, 2017, p. 3). At the time of writing, 85% of global emissions are currently not priced, and about three-quarters of the emissions that are covered are priced well below the target price. The current price levels are therefore incompatible with principles of climate justice. As a result, governments are encouraged to set carbon prices that are truly Paris-compliant.

In addition, environmental integrity must be respected. In the past, carbon markets have relied heavily on offsets, whereby an external project is used to produce emission reduction certificates which are then used within the jurisdiction of the carbon pricing mechanism, either to lessen the tax burden or to reduce the need to procure allowances in a trading system. Offsets have an important role to play in carbon price, but robust accounting rules are needed to restore confidence and prevent double counting of emissions reductions.

2 The vulnerable and marginalised must share in the benefits of the transition to a low-carbon economy and be protected from the negative externalities associated with this transition.

A focus on marginalised and vulnerable communities on the frontline of climate impacts and policy responses is a central tenet to climate justice. This is in part a recognition of the asymmetrical impacts of climate change on women, youth, indigenous peoples, the urban poor, minority populations and those heavily dependent on natural systems for their homes, livelihoods and food (Cameron et al., 2013). Climate justice also places a high value on their lived experience and their capacity to be agents of climate resilience.[2] Focusing on vulnerable communities creates a nexus with international human rights norms. The obligation to respect, protect and fulfil human rights is core to climate justice. As referenced earlier, the nexus between human rights and climate change is the intellectual origin of the climate justice movement. Human rights point societies towards internationally agreed-upon values around which common action can be negotiated and then acted upon (MRFCJ, 2011). The international human rights framework also provides a common legal standard that provides processes conducive to advocacy, the shaping of public policies and the building of resilience; and substantive rights that must be respected in guarding against harm and when crafting appropriate remedies.

The bulk of evidence suggests that climate change is hardest on women as they suffer from intersecting inequalities including high level of dependency on environmental services for livelihoods, food, energy and shelter. Women are often constrained by economic, political, social and cultural norms that prevent them from acquiring appropriate skill sets; restrict their access to assets (including land); prevent them from having adequate access to governance (including access to decision-making and information); place them in inferior social positions; and prevent them from acquiring education and appropriate healthcare (Cameron, 2010). The 1991 cyclone in Bangladesh illustrates many of these issues. More than 90% of the estimated 140,000 fatalities were women; their limited mobility, skill sets and social status exacerbated their vulnerability to this extreme weather event (Oxfam, 2008).

Governments need to consider the social impacts of carbon pricing and ensure that the design of carbon pricing mechanisms include compensating measures to prevent economic disparity. Revenues generated through carbon pricing should be returned to vulnerable populations in the form of "rebates" or "dividends." These can be used to directly lower the energy bills of poor households. Revenues should also be used to reduce the social charges imposed on labour costs. This would counteract the potentially regressive effects of higher carbon prices and help poor people deal with the higher price levels caused by carbon pricing. It also has positive distributional impacts because of the larger share of wages in the total income of poor households (High-Level Commission on Carbon Prices, 2017). Revenues should also be used to finance public goods such as education, health, social safety nets and social mobility. These investments will help overcome the intersecting inequalities that exacerbate vulnerability to climate change and provide funding to support a just transition in communities that will suffer economic dislocation from a movement away from fossil fuels and high-carbon production models.

3   Carbon prices and supporting policies should be developed in a participatory, transparent and accountable manner, with full respect for human rights.

Participatory, transparent and accountable decision-making is key to climate justice. According to the Mary Robinson Foundation Climate Justice, the opportunity to participate in decision-making processes which are fair, accountable and open is essential to the growth of a culture of climate justice (MRFCJ, 2011). This in part rests on the need to provide a voice to vulnerable populations to account for their experience; to provide a means to hold those committing to climate action to account as they seek to honour their pledges; and to create a process that is deemed both legitimate and deliberative. Proponents suggest that climate justice helps to address so-called asymmetries of power, the phenomenon known as "elite capture," and therefore enhances governance, consultation and participation (Darrow and Tomas, 2005).

The author's own work on the interface between climate change and human rights reveals procedural rights, namely those relating to access to information, decision-making and justice, as being the most important for enhancing adaptive capacity. These are critical to helping vulnerable populations anticipate, avoid, absorb and recover from climate impacts and provide a means for those populations to shape public policies in a manner conducive to their resilience (Cameron, 2010).

There is a danger that carbon pricing mechanisms will be designed by bureaucratic elites with too little input from marginalised and vulnerable populations on how to generate and disperse new revenues; too little attention paid to the social cost and economic burdens that carbon pricing could potentially impose upon them; and too much voice provided to vested interests.

Governments should ensure that marginalised and vulnerable communities are provided with full access to information, decision-making and justice to maximise their ability to shape policy alternatives.

4   Bold collective action by all is necessary; with those with the highest capability going further and faster.

Holding global temperatures below 2 degrees Celsius above pre-industrial levels and pursuing efforts to limit the temperature increase to 1.5 degrees Celsius above pre-industrial levels will require tolerating a degree of unfairness and inequality, as communities and countries with little historical responsibility for climate change are asked to contribute to bold collective action by all. Those with the largest footprint and the strongest capabilities should go further faster in emissions reductions. They should also provide incentives and support for universal, if differentiated, action and collaboration (Garibaldi and Arias, 2014). However, climate justice requires all stakeholders to contribute and pursue climate action to their highest possible ambition.

The most divisive dispute within climate justice has concerned historical responsibility. Many proponents of climate justice demand that those who have the most responsibility for the historical and cumulative production of GHG emissions should go further and faster in reducing those emissions, and provide both the financial and technological means for low-carbon development to less prosperous countries. The legitimate goal that those who have the most responsibility for the emissions causing climate change shoulder the greatest responsibility for costs of emissions reduction might ignore what Lord Nicholas Stern calls the "brutal arithmetic" of our current GHG emissions trajectory and what it means for the most vulnerable. This is the simple and unavoidable fact that urgent emissions reductions by all countries will be necessary to hold global mean temperature rises below 2 degrees Celsius above pre-industrial levels (Harvey, 2012). Developed countries, which house only one-seventh of the global population, are the source of around 70% of the cumulative GHG emissions produced since 1950; however, this trend is changing rapidly. As Stern points out, if developing countries see emissions continue to increase at their present annual level of 3% or 4% in 20 years, they will constitute more than 70% of global emissions, and the goal of holding temperatures below 2 degrees Celsius will be out of reach (Stern, 2009). As a result, moving beyond historical responsibility and embracing a vision of bold collective action by all will be a necessary unfairness to avoid the manifest injustice of dangerous climate change.

Conclusions

Forty-five countries and 25 cities, states and provinces use carbon pricing mechanisms. A total of 88 national climate plans include plans or consultations on carbon pricing and/or market mechanisms. In addition, close to 1,400 companies are disclosing their plans or current practice of putting a price on carbon emissions. This represents a small but growing percentage of climate ambition across the globe. Over the coming years, as more stakeholders embrace carbon pricing as the primary means to drive greenhouse gas emissions reductions, aligning the practice of carbon pricing with the principles of climate justice will be critical. Successful alignment will help avoid the manifest injustice of dangerous climate change; ensure that the needs of the marginalised and vulnerable are prioritised; and provide for participatory, transparent and accountable policy-making. It will further incentivise low-carbon investment, production and consumption patterns; stimulate development of clean technology; and raise government revenues.

Notes

1 The Climate Justice Repository is located at: www.gcu.ac.uk/climatejustice/searchresult/
2 The Climate Justice Resilience Fund is available at www.cjrfund.org/who-we-are/

Bibliography

Adeyemi, O.I., and Hunt, L.C., 2007. Modelling OECD industrial energy demand: Asymmetric price responses and technical change. *Energy Economics*, 29, 693–709.

Aglietta, M., et al., 2015. Financing transition in an adverse context: Climate finance beyond carbon finance. *International Environmental Agreements*, 15, 403–420.

Agnolucci, P., 2009. The energy demand in the British and German industrial sectors: Heterogeneity and common factors. *Energy Economics*, 31, 175–187.

Boaz, D., 1998. *Libertarianism: A Primer*. New York: The Free Press.

Bowen, A., 2011. The case for carbon pricing. *Policy Brief*, December, 2012. London: London School of Economics, Grantham Research Institute on Climate Change and the Environment.

Cameron, E., 2010. Human rights and climate change: Moving from an intrinsic to an instrumental approach. *Georgia Journal of International and Comparative Law*, 38(3, Spring), 673–716. Athens: University of Georgia Law School.

Cameron, E., 2011. *Development, Climate Change and Human Rights: From the Margins to the Mainstream?* Social Development Working Papers. Paper No. 123/February 2011. Washington, DC: The World Bank.

Cameron, E., 2016. *Building Climate Justice: An Analysis of How the Nexus Between Climate Change and Human Rights Shapes Public Policy Agendas and Alternatives*. Turku: Åbo Akademi University, Faculty of Social Sciences, Business and Economics, Human Rights.

Cameron, E., and Limon, M., 2012. Restoring the climate by realizing rights: The role of the international human rights system. *Review of European Community & International Environmental Law*, 21(3), 2014–2219. Oxford: Blackwell Publishing Ltd.

Cameron, E., and McMahon, H., 2010. The EU-China partnership: Forging a new space on global climate change. In J. Men (ed.), *Prospects and Challenges for EU-China Relations in the 21st Century*. Brussels: Peter Lang.

Cameron, E., Shine, T., and Bevins, W., 2013. *Climate Justice: Equity and Justice Informing a New Climate Agreement*. World Resources Institute Working Paper Series. Washington, DC: World Resources Institute.

CDP, 2017. *Putting a Price on Carbon: Integrating Climate Risk into Business Planning*. New York: Carbon Disclosure Project (CDP).

Center for International Environmental Law, 2005. *Petition to the InterAmerican Commission on Human Rights: Violations Resulting From Global Warming Caused by the United States*. Washington, DC: CIEL.

Coady, D., Parry, I., Sears, L., and Shang, B., 2017. How large are global fossil fuel subsidies? *World Development*, 91, 11–27. Elsevier.

Corpwatch, 2000. *Alternative Summit Opens With Call for Climate Justice*. San Francisco: Corpwatch Press Release. Available at: www.corpwatch.org/article.php?id=333

CorpWatch, US; Friends of the Earth International; Global Resistance; Greenpeace International Groundwork, South Africa; Indigenous Environmental Network, North America; Indigenous Information Network, Kenya; National Alliance of People's Movements, India; National Fishworkers Forum, India; OilWatch Africa; OilWatch International; Southwest Network for Environmental and Economic Justice, US; Third World Network, Malaysia; and World Rainforest Movement, Uruguay, 2002. *Bali Principles of Climate Justice.* Johannesburg. Available at: www.ejnet.org/ej/bali.pdf

Darrow, M., and Tomas, A., 2005. Power, capture and conflict: A call for human rights accountability in development cooperation. *Human Rights Quarterly*, 27(2), 471–538. Washington, DC: The Johns Hopkins University Press.

The Economist, 2006. Cleaning up. *The Economist*, May 6, 2006, 75.

EDF, and IETA, 2016. *Carbon Pricing: The Paris Agreement's Key Ingredient.* Washington, DC: Environmental Defence Fund.

Garibaldi, J.A., and Arias, G., 2014. *Enhancing Bold Collective Action: A Variable Geometry and Incentives Regime.* Working Paper. Washington, DC: Agreement for Climate Transformation, 2015.

Hallegatte, S., Bangalore, M., Bonzanigo, L., Fay, M., Kane, K., Narloch, U., Rozenberg, J., Treguer, D., and Vogt-Schilb, A., 2015. *Shock Waves: Managing the Impacts of Climate Change on Poverty.* Washington, DC: World Bank.

Harvey, F., 2012. Lord Stern: Developing countries must make deeper emissions cuts. *The Guardian.* December 3, 2012. Available at: www.guardian.co.uk/environment/2012/dec/04/ lord-stern-developing-countries-deeper-emissions-cuts

Hepburn, C., 2006. Regulation by prices, quantities, or both: A review of instrument choice. *Oxford Review of Economic Policy*, 22(2), 226–247.

High-Level Commission on Carbon Prices, 2017. *Report of the High-Level Commission on Carbon Prices.* Washington, DC: World Bank.

Hope, K.R., 2008. *Poverty, Livelihoods, and Governance in Africa: Fulfilling the Development Promise.* New York: Palgrave Macmillan.

Human Rights and Equal Opportunities Commission, 2008. *Human Rights and Climate Change.* Available at: www.hreoc.gov.au/about/media/papers/hrand climate_change.html.

Huntington, H.G., 2006. A note on price asymmetry as induced technical change. *The Energy Journal*, 27(3), 1–7.

Intergovernmental Panel on Climate Change (IPCC), 2012. Summary for policymakers. In *Managing the Risks of Extreme Events and Disasters to Advance Climate Change Adaptation. A Special Report of Working Groups I and II of the Intergovernmental Panel on Climate Change.* Cambridge and New York: Cambridge University Press.

Kaufman, N., Obeiter, M., and Krause, E., 2016. *Putting a Price on "Carbon" Reducing Emissions.* Washington, DC: World Resources Institute.

Kingdon, J., 2003. *Agenda, Alternatives, and Public Policy.* Second edition. New York: Longman.

Kravchenko, S., 2008. Right to carbon or right to life: Human rights approaches to climate change. *Vermont Journal of Environmental Law*, 9, 514–547. South Royalton: Vermont Law School.

Krechowicz, D., 2011. *The Effect of Carbon Pricing on Low-Income Households, and Its Potential Contribution to Poverty Reduction.* Sustainable Prosperity Background Paper. Ottawa: University of Ottawa.

Mary Robinson Foundation Climate Justice, 2011. *Principles of Climate Justice.* New York: MRFC. Available at: www.mrfcj.org/wp-content/uploads/2015/09/Principles-of-Climate-Justice.pdf

Organization of American States, 2008. *Annual Report of the Permanent Council to the General Assembly: Human Rights and Climate Change in the Americas.* Washington, DC: OAS.

Oxfam International, 2008. *Rethinking Disasters: Why Death and Destruction Is Not Nature's Fault but Human Failure.* Oxford: Oxfam.

Rawls, J., 1971. *A Theory of Justice.* Cambridge, MA: Harvard University Press.

Romani, M., Rydge, J., and Stern, N., 2012. *Recklessly Slow or a Rapid Transition to a Low-Carbon Economy? Time to Decide.* London: Centre for Climate Change Economics and Policy/Grantham Research Institute on Climate Change and the Environment.

Rosen, F., 2003. *Classical Utilitarianism from Hume to Mill.* Abingdon: Routledge.

Sen, A., 2009. *The Idea of Justice.* London: Penguin Books.

Stern, N., 2009. *The Global Deal: Climate Change and the Creation of a New Era of Progress and Prosperity.* New York: PublicAffairs.

United Nations, 1972. *Declaration of the United Nations Conference on the Human Environment.* Conference on the Human Environment, Stockholm, Sweden, June 5–16, 1972. U.N. Doc. A/CONF.48/14/Rev.1 (June 14, 1972).

United Nations, 1992. *Framework Convention on Climate Change*. FCCC/INFORMAL/84. New York: United Nations.

United Nations Framework Convention on Climate Change, 2015. *The Paris Agreement*. Conference of the Parties Twenty-First Session, Paris, 30 November to 11 December 2015.

United Nations Office of the High Commissioner for Human Rights, 2014. *An Open Letter From Special Procedures Mandate-Holders of the Human Rights Council to the State Parties to the UN Framework Convention on Climate Change*. Geneva: Office of the United Nations High Commissioner for Human Rights.

US EIA, 2014. *Annual Energy Outlook 2014 With Projections to 2040*. Washington, DC: U.S. Department of Energy.

Walen, A., 2015. Retributive justice. In A. Walen and E. Zalta (ed.), *Stanford Encyclopedia of Philosophy*. Winter, 2016. Stanford, CA: Stanford University.

World Bank, and Ecofys, 2018. *State and Trends of Carbon Pricing 2018*. Washington, DC: World Bank. Washington, DC: World Bank.

World Business Council on Sustainable Development, 2017. *Why Carbon Pricing Matters*. Geneva: WBCSD.

Worster, D., 1994. *Nature's Economy: A History of Ecological Ideas*. Cambridge: Cambridge University Press.

Zehr, H., 2005. *Changing Lenses: A New Focus for Crime and Justice*. Scottdale: Herald Press.

15

Sharing the burden of climate change via climate finance and business models

Emilie Prattico

Why is burden sharing part of the global solution to climate change?

Sharing the burden of climate change involves – for all stakeholders – at once reducing greenhouse gas (GHG) emissions to hold the global mean temperature rise to less than 2 degrees Celsius above pre-industrial levels and recognising that inevitable climate impacts are already locked in as a consequence of the rapid accumulation of GHGs in the atmosphere over many centuries. In the policy context, the burden is shared among countries. However, given that a broader set of stakeholders generates emissions and that the impacts of climate change affect them all, what is their role in burden sharing? In particular, what might this role be for the private sector organisations responsible for moving finance across the globe and for upholding global trade relations, organisations that are themselves emitters and vulnerable to climate change impacts?

Over two decades after the creation of the United Nations Framework Convention on Climate Change (UNFCCC, 1992), parties reached a general political consensus in support of reducing global GHG emissions and of strengthening adaptation measures globally. Indeed, Article 2 defines the Convention's ultimate objective primarily in terms of mitigation, specifically stabilising GHG concentrations to "prevent dangerous anthropogenic interference with the climate system." It also notes that "such a level should be achieved within a timeframe sufficient to allow ecosystems to adapt naturally to climate change, to ensure that food production is not threatened and to enable economic development to proceed in a sustainable manner." The Agreement thus frames parties' obligations about natural adaptation as limits that define the ambition and timeframe of mitigation measures, not as objectives in themselves. Nonetheless, the Agreement does highlight the need for adaptation to occur globally and by all parties. Indeed, burden-sharing issues belong to an extended framework that includes adaptation costs, integrates developing countries and is not limited to GHG emissions.

Article 4 further establishes common but differentiated commitments related to adaptation. In Article 4.1, all parties commit to "formulate, implement, publish, and regularly update national, and where appropriate, regional programs containing . . . measures to facilitate adequate adaptation to climate change," and to "cooperate in preparing for adaptation to the impacts of climate change." Annex II countries in particular commit "to assist the developing country Parties that are particularly vulnerable to the adverse effects of climate change in meetings costs of adaptation to those adverse effects" in Article 4.4 (UNFCCC, 1992).

While focus on burden sharing has strengthened since the adoption of the Convention, the debate continues over how to share the burden of mitigation and adaptation equitably across countries. Complementary to this debate is the notion that other stakeholders play a role in furthering the goal of burden sharing, most notably transnational organisations that redistribute finance – through climate finance vehicles, that is, through different investment methods, or with finance from multinational companies supporting climate-friendly business and procurement models – such as a partnership between French bank BNP Paribas and German sportswear manufacturer Puma to offer financial incentives for PUMA suppliers to improve environmental, health and safety and social standards via a supplier financing program.

Before further analysing the role of climate finance and of business models in sharing the burden of climate change, it is important to understand the questions arising from this debate within the context of the convention. First, the difference between Annex I and non-Annex I countries provides clues as to *how* the burden of climate change can be shared. Annex I countries are a set of 43 Parties to the UNFCCC that are classified as industrialised countries or economies in transition – and had all, apart from the United States, agreed to second-round Kyoto targets. Non-Annex I countries are mostly developing countries, which the Convention recognises as especially vulnerable to the impacts of climate change or to the transition away from fossil fuels. The distinction highlights the inequality in the distributions of the effects of climate change: developing countries will likely feel the negative effects of climate change more severely than their industrialised counterparts, which is due in part to their capability to address the resulting damage (Aldy, 2010). Second, it highlights an imbalance in the way responsibility is attributed for the causes of climate change: for many developing and emergent nations, utilising fossil fuels to industrialise, and hence to burn carbon until they reach higher levels of prosperity, is legitimate, and wealthier countries should take responsibility for the impact they have already made on global climate (Stern, 2008). Third, due to a lack of enforcement of international climate policies and a high level of uncertainty in international collective action as a result – as demonstrated by the USA's announced withdrawal from the Paris Agreement in 2017 –it creates a lack of clarity as to mutual obligations among parties and leaves the door open for them to rescind their obligations, in particular those related to burden sharing (Wiener, 2007; Aldy, 2010).

Another aspect of burden sharing is seen from the vantage of parties collectively benefitting from an international common good – natural resources, biodiversity, clean air, for instance – and agreeing to allocate the costs and benefits of securing access to the good. Indeed, underlying the idea of sharing the burden is the concept of fairness, which is related to the concept of equity. A brief overview of fairness reveals that it has to do with how parties are treated by other parties, and it would also show a requirement that they be treated with equity, that is, with no significant differences between them, unless there are strong reasons to make exceptions in particular cases. In the context of climate change, countries contribute to climate change differently, just like they suffer its impacts differently: these differences count as strong reasons to make differences. Exactly *how* those differences are made, however, remains open for debate.

With this background in view, the role of climate finance and business models in burden sharing becomes more defined. As transnational organisations, the institutions that move finance across the globe are de facto actors of climate justice. Global value chains are a constellation of stakeholders with roles to play in all aspects of managing climate change: from corporations with decision-making authority over procurement of smallholder farmers in developing countries supplying raw materials for production, and including service providers in transport, information technology, or financial services, all actors can contribute to reducing emissions, to increasing climate resilience, and to ensuring that this is achieved by providing broader and more inclusive access to goods, services and to the economy in general. Indeed, communities that share the burden of climate change often share economic or trade relations, which can be shaped to reduce its weight, but building resilience requires investments at scale – far above the promised $100 billion per year in climate finance. The private sector in particular funds project pipelines, incentivises resilience across geographically dispersed supply chains and provides access to its products and services via innovative business models to enable vulnerable communities to rebound from climate impacts.

The following will analyse how climate finance and business models can contribute to fair burden sharing by redistributing finance across the globe to those communities that suffer the effects of climate change most starkly and hence need support in building resilience against them.

What makes burden sharing fair? Three principles of fairness for climate change

The way burden sharing has been treated in global climate policy over the last two decades is undergirded by three norms of fairness: responsibility, capacity and rights. These principles contribute to a definition of fairness in the context of climate change and burden sharing and will shed light on the role of climate finance and business models in it. The norms of responsibility and capacity relate to the distribution of the burdens of providing a common good, whereas rights concern how benefits are allocated.

The part of fairness that is focused on responsibility implies that those who have caused a problem are responsible for solving it. In the context of global environmental policy, it is evidenced, for instance, in Principle 21 of the Stockholm Declaration on the Human Environment (UN, 1972): "States have the responsibility to ensure that activities within their jurisdiction or control do not cause damage to the environment of other States." This raises the question as to the responsibility of private sector organisations that may themselves "cause damage to the environment" outside of their own areas of operation and influence.

Where the norm of capacity is concerned, parties that have greater capacity to solve a joint problem should contribute more than countries with less capacity to do so. This points toward the fact that sharing the burden of the costs of adaptation fairly implies that developed countries take on a larger share than countries that are most vulnerable to the impacts of climate change. Moreover, raising the idea that contributing to addressing the impacts of climate change is proportional to resources, skills and capacity, this norm also thereby raises the question of the role of organisations operating in these geographies.

Finally, fairness is constituted by a norm related to rights. In the context of global climate policy, these rights are sometimes characterised in two different ways. First, the right of all parties and their citizens to access to natural resources such as biodiversity, water and other natural resources that are threatened by climate change. Consequently, developing countries – where these threats are the strongest – would have a claim to protect these from climate change and its impacts. The second implication is that parties have the right to emit an equal amount of GHGs, on the basis of a right to development. The norm underlying this right establishes an equal level of GHG emissions per capita in all countries that is independent of existing emission levels, but rather looks at emissions historically and in aggregate. As a result, this would imply that developing countries, which historically have emitted fewer GHGs than developed countries, would have the right to more per capita emissions, since this supposedly allows them to develop. The burden on developed countries, then, would be larger. This principle takes the form of trading schemes for carbon emissions regulated by countries and other jurisdictions. Indeed, by issuing allowances or credits for emissions, which lie at the basis of trading schemes, countries recognise that emissions are a limited resource to which emitters have a right. In particular, in this case, the right consists in freely disposing of it. For organisations in the private sector with an impact on climate change – via climate finance and business models, notably – the notion of rights to emit GHGs acquires is in tension with the notions of rights to access to natural resources: not only must we determine who is allowed to emit GHGs and by how much, but we must also address the question of the *whom* these emissions will benefit and *for whom* they will restrict the right to access to natural resources. Indeed, if a multinational company with headquarters in a developed country has a supply chain of heavy emitters in a developing country, it is arguable that the latter's emissions to the benefit of the company while as a result of their location they are at the detriment of the suppliers.

In summary, fairness is burden sharing that recognises the responsibility of the organisations and entities involved based on their past actions, that allocates the share of the burden based on their capacity, and that upholds a notion of rights to emission while it also upholds the right to access to resources such as biodiversity and water. Climate finance and business models have a key role in addressing climate change: what follows will explore whether and how they can contribute to fair burden sharing globally.

What role for the private sector in burden sharing?

The national emissions mitigation pledges are collectively insufficient to achieve the Paris Agreement goal of limiting global warming to well below 2 degrees Celsius, let alone 1.5 degrees Celsius (Rogelj, 2016; Robiou du Pont, 2017; UNFCCC, Synthesis Report on the Aggregate Effect of the Intended Nationally Determined). Large investments far above the promised US$100 billion per year in climate finance until 2020 pledged by developed countries in the context of climate change negotiations will be required to build climate resilience (UNFCCC, 2015). According to the IPCC Fifth Assessment Report (2014), electricity and heat production accounts for 25% of global GHG emissions, followed by agriculture, forestry and other land use (24%), industry (21%), transport (14%), other emission sources in the energy sector (9.6%) and buildings (6.4%). Commensurate with the scale of emissions is the potential for mitigation. Strikingly, most multinational companies have emissions profiles that are similar in one respect: most of their emissions are so-called scope 3 emissions.[1] And for most of these companies, scope 3 emissions are located mostly in emerging economies and developing countries.

In the 2000s, the industries and activities that made up global value chains grew significantly in volume and in diversity. They were the backbone of the growth of trade in finished goods and customised intermediates (components and sub-assemblies, for instance), including not only manufacturing but also energy, food production and services that had until then not been traded, call centres, accounting, medical procedures or R&D (Dossani & Kenney, 2003; Engardio, Bernstein, & Kripalani, 2003; Engardio, 2005; Wadhwa, De Vitton, & Gereffi, 2008; Cattaneo, Gereffi, & Staritz, 2010). With the growth of global value chains, scope 3 emissions have grown too, at least until recently, where economic growth and emissions trends decoupled (IEA, 2017).

Specifically, changes are most pronounced in a few concentrated regions. While manufacturing has largely been concentrated in China, services have mostly been traded with India, agricultural and primary commodities with Brazil, and significant amounts of natural resources with Russia. For finished goods that require shorter supply lines such as apparel and automobiles, historical locations such as Mexico and North Africa now compete with Eastern Europe and Southeast Asia.

Central to these global value chains are sets of companies connected by trade relations across borders. In addition, these companies require and benefit from stable and reliable business environments – such as resilient communities – that are partly made possible by global finance. The role of the private sector is thus twofold: (1) by promoting climate-friendly and low-carbon business models through the supply chain and (2) by directing finance to enhance the resilience of business environments in the face of the effects of climate change. In both these regards, the private sector has a critical role to play as its investments will fund project pipelines, its procurement will incentivise adaptation across geographically dispersed supply chains, and access to its products and services will enable vulnerable communities and individuals to rebound from climate impacts – while ensuring that decision-making powers remain within communities. All the available levers that move money around the globe can be mobilised, including public money, private investments and procurement from both the public and the private sector. Corporate procurement as well as investment or finance can be leveraged to build adaptive capacity at a pace and scale that the current predicament calls for. Provided that companies do not strip away decision-making powers from communities, the private sector has the potential to drive adaptation initiatives forward while managing its risk and contributing to building greater climate resilience.

Sharing the burden of mitigation

There is a clear policy signal for investors and financial actors across all jurisdictions to make low-carbon investments, whether through financing projects or investing in new technologies. An extraordinary market shift into renewable energy supply is taking place, with the International Energy Agency (IEA, Perspectives for the Energy Transition, 2017) projecting global investment from national climate plans by 2030 to reach US$3.9 trillion, including US$1.3 trillion in wind, US$1.1 trillion in solar and US$0.9 trillion in hydro. The economic opportunities from energy efficiency are also large: looking out to 2030, the IEA projects that implementing national climate plans will require US$5.4 trillion in energy efficiency investment. In addition, the IEA shows that renewable energy now accounts for 24% of global power generation and 16% of primary energy supply – and that to achieve decarbonisation in line with the Paris Agreement, renewables will have to reach 80% of power generation and 65% of total primary energy supply by 2050 (IEA, Perspectives for the Energy Transition, 2017).

Implementing this will require trillions of dollars in low-carbon investment in order to reach the Paris Agreement goal of 2 degrees Celsius, and pursuing a 1.5 degrees Celsius target will require even more. Developed countries have made a commitment to mobilise US$100 billion per year of climate finance, with public money being used to leverage private sector finance to the highest possible extent (Department of Foreign Affairs and Trade, 2016); pressure on governments to reduce or to remove fossil fuel subsidies is increasing (Chestney, 2016); and carbon pricing is gaining momentum around the globe and in varied jurisdictions (World Bank, 2016). Indeed, much is already in motion within the private sector to contribute to the low-carbon transition.

The We Mean Business coalition, a coalition of business-facing organisations with a mission to accelerate the shift to a deeply decarbonised economy, offers a unique window into the scale of the opportunity represented by and of action already underway towards the energy transition. As of August 2017, 596 companies representing more than US$8.3 trillion in total revenue have made commitments to align their practices, operations and supply chains with climate-compatible growth. At the same time, 183 investors, controlling more than US$20.7 trillion in assets, have pledged to align their investments with the same trajectory. The top three publicly traded companies in the world by market capitalisation – Apple, Google and Microsoft – have all committed to 100% renewable power by 2020 or 2025 depending on the company. The largest private sector employer in the world, Walmart, has made the same commitment, in addition to setting science-based emissions-reduction targets, aiming to reduce their absolute emissions from operations by 18% and Scope 3 emissions by 1 gigatonne by 2025 from 2015 levels (Walmart, 2017). These contributions to the energy transition will require finance and collaborative solutions in innovative ways to achieve scale.

As of early 2018, more than 100 companies committed to powering their operations with 100% renewable energy (RE100), including well-known companies such as Ikea, Nike and Bloomberg (RE100, 2018). Corporations have historically explored a variety of ways to increase renewable energy use, including installing solar panels on their rooftops or wind turbines on their land, but they are increasingly using renewable energy power purchase agreements (PPAs) – long-term contracts for electricity produced by renewable technologies – to show their support for clean energy. Companies added nearly 1.6 gigawatts of such contracts in 2016, which represents a significant increase from only 0.8 gigawatts in 2010 (Business Renewables Center, 2017).

Estimating the impact of these significant shifts in terms of GHG emissions reduction is not easily achieved. However, the scale of corporate commitment signals recognising and taking on a share of the burden of climate change with regards to mitigation. These companies are not acting without regard for self-interest and in all cases will have strong business reasons to shift to low-carbon models: the measure of their impact nonetheless indicates that emissions reductions in line with science and policy cannot be achieved without their contribution.

Sharing the burden of adaptation

The role of climate finance and business models is equally important in adaptation. Companies have an interest in ensuring that their own operations are resilient against the adverse effects of climate change, as well as in contributing to the resilience of partners across their global value chains.

How do companies finance adaptation in their own operations?

- Companies can choose to finance a climate action by making use of **in-house expertise** and embed the project in business operations or channel their contribution through external parties (e.g., local NGOs, experts, etc.) who develop a specific adaptation program. In this case, the company would be the main investor in the project; often this position comes with a hands-on approach of the company characterised by a business interest in the success of the project, regular follow-ups with the executing organisation, etc. For instance, a growing number of water utilities such as Anglian, Severn Trent or the Francisco Public Utilities Commission have used this method to develop vulnerability assessments, mitigation and adaptation planning and building new water infrastructure (Climate Bonds, 2017), thus addressing adaptation at the local level by focusing on water specifically.
- A company's own adaptation financing might be **pooled with other public and private sector resources** first and then directed towards climate projects. In this case, the company is one of several different financiers, which means that the governance structure of such a project would allow the company to either abstain from getting directly involved in the project's decision-making and management or be part of a (private-private or public-private) partnership that requires a hands-on approach to adaptation. Such projects are numerous and range from, for example, Starbucks co-financing vulnerability assessments performed by Conservation International and local cooperatives, to Swiss Re providing financing but also expertise with the World Food Programme and Oxfam, to an insurance scheme for farmers in Africa.

Table 15.1 Financing mechanisms, examples from the private sector, and the necessary conditions for meeting justice.

Financing mechanism	Private sector example	Conditions for justice
Free cash flow investment: This usually means that the adaptation activities are implemented "in-house," i.e., are part of own operations and executed internally. Although somewhat limited in scale, financing through free cash flow is often used for adaptation measures with a genuine business interest and close to the core business of a company.	• Bogota Water and Sewerage Company's investment restored vegetation in the Rio Blanco watershed in order to ensure access to water for its own operations.	• Respect of property and access rights
Green Bonds: The majority of green bonds are issued to promote climate change mitigation actions by financing renewable energy procurement and energy efficiency measures. To date, only 4.3% of bonds' proceeds are used for adaptation financing (Climate Bonds Initiative, 2015). Green bonds offer long-term financing opportunities and market-based pricing. Growth in the green bond market has been outstanding: in 2013, nearly US$11 billion worth of green bonds were issued. In 2014, that number tripled to over US $36 billion(Climate Bonds, 2017).	• In the UK, Anglian and Severn Trent water companies issued bonds to execute their detailed and extensive climate adaptation plans (Climate Bonds Initiative, 2017, Severn Trent, 2012). • The first bond labelled under the Climate Bonds Water Criteria came from the San Francisco Public Utilities Commission in 2016. It raised a total of US$240 million for sustainable water infrastructure.	• Better distribution of bonds to address adaptation
Debt: Debt financing often comes from national or multilateral development banks offering money to a company implementing a medium- to large-scale adaptation project, such as water infrastructure, coastal infrastructure, production plant refitting, etc. This financing can be directly distributed to (large) companies or indirectly distributed, so-called "on-lending," with the help of local banks or non-bank entities targeting micro and small to medium-sized businesses. Estimates are that these contributions, through the EBRD, EIB, IDB and IFC,[i] have triggered around US$5.5 billion of total private and public sector adaptation investments (Vivid Economics, 2015). Agriculture and ecological services (addressing water scarcity) are main beneficiaries with project types such as efficient irrigation, flood and erosion management, crop management, dam upgrades as well as crop resilience.	• The Agricultural Supply Chain and Adaptation Facility, piloted by the Inter-American Development Bank and Calvert Investments, partners with agribusiness companies to give farmers access to finance for climate-resilient investments. At a first stage, during 2014 and 2015, total debt commitments were set to reach US$5 million.	• Inclusion in decision-making

(Continued)

Table 15.1 (Continued)

Financing mechanism	Private sector example	Conditions for justice
Grants: Grants dedicated to climate adaptation often come from the public sector but corporates also hand out grants especially when partnering with public sector stakeholders to push a common adaptation platform or project. These grants are then part of a larger financing schemes involving, for example, debt or equity financing.	• Swiss Re made available US$1.25 million out of a total 9.25 million to kick off the work of R4 Rural Resilience Initiative.	• Inclusion in decision-making
Equity/Portfolio Investment: Private companies and investors might consider investing in equity to strengthen climate adaptation activities. Buying another firm's equity can be a way to support the development of highly innovative climate adaptation products and solutions the target company is developing. This form of cooperation tends to be operational, so that the buying company is, for example, providing access to its marketing channels or R&D. An alternative investment approach targets more mature companies to participate in their success. Such investors increasingly consider climate-related products and services as growth markets and therefore specifically invest in certain companies that are handling climate risks well or having built a business model around climate change (Blackrock Investment Institute, 2016).	• Calvert Investment created a category of funds, e.g., emerging markets (US$116 million, inception: 2012), water (US$434 million, inception: 2008) and energy funds (US$80 million, inception: 2007), which specifically invest in companies that provide solutions to challenges raised by a changing climate (Calvert, 2017).	• Inclusion in decision-making • Avoidance of short-termism in business decision-making

[i] European Bank for Reconstruction and Development (EBRD), European Investment Bank (EIB), Inter-American Development Bank: (IDB) and International Finance Corporation (IFC)

How do companies mobilise finance for adaptation in the supply chain?

Financial flows to the supply chain by procurement decisions, buyer-supplier partnerships and investments in the supply chain have the untapped potential to build further resilience. It is important to remember that companies will always follow a commercial logic, but that some demonstrate efforts to engage and include the smallholders with whom they work.

Procurement of climate-adapted products

Supply chain decisions ultimately drive raw material extraction, all mechanical, chemical or thermal conversion in manufacturing, and all packaging and delivery from source to end consumer. This applies to food, clothing, medicine and machinery as well as all human infrastructure in our communities (O'Marah, 2016). Therefore, procurement decisions are an impactful way to drive change towards climate adaptation through specifically buying climate-adapted products or buying from suppliers having adapted their operations to a changing climate.

Table 15.2 Mechanisms for adaptation in the supply chain along with appropriate private sector examples.

Mechanism for adaptation in supply chains	Private sector example
Procurement of climate-adapted products	• PepsiCo procures specifically climate-adapted potato species from suppliers in South America.
Investment in and cooperation throughout the supply chain	• General Mills invests and engages with suppliers and experts on new seeds, systems and tools, for instance, plant breeding programs providing farmers with seeds that deliver high-yield despite climate variability, develop and distribute tools and systems that monitor climate change at the regional and farm levels. This engagement in particular involves farmers in the development of solutions.
Microfinance and insurance adapted to supply chains	• Centenary Bank's climate risk microfinance for local rice farmers including preferential interest rate for loans used to finance adaptation, weather index insurance as well as dissemination of climate and weather information. • Swiss Re partnered with the R4 Rural Resilience initiative to engineer rainfall index-based insurance for smallholders, giving them the choice to pay the insurance fee by implementing risk-reduction measures. Via this partnership, Swiss Re aimed to include the perspective of farmers as much as possible.
Carbon markets within the supply chain	• Marks and Spencer helping supplier to access carbon finance and allowing them to sell carbon credits to M&S.
Credit enhancement and financing for suppliers	• PUMA, in cooperation with BNP Paribas, allows its suppliers to profit from PUMA's credit rating and an agreed-upon percentage of its due payment upfront from the corporate buyer's bank. The rates and terms partly depend on the supplier's compliance with social and environment standards.

This approach is not entirely new: the public sector has started gaining experience on working in adaptation in their procurement practices (e.g., City of Boston, incorporating climate change adaptation considerations into the City's procurement process). The City's Procurement Guidance states that a procurement officer should assess which aspects of climate change are likely to affect the particular procurement decision and what alternatives are available to reduce that impact (Fievet, 2012).

Companies rolling out this approach on a larger scale often reflect adaptation considerations in their procurement manuals, guidelines and scoring tools, etc., and use specific tools to channel finance to their supply chain. For instance, PepsiCo specifically procures climate-adapted potato species from suppliers in South America. Before starting to procure these species, however, PepsiCo also invested US$3 million in an Agricultural Development Research Center to develop these potatoes and improve practices on efficient water usage.

Investment in and cooperation throughout the supply chain

Efforts by Walmart and General Mills, for instance, show how the Food, Beverage and Agriculture industry leads the way in building resilience in their supply chain by investing in it at scale with explicit adaptation targets (Olson, 2015, 2016). In 2015, General Mills, for instance, set climate targets: absolute reduction of GHG emissions of 28% by 2025 across its value chain; actively build and support adaptation efforts across key commodities and sourcing regions. In addition, the company committed to further improve the ability of its growers and other suppliers to adapt to the inevitable consequences of climate change. Investments in adaptation are projected to amount to close to US$100 million.

Microfinance and insurance products adapted to supply chains

Climate change will amplify, modify or introduce new types of threats, and if people do not have the resources to deal with today's stresses, they are unlikely to be able to deal with the additional impacts of climate change, a predicament known as the "adaptation deficit" (Burton, 2004). Hence, at the forefront of adaptation strategies must be the most vulnerable segments of the supply chain – smallholders and suppliers in at-risk regions.

Microfinance is the delivery of services such as "small loans, typically for working capital; informal appraisal of borrowers and investments; collateral substitutes, such as group guarantees or compulsory savings; access to repeat and larger loans, based on repayment performance; streamlined loan disbursement and monitoring; secure savings products" (World Bank, 1999) to people who do not typically have access to these services. The purpose of microfinance is to enable its users to engage in productive activities, build assets and protect themselves against risk.

Microfinance is typically delivered by public institutions such as development banks but also by credit unions, cooperatives, as well as non-bank entities. Microfinance is used to alleviate poverty and to promote a more inclusive economy by encouraging low-income entrepreneurs to build financial resilience into their enterprises. Studies have shown both the great benefits and potential pitfalls of such products (IISD, 2008). Indeed, many studies have exposed the shortcomings of microfinance and have argued that it does not alleviate poverty by creating new sources of revenue for the poor, and sometimes even worsens this situation by indebting users (DfiD, 2015). As such, it is not seen as a reliable vehicle for furthering adaptation in the context of climate justice.

Micro-insurance can be used to protect smallholders against weather-induced crop failures. For instance, in agriculture, initiatives such as the Fairtrade Insurance Initiative[2] and the JFPS Initiative[3] both use fair-trade premiums to fund a crop insurance scheme. In these models the entity that is ensured is the cooperative, and it disburses finance to smallholders within it. This allows for larger premiums due to a more robust risk profile, better data to improve service, and short- and medium-term solutions to crop losses.

Insurance products for small agricultural suppliers have known the most developments recently. Since standard insurance contracts are either not available, not adapted or too expensive for smallholders in developing countries, insurance companies are developing more and more tailored insurance policies for specific market segments, most prominently the agricultural supply chain. However, more needs to be done by insurers to foster investments in adaptation (Cambridge Institute for Sustainability Leadership (CISL), 2016).

Insurance companies have been the fastest to address climate change risk. The pace at which they have taken up the issue and found adaptation-building solutions is as rapid as the scale of the impact climate change could have on the economic model underpinning the core of their business. According to Henry de Castries, CEO of Axa at the time: "At 4 degrees [temperature increase], the world is uninsurable."[4] Hence, not only is there, from a point of view of insurance companies, an imperative to curb emissions that contribute to increasing temperatures, but also an urgent need to make sure that individuals and companies that are most at risk of climate change impacts can minimise the damage incurred by these risks – that is, that they can be resilient in the face of these risks.

Insurance companies can work at different levels of stakeholders in order to ensure access to insurance against climate risk. For instance, on the micro level, the German insurance company Allianz offers micro insurance products against climate impacts including crop insurance. Over 15,000 farmers in Burkina Faso and Mali took out weather index-based crop insurance policies coupled with a loan for seed purchase policies with Allianz Africa (Allianz Climate Solutions, 2014). "Index-based financial risk-transfer mechanisms" like this one pay out based on weather rather than crop losses. An index of productivity-relevant weather variables such as precipitation onset and intensity, streamflow and temperature determines the pay-out: the insurance pays out, for example, if measured rainfall falls below a specified level (WEF, 2016). At a lower level, insurance and reinsurance companies can work with local governments, as does Swiss Re with the municipal government of Beijing. In this partnership, agricultural insurance is made available to stabilise a farmer's income, for instance (Swiss Re, 2008). On the macro level, the African Risk Capacity is a supranational risk pooling mechanism that aims to cover 150 million people against weather risks until 2020 in 30 countries (Cameron, 2016). Multi-country risk pools or regional catastrophe funds insure countries against disasters, such as droughts or hurricanes. Their benefits include rapid pay-outs, which allow for basic government functions after a catastrophic event to be maintained and rescue efforts to be deployed swiftly.

Carbon markets within the supply chain

Another area where companies can leverage supply chain engagement to strengthen climate adaptation is by providing suppliers with access to carbon markets. Marks and Spencer, for instance, has supported its small-scale suppliers to access carbon finance and sell carbon credits, thus diversifying their income and participating in responsible reforestation programs. Marks and Spencer has set up a reforestation program as part of its own commitment to becoming carbon neutral that includes farmers that are part of its very supply chain for tea and green beans in Kenya. The virtuous circle created by the company – which invests in reforestation projects through the Meru & Nanyuki Kenya Project platform, hence supports some of its suppliers in the area in developing activities that allow them to sell back carbon credits to the company – contributes to strengthening the human, social, financial and natural capital of these communities while also contributing to mitigation activities (Marks and Spencer, 2015).

Conclusion

Sharing the burden of climate change shores up questions of fairness and equity. Typically, these have been the concern of policy and international agreements rather than business. Business is commonly associated with short-term decision-making where profits are prioritised over the longevity and sustainability of suppliers and other stakeholders. On the face of it, this is not compatible with successful adaptation strategies on the ground, which require long-term planning and inclusion of local voices. In addition to not being consistent with building climate resilience instrumentally, the profit-maximising commercial logic of companies in the private sector can run counter to climate justice, which is defined *inter alia* by fairness, inclusion and equity.

One of the main motivations for businesses to build climate resilience is to mitigate risks to the supply chain and risks to the supply and quality of raw materials in particular. Hence, it is unsurprising that considerations related to business risk take precedence over questions of justice for companies. And while some companies are increasingly including consideration of fairness in their resilience-building initiatives, external pressures must maintain the standards of justice for global climate actions. And so, while business is clearly taking on a part of the burden of climate change – whether through finance or business models – it can only be a complement, and not a substitute, to burden-sharing rules at the transnational level that remain bound by ideas of justice. Indeed, questions of legitimacy, checks and balances, and focus on the common good rather than self-interest are at the root of international policy-making, while they are not always the guiding principles of business decisions. Sharing the burden of climate change, then, must rely on business and climate finance, but it must bolster these contributions with robust policy-making.

Notes

1 The GHG Protocol Corporate Standard classifies a company's GHG emissions into three "scopes." Scope 1 emissions are direct emissions from owned or controlled sources. Scope 2 emissions are indirect emissions from the generation of purchased energy. Scope 3 emissions are all indirect emissions (not included in scope 2) that occur in the value chain of the reporting company, including both upstream and downstream emissions.
2 Forum for Agricultural Risk Management in Development: Resilient Supply Chains. See: www.agriskmanagementforum.org/sites/agriskmanagementforum.org/files/farmd_html/farmd/index.html
3 Social Business Network: Holistic Health for Community Development. See: https://thesocialbusinessnetwork.wordpress.com/tag/juan-francisco-paz-silva-coop/
4 Henry de Castries, CEO of Axa, Keynote at the BSR Conference 2015. See: www.youtube.com/watch?v=BdPZwHlBXAY

References

Aldy, J. A. (2010). Designing Climate Mitigation Policy. *Journal of Economic Literature*, 48(4), 903–934.
Allianz Climate Solutions. (2014). *Fourth Annual Meeting San Gorgio Group*. Retrieved from http://climate-policyinitiative.org/wp-content/uploads/2014/11/RUIZ-VERGOTE-PDF.pdf
Blackrock Investment Institute. (2016). *Adapting Portfolios to Climate Change: Implications and Strategies for All Investors*. New York: Blackrock Global Insights.
Burton, I. (2004). *Look Before You Leap: A Risk Management Approach for Incorporating Climate Change Adaptation in World Bank Operations*. Washington, DC: World Bank.
Business Renewables Center. (2017). *Business Renewables Center Deal Tracker*. Retrieved from Business Renewables: www.businessrenewables.org/corporate-transactions/
Calvert. (2017). *A Guide to Calvert's SRI Approaches*. Retrieved from www.calvert.com/NRC/Literature/Documents/TL10036.pdf
Cambridge Institute for Sustainability Leadership (CISL). (2016). *"Investing for Resilience" and "Closing the Protection Gap"*. Retrieved from www.cisl.cam.ac.uk/publications/sustainable-finance-publications/investing-for-resilience
Cameron, E. (2016). *Resilient Business, Resilient World: New Private Sector Vision for the Future at D&C Days*. Retrieved from www.climatecentre.org/news/800/a-resilient-business-resilient-worlda-new-private-sector-vision-for-the-future-at-d
Cattaneo, O., Gereffi, G., and Staritz, C. (2010). *Global Value Chains in a Postcrisis World: A Development Perspective*. Washington, DC: World Bank.
Chestney, N. (2016, June 15). Solar, Wind Costs Could Fall Up to 59 Percent by 2025, Study Says. *Reuters*. Retrieved from www.reuters.com/article/us-renewables-cost-idUSKCN0Z10QD
Climate Bonds. (2015). *2015 Green Bond Market Roundup*. Retrieved from https://www.climatebonds.net/files/files/2015%20GB%20Market%20Roundup%2003A.pdf
Climate Bonds. (2017). *Climate Bonds 2016 Highlights: The Big Issuers: The Big Numbers: The Trends that Count and a 2017 Forecast*. Retrieved from: www.climatebonds.net/2017/01/climate-bonds-2016-highlights-big-issuers-big-numbers-trends-count-and-2017-forecast
Climate Wise and University of Cambridge. (2016). *Insurance Regulation for Sustainable Development: Protecting Human Rights Against Climate Risks and Natural Hazards*. Retrieved from https://cisl.cam.ac.uk/publications/publication-pdfs/insurance-regulation-report.pdf
Department of Foreign Affairs and Trade. (2016). *Roadmap to US$100 Billion*. Retrieved from http://dfat.gov.au/international-relations/themes/climate-change/Documents/climate-finance-roadmap-to-us100-billion.pdf
DfiD. (2015). *What Is the Evidence of the Impact of Microfinance on the Well-Being of Poor People?* Retrieved from www.givedirectly.org/pdf/DFID_microfinance_evidence_review.pdf

Dossani, R., and Kenney, M. (2003). Lift and Shift; Moving the Back Office to India. *Information Technologies and International Development, 1*(2), 21–37.

Engardio, P. E. (2005, March). Outsourcing Innovation. *Business Week*, 47–53.

Engardio, P. E., Bernstein, A., and Kripalani, M. (2003, February). Is Your Job Next. *Business Week*, 50–60.

Fievet, C. (2012). *Guidance for City Procurement to Facilitate Climate Change Adaptation Pursuant to the Mayor's 2007 Executive Order*. Harvard Law School. Retrieved from http://environment.law.harvard.edu/wp-content/uploads/2015/08/climate-adaptation-procurement-guidance.pdf

IEA. (2017, March 17). *IEA Finds CO2 Emissions flat for Third Straight Year Even as Global Economy Grew in 2016*. Retrieved from www.iea.org/newsroom/news/2017/march/iea-finds-co2-emissions-flat-for-third-straight-year-even-as-global-economy-grew.html

IEA. (2017). *Perspectives For The Energy Transition*. Retrieved from https://iea.org/publications/insights/insightpublications/PerspectivesfortheEnergyTransition.pdf

IISD. (2008). *Microfinance and Climate Change Adaptation*. Retrieved from www.iisd.org/sites/default/files/publications/microfinance_climate.pdf

IPCC. (2014). *Contribution of Working Group III to the Fifth Assessment Report of the Intergovernmental Panel on Climate Change*. Cambridge and New York: Cambridge University Press.

Marks and Spencer. (2015). *Global Community Programme*. Retrieved from https://corporate.marksandspencer.com/documents/plan-a-our-approach/global-community-programme-report-june2015.pdf

O'Marah, K. (2016). *Supply Chain Executives Must Lead on Climate Change*. Retrieved from www.scmworld.com/supply-chain-executives-must-lead-climate-change/

Olson, E. (2015). *How General Mills Worked With BSR to Set Ambitious, Science-Based Climate Targets*. Retrieved from www.bsr.org/our-insights/blog-view/how-general-mills-worked-with-bsr-to-set-climate-targets

Olson, E. (2016). *Walmart's Climate Ambition Signals a New Market Reality*. Retrieved from www.bsr.org/our-insights/blog-view/walmarts-climate-ambition-signals-a-new-market-reality

RE100. (2018). Retrieved from http://re100.org/, accessed January 2018.

Robiou du Pont, Y. M. (2017). Equitable Mitigation to Achieve the Paris Agreement Goals. *Journal of Climate Change, 7*, 38–43.

Rogelj, J. M. (2016). Paris Agreement Climate Proposals Need a Boost to Keep Warming Well Below 2°C. *Nature, 534*, 631–639.

SevernTrent. (2012). *Annual Report and Accounts*. Retrieved from https://severntrent.com/content/dam/stw/my-severn-trent/documents/2012-Annual-Report-and-Accounts.pdf

Stern, N. (2008). The Economics of Climate Change. *American Economic Review, 98*(2), 1–37.

Swiss Re. (2008). *Setting Up Sustainable Agricultural Insurance: The Example of China*. Retrieved from http://media.swissre.com/documents/setting_up_sustainable_agricultural_insurance_en.pdf

UN. (1972). *Declaration of the United Nations Conference on the Human Environmen*. Stockholm: United Nations.

UNFCCC. (1992). *United Nations Framework Convention*. Rio de Janeiro: United Nations.

UNFCCC. (2015). *Synthesis Report on the Aggregate Effect of the Intended Nationally Determined*. Retrieved from https://unfccc.int/resource/docs/2015/cop21/eng/07.pdf

Vivid Economics. (2015). *Building an Evidence Base on Private Sector Engagement in Financing Climate Change Adaptation*. Retrieved from http://vivideconomics.com/publications/building-an-evidence-base-on-private-sector-engagement-in-financing-climate-change-adaptation

Wadhwa, V., De Vitton, U. K., and Gereffi, G. (2008). *How the Disciple Became the Guru: Workforce Development in India's R&D Labs*. Ewing Marion Kauffman Foundation.

Walmart. (2017). Retrieved from https://news.walmart.com/2017/04/19/walmart-launches-project-gigaton-to-reduce-emissions-in-companys-supply-chain, accessed January 2018.

WEF. (2016). *The Global Risks Report 2016*, 11th Edition. Retrieved from www3.weforum.org/docs/GRR/WEF_GRR16.pdf

Wiener, J. B. (2007). Climate Change Policy and Policy Change in China. *UCLA Law Review*, 1805.

World Bank. (1999). *Microfinance Handbook: An Instititional and Financial Perspective*. Retrieved from https://openknowledge.worldbank.org/bitstream/handle/10986/12383/18771.pdf

World Bank, E. V. (2016). *State and Trends of Carbon Pricing 2016*. Retrieved from Worldbank.org: https://openknowledge.worldbank.org/handle/10986/25160

Part IV
Just transition

16

From the dirty past to the clean future

Addressing historic energy injustices with a just transition to a low-carbon future

J. Mijin Cha

INTRODUCTION

Transitioning away from fossil fuel use is fundamental to achieving the greenhouse gas emission reductions necessary to stop the worst impacts of climate change. Yet, the inability to reach a meaningful climate accord in Copenhagen in 2009 showed the limitations of focusing solely on greenhouse gas reductions. Della Porta and Parks mark the aftermath of the failure of climate negotiations in Copenhagen as the time when the climate change movement pivoted away from focusing only on greenhouse gas reductions to a broader discussion of climate justice (della Porta and Parks, 2014).

Climate justice looks beyond technical goals, such as emissions reduction targets and limiting global temperature rise, to address underlying issues of marginalisation and inequality. In parallel to the environmental justice movement that preceded it, climate justice addresses the disproportionate burden placed upon marginalised and displaced communities from climate change. These communities will suffer the most from the consequences of climate change, have the least amount of resources to mitigate the harms from climate change, and yet have contributed the least amount of carbon emissions.

While the impact of climate change on marginalised communities is well-established, the impact of moving away from fossil fuels on communities and workers is less well-established as a part of climate justice. The move away from fossil fuels is rightly seen as a positive step, and certainly decreasing fossil fuel use and extraction has many environmental, health and climate benefits. Yet, it is also true that the shift to a low-carbon economy, though necessary, will cause economic distress to regions and workers that rely upon fossil fuel extraction for economic security. Moreover, these communities and workers have long histories of sacrificing life and livelihood to provide the fuel for global economic growth. Addressing the impact on these workers and communities – past, present and future – must be an essential component of climate justice. In other words, issues of livelihood and workers within extractive industries must also be a consideration in climate justice if the transition to a low-carbon economy is to be just. Climate change policy must reduce greenhouse gas emissions *and also* provide a path for fossil fuel communities and workers to successfully transition into a low-carbon future.

Other declining industries have largely failed to successfully transition their workers and communities, leaving little guidance. This fact combined with the dominance of fossil fuels in the current economic system and the scale of transition that will be necessary underscores the need to include transitioning fossil fuel communities and workers into a low-carbon economy as a consideration of climate justice.

This chapter addresses the urgent need of just transition for fossil fuel communities and workers as a consideration of climate justice. The chapter begins with a discussion of environmental justice and climate justice concerns, introduces the concept of just transition, and provides a case study analysis of the formerly coal-dominant region of Ruhr, Germany, one of the few successful examples of just transition, to determine what elements and policies were essential to a successful transition. These findings can inform future just transition programs.

From environmental justice to climate justice

When the climate change movement pivoted to climate justice in the aftermath of the failure of the 2009 Copenhagen climate accords, the shift was reminiscent of the evolution of the environmental justice movement. Traditionally, the mainstream environmental movement[1] revolved around the causes of preservation of nature, resource management and pollution abatement (Bullard, 1993, see also, in general, Bullard, 2003, Taylor, 1993, Lee (1993)). This mainstream movement was primarily supported by white middle to upper middle-class members of society (Bullard, 1993). For decades, the fact that people of colour were facing some of the most severely polluted environments was being ignored. (McGowan, 2003) Traditional environmental groups resisted integrating these social issues of race and class into "environmental" concerns, insisting that environmental advocacy focus on the narrow view of conservation and preservation of nature. Even though evidence showed that environmental concerns cut across racial and class lines, the traditional activist in the mainstream environmental movement came from a background of above-average education, greater access to economic resources and a greater sense of personal power (McGowan, 2003). As a result, expanding the environmental agenda to include the idea of race and class as factors of environmental protection faced significant resistance within mainstream groups, and integrating these issues was a slow process within mainstream environmental groups.

In response, the environmental justice movement arose to address the disproportionate environmental burden and lack of participation in decision-making that people of colour endure. The phrase "environmental injustice" defines the situation where people of colour are forced, through their lack of access to decision-making and policy-making processes, to live with a disproportionate share of environmental harms (Agyeman et al., 2002). For example, communities of colour have higher rates of exposure to air pollutants, which leads to higher rates of asthma and lower health outcomes (Sze, 2004).

Environmental justice recognises that clean air and water and non-toxic living conditions must be viewed as basic civil rights, which are no less important than freedom of speech and the freedom to vote (Solis, 2003). The racial disparity of pollution exposure underscores the need to expand environmental advocacy beyond conversation and preservation of nature. Rather than being separate issues, the consequences of racial and economic injustice are inextricably intertwined with environmental concerns. For example, the lack of decision-making power resulting from political marginalisation leaves communities of colour and low-income communities unable to fight the citation of hazardous waste sites within their communities (Cole and Foster, 2001). These consequences compound and result in communities of colour and low-income communities being exposed to more pollution, leading to poorer health outcomes, which is then exacerbated by a lack of access to adequate healthcare because of racial and economic inequalities (Cole and Foster, 2001). As such, issues of race and class cannot be extricated from environmental concerns.

Similarly, the climate justice movement addressed failures within the mainstream climate change movement by expanding the focus of climate change advocacy beyond the technical view of emissions reductions and limiting global temperature increase to include issues of equity and inequity. Among other claims, climate justice advocacy focuses on the equity and inequity of climate mitigation and climate adaptation. In other words, climate justice asks the questions of who will bear the economic and social burden of the impacts of climate change. Who will bear the economic and social burden of carbon reduction? How can marginalised communities and lower-income countries be protected from both the impacts of climate change and the high cost of climate adaptation?[2]

Within the climate justice discussion, the impact of energy systems (i.e., how energy is produced and distributed) is a particular focus that looks at who will have access to clean energy and what injustices exist within energy systems. Sovacool et al. (2016) propose an energy justice framework that calls for a global energy system that, "fairly disseminates both the benefits and costs of energy services, and one that contributes more to representative and impartial energy decision-making." The principles under this framework include availability, affordability, due process, transparency and accountability, and environmental sustainability. Justice within this context is concerned with the distribution of energy and the environmental impacts of energy systems.

However, the negative impact on fossil fuel communities from extractive industries is not included within these discussions of energy systems. Fossil fuel communities have borne the brunt of economic and environmental burdens of fossil fuel extraction. The environmental devastation that extractive industries expose communities to and the lack of economic benefit to these communities and workers highlight the environmental and economic burden fossil fuel workers and communities have had to bear. Yet, discussions of climate and energy justice focus on who has access to energy and the environmental impact of energy systems and less on the impact of extractive industries on fossil fuel communities and workers. Moreover, the economic and social impact of decarbonisation on fossil fuel communities is also less developed within the climate and energy justice discussions (Healy and Barry, 2017).

The heavy dependence these workers and communities have on fossil fuel extraction means that decarbonisation and the transition to a low-carbon economy will be socially and economically devastating for these workers and communities without a deliberate and targeted intervention. This intervention must be a part of climate and energy justice discussions. Climate and energy justice must address both the sacrifice fossil fuel workers and communities have borne in our extractive fuel-based economy and also the negative consequences decarbonisation will have on fossil fuel communities and workers in order for the transition to a low-carbon economy to be just. The need and importance of transitioning workers and communities away from declining industries, in this case fossil fuel extraction, can be understood through the framework of just transition.

The case for just transition

The disproportionate environmental burden placed upon fossil fuel communities is akin to past environmental justice struggles, where disproportionate environmental burdens were, and continue to be, placed upon low-income and marginalised communities (Newell and Mulvaney, 2013). In addition, while fossil fuel communities and workers bear a disproportionate environmental burden, they also do not reap the majority of the economic benefits of fossil fuel extraction. Rather, fossil fuel corporations and consumers, by way of lower energy prices, benefit from the extractive economy while fossil fuel communities and workers see a disproportionately low portion of the economic benefit. Just transition addresses the economic and environmental side effects of energy extraction and the consequences of decarbonising energy sources and economies and acknowledges the disproportionate environmental burden and also the disproportionate economic burden placed upon fossil fuel communities (Newell and Mulvaney, 2013, see also, in general, Heffron and McCauley, 2017).

The use of fossil fuels, including oil, coal and natural gas, has built economies globally (Environmental and Energy Study Institute, 2017). Yet, it is rarely acknowledged that fossil fuel communities and workers face unjust conditions to fuel this economic development. Many communities that extracted fossil fuels were unable to develop other industries, leaving them particularly vulnerable in the transition away from fossil fuel energy sources (see e.g. Perry, 1982). Fossil fuel companies saw the vast majority of economic benefit from extraction while those living and working in fossil fuel communities reaped a far smaller share of economic gains and faced severe environmental pollution (Mountains of Injustice, 2011).

In the U.S. state of Kentucky, for example, the heavy reliance on coal production pushed out any other local development investment that might reduce access to coal (Perry, 1982). Research shows that counties in Kentucky that were highly dependent on coal production had significantly lower industrial diversification (Perry, 1982). Coal production dominated local politics, and its favoured tax status made other economic activity costlier, further inhibiting the state's ability to diversify its economic activity. The heavy dependence on coal did not economically benefit the workers and communities that grew dependent on extracting the resource. Even in "boom" times, Kentucky counties that were heavily dependent on coal production did not have income levels much higher than those of nearby areas that were not as dependent on coal mining (Perry, 1982). Moreover, the benefits from coal mining are concentrated among coal mine operators and holders of mineral rights.

In addition to the economic marginalisation, fossil fuel communities suffer health consequences and environmental burdens as a result of mining activities. Studies have shown that exacerbated health disparities are a direct result of coal production, for example (Zullig and Hendryx, 2011). In the heaviest coal mining region of the U.S., central Appalachia, residents, "are at greater risk for major depression and several psychological distress compared with other areas of Appalachia or the nation" (Zullig and Hendryx, 2011). Moreover, the environmental impacts of mining are devastating. The environmental impacts range from the destruction of geological formations to access coal, for instance, to the damage caused by mining waste, which can poison water supplies, to the toxins in coal dust that migrates into schoolyards and communities (Mountains of Injustice, 2011).

At the same time that fossil fuel communities bear the economic and environmental burden of extraction, the shift away from fossil fuel use will cause its own devastation. By some estimates, coal consumption will need to decrease by 60% in order to keep global warming under 2 degrees Celsius (Pollin and Callaci, 2016). Coal production is already declining as a result of several factors, including the increased availability of cheap natural gas, and preventing catastrophic global warming will require an even more drastic decline in coal production (Pollin and Callaci, 2016). Given the heavy role that fossil fuels play in creating the climate crisis, the decline necessary in fossil fuel use will mean that fossil fuel-dependent economies will bear the brunt of transitioning away from carbon-intensive fuels.

To be clear, a transition to a low-carbon economy is of fundamental importance. However, just transition requires not only valuing carbon emissions reductions but also mitigating negative impacts from carbon reduction, particularly for vulnerable communities and workers (see, in general, Scott and Smith, 2017; Behles, 2013). Carbon reduction policies will have a significant impact on labour markets and work and will fundamentally shift how economies function. Some impacts will be based on shifting away from fossil fuel production and use, whereas other impacts will be due to a more comprehensive climate mitigation and/or adaptation approach (UNEP, 2008,). The scale of economic and social transformation that needs to occur means that every aspect of our economy and our society will be impacted.

Formulating a just transition

The complexity of just transition efforts highlights the need for several stakeholders to be engaged with just transition efforts. One major constituency, particularly to ensure the protection of workers in the transition to a low-carbon economy, is the labour movement. Currently, a growing leadership within the labour movement understands the urgency of climate change and the role the labour movement can play in guiding environmental policy to protect workers for a just transition. As Annabella Rosemberg, climate and environmental advisor at the International Trade Union Confederation (ITUC) wrote:

> "Just Transition" can be understood as the conceptual framework in which the labour movement captures the complexities of the transition towards a low-carbon and climate-resilient economy, highlighting public policy needs and aiming to maximize benefits and minimize hardships for workers and their communities in this transformation.
>
> *(Rosemberg, 2010)*

Historically, efforts to transition workers away from a declining industry have proven to be largely unsuccessful. As an example, worker transition programs have developed in America to assist workers in several declining industries, including those who were negatively impacted by U.S. trade policies; workers negatively impacted by mechanisation, former Northeast and Midwest railroad workers, and former timber harvesters (Apollo Alliance & Cornell Global Labor Institute, 2009). These programs have had limited success in transitioning workers for many reasons, including limited participation rates and inadequate income and benefit levels. Research shows that rather than successfully transitioning into a new industry, workers in declining industries often end up losing a well-paying job and replacing it with a low-wage job (Public Citizen, 2014).

The scale of the transition to a low-carbon economy combined with the historical failure of transition programs makes understanding and successfully implementing just transition programs an urgent concern. To provide the beginnings of a just transition framework, experts have set out a series of guiding policies that must be put in place to address the complexities of transitioning an entire workforce and community dependent on fossil fuels. Unemployment benefits, fully funded pensions, education and training/re-training, and relocation support are a few of the steps that would be necessary to ensure a just transition for fossil fuel-dependent workers and communities (Olsen, 2009). While these elements are the bare necessity for a successful transition, the case of the Ruhr region offers a more complete and complex picture of what is necessary to transition away from a fossil fuel dominant economy.

The case of the Ruhr region

One of the few examples of successful just transition is the Ruhr region in Germany, which has been undergoing a transition away from fossil fuels for over 50 years. The Ruhr valley is in the state of North-Rhine Westphalia. Steel and coal production dominated the region for decades, and cities within the region developed around coal mines in the 1800s. At one point, the Ruhr region was the largest industrial site in Europe, and coal and steel production were major employers (Stroud, 2014). However, the coal mining and steel production became less and less competitive as cheaper products became available on the global market. As a result, the area has seen rising unemployment and industrial decline for over 50 years. In 1957, coal mining employed 473,000 workers. At the end of 2013, that number fell to 11,448 (European Trade Union Institute, 2016). The share of the economy provided by coal mining fell from 61% in 1960 to 21% in 2014. The federal state has been steadily divesting from coal, and coal subsidies were completely phased out by 2018, making coal mining even more expensive and even less competitive (Deutsche Welle, 2007).

Due to the history of dominance of coal and steel production, there was little economic diversity, and Ruhr's economy was dominated by a few very large firms (Taylor, 2015). This lack of economic diversity meant that once coal production began to decline, there were few options to help counter the resulting economic losses. In addition, there were no technical high schools or universities in the region until 1961, which made skills re-training more challenging (Gotting, 2014). Decades of coal and steel production have left a legacy of air and water pollution, coal mining waste and ground disruption from the underground tunnels used for coal mining causing regular sinkholes in the region (Taylor, 2015).

Coal and steel production oscillated for a few decades during the 1960s to the 1980s, but by the mid-1980s, it became clear that the region could no longer be sustained by coal and steel production. At this time, the State began a series of investment in three areas that were important to the region's future success: (1) investments in infrastructure, particularly intra- and inter-regional public transportation and roads; (2) investment in new universities and technical institutes; and (3) investment in environmental protection (Taylor, 2015). These investments were important because they linked the region to other areas, laid the groundwork for training and re-training opportunities, and dealt with the legacy of pollution, which in turn made the region a more desirable place to vacation and to relocate. The region further transformed in the late 1980s through the 1990s in a period of innovative and technological investment (Taylor, 2015). In 2010, the Ruhr region was Europe's official cultural capital (European Capital of Culture RUHR.2010, n.d.).

To transition an entire region away from fossil fuel requires deliberate and sustained strategies. There are immediate needs of workers facing displacement, and there are longer-term needs associated with economically and socially transitioning an entire region (Taylor, 2015; Thimm, 2010). In the case of the Ruhr region, just transition policies can be categorised into: (a) short-term policies that focused on the needs of displaced workers and (b) long-term actions to diversify the region's economy and employment base. As part of the just transition program, the regional government provided resources to trade unions, company works councils and other non-government bodies to also advance transition strategies.

To deal with the issues that current workers face, short-term policies included wage subsidies, compensation payments and early retirement, or if early retirement was not appropriate, job transfer schemes. Short-term policies help ease the immediate transition from when a mine or plant shuts down. Germany's strong social safety net helped provide economic security for transitioning workers. Fossil fuel workers tend to skew older, so early retirement can cover a large portion of the workforce. For the remaining workers, job transfer schemes are necessary.

Knowing there would be a permanent transition away from coal left decision-makers and advocates with the difficult task of transforming the economic and employment base of the Ruhr region. Long-term policies to diversify the economic and employment base looked to attract investment from high-tech and knowledge-based firms, expand the service sector and promote local entrepreneurship. An example of a long-term project is the transformation of Gelsenkirchen, a town that used to be dominated by the coal industry, into a "solar city" that is the largest supplier of solar energy in Europe (Peterson, 2015). Officials began to develop the city's solar industry in the 1990s, even though coal mining was still dominant. The federal government also invested in building an educational infrastructure to create new technical institutions and universities in the region. Diversifying the economic and employment base prevents the region from becoming overly dependent on one industry and allows for healthier economic growth. Additionally, transforming the region aids the overall community, not just fossil fuel workers. While short-term policies focus on the needs of displaced workers, long-term policies focus on the needs of the community and region in a low-carbon future.

Lessons from Ruhr

The Ruhr region is uniquely successful in being able to transition away from an economy dependent on coal and steel production to a more diversified economy. The Ruhr example provides insight into the difficulty of transitioning workers in declining industries. The Ruhr region also provides evidence that a strong public sector and strong trade union support are necessary for a successful transition.

The disconnect between green jobs and lost jobs

While the Ruhr region has seen success in transforming its economic base, it remains unclear to what extent workers were actually successfully transitioned (Taylor, 2015; Gotting, 2014). Researchers have concluded that it is unlikely that green jobs entirely replaced the jobs lost from coal and steel because the green jobs were created after workers had already been displaced (Stroud, 2014). This reality is important because climate advocates often counter employment losses in the fossil fuel industry with employment gains in the renewable energy industry. However, as the Ruhr example shows, there may be a time delay between when the fossil fuel jobs are lost and when the renewable energy jobs are created. In other regions and countries, there may also be a spatial disconnect between where fossil fuel jobs are lost and where renewable energy jobs are created. As such, job creation policies and efforts must be closely linked geographically and temporarily to where fossil fuel jobs are lost.

Moreover, the new jobs often required new skills. Thus, it may be assumed that the solar jobs that were created in projects like Gelsenkirchen were not at a large enough scale to meaningfully counter coal job losses before workers were displaced. Researchers did conclude, however, that it would be possible for the Ruhr region to make a transition to green jobs with skills development. The skills mismatch raises the importance of strong training programs. The investment in higher education institutions in the Ruhr region was a fundamentally important step in creating a training and re-training pipeline. In addition, partnering with trade unions is a way to ensure access to training and re-training programs, as training is a core component of trade unions. In Ruhr, trade union representatives worked with local politicians to create a plan for compensation and re-training for coal industry workers (Stanley Foundation, n.d.).

The importance of a strong public sector

The ability of the State to provide short-term and long-term plans shows the need for the public sector to guide and provide resources to help transition fossil fuel communities. Short-term support, such as unemployment assistance and other strong social safety net programmes, are most likely administered by the State. Long-term planning is also best grounded within the public sector because private interests have limited incentives, including fiduciary responsibilities to shareholders, to undertake long-term actions with uncertain economic returns. In the Ruhr region, the State set the seeds for regional transformation through investments in infrastructure, higher education institutions and environmental protection. The State was also able to initiate partnerships and programs to tap into innovative and cultural initiatives (Taylor, 2015). The multifaceted approach was necessary to deal with the scale of transformation. The complexity of regional economic transformation is better suited for state agencies with a holistic vision of regional transformation, as highlighted by the Ruhr example.

Beyond logistics and resources, just transition policies should be based in the public sector to help reverse economic and social inequality. The benefits of climate action should be shared broadly and not just reserved for the elite and, similarly, the burdens of climate action should be shared equally. Targeted public policy can redistribute the burdens and benefits of climate harms. For example, emissions reduction should be a public good and not reserved only for those that can afford it. Grounding policies and actions in the public sector can better ensure access to clean energy and emissions reductions benefits for low-income communities and communities of colour that have historically borne the brunt of environmental harms, rather than only for communities that can afford low-carbon technologies (Benton-Connell, et. al., 2015). Grounding policies in the private sector, in contrast, would have to take profit maximisation into account and could make low-carbon technology prohibitively expensive for low-income communities (Benton-Connell, et. al., 2015 and Lydersen, 2016).

The importance of strong trade unions

In addition to the role of trade unions in training and re-training workforces, trade unions, as an entity, were a key to protecting coal miners in the Ruhr (Abraham, 2017). Working with the federal government, the state governments and an energy conglomerate, the Industrial Guild *Bergbau, Chemie, Energie*/Mining, Chemical, Energy (IG BCE) union negotiated an agreement to end all hard coal mining in Germany by 2018 and to provide displaced workers with decent compensation and assistance with job replacement (Abraham, 2017). Workers who worked at least 25 years could retire as early as age 49 and receive a monthly stipend until they qualified for pension benefits. Younger workers could move to another energy or mining job in a different region or enrol in re-training programs to develop new skills while receiving decent pay and job-searching assistance.

The transition assistance for the miners was strong because IG BCE "fought for a degree of democratic industrial planning" (Abraham, 2017), which allowed the union to be a part of industrial policy negotiations, along with governments and business. IG BCE's example shows the importance of strong trade unions to advocate for just transition for their workers. Trade unions are even more important in the transition to a low-carbon future because fossil fuel industries have higher rates of unionisation than other sectors, including the emerging renewable energy sector (Jones and Zabin, 2015; U.S. Dep't of Labor, Bureau of Labor Statistics, 2017). Unionised workers, on average, earn higher wages and are more likely to have benefits. Moving away from fossil fuels to renewable energy leaves workers less protected.

The Ruhr example is particularly relevant because the transition was not just for an isolated community but for an entire region, which shows that successfully transforming entire economies away from carbon-intensive industries is possible. The Ruhr region transformation shows that with advanced and long-term planning, dedicated resources and multi-stakeholder processes, fossil fuel communities and workers can be transitioned into a low-carbon future in a just manner.

Conclusion

While the transition away from fossil fuels is daunting, it is also a natural evolution. Fossil fuel extraction and use built economies around the world. Now, we must move on from the dirty, polluting ways of the past if we have any hope of mitigating the damage of the climate crisis. Yet, while doing so, we must also acknowledge the economic and social harm that has been borne by the very communities that have provided fuel for economic growth worldwide and ensure that the transition away from extractive fuels does not increase economic and social inequality in these regions. Principles of climate and energy justice require that fossil fuel communities and workers transition into a low-carbon future in a way that not only addresses the harms of the past but also includes these communities and workers in the economy of the future.

The case of the Ruhr region offers valuable lessons for future just transition efforts. It must be noted, however, that the Ruhr transformation took several decades, a time horizon that must be shortened for future efforts because of the rapid onset of climate change. While efforts may be advanced more quickly, the substance must remain grounded in protecting extractive communities and workers. Without worker and community protections, there cannot be a just low-carbon future.

Notes

1 The traditional environmental movement discussed here is in the United States, where the ideas of "environmental justice" rose to awareness.
2 These questions and ideas of climate justice were informed, in general, by Carney (2016), Gerrard (2013), Jenkins (2018), Kaswan (2009), Ottinger (2013).

References

Abraham, J. (2017) 'Just Transition for Miners: Labor Environmentalism in the Ruhr and Appalachian Coalfields', *New Political Science*, vol. 29, issue 2, pp. 218–240.

Agyeman, J., Bullard, R., and Evans, B. (2002) 'Exploring the Nexus: Bringing Together Sustainability, Environmental Justice and Equity', *Space and Polity*, vol. 6, issue 1, pp. 77–90.

Apollo Alliance & Cornell Global Labor Institute (2009) 'Making the Transition: Helping Workers and Communities Retool for the Clean Energy Economy', www.climatechange.ca.gov/eaac/comments/2009-12-11_California_Labor_Federation_attachment_2.pdf, accessed 18 April 2018.

Behles, D. (2013) 'From Dirty to Green: Increasing Energy Efficiency and Renewable Energy in Environmental Justice Communities', *Villanova Law Review*, vol. 58, pp. 25–27.

Benton-Connell, K. et. al. (2015) 'Power to the People: Toward Democratic Control of Electricity Generation,' http://unionsforenergydemocracy.org/wp-content/uploads/2015/06/TUED-Power-to-the-Peoplefinal.pdf, accessed 20 September 2018.

Bullard, R. (1993) 'Anatomy of Environmental Racism and the Environmental Justice Movement', in R. Bullard and B. Chavis (eds.), *Confronting Environmental Racism: Voices From the Grassroots*. Boston, MA: Southend Press.

Bullard, R. (2003) 'Environmental Justice for All', *Crisis (the New)*, vol. 110, issue 1.

Caney, S. (2016) 'The Struggle for Climate Justice in a Non-Ideal World', *Midwest Studies in Philosophy*, vol. 40, pp. 9–26.

Climate Justice: An Introduction (2017) Roser, D. and Seidel, C. (eds.). London: Routledge.

Cole, L. and Foster, S. (2001) *From the Ground Up: Environmental Racism and the Rise of the Environmental Justice Movement*. New York: NYU Press.

Della Porta, D. and Parks, L. (2014) 'Framing Processes in the Climate Movement: From Climate Change to Climate Justice', in M. Dietz and H. Garrelts (eds.), *Routledge Handbook of the Climate Change Movement*. London: Routledge.

Deutsche Welle (2007) 'The Rise and Fall of Germany's Coal Mining Industry', www.dw.com/en/the-rise-and-fall-of-germanys-coal-mining-industry/a-2331545, accessed 13 April 2018.

Environmental and Energy Study Institute (2017) 'Fossil Fuels', www.eesi.org/topics/fossil-fuels/description, accessed 30 March 2018.

'European Capital of Culture RUHR.2010' (n.d.) http://archiv.ruhr2010.de/en/home.html, accessed 7 April 2018.

European Trade Union Institute (2016) 'Social Partners and the Collaborative Approach Are Key to the Green Transition of the Ruhr Region', www.etui.org/News/Social-partners-and-the-collaborative-approach-are-key-to-the-green-transition-of-the-Ruhr-region, accessed 10 April 2018.

Gerrard, M. (2013) 'What Does Environmental Justice Mean in an Era of Global Climate Change', *Journal of Environmental and Sustainability Law*, vol. 19, pp. 278–302.

Gotting, A. (2014) 'Structural Change in the Ruhr Region: Problems, Potential and Developments', *IET Working Papers Series*, http://citeseerx.ist.psu.edu/viewdoc/download?doi=10.1.1.877.8402&rep=rep1 &type=pdf, accessed 18 April 2018.

Healy, N. and Barry, J. (2017) 'Politicizing Energy Justice and Energy Systems Transitions: Fossil Fuel Divestment and a "Just Transition"', *Energy Policy*, vol. 108, pp. 451–459.

Heffron, R. and McCauley, D. (2017) 'What Is the "Just Transition"', *Geoforum*, vol. 88, pp. 74–77.

Jenkins, K. et al. (2018) 'Humanizing Sociotechnical Transitions Through Energy Justice: An Ethical Framework for Global Transformative Change', *Energy Policy*, vol. 117, pp. 66–74.

Jones, B. and Zabin, C. (2015) 'Are Solar Energy Jobs Good Jobs?', *UC Berkeley Labor Center*, http://laborcenter. berkeley.edu/are-solar-energy-jobs-good-jobs, accessed 18 January 2018.

Kaswan, A. (2009) 'Greening the Grid and Climate Justice', *Environmental Law*, vol. 39, pp. 1143–1159.

Lee, C. (1993) 'Beyond Toxic Wastes and Race', in R. Bullard and B. Chavis (eds.), *Confronting Environmental Racism: Voices From the Grassroots*. Boston, MA: Southend Press.

Lydersen, K. (2016) 'Clean Power Plan Offers Chance to Right Past Injustices, Advocates Say', *Midwest Energy News*, http://midwestenergynews.com/2016/08/08/clean-power-plan-offers-chance-to-right-past-injustices-advocates-say/ accessed 10 April 2018.

McGowan, A. (2003) 'Environmental Justice for All', *Environment*, vol. 45, issue 5, p. 1.

Mountains of Injustice (2011), Morrone, M. and Buckley, G. (eds.). Ohio: Ohio University Press.

Newell, P. and Mulvaney, D. (2013) 'The Political Economy of the "Just Transition"', *The Geographical Journal*, vol. 179, issue 2, pp. 132–140.

Olsen, L. (2009) 'The Employment Effects of Climate Change and Climate Change Responses: A Role for International Labour Standards?', www.ilo.org/actrav/info/pubs/WCMS_122181/lang – en/index.htm, accessed 13 April 2018.

Ottinger, G. (2013) 'The Winds of Change: Environmental Justice in Energy Transitions', *Science as Culture*, vol. 22, issue 2, pp. 222–229.

Perry, C., (1982) 'Coal Production and Socioeconomic Development in Southern Appalachia: The Case of Eastern Kentucky', *Social Indicators Research*, vol. 11, issue 2, pp. 192–205.

Peterson, E. (2015) 'In Germany, A City Moves Away From Coal', *WFPL News*, http://energyfuture.wfpl. org/in-germany-a-city-moves-away-from-coal/, accessed 13 April 2018.

Pollin, R. and Callaci, B. (2016) 'A Just Transition for U.S. Fossil Fuel Industry Workers', *The American Prospect*, http://prospect.org/article/just-transition-us-fossil-fuel-industry-workers, accessed 13 April 2018.

Public Citizen (2014) 'NAFTA's 20-Year Legacy and the Fate of the Trans-Pacific Partnership', www.citizen. org/sites/default/files/nafta-at-20.pdf, accessed 14 April 2018.

Rosemberg, A. (2010) 'Building a Just Transition, the Linkages Between Climate Change and Employment,' *International Journal of Labour Research*, vol. 2, Issue 2, pp. 125–159.

Scott, D. and Smith, A. (2017) 'Sacrifice Zones in the Green Energy Economy: The "New" Climate Refugees', *Transnational Law and Contemporary Problems*, vol. 26, pp. 371–381.

Solis, H. (2003) 'Environmental Justice: An Unalienable Right for All', *Human Rights*, vol. 5.

Sovacool, B. et al. (2016) 'Energy Decisions Reframed as Justice and Ethical Concerns', *Nature Energy*, vol. 1, issue 4, p. 4.

Stanley Foundation (n.d.) 'Life After Coal', www.stanleyfoundation.org/articles.cfm?id=850, accessed 18 April 2018.

Stroud, D. et al. (2014) 'Skill Development in the Transition to a "Green Economy": A "Varieties of Capitalism" Analysis', *The Economic and Labour Relations Review*, vol. 25, issue 1, pp. 10–27.

Sze, J. (2004) 'Gender, Asthma Politics, and Environmental Justice', in R. Stein (ed.), *New Perspectives on Environmental Justice: Gender, Sexuality, and Activism*. Brunswick, NJ: Rutgers.

Taylor, D. (1993) 'Environmentalism and the Politics of Inclusion', in R. Bullard and B. Chavis (eds.), *Confronting Environmental Racism: Voices From the Grassroots*. Boston, MA: Southend Press.

Taylor, R. (2015) 'Case Study: A Review of Industrial Restructuring in the Ruhr Valley and Relevant Points for China', *Institute for Industrial Productivity*, www.iipnetwork.org/Industrial%20Restructuring%20 in%20the%20Ruhr%20Valley.pdf, accessed 18 April 2018.

Thimm, K. (2010) 'Germany's Ruhr Valley Looks Back to Its Future', *Spiegel Online*, 5 March, www.spiegel. de/international/culture-of-steel-germany-s-ruhr-valley-looks-back-to-its-future-a-681791.html, accessed 18 April 2018.

U.S. Dep't. of Labor, Bureau of Labor Statistics (2017) 'Union Members Summary'.

United Nations Environment Programme (2008) 'Green Jobs: Towards Decent Work in a Sustainable, Low-Carbon World', https://digitalcommons.ilr.cornell.edu/cgi/viewcontent.cgi?referer=www.google.com /&httpsredir=1&article=1057&context=intl, accessed 18 April 2018.

Zullig, K. and Hendryx, M. (2011) 'Health-Related Quality of Life Among Central Appalachian Residents in Mountaintop Mining Counties', *Research and Practice*, www.ncbi.nlm.nih.gov/pmc/articles/ PMC3076406/pdf/848.pdf, accessed 18 April 2018.

17

Just energy? Structures of energy (in)justice and the Indonesian coal sector

Anna Fünfgeld

Introduction: just energy?[1]

Energy is central to struggles over climate justice. Greenhouse gas (GHG) emissions from the energy sector account for around two-thirds of all anthropogenic GHG emissions, with the power sector the biggest contributor (IEA, 2015). This is due to the high proportion of fossil fuels in current energy systems. Oil, coal and gas amounted to around 86% of worldwide energy supply in 2016 (McCauley, 2018), and despite a growth in the share of non-fossil fuel sources, on a global scale fossil fuels are still projected to account for 77% of energy use in 2040 (U.S. EIA, 2017). Thus fossil fuel-based energy generation is regarded as a major source of anthropogenic climate change (Davis et al., 2010) and therefore remains one of the biggest challenges when tackling climate change impacts in the decades to come. On the international level, there has been a growing awareness of the challenges of tackling climate change arising from fossil fuel-related emissions. While international and domestic civil society organisations and countries highly vulnerable to climate change impacts have been emphasising the need to cut emissions from the energy sector for a long time, the problems arising from fossil fuel-based energy systems have only recently been acknowledged by some major industrialised and emerging economies. *Inter alia*, during the latest UN Climate Change Conference held in November 2017 in Bonn, 19 governments (including several U.S. states) announced a goal to phase out coal-based power generation by 2030 in a move initiated by Canada and the United Kingdom.[2] Yet most of the biggest coal producers and consumers (including Indonesia) have not joined this so-called *powering past coal alliance*.[3]

The energy sector therefore remains a major field of struggle in climate justice. However, in order to further understand its importance to questions of (in)justice, it is necessary to look beyond inequalities arising from energy-related emissions. Unequal access to energy affects countless people worldwide, especially with regards to the electricity sector – either because they are not connected to a power grid or because they cannot afford electricity. In Indonesia, this is apparent when considering the spatial disparities: in some of the eastern islands like Papua, around half of the population still lack access to electricity, and even on the country's main island Java, where there is a higher level of electrification, many rural communities suffer from frequent blackouts. Therefore, the current Indonesian government seeks to expand electrification and ensure affordable prices in order to enhance societal equity and generally foster economic growth levels and development. However, in its approach to doing so, the current administration relies heavily on coal-based power production. The mining and firing of coal, in turn, disproportionately affects rural farming and fishing communities living in close proximity to the production sites and thereby aggravates societal inequalities. Certainly, as we shall see, coal-based electricity generation leads to access restrictions to land and coastal areas, severe reductions of harvests, livelihood changes, environmental and health impacts, and (human) rights violations. Therefore, inequality in the energy sector not only tackles the question of who suffers from emission-related climate impacts and who has or does not have access to energy supply. It is also about who profits from specific modes of energy production and who suffers from them. Thus, the energy sector has become a major field of struggle over social justice in countries like Indonesia.

In order to explore the multiple dimensions of (in)justice related to the Indonesian energy sector, this chapter proposes an extended version of recent frameworks on "energy justice." It draws upon empirical field research in two different localities related to coal-based power generation. One is a coal mining site in East Kalimantan province, where the majority of Indonesian coal is extracted. The other is the area surrounding a coal power plant in West Java. The chapter identifies what a social justice perspective can add to our understanding of the energy sector and why it is useful for academic and social movement approaches. The following section develops an extended version of the energy justice framework by drawing on existing approaches to environmental, climate and energy justice, and re-embedding the justice dimensions of redistribution, recognition and participation – which are common to all three frameworks – in Nancy Fraser's justice theory. It furthermore adds a political-economic contextualisation in order to emphasise the importance of considering the interrelationship between fossil fuels and capitalist modes of production and consumption in energy justice approaches. This serves as a theoretical background for better understanding Indonesian coal politics, which are greatly affected by the domestic political-economic structure, as is laid out in the section on "coal-based energy politics in Indonesia." Following that, the justice framework is applied to the local experiences of coal extraction and power production in East Kalimantan and West Java. Finally, the conclusion addresses the questions of whether and why an energy justice framework seems useful for academic and movement approaches to climate justice and points out a number of further challenges to and prospects for energy justice.

Social justice, capitalism and the energy sector

From environmental and climate to energy justice

Efforts towards raising issues of social justice in the environmental field have a long history, both in social movement approaches and in academia. The term "environmental justice" was first coined in the 1980s by movements based in the U.S.[4] Initially, most of their claims focused on the unequal distribution of environmental costs, such as pollution, waste disposal and industrial plants, which due to their locations have disproportionately affected communities of colour and poorer neighbourhoods (Holifield et al., 2009; Walker, 2009; Schlosberg, 2013). Together with other approaches (such as those from the field of Political Ecology), this also contributed to widening our understanding of terms like "environment" or "nature" by emphasising the social and political dimensions underlying and resulting from seemingly mere environmental, non-human matters. Since then, the social movement and scientific concept of environmental justice has significantly expanded. It has gained some further differentiation in terms of considering positionalities that affect the vulnerability of different societal groups. While initially justice was often equated with "equity," later conceptualisations linked the term to multiple dimensions and reasons for (in)justice – most commonly the three core tenets of distributional, recognition and procedural justice. Moreover, linkages have been established, for example, to issues of economic and political rights or basic needs.[5] Environmental justice frameworks have been applied to a broadening range of issues and have expanded to new locations and even the global level. This also allowed for links to various civil society movements, such as civil, labour and indigenous rights groups, to be established (Schlosberg, 2013; Schlosberg and Collins, 2014). Still, quantitatively, the bulk of research in environmental justice remains centred on distributional aspects related to environmental hazards, and is mainly applied to local-level case studies located in the U.S. (Reed and George, 2011).

In contrast, climate justice approaches have been primarily turning to the international/global level by mainly (though not exclusively) targeting differentiated responsibilities and unequal levels of climate change impacts (Schlosberg, 2013). Climate justice approaches are commonly regarded as having emerged from the environmental justice approach and corresponding movements in the early 2000s.[6] For example, one of the earliest documents raising the issue, the *Bali Principles of Climate Justice*, issued by an NGO network in 2002, explicitly took on many aspects of an earlier declaration on environmental justice principles (Schlosberg and Collins, 2014). Similar to more recent concepts of environmental justice, climate justice approaches usually apply a pluralist conceptualisation of social justice by emphasising different dimensions.

Unlike "environmental justice" and "climate justice," which by now have become consolidated terms in social movement and academic discourses (Schlosberg and Collins, 2014), the concept of "energy justice" has only emerged within the last couple of years in a smaller academic circle. Therefore, it is still primarily a scholarly concept that is rarely used in civil society arenas,[7] where energy issues are often subsumed under environmental or climate justice claims. The rather smaller number of (mainly UK-based) researchers working (often jointly) on the topic usually refer to environmental and climate justice approaches, most obviously with respect to the three justice dimensions, which they apply to the energy sector (see, e.g., McCauley et al., 2013; Jenkins et al., 2014; Heffron et al., 2015; Jenkins et al., 2016a; Jenkins et al., 2016b; Bouzarovski and Simcock, 2017; Heffron and McCauley, 2017; LaBelle, 2017; Pesch et al., 2017). Energy justice is mainly understood as the "application of rights (both social and environmental) at each component part of the energy system" (McCauley, 2018: 2). Most scholars in the field perceive the approach primarily as a scientifically informed instrument for policy formulation and thus explicitly target policymakers as their audience. Hence, they have translated the approach into detailed concepts referring to common globalised policy buzzwords (such as affordability, availability, sustainability, etc.) and include checklists (see, e.g., Sovacool and Dworkin, 2015; Sovacool et al., 2016). Thus, some authors have argued that the concept's "lack of anti-establishment past" (Jenkins, 2018) constitutes a strength rather than a weakness as it provides for better connectivity to mainstream policy-making (Jenkins, 2018; McCauley, 2018). They stress that the entanglement of environmental and climate justice approaches with social movements is a major reason why the concepts have not made their way into policy formulation (McCauley, 2018). Yet this claim may be contested by pointing to the fact that there are several examples in which the demands of the respective movements have been applied in policy-making and political discourse (Schlosberg, 2013). Moreover, environmental justice scholars emphasise that despite the mutual benefits arising from exchange between social movements and academia, academia is still often too detached from the articulations and experiences of movements (Schlosberg, 2013). Thus, Schlosberg calls for scholars to "actually learn from the language, demands, and action of movements" (Schlosberg, 2013: 50) as he argues that "the engagement with what is articulated on the ground is of crucial value to our understanding and development of the the the concepts we study" (ibid.).

Nevertheless, the energy justice framework may serve as a valuable starting point for better understanding energy-related policy-making and evaluating it in terms of ethical claims. On this basis it may also provide some new insights into social movements and serve as a basis for argumentation and campaigning. Probably one of the most important contributions of the approach is the demand to take into account entire production chains when evaluating energy policies in light of the principles of justice (McCauley et al., 2013; Jenkins et al., 2014; Jenkins et al., 2016b). This fundamentally challenges the common approach of merely looking at issues of direct energy-related equity, such as electrification levels. As most of the authors refer to environmental justice approaches, they too combine distributional, procedural and recognition justice (see, e.g., McCauley et al., 2013; Jenkins et al., 2014; Jenkins et al., 2016b).[8] The distributional dimension of justice is about the allocation of burdens and benefits – for the energy sector applying to the entire production and consumption chain of energy. Justice of recognition entails appreciating the diversity of those affected by or involved in energy-related processes, including the appreciation that their experiences as well as patterns of disrespect and misrecognition may differ. Procedural justice targets the opportunity to participate in political processes, and the manner in which participation is enabled or disabled (Schlosberg, 2004; McCauley et al., 2013; Jenkins et al., 2014; Jenkins et al., 2016b).

Obviously, there are certain overlaps of the three justice dimensions, which has already been recognised in environmental justice scholarship and movement approaches (Schlosberg, 2004). Still, from a political theory perspective, a major analytical challenge arising from the combination of justice dimensions is their background in distinct philosophical traditions, ranging from liberal (and partly also libertarian), cosmopolitan and communitarian, to recognition-based approaches (McCauley, 2018; Schlosberg, 2004). Therefore, when working with the concept from an academic perspective, it is important to understand the interrelationships and possible inconsistencies arising from the combination of the three justice dimensions from a philosophical as well as an empirical perspective. One approach that includes all mentioned dimensions and sheds light on their interlinkages is to be found in the writings of Nancy Fraser. In response to a broader theoretical debate on the concepts of redistribution and recognition, Fraser (1996) suggests that both aspects may be perceived as two ends of a continuum rather than mutually exclusive claims. According to her, some struggles might be more or less clearly located at one of the two ends. For example, class struggles are obviously in closer relation to demands of redistribution, while struggles over positionalities in the field of sexuality are mainly about recognition. However, according to Fraser, both dimensions are to some extent relevant to all kinds of struggles and may be best understood as being located somewhere in between. This results in Fraser's so-called *bivalent* conception of justice, in which redistribution (related to societal status as opposed to mere identity politics) and recognition are two interrelated solutions for addressing social injustices. What then constitutes the normative core of her concept – and thus brings in the third of the aforementioned dimensions, procedural justice – is called *parity of participation* (Fraser, 1996). This is taken as an essential condition for justice, which according to Fraser "requires social arrangements that permit all (adult) members of society to interact with one another as peers" (Fraser, 1996: 30). It in turn requires standards of legal equality, an allocation of resources that ensures people's independence (redistribution), and institutionalised cultural patterns that express equal respect for everyone (recognition) (Fraser, 1996). This integrative approach therefore transcends a merely additive understanding of different justice dimensions and helps to better elucidate their interlinkages. It therefore seems useful to (re-)consider the theoretical background of the justice dimensions that have been replicated in the different justice frameworks.

Grounding justice in political-economic structures: fossil fuels and the capitalist mode of production

Another aspect that many of the aforementioned justice frameworks often lack is a more thorough understanding of underlying political-economic structures. This is particularly important when looking at the highly fossil fuel-based energy sector that is deeply intertwined with capitalist modes of production and consumption. The important role fossil fuels played in the historical transformation towards capitalism (Huber, 2009) led to path dependencies related to infrastructure development, historical trajectories, and connected business and state interests. Thus, "capitalist social life is profoundly dependent on the abundant provision of fossil fuel energy, for example, coal powered electric power plants, oil powered transportation systems and gas-fired furnaces" (Huber, 2009: 105). Additionally, the centrality of fossil fuels for capitalist industrial development rests on a number of comparative advantages (as compared to biological sources), such as the fact that it is a mobile energy source, thereby making industrial production independent of local availability. It can be used constantly and – in contrast to renewable energy sources where storage problems remain – its intensity is not restricted by certain natural rhythms (Altvater, 2007). This in turn enables mass production that eventually yields consumption (Huber, 2009). However, negative "side effects" of fossil fuel usage are threatening existing ways of life. Therefore, capitalist crisis and climate crisis are closely connected aspects. Moreover, the capitalist system – or what has recently been termed the *imperial mode of living* – is based on highly uneven power relations. It is characterised by an uneven distribution of costs and benefits between and within societies based on spatial and temporal patterns of outsourcing. The unjust distribution of resources is based on the exploitation of labour and nature alike. It is deeply anchored in and enforced through the everyday practices, aspirations and knowledge structures of a transnational consumerist class. It is furthermore stabilised by established physical and material infrastructures and political-economic institutions aiming to extend their basic functioning by advocating neoliberal policies. While this was originally the structural basis of political-economic arrangements in the Global North, similar patterns have been spreading rapidly to countries of the Global South (Brand and Wissen, 2013; I.L.A., 2017). Energy – and especially fossil fuel-based energy generation – may be considered the backbone of these political-economic arrangements. As the major basis of production and consumption, it ensures their steady operation. Dominant modes of fossil fuel-based energy production require the exploitation of labour and nature. They thereby intensify the unequal appropriation of nature on the local and domestic, as well as global, scales. Obviously, this is the case not only for the local impacts of production sites but also for global impacts arising from energy production and consumption. Economistic approaches that usually understand these climate change-related impacts as economic inefficiency and try to measure environmental pollution in terms of its costs and benefits (Bell, 2010) cannot comprehend the underlying patterns of unequal distribution nor the effects they have upon different parts of society. "Economic reductionism" (Bell, 2010) treats all needs and wants – and therefore all costs and benefits – alike and monetises them under the single metric of money in order to identify some supposedly optimal trade-off (Bell, 2010. Those monetarisation efforts and their outcomes therefore have to be challenged by a justice-oriented approach that takes into account different perspectives and positionalities regarding so-called costs and benefits, the incalculable matters in between those concepts, as well as the political-economic structures energy matters are embedded in.

In sum, the chapter proposes an extended version of the energy justice approach, consisting of three core aspects. First, as suggested by other authors, when assessing energy politics in terms of their implications for social justice, we should consider entire production chains. Second, it is important to take into account different dimensions of (in)justice, namely in terms of distribution, recognition and parity of participation. However, this should not be done in an additive fashion: correlations between them have to be assessed in order to allow for a more comprehensive understanding of underlying patterns of injustice. Third, I propose that the political-economic structures underlying injustices arising from the energy sector should be examined. This includes understanding the relation of fossil fuels to general patterns of capitalist production and consumption, but also requires a country-specific assessment of ownership structures, and decision-making and enforcement power. Just as fossil fuels are crucial to the functioning of capitalist modes of production, they are also embedded in political-economic structures and partly constitute domestic configurations of power. For the Indonesian case, this calls for assessing not only current policies in the energy sector, but also the political-economic structures they are embedded in, and an empirically informed evaluation of the impact energy politics has upon specific parts of society. The following sub-chapters centre on the dominant resource in the Indonesian electricity sector, coal, and track its impacts on local communities in extraction and production areas by analysing it along the lines of energy justice.

Energy (in)justice in Indonesia

Coal-based energy politics in Indonesia

Being a densely populated, archipelagic state with great biodiversity and a coastline of staggering length, Indonesia is one of the countries most vulnerable to climate change impacts. At the same time, it is one of the world's largest greenhouse gas emitters.[9] While the Indonesian government has initiated a number of measures in order to reduce deforestation and forest degradation, emissions in other sectors – especially electricity, industry and transportation – are rapidly increasing. It is estimated that while the LULUCF (land use, land use change and forestry) sector still dominates emission levels today, energy-related emissions are going to increase to over 50% of total emissions by 2026–2027, becoming the largest source of GHG emissions (Wijaya et al., 2017). This development is underpinned by fossil fuel-based energy production, largely based on coal, which currently accounts for more than half of the power generated in the country (Cornot-Gandolphe, 2017). Particularly since the mid-2000s, the country has witnessed a massive expansion in both the production and export of coal. This has led to Indonesia's standing as one of the largest producers and exporters of coal worldwide, currently providing almost 28% of global coal exports (IEA, 2017). In order to reach the emission targets included in Indonesia's Nationally Determined Contribution, the government would need to initiate an extensive transformation of the energy sector. While the country's target to reach a share of 23% of renewables in the energy mix by 2025 seems to point in this direction, many stakeholders suggest that it is unlikely to be realised (Bridle et al., 2018). *Inter alia*, this is due to a frequent change of regulations, power purchase prices that are perceived to be too low to recover investments, and the monopoly of the state-owned electricity company PLN (*Perusahaan Listrik Negara*). Moreover, unfavourable conditions for renewables also result from the fact that many powerful stakeholders favour coal-based energy production, which is closely related to current political-economic structures (Bridle et al., 2018).

Generally, Indonesia's economy is best described as a hybrid form of capitalism "characterized by a combination of market-based policies and institutions, direct forms of state intervention, and coordination based on the predatory interests of powerful politico-business families" (Rosser, 2014: 79).[10] The latter refers to a domestic capitalist class that emerged from the powerful politico-bureaucratic families of former president Suharto's *New Order* regime (1966–1998). Despite the implementation of neoliberal policies, the Suharto regime retained some features established under Indonesia's first president Sukarno (1945–1967). This included a number of state-owned corporations controlling key economic sectors such as natural resources. State officials made use of their privileged access to licences, concessions and funds and thereby managed to establish a system of patronage and favour (Robison, 1986; Hadiz and Robison, 2013; Rosser, 2014). From the 1980s onward, these rent-seekers – among them Suharto's own family – started to become directly engaged in business activities and established vast family-run business conglomerates (Robison, 1986; Hadiz and Robison, 2013). In 1997/1998, the Asian economic crisis precipitated the end of the *New Order* regime, leading to the implementation of democratisation and decentralisation reforms. Yet these reforms did not seriously undermine the long-established fusion of political and economic power. The old family conglomerates survived and successfully reorganised themselves within the democratic system. By reinventing themselves as powerful party functionaries and parliamentarians and by forming new alliances with mass organisations, local business and security sector officials, they maintained the oligarchic structure of the *New Order* regime (Robison and Hadiz, 2004). Predatory practices persist and "access to and control of public office and state authority continues to be the key determinant of how private wealth and social power is accumulated and distributed" (Hadiz and Robison, 2013: 35). Still, there is also a reverse flow of influence as new wealthy businesspeople have recently entered the political scene. The political rise of these new second-level politicians with business backgrounds is oftentimes a direct result of their ability to buy their way into political parties, where they use their new political influence in favour of their economic interests (Aspinall, 2013). Hence the Indonesian economic system has also been termed "oligarchic capitalism" (Rosser, 2014).[11]

Thus democratisation and decentralisation reforms did not seriously undermine the long-established fusion of political and economic power. In fact, the transfer of responsibilities to the subnational level opened up new rent-seeking opportunities. Likewise, it appears that the vast number of coal mining concessions is related to the shifting of competencies to local government leaders. Until the reform of the regional autonomy law in 2014, the district and municipality heads were responsible for issuing coal mining concessions.[12] Together with weak law enforcement structures, this allowed for the establishment of a set of various illegal and semi-legal practices connected to patronage, self-enrichment and corruption. Local election candidates have received financial support for their election campaigns that was meant to be recompensed via mining concessions afterwards (Jatam, 2018).[13] However, the close entanglement among politicians, bureaucrats and businesspeople on the local and domestic political level reaches far beyond such immediate relations. Businesspeople have entered politics, and conversely, politicians and bureaucrats have entered the coal mining business, rendering a clear distinction between them difficult. Many government officials, parliamentarians, administrative workers and security personnel are directly involved in the coal business in one way or another, taking advantage of their positions (Fünfgeld, 2016a; Fünfgeld, 2016b).

The implementation of the new Local Government Law No. 23/2014 coincided with a temporary downturn in international coal prices that (together with a sharp decrease in imports by China, Indonesia's most important market for coal) led to a reduction of export rates and caused the bankruptcy of many smaller coal mining companies. Since then, the government's coal policy has focused more on the domestic market, which is underlined by a domestic market obligation and a connected price cap. The bigger coal companies' need for new sales markets seems to go hand in hand with President Joko Widodo's (Jokowi since 2014) political objectives to enhance economic growth and development, which he relates to infrastructure development, amongst others in the electricity sector. One of the fundamental aspirations of the Jokowi administration is to increase electrification levels while providing affordable prices to the citizens. A large share of households in Indonesia – mainly those in rural and rather remote areas located on the eastern islands – are not yet connected to a power grid (Gokkon, 2017). This is reflected in the so-called *35 Gigawatt Programme* as well as in other energy planning documents that are, for example, meant to electrify 2,500 villages that do not yet have access to electricity or are still relying on insecure power supply through diesel generators. In this respect, coal is the energy resource of choice, as government representatives perceive it to be the country's cheapest energy resource.[14] However, these objectives are called into question by civil society activists. They argue that the government's energy planning rather targets economic growth and accommodates industry investments as the vast bulk of coal power plants are to be erected on the islands where electrification levels are already high (especially in Java), while remote areas and especially the eastern islands would not benefit from it.[15] Out of the prospective additional 35 gigawatts, 20 gigawatts shall be based on coal, involving the construction of up to 291 additional power plants. While the target was initially projected to be accomplished by 2019, government representatives predicted some time ago that the deadline might have to be extended (Asmarini, 2015; Sundaryani, 2016; *The Jakarta Post*, 2016), and the state electricity company PLN is slowing down the erection of new power plants due to new calculations of national electricity demand.[16] By late 2017, only 3% of the envisaged additional capacity had been installed (Amelia, 2018). However, several new coal power plants are on the way, and the coal industry still assumes that the program will be realised, albeit over an extended timeframe.[17] If continued, these infrastructure investments indicate a lock-in to fossil fuel-based power generation for decades to come (Chung, 2017). This orientation in energy politics may be regarded as the result of both the political influence of the coal business and the president's strong position and agenda in national energy politics.[18] As Jokowi is perceived to be "a product of *reformasi*" (Muhtadi, 2015: 349), his political success has initially been taken as a sign of the weakening of oligarchic structures. However, Jokowi's choice of cabinet members, as well as many recent political decisions (such as in the energy sector), reveal his dependency on the politico-business elite (Muhtadi, 2015), many of whom are involved in the coal business.[19] Yet Jokowi is still perceived as being the most important decision-maker in national energy politics. Thus, with the next presidential elections in 2019, it is unlikely that the government's orientation in the energy sector will be changing in the upcoming months.[20] This implies a continued and extended dependency on fossil fuels – regardless of societal, ecological and climate change impacts, and Indonesia's repeated promises to tackle greenhouse gas emissions. Moreover, coal mining and coal power plants are likely to exacerbate already existing inequalities in the country, as they lead to the further impoverishment of rural farming and fishing communities, as will be shown in the next section.

Coal and local experiences of injustice in Indonesia

It is characteristic of large-scale energy production and consumption that they connect various locations and people in multiple and complex ways that are difficult to track exactly. In the case of coal-based energy production in Indonesia, this may for example range from a mining site in rural East Kalimantan via the shipping of coal to West Java, where it is burned for electricity generation, up to the usage of electricity at an industrial site that produces a product for the end-user, wherever she may be located. Along this line injustices may be experienced in very different ways by various segments of society. However, when assessing rather concrete local experiences of people who live either in close proximity to a major mine in East Kalimantan, where most of the country's coal reserves are located, or near one of the Javanese coal power plants, experiences are strikingly similar in terms of the tremendous impact energy production has on their livelihoods.

Paradoxically, these rural areas are also among the many Indonesian locations suffering from erratic electricity supply and regular blackouts.[21] Moreover, environmental activists and local communities have pointed out severe problems resulting from the current policy, especially for the people living close to mining sites and power plants. In their view, the costs and burdens arising from coal-based power generation when taking into account the entire production chain far outweigh the advantages claimed by parts of the government and business actors.[22] Besides environmental and health impacts resulting from emissions, burdens are disproportionately shouldered by local communities. One of the major problems is severely reduced income opportunities. In both mining and power plant locations, this is due to restricted access to farm and fishing grounds.[23] Moreover, proximate coal mines lead to a reduction in crop yields and fish breeding as part of the farmland is destroyed (sometimes through mudding), fish ponds are polluted, and water is contaminated.[24] The vast coastal areas often assigned to power plants threaten fishing communities as they cannot enter the areas where they had previously fished and because water temperatures are being altered due to power plants' cooling systems, which reportedly leads to the problem that there is less fish to catch in the area. This is significantly problematic for "small" fishers that fish and/or collect seafood at the shore. In the same community in West Java, some people were also generating income from salt-making. However, since the power plant started operating, most salt-makers have also had to stop their production.[25] Additionally, in both areas, people report an increase in disease, mainly respiratory disease.[26] On top of this, it is not only socio-economic, environmental and health-related costs that render living in coal production areas difficult, but very often issues of human rights violations and the non-granting of citizenship rights are also reported. Most obviously, consultation of affected communities prior to the establishment of mines and power plants, as well as environmental impact assessments, are not being carried out thoroughly or sometimes not at all. The protests of local communities responding to these problems are often criminalised, and they are also reportedly often subject to threats from private and public so-called security forces (sometimes even organised as paramilitary groups).[27] In sum, a set of several intermingled kinds of illegal and semi-legal practices carried out by state personnel and private companies has led to the dramatic increase in the number of coal mining concessions and inhibits law enforcement in the coal sector. These practices range from bribery and corruption to non-compliance with regulations and citizen rights, and criminalisation of local protests (Fünfgeld, 2016a; Fünfgeld, 2016b).

Regarding both examples – coal mining and coal power plants in Indonesia – we may well find injustices connected to both ends, (re)distribution and recognition. However, in interviews and conversations, people directly affected by either coal extraction or coal-based power production far more often directly pointed to problems on the distributional side. Socio-economic problems (or the distribution of costs and benefits) are the primary concerns and claims people mention when asked about the consequences of closely located coal mining sites or power plants. The most severe changes affecting their lives are due to environmental degradation and pollution, as well as restricted access to land and coastal areas, which minimises their harvests (of rice, fruits, salt and fish) and leads to reduced income. Other burdens include environmental destruction and pollution-induced health problems. Moreover, they generally do not benefit from improved electricity supply (in fact, both localities still suffer from regular blackouts) and new income opportunities, for example, through direct employment at the mines or the power plant, remain limited.

Recognitional aspects seem to be far more subtle. These include, for example, the criminalisation of protest activities and related threats. We may perceive this as a matter of misrecognition or non-application of basic human and citizen rights. Another more concrete aspect of legal recognition relates to compensation payments for local fishermen living close to a coal-power plant in Java: only those who own boats received compensation, as shore fishers were not recognised as fishermen. A related dimension connected to the recognition paradigm is a self-perception of being "small people" who do not have access to political channels and representation of their needs. This self-perception may also be part of the reason why affected communities often do not directly demand some kind of recognition or point to the misrecognition of their rights as farming and/or fishing communities, although it seems obvious that their needs tend to be disregarded due to their class position. However, misrecognition in this case may also be related to the preservation of local culture and customs. Many of the members of the affected communities state that they do not seek compensation payments, but would prefer to be able to live and work as they did in the decades before their livelihoods started to change. This is also often connected to cultural ties to the land they work or their use of the sea for fishing or salt-making.[28]

Together, both dimensions, misrecognition and maldistribution, lead to a lack of parity of participation. For example, very often those most affected by coal mining or power plants not only lack adequate information on what is going to happen in their area, but they are also excluded from decision-making processes. Informational events, although formally required, do not take place at all, or the people affected are not invited, or they are framed in incomprehensible technical jargon. Environmental impact assessments, which are also part of the prerequisites for both mining activities and power plant construction, are often not conducted thoroughly, are sometimes issued far too late (for example, after construction has already begun) and are often not publicly accessible.[29] As official mechanisms such as prior community consultation are not being followed, and because many locals do not have legal access rights to farming land and fishing areas, they try to make themselves heard with the support of NGO actors via protest activities, such as blockades or demonstrations. These actions in turn are often criminalised. Thus, the lack of recognition of rural communities as acknowledged stakeholders as well as general distributional effects that allow others to enforce their interests through illegal means, lead to a lack of participation of the ones most affected by coal mining and coal-based power production.

Conclusion: just energy

The necessity of transforming our energy sectors and moving towards a low-carbon future is not only important due to the tremendous and unequally distributed environmental and climate impacts stemming from fossil fuel usage and production. It is also a question of social justice on the local and domestic political levels. In Indonesia, it is especially the farming and fishing communities living in close proximity to production sites such as coal mines and coal power plants that are suffering not only from limited access to electricity but also from deprivation due to reduced harvests, negative health and environmental impacts, and criminalisation and intimidation stemming from coal mining and coal-based power production. Here, people's means of subsistence as well as the continuation of their culture of living and working are at stake. These shortcomings that may well be regarded as effects stemming from maldistribution and misrecognition severely limit their opportunities for political participation and self-determination. Despite these circumstances, many people in affected communities engage in lengthy and often frustrating struggles to prevent a further worsening of their living conditions. Their struggles are especially difficult as it is not the one mining or power plant that they are struggling against, but in fact the whole strategic orientation of the Indonesian energy system, which in turn essentially rests on capitalist market logic. National energy policies are based on centralised decisions such as the *35 Gigawatt Programme*, which are backed by a political-economic structure in which entanglements between the political and the economic sphere work in favour of the coal business. As these characteristics are difficult to tackle for environmental or climate justice approaches alone, it is worthwhile speaking of issues of energy (in)justice in this context. However, a comprehensive energy justice framework needs to take into account the political-economic structures underlying energy decision-making as well as employ a more thorough understanding of the different dimensions of injustice in order to fully grasp the structures of energy injustice in a specific setting. In this way, the energy justice approach may also be considered a potential bridge between environmental and climate justice as it connects the different spatial entities, such as local and global struggles, related to the issue. It may serve as a strategic term in enforcing a stronger focus on energy-related injustices and future visions to tackle them in international as well as domestic struggles. In terms of research, it allows for consideration of the specifics of energy politics as a central concern for nation-states and simultaneously the particular set of characteristics connected to the material basis of energy systems. One of those, for example, is the multiple links and connections it establishes between sites of production, transport and consumption that very often involve various localities and even different countries.

While the case study examples shed light on various injustices arising from coal mining and electricity generation, more research needs to be done with respect to the transportation sector, which is equally important for fossil fuel-based energy systems, as well as other energy sources that might differ in their impacts from the coal example. Notably, what also needs further attention is the question of what a more just energy system should look like. This requires a broader understanding of the interrelationships between fossil fuel-based energy systems and capitalist modes of production, as well as the logic behind this fusion and the contradictions it produces. As Huber stresses: "As the current political economy attests, energy issues are at the epicentre of not only the geopolitics of empire and the global climate crisis, but also the more banal everyday reproduction of capitalist social life" (Huber, 2009: 113).

Therefore, ideas about energy transitions should not only tackle alternative, renewable technologies, but ideally also require a broader social and political change that allows for a more just re-orientation of energy politics. Such a vision could be community-organised and -owned energy production and supply based on small-scale renewables. There are already many projects oriented towards this idea in various parts of the world, and their number is growing.[30] Although their scope ranges from establishing completely self-sufficient, non-market-based, small-scale energy systems to larger cooperatives operating through market mechanisms, they do provide valuable examples for future pathways towards what has been termed *energy democracy* in recent German debates.[31] Indonesia exhibits a huge potential for renewable energy production such as in the fields of solar and small-scale hydro energy. Yet, due to the current prioritisation of coal, these potentials remain underdeveloped, and many regulatory, funding-related and institutional challenges remain. However, several civil society organisations have recently started to elaborate on the question of how to establish small-scale, people-owned renewable energy systems, and are seeking to develop possible roadmaps for a just energy transition in the country.

A possible starting point that is currently under discussion is a newly established village fund, which might serve as a potential funding basis for people-owned renewable energy systems in remote areas.[32] Altogether, it is only in close collaboration with social movements and through profound empirical insights that we will be able to develop a more comprehensive approach to energy justice and possible future pathways towards a socially and ecologically just transition. Thereby, everyone's right to access sufficient energy to live a dignified life as well as a more just distribution of the costs related to energy production have to be ensured. This also requires that affected communities have full access to information, meaningful, non-discriminatory decision-making procedures and legal systems. Moreover, it requires that worker's rights be taken into account in order to prevent new injustices arising from the usage of renewable energy sources.

To consider these aspects and come up with alternative concepts is especially crucial as general developments such as the declining prices of renewable energy technologies and rising awareness of the real costs of fossil fuels indicate that there might be a window of opportunity for a transition towards renewables. Only if the energy justice concept exceeds the academic sphere and grassroots movements are involved in its development can we reach a comprehensive understanding of the ethical challenges arising from energy politics and develop meaningful future visions of a just transformation of the energy sector. In this way, struggles over energy justice on the domestic level may also constitute important stepping stones for enhancing climate justice on the international level.

Notes

1 The chapter draws upon prior publications published with the Rosa Luxemburg Foundation, namely: Fünfgeld, A. (2017) "Claiming Justice Matters in Energy Policy," *Rosa-Luxemburg-Stiftung Policy Paper* 2/2017, and Fünfgeld, A. (2018) "Fossil Fuels and the Question of Justice," *Rosa-Luxemburg-Stiftung Analysen* 44.

2 The original text of the declaration can be retrieved from: www.gov.uk/government/uploads/system/uploads/attachment_data/file/660041/powering-past-coal-alliance.pdf.

3 Further criticisms of this pledge include the fact that some of the members' energy systems are overwhelmingly based on nuclear power (such as France), some engage in other unsustainable energy practices (for example, oil sands/tar sands mining in Canada) and some actually have very low or no coal reserves to be phased out (such as Fiji).

4 The beginnings of the environmental justice movement are usually associated with the 1982 protests by civil rights activists and environmentalists against the disposal of tainted soil at a new landfill in Warren County, North Carolina. However, there have also been earlier cases where exposure of poor and/or black communities towards environmental risks has been mentioned.

5 The latter is often associated with the capabilities approach by Amartya Sen. See: Sen, A. (1985) *Commodities and Capabilities*, North-Holland, Amsterdam.

6 While Hurricane Katrina, which hit the New Orleans region in 2005, is generally regarded as having had a major impact on the rise of climate change–related issues among environmental justice activists and academics, Schlosberg and Collins (2014) point at several intersections between the two approaches that already existed before and stress that environmental justice groups had a major impact upon the conceptualisation of climate justice. For example, the organisation CorpWatch already used the term in 1999 and was involved in the organisation of the Climate Justice summit in The Hague during the COP6 meeting of UNFCCC in 2001.

7 Exceptions include the Energy Justice Network, an American grassroots campaign body advocating clean energy, zero emissions and a zero-waste future (www.energyjustice.net/) and the European Energy Justice Network (www.energyjustice.eu/). The International Energy Justice Council is a consultancy board involving most scholars engaged in the European Energy Justice Network (http://energyjusticecouncil.org/index.html).

8 Reference in this respect is usually taken to the writings of David Schlosberg, building on the writings of Iris Marion Young and Nancy Fraser.

9 In late 2015, when escalating forest and peat fires led to a haze crisis all over Southeast Asia, Indonesia had even become the third largest emitter. Currently, it is ranked the world's fifth largest GHG emitter (Chrysolite et al., 2017).

10 The distinction between liberal market economies and coordinated market economies originates in Hall and Soskice's (2001) publication *Varieties of Capitalism*.

11 From a structural perspective, "oligarchy" is understood as "a system of power relations that enables the concentration of wealth and authority and its collective defence" (Hadiz and Robison, 2013: 37).

12 According to Law No. 4/2009 on Minerals and Coal Mining, the central government is responsible for the issuance of large-scale special mining permits (up to 50,000 ha) and local governments for small-scale mining permits (up to 10 ha). According to the anti-mining NGO Jaringan Advokasi Tambang (Jatam), in 2008 there were around 4,000 mineral and coal mining licenses. However, this number increased rapidly after the enactment of Law No. 4/2009 and had already risen to 10,936 licenses by 2013m translating into almost 7,000 new licenses in 2009–2013. Among these, half were issued for coal mining (3,492 until August 2016) (conversation with Jatam representatives, Jakarta, October 2016).

13 Interview with a law professor, East Kalimantan, 19 November 2011; interview with NGO representative, East Kalimantan, 24 October 2011.

14 These arguments were mentioned in several interviews with Indonesian government stakeholders in 2016, 2017 and 2018.

15 Interview with NGO representative, Jakarta, 24 March 2016; interview with NGO representative, Jakarta, 14 September 2017.

16 Interview with PLN representative, Jakarta, 25 April 2018.

17 Interview with a representative of the Indonesian Coal Mining Association, 6 April 2018, Jakarta.

18 Interview with NGO representative, Jakarta, 11 April 2018; interview with NGO representative/consultant, Jakarta, 3 April 2018.

19 Ibid.

20 Interview with NGO representative, Jakarta, 11 April 2018.

21 Author's observation, also mentioned in several interviews in 2011, 2016 and 2018.

22 This has been stressed in many interviews with NGO representatives and local activists in 2011, 2016, 2017 and 2018.

23 For example, in coal mining areas, some of the farmers did not have legal entitlements to the land they were cultivating and suddenly lost access to it, while others were persuaded to sell it without being fully aware of the impacts on their future economic situation. Moreover, as coal is extracted from open-pit mines, huge areas of East Kalimantan are covered by mining sites. For example, in East Kalimantan's capital Samarinda, coal mining concessions stretch over 71% of the municipal area (Fünfgeld, 2016a; interview with NGO representatives, East Kalimantan, 18 April 2018). As coal power plants are often located next to the sea, ship-less fishermen and -women and collectors of sea animals are especially suffering from restricted access. Coal power plants also go along with a high land consumption, usually using former farmlands. In a location in West Java, local inhabitants reported that they were forced to sell their land for very low rates. Moreover, many farmers received their money either very late or weren't paid at all (Focus group discussion with local community, West Java, 24 October 2016; interview with NGO representative, Jakarta, 27 October 2016; interview with local inhabitants, West Java, 2 September 2017).

24 Focus group discussion with local community, East Kalimantan, 2 November 2011; interview with local inhabitants, East Kalimantan, 16 November 2011; interview with local inhabitants, East Kalimantan, 22 November 2011.

25 Focus group discussion with local community, West Java, 24 October 2016; interview with local inhabitant 1, West Java, 2 September 2017; interview with local inhabitant 2, West Java, 2 September 2017; interview with local inhabitants, West Java, 3 September 2017.

26 Interview with a nurse from a local health centre, East Kalimantan, 21 November 2011; focus group discussion with local community, West Java, 24 October 2016; interview with local inhabitant 2, West Java, 2 September 2017; interview with local inhabitants, West Java, 3 September 2017.

27 Interview with NGO representative, East Kalimantan, 24 October 2011; interview with locals, East Kalimantan, 22 November 2011; interview with NGO representatives, East Kalimantan, 25 November 2011; conversation with local inhabitant, West Java, 3 September 2017; interview with NGO representatives, East Kalimantan, 18 April 2018; conversation with NGO representative, East Kalimantan, 21 April 2018; interview with NGO representative, Jakarta, 29 April 2018.

28 Interview with local inhabitant 2, West Java, 2 September 2017.

29 Focus group discussion with local community, East Kalimantan, 2 November 2011; interview with a law professor, East Kalimantan, 19 November 2011; focus group discussion with local community, West Java, 24 October 2016.

30 One amongst many examples is the initiative of the "power rebels" from Schönau, a small village community in the Black Forest in Germany that started to build up their own energy production and supply system in the wake of the Chernobyl disaster. See the homepage of the Energiewerke Schönau (EWS): www.ews-schoenau.de, and Morris, C. and Jungjohann, A. (2016) *Energy Democracy. Germany's Energiewende to Renewables*, Palgrave Macmillan, Cham.

31 For further information on the concept and descriptions of other cooperatives, see, e.g., Kunze, C. and Becker, S. (2015) *Wege der Energiedemokratie*, ibidem-Verlag, Stuttgart; Weis, L. et al. (2015) "Energiedemokratie. Grundlage und Perspektive einer kritischen Energieforschung," *Studien* 1/2015, Rosa-Luxemburg-Stiftung, Berlin; and Trade Unions for Energy Democracy (ed.) (2015) *Power to the People. Toward Democratic Control of Electricity Generation*, Working Paper No. 4.

32 Interview with NGO representative, Jakarta, 27 April 2018.

References

Altvater, E. (2007) 'The Social and Natural Environment of Fossil Capitalism', *The Socialist Register* 43, pp. 37–59

Amelia, A. R. (2018) 'Hingga November 2017, Hanya 3% Proyek 35 GW Yang Beroperasi. PLN memprediksi proyek 35 GW yang akan beroperasi hingga 2019 mencapai 22 GW', *Katadata*, 10 January 2018, https://katadata.co.id/berita/2018/01/10/hingga-november-2017-hanya-3-proyek-35-gw-yang-beroperasi

Asmarini, W. (2015) 'Indonesia Making Slow Progress on 35 GW Power Programme', *Reuters*, 11 November 2015

Aspinall, E. (2013) 'The Triumph of Capital? Class Politics and Indonesian Democratisation', *Journal of Contemporary Asia* 43(2), pp. 226–242

Bell, D. (2010) 'Justice and the Politics of Climate Change', in C. Lever-Tracy (ed.) *Routledge Handbook of Climate Change and Society*. Routledge, New York, pp. 423–441

Brand, U. and Wissen, M. (2013) 'Crisis and Continuity of Capitalist Society-nature Relationships. The Imperial Mode of Living and the Limits to Environmental Governance', *Review of International Political Economy* 20(4), pp. 687–711

Bridle, R. et al. (2018) 'Missing the 23 Per Cent Target: Roadblocks to the Development of Renewable Energy in Indonesia', *The International Institute for Sustainable Development*, Winnipeg, Manitoba, Canada

Bouzarovski, S. and Simcock, N. (2017) 'Spatializing Energy Justice', *Energy Policy* 107, pp. 640–648

Chrysolite, H. et al. (2017) *Evaluating Indonesia's Progress on Its Climate Commitments*. World Resources Institute, www.wri.org/blog/2017/10/evaluating-indonesias-progress-its-climate-commitments

Chung, Y. (2017) *Overpaid and Underutilized: How Capacity Payments to Coal-Fired Power Plants Could Lock Indonesia Into a High-Cost Electricity Future*, Institute for Energy Economics and Financial Analysis

Cornot-Gandolphe, S. (2017) *Indonesia's Electricity Demand and the Coal Sector*. OIES Paper CL 5, Oxford

Davis, S. J. et al. (2010) 'Future CO2 Emissions and Climate Change From Existing Energy Infrastructure', *Science* 329(5997), pp. 1330–1333

Fraser, N. (1996) *Social Justice in the Age of Identity Politics: Redistribution, Recognition, and Participation*, The Tanner Lectures on Human Values, Stanford University, https://tannerlectures.utah.edu/_documents/a-to-z/f/Fraser98.pdf

Fünfgeld, A. (2016a) *Staatlichkeit als lokale Praxis: Kohleabbau und Widerstand in Indonesien*. LIT Verlag, Berlin

Fünfgeld, A. (2016b) 'The State of Coal Mining in East Kalimantan: Towards a Political Ecology of Local Stateness', *Austrian Journal of South-East Asian Studies (ASEAS)* 9(1), pp. 147–161

Gokkon, B. (2017) 'Indonesia Coal Power Push Neglects Rural Households, Chokes Urban Ones', *Mongabay*, 14 November 2017, https://news.mongabay.com/2017/11/indonesia-coal-power-push-neglects-rural-households-chokes-urban-ones/

Hadiz, V. R. and Robison, R. (2013) 'The Political Economy of Oligarchy and the Reorganization of Power in Indonesia', *Indonesia* 96, pp. 35–57.

Hall, P. A. and Soskice, D. 2001) *Varieties of Capitalism. The Institutional Foundations of Comparative Advantage*. Oxford: Oxford University Press.

Heffron, R. J. and McCauley, D. (2017) 'The Concept of Energy Justice Across the Disciplines', *Energy Policy* 105, pp. 658–667

Heffron, R. J. et al. (2015) 'Resolving Society's Energy Trilemma Through the Energy Justice Metric', *Energy Policy* 87, pp. 168–176

Holifield, R. et al. (2009) 'Introduction. Spaces of Environmental Justice. Frameworks for Critical Engagement', *Antipode* 41(4), pp. 591–612

Huber, M. T. (2009) 'Energizing Historical Materialism. Fossil Fuels, Space and the Capitalist Mode of Production', *Geoforum* 40(1), pp. 105–155

I.L.A. Kollektiv (2017) *Auf Kosten Anderer. Wie die imperiale Lebensweise ein gutes Leben für alle verhindert.* Oekom, München

International Energy Agency (IEA) (2015) *Energy and Climate Change – World Energy Outlook Special Report*. IEA, www.iea.org/publications/freepublications/publication/WEO2015SpecialReportonEnergyandClimateChange.pdf

International Energy Agency (IEA) (2017) *Coal Information: Overview (2017 edition)*. IEA, www.iea.org/publications/freepublications/publication/coal-information-2017-edition-overview.html

Jatam (2018) *Ijon Politik Pilkada Melanggengkan Krisis Sosial Ekologis*. Jaringan Advokasi Tambang, www.jatam.org/2018/03/14/ijon-politik-pilkada-melanggengkan-krisis-sosial-ekologis/

The Jakarta Post (2016) 'Overambitious Power Target', *The Jakarta Post*, 18 November 2016

Jenkins, K. (2018) 'Setting Energy Justice Apart From the Crowd. Lessons From Environmental and Climate Justice', *Energy Research & Social Science* 39, pp. 117–121

Jenkins, K. et al. (2014) 'Energy Justice, a Whole Systems Approach', *Queen's Political Review* II(2), pp. 74–87

Jenkins, K. et al. (2016a) 'The Political Economy of Energy Justice: A Nuclear Energy Perspective', in T. van de Graaf et al. (eds.) *The Palgrave Handbook of the International Political Economy of Energy*. Palgrave Macmillan, London, pp. 661–682

Jenkins, K. et al. (2016b) 'Energy Justice. A Conceptual Review', *Energy Research & Social Science* 11, pp. 174–182

LaBelle, M. C. (2017) 'In Pursuit of Energy Justice', *Energy Policy* 107, pp. 615–620

Lever-Tracy, C. (ed.) (2010) *Routledge Handbook of Climate Change and Society*. New York: Routledge.

McCauley, D. (2018) *Energy Justice: Re-balancing the Trilemma of Security, Poverty and Climate Change*. Palgrave Macmillan, Cham

McCauley, D. et al. (2013) 'Advancing Energy Justice: The Triumvirate of Tenets', *International Energy Law Review* 32(3), pp. 107–110

Muhtadi, B. (2015) 'Jokowi's First Year: A Weak President Caught Between Reform and Oligarchic Politics', *Bulletin of Indonesian Economic Studies* 51(3), pp. 349–368

Pesch, U. et al. (2017) 'Energy Justice and Controversies. Formal and Informal Assessment in Energy Projects', *Energy Policy* 109, pp. 825–834

Reed, M. G and George, C. (2011) 'Where in the World Is Environmental Justice?', *Progress in Human Geography* 35(6), pp. 835–842

Robison, R. (1986) *Indonesia: The Rise of Capital*. Allen & Unwin, North Sydney

Robison, R. and Hadiz, V. R. (2004) *Reorganising Power in Indonesia: The Politics of Oligarchy in an Age of Markets*. RoutledgeCurzon, London and New York

Rosser, A. (2014) 'Indonesia: Oligarchic Capitalism', in M. A. Witt and G. Redding (eds.) *The Oxford Handbook of Asian Business Systems*. Oxford University Press, Oxford, pp. 79–99

Schlosberg, D. (2004) 'Reconceiving Environmental Justice. Global Movements and Political Theories', *Environmental Politics* 13(3), pp. 517–540

Schlosberg, D. (2013) 'Theorising Environmental Justice. The Expanding Sphere of a Discourse', *Environmental Politics* 22(1), pp. 37–55

Schlosberg, D. and Collins, L. B. (2014) 'From Environmental to Climate Justice: Climate Change and the Discourse of Environmental Justice', *WIREs Climate Change* 5, pp. 359–374

Sovacool, B. K. and Dworkin, M. H. (2015) 'Energy Justice: Conceptual Insights and Practical Applications', *Applied Energy* 142, pp. 435–444

Sovacool, B. K. et al. (2016) 'Energy Decisions Reframed as Justice and Ethical Concerns', *Nature Energy* 1(5), p. 16024

Sundaryani, F. S. (2016) 'Indonesia Braces for Defeat in 35 GW Program', *The Jakarta Post*, 17 November 2016

U.S. Energy Information Administration (U.S. EIA) (2017) *International Energy Outlook 2017*. EIA, www.eia.gov/outlooks/ieo/

Walker, G. (2009) 'Beyond Distribution and Proximity. Exploring the Multiple Spatialities of Environmental Justice', *Antipode* 41(4), pp. 614–636

Wijaya, A. et al. (2017) *How Can Indonesia Achieve Its Climate Change Mitigation Goal?* World Resources Institute, Working Paper

18

Climate technology and climate justice

Energy transitions in Germany, India and Australia

James Goodman, Devleena Ghosh and Tom Morton

Introduction

National-level renewable energy targets are now embedded in the UNFCCC climate policy and are being implemented across a wide range of countries as part of the "comprehensive" process of emission reduction launched at the 2015 Paris climate summit. Electricity powered by fossil fuels is the primary source of global greenhouse emissions, and meeting the Paris targets hinges on a global move to renewable energy (IPCC 2014: 8, 21). In practice, though, the task of transition falls to national-level institutions, which have different capacity and varying commitment to renewable energy. In this, national-level questions of climate justice and the wider social legitimacy for renewables have become centrally important. There may be widespread support for renewable energy as a concept, but that breaks down where regressive carbon pricing or climate taxes require low-income consumers to pay for the transition, or where subsidies flow to corporates and incentives are based on ability to pay, creating unjust outcomes. Likewise, large-scale corporate-controlled "wind farms" and "solar parks" can displace livelihood and land use, and may have next-to-zero local benefits (already evident in India; Scheidel and Sorman 2012). These outcomes can be seized upon by fossil-fuel advocates to slow decarbonisation and further entrench the status quo. Questions of social justice and social legitimacy must be addressed if decarbonisation is to occur at the pace and extent required. The chapter compares contrasting country contexts to better understand the socio-ecological relationship between climate change and social justice and its role in generating the process of climate justice.

At least since the 1988 Toronto "Conference on the Changing Atmosphere," there has been an international debate about how to exercise what Mike Hulme calls "purposeful" climate agency (Hulme 2010). That debate has centred on justice issues, and has unfolded and intensified across widening realms of social life. In this respect climate justice cannot easily be defined, except in broad terms as arising from the relationship between the biophysical process of climate disruption and the social process of making justice claims. It is better characterised as a process, not a fixed thing, with clearly defined parameters. While initially framed in terms of greenhouse gases and intergenerational impacts, climate justice has produced a number of distributive questions, across impacts, capacity, responsibility and representation, and has flowed from international to subnational contexts for policy, across sinks and sources, and sites of remediation, adaptation and mitigation. At the same time, conflicts have erupted with existing structures of carbon-intensive production, consumption and waste, and their associated claims to "just transition."

At the core of climate justice, as a process, is the cumulative character of climate change. Unlike other cyclical or episodic crises, with the continued failure to reduce greenhouse gas emissions, climate crisis only intensifies over time. It is, as such, an unmanageable crisis, that produces a hydra of justice claims. Where one claim is addressed only more emerge, swarming across the social field, proliferating in the interaction between social and ecological dimensions. As an ecological biophysical process, climate change has begun to subsume the ecologies on which societies are based; as a social process, produced by and under capitalist relations, it has also begun to subsume questions of social justice and social agency. The subsumption process is conflictual in the first instance, with questions of climate justice defined against prevailing concepts of social justice; under advancing climate change we see a growing re-orientation in how social justice is conceived, which forces a social transformation process, potentially into a new type of social system. This trajectory of climate justice is characterised by urgency and necessity: with new relatively fixed horizons for a climate-constrained future, social agency in the present is forced into a new calendar (Chakrabarty 2009). Climate justice in this context becomes centred, as illustrated in the examples discussed here, on issues of "transition."

This chapter deliberately focuses on transition as a key site where the development of climate justice claims can be tracked, over time and "on the ground." It focuses especially on the justice requirements for energy decarbonisation, comparing energy transition and renewable energy in India, Germany and Australia. The three countries occupy radically different places in the decarbonisation process. As a high-emitting, post-industrial society, Germany positions itself as a front-runner in decarbonisation with its 2011 "Energy Transition" policy. While the fossil fuel sector has protected its share of German electricity generation, the largely community, cooperative and municipality-based renewables sector has played a key political role in legitimising renewables. By contrast, India is a rapidly industrialising country, with up to 40% of its population without access to electricity. The Indian Government's priority is to increase energy capacity, mainly through coal-fired power, but also through nuclear energy and expanded renewables, extending access to low-cost clean energy (Mohan 2015). As a high-income, high-emitting society, Australia is heavily dependent on fossil fuels for electricity and for export income. The renewables sector is relatively marginal both in terms of overall electricity supply and its political influence. Yet renewables have strong public support that can be mobilised, for instance, to protect the Renewable Energy Target (Lowy Institute 2014).

In all three countries, wind and solar power have become the dominant modes of electricity decarbonisation. Germany is most clearly committed, with renewables supplying 33.3% of electricity in 2017, and planned to produce 45% by 2030 (GoG 2015, AG Energiebilanzen 2018). India's non-fossil fuel sector produces 20% of its electricity, and with India's 2015 pledge to the UN, is planned to rise to 40% by 2030 (GoI 2015a). Australia has a target of 23% for renewable electricity generation by 2020, with substantial increases required after that date (GoA 2015a). In each country, the question of how to most effectively advance the production of electricity through the renewables sector has become critical. The chapter investigates the contingent interactions between energy transformations and social and ecological dynamics in the three country contexts as distinct "socio-ecological relations" (Moore 2015).

Decarbonising energy is no mere technical challenge. It is described as "the most thorough and far-reaching structural change since the beginning of the industrial revolution" (Scheer 2007: 5). As such it establishes new relationships between capitalist society and ecological contexts, transforming both (Moore 2015). Here the concept of socio-ecological relations can help in understanding different configurations of electricity generation and distribution, as forms of social organisation distinguished by particular relations with an active biophysical world. The transition to "net zero carbon" can be achieved by very different decarbonisation pathways, each with specific impacts and social relations. Socio-political legitimacy is integral to these energy transitions and to achieving the required emissions "peaking." The social legitimation of decarbonisation is a contested and open-ended process: legitimacy for energy transformation is constructed in the flux of the social process and is embedded in wider socio-political power relations. As such, legitimation is a broad field – not simply a matter of public consent for "energy governance" (Michalena and Maxwell Hills 2013). The ostensibly precautionary state, in seeking to reduce the prospects of climate instability, plays a key role in the transition, but it does so as part of the much wider societal process (Renn 2014).

Energy transitions have both produced and been shaped by large-scale transformations in socio-ecological relations. Biomass, in the form of wood, fed the energy needs of early-modern cities, both constraining urban growth and leading to wholesale forest depletion. The mining and burning of coal catalysed industrial development, provided power for cities and precipitated a mass urban citizenry capable of deepening liberal democracy. The burning of coal for power had serious biophysical impacts at sites of extraction, and with urban smog it became the main cause of death in cities (Freese 2005). The invention of the first power stations during the 1890s then enabled mass electrification and the relocation of coal burning, creating the illusion of pollution-free power (Thorsheim 2006). The subsequent transition from coal to oil diminished dependence on a large industrial workforce to guarantee supplies of energy, and tended to fuel authoritarianism rather than democracy (Mitchell 2011). Oil's biophysical attributes, as a fuel that could be relatively easily transported and transformed into plastics, enabled new forms of social organisation, re-patterning settlement structures across the globe. Its ecological effects were likewise distinct from coal but shared coal's impact on global climate through its CO_2 emissions.

The biophysical attributes of particular regimes of energy production, whether based on biomass, coal or oil, have enabled radically different social formations, with contrasting ecological impacts. In this respect, the means of energy production characterise distinct "socio-ecological relations of energy." Such relations are not made inevitable by the biophysical attributes of the energy source but are enabled by them (Mitchell 2011). Likewise, ecological impacts result from the way the fuel is used, not from the character of coal itself. Electrification displaced coal smog, but the coal is still burnt. Biophysical attributes engender new forms of social agency and entail new forms of ecological change, but these changes are wrought in the social process, not pre-given. Within prevailing capitalist society this process of energy transition sees an entanglement, or a "bundling" as Moore terms it, of particular modes of institutional and corporate power, public involvement and participation, all embedded with the ecological context of particular sites and biophysical impacts, producing distinct socio-ecological relations (Moore 2015: 301). The impacts are far-reaching: as Mitchell argues in relation to renewables, the "building of solutions to future energy needs is also the building of new forms of collective life": "battles over the shape of future energy systems" are crucial for framing future possibilities for energy democracy and climate justice (Mitchell 2011: 238, 267).

With advancing climate change, such battles are embedded in the "negative value" of the current energy regime, in terms of the greenhouse gases it produces (Moore 2015: 277). Uniquely, the current transition is principally a political project designed to overcome the legacy of existing energy systems. The "negative value" of capitalism's fossil fuel dependence is now writ large as a global policy imperative. In this process, "externalised" nature is socialised into the internal logic of accumulation, forcing transformation (see O'Connor 1998 for a discussion of ecological socialisation). As such, the current energy transformation is a distinctively climate transition, driven by the imperative to establish new socio-ecological relations in the face of climate crisis (Moore 2015).

This chapter investigates these transitions, asking what possibilities are opening up for climate justice. There are three sections. First, the theoretical and conceptual structure is further elaborated and the context of the three country cases is presented. Second, the chapter compares the social legitimacy of subnational cases across the three countries. Third, it evaluates the approach in terms of what it reveals about the changing socio-ecological relations of energy.

Background

'Fossil capital' is ubiquitous, entrenched in virtually every aspect of society, able to exert considerable influence on the state (Malm 2016: 391). Governments otherwise committed to decarbonisation compete to minimise, avoid, displace and offset their responsibilities, so as to retain fossil fuel power. There is public opposition to renewables from the beneficiaries of the carbon economy, including from coal-dependent communities and workers' organisations, and from some of those affected by the direct impacts of renewable energy. With "decarbonised" nuclear energy, opposition has a long history based on the specific biophysical dangers of radioactive power generation. With renewable power there is opposition to hydroelectric mega-dams in terms of displacement, impacts on livelihood, water flow and the wider ecology. Large-scale "wind farms" and "solar parks" can similarly displace livelihood and land use, and face opposition (Scheidel and Sorman 2012). Such conflicts can be seized upon to delegitimise decarbonisation and reverse the transition.

With the priority and urgency of decarbonisation, considerable research has been conducted into the politics of expanding renewable electricity (see Edenhofer 2012; Scheer 2007; Toke 2011; Bickerstaff et al. 2013; Sovacool and Dworkin 2014). Much of the research on climate transitions is focused on the policy field, discussing the technical capacity of renewables, the economics of transition and questions of legislative and administrative capacity (Sovacool 2014). There have been some studies of renewable energy initiatives and their social impact, especially in *Renewable and Sustainable Energy Reviews and in Energy Research and Social Science*, but generally not in a comparative perspective, nor addressing questions of social participation: Breukers and Wolsink's comparison of The Netherlands, England and Germany (2007); Hua et al.'s analysis of Australia and China (2016); and Mendonca's U.S.–Danish study are exceptions (2009). There is case study research into the social barriers to decarbonisation (see Agterbosch 2004; Aitken 2010; Wolsink 2012; Praene et al. 2012; Gross 2007; Bridge et al. 2013). Studies into electricity transition as a social process are focused on the question of community or household take-up of low-emissions technology, for instance of rooftop solar, rather than the social questions of larger-scale collective efforts at establishing distributed or de-linked energy supply (see IIASA 2012).

Rarely is climate transition researched in terms of social forces, social conflict and social change (Stirling 2014). There is an established instrumentalist and policy-focused literature on "social acceptance" for energy infrastructures (see Ribeiro et al. 2011), including renewable energy such as wind power (Thygesen and Agarwal 2014). A Special Issue on the topic of "social acceptance of renewable energy innovation" was published in *Energy Policy* in 2007, identifying socio-political, community and market acceptance as key aspects (Wustenhagen et al. 2007). From this perspective the focus is on public acceptance of proposed energy infrastructure, and questions centre on issues of impact assessment, stakeholder involvement and engagement. There is a discussion of how to gain "acceptance" for renewable energy projects (Enevoldsen and Sovacool 2016; see also Devine-Wright 2011), including studies from outside high-income contexts (e.g., in Tunisia, Hammami et al. 2016). Opposition to renewable energy projects is found to vary according to the perceived community benefits and local ownership, and prior perception of the locale, as to whether it is already deindustrialised or is seen as pristine rural landscape (Bidwell 2013). Within this literature there is an emerging focus on the process of institutionalising participation within distributed energy systems where "consumers" become "co-producers," and energy becomes a "commons" where "common pool resources" are collectively managed (Wolsink 2012). Studies suggest that when people "take the initiative for their development, the local and public acceptance of RE projects is higher" (Mignon and Rüdinger 2016: 479–480).

More broadly, it is suggested that renewable energy planning should be embedded with wider concerns about socio-environmental change (Spath and Rohracher 2010). This may respond to the uneven geography of energy systems and of local identification, and leverage wider commitments. This broader lens allows a wider consideration of the institutional and political factors, across scales, including industrial development policy, as setting the framing context for renewables. Reflecting this more macro-level analysis, Jacobson and Lauber identified four aspects in the German experience of wind and solar energy: "institutional changes, market formation, the formation of technology-specific advocacy coalitions, and the entry of firms and other organisations" (2006: 258). Curran identifies the construction of public–political narratives as central to the contestations over renewable energy in Australia, finding four themes: feasibility, security, cost and employment. None of these question the need for renewable energy, but rather cast doubt on its practical application, generating a "reasonable" sceptical stance, creating unease about renewable energy (Curran 2012). Reflecting wider concerns that socio-political barriers pose the most difficult challenge for decarbonisation, voiced by, among others, the World Bank and the United Nations Development Program (World Bank 2012; UNDP 2008), this chapter seeks to develop concrete comparative studies, across social contexts addressing the socio-political forces both in favour of and inhibiting renewables. Comparative analysis is especially important in the context of the Paris Agreement, which defines a global emissions target without creating a roadmap for decarbonisation. Unlike the Kyoto commitments, which centred on legal obligations for the highest emitters, the Paris commitments use UN-endorsed "nationally determined" emissions reductions, to be defined and achieved as national policymakers see fit. Contrasting social conditions and political contexts produce varying possibilities for future development, though there are also wide commonalities, offering rich benefits for comparative analysis.

The envisaged comparison across Australia, Germany and India focuses on social legitimacy as a wide-scale structural social process. Drawing on Olin Wright, legitimacy crises are seen as symptomatic of deeper conflicts in capitalist society (Olin Wright 1978). In this case the focus is on conflicts over sustainability and climate change: as climate change accelerates, and authorities fail to respond adequately, we can anticipate cascading legitimacy crises across a widening social field. In their wake, crises create new forms of contestation, drive new social formations and enable the emergence of alternative relations. Here, contestation over the legitimacy of fossil fuels, exposing otherwise de-contested versions of the "national interest," especially in terms of energy security, is a key aspect, along with efforts to establish new sources of legitimacy for the renewables sector in terms of new relationships with global ecology.

Country cases: India, Germany and Australia compared

India

India has one of the world's lowest per capita greenhouse gas emissions rates, at 1.8 tonnes in 2008, and very low electricity consumption per capita, at about 900 kilowatts per hour (kWh) per person (GoI 2015b). Yet electricity is the most important driver of Indian emissions, at about 44%

in 2010. Indian industrial policy rests on postcolonial developmentalism, and this was reflected in the country's landmark 2008 Climate Action Plan that aligned India's development rights with increased emission of greenhouse gases up to the OECD per capita average (extrapolating to 13gt, against global emissions of 45gt). The Plan stressed uncertainties about the impact of climate change on India, equated fossil-fuel energy consumption with poverty reduction. It therefore planned to expand coal consumption three-fold by 2007–22, to about 1500mt, allowing a two- to three-fold rise in aggregate emissions by 2031 (GoI 2008).

Since the 2008 Plan, India has gradually embraced renewable energy and de-linked its goal of energy justice from fossil fuel dependence (Bickerstaff et al. 2013; Jaeger and Michaelowa 2015). India's "Intended Nationally Determined Contribution" (INDC) for the Paris UNFCCC, subtitled "Working towards Climate Justice," pledged to raise "non-fossil fuel-based" sources to 40% of electric power generation, reducing coal dependency to 53% of overall electricity genera- tion, both by 2030 (GoI 2015a). The following 2017 "Draft National Energy Policy" projected a further reduction in reliance on coal for electricity, to 44–50% by 2040, with renewable energy overtaking at 42–52%, albeit with a doubling of energy-related greenhouse gas emissions to about 4gt (NITI 2017: 98).

The policy realignment is significant as it lent a new dynamism to the energy mix. This is reflected in the series of new energy policies announced by the government from 2014. These were principally designed to reduce coal imports, enable energy security for the grow- ing economy and extend energy access (with decarbonisation as a by-product) (Buckley 2015). The policies envisaged expansion for both coal and renewables, but over time the scale of coal expansion may prove less feasible due to impacts on land, water and air quality (Goodman 2016). Reflecting this, a debate has opened up over whether India is embarking on its own "Energy Transformation" (Buckley 2015). The advocacy NGO, the Prayas Energy, for instance argues that given the difficulties in expanding domestic coal production, renewable energy will "form the most significant share of the incremental capacity addition" into the 2020s (Prayas 2018: 505). Others disagree, arguing that India will probably double its coal-based capacity in a decade given the lack of alternatives at the scale required (Sant and Gambhir 2015: 295). Reflecting this, Jairam Ramesh, a former Environment Minister of India, has insisted there is "no alternative to coal" despite the rush to renewables (Morton 2016).

If coal-fired power falters due to its lack of "social licence," then the renewables sector must be capable of offering a desirable alternative if it is to gain headway. Here, the social legitimacy of renewables as part of a wider industrial strategy is crucial. Since 2012 government incentives have "triggered the resurgence of on-grid solar," centred on eight of the country's 29 States (Moallemi et al. 2017: 242; see also Chandel et al. 2016). The emergent renewables sector is dominated by private financing, often international (Moallemi et al. 2017: 244), and in some parts of India something of a solar rush is underway, fuelled by investor exuberance. One example is the US$20 billion investment announced in 2015 by a group led by Japan's "Softbank" includ- ing Taiwan-based Foxconn, the world's largest IT manufacturer, said to be planning in-country manufacturing. The business case was simple, as the Softbank CEO put it: "India has two times the sunshine (of) Japan . . . the cost of construction of the solar park is half of Japan. Twice the sunshine, half the cost, that means four times the efficiency" (Global Energy News 2015). Supporting this, the Indian Government has created an intergovernmental "International Solar Alliance," with 120 member countries, aiming to raise US$1 trillion in mainly private financing by 2030 (World Bank 2016).

The expansion of large-scale renewables comes with social consequences, especially for land use. Available land for large solar parks is limited (Santhakumari and Sagar 2017), and as state authorities secure land for energy financiers, conflicts over "land grabbing" are already emerging, for instance in Gujarat (Scheidel and Sorman 2012). A more distributed process, at village and community level, may hold greater potential. Paradoxically, this form of socially embedded and distributed transformation may have greater potential to meet the challenge of India's decarbonisation at the scale required than the current focus on centrally directed and corporate-run "ultra-mega" operations. It would also serve to underpin legitimacy for the transition and help delink energy access from coal, and to overcome the false opposition between social justice and decarbonisation.

Germany

Since the 1990s Germany has been strongly committed to the idea of the "green economy." German per capita greenhouse gas emissions fell from 12.6 to 11.5 tonnes CO_2e from 2000 to 2010, although since 2010 there has been little change (Amelang 2017). Electricity remains the key determinant of emissions, at about 40% (GoG 2017). In Germany domestic abatement is supplemented by international offsets, through the UN's "Clean Development Mechanism" and, more important, through growing imports of "embodied carbon," in the form of manufactured goods, mainly from China (Goodman 2016). Renewables are projected to supply 54% of electricity by 2030, up from 18% in 2010 (with coal falling from 41% to 31% of the energy mix) (GoG 2014: 129). Renewable energy is promoted as an alternative to nuclear power, as much as to fossil fuels: following the Chernobyl disaster a series of proposals for a renewable energy feed-in tariff were adopted in a cross-party consensus in 1991, along with a mixture of taxes and subsidies (Jacobsson and Lauber 2006). Efforts by energy industry groups to undermine the tariff saw major counter-mobilisations in 1997, partly enabling the entry of the Greens into coalition government in 1998 and the successful passage of the Renewable Energy Sources Act of 2000, which locked in a national feed-in tariff for 20 years. Rooftop solar power was initiated at the Federal level and taken up by municipalities, linked to an emergent advocacy network comprising ENGOs, renewables companies and associated trade unions. On this basis both wind and solar power made considerable advances (Chalvatzis and Hooper 2009).

The policy was reasserted in the Federal Government's "Energy Concept" (GoG 2010) and in the aftermath of the 2011 Fukushima disaster, with the "Energy Transition Laws" (GoG 2011). Felix Christian Matthes describes the long-term ambition of the *Energiewende* or energy transition as "full decarbonisation of the economy" by mid-century and "the transition to an energy system in which energy supply is almost fully based on renewable energies" (Fabra et al. 2015: 51). The 2011 measures were paired with an ambitious target of 60% renewables by 2050 (GoG 2011). A range of factors facilitate the sector, notably the requirement that grid operators facilitate access for cooperative energy projects; in support of this, public banks provide preferential financing and the feed-in tariff offers a predictable income flow. There is also strong public support, and cooperatives are networked via established and active associations (Mignon and Rüdinger 2016). Over half of the sector is owned by households and cooperatives, and these are increasingly joined by municipalities which have bought back generation capacity and the local grid, and directed it towards renewables (Buchan 2012). Expressing this, renewable power, and especially solar power, has attracted a "high level of legitimacy," since at least the late 1980s (Jacobson and Lauber 2006: 266).

The German energy transition has been variously criticised and delayed, especially by the four privatised energy utilities, which continue to produce three-quarters of Germany's electricity supply and much of the fossil fuel (Eon, Vattenfall, RWE and EnBW) (Buchan 2012). Despite the growth in renewables, a "paradox" of perverse incentives has favoured brown coal as the only source of electricity generation that is cheaper than renewables, though there is evidence this has subsided (Renn and Marshall 2016; AG Energiebilanzen 2018: 28). At the same time, a strong sustainable energy bloc has emerged, across renewables companies and advocacy NGOs, both environment and energy-focused, such as the "German Association for Renewable Energies" established in 1991, and the Klima-Alliance, a climate action NGO with over 10 million members. The two blocs compete for influence over the bureaucracy and over party politics, ensuring that renewable energy policy has become a major stake in political rivalry, dramatically politicising energy policy (Kemfert and Horne 2013).

Yet public support cannot be assumed. Research conducted by the Institute for Advanced Sustainability Studies in 2017 found that public support for the *Energiewende* was conditional on burden-sharing, and that in the long term it had to be of more benefit for low-income groups (IASS 2017). Another study found that two-thirds of citizens believed households should be bearing less of a burden in terms of rising energy prices (Fischer et al. 2016: 1584). On the ground, efforts at exiting from coal-fired power have faced strong opposition in coal-mining regions, including from mining unions. The vigorous and ultimately successful public campaign in 2015 against the "climate contribution" or *Klimaabgabe* (a levy to be paid by older, more heavily polluting coal-fired power plants) was a particularly salient example of this tendency (Morton and Müller 2016). Thus climate justice in Germany is framed primarily in terms of the "costs of transition," as they impact both on consumers and on regions whose economies are structurally dependent on coal mining. Partly in response, in 2017 the Federal Government established a "Commission for Growth, Structural Change and Regional Development" with representatives from unions, industry, local, state and federal government, and other "regional actors," to prepare a blueprint for socially sustainable "just transitions" in coal mining regions (GoG 2018). In Germany decarbonisation depends on maintaining existing levels of citizen support for and involvement in the *Energiewende*, and a greater commitment to climate justice in its implementation, particularly through a more equitable distribution of its costs (Fischer et al. 2016: 1589; Setton et al. 2017).

Australia

Between 1990 and 2013, emissions rose in Australia by about 26% (before taking into account land-use changes). The World Bank databank states CO_2 emissions per capita were static over the period, at 15.4tpp. According to IEA data, in 2016 84% of domestic energy electricity was sourced from coal or gas, 63% from coal; solar and wind power contributed 7% of electricity by 2015, rising from zero in 2000 (IEA 2017). Electricity is the largest single source of greenhouse gas emissions at about one-third of the total, and Australia's coal-fired power stations, which were mainly constructed in the 1970s, are notable for their inefficiency (GoA 2015b). High emissions and fossil fuel dependency reflect Australia's status as a high-income extractivist economy (Goodman 2008). It is one of the world's largest exporters of coal, uranium and (increasingly) gas. Three-quarters of Australian coal is exported. In the context of a coal and gas export boom in 2012 the Government stated fossil fuel exports would address energy poverty and "support higher living standards for billions of people" (GoA 2012: x); three years later the Government announced its strategy of defining Australia as an "energy superpower" through energy exports, including coal, gas and uranium (GoA 2015b).

Australia pursued a successful strategy at the UN in the 1990s to allow the inclusion of land use changes in carbon accounting, giving it windfall emissions reductions from reduced land clearing (Hayley 2009). It also argued successfully that Australia's special dependence on fossil fuels meant it should be permitted to increase its emissions under the Kyoto Protocol (by 8%, 1990–2012). Having insisted on its special status, Australia followed the U.S. in refusing to sign the Protocol, and the country finally joined, in 2007. In 2011 the country introduced a fixed "carbon price," under "Clean Energy Futures" package. The package defined a 5% reduction in emissions on 2000 levels, making deeper reductions dependent on parallel action by competing countries (Lyster 2011). The minimalism was outflanked as the conservative Coalition mobilised social justice concerns against carbon pricing, as the "Great Big Tax on Everything." The 2013 election brought the Coalition to power principally on a platform of dismantling the carbon price. Subsequently Australia's INDC at Paris defined a modest target of 26% below 2005 levels by 2030 (below the EU and U.S. target of about 35%; GoA 2015c).

The energy mix has remained fossil fuel centred, though the renewables sector has benefitted from a relatively mandatory Renewable Energy Target (to 23% by 2020). The key driver for change has been the closure of ageing privately owned coal-fired power stations. Twelve had closed by 2016, accounting for 6.5gw, with a further 15.1gw slated for closure before 2030, leaving about 10gw of coal-fired power remaining post-2030 (Renew Economy 2017). The rapidity of closures was not expected, and it exposed government attempts to shore up coal generation. In this context an active "climate action" movement has become increasingly radicalised (Bulkeley 2000; Baer 2014). Since 2009, and in the midst of a coal boom, a mass-based movement of civil disobedience led by national advocacy organisations such as "Lock the Gate" has emerged, focused on organising farmers in rural areas against new coal mines and especially against coal seam gas (CSG). These campaigns have had some traction in delaying if not halting coal mines, and in preventing the expansion of CSG (Organ 2016).

A parallel effort to promote renewables has had some success. Plans for "100% Renewable" have become mainstreamed, for instance with a 2013 report from the Electricity Market Operator, a federal government agency, that found "no fundamental limits" to reliance on renewable energy (AEMO 2013). With the falling per-unit cost of renewable power now well below that of new coal-fired power, the only "barrier to entry" for 100% renewables is the negligible fixed cost of old (and now closing) coal-fired power stations (Parkinson 2016). In 2015 Federal Labor (in opposition) adopted a target of 50% renewables by 2030, and several State governments adopted the Paris target of net zero emissions by 2050. In 2016 the Australian Council of Trade Unions adopted a more proactive policy of "just transition" for workers and regions dependent on declining fossil fuels (ACTU 2016). At the same time a new industrial lobby was emerging, centred on corporate-owned wind farms and especially on small-scale solar, with 1.4 million or 15% of households having solar PV, one of the highest in the world (Energy Supply Association of Australia 2016).

The fossil fuel energy sector retains considerable influence in Australian political life, but this is not uncontested (Curran 2011; Bell and Hindmoor 2013). Governments have posed climate policy as a threat to livelihood, setting climate policy against social justice (Effendi and Courvisanos 2012), though this strategy has weakened as renewable power becomes cheaper. At the Federal level political incentives for minimalism and denialism have remained high (Byrnes et al. 2013). Yet there are more positive sum developments promoting renewables at the subnational level, as a vehicle for industrial, regional or community renewal. These demonstrate the vitality of renewables as vested in political advocacy coalitions, household and community solar advocacy, and the emerging corporate-renewable sector, linked to State governments. In this context, the challenges posed by the continued leverage of coal and gas, despite waning legitimacy, should not be underestimated.

Conclusion: dynamics of energy and climate justice

Climate justice agendas can and arguably must be enabled to flourish in the transition to decarbonised energy. Energy decarbonisation points to new relationships with biophysical and social forces: most important, it does not depend on exhaustible sources of fossil fuels, and instead taps an inexhaustible biophysical force, and offer strategies for technology-driven economic development beyond resource dependence. Further, the diversity of renewable energy is far greater than for fossil energy. Electricity derived from solar and wind can be generated at multiple scales and consumed with or without distribution from a fixed network. Large-scale renewables may be privately owned by diversified energy corporations, feeding into a centralised grid, or by new configurations of community-owned, locally operated generation and distribution systems. These arrangements are conditioned by government policies that incentivise and plan the transition, by corporate and financial market calculations, and by community campaigns and direct initiatives with strong normative concerns linked to climate change and also to a new vision for distributed energy (IRENA 2015).

The outcome, as outlined, hinges on contests over the meaning, and attainment, of legitimacy. As new players, policy coalitions and political constituencies have emerged, dedicated to decarbonisation, the existing array of fossil fuel interests and infrastructures has become highly visible and politicised. The fossil fuel bloc may retain a capacity, at least in the short term, to block or undermine transition, but this is no longer a technicised and depoliticised process, and instead is highly contested and politicised. The fossil fuel veto may be maintained, but at the cost of a widespread and accelerating crisis of legitimacy for the sector. Even in Australia, where the fossil fuel bloc is especially resilient, reflecting its export orientation, the sector is under assault on a variety of flanks. This is a genuinely new development that comes in the context of growing global uncertainty over the future of carbon-intensive sectors.

Across the three countries questions of climate policy and social justice have become more salient, in some respects have generated climate justice agendas. In Germany, community-level solar has gained its own logic, facilitated by the government's "Energy Transformation," though social justice claims can still be mobilised to threaten climate policy. In Australia household solar has played an important role, and there has been strong community mobilisation for climate justice, against the failure of federal climate policies. In India the nexus between energy justice and fossil fuels is increasingly superseded by an emergent renewable sector, and social justice is increasingly aligned with decarbonisation, albeit corporate-led. In all three countries the transition process is reordering social hierarchies and creating new possibilities for realising both emission reduction and social justice. As argued here, for socially driven take-up to generate transformation at the scale needed, these re-orderings have to be weighted to enable distributed models, meeting finance, technical and administrative requirements for community-level modes of technology and institutionalisation. The three cases, as discussed, demonstrate the centrality of these socio-political frameworks and their relevance to local needs and potential to achieve social transformation at the scale and intensity required.

Overall, in the current period mass-scale distributed renewables offer the best chance of extending the energy transformation to the degree needed to achieve global "net zero carbon" by 2050. They do so as they harness the social legitimacy of renewable energy to a participatory structure that empowers communities and collectivities. That social process is not simply preferred but necessary to achieve the required political and social leverage, as well as the required cross-societal scope for energy transformation. The experience of renewables in Germany demonstrates the vitality and dynamism injected by a socially owned and collectively organised renewables sector. The Australian case offers some potential in this regard, as in part reflected in efforts to organise the existing household sector, through the "solar citizens" initiative for instance, as well as efforts to extend "community power" beyond presently limited social provision. In India the critical issue will be the capacity to downscale the existing "ultra-mega" initiatives and upscale household-based programs. Renewables at the intermediate scale, especially at village, neighbourhood and municipality level, offer real prospects for socialising the energy transformation and extending the social dynamic of its development.

The danger, as noted, across all three countries, is that renewables and associated climate and energy policy become discredited by the forms of disempowerment and stratification that they generate. Renewables "from above" closely replicates the centralised energy management practices derived from the fossil fuel era. There is widespread evidence that corporate and semi-state agencies in the energy sector are now moving to dominate the field and secure their control of renewable energy flows (Glover 2006). Their capacity to monetise renewables hinges on centralising generation and delivery structures, to re-institute their income flow. Household and community renewables, whether on or off-grid, are antagonistic to the centralised model but offer real foundations for a deeper transformation. The challenge of climate change, the necessity for emissions reduction, and the rise of distributed renewable energy, have all dramatically exposed fossil fuel energy, and have politicised energy policy. The newly recognised socio-ecological relations of fossil fuel energy are transforming the policy landscape. The result is a new political dynamism that engages new players and constituencies, and pursues new frameworks for just transitions and climate justice.

References

ACTU Australian Council of Trade Unions (2016) *A Just Transition for Coal-fired Electricity Sector Workers and Communities*. Policy Discussion Paper, 30 November, ACTU, Melbourne.

AEMO (2013) *100 Per Cent Renewables Study: Modelling Outcomes*. Electricity Market Operator, Canberra.

AG Energiebilanzen e.V. (2018) *Energieverbrauch in Deutschland im Jahr 2017*. News Blog, 3 March. www.ag-energiebilanzen.de/20-0-Berichte.html

Agterbosch, S. et al. (2004) 'Implementation of wind energy in the Netherlands: The importance of the social – Institutional setting', *Energy Policy*, vol 32, no 18, pp 2049–2066.

Aitken, M. (2010) 'Why we still don't understand the social aspects of wind power: A critique of key assumptions within the literature', *Energy Policy*, vol 38, no 4, pp 1834–1841.

Amelang, S. (2017) 'Germany set to widely miss climate targets, env ministry warns', *Clean Energy Wire*, 11 October.

Baer, H. (2014) 'A disparate response to climate change and climate politics in a not so lucky country', in Dietz, M. and Garrelts, H. (eds) *Routledge Handbook of the Climate Change Movement*. Routledge, London, pp 147–163.

Bell, S. and Hindmoor, A. (2013) 'The structural power of business and the power of ideas: The strange case of the Australian mining tax', *New Political Economy*, vol 19, no 3, pp 470–486.

Bickerstaff, K., Walker, G. and Bulkeley, H. (2013) *Energy Justice in a Changing Climate*. Zed, London.

Bidwell, D. (2013) 'The role of values in public beliefs and attitudes towards commercial wind energy', *Energy Policy*, vol 58, pp 189–199.

Breukers, S. and Wolsink, M. (2007) 'Wind power implementation in changing institutional landscapes: An international comparison', *Energy Policy*, vol 35, pp 2737–2750.

Bridge, G., Bouzarovski, S., Bradshaw, M. and Eyre, N. (2013) 'Geographies of energy transitions: Space, place and the low-carbon economy', *Energy Policy*, vol 53, pp 330–340.

Buchan, D. (2012) *The Energiewende: Germany's Gamble*. Oxford Institute for Energy Studies, Oxford.

Buckley, T. (2015) *India's Electricity Sector Transformation*. Institute for Energy Economics and Financial Analysis, Cleveland.

Bulkeley, H. (2000) 'Discourse coalitions and the Australian climate change policy network', *Environment and Planning C: Politics and Space*, vol 18, no 6, pp 727–748.

Byrnes, L., Brown, C., Foster, J. and Wagner, L. (2013) 'Australian renewable energy policy: Barriers and challenges', *Renewable Energy*, vol 60, pp 711–721.

Chakrabarty, D. (2009) 'The climate of history: Four theses', *Critical Inquiry*, vol 35, no 2, pp 197–222.

Chalvatzis, C. and Hooper, E. (2009) 'Energy security vs. climate change: Theoretical framework development', *Renewable and Sustainable Energy Reviews*, vol 13, pp 2703–2709.

Chandel, S., Shrivastva, R., Sharma, V. and Ramasamy, P. (2016) 'Overview of the initiatives in renewable energy sector under the national action plan on climate change in India', *Renewable and Sustainable Energy Reviews*, vol 54, pp 866–873.

Curran, G. (2011) 'Modernising climate policy in Australia: Climate narratives and the undoing of a Prime Minister', *Environment and Planning C: Government and Policy*, vol 29, pp 1004–1017.

Curran, G. (2012) 'Contested energy futures: Shaping renewable energy narratives in Australia', *Global Environmental Change*, vol 22, pp 236–244.

Devine-Wright, P. (ed.) (2011) *Renewable Energy and the Public: From Nimby to Participation.* Taylor and Francis, London.

Edenhofer, O. (ed.) (2012) *Renewable Energy Sources and Climate Change Mitigation.* Cambridge University Press, Cambridge.

Effendi, P. and Courvisanos, J. (2012) 'Political aspects of innovation: Examining renewable energy in Australia', *Renewable Energy*, vol 38, pp 245–252.

Energy Supply Association of Australia (2016) *Renewable Energy in Australia: How Do We Really Compare?* ESAA, Canberra.

Enevoldsen, P. and Sovacool, B. (2016) 'Examining the social acceptance of wind energy: Practical guidelines for onshore wind project development in France', *Renewable and Sustainable Energy Reviews*, vol 53, pp 178–184.

Fabra, N., Matthes, F., Newberry, D. and Colombier, M. (2015) *The Energy Transition in Europe: lessons from Germany, France and Spain.* Brussels: Centre on Regulation in Europe.

Fischer, W., Hake, J.-Fr., Kuckshinrichs, W., Schroder, T. and Venghaus, S. (2016) 'German energy policy and the way to sustainability: Five controversial issues in the debate on the "Energiewende"', *Energy*, vol 115, pp 1580–1591.

Freese, B. (2005) *Coal, a Human History.* William Heineman, London.

Global Energy News (2015) 'SoftBank, partners eye $20 billion investment in Indian solar projects', *Reuters*, 22 June.

Glover, L. (2006) 'From love-ins to logos: Charting the demise of renewable energy as a social movement,' in Bryne, J., Toly, N. and Glover, L. (eds) *Transforming Power: Energy, Environment, and Society in Conflict.* Transactions Publishers, New York, pp 249–270.

GoA Government of Australia (2012) *Energy White Paper: Australia's Energy Transformation.* Department of Energy, Resources and Tourism, Canberra.

GoA Government of Australia (2015a) 'Certainty and growth for renewable energy', *Press Release*, 23 June, Canberra.

GoA Government of Australia (2015b) *Energy White Paper.* Department of Energy, Resources and Tourism, Canberra.

GoA Government of Australia (2015c) *Australia's Intended Nationally-Determined Contribution.* GoA, Canberra.

GoG, Government of Germany (2010) *Energy Concept for an environmentally sound, reliable and affordable energy supply.* Federal Ministry for the Environment, Nature Conservation, Building and Nuclear Safety, Berlin.

GoG, Government of Germany (2011) *Energy Transition Laws.* Federal Ministry for the Environment, Nature Conservation, Building and Nuclear Safety, Berlin.

GoG, Government of Germany (2014) *National Communication to the UNFCCC.* Federal Ministry for Economic Affairs and Energy, Berlin.

GoG, Government of Germany (2015) *Making a Success of the Energy Transition.* Federal Ministry for Economic Affairs and Energy, Berlin.

GoG, Government of Germany (2017) *National Communication to the UNFCCC.* Federal Ministry for Economic Affairs and Energy, Berlin.

GoG, Government of Germany (2018) 'Commission on Growth, Structural Change and Employment takes up work'. Press Release, 6 June. Federal Ministry for the Environment, Nature Conservation, Building and Nuclear Safety, Berlin.

GoI, Government of India (2008) *Climate Action Plan.* GoI, New Delhi.

GoI, Government of India (2015a) *India's Intended Nationally-Determined Contribution.* GoI, New Delhi.

GoI, Government of India (2015b) *Growth of Electricity Sector in India From 1947–2015.* Ministry of Power and Central Electricity Authority, New Delhi.

Goodman, J. (2008) 'The minerals boom and Australia's "resource curse"', *Journal of Australian Political Economy*, vol 61, pp 201–220.

Goodman, J. (2016) 'The climate dialectic in energy policy: Germany and India compared', *Energy Policy*, vol 99, pp 184–193.

Gross, C. (2007) 'Community perspectives of wind energy in Australia', *Energy Policy*, vol 35, pp 2727–2736.

Hammami, S., Chtourou, S. and Triki, A. (2016) 'Identifying the determinants of community acceptance of renewable energy technologies: The case study of a wind energy project from Tunisia', *Renewable and Sustainable Energy Reviews*, vol 54, pp 151–160.

Hayley, S. (2009) 'Cheating on climate change? Australia's challenge to global warming norms', *Australian Journal of International Affairs*, vol 63, no 2, pp 165–186.

Hua, Y., Oliphant, M. and Hu, E. (2016) 'Development of renewable energy in Australia and China: A comparison of policies and status', *Renewable Energy*, vol 85, pp 1044–1051.

Hulme, M. (2010) 'Mapping climate knowledge: An editorial essay', *Wiley Interdisciplinary Reviews: Climate Change*, vol 1, no 1, pp 1–8.

IASS, Institute for Advanced Sustainability Studies (2017) 'Social Sustainability Barometer for the Energiewende Shows Broad Support along with Doubts about Implementation'. Announcement, 14 November. IASS, Potsdam.

IEA (2017) *World Energy Outlook 2015*. International Energy Agency, Paris.

IIASA, International Institute for Applied Systems Analysis (2012) *Global Energy Assessment – Toward a Sustainable Future*. Cambridge University Press, Cambridge.

IPCC (2014) *Summary for Policymakers. WG III. Mitigation of Climate Change*. Cambridge University Press, New York.

IRENA (2015) *The Age of Renewable Power: Designing National Roadmaps for Successful Transition*. International Renewable Energy Agency, Abu Dhabi, UAR.

Jacobsson, S. and Lauber, V. (2006) 'The politics and policy of energy system transformation – Explaining the German diffusion of renewable energy technology', *Energy Policy*, vol 34, pp 256–276.

Jaeger, M. and Michaelowa, K. (2015) 'Global climate policy and local energy politics: Is India hiding behind the poor?', *Journal of Climate Policy*, vol 16, no 7, pp 940–951.

Kemfert, C. and Horne, J. (2013) *Good Governance of the Energiewende in Germany: Wishful Thinking or Manageable*? Working Paper. Hertie School of Governance, Berlin.

Lowy Institute (2014) *The Lowy Institute Poll*. Lowy Institute, Sydney.

Lyster, R. (2011) *Australia's Clean Energy Future Package: Are We There Yet*? Sydney Law School Paper 11/85, November.

Malm, A. (2016) *Fossil Capital: The Rise of Steam Power and the Roots of Global Warming*. Verso, London.

Moallemi, E., et al. (2017) 'India's on-grid solar power development', *Renewable and Sustainable Energy Reviews*, vol 69, pp 239–247.

Mendonca, M. (2009) 'Stability, participation and transparency in renewable energy policy: Lessons From Denmark and the United States', *Policy and Society*, vol 27, no 4, pp 379–398.

Michalena, E. and Maxwell Hills, J. (2013) *Renewable Energy Governance*. Springer-Verlag, London.

Mignon, I. and Rüdinger, A. (2016) 'The impact of systemic factors on the deployment of cooperative projects within renewable electricity production – An international comparison', *Renewable and Sustainable Energy Reviews*, vol 65, pp 478–488.

Mitchell, T. (2011) *Carbon Democracy: Political Power in the Age of Oil*. Verso, London.

Mohan, V. (2015) 'India calls for a paradigm shift in global attitudes towards climate change', *The Times of India*, 19 January.

Moore, J. (2015) *Capitalism in the Web of Life: Ecology and the Accumulation of Capital*. Verso, London.

Morton, T. (2016) *Beyond the Coal Rush*. Radio Documentary Series (three hours), Science Show, ABC Radio National, Australian Broadcasting Corporation, Sydney.

Morton, T. and Katja Müller, K. (2016) 'Lusatia and the coal conundrum: The lived experience of the German Energiewende', *Energy Policy*, vol 99, pp 277–287.

NITI (2017) *Draft National Energy Policy, National Institution for Transforming India*. Government of India, New Delhi.

O'Connor, J. (1998) *Natural Causes: Essays in Ecological Marxism*. Guilford Press, New York.

Olin Wright, E. (1978) *Class, Crisis and the State*. New Left Books, London.

Organ, M. (2016) 'New tactics see coal seam gas protests gain the upper hand', *The Conversation*, 28 May.

Parkinson, G. (2016) 'Labor states accuse Turnbull of "ignorant rubbish" on renewable energy', *Renew Economy*, 30 September.

Praene, J. et al. (2012) 'Renewable energy: Progressing towards a net zero energy island, the case of Reunion Island', *Renewable and Sustainable Energy Reviews*, vol 16, no 1, pp 426–442.

Prayas (2018) *Many Sparks But Little Light: The Rhetoric and Practice of Electricity Sector Reforms in India*. PRAYAS Energy, Pune, India.

Renew Economy (2017) 'Australia coal power in free-fall', *Renew Economy*, 14 June.

Renn, O. (2014) 'Towards a socio-ecological foundation for environmental risk research', in Lockie, S. et al. (eds) *Routledge International Handbook of Social and Environmental Change*. Routledge, London, pp 207–220.

Renn, O. and Marshall, J. (2016) 'Coal, nuclear and renewable energyies in Germany: From the 1950s to the "Energiewende"', *Energy Policy*, vol 99, pp 224–232.

Ribeiro, F., Ferreira, P. and Araujo, M. (2011) 'The inclusion of social aspects in power planning', *Renewable and Sustainable Energy Reviews*, vol 15, pp 4361–4369.

Sant, G. and Gambhir, A. (2015) 'Energy development and climate change', in Dubash, N. (ed) *Handbook of Climate Change and India: Development, Politics and Governance*. Routledge, New York.

Santhakumari, M. and Sagar, N. (2017) 'Progressing towards the development of sustainable energy: A critical review on the current status, applications, developmental barriers and prospects of solar photovoltaic systems in India', *Renewable and Sustainable Energy Reviews*, vol 70, pp 298–313.

Scheer, H. (2007) *Energy Autonomy: The Economic, Social and Technological Case for Renewable Energy*. Earthscan and Routledge, London.

Scheidel, A. and Sorman, A. (2012) 'Energy transitions and the global land rush: Ultimate drivers and persistent consequences', *Global Environmental Change*, vol 22, no 3, pp 588–595.

Setton, D., Matuschke, I. and Renn, O. (2017) *Social Sustainability Barometer for the German Energiewende*. IASS, Potsdam.

Sovacool, B. (2014) 'What are we doing here? Analyzing fifteen years of energy scholarship and proposing a social science research agenda', *Energy Research and Social Science*, vol 1, pp 1–29.

Sovacool, B. and Dworkin, M. (2014) *Global Energy Justice: Principles, Problems and Practices*. Cambridge University Press, Cambridge.

Spath, P. and Rohracher, H. (2010) 'Energy regions': The transformative power of regional discourses on socio-technical futures', *Research Policy*, vol 39, pp 449–458.

Stirling, A. (2014) 'Transforming power: Social science and the politics of energy', *Energy Research and Social Science*, vol 1, pp 83–95.

Thorsheim, P. (2006) *Inventing Pollution: Coal, Smoke, and Culture in Britain Since 1800*. Ohio University Press, Athens.

Thygesen, J. and Agarwal, A. (2014) 'Key criteria for sustainable wind energy planning – Lessons from an institutional perspective on the impact assessment literature', *Renewable and Sustainable Energy Reviews*, vol 39, pp 1012–1023.

Toke, D. (2011) 'Ecological modernisation, social movements and renewable energy', *Environmental Politics*, vol 20, no 1, pp 60–77.

UNDP, United Nations Development Programme (2008) *Fighting Climate Change: Human Solidarity in a Divided World*. Human Development Report 2007/8, UNDP, Geneva.

Wolsink, M. (2012) 'The research agenda on social acceptance of distributed generation in smart grids: Renewable as common pool resources', *Renewable and Sustainable Energy Reviews*, vol 16, no 1, pp 822–835.

World Bank (2012) *Turn Down the Heat: Climate Extremes, Regional Impacts and the Case for Resilience*. World Bank, Washington.

World Bank (2016) 'Solar energy to power India of the Future', *World Bank News*, 30 June.

Wustenhagen, R., Wolsink, M. and Burer, M. (2007) 'Social acceptance of renewable energy innovation: An introduction to the concept', *Energy Policy*, vol 35, pp 2683–2691.

19

Big Oil's duty of disgorging funds in the context of climate change

Marco Grasso

Introduction

That climate change is essentially a matter of justice is nothing new (Grasso, 2013). Philosophers and other scholars, as well as politicians, climate activists, religious leaders and many others have long highlighted and explored the numerous ethical considerations and challenges that are inseparable from discussions of the causes, consequences, and potential human responses to anthropogenic climate change (Grasso and Markowitz, 2015). A longstanding concern of climate justice has revolved around the question of "who counts" – that is, which individuals and groups should be at the centre of the ethical debate on climate change? What is the extent of ethical considerations in the context of long-term, global, anthropogenic climate change (Jamieson, 2014, Chapter 5)?

Beyond the predominantly state-centric perspective of the current international system, which basically considers states as the only agents of justice, there is a vigorous ongoing debate about other possible agents. For example, some environmentalist rhetoric focuses on the role of individuals, both in terms of reducing one's own emissions and for advocating larger-scale change. Although this perspective may have gained some traction in recent years, there are normative ethical questions about how much responsibility individuals do have for the harm caused by their (in the big picture, infinitesimal) GHG emissions, as well as positive ethical questions regarding individual responsibility given political and economic constraints on action (Markowitz et al., 2015). Therefore, it is necessary for climate justice to better explore forms of collective responsibility that do not exclude individual responsibility, but are rather able to integrate the two perspectives, with particular attention to novel or neglected collective agents of justice. Among these, given their unique and distinctive role, responsibilities, and duties in the context of climate change, oil and gas companies are possibly the most significant neglected group of agents. Big Oil – or "oil companies" or the "oil industry" – through the emissions generated by the fossil fuels they process, has significantly added to the increase of the concentration of greenhouse gases (GHG), especially carbon dioxide (CO_2) and methane (CH_4), in the atmosphere (IPCC, 2014a). Therefore, Big Oil has notably contributed directly to anthropogenic climate change.[1]

It is worth stressing that this argument does not imply that Big Oil should become the only agent responsible for addressing climate change, or even that oil and gas companies are the most important players. It is not the intent of this chapter to obscure the role of other agents in climate politics. Consumers, civil society, businesses and other stakeholders all have a role and consequent responsibilities in addressing climate change, and they should do their part. Rather, the goal of the chapter is to draw attention to the 'supply-side', in particular to oil and gas companies' responsibilities and duties and the consequent implications for current climate action.

Big Oil should play its part in global climate governance, along with states, individuals, and other agents. That part is significant, since oil and gas companies have a crucial role in causing, shaping, advancing, and defending the current unsustainable fossil fuel-dependent global economy. By continuing to provide fossil fuels to feed the demand, they have been dictating the rules of the game to the global economic system. Based on these considerations, this chapter first outlines the direct contribution that Big Oil made to climate change in terms of global cumulative emissions. Then, it investigates the moral bases of the oil industry's duty of disgorgement, i.e., a duty that implies rectification through relinquishment of funds for its wrongful actions. Finally, the chapter explores some practical issues and challenges that such duty of disgorgement entails for Big Oil.

Big Oil's direct contribution to climate change

Recent studies by Richard Heede and colleagues focused on the contributions of the large carbon producers to global cumulative emissions of the major GHGs, such as carbon dioxide and methane (Heede, 2014; Frumhoff et al., 2016; Heede and Oreskes, 2016). "Carbon majors," as these studies define the big carbon business, are the world's largest public and private investor-owned, state-owned and government-run oil, gas, coal, and cement producers. The primary finding of Heede and colleagues is that 62% of the global industrial emissions of carbon dioxide and methane from 1751 to 2015 can be traced to the activities of 100 currently active carbon majors (41 public investor-owned companies, 16 private investor-owned, 36 state-owned and seven government-run) and eight non-extant ones.[2] Additionally, their data demonstrates that, given also the rapid global industrialisation of the last few decades, the 100 currently operating carbon majors have produced 71% of the global industrial emissions since 1988.[3] A further study by Ekwurzel et al. (2017) extends Heede's (2014) original finding by linking carbon majors' fossil fuel-related activities to atmospheric carbon dioxide and methane *concentrations*, as well as to relevant climate impacts, namely, the *global mean surface temperature* (GMST) and the *global sea level* (GSL). Strikingly, this study found that the historical (1880–2010) and recent (1980–2010) emissions of 90 major carbon producers resulted in "~57% of the observed rise in atmospheric CO_2, ~42–50% of the rise in GMST and ~26–32% of GSL rise over the historical period of 1880–2010 and ~43% (atmospheric CO_2), ~29–35% (GMST), and ~11–14% (GSL) since 1980" (Ekwurzel et al., 2017, p. 579).

Importantly, carbon majors produced more than half of their emissions in the last 25 years, when the global community was already well aware of the potential dangers of climate change.[4] This awareness spread widely after the First Assessment Report of the Intergovernmental Panel on Climate Change (IPCC) in 1990, which announced the global scientific consensus on the negative effects of anthropogenic climate change.

Oil and gas companies are the largest and most numerous carbon majors. In this chapter, Big Oil is a shortcut for "the largest oil and gas companies" or, more precisely, despite the many terminological controversies that possibly reverberate the complexity of the oil world, this term includes those large multinational companies that engage in the exploration, production, refinement and distribution of hydrocarbons, i.e., "conventional oil," "unconventional oil", and "unconventional liquids."

Generally, oil and gas are owned by states or, in weak and failed ones, by the subjects who exert irregular coercive control over them (Wenar, 2015). Yet, the oil industry is the conveyor that moves oil and gas from below the ground irrespective of its ownership and localisation into the global economy. This industry comprises international oil companies (IOCs) and national oil companies (NOCs).[5] IOCs are private entities whose business operations traditionally cover the full cycle from exploration, through production and refinement, to distribution of petroleum products. NOCs are by and large similarly structured, but they are fully or in the majority owned by a national government. The activities of the oil industry are divided into upstream operations of exploration and production, and downstream operations of refining and distribution. Given the high entry costs, the world's largest oil and gas companies are typically integrated, i.e., they carry out both upstream and downstream activities. Exploration includes prospecting, seismic and drilling activities that take place before the development of a proper oilfield; production involves the extraction of oil from below the ground through onshore and offshore drilling; refining concerns the separation of unwanted components in order to obtain clean hydrocarbons marketable into different usable products; finally, in the distribution phase such products are transferred to consumers through pipeline networks, tankers, railway tanks and trucks.

Big Oil's contribution to cumulative emissions of GHGs is, to an extent, impressive. The top 10 companies in terms of cumulative emissions of Heede's (2014) study all belong to the oil industry. The major 60 oil and gas companies contributed to more than 40% of global cumulative industrial emissions in the period 1988–2015; the top ten ones accounted for almost 22%, and the top 20 ones for more than 30%, as evinced by Table 19.1. The oil industry holds fossil fuel

Table 19.1 Big Oil's cumulative GHG emissions 1988–2015, MtCO$_2$e and % of global industrial GHG. Indeed, the largest share (roughly 90%) of oil and gas companies' global industrial GHG emissions originated from downstream combustion (for energy and non-energy purposes) of oil and gas that Big Oil distributed within the global economic system. These emissions are defined by the Greenhouse Gas Protocol of the World Resources Institute (WRI) as "SCOPE 3 EMISSIONS."

Oil Company	Emissions	%	Typology
Saudi Aramco	40,561	4.51%	NOC
Gazprom (Russia)	35,221	3.91%	NOC
National Iranian Oil	20,505	2.28%	NOC
ExxonMobil (USA)	17,785	1.98%	IOC
Pemex (Mexico)	16,804	1.87%	NOC
Royal Dutch Shell (UK/Netherlands)	15,017	1.67%	IOC
China National Petroleum	14,042	1.56%	NOC
BP (UK)	13,791	1.53%	IOC
Chevron (USA)	11,823	1.31%	IOC
PDVSA (Venezuela)	11,079	1.23%	NOC
Abu Dhabi National Oil	10,769	1.20%	NOC
Sonatrach (Algeria)	8,997	1.00%	NOC
Kuwait Petroleum	8,961	1.00%	NOC
Total (France)	8,541	0.95%	IOC
ConocoPhillips (USA)	7,463	0.83%	IOC
Petrobras (Brazil)	6,907	0.77%	NOC
Lukoil (Russia)	6,750	0.75%	IOC
Nigerian National Petroleum Corp	6,491	0.72%	NOC
Petronas (Malaysia)	6,185	0.69%	NOC
Rosneft (Russia)	5,866	0.65%	NOC
TOTAL 20 (Top 10)	**273,559**	**30.41%**	
	(196,629)	**(21.86%)**	

Source: Elaboration from The Carbon Majors Database – 2017 Dataset Release.

reserves that, if burned, will bring the planet well above the 2 degrees Celsius warming increase: to avoid exceeding that threshold, more than one-third of current oil reserves and one-half of gas reserves should, in fact, be kept in the ground (McGlade and Ekins, 2015).

The moral bases of the duty of disgorgement

The prominent role of Big Oil has important implications for climate change. As the evidence provided shows, the activities of Big Oil have *directly* and *profoundly* harmed the planet and humanity (IPCC, 2014a; Oppenheimer and Anttila-Hughes, 2016). For humanity, the effects of climate change have the consequence of threatening food security globally and regionally, increasing risks of food-borne, water-borne as well as vector-borne diseases, increasing displacement of people due migration, increasing risks of violent conflicts, reducing economic growth and poverty eradication, and the emergence of new poverty traps (IPCC, 2014b, pp. 17–21).

This generates the basis for the responsibility of oil companies: "do no harm" is, in fact, one of the clearest and strongest requirements of all notions of morality, which applies to any agents (Shue, 1999). Consequently, oil companies have the responsibility not to act in certain ways in order to prevent or avoid the harm caused by the emissions generated by their activities. Such responsibility provides moral grounds for modifying their behaviour accordingly. Specifically, it is argued that Big Oil has two primary duties: (1) the reduction of its harmful activities and (2) the rectification of the harm already done. These are the duties of decarbonisation and disgorgement, respectively.

Shue (2017) has already investigated the moral bases for grounding the duty of decarbonisation in view of major carbon producers' transition towards non-carbon-based forms of energy, which is an important element of a large-scale change required from these corporations. This chapter focuses instead on the other, so far unexplored, moral aspect of this large-scale change, namely, the duty of Big Oil to rectify the harm done by disgorging funds.

To this end, it is necessary to first emphasise that Big Oil patently infringes on the negative responsibility of doing no harm: this violation assigns it a composite positive responsibility in the context of climate change.[6] To establish and justify such compound positive responsibility, it is necessary to individuate the morally relevant facts (Ekwurzel et al., 2017; Shue, 2017). Such facts help clarify the conduct of oil companies, shape the moral context within which they operate and evince their intentions. The following morally relevant facts provide, therefore, the foundation for assigning composite positive responsibilities and the consequent duties to Big Oil necessary to meet the negative responsibility of doing no harm.

1　The major 60 oil and gas companies contributed to more than 40% of global cumulative industrial emissions in the period 1988–2015 (The Carbon Majors Database – 2017 Dataset Release).
2　Some oil and gas companies had a high level of internal scientific and technical expertise and were aware of the available scientific knowledge about potential harmful effects of burning fossil fuels for the global climate (CIEL, 2017).
3　Most of Big Oil's emissions in the atmosphere were released between 1988 and 2015 (The Carbon Majors Database – CDP Carbon Majors Report, 2017).
4　Big Oil had the possibility to reduce the harmful effects of its business and to adjust its business model to become less carbon-intensive; some investor-owned oil and gas corporations had this opportunity since more than forty years ago (CIEL, 2017).

5   Leading investor-owned oil and gas companies actively opposed and, in many cases, successfully prevented policies towards GHG reduction and in some countries funded climate denial efforts (Oreskes and Conway, 2011; Frumhoff et al., 2016).

6   Oil and gas companies have made substantial profits that have greatly increased the wealth of their shareholders through their activities related to fossil fuels (Frumhoff et al., 2016; Wenar, 2016).

Fact 1 suggests that Big Oil has propelled climate change by exploring, producing, refining, distributing and burning fossil fuels. This fact already establishes causal responsibility, which is a necessary, yet not sufficient, condition for the more stringent notion of moral responsibility. Moral responsibility requires that the agent is aware of the consequences of its action, can form intentions about the action and can carry it out (Miller, 2004). At least since the first IPCC report of 1990, Big Oil knew about the harmful consequences of its business model (Fact 2). Despite this knowledge, the oil and gas companies released most of their emissions in the past three decades (Fact 3), when they were able to limit those harmful actions (Fact 4). In addition, some oil and gas companies intentionally blocked initiatives to address climate change and funded climate denial activities (Fact 5). All oil and gas companies accumulated substantial amounts of wealth through their fossil fuel-related activities (Fact 6). In sum, these facts provide a justification for assigning Big Oil moral responsibility for climate change.

It is necessary to further specify that it is possible to assign oil and gas companies "collective" (moral) responsibility. They are, in fact, conglomerate collectivities, whose "identity is not exhausted by the conjunction of the identities of the persons in the organization" (French, 1984, p. 13). Conglomerate collectivities have the following features: (a) an identity larger than the sum of the identities of their members; (b) decision-making structures that enable the inputs of members' judgements to be translated into collective judgements as outputs; (c) consistency over time; and (d) self-conception as a unit. Accordingly, oil and gas companies are indeed conglomerate collectivities, which can qualify as moral agents and, therefore, can have different forms of responsibility.

The duty of disgorgement intends to guarantee that oil and gas companies rectify the injustice towards those who undeservedly suffered the harm they generated (Vanderheiden, 2011; Shue, 2015). This duty posits that oil and gas companies should "disgorge" part of the money they accumulated by benefitting from their harmful activities to help the "victims" to prevent or adapt to climate impacts, and to compensate those non-adapted or mitigated.

To specify its moral features, it is useful to frame Big Oil's duty of disgorgement through a corrective justice perspective. It requires to identify (1) the moral basis of the injustice, i.e., the moral principles that justify and define rectificatory actions; (2) the types of rectificatory actions required; (3) the forms that rectificatory efforts should take, i.e., the specific actions through which rectification of harm done should be carried out; and (4) the duty recipients, i.e., the subjects entitled to rectification and the modality of the allocation of the rectificatory actions among them envisaged by the duties individuated (Caney, 2006, p. 465).

The moral principles of the duty of disgorgement

The moral justification of rectificatory actions in the context of climate change is usually provided through two backward-looking principles – the "polluter pays principle" (PPP) and the "beneficiary pays principle" (BPP), and a forward-looking one, known as the "ability to pay principle" (APP) (Caney, 2005; Shue, 2015).[7] These principles are generally used independently, even if they in fact all aim at establishing and justifying positive responsibilities for sharing the burden of rectifying the unjust situation created by the actions that produced climate change. This chapter instead espouses the hybrid version developed by Shue for providing a moral argument for climate change action based on these principles. The convergence of the three principles seems to provide appropriate composite moral bases that justify Big Oil's duty of disgorgement (Shue, 2015). Shue (2015, p, 16) argues that "those who contributed heavily to creating the problem of excessive emissions thereby both benefitted more than others and became better able to pay than most others." This is the case of Big Oil. Therefore, the PPP, BPP and APP morally justify oil and gas companies' duty of disgorgement and originate in different ways the related rectificatory actions.

The structure of the duty of disgorgement

Big Oil must rectify the harm its activities generated by supporting affected people. There are different ways to support them, from immaterial approaches, like public acknowledgement and apologies, "naming and shaming," or providing a genuine account of climate change and its implications through, for instance, the establishment of a truth commission (Rotberg and Thompson, 2000), to material rectification of historical wrongdoing (Goodin, 2013; Goodin and Pasternak, 2016). In the context of climate change many practical matters to address its harmful impacts are necessary. Rectification, therefore, must be mainly material and must aim at minimising climate impacts through practical actions.

Given the complexity of climate change, restitution (returning misappropriated things to the rightful owners or their successors) and compensation (compensating the rightful owners or their successors for the harm done) as forms of material rectification are highly problematic, since they both require that the recipient of the rectificatory action be specifically identified (Goodin, 2013). Given substantial temporal and spatial lags between carbon emissions and their impacts, it is almost impossible to identify the rightful recipient or a legitimate successor with certainty.

While restitution and compensation fail, disgorgement seems to be a more useful approach. Disgorgement requires only the relinquishment of the "fruits of historical wrongdoing"; in the case of Big Oil, the "tainted benefits" of its fossil fuel-related activities. Unlike restitution and the even more demanding compensation, the disgorgement form of rectification focuses on the duty bearer and not on the duty recipient and their welfare (Goodin, 2013). Disgorgement does not require the identification of a particular duty recipient, or assumptions over how they would be today had the past wrong not occurred. Therefore, the potential and the advantage of disgorgement lie in its informational parsimony that makes it much more feasible, especially in the complex situations created by climate change.

It is important to note that not all benefits that are ascribable to Big Oil's historical wrongdoing should be viewed as "tainted." Profits are a theoretical proxy and a sound pragmatic measure for oil companies' tainted benefits. In the case of Big Oil, the notion of wrongdoing reasonably applies to their fossil fuel-related activities undertaken after 1990, as previously mentioned. After 1990, their ignorance about the consequences of carbon emissions and alleged impotence of oil and gas companies to reduce their contribution becomes inexcusable. Profits of Big Oil since 1990 can be therefore understood as a practical measure of the tainted benefits that they should disgorge.

The indication of the form that rectificatory actions should take

In practical terms, disgorgement can take the form of a fund similar in its objectives to the Earth Atmospheric Trust envisaged by Barnes et al. (2008) for financially supporting people affected by climate change and most socially vulnerable to its impacts. This fund should be gradually replenished through the profits disgorged by oil and gas companies, as explained below.

The individuation of duty recipients

A further specification of the duty of disgorgement and a fundamental issue of corrective justice requires identifying those among whom the disgorged funds should be distributed. In relation to climate change, agents who are most socially vulnerable to its harmful impacts are the rightful duty recipients. The degree of vulnerability can be used for defining their level of entitlement to the disgorged funds: the greater the vulnerability, the larger the rectification through disgorged funds. A stringent normative imperative of putting the most vulnerable first is given by Shue's third general principle of equity (Shue, 1999). This principle, known as "guaranteed minimum," states that those who have less than enough for a decent human life should be given enough resources and means for living decently. In this light, being vulnerable indicates being deprived and having far less than enough. More vulnerable agents, therefore, should be given the rectification means (the funds, in this case) necessary to attain a level sufficient for them to cope with, and to recover from, climate impacts.

Practical issues and challenges of the duty of disgorgement

The strong moral imperative outlined here that requires Big Oil to disgorge funds that are the fruit of historical wrongdoing should be translated into practical steps in order to bring about a more just arrangement of global climate governance. In this light, a number of practical issues related to the duty of disgorgement require clarification.

First, there is the issue of the form disgorged funds should take. More specifically, if the international community accepts the duty of disgorgement, how should the process be organised and managed? Theoretically, as underlined in the previous section, the disgorged funds should go back to an impersonal common pool to be allocated to most vulnerable people. However, it seems impossible that oil and gas companies relinquish all the profits made since 1990 until today. This would shatter the financial stability of the oil industry and even of some states, and severely disrupt the international order. The only feasible alternative is to use current, ongoing profits. However, also in this case, to avoid immediate bankruptcy of oil and gas companies, it is necessary to proceed gradually. Initially, these companies should disgorge only the portion of current profits usually employed for paying dividends to shareholders or investing in the exploration and development of new locations for fossil fuels, and retain the rest. Gradually, over the next decades, oil and gas companies should come to disgorge all current profits.

Second, it is important to clarify how vulnerability should be understood and employed to serve as a useful criterion for disgorging funds. Intuitively, the most appealing benchmark seems to be a notion of vulnerability intended as the degree to which agents are susceptible to, or unable to cope with, negative impacts of climate change. However, such *biophysical* notion of vulnerability alone does not give any information on the ability of peoples and communities to deal with climate change and cannot be a conclusive referent for the allocation of funds, which must be directed specifically for coping with climate impacts (Kelly and Adger, 2000; O'Brien et al., 2004). To this end, it is more useful to adopt a notion of *social* vulnerability defined as a state of wellbeing pertaining directly to individuals and social groups, whose causes are related to social, institutional and economic factors, such as poverty, class, race, ethnicity, gender, etc., as well as to climate impacts (Paavola and Adger, 2006; Grasso et al., 2014). Such notion of social vulnerability would also have the further advantage of being practically measurable at the community level through an opportune index framed in terms of different basic determinants, for instance economic welfare, social wellbeing, infrastructure and technology, and the structure of the economy (Grasso et al., 2014). In brief, for distributing disgorged funds among more vulnerable agents, an index of social vulnerability should be used.

Third, despite the moral robustness of Big Oil's duty disgorgement, taking action to hold them responsible for their historical wrongdoing poses unprecedented challenges for several reasons. The general recognition and self-perception of oil and gas companies as the corporate entities first and foremost responsible for the climate crisis may be problematic. Pre-philosophical common-sense morality would suggest that other businesses (e.g., automotive, chemical or construction industries) are also similarly responsible for climate change, as they also continued the use of fossil fuels after the consensus on the harmfulness of carbon emissions was established. To address this challenge, it is necessary to further emphasise the unique role of Big Oil in the current socio-economic system. Oil and gas companies are the corporate entities that have been dictating the rules of the game in terms of reliance on fossil fuels to other businesses. Through their informed choice to continue the extraction, refinement and distribution of fossil fuels in the 1990s, Big Oil created a dependency of other industries, which had to shape their business models around fossil fuels. Therefore, oil and gas companies should be considered the primary duty-bearers. Other industries, which depend on the supply from oil companies, should be attributed fossil fuel-related duties only after the "rule shapers" (i.e., Big Oil) have met theirs. Identifying Big Oil as a stand-alone group, with very particular and unique moral responsibilities, is crucial to advancing the efforts to combat climate change. This recognition, in turn, should prompt the emergence of a new social norm delegitimising Big Oil's behaviour. Delegitimisation of once deeply socially entrenched practices and behavioural patterns through a change in social norms has happened in the past (e.g., slavery, tobacco). The recognition of the activities of Big Oil as morally inadmissible should favour the global acceptance of the duty of disgorgement and to its actual operationalisation.

The disruptive nature of the process of holding oil and gas companies responsible and accountable for their actions poses a further major practical challenge. This issue lies in the novelty of the problem. States have been the main units of international action against climate change for decades. Holding private and and more generally non-state agents accountable for their harmful activity usually falls within the jurisdiction of national and international courts. Recognising oil and gas companies from different countries as morally responsible for climate change, as a group and as individual entities, capable of disgorging funds for their historical wrongdoing, would set a precedent and disrupt the status quo of the international system. There is no existing institutional structure which could accommodate the new arrangement and facilitate the disgorgement process. Creating a new structure to collect and manage disgorged funds would raise questions about justice and legitimacy, the mode of participation and the extent of private agents' obligations and rights. Yet, it seems the only viable solution. Moreover, having a state-centred system that imposes constraints and conditions onto business entities would also challenge the dominant paradigms on the role of the state. These are specific about the role of the state and its relationship to business, permitting little infringement of corporate autonomy under a "business-as-usual" scenario. Even though climate change is not business-as-usual, there is likely to be a strong resistance against the idea of states dictating that the most powerful global corporations share substantial parts of their profit (and gradually all of it) for moral reasons, because "it is the right thing to do."

This introduces another critical challenge, a motivational problem. In some instances, there is the problem of the most influential shareholders and board members, who are interested in maintaining a business-as-usual approach for self-interest reasons, controlling the activities of oil and gas companies. These behaviours should be condemned on moral grounds, since they prioritise the wealth and power of few over the lives, health and wealth of many. However, it is not always a clear-cut case of greed against virtue. A blurry line between private and public interests and ownership structures – i.e., IOCs vs. NOCs – in many oil and gas companies complicates the matter since fossil fuel exports strongly affect the development of several natural resource-dependent economies, like Saudi Arabia, Russia, and Brazil. Resistance to any attempts to dissolve a corporation, which is the primary source of economic growth and of fiscal revenue, is inevitable since such actions would directly endanger the economies of these states.

Conclusions

Recently, scholars have started to address the ethical issues raised by climate change also from a descriptive rather than an exclusively normative perspective. This growth and widening of climate justice seems critical to bridge the gap between positive and normative theorisation and real-world climate decision-making. In this regard, this chapter offers a novel ethical inquiry into the (thorny) notions of responsibilities and duties of non-state, collective agents of justice – oil and gas companies – with significant implications for a world severely threatened by climate change (Brown and Caldeira, 2017).

This study was prompted by the general disregard of Big Oil's responsibilities and duties in climate change. It seems, in fact, that the international community is ignoring the elephant in the room of the global climate debate. Failure to engage these agents is particularly evident in the light of the constant shortage of financial resources to combat climate change. Oil and gas companies are directly responsible for the problem and financially capable of assisting in the global climate change efforts. The normative analysis carried out indicates and clarifies the moral role of oil and gas companies; the ensuing descriptive analysis addresses some practical issues concerning the operationalisation of their duty of disgorgement. Altogether, this work emphasises that the inclusion of Big Oil among the direct agents of climate justice can propel global collaboration on climate change by adding the necessary resources to pursue the ambitious goals set by the Paris Agreement, and distributing such resources in a more equitable manner than in the current international system.

Notes

1 The official definition of anthropogenic climate change can be found at article 2 of the 1994 United Nations Framework Convention on Climate Change – UNFCCC (http://unfccc.int/key_documents/the_convention/items/2853.php).
2 The emissions traced to carbon majors are calculated based on the carbon content of fuels marketed (subtracting non-energy uses), CO_2 from cement production process, CO_2 from flaring, venting, own fuel use and fugitive or vented CH_4.
3 According to Heede's figures, the top emitters and the large majority of producers are fossil fuel corporations (IOCs, NOCs and coal companies), whereas cement producers are a small minority among carbon majors. The original 2014 database, for instance, included only seven cement producers whose emissions amounted to 1.45% of carbon majors cumulative total (Heede, 2013, Table 4, p. 17). The moral analysis of this chapter is applicable only to the still existing oil and gas companies, since in the case of climate change the attribution of responsibilities for rectifying the harm done to non-existing entities is not possible according to the relevant literature of climate ethics (e.g., Caney, 2006).
4 833 Gt CO_2 (50.4%) of the emissions associated with carbon majors' activities were produced since 1988, whereas 820 Gt CO_2 (49.6%) in the period between 1750 and 1987 (The Carbon Majors Database – CDP Carbon Majors Report 2017, p. 7). More generally, Heede (2014, p. 234) claims that "[O]f the emissions traced to carbon major fossil fuel and cement production, half has been emitted since 1986."
5 This analysis excludes two other typologies of oil and gas companies, given their irrelevance in terms of contribution to global GHG emissions: the so-called independents, smaller companies that operate only in the upstream segment of the oil industry's operations, and oilfield service companies that provide services and outsourcing needs to the oil industry.
6 "If one does contribute to harm, in violation of the negative responsibility, it becomes one's positive responsibility to correct it – and perhaps compensate for it as well" Shue (2017, p. 593). In other words, responsibility can be "negative" and compel agents not to act or "positive" and demand that agents act in certain ways: generally, the first kind of responsibility provides the moral basis for and "triggers" the second kind.

7 The PPP distributes the financial and other burdens associated with rectificatory actions in proportion to past contributions that agents have made to the overall level of emissions. The BPP holds instead that proportionality in such distribution should be calculated on the basis of the benefits that agents have derived from activities generating emissions. The APP posits that the quota of burdens should be proportional to the agents' relative capacity to bear such burdens (Caney, 2005; Shue, 2015).

References

Barnes, P., et al. (2008) 'Creating an earth atmospheric trust', *Science*, vol 319, no 5864, pp 724–724.

Brown, P. T. and Caldeira, K. (2017) 'Greater future global warming inferred from Earth's recent energy budget', *Nature*, vol 552, no 7683, pp 45–50.

Caney, S. (2005) 'Cosmopolitan justice, responsibility, and global climate change', *Leiden Journal of International Law*, vol 18, no 4, pp 747–775.

Caney, S. (2006) 'Environmental degradation, reparations, and the moral significance of history', *Journal of Social Philosophy*, vol 37, no 3, pp 464–482.

CDP (2017) *The Carbon Majors Database – CDP Carbon Majors Report 2017*. www.cdp.net/en//articles/media/new-report-shows-just-100-companies-are-source-of-over-70-of-emissions.

CIEL (Center for International Environmental Law) (2017) *Smoke and Fumes. The Legal and Evidentiary Basis for Holding Big Oil Accountable for the Climate Crisis*. CIEL, Washington, DC, and Geneva.

Ekwurzel, B., Boneham, J., Dalton, M. W., Heede, R., Mera, R. J., Allen, M. R., and Frumhoff, P. C. (2017) 'The rise in global atmospheric CO_2, surface temperature, and sea level from emissions traced to major carbon producers', *Climatic Change*, vol 144, no 4, pp 579–590.

French, P. A. (1984) *Collective and Corporate Responsibility*. Columbia University Press, New York.

Frumhoff, P. C., Heede, R., and Oreskes, N. (2016) 'The climate responsibilities of industrial carbon producers', *Climatic Change*, vol 132, no 2, pp 157–171.

Goodin, R. E. (2013) 'Disgorging the fruits of historical wrongdoing', *American Political Science Review*, vol 107, no 3, pp 478–491.

Goodin, R. E. and Pasternak, A. (2016) 'Intending to benefit from wrongdoing', *Politics, Philosophy & Economics*, vol 15, no 3, pp 280–297.

Grasso, M. (2013) 'Climate ethics: With a little help from moral cognitive neuroscience', *Environmental Politics*, vol 22, no 3, pp 377–394.

Grasso, M. and Markowitz, E. M. (2015) 'The moral complexity of climate change and the need for a multidisciplinary perspective on climate ethics', *Climatic Change*, vol 130, no 3, pp 327–334.

Grasso, M., Moneo, M., and Arena, M. (2014) 'Assessing social vulnerability to climate change in Samoa', *Regional Environmental Change*, vol 14, no 4, pp 1329–1341.

Heede, R. (2013) *Carbon Majors: Accounting for Carbon and Methane Emissions 1854–2010*, Methods and Results Report.

Heede, R. (2014) 'Tracing anthropogenic carbon dioxide and methane emissions to fossil fuel and cement producers', 1854–2010', *Climatic Change*, vol 122, no 1–2, pp 229–241.

Heede, R. and Oreskes, N. (2016) 'Potential emissions of CO_2 and methane from proved reserves of fossil fuels: An alternative analysis', *Global Environmental Change*, vol 36, pp 12–20.

IPCC (2014a) *Climate Change 2014: Synthesis Report. Contribution of Working Groups I, II and III to the Fifth Assessment Report of the Intergovernmental Panel on Climate*. Cambridge University Press, Cambridge and New York.

IPCC (2014b) *Working Group II, Impacts, Adaptation, and Vulnerability, Synthesis for Policy Makers*. www.ipcc.ch/pdf/assessment-report/ar5/wg2/ar5_wgII_spm_en.pdf

Jamieson, D. (2014) *Reason in a Dark Time: Why the Struggle Against Climate Change Failed – And What It Means for Our Future*. Oxford University Press, New York.

Kelly, P. M. and Adger, W. N. (2000) 'Theory and practice in assessing vulnerability to climate change and facilitating adaptation', *Climatic Change*, vol 47, no 4, pp 325–352.

Markowitz, E. M., Grasso, M. and Jamieson, D. (2015) 'Climate ethics at a multidisciplinary crossroads: Four directions for future scholarship', *Climatic Change*, vol 130, no 3, pp 465–474.

McGlade, C. E. and Ekins, P. (2015) 'The geographical distribution of fossil fuels unused when limiting global warming to 2°C', *Nature*, vol 517, no 7533, pp 187–190.

Miller, D. (2004) 'Holding nations responsible', *Ethics*, vol 114, no 2, pp 240–268.

O'Brien, K., Leichenko, R., Kelkar, U., Venema, H., Aandahl, G., Tompkins, H., Javed, A., Bhadwal, S., Barg, S., Nygaard, L., and West, J. (2004) 'Mapping vulnerability to multiple stressors: Climate change and globalization in India', *Global Environmental Change*, vol 14, no 4, pp 303–313.

Oppenheimer, M. and Anttila-Hughes, J. K. (2016) 'The science of climate change', *The Future of Children*, vol 26, no 1, pp 11–30.

Oreskes, N. and Conway, E. M. (2011) *Merchants of Doubt: How a Handful of Scientists Obscured the Truth on Issues From Tobacco Smoke to Global Warming*. Bloomsbury Publishing, New York.

Paavola, J. and Adger, W. N. (2006) 'Fair adaptation to climate change', *Ecological Economics*, vol 56, no 4, pp 594–609.

Rotberg, R. I. and Thompson, D. (Eds.). (2000) *Truth v. Justice: The Morality of Truth Commissions*. Princeton University Press, Princeton.

Shue, H. (1999) 'Global environment and international inequality', *International Affairs*, vol 75, no 3, pp 531–545.

Shue, H. (2015) 'Historical responsibility, harm prohibition, and preservation requirement: Core practical convergence on climate change', *Moral Philosophy and Politics*, vol 2, no 1, pp 7–31.

Shue, H. (2017) 'Responsible for what? Carbon producer CO_2 contributions and the energy transition', *Climatic Change*, vol 144, no 4, pp 591–596.

Vanderheiden, S. (2011) 'Globalizing responsibility for climate change', *Ethics & International Affairs*, vol 25, no 1, pp 65–84.

Wenar, L. (2015) 'Coercion in cross-border property rights', *Social Philosophy and Policy*, vol 32, no 1, pp 171–191.

Wenar, L. (2016) *Blood Oil: Tyrants, Violence, and the Rules that Run the World*. Oxford University Press, New York.

20

Climate justice and REDD+

A multiscalar examination of the Norwegian-Ethiopian partnership

David Brown

Background

In recent years, increasing attention has been paid to the role of forests in stabilising the Earth's climate. The role of forests in climate change is unique in that they act as a source of GHG emissions as well as a land-based carbon sink (Savaresi, 2016; Dooley and Gupta, 2017). By reducing deforestation rates, climate change policymakers and practitioners aim to curb GHG emissions while simultaneously expanding the space for carbon sequestration. Recent interest in forests in international climate change negotiations and agreements has been driven by the importance placed upon reducing deforestation rates in tackling climate change in the Stern report (2007). The IPCC (2014) propose that the land-based sector accounts for approximately 24% of global GHG emissions, of which deforestation is a key element, although more recent scientific research suggests that the actual contribution of land-based emissions and deforestation may be somewhat lower in reality (Tubiello et al., 2015).

Post-Kyoto, policymakers and negotiators have increasingly integrated tropical deforestation interventions and sustainable forestry initiatives into international climate change agreements (Dooley and Gupta, 2017; Krug, 2018). Most prominently, REDD+, or "Reducing Emissions from Deforestation and forest Degradation," is an international policy framework that has emerged since 2007 as a way of combatting climate change through reductions in tropical deforestation and degradation. Aligning with a Payment for Ecosystem Services (PES) set-up, REDD+ works by rewarding and incentivising tropical-forested nations for reducing deforestation levels below a given baseline and for sustainably managing their forest stocks (Savaresi, 2016; Angelsen, 2016).

The idea is that REDD+ funds, deriving from both bilateral and multilateral sources, are transferred to tropical-forested nations in the Global South on the basis of verified reductions in deforestation and forest degradation. Falling under the UN-REDD framework, the REDD+ agenda has gained high-profile and significant momentum in recent international climate change agreements, as a voluntary and fragmented approach to GHG emissions reductions. As well as acting as a potential source of significant reductions in global GHG emissions, REDD+ is also proposed to offer synergistic social and economic benefits for local forest-dependent communities in the Global South (Okereke and Dooley, 2010; Savaresi, 2016).

A broad evolution of REDD+ since its initial conceptualisation and formulation can be noted, with environmental and social safeguards increasingly integrated into the UN-REDD framework following the Cancun COP in 2010 (Jagger et al., 2012; McDermott et al., 2012; Angelsen, 2016). These attempt to ensure basic environmental and social protections in the implementation of REDD+ in tropical-forested nations. Socially, the safeguards aim to realise "non-carbon benefits" at the community level, to enhance the participatory rights of local-level actors and to address conflicts in land tenure (Agrawal et al., 2011).

However, concerns have been raised in the literature that REDD+ may have negative impacts upon the rights, needs and interests of marginalised forest-dependent communities (Paladino, 2011; Beymer-Farris and Bassett, 2012; Forsyth and Sikor, 2013). The extent to which the proposed "safeguards" in the UN-REDD framework can adequately address these issues has been questioned. REDD+ scholars are concerned with community-level retainment of benefits from forest conservation practices and the sufficient and actual participation of local-level actors in REDD+ decision-making (Sikor et al., 2014; Martin et al., 2014). Early evidence suggests that the design and implementation of REDD+ are unlikely to be in the interests of the affected forest-dependent communities, without significant shifts in attention among REDD+ policymakers, and that the safeguards do not go far enough in protecting the rights, needs and interests of vulnerable local-level actors in the Global South (Paladino, 2011; Beymer-Farris and Bassett, 2012).

The empirical research in this chapter builds upon these community-centric critiques of REDD+ to put forward a specifically climate justice-led and multiscalar analysis of the initiative. It has been highlighted that particular justice dilemmas emanate from the protection and conservation of tropical forests, as an international climate change mitigation strategy (Martin et al., 2014). Indeed, the success of REDD+ in realising synergistic "co-benefits" with REDD+ and positively impacting upon the livelihoods of forest-dependent communities is likely to be determined by how issues of justice are dealt with in the REDD+ negotiations and policy (Okereke and Dooley, 2010). Thus, this research questions whether REDD+ can form part of a "just transition."

The adoption of a multiscalar climate justice framework in examining REDD+ responds to two key gaps in extant research. Firstly, while there has been significant theorisation of climate justice on an abstract level (e.g., "ideal" distribution of climate burdens), it has been less considered how such abstract conceptualisations map onto currently existing policy practices, such as REDD+. There is a need to better understand how notions of climate justice are constructed in the actual practice of climate action, considering the ways in which justice norms underpin or justify responses to climate change (Okereke, 2008; Burnham et al., 2013). Despite the considerable debate surrounding REDD+, particularly at the community level, there is a dearth of analysis that examines REDD+ through a specifically climate justice lens. Thus, this research builds upon previous justice-centric analyses of REDD+ and "avoided deforestation" (Okereke and Dooley, 2010; Page, 2016).

Secondly, there is currently insufficient research that examines climate justice issues on a multiscalar level, whereby the international, national and subnational levels have thus far been examined in isolation. Accordingly, Barrett (2013) proposed the need for a refined, scalar analysis of climate justice, which considers the commonalities and divergences across and between scales of climate governance. With REDD+, the local-level issues have not generally been understood in relation to broader contexts. A multiscalar analysis of REDD+ is pertinent considering its fundamental structure, which interconnects actors on multiple levels of governance (Korhonen-Kurki et al., 2012; Schroeder and McDermott, 2014).

Thus, in this chapter, the construction of climate justice norms in REDD+ discourse is examined using a multiscalar framework (see Figure 20.1), whereby actors on international, national and local levels of REDD+ governance are analysed through a climate justice lens.

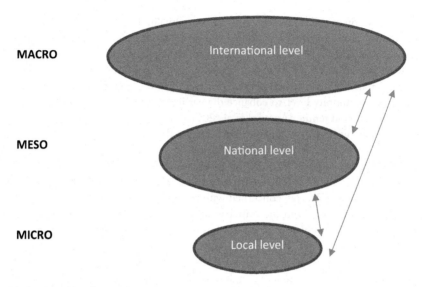

Figure 20.1 A multiscalar analysis of climate justice.

Source: Author's own analysis.

Case study

The examined case study in this research is the REDD+ partnership between Norway and Ethiopia. Norway plays a prominent and leading role in REDD+, acting as by far the largest bilateral financial supporter of the REDD+ initiative globally. As of 2016, Norway's International Climate and Forest Initiative (NICFI) accounts for approximately 73% of pledged REDD+ funds (around $500 million per year) and is the largest donor to the UN-REDD programme (Climate Funds Update, 2016; Angelsen, 2016). Given the key role that Norway plays in developing the REDD+ agenda internationally, it is necessary to critically examine and assess the notions of climate justice that underpin and justify its REDD+ policy discourse.

Meanwhile, since 2011, the Ethiopian government has placed REDD+ centrally in its ambitious green growth strategy, known as the "Climate Resilient Green Economy" (CRGE) strategy (Bekele et al., 2015). The government is aiming to become a middle-income country by 2030, while maintaining domestic GHG emissions at 2010 levels (NICFI, 2016). Driven by the long-term, persistent and acute deforestation in the country (a rate of around 1.0–1.5% annually) and an acknowledgement of the key role that forests play in regulating the climate (with the forest sector accounting for around 40% of GHG emissions in Ethiopia), Ethiopia has made a concerted and institutionalised effort to sustainably manage its forests (Bekele et al., 2015; FAO, 2015, Moges et al., 2010). Bilateral and multilateral REDD+ funds are seen to be key in financing the CRGE strategy.

Existing since 2013, the Norwegian-Ethiopian REDD+ partnership includes technical and financial support from Norway as part of the "Readiness" phase of REDD+ in Ethiopia, which aims to enhance the institutional and monitoring capacities of Ethiopian forest governance and to lay the foundations for the forthcoming implementation of REDD+ practices (Bekele et al., 2015). Additionally, although the specific details are as yet unclear, the agreement incorporates the future purchasing of verified emissions reductions from deforestation. Here, Norway acts as the largest financial contributor to Ethiopia's REDD+ initiative, through both bilateral and multilateral channels (see Table 20.1).

Table 20.1 Sources of REDD+ funding in Ethiopia.

Funding Body	Amount pledged (in US$)
NICFI (Norwegian Government)	$8 million
DFID (UK Government)	$6.6 million
FCPF (Forest Carbon Partnership Facility)	$3.6 million
FAO (Food and Agriculture Organization)	$830,000

Source: Climate Funds Update (2016).

Outside of the Norwegian and Ethiopian governments, other actors also play a key role in the design and implementation of REDD+ in Ethiopia (see Figure 20.2 for a multiscalar dissection of the key actors involved in the Norwegian-Ethiopian REDD+ partnership). On an international level, multilateral institutions provide technical and financial support for REDD+ processes in Ethiopia, notably the UN and the World Bank. Since 2012, the World Bank has contributed funds to the REDD+ readiness process in Ethiopia, with an initial grant of $3.6 million, as well as agreeing to pay for future verified emissions reductions (Bekele et al., 2015). Meanwhile, the UNDP and UNEP provide primarily technical support in Ethiopia, including giving advice on the design of the national REDD+ strategy and carrying out an economic evaluation of the value of Ethiopia's forests.

Additionally, environmental NGOs from both Norway (e.g., The Rainforest Foundation, Friends of the Earth Norway, The Development Fund) and Ethiopia (e.g., Farm Africa, Ethio Wetlands and Natural Resources Association) play a key role in the local- and regional-level implementation of REDD+ projects. Primarily, these projects have taken place within Oromia, the state that has been designated as the REDD+ pilot region in Ethiopia. Given this status and the high presence of forest governance and REDD+ infrastructure there (Moges et al., 2010), Oromia was selected as the examined region in this research. Based on FAO (2010) estimates, Oromia contains by far the most forest cover in the country (approximately 6.9 million hectares).

The particular focus in this research is upon a REDD+ project being implemented by Ethio Wetlands and Natural Resources Association (EWNRA), a domestic environmental NGO that works on natural resource and forest management at project level in Ethiopia using a Participatory Forest Management (PFM) approach. EWNRA's project is financially supported by the Norwegian government, with funding channelled through the Development fund, a Norwegian NGO and partner organisation. The field site is located in two villages (Gago and Yakama) in the Nono Sele district of Illubabor in Southwest Oromia. The district was selected due to the majority of Oromia's high forests being located there and it being one of the zones where forest loss has been most severe in the state (Hailu et al., 2000), while the villages were chosen in coordination with EWNRA, on the basis of pragmatic reasons: the availability of a translator and the presence of NGO workers to aid with the fieldwork.

In this research, the Norwegian-Ethiopian REDD+ partnership was examined in order to identify and assess the underlying climate justice norms present in the policy and community-level discourse on a multiscalar level. The research was driven by two primary research questions: (a) *How is climate justice constructed in the REDD+ policy discourse and what implications does this have for current and future REDD+ practices?* and (2) *How do the identified (climate) justice constructions in REDD+ policy discourse synergise and diverge across and between multiple scales and actors?*

The data was primarily collected through document analysis and in-depth interviews. Regarding the former, a number of key policy documents from the REDD+ actors, comprising of policy

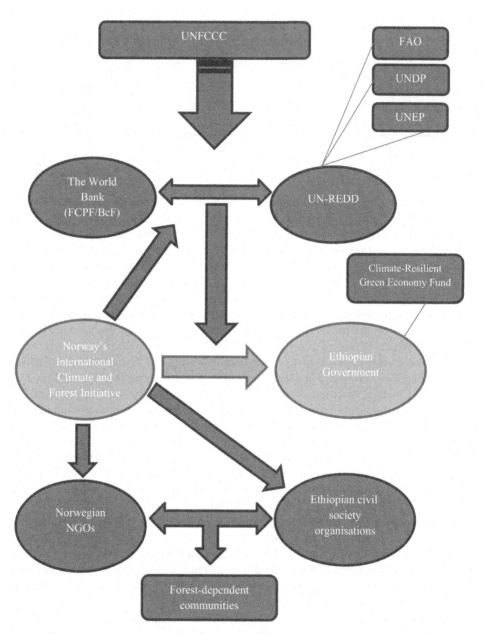

Figure 20.2 The multiscalar actors interconnected in the Norwegian-Ethiopian REDD+ Agreement.

Source: Author's own analysis.

reports, presentations and memos, were examined. To supplement this data, 16 in-depth interviews were carried out with representatives from the policy institutions, alongside 20 interviews with members of the forest-dependent communities in Ethiopia. Critical discourse analysis was used in this project, whereby the content and underlying linguistic devices and mechanisms of the policy texts and interview transcripts were critically assessed and interrogated in line with the research enquiries.

"Trade-offs" in REDD+

The findings suggest that the REDD+ policymakers in the Norwegian-Ethiopian partnership are primarily driven by the cost-effective and large-scale reductions in GHG emissions. To varying extents, NICFI, the UN and the World Bank all demonstrate this as being the ultimate overriding factor in their REDD+ engagement throughout the policy discourse. NICFI most clearly demonstrates its primary motivations for REDD+ engagement in its stated "core objectives":

1 To work towards the inclusion of emissions from deforestation and forest degradation in a new international climate regime;
2 To take early action to achieve cost-effective and verifiable reductions in greenhouse gas emissions;
3 To promote the conservation of natural forests to maintain their carbon storage capacity.

In the first two objectives, NICFI clearly and explicitly position the reductions of GHG emissions and deforestation rates as the institution's priority in designing REDD+. It promotes the use of the forest sector in realising significant GHG emissions reductions as the key driver of REDD+, forming part of a "new international climate regime." However, in none of the NICFI's core objectives are the development, poverty alleviation or livelihoods benefits of REDD+ present. This is in line with what was found in the policy discourse more broadly, whereby these aspects of REDD+ tend to be discussed or highlighted to a much lesser extent than are the carbon-oriented goals.

Through a number of linguistic devices and discursive structures, the development or poverty alleviation potential of REDD+ is side-lined and rendered secondary in the policy discourse. The development aspects of REDD+ are largely referred to in the form of "co-benefits" or "non-carbon benefits." Labelling these as "co-benefits" or "non-carbon benefits" in itself necessarily distinguishes the development aims of REDD+ as supplementary: benefits which can be achieved where possible but are not prioritised (i.e., the marginalising of "non-carbon benefits" in comparison to the primary intended outcomes of "carbon benefits").

Additionally, emphasis is placed upon the importance of cost-effectiveness in designing REDD+ strategies throughout NICFI's policy texts. In line with an economic framing of REDD+ that has existed since Stern's (2007) report, cost-effectiveness appears to act as a key indicator of progress in REDD+, rather than equitable outcomes. It highlights NICFI's ultimate priority: the reduction of international GHG emissions, wherever these may be the cheapest, which is likely to conflict with the realisation of the development or poverty alleviation potential of REDD+. Indeed, climate justice scholars have raised concerns over the potential trade-offs between efficiency and equity, with Traxler (2002) proposing that a cost-effective climate change mitigation strategy may lead to countries with higher opportunity costs being allocated greater or earlier climate burdens.

Moreover, all of the policymakers, to varying extents, indicate the importance of measuring and monitoring the rates of deforestation in the recipient nation and refer continually to "verified" emissions reductions. The detailed and concrete outline of the emissions monitoring and measurements acts in contrast to the lack of clarity surrounding the wider potential development-oriented benefits of REDD+. It is rarely discussed how the perceived "co-benefits" of REDD+ may be achieved nor how they may be measured. This again acts to demonstrate what is of ultimate priority for the policymakers, with the progress of REDD+ being determined by the metrics of deforestation rates and GHG emissions.

Additionally, NICFI indicate the importance of tropical forest conservation as a way to "maintain their carbon storage capacity," indicating the value and orientation of the tropical forests for the institution: as a cost-effective form of carbon sequestration. Indeed, throughout the REDD+ policymakers' discourse, forests are referred to as "carbon stocks" or "carbon sinks" to a much greater extent than as a source of livelihoods for the communities. This acts to define forests primarily for their carbon-sequestering abilities rather than for their role in development or poverty alleviation.

More broadly, the discussions of poverty alleviation that are present in the REDD+ policy discourse tend to concern the impacts that this may have upon deforestation rates. Throughout, the policymakers propose that if the deforestation rates are to be reduced in the recipient natures, poverty necessarily needs to be simultaneously tackled. Thus, the motivations for discussions of poverty alleviation and development by the REDD+ policymakers appear to be for their instrumental rather than intrinsic values, again acting to demonstrate the institutions' overriding priorities.

Accordingly, the "supplementary" nature of the development or poverty-oriented benefits of REDD+ in the policy discourse suggests that these are not an active priority for the policymakers. Success is not determined by these; if the "non-carbon benefits" can arise simultaneously alongside reductions in GHG emissions, then the policymakers will celebrate these, but they are unlikely to pursue them in the first place. The lack of prioritisation of development objectives perhaps reflects the funders' confidence that these will occur organically when implementing REDD+ policy. However, livelihood or development aspects are only likely to be pursued if they are symbiotic with achieving cost-efficient and significant reductions in deforestation levels and GHG emissions.

For the Ethiopian government, the development or poverty alleviation aspects of REDD+ also tend to be side-lined, but to a lesser extent than the other policymakers and in a distinctive form, in line with the country's CRGE strategy. The CRGE strategy dictates a drive towards agricultural expansion as the key element of Ethiopia's economic development alongside concentrated efforts to reduce deforestation and forest degradation rates in the country. However, current research suggests that large-scale and smallholder agricultural expansion act as one of the key drivers of deforestation in Ethiopia (FAO, 2015, Bekele et al., 2015), suggesting a likely tension between the two in the implementation of REDD+ in the country.

In line with this, the Ethiopian government emphasises the role that agriculture plays as a "major" or "primary" driver of deforestation in the country throughout its policy reports, to a much greater extent than other identified drivers. For instance, in one of the Ethiopian governments' assessment reports it is stated:

> Ever increasing scarcity of land resources for agricultural practices in the region has escalated the problem of encroachment for cultivation, grazing and settlement in and around forested landscapes in the region.
>
> *(MEF, 2015: 95)*

In this quote, the Ethiopian government highlights the role of "agricultural practices" in deforestation in Ethiopia, while also framing land resources as "scarce." The latter implies the limited capacity of land to manage with the needs of both forest conservation and agricultural development in Ethiopia, suggesting an inbuilt or inherent conflict of land use in the country. Due to limited space, agricultural expansion necessarily reduces space for forested land and presents a challenge for forest conservation. Additionally, the use of "encroachment" in the policy text is significant, acting to somewhat negatively frame the increasing expansion of agriculture in Ethiopia.

Moreover, the Ethiopian government also frequently highlights the importance of multi-sectoral coordination and the progression in enhancing this following the establishment of the Ministry of Environment, Forests and Climate Change (MEFCC) in the country. The argument is that progress in REDD+ in the country hinges upon the extent to which different sectors of the government (with different interests) work effectively together, notably the MEFCC and the Ministry of Agriculture. The synergies and coordination between the sectors are seen as ways of addressing conflicts in land use.

However, while multi-sectoral tensions are highlighted, the underlying reasons for such tensions are left unexamined, i.e., the conflict in land use between agricultural development and forest conservation. This conflict is unlikely to be addressed by multi-sectoral coordination alone. Additionally, while agricultural expansion is consistently indicated to be a key driver of deforestation in Ethiopia, the government do not indicate an inherent conflict in land use, which would act to challenge the fundamental bases of the government's CRGE strategy and the ease with which it can be implemented.

The international policymakers are similarly reluctant to highlight inherent or contradictory challenges in meeting both agricultural and forest conservation needs in Ethiopia. For instance, the UN only once uses the phrase "trade-off" when discussing conflicts in land use. It is likely that a general reluctance to use the term in the policy discourse stems from its perceived implications: that something is being "lost" in the REDD+ implementation process. Instead of using "trade-off," the policymakers tend to be much more positive in their framing of multi-sectoral tensions, making use of terms such as "synergies," "coordination" or "collaboration," which mask underlying conflicts in land use.

Simultaneously, the REDD+ policymakers, particularly the Ethiopian government, frequently assume that the multiple aims of REDD+ are complimentary and do not necessarily need to be traded off. Thus, a contradiction exists in the REDD+ policy discourse which, on the one hand, claims that REDD+ can realise a "win-win-win" in its implementation that, without compromise, allows agricultural development to occur alongside forest conservation while, on the other hand, consistently positions agricultural expansion as a key driver of deforestation.

In contrast to the other policymakers, the Ethiopian and Norwegian environmental NGOs were generally found to integrate the development or livelihood aspects of REDD+ into their core objectives. In line with their broader missions, the NGOs examined in this research place the livelihoods or development-oriented aims centrally in the design of their REDD+ strategies; pertinently, these appear to be pursued for their inherent worth, rather than for the benefits they can provide in facilitating the effective reductions of deforestation levels and GHG emissions. This includes an explicit and clear focus on strengthening the rights of indigenous peoples in forested communities and enhancing communities' livelihood strategies.

Additionally, during the interviews with the Norwegian NGOs, a number of criticisms were raised over the orientation of NICFI's REDD+ strategy. Here, there were suggestions that the livelihood or poverty alleviation needs of forested communities should be more closely integrated into NICFI's as part of a more positive approach to REDD+ that would encompass a "broader development agenda." Thus, despite the proposals in the literature that the Norwegian government and the NGOs have reached a broad consensual agreement over REDD+ in domestic politics (Okereke and Dooley, 2010; Hermansen et al., 2017), there are nevertheless key points of departure between the two in terms of focus.

Despite their overarching priorities and core objectives, NICFI's more recent policy documents demonstrate an enhanced willingness to engage with the livelihood or development aims of REDD+ and a more holistic integration of these into the design of their REDD+ strategies, in line with a broader noted evolution in REDD+ policy (Angelsen, 2016; Savaresi, 2016). Considering this, increased engagement with development concerns in Norwegian REDD+ policy is arguably an outcome of continued domestic negotiations with participating NGOs and the typically close, "insider" relationship that the NGOs tend to have with the Norwegian government, rather than a fundamental shift in the values of NICFI, as Hermansen and Kasa (2014) have previously suggested.

For the forested communities in Nono Sele, the interviews suggested that what is of highest importance in the ground-level REDD+ strategies are the livelihood aspects of REDD+. For instance, interviewees consistently highlighted the benefits received in their coffee farming since the implementation of the REDD+ project. The importance of REDD+ is rarely linked to the carbon sequestration potential of the forests in Ethiopia or the broader climate change mitigation aims of the REDD+ policymakers. Alongside the livelihood aspects of the project, the communities also tended to be motivated by the protection of the local environment and the sustainable, long-term management of the forests. In many ways, the communities' responses aligned with the NGOs discourse: a more integrated and less carbon-centric framing of REDD+.

Overall, in contrast to the views of the communities and the NGOs, the cost-effective and large-scale reductions of GHG emissions are the focal point and priority for the REDD+ policymakers, with the livelihood or development aspects of REDD+ side-lined or rendered secondary. It has been well-highlighted in the literature that trade-offs are likely to take place in the ground-level implementation of REDD+ (Paladino, 2011; Pokorny et al., 2013). Accordingly, the lack of priority given to the livelihood or development concerns in the policy discourse suggests that it would be likely that these would be traded off in the implementation of REDD+ in Ethiopia.

This framing of REDD+ has significant implications for climate justice. It is likely to mean that forested communities bear an unfair and disproportionate climate burden in their efforts to conserve tropical forests: those who have little responsibility for climate change or capabilities to deal with its impacts. Page (2016) argues that a just integration of tropical forest conservation into international climate change mitigation strategies requires that the burdens of such conservation do not fall unfairly onto those who are making the sacrifices to reduce deforestation levels.

In Ethiopia, government-community relations are currently unstable, with many rural communities, particularly in Oromia, not feeling the effects of the nation's recent strong economic growth. The inequitable distribution of wealth and power in Ethiopia is not conducive to community receipt of benefits from REDD+. Additionally, there exists a contradiction in the Ethiopian government's discourse between the ease of achieving its CRGE strategy and the conflict between agricultural expansion and forest conservation. Without active and reflexive engagement of the immense challenges of meeting the needs of both agricultural development and forest conservation, it is unlikely that the issue will be organically resolved in a just way that acknowledges the multiple land uses of the rural poor.

Even if the forested communities are adequately financially compensated for their forest conservation efforts, there are likely to be opportunity costs without sufficient attention being paid to the development or livelihood aspects of REDD+. The examined REDD+ policy discourse indicates forest conservation initiatives which work against the needs, interests and rights of the rural communities in Ethiopia, as well as enacting a "shrinking of development space" for the country (Wade, 2003, p. 622). In such a way, REDD+ acts as a way for the developed nations to partially offset their climate burdens onto the Global South, as part of a "cost-effective" narrative. This has been a cornerstone of Norway's environmental positioning since the early 1990s (Okereke and Dooley, 2010; Hermansen and Kasa, 2014; Angelsen, 2016).

Conceptions of responsibility for climate change

The findings suggest that the REDD+ policymakers minimally engage with the notion of responsibility for climate change. Where there is engagement with the notion, it tends to be vague and inconsistent. On only two occasions during the in-depth interviews does NICFI refer explicitly to responsibility or burden-sharing. Notably, one NICFI representative vividly highlights the responsibilities of the developed nations for bearing the burdens of climate change:

> because they might say we are trying to combat climate change, the climate change that you imposed on us by your extremely consumerist societies and now you are meddling with how we deal with our internal affairs.

This quote demonstrates an explicit recognition of the idea that Northern countries have historically over-used their share of atmospheric space, resulting in unfairly imposed climate change impacts in the developing world. The phrasing of "extremely consumerist" is vivid and stark, while "imposed" implies active agency on the part of the Global North in GHG emissions. However, the interviewee simultaneously distances themselves from such an assertion and avoids attributing themselves to such a viewpoint, stating clearly that, "they might say . . . ." Nevertheless, this is a rare, explicit recognition of Norway's responsibility for climate change and its engagement in REDD+.

For Norway, their climate change responsibility is based on the country's economic dependence on the extraction and exportation of fossil fuels, rather than what is typically discussed by climate justice scholars: the wealth generated by industrialised nations' *domestic* GHG emissions. Norway continues to maintain and even expand its petroleum industry which, according to Moss's (2016) recent paper, should be encompassed as part of a conceptualisation of countries' responsibilities for climate change. Moss (2016) asserts that the harms of climate change impacts and the distributive injustices tied up with fossil fuel exports and the GHG emissions produced elsewhere demand that this forms part of nations' carbon budgets.

In these findings, it was identified that, as suggested elsewhere (Hermansen and Kasa, 2014; Angelsen, 2016), REDD+ acts as a form of "political offsetting" for Norway. This means that by focusing its climate change policy efforts on REDD+, the Norwegian government can divert attention away from the lack of action taken on scaling back its expansive petroleum industry. Throughout their policy discourse, NICFI is keen to underline the "substantial" commitments that Norway has made towards the international REDD+ agenda, including the significant REDD+ funding that the country has provided. For instance, the following statement in their most recent evaluation report is typical of comments made throughout NICFI's REDD+ discourse:

> NICFI is the largest REDD+ donor globally, supporting all available multilateral channels and seven bilateral programmes across Africa, Asia, Central and South America. NICFI has pledged the majority of global funds for REDD+ and is a major donor to each of the multilateral REDD+ institutions.
>
> *(Norad, 2014: xx)*

Here, the high level of funding provided for REDD+ by the Norwegian government is seen to be symbolic of the leading role that the country has played in advancing the REDD+ agenda internationally. This is supported by the emphasis placed on Norway's contribution to the wider development of the international REDD+ agenda and architecture and the progress of REDD+ in the UNFCCC negotiations. Throughout the policy documents, NICFI uses leading and persuasive language to highlight the country's role in international REDD+ politics: making a "substantial" contribution to REDD+; acting as a REDD+ "pioneer"; enacting an "instrumental" role in the initiative. NICFI's policy discourse largely aligns with Lahn and Wilson Rowe's (2014) understanding of Norway's "status-seeking" initiative in international environmental politics, whereby the country's political action on climate change is driven by a desire to be perceived as "front-runner" in international environmental politics.

Meanwhile, in their REDD+ policy documents, NICFI does not once mention their role in extracting and exporting fossil fuels (and therefore GHG emissions) worldwide. While placing considerable emphasis on the significant, multifarious contributions that it has made to the international REDD+ agenda, the Norwegian government avoids discussion of the country's dependence on the petroleum industry. This implies that, to a certain extent, NICFI is acting to "politically offset" the lack of attention taken by Norway in scaling back its expansive petroleum industry by diverting attention towards its proposed leadership on REDD+, while simultaneously acting to strengthen Norway's status in the hierarchy of international environmental politics.

For the other REDD+ policy actors, there is also limited discussion of responsibility for climate change and burden-sharing, alongside an identified discourse of "shared responsibility." This implies that each country has responsibilities for climate change mitigation. Although these burdens may be differentiated according to a country's capabilities, the prevalence of "shared responsibility" in the REDD+ policy discourse acts to shift the focus away from the Global North's responsibility for climate change.

In particular, during interviews with the UN representatives, frequent mentions were made of adopting a more "diversified" approach to funding REDD+, which partially referred to a proposed enhanced role for the private sector in implementing the sustainable forestry management and partially to a greater contribution of resources and finance by the tropical-forested nations in REDD+. There is a sense here that REDD+ cannot progress to a significant extent without enhanced contributions from the recipient countries, partly due to the fluctuating, unreliable and limited nature of international funding. For the policymakers, the "shared responsibility" discourse justifies REDD+ funds based on Ethiopia's limited financial and institutional capacities, rather than responding to climate injustices or responsibilities of the Global North.

Additionally, evident in the multilateral institutions' discourse, as well as that of the Ethiopian government, is an emphasis on the tropical-forested nation as *beneficiaries* of REDD+, implying that the agreements are akin to an equal deal, with both sides profiting from the arrangement. The idea that without sufficient focus and pro-poor orientation, Ethiopia can act as the beneficiaries of REDD+ to the same extent as Norway or other REDD+ funding nations contradicts much of what has been outlined in recent climate justice research (Blomfield, 2016; Page, 2016; Armstrong, 2016). Here, scholars propose that while the whole world benefits from climate change mitigation, the industrialised nations particularly profit from REDD+ engagement as it facilitates the cost-effective and large-scale reductions of GHG emissions outside of its borders.

However, in contrast to the other policymakers, the Norwegian and Ethiopian environmental NGOs implicated in the Norwegian-Ethiopian REDD+ partnership more clearly and explicitly express support for responsibility on behalf of the Global North. Rather than side-lining historical responsibility, the documents and in-depth interviews suggest that the NGOs wish to place it centrally in REDD+. Specifically, one of the Norwegian NGO representatives asserted:

> We have also been discussing a lot on the whole net zero emissions discourse that is going on the table in Paris, where we believe that you have to go- that Norway has to take- that the countries with historical responsibility have to take their share of reducing emissions and also not paying for it.

The interviewee makes a clear, bold case here for Norway to take their share of climate burdens, explicitly driven by historical responsibility, using language that is firm, emotive and moralistic in nature: "we believe," "Norway has to take its share." Elsewhere, other NGO interviewees suggest that there is an immorality in Norway continuing extraction and exportation of fossil fuels; unlike the Norwegian government, the NGOs are willing to tackle the paradoxical nature of

Norway's environmental "leadership." As highlighted previously, the underpinning philosophies and motivational drivers of the Norwegian NGOs' engagement in REDD+ appear to differ significantly from that of NICFI.

Overall, the policymakers do not place responsibility for climate change as central to the design of the REDD+ policy. Instead, a discourse of "shared responsibility" appears to be more prominent, which emphasises the benefits that the tropical-forested nations are likely to gain from engagement in REDD+. However, considering the evident priorities of the policymakers, it appears more likely that the tropical-forested nations and forested communities in the Global South will bear the greatest burdens of REDD+, whereas the benefits are as yet unclear.

The Global North's historical responsibility for climate change is rarely engaged with by NICFI, the Ethiopian government and the multilateral organisations, and the promise of REDD+ funds is justified primarily based on the insufficient financial, institutional or technical capacities of the tropical-forested nation to implement REDD+ (i.e., "ability to pay" theory). More specifically, the Norwegian government is evidenced to "politically offset" its specific responsibility for climate change: by emphasising its leadership, ambition and significant contributions to REDD+, it diverts attention away from its economic dependence on an expansive petroleum industry.

Concluding thoughts and reflections

Overall, the analysis suggests that, rather than a sense of responsibility or responding to climate justice concerns, the policymakers are primarily driven in their REDD+ engagement by a motivation to cost-effectively reduce global GHG emissions. The livelihood or development aspects of REDD+ are largely de-valued and side-lined in the policy discourse. Such a framing of REDD+ appears to primarily benefit the industrialised nations, including Norway, in "politically offsetting" its responsibility to scale back its expansive petroleum industry. Given the multiscalar divergences in discursive constructions of climate justice norms, the interests and needs of the forested communities in Ethiopia do not appear to be sufficiently represented in the policy discourse. For the communities and the environmental NGOs, what is of importance is the support that the REDD+ funders can provide in developing a livelihood-led sustainable forest management strategy.

Without a shift towards a pro-poor approach and away from a primarily carbon-centric approach, it is unlikely that the design of REDD+ frameworks will adequately reflect these needs and interests. Thus, despite the evolution in REDD+ policy and the integration of safeguards and non-carbon benefits into the international REDD+ framework, analysis of the policy discourse suggests that significant and undue burdens are to be placed upon tropical-forested nations and forested communities in Ethiopia – those who have little responsibility for climate change and have limited capacity to deal with its impacts. The findings suggest that the role of NGOs and other non-state actors in REDD+ policy design is likely to be key in determining the orientation of REDD+ and the underpinning equity principles.

A multiscalar and climate justice-led framework has allowed an in-depth and critical examination of the discourse evident in the REDD+ framework, as well as the community, ground-level discourse. It can allow researchers to better consider the alignment or divergences between and across REDD+ actors based on climate justice norms and subsequently the underlying reasons behind conflicts in international forest governance. While it is increasingly urgent to formulate and implement strategies to combat climate change on a global scale in order to effectively limit dangerous climate change and meet the 1.5 to 2 degrees Celsius internationally agreed-upon climate change targets, there is a simultaneous need to ensure that these strategies are fair and equitable in nature and serve the interests of everyone (Klinsky et al., 2017). This REDD+ policy analysis suggests that the framework has significant work to do to ensure that it can form part of a just transition, but further research is required at later stages of REDD+ (i.e., when the performance-based payments for emissions reductions have begun) and in other contexts of REDD+.

References

Agrawal, A., Nepstad, D. and Chhatre, A. (2011) 'Reducing Emissions From Deforestation and Forest Degradation', *The Annual Review of Environment and Resources*, vol 36, pp 373–396.

Angelsen, A. (2016) 'REDD+ as Result-based Aid: General Lessons and Bilateral Agreements of Norway', *Review of Development Economics*, pp 1–28.

Armstrong, C. (2016) 'Fairness, Free-riding and Rainforest Protection', *Political Theory*, vol 44, issue 1, pp 106–130.

Barrett, S. (2013) 'The Necessity of a Multiscalar Analysis of Climate Justice', *Progress in Human Geography*, vol 37, issue 2, pp 215–233.

Bekele, M., Tesfaye, Y., Mohammed, Z., Zewdie, S., Tebikew, Y., Brockhaus, M. and Kassa, H. (2015) *The Context of REDD+ in Ethiopia*. CIFOR, Bogor.

Beymer-Farris, B. and Bassett, T. (2012) 'The REDD Menace: Resurgent Protectionism in Tanzania's Mangrove Forests', *Global Environmental Change*, vol 22, issue 2, pp 332–341.

Blomfield, M. (2016) 'Historical Use of the Climate Sink', *Res Publica*, vol 22, pp 67–81.

Burnham, M., Radel, C., Ma, Z. and Laudati, A. (2013) 'Extending a Geographic Lens Towards Climate Justice, Part 1: Climate Change Characterization and Impacts', *Geography Compass*, vol 7, issue 3, pp 239–248.

Climate Funds Update (2016) *The Latest Information on Climate Funds*. www.climatefundsupdate.org, accessed 13 August 2016.

Dooley, K. and Gupta, A. (2017) 'Governing By Expertise: The Contested Politics of (Accounting for) Land-based Mitigation in a New Climate Agreement', *International Environmental Agreements: Politics, Law and Economics*, vol 17, issue 4, pp 483–500.

FAO (2010) *Global Forest Resources Assessment 2010 – Country Report Ethiopia*. UN Food and Agriculture Organisation (FAO), Rome.

FAO (2015) *Global Forest Resources Assessment 2015. Country Report: Ethiopia*. UN Food and Agriculture Organization (FAO), Rome.

Forsyth, T. and Sikor, T. (2013) 'Forests, Development and the Globalisation of Justice', *The Geographical Journal*, vol 179, issue 2, pp 114–121.

Hailu, A., Dixon, A.B. and Wood, A.P. (2000). 'Nature, extent and trends in wetland drainage and use in Illubabor Zone, South-west Ethiopia'. *Report for the Ethiopian Wetlands Research Programme*. Sustainable Wetland Management in Illubabor Zone, South-West Ethiopia.

Hermansen, E.A., McNeill, D., Kasa, S. and Rajão, R. (2017) 'Co-Operation or Co-Optation? NGOs' Roles in Norway's International Climate and Forest Initiative', *Forests*, vol 8, issue 64, pp 1–27.

Hermansen, E. and Kasa, S. (2014) *Climate Policy Constraints and NGO Entrepreneurship: The Story of Norway's Leadership in REDD+ Financing*. CGD Working Paper 389. Center for Global Development, Washington, DC.

IPCC (Inter-governmental Panel on Climate Change) (2014) *Mitigation of Climate Change*. Contribution of Working Group III to the Fifth Assessment Report of the Intergovernmental Panel on Climate Change. Cambridge University Press, Cambridge and New York.

Jagger, P., Lawlor, K., Brockhaus, M., Gebara, M.F., Sonwa, D.J. and Resosudarmo, I. (2012) 'REDD+ safeguards in national policy discourse and pilot projects', in A. Angelsen, M. Brockhaus, W.D. Sunderlin and L. Verchot (eds) *Analysing REDD+: Challenges and Choices*. CIFOR, Bogor.

Klinsky, S., Roberts, T., Huq, S., Okereke, C., Newell, P., Dauvergne, P. and O'Brien, K. (2017) 'Why equity is fundamental in climate change policy research', *Global Environmental Change*, vol 44, pp 170–173.

Korhonen-Kurki, K., Brockhaus, M., Duchelle, A.E., Atmadja, S. and Pham, T. (2012) 'Multiple levels and multiple challenges for REDD+', in A. Angelsen, M. Brockhaus, W.D. Sunderlin and L. Verchot (eds) *Analysing REDD+: Challenges and Choices*. CIFOR, Bogor.

Krug, J.H. (2018) 'Accounting of GHG emissions and removals from forest management: A long road from Kyoto to Paris', *Carbon Balance and Management*, vol 13, issue 1, pp 1–11.

Lahn, B. and Rowe, E.W. (2014) 'How to be a "front-runner": Norway and international climate politics', in B. Carvalho and I. Neumann (eds) *Small States and Status Seeking: Norway's Quest for International Standing*. Routledge, Oxford.

Martin, A., Gross-Camp, N., Kebede, B., McGuire, S. and Munyarukaza, J. (2014) 'Whose environmental justice? Exploring local and global perspectives in a payments for ecosystem services scheme in Rwanda', *Geoforum*, vol 54, pp 167–177.

McDermott, C.L., Coad, L., Helfgott, A. and Schroeder, H. (2012) 'Operationalizing social safeguards in REDD+: Actors, interests and ideas', *Environmental Science & Policy*, vol 21, pp 63–72.

Ministry of Environment and Forest (MEF). (2015) Strategic Environmental and Social Assessment (SESA) for the Implementation of REDD+ in Ethiopia including the Oromia Forested Landscape Program (OFLP) Social Assessment (SA). Addis Ababa, Ethiopia. https://www.biocarbonfund-isfl.org/sites/biocf/files/documents/Ethiopia%20SESA.pdf, accessed 02 February 2018.

Moges, Y., Eshetu, Z. and Nune, S. (2010) *Ethiopian Forest Resources: Current Status and Future Management Options in View of Access to Carbon Finances*. Ethiopian Climate Research and Networking, Addis Ababa.

Moss, J. (2016) 'Mining, morality and the obligations of fossil fuel exporting countries', *Australian Journal of Political Science*, vol 51, issue 3, pp 496–511.

Norway's International Climate and Forest Initiative (NICFI) (2016) *Ethiopia*. www.regjeringen.no/en/topics/climate-and-environment/climate/climate-and-forest-initiative/kos-innsikt/Ethiopia/id751782/, accessed 09 September 2017.

Norwegian Agency for Development Cooperation (Norad) (2014) Real-Time Evaluation of Norway's International Climate and Forest Initiative. Synthesising Report 2007–2013. https://www.norad.no/en/toolspublications/publications/2014/real-time-evaluation-of-norways-international-climate-and-forest-initiative.-synthesising-report-2007-2013/, accessed 09 September 2017.

Okereke, C. (2008) *Global Justice and Neoliberal Environmental Governance: Ethics, Sustainability and International Co-operation*. Routledge, London.

Okereke, C. and Dooley, K. (2010) 'Principles of justice in proposals and policy approaches to avoided deforestation: Towards a post-Kyoto climate agreement', *Global Environmental Change*, vol 20, issue 1, pp 82–95.

Page, E. (2016) 'Qui bono? Justice in the distribution of the benefits and burdens of avoided deforestation', *Res Publica*, vol 22, issue 1, pp 83–97.

Paladino, S. (2011) 'Tracking the fault lines of pro-poor carbon forestry', *Culture, Agriculture, Food and Environment*, vol 33, issue 2, pp 117–132.

Pokorny, B., Scholz, I. and de Jong, W. (2013) 'REDD+ for the poor or the poor for REDD+? About the limitations of environmental policies in the Amazon and the potential of achieving environmental goals through pro-poor policies', *Ecology and Society*, vol 18, issue 2.

Savaresi, A. (2016) 'A glimpse into the future of the climate regime: Lessons from the REDD+ Architecture', *Review of European, Comparative & International Environmental Law*, vol 25, issue 2, pp 186–196.

Schroeder, H. and McDermott, C. (2014) 'Beyond carbon: Ensuring justice and equity in REDD+ Across levels of governance', *Ecology and Society*, vol 19, issue 1, Editorial.

Sikor, T., Martin, A., Fisher, J. and He, J. (2014) 'Toward an empirical analysis of justice in ecosystem governance', *Conservation Letters*, vol 7, pp 524–532.

Stern, N.H. (2007) *The Economics of Climate Change: The Stern Review*. Cambridge University Press, Cambridge.

Traxler, M. (2002) 'Fair chore division for climate change', *Social Theory and Practice*, vol 28 issue 1, pp 101–134.

Tubiello, F.N., Salvatore, M., Ferrara, A.F., House, J., Federici, S., Rossi, S., Biancalani, R., Condor Golec, R.D., Jacobs, H., Flammini, A. and Prosperi, P. (2015) 'The contribution of agriculture, forestry and other land use activities to global warming, 1990–2012', *Global Change Biology*, vol 21, issue 7, pp 2655–2660.

Wade, R. (2003) 'What strategies are visible for developing countries today? The world trade organisation and the shrinking of development space', *Review of International Political Economy*, vol 10, issue 4, pp 627–644.

Part V

Urban Climate Justice

21

The climate-just city

Wendy Steele, Jean Hillier, Donna Houston,
Jason Byrne and Diana MacCallum

Introduction

Climate change poses significant implications for urban justice (Steele et al. 2012). The convergence of rapid urbanisation and anthropogenic climate change results in disproportionately negative effects on the urban poor and those already most marginalised (Houston et al. 2016). The more affluent in our society are less vulnerable, with the impacts of climate change felt most by the most marginalised groups, which include (but are not limited to) the urban poor, children, women and the elderly (Ambrey et al. 2017). Climate change also disproportionately impacts non-human individuals, species and worlds, where diminishing biodiversity and the loss of resilience contributes to socio-ecological instability (Houston 2008; Steele et al. 2015). Climate change is therefore an urban, cultural and environmental crisis, and the response demands unprecedented redistribution efforts by those least affected and largely responsible. Society, economy and nature are all reconfigured by the ways these connections are played out in climate hotspots around the globe.

In this chapter we focus on the application of "the climate-just city" as a conceptual framework for taking the urban equity agenda forward within the context of climate change, with specific reference to Australian cities at the local scale (Steele et al. 2012). Climate justice within the Australian city context has been historically "a chronically underdeveloped area of thinking" (Garnaut 2009, p. 1). We argue that adopting an eco-cultural-political approach through the climate-just city framework helps keep sight of the complexity of climate-induced injustice and fosters a climate-just imaginary for our times – one that is able to offer both critique and a constructive vision that supports and promotes the possibility of achieving more equitable urban environments.

The aims of the chapter are three-fold. The first is to extend the idea of "the just city" to include a more overt equity focus to climate change in cities through the "climate-just city" framework. Secondly, we highlight examples of socially innovative responses to issues of climate equity at the local scale, drawing on empirical research in the Australian context. In the third section of the chapter the justice implications of framing for mobilising the climate-just city in practice is emphasised. In our normative quest for the climate-just city, the principles of climate justice and equity must come first – not last – within climate adaptation policies and planning practices.

Urban climate justice

Within the context of climate change, ideas about the just city include not only questions of democracy, equity and economic distribution, but also questions of how human actions are impacting the non-human world. Of particular note is that this straddles political-economic, socio-cultural and ecological spheres, thus broadening the socio-spatial scope, impact and implications for justice. As Mike Hulme (2010, p. 274) highlights:

> climate change is reminding us . . . that we are intimate co-workers with the non-human in the mutual shaping of our present and future worlds, rather than being lords of all we can see . . . and that our identities and our interpretations of the world around us can never fully escape encounters with place and materiality.

The just-city conceptualisation (see Fainstein 2010) builds on an eclectic mix of philosophical thinking around questions of democracy, equity and diversity through the work of John Rawls (1999), Amartya Sen (1999), Martha Nussbaum (2000), Iris Marion Young (1990) and Henri Lefebvre (1996) to highlight issues of social fairness, equitable distribution of capital and resources. Within the "just city" literature, the state, human activity and citizenry are the key foci for research, advocacy and analysis that centres on the injustices that occur for marginalised people within human environments. This involves changing the civic dialogue around planning praxis and enlarging the boundaries of dialogue and action "so that demands for equity are no longer marginalised as a first step towards reversing the current tendency that excludes social justice from the aims of urban policy" (Fainstein 2006, p. 26). But the interplay between human and natural and non- human environments and how these relations define and shape dimensions of justice in the city are largely ignored. We argue that the key tenets of the just city around democracy, diversity, recognition and equity must more explicitly take into account the complex links among human society, urban settlements and the natural environment.

Understandings of urban and political ecology highlight cities as "metabolic" systems in which practices of production and consumption continually alter both "nature" and "culture" (Swyngedouw and Heynen 2003). Seeing these systems in their institutional contexts means critically engaging with the stories, ethics and practices shaping relations between humans and non-humans, a crucial task when faced with crises such as climate change (Waitt et al. 2006). For a growing number of urbanists, humanitarian justice scholars, environmental and ecological advocates, addressing the issues of what is being termed "climate justice" has become the moral and ethical imperative of the times (Bell 2010).

A climate-just city makes explicit that in the face of potentially catastrophic climatic change, significant challenges have emerged that threaten the human world, the non-human world, sustainability and governance and decision-making more generally (Adger et al. 2006). Barnett (2006, p. 115) identifies five key aspects to understanding climate justice: (1) the responsibility for climate change is not equally distributed; (2) climate change will not affect all people equally, with some people and groups more vulnerable; (3) this vulnerability is determined by political-economic processes that benefit some more than others; (4) climate change will compound under-development because of the processes of disadvantage embedded within the (neo) liberal political-economic status quo; and (5) climate change policies may create unfair outcomes by exacerbating, maintaining or ignoring existing or future inequalities.

Approaches, frameworks and practices associated with the climate-just city break down established planning processes that separate nature from culture and risk from justice, recognising that climate adaptive practices – particularly those associated with low-carbon energy transitions and urban greening – are not in and of themselves inherently "just" (Bulkeley et al. 2014; also see Mitchell and Chakraborty, this volume). Urban political ecologists have long asserted the historically and spatially uneven processes of "urban metabolism" where environmental harms and benefits are reflected in relations of race, class, gender and power (Holifield 2009). Heynen et al. (2006), for example, demonstrated that unequal distribution of urban canopy cover in Milwaukee, with urban forest tree-planting programs privileging private-property owners who are more likely to be white and middle class. Studies in Australia on urban forest cover in Australia (Davison and Kirkpatrick 2014 and green infrastructure and suburban disadvantage (Ambrey et al. 2017) highlight the need to address inequity and participation in developing responses to urban climate risks such as heat stress.

The climate-just city framework offers an emergent conceptual lens, whereby the emphasis is placed on the need to integrate considerations of social justice (people), environmental justice (places) and ecological justice (non-humans). The focus is on finding and embedding new methods for incorporating the principles of climate justice within existing mainstream urban governance processes, actively engaging with alternative practices and making public unjust practices and contexts. Central to this is recognition that the struggles surrounding urban exclusion, and the transfer of negative externalities from rich to poor, co-evolve through material effects and public discourses. This is a deliberate emphasis on key justice questions such as: "who dominates?," "who benefits?," and "who gets left behind? ."

This framing approach to urban climate adaptability and change emphasises the need to attend to the stories and visions of different actors and to identify practical pathways for action. To this end, new, practically oriented strategies and frameworks for knowledge production are required – ones that engage directly with the practices, stories and perspectives of those that have been traditionally excluded from mainstream planning policies and practices. Specifically this involves: (a) advancing an understanding of how actors (e.g., policy and decision makers, advocacy and service practitioners and vulnerable people) imagine, conceptualise and practice climate justice at various scales; (b) explaining how these actors shape their imaginaries, issue-framing and practice across multiple scales; and (c) developing and applying innovative methods for putting climate justice into urban policy and community practice. The climate-just city lens is thus designed to apply to contexts which have a cultural, historical and institutional fabric specific to particular places and spaces. The ground-truthing of the climate-just city framework occurs within the situated stories and practices involving activists, citizens and policymakers.

From principles to practice in the Australian city context

Our framing of the climate-just city is informed by a three-year research project on the relationship between social innovation (broadly defined as innovative practices operating in both formal and informal contexts) and local climate adaptation in four Australian cities. The research has involved three specific empirical phases, including: (1) a comprehensive audit of local government, community-based initiatives and identification of case studies (2015); (2) case study investigation and analysis in the four Australian cities including interviews and focus groups (2015–2017); and (3) crosscutting analysis and synthesis across the project data collected (2017–2018). This study has sought to understand the dynamics and tensions between the risk-based assessments of local climate agencies and innovations by local groups, NGOs and the private sector.

Australia, as one of the world's driest continents and with a population perched precariously in coastal cities that are highly vulnerable to sea-level rise, is one such urban hotspot at the frontline of climate change responses within the developed world (IPCC 2007). The highly concentrated nature of the urban population in Australia, coupled with the relatively fixed nature of much of the metropolitan built form, serves to magnify climate-related risks and vulnerabilities from extreme weather and natural disasters (i.e., sea-level rise, heatwaves and drought). The impacts of climate change serve to often compound existing urban vulnerabilities such as poverty, inadequate public infrastructure, loss of biodiversity or environmental degradation. Yet the response to these issues is locked into processes that are largely hardwired into dry economic models of growth and development. Within Australian cities a focus on issues of climate justice is barely part of the urban policy or planning vernacular. The emergent climate justice agenda has only recently begun to penetrate political discourses surrounding cities. Within urban planning, fixated upon a staircase model of economic growth, making the necessary justice links among economic, social and ecological vulnerability remains on the margins.

Our research confirms the significance of applying urban climate justice to diverse local climate projects and initiatives (Houston et al. 2016). The emphasis was a critical focus on the ideas and practices that shape the climate-just city, including: the stories of climate justice that make the connections between people and the material and natural world; the benefits or detriments of the climate-just city for marginalised communities within particular urban contexts; how climate justice challenges, compliments or replaces current rights and existing privileges in cities; and how climate justice must incorporate ethics and responsibilities that recognise the ways non-humans participate in climate adaptation and governance. We found that "just" outcomes in local climate adaptation – that is, outcomes that enhanced urban resilience and adaptability by engaging marginalised, under-represented and disadvantaged communities – were seen by local governments, the private sector and NGOs as being particularly "innovative."

For example, *Blacktown* Local Government Area (LGA) in Sydney's West is one of the largest LGAs in Sydney in terms of area (240 sq. km.) and population (332,424). The main climate impacts on Blacktown are increased risks from heat, fire and drought: increases in deterioration of infrastructure, energy demands for cooling, heat-stress/heat-related deaths; longer, more intense heatwaves; and spread of vector-, water- and food-borne disease. It is also a region with an ethnically diverse and socio-economically vulnerable population. Prioritising climate action in areas of disadvantage as a justice agenda is complex in councils such as Blacktown, as this local government planner articulates:

> [I]n my experience, areas that are disadvantaged have other priorities. They've got bigger problems in their life than whether the streets have trees, whether climate change is actually occurring, whether their streets are getting hotter, whether that's an issue . . . for example, a lot of the housing is old Defence housing. So it's asbestos panels, no air conditioning, no insulation. . . . So in summer they cook and in winter they freeze, but it is still very hard to engage with them on the subject of climate change and adaptation. It's really, really hard. You'd need to offer them something, because they have other priorities, especially in areas where you have community housing, whether it be government or otherwise.

Blacktown council hosts a community-focused Sustainability Workshop series comprised of education and awareness-raising programs focusing on local fauna ecologies, "green" baby care workshops, waste-processing awareness, "upcycling" second-hand goods, community-wide garage sale events, backyard food security, suburban bee-keeping, sustainable kitchen and cooking programs and urban forestry programs such as tree give-away schemes and adoption of public tree-stock. The council also partners with the local TAFE Outreach College to deliver community courses on horticulture and eco-living.

One program the Council identified as being particularly innovative was the "Cool Streets" pilot program. Cool Streets integrated a community engagement and scientific tool for street planting where local residents participate in urban forestry at the street level and have a final say in the design of their street. In mixing scientific approaches to improving urban forest cover with participatory elements, the "Cool Streets" program is an example of bringing together a range of issues (the relationship between urban tree canopy cover and social class) with local climate adaptation.

> It's the only project I can think of that's not just about planting trees, it's about engaging with the community about planting those trees and showing them what those trees are going to do, change the liveability of their street and talk to them before you put the trees in, and talking to them face to face in their street about where the trees are going and what they want for their street first before you do it. It's labour intensive, but it's the only project I know of that's doing stuff like that.
>
> *(Local government planner)*

The City of *Darebin* is located 5 kilometres north of Melbourne. Darebin has one of Australia's most diverse communities, with a large number of pensioners (both aged and those with social disadvantage), low-income households and people who are socially isolated or disadvantaged. The Council's adaptation focus is heat-stress response and reflects the vulnerable status of many social groups within its community who are unable to afford and access air conditioning or heat-stress management options in times of extreme heat. One of Darebin's key adaptation initiatives is the "Solar $aver Program," which won an environmental justice award in 2014. This program enables pensioners to instal solar power to their homes with no upfront cost and instead pay the system off through their Council rates over 10 years, interest free. The City developed an arrangement for financing solar panels on interest-free terms, recouping costs through a surcharge on annual rates notices, calculated to be lower than residents' estimated power bills in the absence of the solar panels. In this way the program responds to several climate justice concerns: the management of health risks associated with heatwaves especially for elderly citizens, the avoidance of maladaptive responses, the transition to renewable energy and distributional justice across the local government area by targeting disadvantaged groups such as pensioners.

> I always felt comfortable arguing that heat stress impacts on disadvantaged communities, and we have a significant proportion of those in Darebin – typically older post war migrants who've settled here. They're in small old house but their houses are not thermally efficient . . . They are worse in rental communities. We understand that's an impact and we can't just walk away and say we have no responsibility for elderly people or those who are sick. . . . The quickest and simplest way was perhaps to add an air conditioner but what that did was exacerbate the electricity bill so you go in a horrible spiral and if it's powered by black power you're adding to climate change. So you might deal with the heat wave issue one way but you're spiralling – you're getting a terrible, negative result . . . it's an adverse effect of an adaptation mechanism that creates an even worse problem.
>
> *(Local government climate officer)*

An important "side effect" of the Solar $aver Program is that owning solar panels and a commitment to renewable energy now plays a role in building political support for a reconfigured State energy regime that privileges renewables over fossil fuels. The strong publicity the solar program has received has prompted similar local government initiatives in Victoria and beyond, helping to refocus attention on the equity implications of climate change, and climate change responses, at scales below the global.

Solar $aver remains an exception, even in Darebin, but it shows that it is possible to respond sensitively and effectively to uneven vulnerabilities at the municipal level, albeit without seriously challenging neoliberal discourses of individualism or market-led growth. In contrast, most urban forest and green infrastructure strategies in Australian state and local jurisdictions – also consistently documented as a means of managing heat – do not appear to be targeted to poor areas, in spite of these areas often being poorly serviced by parks (Byrne et al. 2016). They have instead become linked to city-making and branding projects that legitimise more intensive development of the urban core, without addressing indirect impacts such as urban heat island effects (see Mitchell and Chakraborty, this volume). As Ambrey et al. 2017 note, urban greening can under some circumstances further entrench, rather than lessen, urban inequalities (e.g., shifting maintenance costs to low-income earners).

While salient examples of social innovation for climate adaptation across all sectors may become a point of departure for climate justice to play a greater role in a wider range of adaptation measures, we found little evidence that these considerations are shaping other areas of adaptive activity within Australian local governments. In other words, such initiatives have tended to be "stand-alone" projects or bolted on to existing "community initiatives" rather than changing core business models or operational activities.

Framing climate justice in cities: the implications for practice

Framing indicates a set of organising principles through which meanings and beliefs are constructed and maintained (Alkon et al. 2013; de Boer et al. 2010). They act as sense-making devices. Frames allow certain questions to be asked while others get silenced (O'Brien et al. 2007). This means that policies are developed along particular normative and conceptual lines, which influences goals and the range of options that are taken into consideration for addressing the issue.

Justice, in the contemporary climate of economic, environmental and social change, is continually being framed and re-framed in relation to people, places and species. The idea of the "just city" is not new to urban policy and planning. From its earliest conception, planning has sought to correct harms arising from living in cities and to advance a better quality of life for urban residents (Hall 2002). In its formative days the discipline and profession worked to redress material expressions of inequality through spatial fixes and design interventions, but much of this period was focused on achieving "design solutions" rather than on redressing the causes of socio-ecological problems. Urban policies and plans, however, have often served to compound rather than improve conditions of poverty, homelessness, access to basic services and ecological integrity, due to an institutional emphasis on growth and efficiency.

Within the Australian context, current approaches to planning in climate change continue to be framed by an orientation to risk management (financial, environmental and political), rather than to social, ecological or environmental justice (Byrne et al. 2009). Since 2006, risk management approaches to climate change adaptation have been formally encouraged in the Australian private and public sectors by the Australian Government, as outlined in the influential guide on *"climate change impacts and risk management"* (Australian Government 2006). Fünfgeld and McEvoy (2014, p. 53) state that: "One of the strengths of risk assessment approaches to climate change is that they can fit with existing organizational procedures and can readily be integrated into existing risk management systems and structures."

However, as our research discovered, climate change responses are dominated by risk framing. The implementation of risk assessment processes tends to be focused inwardly, onto corporate assets and so on, sometimes to the neglect of external human and non-human stakeholders. As Evans and Reid (2013) suggest, this form of risk framing can silence and disempower those who are not aligned with the interests of the urban elite (e.g., land and property developers, asset owners). Corporations are increasingly shoring up their exposure to climate change impacts on the basis of "fiduciary responsibility," but others "at risk" (e.g., homeless, low-income earners, recent migrants) are left to "fend for themselves."

Our empirical work included an audit of published Local Government Authority adaptation strategies across all Australian metropolitan capital regions and detailed document analysis of two published strategies in four metropolitan regions – Melbourne, Sydney, Perth and South East Queensland (a conurbation of cities around Brisbane). Of interest was the way in which these documents framed notions of climate change and adaptation, localness, agency and responsibility, vulnerability and difference, and inclusiveness of the process of writing the strategy. As Table 21.1 highlights, risk is the key framing device for climate impacts within metro local governments, with a large focus on assets and infrastructure, relatively minimal attention to vulnerable human populations and inclusive processes, and no consideration of non-human species concerns as part of a broader climate equity and justice agenda.

There is an unequal landscape of risk; as we are aware from the aftermath of Hurricane Katrina in New Orleans (Comfort 2006), the poor bear the brunt of risk, which may be institutionalised as "tolerable" for the city as a whole, but not for their personal lives in particular. Climate change strategies are in danger of "being tied to a neoliberal ideology that clouds racial, cultural and

Table 21.1 Climate adaptation framing in selected local government strategic documents.

Climate Change	Adaptation	Local	Agency	Vulnerabilities	Process
Scientific fact	Response to risk assessment	Locus of felt impacts	Local government has a key role and strong agency	Age-related (children and elderly)	No evidence of public involvement in developing the strategy, beyond standard call for comment – largely confirmed by interviews
Future impacts – extreme weather, goods and services, health	Needed now regardless of timeframe for CC itself	Embedded in larger scales of governance	Local government needs to show leadership	Services to community	
Timeframes in decades	Timeframes in years	Positively construed as an appropriate scale of action	Responsibility across several departments, including planning	Assets and infrastructure	
Environmental problem with largely environmental and economic impacts	Explicitly or implicitly Contrasted with mitigation	Particular resources (natural, built, and/or social) identified as valuable	Funding, coordination, education and research	Heatwaves Greening public spaces	
RISK is key framing device for impacts	BUT energy a key issue for adaptation		Community – needing education on issues and preparedness		
Both threats and opportunities (economic)	Dominated by "prepare" and "defend" strategies; "retreat" very rare				
Unpredictable, but rendered manageable			Civil society barely mentioned, if at all		

gendered discriminations by the smokescreen of objective risk assessments" (Evans and Reid 2013, p. 97). As Gurstein and Vilches (2010, p. 433) make clear, the "unjust city" abounds:

> we rewrite both activity and citizenry as exclusive domains of those who conform to standards of market production and consumption. . . . Those who do not conform are forced to inhabit a residual city that operates beyond the official city and lacks the supports needed to thrive.

We are concerned by this framing gap and its application within Australian climate adaptation policy and planning approaches and practices. We contend that this represents a failure in imagination: where the segregation of social and ecological equity and justice concerns from the environmental/economic imperatives of climate change crisis impede action toward sustainable and just urban futures (Houston et al. 2016). We also contend that normative dimensions of urban climate change policy, largely framed by risk management, can only have limited purchase in grasping present eco-geo-social realities in contemporary cities.

In the face of such marked social and ecological disparity, work by Edwards et al. (2009) has highlighted a number of propositions that seek to support and promote a more equitable approach to climate change policy in Australia, including: (a) the need to take urgent action to prevent dangerous climate change and business and politics as usual is not an option; (b) that action to prevent climate change is a responsibility of all Australians and all sectors of society to develop climate justice responses; and (c) that the community has a vital role and responsibility in advocating urgent action and ensuring equitable approaches to mitigation and adaptation.

Informed by the framework of "the climate-just city," our research into socially innovative responses to climate adaptation at the local scale in Australian metropolitan contexts has emphasised the need to focus on the variety of ways a climate justice approach to the city is being imagined and enacted – whereby even if the practices and language are diverse (e.g., at scale/sector), the framing is clear. In this case there is demonstrated action around the following: responsiveness to local conditions; meeting genuine needs; empowerment of communities; potential transformation of social relations; community engagement in preparation and delivery of strategy and initiatives; and inclusion of the vulnerable and non-human. Connectivity and communication across sectors underpinned by a justice and equity framing agenda in the face of climate change are the key.

The Gold Coast and Hinterland Environment Council (Gecko), for example, is the Gold Coast's peak non-government not-for-profit environment group. Gecko networks with a wide range of volunteers and organisations in Queensland who work together to protect and enhance the Gold Coast's natural and environmental assets. Gecko's primary goal is to anticipate and assess impacts prior to projects being approved, to ensure development is undertaken without risks to biodiversity, the ecological system and the liveability of the region. Gecko are committed to equitable action on climate change at a local level. The organisation's initiatives comprise both advocacy and education. For example, Gecko initiated a local climate adaptation "conference" that brought together key stakeholders across local government, state government and the private sector (e.g., ethical investment) to try to progress socially just and economically responsible climate change adaptation initiatives. Many of these initiatives are predicated upon justice, human rights and sustainable development (as articulated in various international protocols) and seek to advance alternatives to "endless growth in a finite world" (see http://gecko.org.au/).

As these and other socially innovative agenda highlight, land use planning generally, and climate adaptation planning specifically, operates in a context of radical indeterminacy and uncertainty. To take action in such a context requires rethinking the way planning operates. Attention must thereby be diverted from damage repair and provision of "resilient" infrastructure to the vulnerabilities of particular humans and non-humans. Whilst an emphasis on risk and repair can be leveraged within organisations as a means for achieving some change, this framing greatly limits the capacity of community to transition beyond the current status quo to more transformative and equitable urban climate change practices. As Shove (2010, p. 278) states: "climate change policy proceeds on the basis of an extraordinarily limited understanding of the social world." This understanding of the social and ecological world is limited by a neoliberal risk framing, and can be greatly strengthened if is framed instead by the principles and practices of the climate-just city.

Conclusion

Climate change is now manifest in cities. In this chapter we have argued that the imperative of climate change adds urgency to the longstanding equity agenda in urban and regional planning, yet at the same time exacerbates that agenda's increasing marginalisation within contemporary planning debates and discourses. However, locally based urban climate justice work already underway reflects stories and practices that will actively shape the future of our cities. What these community-based actions suggest is that there is already active work engaging with the kind of relational thinking and foresight that is often missing from national planning and policy responses to climate change. There is a pressing need to open back up land use planning and policy-making in Australia to broader community involvement. Over the past decade or so, neoliberal governance has restrained marginalised and vulnerable populations from meaningfully participating in planning. The daily practices of development control do not include mechanisms for responding directly to both climate change and social justice imperatives; this is typically left to strategic planning exercises, which occur at a scale too broad for local residents to identify local impacts and their implications.

If we are to advance cities that are "fair," then creative, multidisciplinary approaches to justice and equity must be embedded deep within the collective practices of disciplines such as urban planning. This entails wider recognition of the socio-spatial constraints that work to impede those already impoverished and suffering hardship within our society. The need to create an inclusive city based upon a different ordering of rights and different political-ecological practices and more engaged citizenship is pressing. Better understanding of how our policy responses can "hurt people" (Friends of the Earth 2010, p. 1), by concentrating, entrenching and reproducing social, spatial and ecological inequality, as well as the possibilities for socially innovative planning practices, offers a way forward.

Climate change has intensified the need to find creative, meaningful ways to address issues of climate justice as the relationship among humans, non-humans and nature is continually redefined. Yet climate justice in cities remains chronically misunderstood, marginalised and underresearched, in part because of a lack of analytical, conceptual and practical tools within urban studies and policy sciences for engaging with discourse and difference. Processes of social learning and interconnection underpin local climate actions that actively seek to transform our cities in socially and ecologically just ways. It also requires exploring and disseminating creative ways to embed the concept of climate justice into the mainstream. Imagining a climate-just city will entail making better policy and planning connections among environmental, ecological and social concerns in order to create more equitable urban futures.

References

Adger, W.N., Paavola, J., Huq, S. and Mace, M. (Eds.) (2006) *Fairness to adaptation to climate change.* Cambridge: Massachusetts Institute of Technology.

Alkon, A., Cortez, M. and Sze, J. (2013) 'What is in a name? Language, framing and environmental justice activism in California's Central Valley'. *Local Environment: The International Journal of Justice and Sustainability*, 18(10): 1167–1183.

Ambrey, C., Byrne, J., Matthews, T., Davison, A., Portanger, C. and Lo, A. (2017) 'Cultivating climate justice: Green infrastructure and suburban disadvantage in Australia'. *Applied Geography*, 89: 52–60.

Australian Government (2006) *Climate change impacts and risk management: A guide for business and government.* Canberra: Commonwealth of Australia.

Barnett, J. (2006) 'Climate change, insecurity and injustice'. In W. Adger, J. Paavola, S. Huq and M. Mace (Eds.) *Fairness to adaptation to climate change.* Cambridge: Massachusetts Institute of Technology.

Bell, D. (2010) 'Ethics, justice and climate change'. *Environmental Politics*, 19(3): 475–479.

Bulkeley, H. Edwards, G. and Fuller, S. (2014) 'Contesting climate justice in the city: examining politics and practice in urban climate change experiments'. *Global Environmental Change*, 25:31–40.

Byrne, J., Ambrey, C., Portanger, C., Lo, A., Matthews, T., Baker, D. and Davison, A. (2016) 'Could urban greening mitigate suburban thermal inequity?: The role of residents' dispositions and household practices'. *Environmental Research Letters*, 11(9): (online)095014.

Byrne, J., Gleeson, B., Howes, M. and Steele, W. (2009) 'Climate change and Australian urban resilience: The limits of ecological modernization as an adaptive strategy'. In S. Davoudi, J. Crawford and A. Mehmood (Eds.) *Planning for climate change: Strategies for mitigation and adaptation for spatial planners.* London: Earthscan, 136–154.

Comfort, L.K. (2006) 'Cities at risk: Hurricane Katrina and the drowning of New Orleans'. *Urban Affairs Review*, 41(4): 501–516.

Davison, A. and Kirkpatrick, J.B. (2014) 'Re-inventing the urban forest: the rise of arboriculture in Australia'. *Urban Policy and Research*, 32: 145–162.

De Boer, J., Wardekker, J. and Van der Sluijs, J. (2010) 'Frame-based guide to situated decision-making on climate change'. *Global Environmental Change*, 20(3): 502–510. Edwards, T., Ftize, J. and Wiseman, J. (2009) 'Community well-being in a changing climate: Challenges for the Australian community sector'. *Just Policy*, 50: 80–86.

Evans, B. and Reid, J. (2013) 'Dangerously exposed: The life and death of the resilient subject'. *Resilience: International Policies, Practices and Discourses*, 1(2): 83–98.

Fainstein, S. (2006) *Planning and the just city.* Searching for the Just City Conference, Columbia University, New York, April 29.

Fainstein, S. (2010) *The just city.* Cornell: Cornell University Press.

Friends of the Earth. (2011) *What is climate justice?* http://www.foe.org.au/climate-justice/issues [accessed 2/11/2011].

Fünfgeld, H. and McEvoy, D. (2011) *Framing climate change adaptation in policy and practice.* Working Paper 1, Framing Adaptation in the Victorian Context, VCCCAR, Melbourne. www.vcccar.org.au/publication/working-paper/framing-climate-change-adaptation-in-policy-and-practice [accessed 23/03/2018].

Fünfgeld, H. and McEvoy, D. (2014) 'Frame divergence in climate change adaptation planning: A case study in Australian local government'. *Environment and Planning C*, 32: 603–622

Garnaut, R. (2009) 'Foreword: Climate change as an equity issue'. In J. Moss (Ed.) *Climate change and social justice.* Melbourne: Melbourne University Press.

Gurstein, P. and Vilches, S. (2010) 'The just city for whom? Re-conceiving active citizenship for lone mothers in Canada'. *Gender, Place & Culture: A Journal of Feminist Geography*, 17(4): 421–436.

Hall, P. (2002) *Cities of tomorrow: An intellectual history of urban planning and design in the twentieth century.* Malden: Blackwell Publishing.

Heynen, N., Perkins, H., Roy, P. (2006) 'The political ecology of uneven urban green space: The impact of political economy on race and ethnicity in producing environmental inequality in Milwaukee'. *Urban Affairs Review*, 42(1): 3–25.

Holifield, R., Porter, M. and Walker, G. (2009) 'Introduction spaces of environmental justice: Frameworks for critical engagement'. *Antipode*, 41(4): 591–612.

Houston, D. (2008) 'Crisis and resilience: Cultural methodologies for environmental sustainability and justice'. *Continuum*, 22: 179–190.

Houston, D., MacCallum, D., Steele, W. and Byrne, J. (2016) 'Climate cosmopolitics and the possibilities for urban planning'. *Nature + Culture*, 11(3): 1–29.

Hulme, M. (2010) 'Cosmopolitan climates: Hybridity, foresight and meaning'. *Theory, Culture and Society*, 27(2): 267–276.

IPCC (2007) *Impacts, adaptation and vulnerability*. Intergovernmental Panel on Climate Change Working Group II Report. United Nations, New York.

Lefebvre, H. (1996) *Writings on cities*. Cambridge: Blackwell Publishing.

Nussbaum, M. (2000) *Women and human development*. New York: Cambridge University Press.

O'Brien, K., Eriksen, S., Nygaard, L. and Schjolden, A. (2007) 'Why different interpretations of vulnerability matter in climate change discourses'. *Climate Policy*, 7(1): 73–88.

Rawls, J. (1999) *A theory of justice*. Cambridge: Bellnap Press.

Sen, A. (1999) *Development as freedom*. Oxford: Oxford University Press.

Shove, E. (2010) 'Social theory and climate change: Questions often, sometimes and not yet asked'. *Theory, Culture and Society*, 27(2–3): 277–288.

Steele, W., MacCallum, D., Byrne, J. and Houston, D. (2012) 'Planning the climate-just city'. *International Planning Studies*, 17(1): 67–83.

Steele, W., Mata, L. and Funfgeld, H. (2015) 'Urban climate justice: Creating sustainable pathways for humans and other species'. *Current Opinion in Environmental Sustainability*, 14: 121–126.

Swyngedouw, E. and Heynen, N. (2003) 'Urban political ecology, justice and the politics of scale'. *Antipode*, 35(5): 898–918

Waitt, G., Head, L. and Gill, N. (2006) 'Introduction: Applied natures: Cultural engagements with Australian environmental management'. *Australian Geographer* 37: 1–3.

Young, I.M. (1990) *Justice and the politics of difference*. Princeton: Princeton University Press.

22

Configuring climate responsibility in the city

Carbon footprints and climate justice in Hong Kong

Sara Fuller

Introduction

Carbon footprints have been widely adopted in debates about responsibility for addressing climate change (Wiedmann and Minx 2008). The adoption of this term has been driven by corporate, governmental and non-governmental organisations as a means to represent an amount of greenhouse gas (GHG) emissions associated with a certain activity, product or population (Wright et al. 2011). While they form part of a variety of methodologies for assessing emissions at an urban scale (Bulkeley 2013; Minx et al. 2013), there is however no consensus on how to measure or quantify a footprint (Wiedmann and Minx 2008), and the outcomes depend on the underlying assumptions and methodological approach employed. Nonetheless, the growing interest in understanding emission drivers via carbon footprints is significant, not only because such measurements allow emissions to be quantified but because they allow emissions to be linked to activities and behaviour (Kennedy et al. 2014; Peters 2010). Carbon footprints and associated practices of carbon calculation thus draw attention to consumption practices that are deemed to be problematic and unsustainable in the long term.

More importantly, however, such mechanisms seek to invoke action through an allocation of responsibility for carbon reduction. In so doing, the process of carbon footprinting raises a series of questions for climate justice in terms of how such moral and political responsibility is configured and distributed within the city and how the everyday lives of populations are incorporated into practices associated with carbon mitigation. This chapter argues that carbon footprints offer important opportunities for measuring the impacts of carbon-intensive activities and generating discussions about the allocation of responsibility for addressing climate change. However, it also shows that such metrics distribute moral and political responsibility evenly across a city on the basis of an imagined population of carbon consumers. In so doing, it suggests that carbon footprints not only serve to ignore the uneven nature of carbon emissions but also obscure important questions about the roles and responsibilities of other actors. Overall, it proposes an approach drawing on the principle of common but differentiated responsibilities, whereby the duty to respond to climate change applies across all parties but with explicit recognition that different demands can be made on different parties (Caney 2005).

This chapter draws on a case study of carbon footprinting in Hong Kong. While measuring the GHG emissions of specific cities is complex and contested (Bulkeley 2013), evidence suggests that Hong Kong's overall per capita carbon footprint is significant and increasing over time (WWF Hong Kong 2013; Harris 2012). The chapter explores the ways in which carbon footprinting configures responsibility for climate action by juxtaposing carbon footprints and the associated techniques of quantification alongside a discussion of the everyday experiences and practices of residents in a low-income neighbourhood in Hong Kong. This represents a novel starting point, as there is currently little understanding about the impact that metrics such as carbon footprints might have on low-income (and hence low-consuming) residents, beyond a recognition that they are likely to generate lower emissions overall. More significantly, it draws attention to questions about appropriate levels of consumption and whether interventions that rely on universal targets for carbon reduction can ever be equitable. As such the chapter contributes to the nascent academic literature, which seeks to draw out the complex justice issues intimately bound up in urban climate interventions.

The chapter first reviews debates about individual responsibility in the context of climate change before exploring how carbon footprints serve to assign responsibility for carbon reduction. In so doing, it identifies three normative assumptions that underpin per capita carbon footprints: individuals as appropriate climate actors, the existence of equal carbon responsibility and the capacity of individuals to make changes. Next, it reflects on the significance and implementation of carbon footprints in practice through a case study of Hong Kong. Finally, it draws conclusions about how this calculation of carbon footprints – and associated allocation and enactment of responsibility – brings significant implications for climate justice in the city.

Responsibility, carbon footprints and climate justice: positioning the individual

While responsibility for addressing climate change has typically been considered at the national and international scale (Gardiner 2004; Page 2008; Roberts and Parks 2007), recent work has broadened this focus to consider the allocation of responsibilities to other actors. Emerging conceptions of climate responsibility echo Caney (2005, 756), who advocates for "a fine-grained analysis which traces the contributions of individuals, corporations, states and international actors and which accordingly attributes responsibilities to each of these." Such calls resonate with the well-established body of literature on individual responsibility and environmental action, which not only explores consumption in terms of attitudes, behaviours and choices but also considers how such consumption is mediated socially and technically (Barnett et al. 2005; Gibson et al. 2011; Hobson 2013). In this context, carbon footprinting offers a valuable lens to explore how individual climate responsibility is configured in the broader context of environmental consumption practices.

Mechanisms such as carbon footprints are rooted in an ongoing process of "individualisation," where action and practices are related to a specific configuration of responsibility and individuals are mobilised to govern their own emissions (Maniates 2001; Paterson and Stripple 2010). This is underpinned by a process of quantification (or carbon calculation) that seeks to allocate individual responsibility through behaviour change metrics. In practice, this is enabled by technologies such as personalised carbon calculators, often available online, that allow individuals to measure the environmental impact of their personal consumption practices (such as food, home energy efficiency, transportation or recycling). By linking emissions to these activities and behaviours, it is argued that people can visualise their responsibility for climate change and, in so doing, consider how they might modify their behaviour. Fundamentally, this assumes that individuals are appropriate actors to take action on carbon reduction. However, this raises questions about the implications of placing responsibility upon individuals for their own emissions at the expense of other actors – including, for example, the state or private corporations.

Furthermore, such calculative practices are not without normative values. As Paterson and Stripple (2010) highlight, practices such as footprinting serve to render some things visible and others invisible. This raises questions about the principles underpinning such mechanisms in terms of, for example, the types of emissions that are included or excluded. They further argue that numbers generated through a process of carbon calculation "represent immediately moralised activities on which the footprinter is invited, exhorted to act" (Paterson and Stripple 2010, 350). Despite this, there has been little consideration of how questions of justice and fairness might intersect with individual climate responsibility across different social groups. As such, the moral and political values at the heart of such calculative devices need to be more fully interrogated.

Alongside moral and political principles, it is also critical to consider patterns of unequal carbon consumption across the city. While it is acknowledged that the size of household carbon footprints is associated with income (Kennedy et al. 2014), such per capita calculations may nonetheless ignore vast differences among individuals in terms of structural patterns of advantage and disadvantage (Bulkeley et al. 2014). The assumption of equal carbon responsibility across the city – implicit with per capita calculations and common reduction targets – raises questions about the equity of asking all individuals to reduce their carbon consumption. This is particularly significant in light of debates about "underconsumption" and the complex role that energy services play in enabling or producing wellbeing (Day et al. 2016).

A related assumption here is whether individuals do, in fact, have the capacity to make changes in their lifestyles. This highlights the need to more carefully explore consumption practices in relation to "everyday" life (Gibson et al. 2011). For example, while increased use of air conditioning is often predicted to be a key response to warmer climates (Winter 2013), research on adaptation to heat finds everyday activities, such as clothing and flexible routines, to be as important as cooling technologies (Fuller and Bulkeley 2013). As Lövbrand et al. (2015, 216) argue, a pressing analytical task is to examine "how a changing environment is interpreted, lived and enacted across multiple socio-political contexts." This suggests that any process of carbon calculation needs to engage with the non-linearity of everyday practices in order to more carefully understand opportunities for action.

In summary, carbon footprints have gained traction as a means of quantifying individual responsibility for climate change and for motivating individual action through changes in behaviour. There is, however, little research that explicitly interrogates the normative assumptions underpinning such mechanisms, namely that individuals are appropriate actors to take action on climate change, the existence of equal carbon responsibility across the city and the capacity of individuals to take climate action. This raises wider questions for climate justice in terms of how this process of assigning responsibility is operationalised, if and how mechanisms such as carbon footprints account for everyday life, and the wider moral and political implications of this allocation of individual responsibility. In this context, the chapter now explores carbon footprinting in practice in Hong Kong.

Carbon footprints and the configuration of climate responsibility in Hong Kong

Hong Kong's per capita carbon footprint is the largest component (at around 60%) of the city's overall ecological footprint (WWF Hong Kong 2013). Despite this, Hong Kong lacks a coherent climate policy, and the limited and fragmented government response to date is deemed by many to be both inadequate and ineffective (Chu and Schroeder 2010; Francesch-Huidobro 2012; Harris 2012; Higgins 2013; Mah et al. 2012). In this context, civil society has been crucial in terms of organising environmental programmes and shaping the climate policy agenda – particularly major NGOs such as Oxfam Hong Kong, Greenpeace China and WWF Hong Kong (Cheng and So 2015; Mah and Hills 2016). As such, any exploration of climate responsibility in Hong Kong needs to foreground the role of civil society. One important example is the WWF Hong Kong Climate Programme – Climateers – which launched in 2007. The programme comprises a set of actions – both online and community projects – that serve to connect information with practical action, one of which is Hong Kong's first carbon calculator. This section first explores the significance of carbon footprints in Hong Kong, before examining the justice implications of footprints in practice.

The role of carbon footprints in Hong Kong

The World Wildlife Fund (WWF) launched Hong Kong's first carbon calculator "to allow everyone in Hong Kong to assess the climate change impacts of their daily lives, by providing a personalised 'carbon footprint', calculating the carbon dioxide emissions resulting from their homes and travel patterns" (WWF Hong Kong 2007). The calculator is available online and comprises a series of questions about different lifestyle activities: home energy and water consumption, frequency of recycling, local transport and air travel. Based on individual responses, it generates a report that indicates the total amount of carbon dioxide produced from these activities. In essence, WWF argues that bringing together awareness, personal commitment and opportunities for action creates a citizen consumer who can take personal responsibility to "slim down their carbon figure" (WWF Hong Kong no date-a). While several other calculators now exist in Hong Kong, this specific example serves as a productive mechanism for an analysis of this type, as it was the first such calculator in the city and the only one designed to be specific to Hong Kong (WWF Hong Kong 2010). It was also enabled by corporate support (e.g., HSBC) and has served as an impetus for a multiplicity of carbon calculation initiatives across the city (Bulkeley et al. 2015; Bulkeley et al. 2014), thus demonstrating its wider significance.

In order to understand how this process of carbon calculation serves to allocate responsibility across the city, the remainder of this chapter reviews its specific characteristics and considers its application in a low-income neighbourhood in Hong Kong. This is important not only because low-income neighbourhoods provide an important lens for understanding the justice implications of climate mitigation interventions such as carbon footprints, but also because evidence suggests that WWF has operationalised their Climateers programme in low-income neighbourhoods (Bulkeley et al. 2015). The specific neighbourhood is Shek Kip Mei, a public rental housing estate within the Sham Shui Po district of Kowloon. Comprising 17 blocks with approximately 9,000 households, the estate has a combination of older 1970s housing alongside modern flats completed in the last ten years. Like much high-rise housing in Hong Kong, the flats on the estate are often small; sizes range from 11.5 to 55.7 square metres. Official census figures show a lower-than-average median monthly income, which implies that many residents in Shek Kip Mei are living low-consuming and hence low-carbon lives.

As part of a wider project that sought to understand opportunities and challenges for carbon reduction, questionnaires and observations were undertaken in flats across Shek Kip Mei in both older and more modern blocks. Using the WWF calculator as a baseline, the questionnaires gathered background data (number of residents, size of apartment and recent charges for electricity, gas and water) alongside information about current living practices in relation to energy and water use, air quality and environmental awareness. Additionally, each visit included an observation "check list" to assess the physical condition of the flat in terms of natural light, indoor temperature and ventilation, and the existence of energy efficiency labels on household appliances. The questionnaires and observations generated quantitative data (e.g., number of light bulbs, weekly hours of air conditioning use and frequency of recycling practices) alongside qualitative data (e.g., reflective comments on adequacy of natural light and reasons for poor ventilation). Data analysis involved the use of descriptive statistics to highlight key trends, which were subsequently cross-referenced with the qualitative reflections.

While the study focused on an array of everyday living practices, this chapter specifically emphasises the use of air conditioning to demonstrate the justice implications of the carbon footprint approach in practice. This is particularly cogent because, similar to other cities in Asia (Winter 2013), air conditioning is one of Hong Kong's largest contributors to energy consumption (Electrical and Mechanical Services Department 2015). The following section explores the assumptions raised, namely the extent to which individuals are appropriate actors to take action on carbon reduction, the existence of equal carbon responsibility across the city and whether individuals have the capacity to make changes.

Climate justice and carbon footprints in practice

In the context of debates about individualisation, it is important to reflect on how and where carbon emissions are generated in Hong Kong. Statistics show that 90% of GHG emissions in the city originate from energy use (Electrical and Mechanical Services Department 2015), both local emissions through electricity generation for buildings and fossil fuels for transportation and embodied emissions in imported goods (Harris 2012). A persistent rise in energy consumption is attributed to population growth, economic growth, change in lifestyles and the expansion of the services sector (Choy et al. 2013; To et al. 2012). Residential energy use – particularly cooking, space conditioning and hot water – comprises 21% of total energy use in Hong Kong (Electrical and Mechanical Services Department 2015). The commercial (42%), transport (32%) and industrial (5%) sectors account for the remainder of energy use (Electrical and Mechanical Services Department 2015). These statistics suggest that individuals do make a significant contribution to Hong Kong's GHG emissions through their consumption practices – both at home and in their use of commercial and transport services – but it is also clear that a range of other actors have responsibilities associated with their energy consumption.

Furthermore, while individual carbon footprints mandate a reduction in energy use, this is in the face of an energy market that favours commercial and industrial customers. There are two electricity companies in Hong Kong – the Hong Kong Electric Company and CLP Power Hong Kong Limited. These private companies are regulated under a scheme of control which dictates the price of electricity and establishes a standard rate of return on capital invested by electricity companies while also preserving each power company's monopoly (Harris 2012). This guaranteed rate of return gives power companies an incentive to maximise electricity demand (Harris 2012) through regressive rates for industrial customers (Choy et al. 2013), which creates a disincentive for energy efficiency (Mah et al. 2012). This allocation of responsibility to individuals may thus serve to downplay the responsibility of other actors who may be more responsible for rising energy use across the city.

The diverse range of actors with climate responsibilities serves to complicate the assumption of equal carbon responsibility in the city. The WWF calculator was designed to be specific to Hong Kong and to reflect the lifestyles and facilities available for Hong Kong residents, as noted:

> Many carbon calculators that are built in other countries are not appropriate because . . . they are applicable to cooler climates, or because the power stations use different fuels. The

WWF Climateers specifically uses data gathered in Hong Kong to build a carbon calculator that reflects Hong Kong living.

(WWF Hong Kong, no date-b)

The specificity of this calculator, namely that it is designed to reflect local circumstances, is imbued with an implicit sense of fairness. The positioning to reflect lifestyles led in Hong Kong suggests (a) that the lifestyles being measured are those experienced by all within the city and (b) that the footprint mechanism provides an appropriate means to capture this activity. However, like many cities, Hong Kong displays distinctive patterns of social and spatial inequalities (Higgins 2013), with one of the world's highest levels of income inequality. This results in variable consumption patterns, where some sections of the population lead "highly polluting lives, flying frequently and consuming large quantities of emissions-intensive products" whereas "others lead lives that result in quite limited GHG pollution" (Harris 2012, 195).

The presence of these income – and hence consumption – differentials is significant for understanding the political and moral implications of carbon footprinting in Hong Kong. This is primarily because the carbon calculator is based on the notion of universal overconsumption, demanding quantifiable action in response – namely a specified percentage reduction in carbon-generating activities: "If each of us reduce 10% of our basic carbon footprint, we can aggregate a saving of 4.7 million tonnes of emissions" (WWF Hong Kong no date-b). This sense of collective responsibility – validated by a common target – implies that carbon consumption is equal across the city. This assumption becomes even more visible through the inclusion of an "add-on" which adds 2.7 tonnes of carbon dioxide to *everyone's* footprint representing emissions from Hong Kong's industrial, commercial and government sectors (WWF Hong Kong no date-b). This is based on the notion that these sectors – including shopping centres and government offices – provide employment, goods and services equally to Hong Kong residents. The resulting outcome therefore is that the carbon from these sectors is divided and distributed equally. While allocating moral responsibility evenly across the city, the calculator does not therefore adequately reflect how, where and by whom carbon emissions are actually generated.

Furthermore, such measurements do not take into consideration that some people consume significantly less carbon than others. This is demonstrated with our empirical research in Shek Kip Mei, which showed that a significant proportion of households were under- rather than overconsuming. Nearly 50% of flats surveyed had an indoor temperature that was uncomfortable (around 30 degrees Celsius). In these cases, people either did not have access to air conditioning or chose not to use air conditioning due to high electricity costs. This suggests that they were limiting their carbon consumption activities due to financial scarcity rather than a sense of moral responsibility. It is clear, then, that mechanisms of carbon calculation such as footprints do not accurately reflect the material circumstances of poverty within which people are living. In this situation, the requirement to reduce emissions by 10% or be held accountable for the "add on" appears unjust, both in principle and in practice.

Moving beyond questions about the desirability of making changes, there are also questions about the capacity of individuals to act to reduce their carbon emissions. At the household scale, our research highlighted residents' limited ability to control the material circumstances of their living environments. The questionnaires and observations demonstrated that the use of air conditioning was complicated by several factors. First, most flats only had windows on one side of the building and not in all rooms. This was particularly the case for older blocks and often resulted in poor ventilation – a factor completely out of the residents' control. Due to poor ventilation, there was a more pressing need to use air conditioning in these flats than was observed in the newer blocks. Secondly, the small flat size often meant that there was very limited storage space.

As a result, windows were often blocked with furniture or personal belongings as there was no other space available. Again, these conditions affected the potential for natural ventilation and the desire to use air conditioning. While this could be read as a "choice" to store items in this way, the lack of space within individual flats had important consequences for the ability of residents to use natural ventilation instead of air conditioning. Both factors are largely out of residents' control, suggesting that carbon footprints fail to capture their lived reality because their carbon consumption and ability to reduce their carbon emissions are deeply embedded in their spatial surroundings and financial circumstances.

Overall, therefore, the situation in Hong Kong, and Shek Kip Mai specifically, challenges the assumptions that individuals have equal climate responsibility and that carbon consumption is equally distributed across the city. It also undermines the argument that air conditioning has risen universally across Hong Kong. Without taking socio-economic inequalities into consideration, this assumption of rising air conditioning use conceals the ways in which some groups benefit from cooling technologies more than others. It is apparent, therefore, that while carbon footprinting seeks to quantify moral responsibility, doing so on a per capita basis ignores vast differences among individuals within the city and obscures inequalities in terms of individual contributions to carbon emissions and capacity to act.

Conclusions

This chapter has sought to broaden understandings about how, and with what effects, carbon footprints allocate responsibility for carbon production and consumption at an everyday level. In so doing, it has explored the case of Hong Kong and demonstrated the considerable challenges in using carbon footprint measurements as a means of quantifying and distributing individual responsibility and motivating action. The chapter concludes by reflecting on broader questions of moral and political responsibility and the implications for urban climate justice.

It is clear that carbon footprints, with their inherent focus on individual behaviour change, support projects and discourses of ecological modernisation. Such individual mechanisms not only have limited capacity to challenge development models that are sustained by high consumption, but they also demonstrate the degree to which prevailing governmental logics of calculation are shaping the way that organisations attempt to intervene in environmental transformation at the level of individual behaviour (Ong 2007). Overall, the measurement of carbon footprints on a per capita basis ignores wider structural differences among individuals within the city – a crucial concern for justice. This is significant as it masks fundamental inequalities both in terms of contribution to the carbon footprint and ability to act.

There is nonetheless a value in how carbon footprints serve to make injustices in consumption more visible. As noted, the existence of social and spatial inequalities in Hong Kong creates wide disparities in carbon consumption (Higgins 2013). Per capita carbon footprints are significant for individuals in low-income neighbourhoods, not least because they highlight that the expectation of a reduction in emissions is inequitable. Given the complex interrelationships between energy consumption and wellbeing, this observation raises questions about whether in fact an increase in emissions might be "just" for these social groups in relation to specific sectors or practices. This perspective also has implications for higher-income groups in the city and whether they should be expected to reduce emissions to a much larger extent. Therefore, while carbon footprints are used to motivate individual action by raising awareness of personal responsibility, this moral dimension is fraught with difficulty in practice, in terms of its ability to fully capture the uneven nature of carbon emissions within the city.

The quantification of carbon in terms of how it is used to calculate consumption and by extension, responsibility, clearly invokes a moral and ethical incentive for action. As the chapter highlights, calculators assign responsibility to individuals based on carbon footprints comprised of elements beyond their control, either due to wider institutional structures or individual social and material constraints. Thus, holding individuals responsible for acting on anything more than a small portion of their own carbon footprint is problematic. Moreover, there is a clear disconnection between quantified carbon footprints and the non-linearity of everyday practices. Bringing this juxtaposition to the forefront allows a different and more nuanced framing of what it means to act in the context of environmental change – both in terms of mundane political practices and the opportunities for more radical action.

In a broader sense, the creation of individual carbon footprints downplays the responsibility of government or industry in Hong Kong. This is particularly cogent given the rising energy use across other sectors of the city and in the absence of any coherent climate change strategy. Without a clear understanding of the institutional drivers of carbon consumption in specific commercial or industrial sectors, it becomes difficult to mobilise appropriately and transform those sites, spaces and activities that are most carbon intensive. This raises questions about the configuration of responsibility within the city, not only the appropriateness of allocating responsibility to individuals in the face of perceived inadequacy of government responses, but also the outcome of individual action. It is thus critical to foreground questions about justice in any configuration of responsibility.

In acknowledging the need for a socially and politically differentiated response to the challenges of climate change, the chapter calls, in conclusion, for a more considered approach to questions of responsibility within urban areas; a challenge, as Houston (2013) reminds us, of developing new understandings of how everyday realities might be reimagined in environmentally just ways. It is clear that any configuration of responsibility needs to be finely nuanced in terms of capturing the specificity of people and place while also being guided by an ethical framework that invokes a moral and political obligation to act. An approach centred on the principle of common but differentiated responsibilities might therefore facilitate a more just response towards the challenges of addressing climate change in the city.

Acknowledgements

A version of this chapter was previously published in *Area* (Fuller, 2017). It is reproduced here with kind permission from John Wiley and Sons.

References

Barnett C, Cloke P, Clarke N and Malpass A 2005. Consuming Ethics: Articulating the Subjects and Spaces of Ethical Consumption. *Antipode* 37 23–45

Bulkeley H 2013. *Cities and Climate Change.* Routledge, Oxon

Bulkeley H, Castán Broto, V and Edwards G A S 2015. *An Urban Politics of Climate Change.* Routledge, Oxon

Bulkeley H, Edward, G A S and Fuller S 2014. Contesting Climate Justice in the City: Examining Politics and Practice in Urban Climate Change Experiments. *Global Environmental Change* 25 31–40

Caney S 2005. Cosmopolitan Justice, Responsibility, and Global Climate Change. *Leiden Journal of International Law* 18 747–775

Cheng, N-Y I and So, W-M W 2015 Environmental Governance in Hong Kong – Moving Towards Multi-level Participation. *Journal of Asian Public Policy* 8 297–311

Choy L H T, Ho W K O and Mak S W K 2013. Toward a Low Carbon Hong Kong: A Proposal From the Institutional Perspective. *Habitat International* 37 124–129

Chu S Y and Schroeder H 2010. Private Governance of Climate Change in Hong Kong: An Analysis of Drivers and Barriers to Corporate Action. *Asian Studies Review* 34 287–308

Day R, Walker G and Simcock N 2016. Conceptualising Energy Use and Energy Poverty Using a Capabilities Framework. *Energy Policy* 93 255–264

Electrical and Mechanical Services Department 2015. *Hong Kong Energy End Use Data 2015.* Electrical and Mechanical Services Department, Hong Kong

Francesch-Huidobro M 2012. Institutional Deficit and Lack of Legitimacy: The Challenges of Climate Change Governance in Hong Kong. *Environmental Politics* 21 791–810

Fuller S 2017. Configuring Climate Responsibility in the City: Carbon Footprints and Climate Justice in Hong Kong. *Area* 49 519–525

Fuller S and Bulkeley H 2013. Changing Countries, Changing Climates: Achieving Thermal Comfort Through Adaptation in Everyday Activities. *Area* 45 63–69

Gardiner S M 2004. Ethics and Global Climate Change. *Ethics* 114 555–600

Gibson C, Head L, Gill N and Waitt G 2011. Climate Change and Household Dynamics: Beyond Consumption, Unbounding Sustainability. *Transactions of the Institute of British Geographers* 36 3–8

Harris P G 2012. *Environmental Policy and Sustainable Development in China: Hong Kong in a Global Context.* Policy Press, Bristol

Higgins P 2013. From Sustainable Development to Carbon Control: Urban Transformation in Hong Kong and London. *Journal of Cleaner Production* 50 56–67

Hobson K 2013. On the Making of the Environmental Citizen. *Environmental Politics* 22 56–72

Houston D 2013. Crisis Is Where We Live: Environmental Justice for the Anthropocene. *Globalizations* 10 439–450

Kennedy E H, Krahn H and Krogman N T 2014. Egregious Emitters: Disproportionality in Household Carbon Footprints. *Environment and Behavior* 46 535–555

Lövbrand E, Beck S, Chilvers J, ForsyTh T, Hedrén J, HulMe M, Lidskog R and VasilEiadou E 2015. Who Speaks for the Future of Earth? How Critical Social Science Can Extend the Conversation on the Anthropocene. *Global Environmental Change* 32 211–218

Mah D N-Y and Hills P 2016. An International Review of Local Governance for Climate Change: Implications for Hong Kong. *Local Environment* 21 39–64

Mah D N-Y, Van Der Vleuten J M, Hills P and Tao J 2012. Consumer Perceptions of Smart Grid Development: Results of a Hong Kong Survey and Policy Implications. *Energy Policy* 49 204–216

Maniates M F 2001. Individualization: Plant a Tree, Buy a Bike, Save the World? *Global Environmental Politics* 1 31–52

Minx J, Baiocchi G, Wiedmann T, Barrett J, Creutzig F, Feng K, Förster M, PicHler P P, Weisz H and Hubace K K 2013. Carbon Footprints of Cities and Other Human Settlements in the UK. *Environmental Research Letters* 8 1–10

Ong A 2007. Neoliberalism as a Mobile Technology. *Transactions of the Institute of British Geographers* 32 3–8

Page E A 2008. Distributing the Burdens of Climate Change. *Environmental Politics* 17 556–575

Paterson M and Stripple J 2010. My Space: Governing Individuals' Carbon Emissions. *Environment and Planning D: Society and Space* 28 341–362

Peters G P 2010. Carbon Footprints and Embodied Carbon at Multiple Scales. *Current Opinion in Environmental Sustainability* 2 245–250

Roberts J and Parks B 2007. *A Climate of Injustice: Global Inequality, North-South Politics, and Climate Policy.* MIT Press, Cambridge MA

To W M, Lai T M, Lo W C, Lam K H and Chung W L 2012. The Growth Pattern and Fuel Life Cycle Analysis of the Electricity Consumption of Hong Kong. *Environmental Pollution* 165 1–10

Wiedmann T and Minx J 2008. A Definition of 'Carbon Footprint'. In Pertsova C C ed *Ecological Economics Research Trends.* Nova Science Publishers, Hauppauge NY 1–11

Winter T 2013. An Uncomfortable Truth: Air-conditioning and Sustainability in Asia. *Environment and Planning A* 45 517–531

Wright L A, Kemp S and Williams I 2011. 'Carbon Footprinting': Towards a Universally Accepted Definition. *Carbon Management* 2 61–72

WWF Hong Kong 2007. *WWF Climateers Put Their Foot Down to Stop Climate Change* (www.wwf.org. hk/en/news/press_release/?1332/WWF-Climateers-put-their-foot-down-to-stop-Climate-Change) Accessed 10 January 2016

WWF Hong Kong 2010. *WWF Reveals the Latest Carbon Footprint Data Average Carbon Footprint of Hong Kong Citizen is 13.44 Tonnes, Air Travel to Blame* (www.wwf.org.hk/en/?2560/WWF-Reveals-the-Latest-Carbon-Footprint-Data) Accessed 10 January 2016

WWF Hong Kong 2013. *Hong Kong Ecological Footprint Report 2013.* WWF Hong Kong, Hong Kong

WWF Hong Kong no date-a. *Be A Climateer* (www.wwf.org.hk/en/whatwedo/footprint/climate/examples_of_individual_actions/climateers/beaclimateer) Accessed 10 January 2016

WWF Hong Kong no date-b. *About Calculator* (www.climateers.org/eng/contents/about_calculator.php) Accessed 10 January 2016

23

The shifting geographies of climate justice

Mobile vulnerabilities in and across Indian cities

Eric Chu[1] and Kavya Michael[2]

Situating climate justice in the Global South

Scholars of climate change justice have explored the need to delineate global mitigation responsibilities and share adaptation resources (Ciplet, Roberts, and Khan 2015; Caney 2014). At the local level, recent literature on climate justice has focused on diagnosing injustices or articulating normative ideals for how justice priorities can be operationalised into policies (Shi et al. 2016; Hughes 2013). In this chapter, we unpack the justice implications of urban climate change adaptation and resilience in development contexts. This literature especially notes the importance of including vulnerable actors in managing risks and adaptation benefits (Archer et al. 2014; Chu, Anguelovski, and Carmin 2016; Ziervogel et al. 2017), as well as assessing the social, economic and political implications of particular adaptation interventions (Anguelovski et al. 2016). In the Global South, however, justice considerations are often complicated by the material frames of daily life, which are mostly cast through the prism of economic production and investment (Betsill and Bulkeley 2007; Boyce 2002). In this context, *economy* is by far the most important development paradigm driving climate actions. We see this in how climate adaptation or resilience is packaged as a constituent element of urban economic competitiveness (Vale 2014; Meerow, Newell, and Stults 2016; Harris, Chu, and Ziervogel 2017) and in how adaptation and risk management are used as tools for enabling gentrification (Anguelovski et al. 2018).

This chapter takes the cases of Bangalore and Surat in India to examine how the reorganisation of labour – together with its associating economic networks and spatial infrastructure – is emblematic of the shifting interconnections between uncertain climate change risks and experiences of local economic transformations. We draw on a mixed-methods qualitative methodology (primarily semi-structured interviews, household surveys and gender-differentiated focus groups) to evaluate how rural-urban migrants in India experience the compounding and transboundary impacts of climate change and contemporary economic transformations. In particular, the case studies from Bangalore and Surat highlight the *shifting* dynamics of climate injustice in cities of the Global South. The idea of *shifting* not only speaks to the mobile and constantly evolving nature of how risks and vulnerabilities are experienced in and across space, but it also points to a need to renew our conceptual approach to identifying, delineating and evaluating climate (in)justice in cities. The mobility of risks points to how urban climate injustices are situated within intersecting forms of socio-economic marginality beyond the immediate borders of the city *and* are simultaneously reconstructed in situ due to the overlapping vulnerabilities posed by employment insecurity, housing precariousness and emerging climate change risks.

Our chapter informs climate justice theories by documenting the shifting geographies of climate injustice within and across the ill-defined boundaries of the "urban" in the Global South. In particular, the case studies highlight a clear connection between the urbanisation of economic production (Brenner and Theodore 2002; Brenner 2004) and the reproduction of environmental vulnerability among the poor (Michael, Deshpande, and Ziervogel 2017; Walker 2012). We note that first, spatially and temporally "static" definitions of climate justice fail to account for the mobility of people and transfer of vulnerabilities across space. Second, climate justice theories should encompass priorities to transform economic structures underlying economic informality. We must therefore further examine the multiple intersections – or the double exposures (see Leichenko and O'Brien 2008) – of urban labour and economic marginalisation under climate change in the Global South.

Theories of climate justice in and across cities

Issues of climate change adaptation and resilience are inherently engrained within questions of equity, inclusion and justice (Pelling 2010; Parks and Roberts 2010; Beckman and Page 2008). In the context of cities in the Global South, one must balance the reality that many are seeking to embark on resource-intensive development pathways while simultaneously experiencing inadequate infrastructure to deal with uncertain climate change impacts. This inevitably yields questions about adaptation and resilience *for whom, through what mechanism* and *to what end* (Meerow and Newell 2016; Shi et al. 2016; Sovacool, Linnér, and Goodsite 2015). Many existing studies focus on issues of social inclusion in climate adaptation planning and policy-making processes, which posit that adequate representation and participation of vulnerable communities will yield more equitable solutions (Chu, Anguelovski, and Carmin 2016; Chu, Schenk, and Patterson 2018). Simultaneously, some studies have begun to show how existing or pipeline climate adaptation or resilience-building actions are resulting in negative impacts for urban communities, such as displacing low-income groups, incentivising unaffordable or privatised public services, or prioritising economic investment opportunities over providing collective welfare needs (Anguelovski et al. 2016; Pearsall 2012; Anguelovski and Martínez Alier 2014). Though many of these studies are normative in nature, they do show that poor communities are differentially impacted, experience less adaptive capacity due to lower access to social, political and economic capital, and are typically not the focus of wide-ranging urban climate change actions.

Despite an emerging scholarship on urban climate justice, these assessments tend to focus on the instruments, strategies and actions required to rectify immediate inequalities rather than diagnose the structural factors contributing to social, economic and political marginality at-large (Parks and Roberts 2010; Schlosberg 2012; Bulkeley et al. 2013). To achieve the latter, we must expand the scope of our interrogations to include intersectional injustices – i.e., in terms of ethnicity, caste, gender, etc. (see Terry 2009; MacGregor 2010; Arora-Jonsson 2011) – as well as spatialise our theories to encompass extra-urban and trans-boundary contributors to urban climate injustice (Shi et al. 2016; Fisher 2015). In this chapter, we critically evaluate the issue of migration as an entry point to analysing this spatial "turn" to urban climate justice. Migration patterns are attributed to a complex interplay of economic, social, political and demographic factors, though disentangling the role of climate change as a particular driver is difficult (IPCC 2014; Scheffran, Marmer, and Sow 2012; Faist and Schade 2013; Hunter, Luna, and Norton 2015).

Researchers in India have also identified gaps in understanding how migration affects wellbeing at the sources and destinations of migrants (Deshingkar 2004; Chandrasekhar and Sharma 2014). Earlier assessments of migration from the perspective of economic geography saw it as a movement of people from less to well economically developed areas through push factors – including those attributed to poverty and deprivation – and pull factors such as better wages (Deshingkar 2004). However, more recently, scholars have documented forms of involuntary migration (or migration for survival). As such, Deshingkar (2004) argues that we should not only examine productivity and labour demand as the sole determinants of migration patterns. In fact, migration is also structured around people's access to resources, the environment, intra-household relations and wider social divisions.

Migration is not only an integral livelihood strategy for the rural poor; it also allows for researchers to document rural-urban dynamics (Satterthwaite and Tacoli 2002). Climate change and its associating environmental impacts often dictate migration decisions only after being filtered through social, political and economic conditions on the ground (Michael, Deshpande, and Ziervogel 2017). In India, climatic factors such as increased drought frequency and changing temperature and rainfall patterns significantly drive temporary forms of migration, although they exert lesser influence on permanent migration (Kavi Kumar and Viswanathan 2013). Furthermore, 60% of the Indian population depends on agriculture, so large landholders with strong social capital and large asset bases are able to resist climate change-induced stresses while small-scale landowners, marginal farmers and landless labourers are forced to migrate (Viswanathan and Kavi Kumar 2015). Such groups of marginalised, landless and unskilled migrants – often with poor access to social networks and political agency – travel to cities and end up in precarious or insecure jobs and congregate in informal squatter settlements.

Reminiscent of the recent history of cities across the Global South, urbanisation patterns in India have largely been forged by neoliberal practices of market-oriented governance – and subsequently enabled through privatisation and urban entrepreneurialism (Smith 2002; Harvey 1989; Miraftab 2004) – that resulted in benefits for a particular socio-economic class and yielded uneven power relations across society (Whitehead 2013; Vakulabharanam and Motiram 2012; Corbridge, Harriss, and Jeffrey 2013). Since liberalisation reforms were implemented in 1991, the Indian state has rapidly transformed from being a land regulator to becoming an active agent for private interests (Shrivastava and Kothari 2012; Chibber 2003). Many from the rural areas began moving into cities in search of employment opportunities after experiencing land expropriation and falling welfare (Viswanathan and Kavi Kumar 2015). However, many found themselves in mushrooming informal settlements. This high concentration of informality represents one of the starkest manifestations of urban poverty and inequality – trends that are exacerbated due to the compounding effects of climate change on social precariousness and informality (Michael, Deshpande, and Ziervogel 2017).

Recent research on cities in the Global South increasingly focuses on urban processes that span urban-rural continuums rather than the spatial confines of urban spaces and structures (Roy 2016; Swyngedouw and Heynen 2003; Heynen 2013). In India, Gururani and Dasgupta (2018) argue that the rural and urban are in fact materially and symbolically co-produced, while the contested politics of urbanisation is shaped by processes of urban-to-rural migration. In particular, decreasing rates of social provisioning by the state and declining access to rural commons have created an increased appetite for migration to cities (Rao and Vakulabharanam 2018). Migration therefore entails giving up land – whether voluntarily or involuntarily – as well as long-held employment practices, livelihood strategies and kinship and social relations. As rates of rural-urban migration have increased since liberalisation in 1991, conflicts around access to real estate, land and infrastructure have intensified due to highly unequal opportunities shaping socio-political inclusion and exclusion (Corbridge, Harriss, and Jeffrey 2013). Rao and Vakulabharanam (2018) note that India has entered into a migration crisis, which is characterised by three overlapping social crises: an agrarian crisis, an employment crisis and a crisis of social reproduction. Due to a drastic reduction of public investment in agriculture, decreased state support for small and marginal farmers (with both male and female heads of households), and the consequent loss of livelihood opportunities for small farmers and wage labourers (Vakulabharanam and Motiram 2012), the reordering of productive and reproductive labour across space has signified a deep transformation in Indian society (Rao and Vakulabharanam 2018). The agrarian crisis exacerbated rural poverty and pushed a large number of rural families to seek employment elsewhere (Shrivastava and Kothari 2012). However, due to the lack of high-quality and regular formal jobs and the mismatch of skills requirements in the formal sector, most migrant workers find refuge in the informal sector.

The economic vulnerability of informal sector workers in Indian cities is compounded by heightened exposures to climate change and disaster risks (Mukhopadhyay and Revi 2012). Climate hazards can cause loss of land and livelihoods, putting pressure on the city's existing urban infrastructure (Michael, Deshpande, and Ziervogel 2017; Revi 2008). In the Indian context, the informal economy is largely constituted of the excluded masses that subsidise and feed the formal economy by providing various cheap inputs in the form of labour or commodities, all the while being periodically dispossessed by the elite. For example, male urban informal workers often find it impossible to provide basic needs and care work, ultimately leading to increased reliance on unpaid labour performed by women (Rao and Vakulabharanam 2018). The growing importance of unpaid female labour entrenches traditional gender norms and supports the survival of male migrants in hostile urban conditions by allocating care activities and provisioning of basic needs like cooking, cleaning and fetching water to women (Folbre 2002; Rao 2017; Razavi 2007). From a climate justice point of view, groups that are marginalised – such as women in the informal economy – are likely to have fewer opportunities to influence policy-making, so decisions made by governments are unlikely to benefit them (Chu, Anguelovski, and Carmin 2016). As a result, the challenge of climate injustice in Indian cities is embedded within the structural economic, political and social disenfranchisements experienced by the poor over the past several decades of neoliberal reform.

Under climate change, projected ecological risks and vulnerabilities will inevitably be embodied by labourers in their daily interactions with the various hazards of economic production. This may include their double exposure to climate impacts and local economic transformations (Leichenko and O'Brien 2008) to smaller-scale risks such as working outdoors in extreme temperatures, living in precarious housing conditions, and being prevented from accessing adequate education and capacity-building programmes (Revi 2008; Michael, Deshpande, and Ziervogel 2017). In India and across the Global South, forms of urban marginalisation are the outcomes of historic development pathways that have yielded highly unequal processes and patterns of allocating resources and access to spaces within the city (Fernandes 2004; Watson 2009). Social divisions and hierarchies based on caste or gender make exploitation even more stark (Desai and Sanyal 2012). As these patterns of social exclusion are replicated across rural and urban areas (Bhagat 2017), an analysis of urban labourers and their experience of political, social and environmental marginality must also be understood within the larger context of the rural-urban continuum (Rao and Vakulabharanam 2018).

As articulated in this section, there is a significant gap in the literature on understanding how the *spatial* process of migration and accelerating urbanisation affects existing inequities in resource distribution and access, as well as shapes the vulnerability of migrants to climate change. In this chapter, we illustrate these contending dynamics through evaluating the experiences of the cities of Bangalore and Surat. The Bangalore case highlights how vulnerability is transferred in a circular manner between urban and rural spaces, while the Surat case illustrates how transboundary ideas are enacted across the urban space. Both unpack the heightened climate vulnerabilities for migrants who experience little to no citizenship rights and remain excluded from the unfolding benefits of neoliberal urbanisation.

Bangalore: a case of rural-urban disenfranchisement

The city of Bangalore is located in the southeastern dry zone of Karnataka and is characterised by a semi-arid climate (Basu and Bazaz 2016). Bangalore has experienced significant changes in climatic conditions, including increasing temperature, significant decline in annual precipitation and erratic rainfall patterns. These climatic conditions intersect with the existing exclusionary development pattern in Bangalore and often define vulnerabilities for the lower echelons of society (Michael, Deshpande, and Ziervogel 2017). Bangalore is one of India's fastest growing metro cities and is an ideal representation of the pattern of contemporary urbanisation in India. Bangalore was known as a comfortable middle-class town dominated by secure union jobs and manufacturing firms till the early 1990s (Goldman 2011). The city was noted for its distinctive local economy that catered to poor and middle-income groups (Benjamin 2000). However, following liberalisation, Bangalore experienced an influx of transnational corporations that paved the way for the city's transformation into a "world-class" city, with infrastructure and public services catering for the emerging information communication technology (ICT) industry (Basu and Bazaz 2016; Goldman 2011). This development was also accompanied by accelerating patterns of socio-economic inequality, mass displacement and dispossession, the proliferation of slum settlements, increased communal and ethnic violence and tensions, and epidemic public health crises due to severe water supply and sewage problems, particularly in poor and working-class neighbourhoods (Goldman 2011).

Like many cities across the Global South, Bangalore has pursued the idea of building a "world-class city," which has led to mass displacement of the urban informal settlement dwellers. The allocation of land and funds by the state or debt-financed para-statals – who are accountable only to their international donor organisations – are highly discriminatory and largely favour transnational corporations (Benjamin 2000). The mega city projects executed under key schemes such as the Bangalore-Mysore Infrastructure Corridor (BMIC), the IT corridor and the Bangalore International Airport and its surrounding development area (BIAL) all clearly show how para-statal agencies serve as active agents of land speculation (Goldman 2011). These large-scale projects attract both highly skilled as well as numerous distressed migrants, who often find refuge in burgeoning informal settlements in and around the city, where they are exposed to insecure and fragile livelihoods and living conditions (Michael, Deshpande, and Ziervogel 2017).

Bangalore attracts both migrants from within Karnataka (i.e., intra-state migrants) as well as those from Uttar Pradesh, Bihar and West Bengal. To comprehend the shifting nature of vulnerabilities experienced by these migrants, it is critical to assess the socio-economic, political and climatic factors that triggered their decision to migrate. Based on our field research findings, while inter-state migrants identified severe socio-economic marginalisation in their homelands as the primary driver of migration, those from West Bengal also attributed their decision to flash floods that occurred in 2000. Intra-state migrants similarly noted the impacts of looming drought and agrarian crises in their home districts – notably Raichur, Gulbarga, Yadgiri, Bijapur, Bellary, Haveri and Koppala – as primary drivers of migration to Bangalore in search of alternate livelihood options. Many of these rural-urban migrants are landless agricultural labourers or small/marginal farmers belonging to socio-economically disadvantaged groups, who are further disadvantaged due to falling land productivity, severe indebtedness and the lack of support from recent agrarian reforms.

As noted by Breman (2013), intra-state migrants fit aptly into the category of footloose or nomadic labour who circulate between the village and the city. These workers are often unable to find viable livelihood options in agriculture, while their temporary status prevents them from attaining a foothold in the city (Vakulabharanam and Motiram 2012). This creates circular forms of migration because they are displaced from the rural-urban continuum. Inter-state migrants, however, often do not have any fall-back options in their villages and so live a disconnected and isolated life in the city. The linguistic gap adds an additional layer of vulnerability for inter-state migrants as it leads to their total alienation from public services, social networks and political voice (Michael, Deshpande, and Ziervogel 2017). Inter-state migrants typically engage in waste-picking and informal construction, although the municipal government does not fully recognise many of them, and the stigma attached to their occupation often results in detrimental impacts on their sense of dignity. Some level of labour exploitation is common, as Vakulabharanam and Motiram (2012) note how there tends to be a deliberate strategy of employing a voiceless and pliable labour force. Migrants also are unable to avail subsidies from the public distribution system since ration cards are invalid if they are not procured locally in Bangalore. The lack of citizenship rights means that migrants are under a constant threat of eviction, where their illegal status yields a pervasive sense of fear and insecurity. In sum, these examples highlight how in Bangalore, migrants' previous experiences with the trauma of land expropriation are then compounded with the distress of marginal economic, political and social life in the city.

In assessing the environmental vulnerability of migrants in Bangalore, it is clear that they experience inadequate access to basic services and infrastructure (Basu and Bazaz 2016). Migrants usually settle in newer parts of the city where informal settlements have existed for less than ten years. Such areas tend to be undeclared settlements and therefore do not receive any government support. Housing conditions are often poor, where dwellings are typically made of unsteady and temporary metal or tarpaulin sheets and unbaked bricks. Since many of these settlements lack adequate drainage or sewerage systems despite their low elevation, many are severely flooded during heavy rains. In the face of climate change, these settlements are exposed to additional flooding, heat island effects, and periods of water scarcity (Revi 2008), which not only causes detrimental effects on public health but also prevents migrants from earning an adequate daily wage. Furthermore, they have little or no negotiating power in the city and are ignored by many government and civil society programmes. In this case, climate-related risks are experienced by vulnerable migrants in ways that intersect with multiple forms of socio-economic marginalisation and livelihood insecurity that span across their rural origins and urban destinations.

Surat: a case of exclusion and displacement

With a population of 4.5 million, Surat is the eighth largest city in India. The city is situated on the Tapi River in the state of Gujarat, near to the point where it meets the Arabian Sea. Surat has served as a major trading hub since the 16th century, when it emerged as a notable shipping and sea-trading node. Since then, the city has retained its identity as a major commercial hub, and now is home to large concentrations of diamond cutting and polishing, textiles and petrochemical industries. As India's economy began to liberalise starting in the early 1990s, Surat experienced a major population boom on account of its economic centrality, with some estimates showing 40–50% population growth per decade over the past 30 years (ACCCRN 2011). With this growth, Surat has transformed itself from a medium-sized regional trading town to a major global and national hub for diamonds and textiles. The municipal government of Surat has recognised the city's economic strengths and has facilitated investment-friendly policies to attract small- and medium-sized enterprises (SMEs) as well as larger petrochemical and information technology firms.

As with Bangalore, the growth of Surat's economic base over the past three decades has led to high levels of migration. The city attracts labourers from eastern India, primarily from rural areas in Odisha, Bihar and Jharkhand, who flock to the city in search of opportunities in Surat's many diamond and textile factories. In response, the Surat municipal government (the Surat Municipal Corporation or SMC) has partnered with the Surat Urban Development Authority (SUDA) to respond to this growing housing need. Although additional housing units have been built in the northern and western zones of the city, this development has not been able to meet the growing demand, particularly since many of the migrants are low-wage earners and so are not able to afford newly built units. As a result – and as common to many of India's large cities – low-income migrants start to congregate in informal settlements. For Surat, such areas include the Tapi River flood zones and on marginal lands in the city's periphery, all of which are environmentally precarious and lack adequate access to public services and infrastructure.

In addition to promoting investment and industrial development, a unique aspect of Surat's development over the past decade has been a focus on environmental management. Surat has experienced a number of disasters, including a plague epidemic in 1994 that led to one of India's first comprehensive urban sanitation and public health programmes. Another is a major flood disaster in 2006, which again caused a major public health crisis due to the way stagnant water promotes vector-borne diseases (including leptospirosis and dengue fever) and gastrointestinal maladies such as cholera. The 2006 floods also caused major infrastructural damage to the city centre (Bhat et al. 2013). The twin disasters not only led Surat to focus on improving its public health standards and policies – such as through developing a vector-borne diseases surveillance unit within the SMC – but it also catalysed initial ideas around the need for a more comprehensive disaster risk management and resilience-building approach for the city (Anguelovski, Chu, and Carmin 2014). This latter point was seen as particularly important due to the city's interest in fostering an entrepreneurial spirit among its residents.

In 2009, the Rockefeller Foundation identified Surat as a pilot city for their new Asian Cities Climate Change Resilience Network (ACCCRN) programme. The Rockefeller Foundation had recently identified tackling climate change as an institutional priority, and looked into opportunities for building climate resilience in small- and medium-sized urban centres across South and Southeast Asia (Moench, Tyler, and Lage 2011). As one of three ACCCRN pilot cities in India, Surat was selected because of its high governance capacity, high public awareness of emerging environmental risks and high levels of private sector interest in building resilience (Sharma, Singh, and Singh 2014; Chu 2016a; Brown, Dayal, and Rumbaitis Del Rio 2012). In particular, the Rockefeller Foundation noted Surat's prior experience in large-scale public projects to address public health crises and natural disasters, and therefore saw the city as a unique case to pilot more comprehensive risk and vulnerability assessments and more collaborative, cross-sectoral planning and policy-making methodologies.

Notably, the primary focus of ACCCRN's interventions in Surat was not on the justice or equity dimensions of climate change resilience action. Between 2010 and 2014, most of the resources offered through the ACCCRN programme were channelled into building local government capacities around assessing climate change risks and vulnerabilities, identifying relevant public sector institutional partnerships and designing specific upgrade projects to improve the adaptive capacity of critical infrastructure sites (Chu 2016a). Examples of interventions include comprehensive flood risk assessments across the city, installing water gauges along the Tapi River to create a unified early warning system and strengthening flood protection systems (ACCCRN

2011; Chu 2016b). Beyond the initial priorities around building capacity for public health and flood risk management, the city also began to envision more inclusive decision-making pathways to ensure adequate representation and voice for more disadvantaged people in evaluating and prioritising resilience projects. These included designing more climate-sensitive housing units with natural sources of cooling, building a vulnerable peoples database to inform emergency services in the event of disasters, and embarking on different "shared-learning dialogue" workshops to gather citizen ideas, priorities and interests during the climate change planning process (ISET 2010; Chu 2016b). As climate change discourses were relatively new for both the local government and residents, the ACCCRN programme focused on inclusiveness by increasing public awareness of climate change risks, impacts and priorities for building resilience (Chu, Anguelovski, and Carmin 2016). Strategically, ACCCRN interventions emphasised mainstreaming emerging climate change priorities into pre-existing development strategies around public health, economic competitiveness and infrastructure upgrading.

Financial support from the Rockefeller Foundation concluded in 2014, so the city established the Surat Climate Change Trust (SCCT) to formalise many of the earlier pilot interventions. As the SCCT was registered as a philanthropic trust, it could pool and channel financial resources in a more efficient manner compared to the municipal authority (Cook and Chu 2018). Many of the former members of the city advisory committee for ACCCRN were also brought on as trustees for the SCCT. This included representatives from the Surat Municipal Corporation (SMC), Surat Urban Development Authority (SUDA), as well as the Southern Gujarat Chamber of Commerce and Industry (SGCCI). The leadership role played by the Chamber of Commerce not only reflects the priority of integrating environmental and economic resilience across the city, but it also reflects the historical role that industrial and trading classes have played in directing Surat's development trajectory. The SCCT subsequently built upon previous ACCCRN-supported interventions around public health resilience, disaster risk early warning systems and raising awareness of climate change risks and vulnerabilities among local government actors.

From a climate justice point of view, Surat's experience highlights concerted efforts to enhance procedural equity and inclusiveness in the initial planning and piloting phases (Chu, Anguelovski, and Carmin 2016). Notably, the *Surat City Resilience Strategy* (2011) highlighted the importance of achieving social cohesion through the resilience-building process (ACCCRN 2011). Embedded in this is the assumption that collective actions would increase adaptive capacity in times of disasters, such as during the 1994 plague and 2006 flood events. The focus on social cohesion is also rooted in Surat's socio-cultural identity, where entrepreneurial classes often shaped around kinship, caste, ethnic and religious communities have historically contributed to the economic development of the city (Chu 2016a). The Rockefeller Foundation saw an opportunity to harness existing ideals around social cohesiveness and economic innovation to further local initiatives around improving public health, urban infrastructure and disaster warning under climate change.

Although Surat's experience is often hailed as a success in urban resilience action, the structured planning and participatory process has been critiqued. In particular, from a procedural equity standpoint, the selection of participants in the various adaptation and resilience projects have been limited to expert decision-makers and notable city leaders, such as those representing major economic bodies (Harris, Chu, and Ziervogel 2017). This selection process made sense at the time because general awareness of climate change was low. However, it soon became clear that the process lacked broad representation from the different affected communities. Second, as the planning process lacked a voice from poor and vulnerable citizens, the subsequent interventions also neglected to account for the interests of the marginalised. For example, the various infrastructure upgrade projects in response to emerging climate risks – including fortifying river embankments and upgrading pipelines – were built in ways that displaced communities living in the floodplains, which housed many of the city's migrant labour population (Anguelovski et al. 2016). From a public health perspective, in contrast, many of the disease-monitoring systems supported by the SCCT did explicitly target lower-income neighbourhoods that disproportionately suffered from dengue, leptospirosis and gastrointestinal disease outbreaks during floods. These examples highlight an uneven treatment of climate inequalities when poor communities are not involved in the decision-making process from the outset.

For those who were displaced by Surat's climate change infrastructure, the results point to a "double exposure" to climate vulnerability and economic precariousness (see Leichenko and O'Brien 2008). As migrants arrived in Surat in search of jobs in the city's flourishing diamond and textile factories, their lack of economic security often meant that they congregated on marginal lands. In Surat, this often meant low-lying floodplain zones that were vulnerable to flooding and inundation, which are projected to worsen under climate change (ACCCRN 2011). At the same time, as shown through the Rockefeller Foundations engagement between 2009 and 2014, the city recognised the imminent risks of climate change, and therefore devised planning strategies to address them with the help of notable and economically powerful actors. This eventually led to a policy discourse where climate change was seen as an opportunity to strengthen and render the city's economic base more competitive through upgrading infrastructure, improving environmental quality and enabling wider economic competitiveness. Though many of the ACCCRN-supported interventions pay some attention to the unequal distribution of climate change risks across the urban landscape, the eventual infrastructural outcomes shifted climate risks from economically valuable industries to economically marginalised slums.

Theorising the shifting geographies of urban climate justice

The case studies from Bangalore and Surat highlight the *shifting* dynamics of climate injustice in cities of the Global South. This idea speaks to the mobile, trans-boundary and constantly evolving nature of how risks and vulnerabilities are experienced within and across space. It also points to a need to renew our conceptual approach to identifying, delineating and evaluating climate injustices in cities. These arguments are exemplified through our two case studies, where we see a transfer of socio-economic precariousness from rural to urban spaces due to the introduction of neoliberal policies and the transformation of economic production in India over recent decades. This mobility of risk points to how urban climate injustices are tied to intersecting forms of socio-economic marginality beyond the immediate borders of the city *and* are simultaneously reconstructed in-situ due to the overlapping vulnerabilities posed by employment insecurity, housing precariousness and emerging climate change risks.

Our discussion of the *shifting* geographies of climate justice also points to a need to renew our methodological approach to unpacking the sources, experiences and consequences of climate injustice in cities. Our brief investigations into Bangalore and Surat – both cities with extraordinarily high population growth rates over the past several decades – highlight the need to examine climate (in)justice through the pathways and flows of human and capital movement across space. In India and across much of the Global South, cities have been nodes of transformation amidst a wider network of economic, social and political change. Both Bangalore and Surat have experienced the liberalisation of their economic bases since the early 1990s, as well as an influx of speculative land management policies – often advocated by firms and government agendas beyond the city itself – which have resulted in mostly unregulated spaces of extreme inequality. When combined with emerging understandings on the multiscalar and trans-boundary nature of climate change risks (see Bulkeley and Betsill 2005; Bulkeley, Castán Broto, and Edwards 2015; Hughes, Chu, and Mason 2018), theories of climate justice must also interrogate the structural changes experienced by Indian cities over the past decades. To conclude this chapter, we offer several insights on theorising climate justice through this lens.

First, at a descriptive level, both case studies highlight how climate change actions target specific spaces for vulnerability reduction, adaptation and resilience building (see Shi et al. 2016). The example from Bangalore highlights how climate vulnerabilities are mobile for poor migrants across rural and urban areas, while the case from Surat illustrates how trans-boundary ideas of adaptation and resilience are selectively enacted across economically valuable urban spaces. Such spaces are delineated based on rhetoric and ideals that are external to the space itself. In India, this rhetoric includes opportunities for increasing economic competitiveness, enhancing capital speculative potential and improving environmental quality for middle-class consumers. These political-economic ideals are now further couched within the emerging climate change priorities, and offer a utopian vision of economic growth, environmental sustainability and human wellbeing. However, as both case studies show, this process simultaneously exacerbates vulnerabilities for migrants who experience little to no citizenship rights. Those who were marginal or invisible to the benefits of urban development in the past continue to be marginalised and invisibilised in the implementation of climate change actions.

Second, a geographical approach to theorising climate justice calls for a consideration of how cities – particularly marginalised and vulnerable residents – are "doubly exposed" to environmental changes and socio-economic transformations of modern society (Leichenko and O'Brien 2008; Parks and Roberts 2006). Migrant labourers are particularly at the whims of economic transformation (i.e., a heightened preciousness of the poor due to entrenched economic insecurity and informality) and climate change impacts. An analysis into the unjust distribution of infrastructure or the exclusion of vulnerable populations from decision-making must be tied to larger issues of urban entrepreneurialism, the revanchist city, rural land reform, a diminishing social welfare system and the gradual deconstruction of state authorities in modern India. This therefore relates to the shifting interconnections between uncertain climate change risks and experiences of local economic transformations, and speaks to how climate justice scholarship can be better theorised against more foundational concepts in urban and environmental justice.

Finally, our focus on trans-boundary migrants as those experiencing heightened forms of climate and socio-economic injustices highlights how, in reality, vulnerabilities are mobile across space. This therefore requires a more nuanced understanding of the "urban" whereby the politics, processes, actors and resources associated with climate change also span across space (see Hughes, Chu, and Mason 2018). Movement is sometimes forced (i.e., displacement) but other times voluntary. The case studies from Bangalore and Surat illustrate that migration outcomes are largely determined by complex social processes, power dynamics, identity politics and the reorganisation of labour across gender and class lines. Addressing climate change vulnerabilities on a city scale thus calls for due recognition and participation of the expanding unskilled migrant groups in cities, who remain spatially disengaged from broader urban systems and remain excluded from mainstream or formal urban opportunities. As such, theories of climate justice are not only about the actors and the sites of inequality and marginality, but they are also about the flows, exchanges and processes of reconstituting risks and vulnerabilities across space.

Acknowledgments

Research in Surat was supported by the David L. Boren Fellowship of the U.S. National Security Education Program and the MIT Center for International Studies. Research in Bangalore was carried out under the Adaptation at Scale in Semi-Arid Regions (ASSAR) project. ASSAR is one of the five research programmes funded under the Collaborative Adaptation Research Initiative in Africa and Asia (CARIAA), with financial support from the UK Government's Department for International Development (DfID) and the International Development Research Centre (IDRC), Canada.

Notes

1 School of Geography, Earth and Environmental Sciences, University of Birmingham (UK).
2 The Energy and Resources Institute, New Delhi (India).

References

ACCCRN. 2011. *Surat City Resilience Strategy*. Surat, India: Asian Cities Climate Change Resilience Network (ACCCRN) and TARU-Leading Edge.

Anguelovski, Isabelle, Anna Livia Brand, Eric Chu, and Kian Goh. 2018. "Urban Planning, Community (Re)Development, and Environmental Gentrification: Emerging Challenges for Green and Equitable Neighborhoods." In *The Routledge Handbook of Environmental Justice*, edited by Ryan Holifield, Jayajit Chakraborty, and Gordon Walker, 449–462. Oxford: Routledge.

Anguelovski, Isabelle, Eric Chu, and JoAnn Carmin. 2014. "Variations in Approaches to Urban Climate Adaptation: Experiences and Experimentation From the Global South." *Global Environmental Change* 27: 156–167. doi:10.1016/j.gloenvcha.2014.05.010.

Anguelovski, Isabelle, and Joan Martínez Alier. 2014. "The 'Environmentalism of the Poor' Revisited: Territory and Place in Disconnected Glocal Struggles." *Ecological Economics* 102: 167–176. doi:10.1016/j.ecolecon.2014.04.005.

Anguelovski, Isabelle, Linda Shi, Eric Chu, Daniel Gallagher, Kian Goh, Zachary Lamb, Kara Reeve, and Hannah Teicher. 2016. "Equity Impacts of Urban Land Use Planning for Climate Adaptation." *Journal of Planning Education and Research* 36(3): 333–348. doi:10.1177/0739456X16645166.

Archer, Diane, Florencia Almansi, Michael DiGregorio, Debra Roberts, Divya Sharma, and Denia Syam. 2014. "Moving Towards Inclusive Urban Adaptation: Approaches to Integrating Community-Based Adaptation to Climate Change at City and National Scale." *Climate and Development* 6(4): 345–356. doi:10.1080/17565529.2014.918868.

Arora-Jonsson, Seema. 2011. "Virtue and Vulnerability: Discourses on Women, Gender and Climate Change." *Global Environmental Change* 21(2): 744–751. doi:10.1016/j.gloenvcha.2011.01.005.

Basu, Ritwika, and Amir Bazaz. 2016. *Assessing Climate Change Risks and Contextual Vulnerability in Urban Areas of Semi-Arid India: The Case of Bangalore*. CARIAA-ASSAR Working Paper. Ottawa and London.

Beckman, Ludvig, and Edward Page. 2008. "Perspectives on Justice, Democracy and Global Climate Change." *Environmental Politics* 17(4): 527–535. doi:10.1080/09644010802193393.

Benjamin Solomon. 2000. "Governance, Economic Settings and Poverty in Bangalore." *Environment and Urbanization* 12(1): 35–56. doi:10.1177/095624780001200104.

Betsill, Michele M., and Harriet Bulkeley. 2007. "Looking Back and Thinking Ahead: A Decade of Cities and Climate Change Research." *Local Environment* 12(5): 447–456. doi:10.1080/13549830701659683.

Bhagat, R B. 2017. "Migration, Gender and Right to the City." *Economic and Political Weekly* 52(32): 35–40.

Bhat, G K, Anup Karanth, Lalit Dashora, and Umamaheshwaran Rajasekar. 2013. "Addressing Flooding in the City of Surat Beyond Its Boundaries." *Environment and Urbanization* 25(2): 429–441. doi:10.1177/0956247813495002.

Boyce, James K. 2002. *The Political Economy of the Environment*. Cheltenham and Northampton: Edward Elgar Publishers.

Breman, Jan. 2013. *At Work in the Informal Economy of India: A Perspective From the Bottom Up*. New Delhi, India: Oxford University Press.

Brenner, Neil. 2004. *New State Spaces: Urban Governance and the Rescaling of Statehood*. Oxford and New York: Oxford University Press.

Brenner, Neil, and Nik Theodore. 2002. "Cities and the Geographies of 'Actually Existing Neoliberalism'." *Antipode* 34(3): 349–379. doi:10.1111/1467-8330.00246.

Brown, Anna, Ashvin Dayal, and Cristina Rumbaitis Del Rio. 2012. "From Practice to Theory: Emerging Lessons From Asia for Building Urban Climate Change Resilience." *Environment and Urbanization* 24(2): 531–556. doi:10.1177/0956247812456490.

Bulkeley, Harriet, and Michele M. Betsill. 2005. *Cities and Climate Change: Urban Sustainability and Global Environmental Governance.* London and New York: Routledge.

Bulkeley, Harriet, JoAnn Carmin, Vanesa Castán Broto, Gareth A. S. Edwards, and Sara Fuller. 2013. "Climate Justice and Global Cities: Mapping the Emerging Discourses." *Global Environmental Change* 23(5): 914–925. doi:10.1016/j.gloenvcha.2013.05.010.

Bulkeley, Harriet, Vanesa Castán Broto, and Gareth A. S. Edwards. 2015. *An Urban Politics of Climate Change: Experimentation and the Governing of Socio-Technical Transitions.* New York and London: Routledge.

Caney, Simon. 2014. "Two Kinds of Climate Justice: Avoiding Harm and Sharing Burdens." *Journal of Political Philosophy* 22(2): 125–149. doi:10.1111/jopp.12030.

Chandrasekhar, S, and Ajay Sharma. 2014. *Internal Migration for Education and Employment Among Youth in India.* Working Paper-2014-004 Mumbai: Indira Gandhi Institute of Development Research.

Chibber, Vivek. 2003. *Locked in Place: State-Building and Late Industrialization in India.* Princeton and Oxford: Oxford University Press.

Chu, Eric. 2016a. "The Political Economy of Urban Climate Adaptation and Development Planning in Surat, India." *Environment and Planning C: Government and Policy* 34(2): 281–298. doi:10.1177/0263774X15614174.

Chu, Eric. 2016b. "The Governance of Climate Change Adaptation Through Urban Policy Experiments." *Environmental Policy and Governance* 26(6): 439–451. doi:10.1002/eet.1727.

Chu, Eric, Isabelle Anguelovski, and JoAnn Carmin. 2016. "Inclusive Approaches to Urban Climate Adaptation Planning and Implementation in the Global South." *Climate Policy* 16(3): 372–392. doi:10.1080/14693062.2015.1019822.

Chu, Eric, Todd Schenk, and James Patterson. 2018. "The Dilemmas of Citizen Inclusion in Urban Planning and Governance to Enable a 1.5 °C Climate Change Scenario." *Urban Planning* 3(2): 128–140. doi:10.17645/up.v3i2.1292.

Ciplet, David, J. Timmons Roberts, and Mizan Khan. 2015. *Power in a Warming World: The New Global Politics of Climate Change and the Remaking of Environmental Inequality.* Cambridge, MA: MIT Press.

Cook, Mitchell J., and Eric K. Chu. 2018. "Between Policies, Programs, and Projects: How Local Actors Steer Domestic Urban Climate Adaptation Finance in India." In *Climate Change in Cities: Innovations in Multi-Level Governance,* edited by Sara Hughes, Eric Chu, and Susan Mason, 255–277. Cham, Switzerland: Springer. doi:10.1007/978-3-319-65003-6_13.

Corbridge, Stuart, John Harriss, and Craig Jeffrey. 2013. *India Today: Economy, Politics and Society.* Malden and Cambridge: Polity Press.

Desai, Renu, and Romola Sanyal, eds. 2012. *Urbanizing Citizenship: Contested Spaces in Indian Cities.* New Delhi, India: Sage Publications.

Deshingkar, Priya. 2004. *Understanding the Implications of Migration for Pro-Poor Agricultural Growth.* London: Overseas Development Institute.

Faist, Thomas, and Jeanette Schade, eds. 2013. *Disentangling Migration and Climate Change.* Dordrecht: Springer Netherlands. doi:10.1007/978-94-007-6208-4.

Fernandes, Leela. 2004. "The Politics of Forgetting: Class Politics, State Power and the Restructuring of Urban Space in India." *Urban Studies* 41(12): 2415–2430. doi:10.1080/00420980412331297609.

Fisher, Susannah. 2015. "The Emerging Geographies of Climate Justice." *The Geographical Journal* 181(1): 73–82. doi:10.1111/geoj.12078.

Folbre, Nancy. 2002. *The Invisible Heart: Economics and Family Values.* New York: New Press.

Goldman, Michael. 2011. "Speculative Urbanism and the Making of the Next World City." *International Journal of Urban and Regional Research* 35(3): 555–581. doi:10.1111/j.1468-2427.2010.01001.x.

Gururani, Shubhra, and Rajarshi Dasgupta. 2018. "Frontier Urbanism: Urbanisation Beyond Cities in South Asia." *Economic and Political Weekly* 53(12): 41–45.

Harris, Leila M., Eric K. Chu, and Gina Ziervogel. 2017. "Negotiated Resilience." *Resilience,* July. Routledge, 1–19. doi:10.1080/21693293.2017.1353196.

Harvey, David. 1989. "From Managerialism to Entrepreneurialism: The Transformation in Urban Governance in Late Capitalism." *Geografiska Annaler* 71(1): 3–17.

Heynen, Nik. 2013. "Urban Political Ecology I: The Urban Century." *Progress in Human Geography* 38(4): 598–604. doi:10.1177/0309132513500443.

Hughes, Sara. 2013. "Justice in Urban Climate Change Adaptation: Criteria and Application to Delhi." *Ecology and Society* 18(4): 48. doi:10.5751/ES-05929-180448.

Hughes, Sara, Eric K. Chu, and Susan G. Mason, eds. 2018. *Climate Change in Cities: Innovations in Multi-Level Governance.* The Urban Book Series. Cham, Switzerland: Springer. doi:10.1007/978-3-319-65003-6.

Hunter, Lori M., Jessie K. Luna, and Rachel M. Norton. 2015. "Environmental Dimensions of Migration." *Annual Review of Sociology* 41(1): 377–397. doi:10.1146/annurev-soc-073014-112223.

IPCC. 2014. *Climate Change 2014: Impacts, Adaptation, and Vulnerability. Contribution of Working Group II to the Fifth Assessment Report of the Intergovernmental Panel on Climate Change.* Edited by C. B. Field, V. R. Barros, D. J. Dokken, K. J. Mach, M. D. Mastrandrea, T. E. Bilir, M. Chatterjee, et al. Cambridge and New York: Cambridge University Press.

ISET. 2010. *The Shared Learning Dialogue: Building Stakeholder Capacity and Engagement for Climate Resilience Action.* Climate Resilience in Concept and Practice Working Paper Series. Boulder: Institute for Social and Environmental Transition.

Kavi Kumar, K S, and Brinda Viswanathan. 2013. "Influence of Weather on Temporary and Permanent Migration in Rural India." *Climate Change Economics* 4(2): 1350007. doi:10.1142/S2010007813500073.

Leichenko, Robin M., and Karen L. O'Brien. 2008. *Environmental Change and Globalization: Double Exposures.* Oxford and New York: Oxford University Press.

MacGregor, Sherilyn. 2010. "A Stranger Silence Still: The Need for Feminist Social Research on Climate Change." *The Sociological Review* 57(SUPPL. 2): 124–140. doi:10.1111/j.1467-954X.2010.01889.x.

Meerow, Sara, and Joshua P. Newell. 2016. "Urban Resilience for Whom, What, When, Where, and Why?" *Urban Geography*: 1–21. doi:10.1080/02723638.2016.1206395.

Meerow, Sara, Joshua P. Newell, and Melissa Stults. 2016. "Defining Urban Resilience: A Review." *Landscape and Urban Planning* 147: 38–49. doi:10.1016/j.landurbplan.2015.11.011.

Michael, Kavya, Tanvi Deshpande, and Gina Ziervogel. 2017. "Examining Vulnerability in a Dynamic Urban Setting: The Case of Bangalore's Interstate Migrant Waste Pickers." *SSRN Electronic Journal* id2924375: 1–19. doi:10.2139/ssrn.2924375.

Miraftab, Faranak. 2004. "Public-Private Partnerships: The Trojan Horse of Neoliberal Development?" *Journal of Planning Education and Research* 24(1): 89–101. doi:10.1177/0739456X04267173.

Moench, Marcus, Stephen Tyler, and Jessica Lage, eds. 2011. *Catalyzing Urban Climate Resilience: Applying Resilience Concepts to Planning Practice in the ACCCRN Program (2009–2011).* Boulder: Institute for Social and Environmental Transition (ISET).

Mukhopadhyay, Partha, and Aromar Revi. 2012. "Climate Change and Urbanization in India." In *Handbook of Climate Change and India: Development, Politics and Governance,* edited by Navroz K. Dubash, 303–316. London and New York: Earthscan.

Parks, Bradley C., and J. Timmons Roberts. 2006. "Globalization, Vulnerability to Climate Change, and Perceived Injustice." *Society & Natural Resources* 19(4): 337–355. doi:10.1080/08941920500519255.

Parks, Bradley C., and J. Timmons Roberts. 2010. "Climate Change, Social Theory and Justice." *Theory, Culture & Society* 27(2–3): 134–166. doi:10.1177/0263276409359018.

Pearsall, Hamil. 2012. "Moving Out or Moving in? Resilience to Environmental Gentrification in New York City." *Local Environment* 17(9): 1013–1026. doi:10.1080/13549839.2012.714762.

Pelling, Mark. 2010. *Adaptation to Climate Change: From Resilience to Transformation.* London and New York: Routledge.

Rao, Smriti. 2017. "Women and the Urban Economy in India: Insights From the Data on Migration." In *Gender and Time Use in a Global Context: The Economics of Employment and Unpaid Labor,* edited by Rachel Connelly and Ebru Kongar, 231–257. New York: Palgrave Macmillan US. doi:10.1057/978-1-137-56837-3_9.

Rao, Smriti, and Vamsi Vakulabharanam. 2018. "Migration, Crises and Social Transformation in India Since the 1990s." In *Handbook of Migration Crises,* edited by Cecilia Menjivar, Marie Ruiz, and Immanuel Ness. Oxford: Oxford University Press.

Razavi, Shahra. 2007. *The Political and Social Economy of Care in a Development Context: Conceptual Issues, Research Questions and Policy Options.* Paper Number 3. Gender and Development Programme, Geneva.

Revi, Aromar. 2008. "Climate Change Risk: An Adaptation and Mitigation Agenda for Indian Cities." *Environment and Urbanization* 20(1): 207–229. doi:10.1177/0956247808089157.

Roy, Ananya. 2016. "What Is Urban About Critical Urban Theory?" *Urban Geography* 37(6): 810–823. doi:10.1080/02723638.2015.1105485.

Satterthwaite, David, and Cecilia Tacoli. 2002. "Seeking an Understanding of Poverty that Recognizes Rural – Urban Differences and Rural – Urban Linkages." In *Urban Livelihoods: A People-Centred Approach to Reducing Poverty,* edited by Tony Lloyd-Jones and Carole Rakodi, 52–70. London: Routledge.

Scheffran, Jürgen, Elina Marmer, and Papa Sow. 2012. "Migration as a Contribution to Resilience and Innovation in Climate Adaptation: Social Networks and Co-Development in Northwest Africa." *Applied Geography* 33: 119–127.

Schlosberg, David. 2012. "Climate Justice and Capabilities: A Framework for Adaptation Policy." *Ethics & International Affairs* 26(4): 445–461. doi:10.1017/S0892679412000615.

Sharma, Divya, Raina Singh, and Rozita Singh. 2014. "Building Urban Climate Resilience: Learning From the ACCCRN Experience in India." *International Journal of Urban Sustainable Development* 6(2): 133–153. doi:10.1080/19463138.2014.937720.

Shi, Linda, Eric Chu, Isabelle Anguelovski, Alexander Aylett, Jessica Debats, Kian Goh, Todd Schenk, et al. 2016. "Roadmap Towards Justice in Urban Climate Adaptation Research." *Nature Climate Change* 6(2): 131–137. doi:10.1038/nclimate2841.

Shrivastava, Aseem, and Ashish Kothari. 2012. *Churning the Earth: The Making of Global India.* New York: Penguin.

Smith, Neil. 2002. "New Globalism, New Urbanism: Gentrification as Global Urban Strategy." *Antipode* 34(3): 427–450. doi:10.1111/1467-8330.00249.

Sovacool, Benjamin K., Björn-Ola Linnér, and Michael E. Goodsite. 2015. "The Political Economy of Climate Adaptation." *Nature Climate Change* 5(7): 616–618. doi:10.1038/nclimate2665.

Swyngedouw, Erik, and Nikolas C Heynen. 2003. "Urban Political Ecology, Justice and the Politics of Scale." *Antipode* 35(5): 898–918. doi:10.1111/j.1467-8330.2003.00364.x.

Terry, Geraldine. 2009. "No Climate Justice Without Gender Justice: An Overview of the Issues." *Gender & Development* 17(1): 5–18. doi:10.1080/13552070802696839.

Vakulabharanam, Vamsi, and Sripad Motiram. 2012. "Understanding Poverty and Inequality in Urban India Since Reforms: Bringing Quantitative and Qualitative Approaches Together." *Economic and Political Weekly* 47(47/48): 44–52.

Vale, Lawrence J. 2014. "The Politics of Resilient Cities: Whose Resilience and Whose City?" *Building Research & Information* 42(2): 191–201. doi:10.1080/09613218.2014.850602.

Viswanathan, Brinda, and K S Kavi Kumar. 2015. "Weather, Agriculture and Rural Migration: Evidence From State and District Level Migration in India." *Environment and Development Economics* 20(4): 469–492. doi:10.1017/S1355770X1500008X.

Walker, Gordon. 2012. *Environmental Justice: Concepts, Evidence and Politics.* London and New York: Routledge. doi:10.4324/9780203610671.

Watson, Vanessa. 2009. "'The Planned City Sweeps the Poor Away . . .': Urban Planning and 21st Century Urbanisation." *Progress in Planning* 72(3): 151–193. doi:10.1016/j.progress.2009.06.002.

Whitehead, Mark. 2013. "Neoliberal Urban Environmentalism and the Adaptive City: Towards a Critical Urban Theory and Climate Change." *Urban Studies* 50(7): 1348–1367. doi:10.1177/0042098013480965.

Ziervogel, Gina, Mark Pelling, Anton Cartwright, Eric Chu, Tanvi Deshpande, Leila Harris, Keith Hyams, et al. 2017. "Inserting Rights and Justice Into Urban Resilience: A Focus on Everyday Risk." *Environment and Urbanization* 29(1): 123–138. doi:10.1177/0956247816686905.

24

Fair for whom? How residents and municipalities evaluate sea-level rise policies in Botany Bay, Australia

Anne Maree Kreller and Sonia Graham

Introduction

Increased coastal flooding, resulting from sea-level rise (SLR) and stronger tropical storms, is one of the most certain impacts of climate change (Clark et al., 2016). Such coastal hazards are concerning because 10% of the world's population and 13% of the world's urban population live in the low-elevation coastal zone – the contiguous and hydrologically connected area along the coast less than 10 meters above sea level (McGranahan et al., 2007). The urban population is particularly prone to coastal disasters because of high and increasing urban population densities, which place a concentration of infrastructure at risk (Neumann et al., 2015) and degrade ecosystem services that could otherwise ameliorate some of the impacts of climate change (McGranahan et al., 2007). Thus, urban policymakers face the considerable challenge of developing climate-resilient cities that meet the economic, environmental and social needs of their populations (Kamal-Chaoui, 2008).

The emerging climate justice literature argues that it is not enough for adaptation policies to accommodate the diverse values and priorities of permanent and temporary residents; policymakers need to explicitly consider whether adaptation processes and outcomes are fair (Bulkeley et al., 2013; Hughes, 2013). This involves designing and implementing adaptation processes that engage and mobilise citizens, give a voice to marginalised people in adaptation decision-making (Hughes, 2013) and ensure that the most vulnerable urban populations are not rendered more vulnerable through adaptation actions (Adger et al., 2006; Hughes, 2013; Forsyth, 2014; Zografos et al., 2016). Now is an ideal time to evaluate the integration of justice principles into climate adaptation planning because many urban adaptation plans are in their infancy. While growing numbers of municipalities have or are developing adaptation plans, few have taken action and rarely consider justice in planning (Bulkeley et al., 2013; Araos et al., 2016). Studying nascent SLR adaptation efforts provides an excellent opportunity to observe how concepts of justice are incorporated into adaptation plans and whether such plans are evaluated as fair by communities so as to inform plans before implementation.

In recent years, researchers have begun investigating how adaptation occurs at local scales, with some focusing on how municipalities include fairness considerations into their adaptation planning (e.g., Hughes, 2013; McManus et al., 2014; Chu et al., 2016; Graham and Barnett, 2017). Yet such studies are predominantly situated in regional coastal areas, rather than cities, or in developing, rather than developed, countries (for a notable exception, see the evaluation of 75 climate adaptation initiatives in global cities by Bulkeley et al., 2013). There is also little explicit consideration of how urban residents evaluate the fairness of adaptation policies. When residents have been asked to evaluate adaptation policies, the methods have involved qualitative interviews with small sample sizes, often with fewer than 20 interviewees per place (e.g., McManus et al., 2014; Graham et al., 2015).

To address these gaps, this study aimed to investigate: (1) how two Australian local councils with vulnerable urban coastal communities explicitly or implicitly incorporated fairness into SLR adaptation policies; and (2) how residents evaluated the fairness of council policies. The following sections explain how fairness was conceptualised, how the research was undertaken, the key findings and how the results expand our understandings of urban climate justice.

Justice and fairness in urban climate adaptation

Discourses about justice and fairness are increasingly prominent in climate change research and management. Much of the climate justice scholarship focuses on the global scale of governance and involves attributing responsibility for mitigating emissions (Adger et al., 2006; Paavola and Adger, 2006) and paying for adaptation efforts (Bulkeley et al., 2013). There has been growing interest in how climate justice applies at the local scale, where adaptation policies are being designed and implemented. It is at the local scale that the concept of fairness has emerged as distinct from justice. For example, Grasso (2007) argues that justice principles are those that apply independently of any personal or interpersonal judgement process, while fairness relates to individual-level evaluations of a process or outcome. In this chapter we use the term *fairness* because we are interested in staff and residents' personal evaluations of SLR adaptation planning.

The emerging body of urban climate justice research has focused on justice principles rather than individual-level evaluations of fairness. For example, Bulkeley et al. (2013) explored the extent to which distributive and procedural justice principles were evident in 627 mitigation and adaptation initiatives in global cities. Hughes (2013) described four mechanisms – thick injustice, the political economy of poverty, technocratic governance and institutional capacities – that contribute to injustices in cities and how they apply in Delhi, India. Whilst these are important studies, research on coastal adaptation planning suggests that it is also important to consider personal perspectives of fairness. For example, Schlosberg et al. (2017) engaged with residents of the City of Sydney council to assess their perspectives on the processes and impacts of climate change for the purposes of designing a fair adaptation policy. They found communities are interested in addressing social justice concerns through adaptation by enhancing the basic capabilities of vulnerable urban residents. We aim to build on the work by Schlosberg et al. (2017) by focusing on perspectives of fairness of vulnerable urban residents in another part of Sydney.

There are six dimensions of fairness – distributive, procedural, interpersonal, informational, spatial and temporal – that have been identified as important in climate adaptation research largely beyond the urban sphere. These six dimensions of fairness have been defined elsewhere (see Graham et al., 2015), so here we focus on how these dimensions of fairness have been found to differ when considered from the perspectives of local adaptation policymakers compared to their constituents.

The two dimensions that have received the most attention are distributive and procedural fairness. Distributional fairness involves evaluations of the *distribution* of costs and benefits of adaptation. From the perspectives of decision-makers, distributive fairness involves analysing who will bear the burdens of climate change and what kind of assistance can be offered to offset these burdens (Bulkeley et al., 2013). For SLR, this involves considering the impact of flooding on property prices but also impacts to livelihoods and sense of community (Graham and Barnett, 2017). From the perspective of communities, distributive fairness is about whether adaptation policy decision-makers recognise the varied and localised impacts of climate change on their everyday lives (Padawangi, 2012; Graham et al., 2015). Residents recognise that fair policies need to address different types of vulnerability, determined by both social disadvantage and exposure to climate risks, like SLR (McManus et al., 2014).

Procedural fairness involves evaluations of the adaptation *process*. Decision-makers are interested in ensuring that all interest groups are represented in adaptation decision-making, that citizens are engaged, empowered and mobilised (Bulkeley et al., 2013; Hamin et al., 2014; Graham and Barnett, 2017). Studies are finding that decision-makers are struggling to engage local communities because residents don't believe climate change is occurring (Graham and Barnett, 2017), and denying the risks can underscore why private property interests oppose taking action now (Hamin et al., 2014). From the perspectives of citizens, procedural fairness not only means being involved in transparent decision-making processes (McManus et al., 2014) and being able to voice their opinions, as per the "voice effect" (Lind et al., 1990), but seeing their contributions integrated into final adaptation plans (McManus et al., 2014; Graham et al., 2015).

Closely related to procedural fairness are the concepts of interpersonal and informational fairness. These concepts relate to the perceptions of behaviour during decisions and procedures, such as politeness and respectful interactions between parties (Usmani and Jamal, 2013) and exchanging information (Lukasiewicz et al., 2013). While some authors consider these two types of fairness to be subtypes of interactional fairness, we follow Graham and Barnett (2017) in treating them separately.

Interpersonal fairness relates to being treated with dignity and respect, and is consistent with the "dignitary process" effect described in social psychology research (Lind and Earley, 1992). From the perspective of decision-makers, interpersonal fairness is about establishing mutual trust with citizens (Graham and Barnett, 2017). Not only do decision-makers want residents to trust them, but they also want residents to respect them during difficult decision-making (Graham and Barnett, 2017). From the perspective of citizens, interpersonal fairness involves being engaged with honestly and directly by governments on matters that affect their community and feeling that the time that they dedicate to community engagement processes is valued (Graham et al., 2015).

The legitimacy of SLR adaptation policies may be undermined by uncertainty about the future effects, which can be addressed by assessing informational fairness. This concept is generally understood as the exchange of information between parties during decisions (Usmani and Jamal, 2013). For local government decision-makers, informational fairness is as much about getting high-quality and timely information from upper tiers of governments and scientists, as being careful about sharing information with communities so that it doesn't cause unnecessary concern about SLR impacts (Hamin et al., 2014; Graham and Barnett, 2017). For local communities, informational fairness is not only about being provided with information and explanations about climate change predictions and plans, but also knowing who to talk to in council to obtain such information (Graham et al., 2015).

The impacts of SLR will worsen over time, and questions arise about which generations will bear the costs of adaptation. Temporal fairness is about the speed with which adaptation decisions and plans are implemented (Burton et al., 2002) as well as considering fairness across generations (Adger and Nelson, 2010). In past coastal research, adaptation decision-makers have expressed concern about how to make decisions for the future while they only have information about current conditions (Hamin et al., 2014). Communities are also seeking assurances that they won't be forced to bear the burden of adapting to future climate changes that they may not experience in their lifetime (Graham et al., 2015). The pathways approach to adaptation has evolved partly to address these concerns by decision-makers and communities, so that decisions can be made at a pace that is commensurate with environmental and social changes (Barnett et al., 2014; Fincher et al., 2015; Abel et al., 2016).

SLR is not experienced equally across the globe, meaning the burden of decision-making falls on some local communities more than others. Spatial fairness is about ensuring that access to socially valued resources is equitable across space (Shi et al., 2016), but decision-makers and residents may have different ideas about this concept. From the perspective of policymakers, spatial fairness is about ensuring that adaptation plans are designed to meet the needs of geographically diverse communities as well as ensuring that vulnerable people are not worse off (Graham and Barnett, 2017). Regional communities want assurances that they will be treated commensurately with urban centres (Graham et al., 2015).

The discussion of the six dimensions of fairness above draws heavily on a small number of qualitative studies based in regional urban areas. We seek to extend this current understanding of fair adaptation through a mixed-methods case study based in a large coastal city. In doing so, we are also making a methodological contribution, by developing and testing a survey instrument that operationalises these key concepts from the perspectives of vulnerable residents.

The physical and social vulnerability of Botany Bay, Australia

If adaptation policies are to put the most vulnerable first (Paavola and Adger, 2006), then it is necessary to identify and work with vulnerable populations. In 2008, the Sydney Coastal Councils Group (SCCG) – a collective of ten coastal councils – partnered with scientists to map climate change vulnerability in the Sydney Region. The project revealed that the area most physically and socially vulnerable to SLR is the region encompassed by the City of Botany Bay and Rockdale City Council boundaries (Preston et al., 2008), otherwise known as Botany Bay. Here we explain how the bay's morphology, urban development and institutional history have enabled these vulnerabilities to evolve.

Botany Bay is a marine estuary system 13 kilometers south of the Sydney central business district, with a population of just over 156,000 people (ABS, 2016). Botany Bay is highly urbanised and subject to intense industrial development along the foreshore, such as an oil refinery, working port and Sydney Airport. The bay is subject to vigorous wave activity, erosion and flooding (Frost, 2011; Brakell et al., 2012), and construction of groynes along the foreshore have had little effect on coastal erosion, which has been attributed to changing hydrodynamics in the bay (Frost, 2011). Thus, urban development in Botany Bay is highly vulnerable to storm surges and SLR, despite protective coastal policies.

Botany Bay is also socially vulnerable to SLR. Preston et al. (2008) found that Botany Bay has a lower adaptive capacity compared to other regions in Sydney because of lower levels of household income, available financial resources, education and internet access, and higher proportions of people who speak languages other than English.

There are also institutional barriers to SLR adaptation in Botany Bay. Until September 2016 Botany Bay was managed by two local councils, City of Botany Bay (Botany) and Rockdale Council (Rockdale). Rockdale engaged in limited community consultation, asking if residents were satisfied with council management of SLR, but did not formulate an adaptation policy (Rockdale City Council, 2013). Botany had an SLR policy with no evidence of community input (City of Botany Bay Council, 2015). In September 2016, just after data collection ended, the two councils amalgamated to form a large coastal council called Bayside Council. At present, no new SLR policy or process has been released. Furthermore, in November 2016, the NSW state planning authority released plans for the Bayside West Precincts – a large residential and commercial development in Rockdale Council, which included development along the Cooks River foreshore (NSW Department of Planning and Environment, 2016), a major tributary discharging into the bay. At the time of writing, SLR was not taken into consideration for development plans.

Methods

An online questionnaire was developed for Botany and Rockdale residents. The survey included 16 statements designed to elicit residents' perspectives on the six dimensions of fairness (Figure 24.1). Question wording was based on past survey research on climate and environmental fairness. The statements relating to distributive fairness and community consultation were adapted from Graham's (2002) study of attitudes towards environmental flows, and the statements on transparency and clarity are consistent with McManus et al.'s (2014) study of equity in climate adaptation. Where we could not find survey questions from a climate or environmental policy context, we looked to other fields of research that have operationalised these dimensions of fairness. The statements relating to being heard (procedural fairness), being treated with respect (interpersonal fairness) and being offered explanations that make sense and clearly explained policy decisions (informational fairness) were adapted from Usmani and Jamal's (2013) study on job satisfaction. Questions about temporal and spatial fairness were derived from Graham et al.'s (2015) qualitative study about fair adaptation in coastal Victoria, Australia. Responses to the 16 statements were provided on a Likert scale – strongly agree, agree, neutral, disagree, strongly disagree – as per Graham (2002) and Usmani and Jamal (2013). We also included a "don't know" option because McManus et al. (2014) found that many interviewees were unsure or couldn't answer questions about whether climate change responses were fair.

The survey also asked questions about residents' beliefs about SLR, specifically whether they are concerned about it, whether they perceive it to be a local problem and the timescale at which it will be problematic (questions adapted from Hine et al., 2013). These questions were asked because past research has found that decision-makers find it hard to engage with communities who do not believe climate change is happening (e.g., Hamin et al., 2014; Graham and Barnett, 2017). Demographic questions were also included to evaluate the representativeness of the sample.

A pilot survey was distributed to check the question wording as well as the reliability and credibility of the data obtained. Feedback was incorporated prior to administering the questionnaire. Ethical approval for the survey was obtained from the UNSW Human Research Ethics committee. The survey was open between 20 May and 14 July 2016. The survey was advertised by contacting publicly listed community groups and local political organisations, residents of the two council areas through Facebook advertising and via an article about the study published in the local newspaper, *The St George Leader.*

A guide was formulated for the semi-structured interviews with council staff. Council staff at both councils who had a role in adaptation planning and consultation were invited to participate in the study, and four staff agreed to be interviewed. Interview questions asked staff about their roles in council and the way in which the councils undertake planning and consultation processes in general, and specifically for SLR. Questions were designed to cover the various dimensions of fairness (see Kreller 2016 for questions). Interviews were digitally recorded, transcribed, de-identified and uploaded to NVivo qualitative data analysis software. Data analysis involved a combination of thematic analysis and iterative categorisation (Braun and Clarke, 2006; Neale, 2016). The text was read to identify words and phrases relating to the dimensions of fairness. Nodes relating to the six dimensions were created, and then inductive coding allowed for

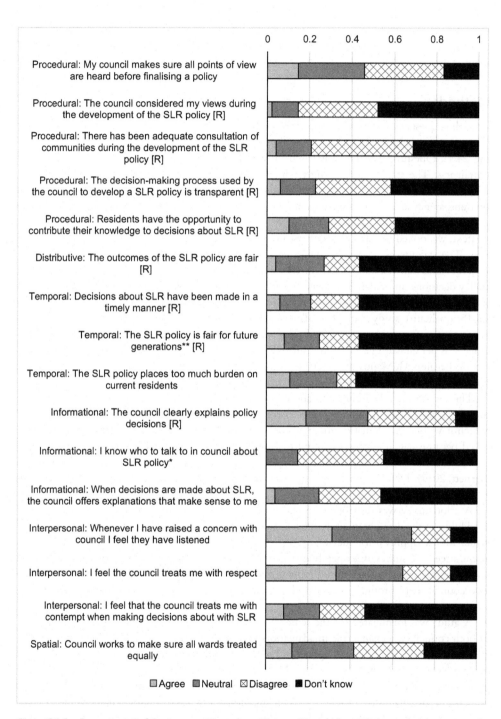

Figure 24.1 Responses to fairness questions (n = 48, *n = 47 and **n = 45 due to non-responses). [R] indicates that all the respondents who agreed with a statement were from Rockdale.

discovery of additional nuances in the data. Because of the sensitive nature of the information discussed, participants' identities and roles in council have been de-identified.

Results

Overall, 49 residents living around Botany Bay responded to the survey: nine from Botany and 40 from Rockdale. This is comparable to the 42 survey responses that McManus et al. (2014) received in their study of fair adaptation in Lake Macquarie, Australia. Given the small sample size, we present the results for the whole sample, but identify where there were differences between residents in the two councils.

The sample was comparable to the demographics of the Botany Bay region with respect to household income, home ownership, gender, people aged 18–24 years of age, those aged between 35 and 44, and those over 65 (Table 24.1). The sample was over-represented by residents who

Table 24.1 Demographic comparison between respondents and Botany Bay region.

	Survey respondents	Botany Bay region[a]
Gender		
Female	53%	50%
Male	47%	50%
Age range		
18–24	10%	8%
25–34	10%	19%
35–44	14%	15%
45–54	31%	12%
55–64	24%	10%
65+	10%	14%
Education		
Bachelor degree level and above	40%	27%
TAFE or other vocational certificate	44%	20%
Year 12 or equivalent	8%	20%
Year 11 or equivalent	2%	3%
Year 10 or below	4%	16%
Language		
English only at home	78%	43%
More than one language	22%	54%
Housing status		
Owned outright	33%	27%
Buying with a mortgage	44%	29%
Renting and rent free	23%	40%
Annual household income		
Nil to $40,000	16%	Median household
$40,001 to $80,000	31%	incomes were $81,744
$80,001 to $150,000	22%	and $84,522 for Rockdale
Over $150,000	29%	and Botany, respectively.

[a] ABS (2016)

hold university and secondary technical qualifications. Around 2.2% of people living around Botany Bay identify as indigenous, whereas no respondents identified as such. The sample was over-represented by native English speakers and established residents between 45 and 64 years of age. This suggests that the sample may not reflect the most vulnerable residents of Botany Bay and that further efforts are required to elicit their perspectives.

Beliefs about SLR

Over half (55%) of the sample were very or fairly personally concerned about SLR (Table 24.2). A similar proportion (57%) believed SLR will have somewhat or very serious effects on Botany Bay. Almost half (47%) believe the effects are already being felt or will be felt within the next 10 years.

Fair adaptation policy

Responses to questions about fairness showed some consistent views across the sample. When asked about *procedural* fairness, almost half (48%) the respondents disagreed that there was adequate consultation of the community (Figure 24.1). Only one-sixth (15%) of the sample agreed with the statement that council ensures all points of view are heard before finalising policy. For the three remaining statements about procedural fairness, about two-fifths of respondents indicated that they did not know whether their views were considered by council (48%), whether residents had had an opportunity to contribute their knowledge to decisions about SLR (40%), or whether the process their council used to develop SLR policy is transparent (42%). Those that did know were more likely to perceive the process to be unfair, than fair.

When asked about *informational* fairness, no respondent agreed that they know who to talk to about the issue in council. Likewise, only two people agreed with the statement that decisions about SLR make sense to them, and only one-fifth (19%) agreed that council clearly explains policy.

Table 24.2 Percentage of Botany Bay respondents' beliefs about SLR (n = 49).

Considering the personal effects of SLR	
Very concerned	22% (11)
Fairly concerned	33% (16)
Not very concerned	29% (14)
Not at all concerned	10% (5)
Don't know	4% (2)
No opinion	2% (1)
Considering the effects of SLR on Botany Bay	
Very serious	57% (28)
Somewhat serious	29% (14)
Not so serious	8% (4)
Not serious at all	6% (3)
When will Botany Bay feel the effects of SLR?	
We are already feeling the effects	22% (11)
Within the next 10 years	24% (12)
Within the next 25 years	5% (10)
50 years+	20% (10)
Never	4% (2)
Don't know	18% (9)

Of all the fairness statements, residents were most likely to perceive that the council achieved *interpersonal* fairness. About one-third of residents agreed that they feel that council has listened when they raised concerns (31%) and that council treats them with respect (33%). Over half (53%) of respondents don't know if council treats them with contempt.

The most frequent response to questions about distributional and temporal fairness was "don't know." The majority (56%) of the sample did not know if the outcomes of the SLR policy are fair (*distributional*); whether the policy is fair for future generations (56%); if decisions are being made in a timely manner (56%); or if the policy places burden on current residents (58%) (*temporal*).

Botany residents were less likely than Rockdale residents to agree to the fairness statements. None of the Botany residents agreed to eight of the procedural, distributive and temporal fairness statements (Figure 24.1).

Qualitative interviews with council adaptation staff

Council staff discussed a range of concerns about how to engage with their communities. In doing so, they primarily focused on procedural, informational and temporal dimensions of community engagement. There was limited discussion of interpersonal relationships with individual community members or spatial or distributive fairness. The following sections explain how the six dimensions of fairness emerged in the interviews.

Distributional

Staff in both councils acknowledged that the impacts of SLR, storm surges and flooding are experienced by a small number of residential homes around Botany Bay: "There are not a huge number of houses in Rockdale that would be impacted by sea-level rise. . . . There are less than 100 really I think from memory . . . that is potentially severe for small areas for a small number of people," so the impacts of SLR were seen to be spatially constrained. There was no consideration of the socio-economic characteristics of the people likely to be directly affected. In Rockdale, there was some acknowledgement that a larger number of people will be affected by other coastal hazards, such as storms. Staff indicated that their resources were being invested in climate change problems that have a "more severe effect on a greater number of people than sea-level rise." Thus distributional impacts were used to evaluate where to invest climate adaptation resources.

Procedural

Each council had a unique approach to community engagement. In Rockdale, the emphasis was on creating a range of fora that enable community members to identify what they collectively need council to provide as well as for council to inform the community of what they are doing. For example, the council has a Mayoral forum every six months to enable the community to ask questions and have them answered: "That is a genuine attempt to allow that discussion." The staff are proactive about identifying community needs through their Youth Council, precinct committees and by "monitor[ing] social media, the papers, the community networks." They organise a range of activities – focus groups, monthly workshops and online surveys – to explore current issues and how they can be addressed. For SLR, they had a meeting with residents to ask for their opinions about the issue, but found it difficult to "pin-point adaptation actions." Thus, although there is no SLR policy in Rockdale, there is an emphasis on engaging with groups within the community to jointly develop plans.

Botany had a more individualistic approach to engagement. For example, they delivered brochures to all residents about their Local Environmental Plan and invited individual submissions, of which they only received 20. They occasionally run workshops and exhibitions but do not have any precinct committees. In the case of SLR, the decision to include information about SLR on property titles (known as a Section 149 Certificate, which contains information about restrictions on development that may apply to a property) was advertised in the local paper, at the library and on the council website. Individuals were expected to independently find and respond to the information. As a result, they only had one submission about the proposed policy. Staff acknowledged that individuals are likely to find out about the policy when they lodge a development application and are told that they need to take SLR into account.

Common to both councils was concern about how to ensure that a diversity of interests are included in local government planning. At Rockdale, staff acknowledged that community engagement is "about democracy," and even though they use various methods to reach different groups within the community, they find it "hard to get a good cross section [of the community]." In part, this is because "You always have a group of 50 people who are involved in everything council does. How do you talk to other people?" To address this challenge they have started using an independent recruitment agency to engage with diverse groups and reach communities with language barriers who may be trying to establish themselves in a new country.

In Botany, the staff were concerned about the lack of engagement by their residents and that the small number who do make submissions are the same "couple of people who always write in." They compared the number of submissions they received with other councils and suggested that Botany is a "lethargic community" that has low levels of engagement because of the socio-economic characteristics of the community. The benefit of having so few submissions meant that the local government could introduce SLR reforms that other councils avoided because of actual or potential community opposition.

Interpersonal

All staff briefly discussed their personal interactions with residents, and in Rockdale both staff emphasised the importance of managing community emotions. At Rockdale staff recognised that community engagement is about "people having a voice" and that trust needs to be built by showing them that the information they provide is used by council. They acknowledged that part of giving residents a voice means understanding that there need to be avenues for residents to express their concerns and frustrations with council.

Informational

Staff of both councils discussed sharing information, in the context of developing SLR flood risk maps with the SCCG as well as sharing that information with their communities. In Rockdale a decision had been made not to make it public. In Botany, "We adopted a policy late last year. It [the policy] is on our website along with the maps that have been done by the SCCG." In both cases, staff identified that they had obtained legal advice about releasing the maps on their websites. The legal advice pertained to their duty of care to release information to the public about coastal hazards.

Aside from deliberations about whether to make SLR risk maps available to the public online, staff discussed legislative requirements to inform communities about flood risks. More generally, in Rockdale staff mentioned a "statutory requirement within that flood modelling process to inform the community. They have to do community information and consultation . . . [but] they have not got around in doing that yet." Similarly, in Botany staff mentioned: "At the moment it is a coastal hazard, we are obliged under legislation that if we have got information, to say there is a hazard now or in the future." Thus part of the motivation for sharing information with the public came from their legislated responsibilities.

Temporal

There were three aspects to temporal fairness that emerged in the interviews relating to past, present and future generations and decisions. One Rockdale staff member reflected on past decisions and the impact that had on current generations.

> That is the argument. To protect your house, why should the council or ratepayers pay for something to protect private property? Those houses should never have been built there 100 years ago. Anywhere on those places that have been affected, up on the north coast or even here. Now probably would never happen because people understand dune dynamics are areas that move back and forth and we should have left a 200m buffer between the high water mark and the first houses, but that is too late now.

This example highlights how future generations may evaluate decisions being made by councils today.

In Rockdale, staff debated the need to inform current residents about future flood risks, reflecting on other councils who had put information about SLR on Section 149 Certificates:

> Some councils have done that. In Wyong [a regional council] they did it and there was a complete uproar because it reduced your house value . . . If you are in a current flood zone it has to be on there [the Section 149 Certificate] but it is something that might happen in 50 years' time. I don't believe we have to put that on our 149 Certificates.

Here the temporal and informational dimensions of fairness intersect, with a question arising about when is the best time to share information about SLR with communities, given its impacts on current residents.

In Rockdale staff recognised that SLR will mostly affect subsequent generations but did not know how to effectively engage young people. While Rockdale Council has a youth council and holds an annual youth week, SLR is not explicitly discussed with young people. In Botany, staff expected an increase in interest about SLR from new residents rather than from the "average working-class person who has been here for 20 years." This indicates the importance of keeping abreast of changing community demographics and ways of engaging with them through time.

Spatial

At the sub-municipal scale, staff discussed the different costs associated with protecting stretches of coastline within their council as well as different levels of success engaging residents in diverse parts of the municipality. They were also critical of the requirements that require local councils to plan for, fund and engage the community about SLR but not private and state-owned corporations, such as Sydney Airport and NSW Ports. At the municipal scale, staff compared approaches to adaptation by various councils within and beyond Sydney – including the listing of SLR risks on Section 149 Certificates and the sharing of the SCCG maps with residents.

Staff acknowledged that adaptive action across councils was related to multiscalar spatial discrimination. Three staff members expressed concern that councils bear the responsibility for SLR decision-making after the previous state government disbanded the state-wide SLR policy.

> So much about council government is about leadership so if the leadership is not interested in doing it then they won't do it. . . . If there is leadership from state or federal government that often helps. But what happened in the case of the state government removing the sea-level rise policy there was a vacuum in leadership . . . and then it came down to individual councils what their leadership decided to do. Some that were not climate change deniers went forward with it and others who were thought: "Great we don't have to do anything now."

Here it is possible to see how decisions at various scales affect the implementation of SLR adaptation planning at the local scale. This intersects with informational fairness where the absence of clear state guidelines results in patchy distribution of information about SLR risks to residents.

Discussion

Residents of Rockdale and Botany were knowledgeable and satisfied with the fairness of council decision-making processes, information sharing and interpersonal interactions when they do not specifically pertain to SLR. This was despite different – collective versus individualistic – approaches between the two councils with respect to community engagement. Part of council staff justifications for not engaging more with residents about SLR was because there are other climate change issues that affect more residents, that residents are not interested, or don't have the time to engage. Yet, more than half of the residents were personally concerned about SLR, and the levels of dissatisfaction with SLR-specific policy procedures indicate a desire for greater engagement. The following discussion considers why such disparities exist, in the context of past research, and the implications this has for the amalgamated council. Consideration is also given as to how the dimensions of fairness researched here extend our understanding of climate fairness more generally and how the method implemented here can inform future applied research.

Comments made by council staff indicated that they were more concerned with *who* to involve and on *what* topic than on *how* to engage. While staff didn't explicitly consider justice principles, their approaches reflect the ideas of "equal participation of all" (Paavola and Adger, 2006) and the utilitarian principle of achieving the greatest good for the greatest number (Leichenko and O'Brien, 2006). Their lack of consideration of how to achieve "meaningful inclusion" (Few et al., 2007) is evident in residents' perceptions that procedural fairness has not been achieved by either council with respect to SLR planning; residents don't feel they've had the opportunity to contribute or that their views have been heard (Figure 24.1). Indeed, looking to the community engagement literature more broadly, the participatory processes described by the councils constitute "consultative participation" because residents participate by being consulted on topics defined as important by the council, and there is no evidence that either council concedes any share in decision-making (Pimbert and Pretty, 1996). Thus, the question staff need to ask is not only how to bring diverse interests to the table but how to share decision-making power on issues that residents prioritise.

The development of a new SLR policy for the amalgamated council requires cooperative decision-making tools where the council trusts the deliberative capacities of stakeholders to propose plans that are effective and equitable (Few et al., 2007). For example, the nearby City of Sydney council has started considering how to include the most vulnerable people into community-based adaptation planning (Schlosberg et al., 2017). The amalgamated council may benefit from experimenting with novel methods that researchers have developed to achieve such meaningful engagement and co-management for climate adaptation. Methods such as sense-making perspectives (Larsen et al., 2012), scenario planning (Butler et al., 2016) and group-based organisations (Chowdhury et al., 2016) are specifically designed to accommodate scientific uncertainty around climate change and help ensure that "hard to reach" populations are effectively engaged in an ongoing dialogue over the long timeframes of adaptation (Few et al., 2007). If the council doesn't meaningfully engage with its community about coastal hazards now, it might find it more difficult to implement sensitive adaptation responses in the future (Costas et al., 2015).

If the council is to move toward such a collaborative approach, it needs to recognise that although few homes might be directly impacted by SLR, there is broader concern among the community. Niven and Bardsley (2013) found that staff in coastal municipalities regard heatwaves and bushfires as more urgent planning issues than SLR, which is consistent with the findings here. Compared to the study of coastal residents in Lake Macquarie (McManus et al., 2014), Botany Bay residents were much more likely to be concerned about SLR (55% compared to 33%). McManus et al. (2014) also asked residents about their concern for multiple climate change impacts and found that coastal residents were more concerned about SLR than floods and heatwaves. Thus the new council could benefit from investigating residents' concern about various climate change impacts to ensure adaptation planning focuses on the issues residents believe will have the greatest impact on their everyday lives. Such information may also reveal that there is more consensus and concern among residents about specific climate change issues, thereby helping councils to identify whether conflict is more or less likely.

Overall, the ways in which staff interpreted procedural, interpersonal, informational and distributive fairness was largely consistent with other research in regional Australia. Yet the staff expanded the scope of what temporal and spatial fairness involve. In this study temporal fairness not only pertained to thinking about future residents, consistent with the regional council staff perspectives described by Graham and Barnett (2017), but also looking back and reflecting on how past decisions have created the conditions that put current residents at risk. Previously, considerations of temporal fairness in the context of climate adaptation and mitigation (Puaschunder, 2016), as per the scholarly literature more generally, have been forward looking. For example, in Hockett's (2009) critique of intertemporal justice, the focus was on "those who do not yet live, but indeed shall live in future" (p. 1149). The comments made by Botany staff reflect the importance of situating current SLR planning decisions and rationales in the context of past coastal decisions. Such a longer-term perspective provides a different baseline for evaluating the fairness of current adaptation decisions and the burdens that are being placed on current generations. It reinforces the importance of taking a measured approach to adaptation, where decisions are made at a pace that allows for such inequalities to be addressed through time (Fincher et al., 2015).

Past empirical research on spatial fairness in the context of climate adaptation has focused on comparing units within a particular scale, i.e., making sure opportunities to access and use resources are equitably allocated across space (Shi et al., 2016). In practice, such fairness evaluations have involved comparing decisions across localities within a municipality or across municipalities within a region (Graham and Barnett, 2017), country or internationally (Shi et al., 2016). In this study, spatial fairness also involved evaluations across different spatial scales, from the local to the federal. This lends support to Barrett's (2013) calls for climate justice research that is multiscalar and Shi et al.'s (2016) call for research that examines the effects of multiple levels of adaptation policy-making on social equity.

Beyond the conceptual contributions, this study is also the first we know of that quantifies the perceived fairness of climate adaptation decisions beyond procedural and distributive dimensions (e.g., McManus et al., 2014). As per McManus et al. (2014), we found that a large proportion of residents selected the "don't know" option, ranging from 10% to 58% of respondents, depending on the statement. The lowest "don't know" responses pertained to the five general questions about how councils engage with residents that did not specifically mention SLR. The highest "don't know" responses pertained to the five statements about distributive and temporal fairness and the remaining statement about interpersonal fairness. Over two-fifths of respondents (40%) answered "don't know" to all five of these specific SLR statements. There were no clear socio-demographic or interest-driven characteristics of this sub-sample to explain the noncommittal response pattern (Durand and Lambert, 1988). Given that McManus et al. (2014) found that residents equivocate when answering questions about adaptation fairness in individual interviews, group-based research may be required to understand how climate fairness is socially constructed.

Conclusion

Two justice principles were evident in adaptation planning in Botany Bay. These were: (1) the utilitarian principle of providing the greatest good to the greatest number, by focusing on climate impacts that staff believe will affect the greatest number of residents; and (2) equal participation of all, by ensuring that everyone gets the same information (Botany) and ensuring that even hard-to-reach segments of the community are consulted (Rockdale). Yet residents' responses indicate that they have different understandings of SLR risk and are more concerned about SLR than is recognised by council staff, thus raising the question of how to prioritise which climate risks to plan for first. Residents' evaluations of fairness also indicate that they do not feel that they have been meaningfully included in SLR planning processes. The consultative participatory processes implemented by each council for SLR can be considered to be doing little. The rationale in Rockdale was that doing something would result in considerable community angst, yet doing little is undermining their relationship with residents. Meaningful engagement processes are needed that enable residents to inform and influence council decision-making. Given the uncertainty among residents about what constitutes fair SLR adaptation, explicit conversations are also needed to develop a shared understanding of how fairness can be delivered across the six dimensions considered here.

Acknowledgments

We would like to thank all the people who took the time to respond to the survey and participate in the interviews. Dr Graham acknowledges the financial support from the Spanish Ministry of Economy and Competitiveness, through the "María de Maeztu" program for Units of Excellence (MDM-2015–0552).

References

Abel, N., Wise, R., Colloff, M., Walker, B., Butler, J., Ryan, P., Norman, C., Langston, A., Anderies, J., Gorddard, R. and Dunlop, M. (2016) 'Building resilient pathways to transformation when "no one is in charge": Insights from Australia's Murray-Darling Basin', *Ecology and Society*, vol 21, no 2

ABS (2016) *Census of population and housing.* Australian Bureau of Statistics, Canberra

Adger, W. N. and Nelson, D. R. (2010) 'Fair decision making in a new climate of risk', in K. L. O'Brien, A. L. Clair, and B. Kristoffersen (eds) *Climate change, ethics and human security.* Cambridge University Press, Cambridge, pp 83–94

Adger, W. N., Paavola, J. and Huq, S. (2006) 'Toward justice in adaptation to climate change', in W. N. Adger, J. Paavola, S. Huq, and M. J. Mace (eds) *Fairness in adaptation to climate change*. MIT Press, Cambridge, MA, pp 1–19

Araos, M., Berrang-Ford, L., Ford, J. D., Austin, S. E., Biesbroek, R. and Lesnikowski, A. (2016) 'Climate change adaptation planning in large cities: A systematic global assessment', *Environmental Science and Policy*, vol 66, pp 375–382

Barnett, J., Graham, S., Mortreux, C., Fincher, R., Waters, E. and Hurlimann, A. (2014) 'A local coastal adaptation pathway', *Nature Climate Change*, vol 4, no 12, pp 1103–1108

Barrett, S. (2013) 'The necessity of a multiscalar analysis of climate justice', *Progress in Human Geography*, vol 37, pp 215–233

Brakell, K., Bearsley, C., Stephens, K. and Callipari, C. (2012) 'In the beginning there was the flood study', in *Hydrology and Water Resources Symposium 2012*. Engineers Australia, Barton, pp 316–324

Braun, V. and Clarke, V. (2006) 'Using thematic analysis in psychology', *Qualitative Research in Psychology*, vol 3, no 2, pp 77–101

Bulkeley, H., Carmin, J., Castán Broto, V., Edwards, G. A. S. and Fuller, S. (2013) 'Climate justice and global cities: Mapping the emerging discourses', *Global Environmental Change*, vol 23, no 5, pp. 914–925

Burton, I., Huq, S., Lim, B., Pilifosova, O. and Schipper, E. L. (2002) 'From impacts assessment to adaptation priorities: The shaping of adaptation policy', *Climate Policy*, vol 2, pp 145–159

Butler, J. R. A., Suadnya, W., Yanuartati, Y., Meharg, S., Wise, R. M., Sutaryono, Y. and Duggan, K. (2016) 'Priming adaptation pathways through adaptive co-management: Design and evaluation for developing countries', *Climate Risk Management*, vol 12, pp. 1–16

Chowdhury, A., Maiti, S. K. and Bhattacharyya, S. (2016) 'How to communicate climate change "impact and solutions" to vulnerable population of Indian Sundarbans? From theory to practice', *SpringerPlus*, vol 5, no 1, p 1219

Chu, E., Anguelovski, I. and Carmin, J. (2016) 'Inclusive approaches to urban climate adaptation planning and implementation in the Global South', *Climate Policy*, vol 16, no 3, pp. 372–392

City of Botany Bay Council. (2015) 'Council policy on SLR', www.botanybay.nsw.gov.au/Environment/Sustainable-Council/Sea-Level-Rise

Clark, P. U., Shakun, J. D., Marcott, S. A., Mix, A. C., Eby, M., Kulp, S., Levermann, A., Milne, G. A., Pfister, P. L., Santer, B. D., Schrag, D. P., Solomon, S., Stocker, T. F., Strauss, B. H., Weaver, A. J., Winkelmann, R., Archer, D., Bard, E., Goldner, A., Lambeck, K., Pierrehumbert, R. T. and Plattner, G. K. (2016) 'Consequences of twenty-first-century policy for multi-millennial climate and sea-level change', *Nature Climate Change*, vol 6, no 4, pp 360–369

Costas, S., Ferreira, O. and Martinez, G. (2015) 'Why do we decide to live with risk at the coast?', *Ocean and Coastal Management*, vol 118, pp 1–11

Durand, R. M. and Lambert, Z. V. (1988) 'Don't know responses in surveys: Analyses and interpretational consequences', *Journal of Business Research*, vol 16, no 2, pp 169–188

Few, R., Brown, K. and Tompkins, E. L. (2007) 'Public participation and climate change adaptation: Avoiding the illusion of inclusion', *Climate Policy*, vol 7, no 1, pp 46–59

Fincher, R., Barnett, J. and Graham, S. (2015) 'Temporalities in adaptation to SLR', *Annals of the Association of American Geographers*, vol 105, no 2, pp 263–273

Forsyth, T. (2014) 'Climate justice is not just ice', *Geoforum*, vol 54, pp 230–232

Frost, G. (2011) *Review of coastal processes and evaluation of the impact of the constructed groynes along Lady Robinsons Beach, Botany Bay, New South Wales, Australia*. Honours thesis, University of Wollongong, Australia

Graham, S. (2002) *Being green when you're in the red: The attitudes of rice and grape growers towards environmental flows for wetlands*. Honours thesis, The University of Sydney, Australia

Graham, S. and Barnett, J. (2017) 'Accounting for justice in local government responses to SLR: Evidence from two local councils in Victoria, Australia', in A. Lukasiewicz, S. Dovers, L. Robin, J. M. McKay, S. Schilizzi, and S. Graham (eds) *Natural resources and environmental justice Australian perspectives*, CSIRO Publishing, Melbourne, pp 91–104

Graham, S., Barnett, J., Fincher, R., Mortreux, C. and Hurlimann, A. (2015) 'Towards fair local outcomes in adaptation to SLR', *Climatic Change*, vol 130, no 3, pp 411–424

Grasso, M. (2007) 'A normative ethical framework in climate change', *Climatic Change*, vol 81, no 3–4, pp 223–246

Hamin, E. M., Gurran, N. and Emlinger, A. M. (2014) 'Barriers to municipal climate adaptation: Examples from coastal Massachusetts' smaller cities and towns', *Journal of the American Planning Association*, vol 80, no 2, pp 110–122

Hine, D. W., Phillips, W. J., Reser, J. P., Cooksey, R. W., Marks, A. D. G., Nunn, P. D., Watt, S. E. and Ellul, M. C. (2013) *Enhancing climate change communication: Strategies for profiling and targeting Australian interpretive communities*. National Climate Change Adaptation Research Facility, Gold Coast, Australia

Hockett, R. C. (2009) 'Justice in Time', *Cornell Law Faculty Publications, Paper 123*, http://scholarship.law.cornell.edu/lsrp_papers/123

Hughes, S. (2013) 'Justice in urban climate change adaptation: Criteria and application to Delhi', *Ecology and Society*, vol 18, no 4, pp 1–15

Kamal-Chaoui, L. (2008) *Competitive cities and climate change: An introductory paper*, Competitive Cities and Climate Change OECD Conference proceedings, pp. 29–47

Kreller, A. (2016) *Pulling our heads out of the sand: The values, beliefs about sea-level rise and perceptions of fairness of Botany Bay residents*. Honours thesis, The University of New South Wales, Australia

Larsen, R. K., Swartling, Å. G., Powell, N., May, B., Plummer, R., Simonsson, L. and Osbeck, M. (2012). 'A framework for facilitating dialogue between policy planners and local climate change adaptation professionals: Cases from Sweden, Canada and Indonesia', *Environmental Science and Policy*, vol 23, pp 12–23

Leichenko, R. and O'Brien, K. (2006) 'Is it appropriate to identify winners and losers?', in W. N. Adger, J. Paavola, S. Huq and M. J. Mace (eds) *Fairness in adaptation to climate change*. MIT Press, Cambridge, MA, pp 1–19

Lind, E. A. and Earley, P. C. (1992) 'Procedural justice and culture', *International Journal of Psychology*, vol 27, no 2, pp 227–242

Lind, E. A., Kanfer, R. and Earley, P. C. (1990) 'Voice, control and procedural justice: Instrumental and noninstrumetnal concerns in fairness judgments', *Journal of Personality and Social Psychology*, vol 59, no 5, pp 952–959

Lukasiewicz, A., Bowmer, K., Syme, G. J. and Davidson, P. (2013) 'Assessing government intentions for Australian water reform using a social justice framework', *Society and Natural Resources*, vol 26, no 11, pp 1314–1329

McGranahan, G., Balk, D. and Anderson, B. (2007) 'The rising tide: Assessing the risks of climate change and human settlements in low elevation coastal zones', *Environment and Urbanization*, vol 19, no 1, pp 17–37

McManus, P., Shrestha, K. K. and Yoo, D. (2014) 'Equity and climate change: Local adaptation issues and responses in the City of Lake Macquarie, Australia', *Urban Climate*, vol 10, pp 1–18

Neale, J. (2016) 'Iterative categorization (IC): A systematic technique for analysing qualitative data', *Addiction*, vol 111, no 6, pp 1096–1106

Neumann, J. E., Price, J., Chinowsky, P., Wright, L., Ludwig, L., Streeter, R., Jones, R., Smith, J. B., Perkins, W., Jantarasami, L. and Martinich, J. (2015) 'Climate change risks to US infrastructure: Impacts on roads, bridges, coastal development, and urban drainage', *Climatic Change*, vol 131, no 1, pp 97–109

Niven, R. and Bardsley, D. (2013) 'Planned retreat as a management response to coastal risk: A case study from the Fleurieu Peninsula, South Australia', *Regional Environmental Change*, vol 13, no 1, pp 193–209

NSW Department of Planning and Environment (2016) *Bayside West precincts: Key actions and documents*. NSW Government, Sydney, Australia

Paavola, J. and Adger, W. N. (2006) 'Fair adaptation to climate change', *Ecological Economics*, vol 56, no 4, pp 594–609

Padawangi, R. (2012) 'Climate change and the north coast of Jakarta: Environmental justice and the social construction of space in urban poor communities', in W. G. Holt (ed) *Urban areas and global climate change*. Emerald Group Publishing Limited, Bingley, UK, pp 321–339

Pimbert, M. and Pretty, J. (1996) 'Parks, people and professionals: Putting "participation" into protected area management', in K. Ghimire and M. Pimbert (eds) *Social change and conservation*, Earthscan, London, pp 297–330

Preston, B. L., Smith, T. F., Brooke, C., Gorrdard, R., Measham, T. G., Withycombe, G., McInnes, K., Abbs, D., Beveridge, B. and Morrison, C. (2008) *Mapping climate change vulnerability in the Sydney Coastal Councils Group*. Australian Government Department of Climate Change, Canberra, Australia

Puaschunder, J. M. (2016) 'Intergenerational climate change burden sharing: An economics of climate stability research agenda proposal', *Global Journal of Management and Business Research (B)*, vol 16, pp 31–38

Rockdale City Council (2013) *Rockdale City Council community research*. Micromex Research, Tuggarah, Australia

Schlosberg, D., Collins, L. B. and Niemeyer, S. (2017) 'Adaptation policy and community discourse: Risk, vulnerability, and just transformation', *Environmental Politics*, vol 26, no 3, pp 413–437

Shi, L., Chu, E., Anguelovski, I., Aylett, A., Debats, J., Goh, K., Schenk, T., Seto, K. C., Dodman, D., Roberts, D. and Roberts, J. T. (2016) 'Roadmap towards justice in urban climate adaptation research', *Nature Climate Change*, vol 6, no 2, pp 131–137

Usmani, S. and Jamal, S. (2013) 'Impact of distributive justice, procedural justice, interactional justice, temporal justice, spatial justice on job satisfaction of banking employees', *Review of Integrative Business and Economics Research*, vol 2, no 1, pp 351–383

Zografos, C., Anguelovski, I. and Grigorva, M. (2016) 'When exposure to climate change is not enough: Exploring heatwave adaptive capacity of a multi-ethnic, low-income urban community in Australia', *Urban Climate*, vol 17, pp 248–265

25

Thermal inequity

The relationship between urban structure and social disparities in an era of climate change

Bruce C. Mitchell and Jayajit Chakraborty

Introduction

Since public debate over responses to climate change began in the 1980s, scientific consensus on the consequences and hazard risks of "global warming" has increased in both depth and scope. Establishment of the Intergovernmental Panel on Climate Change (IPCC) in 1988 created the framework for an international consensus of scientific opinion through periodic Assessment Reports. The IPCC assessments have identified a wide range of impacts on physical and biological systems from a rising global temperature baseline, including sea-level rise and increased damage from coastal flooding, changes in the amount of rainfall, and increases in both the frequency and intensity of heatwaves (2007). These changes are occurring at the continental and regional scale, but the impacts are felt by communities at the local scale. The multiple hazards and global scope of climate change require researchers to consider interlocking relationships that cut across scales, to understand what Walker terms the "compounding forms of injustice" to "environmentally marginalized people" that are at the centre of climate justice concerns (2012, p. 179). Thermal inequity is an example of this interrelation: built structure and social structure increase the vulnerability of socially disadvantaged people to a combination of the urban heat island effect and a rising temperature baseline, which intensifies urban heat in specific locations and increases the frequency of heatwaves.

This chapter presents thermal inequity as a distributive justice concern where socially marginalised communities that are least equipped for adapting to and mitigating the effects of a changing temperature baseline cope with the most adverse impacts. We first introduce thermal inequity as a fundamental example of a distributive injustice related to anthropogenic climate change. Next, the role of built structure and social structure in urban formation and in the increased risk of exposure to urban heat is considered. This includes an overview of the research literature which developed theories of urban heat "riskscapes" and the "climate gap." Finally, empirical studies and methods used to assess thermal inequity in advanced industrial economies are reviewed, with a presentation of findings from several recent case studies.

Thermal inequity and distributive justice

While the debate over the certainty and causes of global climate change has occupied public attention in the U.S., research on the inequitable distribution of the adverse effects of climate change has grown in recent years (Schlosberg and Collins, 2014). Social inequities in vulnerability to climate change is a concern both within and between nations, though the international dimensions have earned greater attention due to a series of high-level conferences and summits after the United Nations Framework Convention of Climate Change (UNFCCC) was adopted in 1992. In 2001, the Environmental Justice and Climate Change Initiative began as a result of UNFCCC conferences, and the following year established 10 principles for climate change policies in the U.S. Its second principle recognises disparities, both in the effects of climate change and in the ability of vulnerable communities to adapt. Since the beginning of the climate justice movement, an emphasis has been placed on the national, racial/ethnic and socio-economic disparities in exposure and vulnerability, and also on the power relations shaping public policy. This understanding was derived from the experiences of environmental justice communities over the preceding decades which informed climate justice scholarship and activism (Schlosberg and Collins, 2014).

In the U.S., there was additional recognition of social disparities in exposure to climate change when the Congressional Black Caucus (CBC) issued a report titled *Blacks and Climate Change: An Unequal Burden* (2004). The CBC report utilises distributive justice arguments to emphasise that the burdens imposed by climate change intensify already existing racial disparities. While the report lists a number of adverse health and socio-economic burdens, the very first topic of the report addresses the disproportionate mortality rate of Black residents during heatwaves. The urban context and racial disparity in rates of mortality had become apparent after several heatwaves in cities located in the northern U.S., particularly the 1995 Chicago heatwave (Semenza *et al.*, 1996; Whitman *et al.*, 1997). The CBC report points to racial disparity and socio-economic disadvantage as elements of climate injustice specifically relating to heatwaves, but stops short of conceptualising thermal inequity as a topic. Thermal inequity is a form of distributive injustice rooted in the spatial structure and segregated residential patterns of cities, in which racial/ethnic minorities and individuals of lower socio-economic status are disproportionately exposed to the risks posed by urban heat islands and climate change.

Built structure, social structure and their role in thermal inequity

A key element of thermal inequity is its origin in human activities which impact the physical environment and relationships that shape our social structure. It is not just a concern of environmental justice, and its study must be informed by scholarship in geography, climatology and urban sociology with implications for public health and hazards research. Geographers, going back to Humboldt (1819) and Sauer (1925), have recognised that human alteration of the environment is a social process. Both climate change (Arrhenius, 1896) and urban heat island (Howard, 1820; Renou, 1868) research have their origins in the 19th century. Public health and hazards researchers recognised connections between increased mortality rates and urban heat islands and heatwaves in the 1970s (Buechley *et al.*, 1972; Clark, 1972). The work of urban sociologists from Burgess and Park (1925) through Massey and Denton (1989) has outlined (and sometimes perpetuated) the dynamics of economic and racial residential segregation that shape the social structure of cities. All of these disciplinary approaches have contributed to our understanding of the causes and consequences of social disparities in exposure to urban heat. This highlights the need for a cross-disciplinary approach when analysing the role of built structure and social structure in thermal inequity.

Built structure

The technological basis of thermal inequity arises from the industrial processes which produce greenhouse gases and the urbanisation of the landscape that cause the urban heat island effect (UHI). Patterns of human habitation have become increasingly urbanised, so that worldwide the proportion of people living in cities exceeded 50% around 2008 (UNDESA, 2011). These changes are occurring simultaneously with an increasing global temperature baseline, resulting in a changing climate and more variable local weather patterns which are subject to greater extremes (IPCC, 2007). A global study of 217 cities by Mishra *et al.* (2015) indicated that half of them had experienced increases in extremely hot days in the period 1973–2012. There are indications in different regions of the world of increases in both the baseline temperature and heatwaves. Studies in rapidly urbanising regions of East Asia (Choi *et al.*, 2009) and South Asia (Rohini *et al.*, 2016) and already urbanised Europe (Barriopedro *et al.*, 2011) and North America (Meehl and Tebaldi, 2004) indicate that large population centres have experienced greater temperature extremes in recent decades. The sprawl of urbanisation transforms rural areas, increasing population and structural density and industrial activity. Processes of industrial production create the greenhouse gases which change not only the chemical balance of our global atmospheric commons but also impact local landscapes.

There are two contributors to the physical risk of urban heat: (1) a rising global temperature baseline causing more intense and frequent heatwaves, and (2) the UHI which varies the distribution of heat across neighbourhoods. The morphology of cities, with their increased structural density and reduced vegetation, results in the UHI. Linkages between the elevated temperature of urban areas and their greater structural density have been understood since the early 19th century when Luke Howard (1820) first described the differences in temperature measurements within the city of London and the surrounding countryside. Howard ascribed these to the industrial processes taking place in the city, growing population density and the greater thermal storage capacity of the buildings. It was not until the 1960s that the term "urban heat island" came into use, and its physical basis had been fully described by the late 1980s (Chandler, 1965; Landsberg, 1981; Oke, 1982). Not only are cities generally sites of increased industrial activity, but the built structure of cities transforms vegetated areas into a landscape of asphalt, brick and concrete. These materials have higher thermal mass with greater capacity to store and emit heat (Golden, 2004). Loss of vegetation decreases cooling of the air through evapotranspiration and reduces shade. This alters the thermal exchange between the land surface and lower atmosphere at the local level. Variations in the thermal exchange are evident at the neighbourhood level and are contingent on land cover differences (Voogt and Oke, 2003). This is most apparent in imagery of land surface temperature (LST) patterns taken utilising high-resolution remote-sensing instruments. "Micro-urban heat islands" were first discussed by Aniello *et al.* (1995), although neighbourhood-level atmospheric temperature differences had been identified much earlier in temperature transect studies of cities (Schmidt, 1927; Middleton and Millar, 1936; Sundborg, 1950). Micro-urban heat islands are evident as LST "hotspots" with a surrounding temperature gradient. There are also distinctive "cool-island" features that are centred on water features and densely vegetated areas, which lower the temperature of the area. While overall urban temperatures are elevated above those of the surrounding countryside, differences in urban land cover create a patch-like LST pattern in cities, creating the conditions for variable exposure to the physical risk of urban heat.

Social structure

Neighbourhoods that are most exposed to higher levels of urban heat are often inhabited by socially vulnerable residents. In this context, social vulnerability refers to "the characteristics of a person or group and their situation that influence their capacity to anticipate, cope with, resist and recover from the impact of a natural hazard" (Blaikie et al., 2004, p. 11). Socially vulnerable communities are exposed to greater risk due to their reduced capacities to adapt to or mitigate the effects of heat-related hazards. Poverty and lack of economic resources is one element of social vulnerability, and as Ribot et al. note for many, "their everyday conditions are unacceptable even in the absence of climate stress" (2017, p. 50). Individuals of lower socio-economic status are often clustered in neighbourhoods with antiquated and dilapidated housing, which is difficult to cool during heatwaves (Klinenberg, 2002). Inadequate housing and reduced ability to access air conditioning increase vulnerability to the hazard of urban heat for people of low socio-economic status.

In the U.S. and elsewhere, patterns of urban settlement and residential development reflect the social and technological currents of specific historical eras. Whether one neighbourhood of a city is cooler than another may be low on the list of considerations when searching for a residence, but amenities like parks and waterfront locations are important considerations which increase neighbourhood desirability and property prices. It just so happens that these same amenities are also protective factors from urban heat exposure. Historically, the settlement patterns of racial/ethnic minorities in the U.S. were shaped by different constraints than those of the majority White population. Minorities not only faced normal constraints like affordability, proximity to work and personal preferences, but they also contended with residential steering and institutional discrimination (Galster, 1988). These factors were especially important in the establishment of segregated neighbourhoods until adoption of the Fair Housing Act of 1968 made these practices illegal. Residential segregation was imposed through widespread restrictive covenants and deeds, exclusionary zoning, real estate steering and redlining (Rothstein, 2017). These segregationist practices played an important role in the creation of inequitable residential settlement patterns which persist to this day.

Additionally, many cities underwent considerable suburbanisation during the post-war period. The expansion of transportation networks into areas surrounding cities increased the availability of cheap land, leading to sprawling subdivisions, distant from the previously established urban core (Cohen, 2004). The era of suburbanisation initiated a large-scale abandonment of many central cities by White middle-class families termed "White-flight" (Frey, 1979). While "White-flight" characterised an earlier era, many downtowns are now undergoing gentrification and a demographic inversion, which is the converse of suburbanisation (Ehrenhalt, 2012). The downtowns of many prosperous cities are being structurally and socially transformed by this process. The consequence of these settlement flows is that minority neighbourhoods are often situated in the least desirable and most structurally antiquated areas of cities in the U.S., places that often increase physical exposure to higher levels of urban heat.

As a final note, while socio-economic status and racial/ethnic segregation are important aspects of social vulnerability, other factors such as group perceptions influence responses to urban heat and heatwaves. Although it may appear somewhat counterintuitive, social vulnerability can be exacerbated by social cohesion. According to a study of elderly residents conducted by Wolf et al. (2010) in London and Norwich, strong social networks reinforced narratives that heatwaves are manageable events which do not require special precautions or preparation for risk mitigation. Attitudes reinforced by a social network can dissuade respondents from taking advice from emergency planning authorities. This indicates that it is insufficient to simply provide emergency cooling shelters during heatwaves and that misperceptions of risk must also be addressed.

Heatwaves, "riskscapes" and the "climate gap"

As mass casualty events, heatwaves have long been recognised as a public health concern, and the literature pertaining to heatwaves indicates a growing emphasis on social disparities in the spatial distribution of this hazard. The earliest literature relating the urban heat island with heatwave mortality appeared in the work of Buechley *et al.* (1972) and Clark (1972). High mortality rates from heatwaves in the summer of 1980, and especially as a result of a 1995 Chicago, Illinois heatwave, increased public health awareness of the issue. The death toll during the Chicago heatwave was particularly shocking, with 536 deaths in a five-day period (ILDPH, 1997). The resulting outcry compelled public officials to recognise social disparities in the impact of urban heat on vulnerable groups. *Heat Wave: A Social Autopsy of Disaster in Chicago*, by Eric Klinenberg (2002), brought attention to social disparities in exposure to urban heat. Socially vulnerable groups, including Blacks, people living below the poverty level, older people living alone in anti-quated "single room occupancy" apartment units, and people with medical conditions, suffered higher rates of mortality during the heatwave. Klinenberg argued that the Chicago heatwave was a disaster because public policy failed to recognise and protect the most vulnerable members of society, who were invisible to the municipal emergency planning structure of the time. The Chicago heatwave was not just a natural disaster, but a disaster created by social systems which fostered vulnerability, then failed to provide adequate protection. While *Heatwave* articulates many of the components of a climate justice argument, its approach is sociological, and it stops short of linking the 1995 Chicago event with environmental inequities.

The extensive studies of urban heat conducted in the Phoenix metropolitan area of Arizona by Harlan *et al.* (2006) and Jenerette *et al.* (2016) represent the first attempt to utilise an interdisciplinary framework combining urban climatology, natural hazards and sociological approaches to explicitly discuss disproportionate exposure to urban heat as an environmental justice issue. A series of studies compares patterns of urban heat in Phoenix and the socio-demographic composition of the city, finding significant associations between increased temperature and neighbourhoods with weaker social networks, lower median income and higher proportions of Hispanic residents. Harlan's study (2013) also noted that structural and historical forces left "poor and minority populations" in "deteriorated urban spaces" which were not amenable to environmental improvement. Subsequently, another study by Jenerette *et al.* (2011) suggested that lack of environmental amenities and cooling vegetation in warmer urban areas of Phoenix creates a "heat riskscape" with varying risk exposure and human vulnerability in the urban environment. Chow *et al.* (2012) extended Harlan's methodological approach in another study of Phoenix, calculating summer maximum and minimum temperatures and an index of vegetation abundance for two periods: 1990 and 2000. Their findings supported the previous evidence that higher temperatures and lower amounts of vegetation were associated with higher numbers of Hispanic and elderly residents, as well as lower socio-economic status. Chow *et al.* concluded that economically affluent Phoenicians are better able to control their environment through lower structural density, increased landscaping and the use of air conditioning (2012). In other words, economically affluent residents mitigate the effect of urban heat through environmental modifications that less-affluent residents are not able to afford. Each of these studies in Phoenix has moved toward a more comprehensive framing of urban heat and the factors associated with social vulnerability as environmental justice concerns.

The concept of urban "heat riskscapes" links the historical development of city landscapes, minority settlement and elevated exposure to the urban heat island using case studies of Phoenix, Arizona, one of the hottest major cities in the U.S. More general climate justice concerns are evident in "climate gap" studies (Shonkoff *et al.*, 2009). The "climate gap" refers to the way in which racial/ethnic minority and lower socio-economic status residents are simultaneously exposed to climate change and possess inadequate resources to mitigate or adapt to its adverse effects (Grineski *et al.*, 2012, 2013). The impacts of climate change have both health and economic ramifications for minorities and lower-income groups. Because these groups are often employed in physically demanding outdoor work, their exposure is increased as temperatures rise. Additionally, sectors of the economy like agriculture are expected to face dramatic shifts in their areas of production, causing disruption in employment patterns and job loss (Shonkoff *et al.*, 2011). The climate gap has distributive justice implications both in how the physical impacts of climate change are dealt out and to the different abilities of vulnerable communities to adapt to and mitigate the effects of urban heat. Climate gap studies are particularly pertinent to transnational issues, as seen in Grineski *et al.*'s study of the El Paso, Texas and Ciudad Juarez, Mexico border area, where economic conditions reflect the effects of globalisation and criminal activities, intensifying cross-border disparities. Both "heat riskscapes" and the climate gap are aspects of the broader concern over thermal inequity. The "riskscape" concept presents a theory of how historical settlement patterns and economic deprivation create the circumstances for neighbourhood-level exposure to urban heat. The climate gap is a broader theory of the socio-economic impacts of climate change on communities. Thermal inequity is descriptive of these two patterns: neighbourhood structure and socio-economic deprivation combining with local and global-level modifications of the urban climate in the amplification of exposure and risk.

Thermal inequity case studies

Since distributive injustice arises from spatial patterns in human activity, quantitative and spatial analytical methods are particularly useful for establishing whether urban heat risks are disproportionately distributed with respect to the social characteristics of the population. Spatial analysis is suited for the evaluation of geographic relationships because it allows different location patterns to be examined and evaluated through the overlay of multiple layers of data using geographic information systems (GIS). This approach is ideal for building and assessing the validity of statistical models containing physical and socio-demographic data related to the population of an area. Two primary methods of analysis have emerged, which include direct assessment of the coincidence of LST to socially vulnerable groups using regression models (Johnson *et al.*, 2011; Dousset et al., 2011; Grineski *et al.*, 2012), and the use of a heat vulnerability index (HVI), which combines indicators of both physical vulnerability and social vulnerability for "heat risk mapping" (Reid *et al.*, 2009; Harlan *et al.*, 2013; Wolf and McGregor, 2013). Both regression and factor analysis-based studies established the use of physical indicators of urban heat, such as LST, lack of vegetation, or impervious surface prevalence, and specific socio-demographic variables as predictive of greater exposure to risk of urban heat. While socio-economic variables have shown fairly consistent associations across urban areas, demographic variables, especially those indicative of race and ethnicity, are simplified to "minority status" and typically have not examined differences among specific minority groups. The following studies (Mitchell and Chakraborty, 2014, 2015, 2018) employ cutting-edge analytical techniques such as spatial regression and multi-level modelling to examine the statistical association of urban heat with a wide range of socio-demographic explanatory variables. These thermal inequity studies are described in more detail in the following subsections and summarised in Table 25.1.

Pinellas County study

The first study of thermal inequity examined racial/ethnic and socio-economic disparities in the spatial distribution of LST in Pinellas County, Florida, which is located on the Pinellas peninsula of the Tampa Bay metropolitan statistical area (MSA) in the U.S. (Mitchell and Chakraborty, 2014).

Pinellas County is the most densely populated county in Florida, with 76% of the land urbanised and is "built-out," having exhausted all commercially available land for development. The history of modern settlement of the Pinellas peninsula was shaped by its attractiveness as an amenity destination for vacationers and retirees, who enjoyed the winter climate and proximity to beaches and the water (Arsenault, 1988). Coastal areas of the peninsula saw extensive environmental modification through drainage projects and dredging to accommodate development along the Gulf of Mexico and Tampa Bay (Stephenson, 1997). While economically affluent residents occupied waterfront properties, less affluent residents and a segregated Black service class, who were drawn by employment opportunities in hotels and the construction industry, occupied interior areas away from the waterfront. Unless they were associated with maritime activities or commerce, light industrial and commercial districts also tended to locate in the interior of the peninsula. Pinellas also has high rates of Black/White segregation, with a dissimilarity index[1] of 0.625, compared to neighbouring Hillsborough County (location of the City of Tampa), which was 0.437 in 2010. This implies that the Black and White residents are not as evenly distributed relative to each other in Pinellas County as in Hillsborough. Additionally, Pinellas has the second largest community of Southeast Asian residents in Florida: Cambodian, Hmong and Vietnamese, many of whom are clustered in the centre of the peninsula. While the Asian to White dissimilarity index is lower in the Tampa MSA at 0.395, it has increased with growth of the Asian population since 1990 (CensusScope, 2010).

Settlement patterns in Pinellas County, with different land cover, land uses and structural densities along the coasts and interior, establish a thermal pattern which is evident when viewing remote-sensing imagery. At larger scales, LSTs resolve into a temperature gradient which increases toward the interior of the peninsula (Figure 25.1). At smaller scales, however, LST differences are apparent

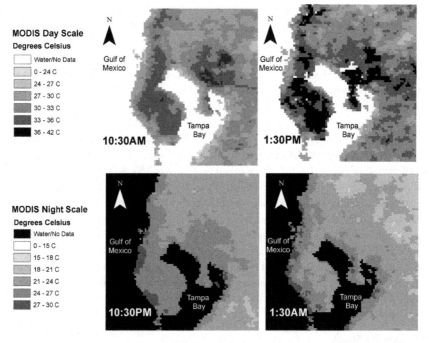

Figure 25.1 Indications of the formation of an urban heat island in the central portion of the Pinellas peninsula during the afternoon.

Source: MODIS Aqua and Terra satellite eight-day composite land surface temperature image at 1km spatial resolution. September 14–21 2010

as a patch-like pattern, with numerous "cool islands" where land cover consists of parkland or water, and "micro-urban heat islands" consisting of large industrial structures or commercial strips lining major roadways (Figure 25.2). With a population size ranging from 2,500 to 8,000, census tracts are convenient proxies for neighbourhoods in the U.S. The results of a census tract-level analysis in Pinellas indicate that densely populated tracts with higher percentages of low-income and Asian residents are more exposed to urban heat as measured by LST. This pattern illustrates

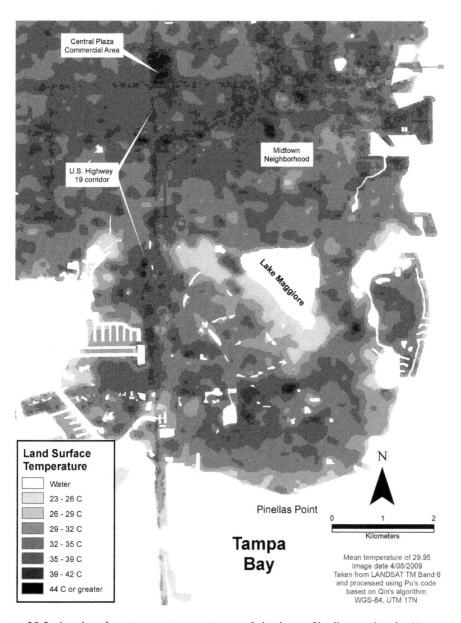

Figure 25.2 Land surface temperature patterns of the lower Pinellas peninsula. Numerous "cool islands" and "micro-urban heat islands" are evident, as is a thermal gradient extending from the coast inland.

the inequitable exposure of residential communities and thus represents "a landscape of thermal inequity." This implies that the built landscape of Pinellas County, with its greater structural density in many interior areas, causes an increase of LST, which in turn intensifies the urban heat island effect in neighbourhoods. For example, an area of the inner peninsula known as Lealman contains a small and highly clustered Asian community, whose members are exposed to higher levels of urban heat. The human-constructed structural landscape and the social arrangement of neighbourhoods have thus contributed to greater physical and social vulnerability for specific communities in this urban area. Economically affluent residents who reside in less dense and more vegetated areas or along waterfront areas with sea breezes are more protected and face lower exposure to urban heat.

Study of the largest U.S. cities: Chicago, Los Angeles and New York

While the Pinellas County study examined thermal inequity at a smaller scale in a specific regional context, the existing literature seemed to indicate that similar issues of thermal exposure and social vulnerability would be evident across larger regions and in more populous urban areas of the U.S. with different settlement patterns. To confirm this, a three-city study was undertaken to examine urban heat and social vulnerability in three of the largest U.S. cities: New York City, New York; Chicago, Illinois; and Los Angeles, California (Mitchell and Chakraborty, 2015). Instead of consolidating indicators of physical and social vulnerability into a single indicator like the HVI, a different approach utilising an indicator of urban heat as the dependent variable was developed. An index of landscape-related factors which collectively indicate areas with elevated urban heat was developed into an Urban Heat Risk Index (UHRI). This combines three characteristics of the urban thermal landscape: land surface temperature (LST), vegetation abundance (NDVI) and the structural density (NDBI) of the built urban environment. All three variables can be calculated utilising a single remote-sensing image from the LandsatThematic Mapping (TM) sensor (Figure 25.3) achieving temporal consistency of the data.

Each study area had differences in the natural and built land cover which impacted the spatial distribution of the UHRI scores. Los Angeles, in particular, has large desert areas north of the San Gabriel Mountains, where the Mojave Desert and Antelope Valley are located. This natural area of desert has very low population density, but high LST, sparse vegetation, and extensive impervious surface of exposed rock and barren soil. As a consequence, the desert areas of Los Angeles, and census tracts with under 500 population, were excluded from the calculations. In contrast, the cities of Chicago and New York are extensively vegetated with Chicago also having lower mean structural density, greater mean vegetation and lower mean LST than the other cities. LST in the New York study area varied widely and the land cover ranges from marshes to concrete and asphalt. However, unlike Los Angeles, the hottest areas still contain large populations who were exposed to urban heat. While the landscape of Los Angeles may have greater extremes in temperature and less vegetation, the population densities in the hottest areas are lower compared to those in Chicago and New York.

A variety of indicators of social vulnerability at the census tract level were utilised in the three-city study. Demographic variables included population density, percentage race/ethnicity, age and disability status. Socio-economic indicators included median household income, percentage home owner occupancy, percentage with high school educations, an indicator of linguistic isolation and the Gini coefficient for economic inequality. Synthesising across the three study areas, there are consistent and significant associations between the risk factors of urban heat and lower socio-economic status of urban residents, which are similar to those reported in previous studies of other U.S. cities (Semenza et al., 1996; Whitman et al., 1997; Harlan et al., 2006; Uejio et al., 2011). The greatest consistencies in association were present in the socio-economic

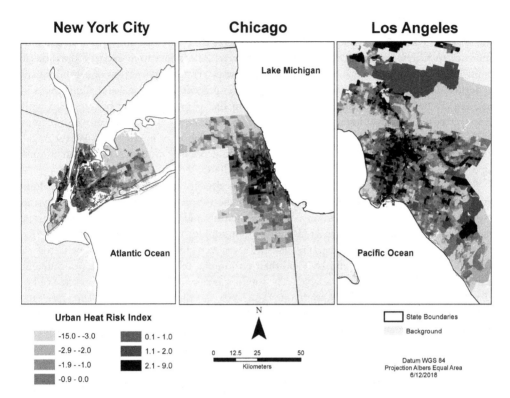

Figure 25.3 Urban Heat Risk Index for three cities calculated from land surface temperature, structural density and vegetation abundance using LandsatTM multispectral imaging taken in 2010.

Source: USGS Landsat 5 TM imagery

variables related to household income ($p < .01$), home ownership ($p < .01$, except in Chicago) and economic inequality ($p < .01$). The demographic variables suggest that local patterns in the distribution of racial/ethnic minority groups influence the relationship between heat exposure and social vulnerability. Higher percentages of Asian residents were significantly and positively related to the UHRI in all three cities ($p < .001$ to $p < .01$). Higher percentages of Black and Hispanic residents were positive and significant with respect to the UHRI in Chicago ($p < .01$ and $p < .001$) and Los Angeles (both $p < .01$), but not in New York City. Analysis of a more restricted set of "core" urban census tracts also indicated that scale and spatial extent of the study area are important considerations when analysing thermal inequity.

Twenty-city study of thermal inequity and segregation

Previous studies of urban heat have examined its relation at the census tract level to variables related to the demographic and socio-economic characteristics of residents. There has not, however, been an examination of the spatial relationships with broader social indicators such as residential segregation and urban heat at large scales across the U.S. Racial and ethnic segregation is a key element in the settlement patterns and social structure of U.S. cities. A study to examine inequities in the distribution of urban heat in 20 of the largest U.S. cities, many of which are typified by conditions of extreme segregation, or "hypersegregation" (Massey and Denton, 1989), was recently conducted (Mitchell and Chakraborty, 2018). This case study took a different approach to analyse thermal inequity and utilised several innovations to re-examine the issue. A multi-level model was constructed to test two hypotheses: (1) that higher levels of urban heat are associated with lower socio-economic status and larger percentages of racial and ethnic minorities; and (2) the level of racial ethnic segregation in the urban area would be associated with greater exposure to urban heat. Multi-level modelling techniques allow variables with different units of aggregation to be examined. In this case the association of metropolitan-level segregation, with neighbourhood-level racial/ethnic and socio-economic disparities in exposure to one aspect of climate change: urban heat denoted by the UHRI.

Selection of study areas for this 20-city study was driven by several considerations, including population size and regional distribution across the U.S. Another key criterion was by the exposure to increased extreme heating days projected by mid-century using simulations from the National Center for Atmospheric Research, Community Climate System Model (NCAR/CCMS, 2014). Examination of maps for each city revealed patterns between landscape factors of vegetation, structural density and LST and their positioning relative to percentages of different minorities and socio-economic variables. The top four images (Figure 25.4) indicate the overlap of some of these factors in the Washington D.C. MSA and the combination of landscape factors which comprise the UHRI. Below those are maps indicating median income levels and the percentages of different racial and ethnic groups. The images suggest an association of increased

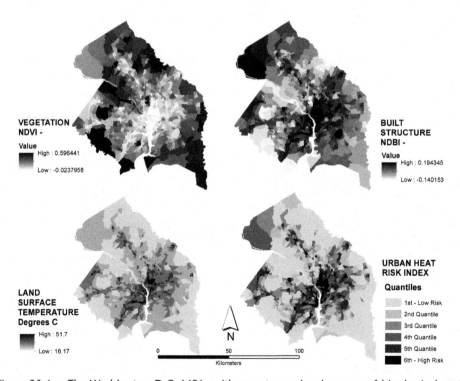

Figure 25.4a The Washington D.C. MSA, with remote-sensing imagery of biophysical attributes of vegetation, structural density and land surface temperature consolidated as an Urban Heat Risk Index (top).

Source: USGS Landsat 5 TM imagery, 2010

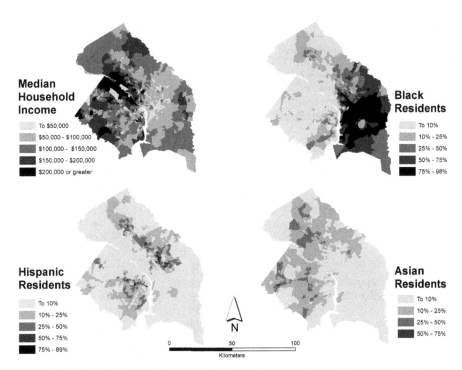

Figure 25.4b The Washington D.C. MSA, with socio-economic and demographic data at the tract level (bottom).

Source: U.S. Census ACS 5-year Summary File 2010–2014

UHRI and lower median income and greater percentages of Black residents in the Washington D.C. MSA.

The 20-city multi-level study suggests that social processes such as segregation which affect the urban distribution of racial/ethnic minorities are an additional factor in establishing the exposure to risk for socially vulnerable communities. Segregation is a multifaceted social process, involving not only the separation of people based on race or ethnicity but also other spatial characteristics, such as the unevenness of distribution between groups measured by the dissimilarity index, clustering, concentration, proximity to the central business district or centrality, and isolation from other groups (Massey and Denton, 1989). As such, it directly affects the inequitable exposure of racial/ethnic minorities, especially those with lower incomes, to a wide range of environmental hazards and risks. Segregation data for the five measures was calculated at the metropolitan area level for each city. A two-level model was then constructed to test the associations at census tract and metropolitan scales.

The multi-level analysis of tract-level variables indicated highly significant associations between the UHRI and all socio-economic variables: median household income, percentage of high school graduates and home ownership rate (all $p < .001$). For the demographic variables, highly significant and positive associations were observed for percent Black ($p < .001$) and percent Asian ($p < .001$), while the percent Hispanic indicated a significant ($p < .10$) negative association, even after controlling for population density. These results indicate that at the tract level, socio-economic indicators and higher percentages of Black and Asian residents are very strong predictors of increased urban heat exposure. The negative association for Hispanic residents may

341

Table 25.1 Results of three studies across different geographies with associations to urban heat.

Variables	Pinellas County Study	Largest Cities Study: Chicago, Los Angeles, New York City	Twenty-City Study
Statistical Method	Conventional Statistics and Spatial Autoregressive Methods	Conventional Statistics and Spatial Autoregressive Methods	Multi-level Modelling
Dependent Variable	Land Surface Temperature (LST)	Urban Heat Risk Index = LST – Land Surface Temperature NDBI – impervious surface NDVI – vegetation	Urban Heat Risk Index = LST – Land Surface Temperature NDBI – impervious surface NDVI – vegetation
Socio-economic Variables – Significant	% Owner Occupancy % Poverty	% Owner Occupancy[3] Median HH Income % High School Grad[1] % Non-English Speaking[2] Gini Coefficient	% Owner Occupancy Median HH Income % High School Grad
Demographic Variables – Significant	Population Density Race – % Asian	Population Density Race – % Asian Race – % Black[6] Ethnicity – % Hispanic[7] (neg)[8] (pos) % Age <5 years (pos[4],. neg[5]) % Age>65 years[6] (neg) Disabled[9]	Population Density Race – % Asian Race – % Black Ethnicity – % Hispanic
Segregation Variables – significant	N/A	N/A	Dissimilarity Index – Black & Hispanic Clustering – Hispanic (neg) Concentration – Asian

[1] = Los Angeles; [2] = Chicago & New York; [3] = Los Angeles & New York; [4] = Chicago (pos); [5] = Los Angeles & New York (neg); [6] = Chicago & Los Angeles; [7] = Chicago & Los Angeles (pos); [8] = New York (neg); [9] = Los Angeles

reflect greater levels of Hispanic suburbanisation, with 45% of Hispanics living in urban areas outside of the downtown core, compared to only 39% of Blacks (Massey and Tannen, 2017). Metropolitan-level segregation indicators were significant for the dissimilarity index between Whites and Blacks ($p < .01$), and the Whites and Hispanic ($p < .10$) groups, while the indicator of concentration for Asians was significant ($p < .001$), and the indicator of clustering was significant ($p < .01$) and negative in the Hispanic model. These results suggest not only that minority exposure to urban heat differs significantly among racial/ethnic groups but also that patterns of segregation are an additional contributor to inequitable exposure.

The results of the three case studies, summarised in Table 25.1, collectively indicate consistent relationships between urban heat and socio-economic variables, but differences in association for demographic variables. Specifically, exposure to significantly higher levels of urban heat is observed for neighbourhoods with lower median income and lower percentages of home owner occupancy and high school graduates, respectively, across these studies. As for the racial/ethnic variables, higher population density and higher percentages of Asian and Black residents are consistently and significantly related to greater urban heat exposure. Statistical associations are less consistent for the percentage of Hispanic residents at the neighbourhood level. These findings suggest that the historical settlement patterns of minority groups within urban systems of the U.S. differ considerably, and that caution should be taken when using generalised variables like "minority status" in the assessment of heat exposure. Our results also indicate that other factors in the spatial arrangement of minorities relative to the majority population, such as residential segregation, significantly influence the assessment of exposure to urban heat, as well as other adverse environmental exposures.

Conclusion

This chapter has outlined the circumstances of thermal inequity which impact residents of urban areas with different intensities. Our conclusions point to the heightened exposure of socially vulnerable residents living in areas of cities with the least greenspace and highest densities – both in terms of population and structures. The statistical associations revealed in our case studies of U.S. urban areas can be typified as "hottest, densest and poorest." In addition, we found strong evidence of higher exposure for racial/ethnic minority groups, which vary from one metropolitan area to another. Thermal inequity can be expected to increase as the socio-economic gap intensifies between the lower and higher-income households, as well as between specific minority groups and Whites. It can also be expected to amplify as the biophysical drivers of urban heat, climate change and an expanding urban heat island "footprint" of cities increase. The trend of minority and low-income suburbanisation, however, may mitigate heat exposure in some areas. These conclusions are consistent with those of researchers who have approached the issue of heatwave morbidity and mortality from different disciplinary perspectives (Semenza et al., 1996; Whitman et al., 1997; Klinenberg, 2002; Hondula et al., 2012; Harlan et al., 2013).

Although previous research and case studies discussed in this chapter have relied primarily on aggregated data and neighbourhood-level associations, future studies need to examine individual or household factors that potentially influence exposure to heat risk. Recent work by Byrne et al. (2016) demonstrates the usefulness of household-level surveys in assessing the impacts of increasing urban density and perceptions of climate change for socially vulnerable residents and their attitudes regarding mitigating factors like green infrastructure. Additionally, Byrne's work expands the context of thermal inequity as a distributive justice issue internationally. While the collection of data in informal settlements in rapidly developing urban areas may present a data acquisition challenge, these cities present increasing exposure to risk due to their expanding area and growing population. The death toll from a 2015 Indian heatwave, for instance, is reported to have exceeded 2,500 (Wehner et al., 2016). Additionally, the use of indicators of broader social significance will increase the validity of results. Continued exploration of metropolitan-level social indicators such as segregation and income inequality using multi-level modelling can provide more insights on disparities in exposure as a distributive justice concern. Thermal inequity presents an expanding challenge of exposure and social vulnerability as urban areas continue to grow and the global temperature baseline increases.

Note

1 The Dissimilarity Index is a common measure used to quantify the segregation between two racial/ethnic or economic groups in an area. It provides a measure of the evenness of distribution between groups over an area. The value of the index provides the percentage of population of the group which would have to move in order to achieve an even distribution, with 0.0 being a completely even distribution and 1.0 absolute segregation.

References

Aniello, C., Morgan, K., Busbey, A., and Newland, L. (1995) Mapping micro-urban heat islands using LANDSAT TM and a GIS. *Computers and Geosciences*, 21(8), 965–969.

Arrhenius, S. (1896) XXXI. On the influence of carbonic acid in the air upon the temperature of the ground. *The London, Edinburgh, and Dublin Philosophical Magazine and Journal of Science*, 41(251), 237–276.

Arsenault, R.O. (1988) *St. Petersburg and the Florida Dream*. Norfolk: Conning Co.

Barriopedro, D., Fischer, E.M., Luterbacher, J., Trigo, R.M., and García-Herrera, R. (2011) The hot summer of 2010: Redrawing the temperature record map of Europe. *Science*, 332(6026), 220–224.

Blaikie, P., Cannon, T., Davis, I. and Wisner, B., 2004. *At risk: natural hazards, people's vulnerability and disasters*. London: Routledge.

Buechley, R.W., Van Bruggen, J., and Truppi, L.E. (1972) Heat island = Death island? *Environmental Research*, 5(1), 85–92.

Burgess, E.W., McKenzie, R.D., and Park, R.E. (1925) *The City*. Chicago: University of Chicago Press.

Byrne, J., Ambrey, C., Portanger, C., Lo, A., Matthews, T., Baker, D., and Davison, A. (2016) Could urban greening mitigate suburban thermal inequity?: The role of residents' dispositions and household practices. *Environmental Research Letters*, 11(9), 095014. http://iopscience.iop.org/article/10.1088/1748-9326/11/9/095014/pdf

CensusScope. (2010) *Social Sciences Data Analysis Network (SSDAN)*. www.censusscope.org/index.html

Chandler, T. (1965) *The Climate of London*. London: Hutchinson.

Choi, G., Collins, D., Ren, G., Trewin, B., Baldi, M., Fukuda, Y., Afzaal, M., Pianmana, T., Gomboluudev, P., Huong, P.T.T., and Lias, N. (2009) Changes in means and extreme events of temperature and precipitation in the Asia-Pacific Network region, 1955–2007. *International Journal of Climatology*, 29(13), 1906–1925.

Chow, W., Chuang, W.C., and Gober, P. (2012) Vulnerability to extreme heat in metropolitan Phoenix: Spatial, temporal, and demographic dimensions. *The Professional Geographer*, 64(2), 286–302.

Clarke, J.F. (1972) Some effects of the urban structure on heat mortality. *Environmental Research*, 5(1), 93–104.

Cohen, L. (2004) A Consumers' Republic: The politics of mass consumption in postwar America. *Journal of Consumer Research*, 31(1), 236–239.

Congressional Black Caucus Foundation, Inc. (2004) *African Americans and Climate Change: An Unequal Burden*. http://sustainablecommunitydevelopmentgroup.org/wordpress/wp-content/uploads/2013/06/African-Americans-Climate-Report-l.pdf

Dousset, B., Gourmelon, F., Laaidi, K., Zeghnoun, A., Giraudet, E., Bretin, P., Mauri, E., and Vandentorren, S. (2011) Satellite monitoring of summer heat waves in the Paris metropolitan area. *International Journal of Climatology*, 31(2), 313–323.

Ehrenhalt, A. (2012) *The Great Inversion and the Future of the American City*. New York, NY: Vintage Books.

Frey, W.H. (1979) Central city white flight: Racial and nonracial causes. *American Sociological Review*, 425–448.

Galster, G. (1988) Residential segregation in American cities: A contrary review. *Population Research and Policy Review*, 7(2), 93–112.

Golden, J.S. (2004) The built environmental induced urban heat island effect in rapidly urbanizing arid regions-a sustainable urban engineering complexity. *Environmental Sciences*, I(4), 321–349.

Grineski, S.E., Collins, T.W., Ford, P., Fitzgerald, R., Aldouri, R., Velásquez-Angulo, G., and Lu, D. (2012) Climate change and environmental injustice in a bi-national context. *Applied Geography*, 33, 25–35.

Grineski, S.E., Collins, T.W., McDonald, Y., Aldouri, R., Aboargob, F., Eldeb, A., Romo Aguilar, L., and Velázquez-Angulo, G. (2013) Double exposure and the climate gap: Changing demographics and exposure to extreme heat in Ciudad Juárez, Mexico. *Local Environment*, 20(2), 180–201.

Harlan, S.L., Brazel, A.J., Prashad, L., Stefanov, W.L., and Larsen, L. (2006) Neighborhood microclimates and vulnerability to heat stress. *Social Science and Medicine*, 63(11), 2847–2863.

Harlan, S.L., Declet-Barreto, J.H., Stefanov, W.L., and Petitti, D.B. (2013) Neighborhood effects on heat deaths: Social and environmental predictors of vulnerability in Maricopa County, Arizona. *Environmental Health Perspectives (Online)*, 121(2), 197.

Hondula, D.M., Davis, R.E., Leisten, M.J., Saha, M.V., Veazey, L.M., and Wegner, C.R. (2012) Fine-scale spatial variability of heat-related mortality in Philadelphia County, USA, from 1983–2008: A case-series analysis. *Environmental Health*, 11(1), 16.

Howard, L. (1820) *The Climate of London Deduced from Meteorological Observations Made at Different Places in the Neighborhood of the Metropolis*. London: W. Phillips, George Yard, Lombard Street.

Humboldt, A.V. (1819) *Personal Narrative of Travels to the Equinoctial Regions of the New Continent During the Years 1799–1804*. Ed by Alexander de Humboldt and Aime Bonpland, Volume 4. London: Longman, Hurst, Rees, Orme, and Brown.

Illinois Department of Public Health. (1997) *Heat-Related Mortality in Chicago*, Illinois, July 1995. www. idph.state.il.us/cancer/pdf/HEAT.PDF (last accessed 18 April 2017)

Intergovernmental Panel on Climate Change. (2007) *Climate Change 2007: The Physical Science Basis. Contribution of Working Group I to the Fourth Assessment Report of the Intergovernmental Panel on Climate Change.* Ed. by S. Solomon, D. Qin, M. Manning, Z. Chen, K.B. Marquis, M. Averyt, M. Tignor, and H.L. Miller. New York: Cambridge University Press.

Jenerette, G.D., Harlan, S.L., Buyantuev, A., Stefanov, W.L., Declet-Barreto, J., Ruddell, B.L., and Li, X. (2016) Micro-scale urban surface temperatures are related to land-cover features and residential heat related health impacts in Phoenix, AZ USA. *Landscape Ecology*, 31(4), 745–760.

Jenerette, G.D., Harlan, S.L., Stefanov, W.L., and Martin, C.A. (2011) Ecosystem services and urban heat riskscape moderation: Water, green spaces, and social inequality in Phoenix, USA. *Ecological Applications*, 21(7), 2637–2651.

Johnson, D., Lulla, V., Stanforth, A. and Webber, J., (2011). Remote sensing of heat-related health risks: The trend toward coupling socioeconomic and remotely sensed data. *Geography Compass*, 5(10), pp.767–780.

Klinenberg, E. (2002) *Heat Wave: A Social Autopsy of Disaster in Chicago.* Chicago: University of Chicago Press.

Landsberg, H.E. (1981) *The Urban Climate*, Volume 28. New York, NY: Academic Press.

Massey, D.S., and Denton, N.A. (1989) Hypersegregation in US metropolitan areas: Black and Hispanic segregation along five dimensions. *Demography*, 26(3), 373–391.

Massey, D.S., and Tannen, J. (2017) Suburbanization and segregation in the United States: 1970–2010. *Ethnic and Racial Studies*, 1–18.

Meehl, G.A., and Tebaldi, C. (2004) More intense, more frequent, and longer lasting heatwaves in the 21st century. *Science*, 305(5686), 994–997.

Middleton, W.E.K., and Millar, G. (1936) Temperature profiles in Toronto. *The Journal of the Royal Astronomical Society of Canada*, 265–172.

Mishra, V., Ganguly, A.R., Nijssen, B., and Lettenmaier, D.P. (2015) Changes in observed climate extremes in global urban areas. *Environmental Research Letters*, 10(2), 024005.

Mitchell, B.C., and Chakraborty, J. (2014) Urban heat and climate justice: A landscape of thermal inequity in Pinellas County, Florida. *Geographical Review*, 104(4), 459–480.

Mitchell, B.C., and Chakraborty, J. (2015) Landscapes of thermal inequity: Disproportionate exposure to urban heat in the three largest US cities. *Environmental Research Letters*, 10(11), 115005.

Mitchell, B.C., and Chakraborty, J. (2018) Exploring the relationship between residential segregation and thermal inequity in twenty U.S. cities. *Local Environment*, 1–8.

Morello-Frosch, R., and Lopez, R. (2006) The riskscape and the color line: Examining the role of segregation in environmental health disparities. *Environmental Research*, 102(2), 181–196.

National Center for Atmospheric Research, Community Earth System Model (NCAR/UCAR, CESM). (2014). www.cesm.ucar.edu/models/ (last accessed 18 April 2017).

Oke, T.R. (1982) The energetic basis of the urban heat island. *Quarterly Journal of the Royal Meteorological Society*, 108(455), 1–24.

Pu, R., Gong, P., Michishita, R., and Sasagawa, T. (2006) Assessment of multi-resolution and multi-sensor data for urban surface temperature retrieval. *Remote Sensing of Environment*, 104(2), 211–225.

Reid, C.E., O'Neill, M.S., Gronlund, C.J., Brines, S.J., Brown, D.G., Diez-Roux, A.V., and Schwartz, J. (2009) Mapping community determinants of heat vulnerability. *Environmental Health Perspectives*, 117(11), 1730.

Renou, E. (1868) Différences de température entre la ville et la campagne. *Annuaire Societe Meteorologie de France*, 83–97.

Ribot, J. (2017) Vulnerability does not just fall from the sky. *Risk Conundrums*, Volume 224, No. 242, 224–242). Routledge in Association with GSE Research. https://www.ingentaconnect.com/content/rout/26bxfh

Rohini, P., Rajeevan, M., and Srivastava, A.K. (2016) On the variability and increasing trends of heatwaves over India. *Scientific Reports*, 6, 26153.

Rothstein, R. (2017) *The Color of Law: A Forgotten History of How Our Government Segregated America.* New York and London: Liveright Publishing.

Sauer, C.O. (1925) *The Morphology of Landscape.* Berkeley: University of California Publications in Geography 2, 19–54.

Schlosberg, D., and Collins, L.B. (2014) From environmental to climate justice: Climate change and the discourse of environmental justice. *Wiley Interdisciplinary Reviews: Climate Change*, 5(3), 359–374.

Schmidt, W. (1927) Die Verteilung der Minimum temperaturen in der Frostnacht des 12 Mai 1927 im Gemeindegebiet von Wien. *Fortschritte der Landwirstschaft*, 2, 681–686.

Semenza, J.C., Rubin, C.H., Falter, K.H., Selanikio, J.D., Flanders, W.D., Howe, H.L., and Wilhelm, J.L. (1996) Heat-related deaths during the July 1995 heatwave in Chicago. *The New England Journal of Medicine*, 335(2), 84–90.

Shonkoff, S.B., Morello-Frosch, R., Pastor, M. and Sadd, J., (2009). Minding the climate gap: Environmental health and equity implications of climate change mitigation policies in California. *Environmental Justice*, 2(4), pp.173–177.

Shonkoff, S.B., Morello-Frosch, R., Pastor, R., and Sadd, J. (2011) The climate gap: Environmental health and equity implications of climate change and mitigation policies in California – A Review of the Literature. *Climatic Change*, 109(1), 485–503.

Stephenson, R.B. (1997) *Visions of Eden: Environmentalism, Urban Planning, and City Building in St. Petersburg, Florida, 1900–1995*. Columbus: The Ohio State University Press.

Sundborg, A. (1950) Local climatological studies of the temperature conditions in an urban area. *Telus*, 222–232.

Uejio, C.K., Wilhelmi, O.V., Golden, J.S., Mills, D.M., Gulino, S.P., and Samenow, J.P. (2011) Intra-urban societal vulnerability to extreme heat: The role of heat exposure and the built environment, socioeconomics, and neighborhood stability. *Health and Place*, 17(2), 498–507.

UNDESA. (2011) *World Urbanization Prospects, the 2011 Revision*. United Nations Department ot Economic and Social Affairs Population Division, New York.

United States Census Bureau. (2015) *Summary File 2010–2014 American Community Survey*. www2.census.gov/programs-surveys/acs/summary_file/2014/data/

United States Geological Survey. *EarthExplorer*. LANDSAT 5 TM. https://landsat.usgs.gov/landsat-data-access (last accessed 18 April 2017).

U.S. Census Bureau's American Community Survey Office. (2010) *2010 Census*. www.census.gov/2010census/data/ (last accessed 18 April 2017).

U.S. Census Bureau's American Community Survey Office. (2014). http://ftp2.census.gov/ (last accessed 18 April 2017).

Voogt, J.A., and Oke, T.R. (2003) Thermal remote sensing of urban climates. *Remote Sensing of Environment*, 86(3), 370–384.

Walker, G. (2012) *Environmental Justice: Concepts, Evidence, and Politics*. London and New York: Routledge.

Wehner, M., Stone, D., Krishnan, H., Rao, K., and Castillo, F. (2016) The deadly combination of heat and humidity in India and Pakistan in summer 2015. *Bulletin of the American Meteorological Society*, 97(12), S81–S86.

Whitman, S., Good, G., Edmund, R., Benbow, N., Shou, W., and Mou, S. (1997) Public health briefs: Mortality in Chicago attributed to the July 1995 heatwave. *American Journal of Public Health*, 87(9), 1515–1518.

Wolf, J., Adger, W.N., Lorenzoni, I., Abrahamson, V., and Raine, R. (2010) Social capital, individual responses to heat waves and climate change adaptation: An empirical study of two UK cities. *Global Environmental Change*, 20(1), 44–52.

Wolf, T., and McGregor, G. (2013) The development of a heat wave vulnerability index for London, United Kingdom. *Weather and Climate Extremes*, 1, 59–68.

Part VI
Climate Justice and Gender

26

Climate justice, gender and intersectionality

Patricia E. Perkins

Climate justice, gender and intersectionality

While climate change is often seen as an "Anthropocene" or human species-induced problem, climate change affects different people differently, and certain humans are more responsible than others for causing it; some even benefit from climate change. Furthermore, some people have much greater ability than others to influence climate change policies. These differences – which together underlie *distributive* and *procedural* climate injustices – are deeply gendered[1] everywhere in the world; denying or disregarding this reality both heightens longstanding injustices and hampers efforts to address climate change (Moosa and Tuana 2014; Macgregor 2017; Buckingham and Kulcur 2017; Tschakert and Machado 2012). There are other aspects of climate justice which also are gendered: *intergenerational justice* (the rights of those who are not yet born to inherit a liveable Earth, and the responsibilities of people who are alive now for the future impacts of current decisions and consumption which will have long-term impacts on those not yet born), *interspecies justice* (consideration for non-human species and for protecting biodiversity), and *corrective, retributive,* or *restorative justice* (fairness in the measures taken to address unjust situations).

The ethical argument for emphasising gender in climate justice is that women make up half of humankind, so the well-documented disproportional impacts of climate change on women must be addressed as an urgent matter of equity.

Moreover, since women have large biological and cultural roles in human reproduction and livelihood production, even small gender-linked differentials have huge impacts on humanity as a whole. Gender is the most crucial category of climate injustice. This chapter briefly summarises why an intersectional gender perspective on all types of climate justice is not only ethically vital, but also efficient, strategic, theoretically fundamental and inspiring.

The effects of climate change are gendered

In all countries, women on average tend to be less educated, poorer, less mobile and more long-lived than men (Röhr et al. 2010; Nagel 2015: 5) – all risk factors for vulnerability to climate change (Terry 2009; Alston and Whittenbury 2013; Weiss 2012). In many countries, agriculture and food production, cooking, care for children and other family/community members and obtaining water for the household are almost exclusively women's responsibilities, due to gendered social roles. Climate change increases the (usually unpaid) work associated with these responsibilities. Sometimes girls must leave school to do this extra work, or women are forced to switch away from paid work, which further reduces their earning potential, incomes and relative economic position (Denton 2002; Dankelman 2010; UNDP 2008; Nagel 2015: 34–39; Rodenberg 2009; Habtezion 2013). So gendered climate vulnerability involves self-reinforcing feedbacks that increase its impacts over time and over generations.

Disasters such as floods, droughts, wildfires and other extreme events triggered by climate change often cause surges in gender-based violence (Enarson 2012; Dunn 2009; IFRC 2007). Women and children are disproportionately forced to migrate because of such extreme events, and they are more at risk (Roberts 2009; Black 2016: 174–175; Neumayer and Plümper 2007; WHO 2014: 16; Dasgupta et al. 2010). Women – especially older women – are more likely than men to die in heatwaves (Nagel 2015: 30; Rainham and Smoyer-Tomic 2003) despite their deeper social networks compared to men, which can help women's climate resilience (Global Gender and Climate Alliance 2016: 24).

Women's health, especially reproductive health, may be gravely affected by fossil fuel extraction, processing, transport and other forms of pollution related to climate change (Klein 2014 428–430; WEA & NYSHN 2016 de Onís 2012; WHO 2012; WHO 2014). Climate change also produces mental health impacts for women that are most pronounced during and after extreme weather events (Clayton et al. 2014). Pregnant women may be at special risk during extreme weather events, because anxiety and stress can induce obstetric complications. Women may also be more vulnerable to psychosocial health impacts due to multiple demands they face following extreme events during the processes of moving, caring for families, cleaning up, resettling and recovering (Duncan 2008; Nagel 2015: 62; Toronto Public Health 2009: 8). Insofar as these health impacts (e.g., cancer, miscarriages, genetic damage to foetuses, etc.) affect future generations, they represent *intergenerational injustice* due to climate change.

Since women make up the majority of healthcare workers, both formally and informally, the health impacts of climate change have implications for many women's home and work lives, besides their devastating implications for those who are directly affected (WomenWatch 2010; WEI 2015).

The causes and "benefits" of climate change are gendered

Partly because of their relative poverty compared to men, women's lower consumption levels make them less responsible for fossil fuel consumption (Cohen 2017) and less likely to profit or benefit from the economic systems which produce and perpetuate climate change (Moosa and Tuana 2014; Klein 2014 Lambrou and Piana 2006: 2). For example, 79% of Fortune 500 corporations' board members and 95% of their CEOs are men (Lindzon 2016; Mather 2015); six of the top ten firms are involved primarily in fossil fuels (Danaher et al. 2007: 192). Of course, gender is not the only important measure of climate change responsibilities and benefits – age, income, skin colour, ethnicity, sexuality, class, location, country and many other aspects of individual identity and position are involved, as discussed later (Kaijser and Kronsell 2014: 421) – but gender differences are economically ubiquitous and notoriously resistant to change.

Also due to gendered socio-economic positions and roles, women are generally made responsible for the decisions and work required to "green" the economy household by household, for example, by composting and recycling wastes, planning energy-saving, reducing carbon-intensive practices such as meat consumption and organising community-based environmental initiatives.

As noted earlier, these responsibilities take women's time away from other potential activities and have costs for the women themselves, which are often not recognised or compensated.

In polls, women consistently express more knowledge and concern than men do about climate change, stronger pro-environmental attitudes and greater willingness to take action and vote for climate policies (Nagel 2015: 166–182; Perkins 2017b). Men's lower rates of concern and activism are often understood as being related to their relative social position and sense of invulnerability (Nagel 2015: 168; Goldsmith et al. 2013: 161). The resulting delays in developing and implementing effective climate change policies increase the intensity and impacts of climate change – another intergenerational injustice feedback loop.

Climate-related policy development is gendered

From local communities to the United Nations, despite the growing literature on gender and climate change, attention to gender in climate change policy is still largely absent (Alber 2009; Bonewit 2015; Nagel 2015; McNutt and Hawryluk 2009; Skutsch 2002). A 2012 report found that "women's involvement in climate change decision-making at national, European and international levels is still low" and that women are a low proportion of graduates in scientific and technological fields deemed important for climate change response (EIGE 2012: 3; Hemmati 2008; Morrow 2012). The moment an emergency is declared by government bodies (e.g., when there is an extreme weather event or power outage caused by a storm), the institutions that take over are the ones that are the most top-down and male-dominated: the army, police, power authorities, firefighters and disaster-relief organisations (Enarson 2012). Climate finance – decisions about how to use funds directed locally, regionally or globally for climate change mitigation and adaptation – usually ignores the needs and views of women, which is inefficient at the very least (Schalatek 2009).

Both at the level of representation – policymakers are mostly men and the insights from women's lived experience with climate change are under-represented (Alber et al. 2017; Morrow 2012) – and at the level of theory, feminist ethical and ontological frames and methods are usually ignored in policy circles (Nelson 2012; Beuchler and Hanson 2015; Moosa and Tuana 2014; Nagel 2015; MacGregor 2010); climate change policy remains gendered in ways that ignore and undermine women's interests.

Intersectionality can heighten the effects of gender

Gender and climate researchers emphasise the importance of an intersectional standpoint, recognising that each person's complex identity affects how they are implicated and affected by climate change (Godfrey and Torres 2016; Kaijser and Kronsell 2014; Moosa and Tuana 2014; Osborne 2015; Rodriguez 2015). This means recognising the importance of power relations, situated contexts for different people and how social groupings affect material outcomes. For example, studies of Hurricane Katrina in New Orleans have found that material vulnerability increased in proportion to people's intersecting types of marginality: "race," gender, class, economic situation, sexuality, education level, etc. (Luft 2009; Tuana 2008; Pyles and Lewis 2010). Indigenous peoples, in particular, have been excluded from climate decision-making bodies and consultation, despite evidence that they bear extreme risks and damages from fossil fuel extraction and climate change, and despite Indigenous women's activism and powerful leadership (Walsh 2016; Gorecki 2014; Narine 2015; Nixon 2015; Perkins 2017b). As emphasised in feminist theory (Spencer et al. 2018), a gendered perspective on climate justice involves attention to all aspects of social difference and their interrelationships, since power relations create marginality along many intersecting dimensions (Ravera et al. 2016; Wilson 2017; Godfrey and Torres 2016).

Efficiency in policy approaches requires attention to vulnerability and gender

Women's lived experience, responsibilities and skills often make them experts on the best ways to use limited resources to address climate-related challenges. Including their views is economically efficient and a shortcut to effective climate policies (Perkins 2017a; Isla 2009; Perera 2012).

> Time and again, experience has shown that communities fare better during natural disaster when women play a leadership role in early warning systems and reconstruction. Women tend to share information related to community well-being, choose less polluting energy sources, and adapt more easily to environmental changes when their family's survival is at stake. Women trained in early warning disaster reduction made a big difference in La Masica, a village in Honduras that, unlike nearby communities, reported no deaths during Hurricane Mitch in 1998. Integrating gender perspectives in the design and implementation of policies and laws also helps meet the gender-differentiated impacts of environmental degradation – shortage of water, deforestation, desertification – exacerbated by climate change.
>
> *(ILO 2008: 3)*

Recommends the International Labour Organization, for example:

Actions to promote climate change adaptation and mitigation [should include]:

- Tapping into the vast knowledge and natural resource management abilities of women when devising adaptation and mitigation policies and initiatives for climate change.
- Mainstreaming gender perspectives into international and national policies.
- Ensuring that women and men participate in decision- and policy-making processes.
- Promoting participatory approaches in local and community planning activities.
- Creating opportunities at the national and local level to educate and train women on climate change, stimulate capacity building and technology transfer and assign specific resources to secure women's equal participation in the benefits and opportunities of mitigation and adaptation measures.
- Gathering new sex-disaggregated data and gender analysis in key sectors such as agriculture, tourism, forestry, fishing, energy and water usage to further understand how climate change impacts on women's lives.

(ILO 2008: 5)

Gender perspectives generate rich theoretical insights

To facilitate "gender justice as climate justice," better research and policy are needed. Virtually all studies on gender and climate call for more research, better data collection, and more attention to the gender equity and justice implications of climate change.

Much better equity-focused and gender-disaggregated data is necessary in order to measure and acknowledge distributional impacts and inequities. Collaboration and interdisciplinary work, including the fields of political ecology, public health, social work, disaster and risk management, economics, anthropology, sociology, ecology, toxicology, medicine and gender studies, is needed.

Gender budgeting can serve as a model for considering various justice interests and priorities related to climate change, including those resulting from adaptation strategies (Terry 2009: 12–13).

From the perspective of *procedural justice*, women's stronger risk perceptions, smaller carbon footprints and protective environmental policy activities are useful in the struggle to strengthen climate change policies (Terry 2009: 8–9); as their voices, political agency and representation become stronger, women's perspectives and activism are crucial. There are many potential contributions of gender perspectives for climate change research and policy development: intersectional analysis provides more detail for better policy; studying relationships among people and their interdependence is more realistic than just considering individuals; seeing "facts" as driven by the desires of investigators and "reality" as situated, not universal, is more accurate (Kronsell 2017; Tuana 2013; Israel and Sachs 2013; Bell 2013; Bee et al. 2013).

For example, human connections with and reliance on other species and complex ecosystems brings *interspecies justice* into focus as a key component of climate justice (Moosa and Tuana 2014: 688; Plumwood 1994).

Strategic climate action must be gendered

From a policy perspective, climate change heightens the importance of pay equity, affirmative action, training of women and men for jobs across the spectrum of employment, and a broader view of what work should be paid work and how it should be compensated – traditional and longstanding labour market challenges. This parallels the heightened importance of income distribution, development and poverty-reduction priorities in general, especially in times of climate change, and is true in both the Global North and the Global South.

For women to be able to assume a fair share of the jobs and responsibilities connected with global change, the following elements must be in place for them:

* access to education, training and upgrading
* access to and control over productive resources including access to land and ownership rights
* access to markets (land, labour, financial and product markets)
* access to services
* benefits from the use of public funds, particularly for infrastructure, and access to public goods
* means of enforcing claims for unpaid/reproductive work and redistribution/remuneration for such work
* the possibility of generating income from the use of their own labour

(Bäthge 2010: 7; see also ILO 2016)

Climate change throws into stark relief the gendered costs of capitalism, industrialised globalisation and economic "development," over the same time period when fossil fuel emissions have skyrocketed worldwide, heating up the Earth (Mies 1986; Mellor 1992; Buckingham and Le Masson 2017; Arora-Jonsson 2011). This is one reason why "climate justice and gender justice" overlap so closely with "gender and development" imperatives. Calls for climate justice and gender justice are in effect a reiteration that problems inherent in the expansion of the global capitalist system (worsening income distribution, intractable poverty, resource wars, violence against women, migration and environmental devastation, along with climate change) cannot sustainably be addressed from within the system; fundamental system transformations grounded in place-based democracy, transparency, equitable civic rights for all, diversity and public action are imperative (Klein 2014; Awâsis

2014; Buckingham and Le Masson 2017; Salleh 2009; Gibson-Graham 2006; Kaufman 2012). In fact, many women activists are working toward and leading such transformations.

Women's leadership and activism catalyses system change and climate justice

For all these reasons, women have long been leaders in environmental movements and activism (Perkins 2013; Mellor 1997). Global solidarity and gendered partnerships are modelling how to build progressive, alternative governance structures capable of addressing climate change equitably, especially at the local/urban level (Perkins 2017a; Röhr et al. 2008; Alber et al. 2017; Röhr et al. 2010; Ostrom 2014). Such initiatives and models include equitable local-economy institutions, cooperatives and land trusts, community gardens and food programmes, childcare and elder care cooperatives, support for victims of gender-based violence, water-harvesting schemes, community shelters, agroforestry projects and many other collective livelihood and care initiatives, which are appropriate for local socio-ecological conditions (Kaufman 2012; Gibson-Graham 2006; Klein 2014). All bring people together to build community resilience in the face of climate change while developing the skills and relationships necessary for equitable and sustainable commons governance. As noted by Elinor Ostrom (2014), the winner of the 2009 Nobel Prize in Economic Science, successfully managed commons in polycentric networks allow people to reduce their dependence on both markets and the state, thus increasing their climate resilience by creating new collective, environmentally based governance structures.

The successes of Indigenous women's activism on climate change, extraction and environmental damage (Perkins 2017a), and their clear distinction that for many this activism is grounded not in feminism so much as in "Indigenous womanism" and Indigenous land-based cultures, are an indication that the gendered meanings and implications of climate change (among other "Anthropocene" phenomena) are transformative and emergent (Perkins 2017b; Fortier 2017; Trosper 2009; Godfrey and Torres 2016). These changes cannot be grasped without a respectful, intersectional understanding that also recognises the deep connections between Indigenous cultures and responsibilities to the land and water (Horn-Miller 2017; WEA & NYSHN 2016; Awâsis 2014; White 2014).

An intersectional perspective on climate justice thus involves a great deal more than rectifying – for ethical reasons – the inequitable impacts of climate change on the female half of humanity in terms of *distributional, procedural,* and *corrective justice.* When women's situated experiences and expertise, diversity and gendered roles in production and reproduction are taken into account, climate justice for women increases the welfare of all humans – economically, socially and politically, both *intra-generationally* and *inter-generationally.* Moreover, the cultural expertise of Indigenous women and the activist leadership of marginalised and highly impacted women are replacing the unsustainable systems that produced climate change in the first place, building *intra-species and inter-species resilience* that has great potential for restorative transformation of the Earth.

Note

1 Gender is the range of characteristics which differentiate between masculinity and femininity, including biological sex or physical appearance, sex-based social structures and roles and culturally formed gender identity. When something is "gendered," it reflects or involves gender differences, prejudices or roles.

References

Alber, G., 2009. Gender and climate change policy. *In:* J.M. Guzmán, G. Martine, G. McGranahan, D. Schensul, and C. Tacoli, eds. *Population Dynamics and Climate Change.* New York/London: United Nations Population Fund/International Institute for Environment and Development, 149–163.

Alber, G., Cahoon, K., and Röhr, U., 2017. Gender and urban climate change policies: Tackling cross-cutting issues towards equitable, sustainable cities. *In:* S. Buckingham and V. Le Masson, eds. *Understanding Climate Change Through Gender Relations.* Oxon/New York: Routledge, 64–86.

Alston, M. and Whittenbury, K., eds., 2013. *Research, Action and Policy: Addressing the Gendered Impacts of Climate Change.* Dordrecht: Springer.

Arora-Jonsson, S. 2011. Virtue and vulnerability: Discourses on women, gender, and climate change. *Global Environmental Change* 21 (2), 744–751.

Awâsis, S., 2014. Pipelines and resistance across Turtle Island. *In:* T. Black, S. D'Arcy, T. Weis, and J.K. Russell, eds. *A Line in the Tar Sands: Struggles for Environmental Justice.* Toronto/Oakland: Between the Lines/PM Press, 253–266.

Bäthge, S., 2010. *Climate Change and Gender: Economic Empowerment of Women Through Climate Mitigation and Adaptation?* Eschborn, Germany: OECD Governance and Democracy Division/GTZ.

Bee, B., Biermann, M., and Tschakert, P., 2013. Gender, development, and rights-based approaches: Lessons for climate change adaptation and adaptive social protection. *In:* M. Alston and K. Whittenbury, eds. *Research, Action and Policy: Addressing the Gendered Impacts of Climate Change.* Dordrecht: Springer, 95–108.

Bell, K., 2013. Post-conventional approaches to gender, climate change and social justice. *In:* M. Alston and K. Whittenbury, eds. *Research, Action and Policy: Addressing the Gendered Impacts of Climate Change.* Dordrecht: Springer, 53–62.

Black, T., 2016. Race, gender, and climate injustice: Dimensions of social and environmental inequality. *In:* P. Godfrey and D. Torres, eds. *Systemic Crises of Global Climate Change: Intersections of Race, Class and Gender.* New York: Routledge, 172–184.

Bonewit, A., 2015. *The Gender Dimension of Climate Justice: In-Depth Analysis for the FEMM Committee.* European Parliament, Directorate – General for Internal Policies. www.europarl.europa.eu/RegData/etudes/IDAN/2015/536478/IPOL_IDA(2015)536478_EN.pdf (accessed 31 January 2018).

Buckingham, S. and Kulcur, R., 2017. It's not just the numbers: Challenging masculinist working practices in climate change decision-making in UK government and non-governmental organizations. *In:* M.G. Cohen, ed. *Climate Change and Gender in Rich Countries: Work, Public Policy and Action.* London/New York: Routledge/Earthscan, 35–51.

Buckingham, S. and Le Masson, V., 2017. *Understanding Climate Change Through Gender Relations.* Oxon/New York: Routledge.

Clayton, S., Manning, C., and Hodge, C., 2014. *Beyond Storms and Droughts: The Psychological Impacts of Climate Change.* Washington, DC: American Psychological Association and ecoAmerica.

Cohen, M.G., 2015. Gendered emissions: Counting greenhouse gas emissions by gender and why it matters. *In:* C. Lipsig-Mummé and S. McBride, eds. *Working in a Warming World.* Montreal, QC and Kingston, ON: McGill – Queen's University Press, 59–81.

Cohen, M.G., ed., 2017. *Climate Change and Gender in Rich Countries: Work, Public Policy and Action.* New York/London: Routledge.

Danaher, K., Biggs, S., and Mark, J., 2007. *Building the Green Economy: Success Stories From the Grassroots.* London/New York: Routledge.

Dankleman, I., ed., 2010. *Gender and Climate Change: An Introduction.* London/New York: Earthscan/Routledge.

Dasgupta, S., Siriner, I., and De, P.S., eds., 2010. *Women's Encounter With Disaster.* London: Frontpage Publications.

Denton, F., 2002. Climate change vulnerability, impacts, and adaptation: Why does gender matter? *Gender and Development* 10 (20), 10–20.

De Onís, K.M., 2012. 'Looking both ways': Metaphor and the rhetorical alignment of intersectional climate justice and reproductive justice concerns. *Environmental Communication* 6 (3), 308–327.

Duncan, K., 2008. Feeling the heat: Women's health in a changing climate. *Canadian Women's Health Network,* 10 (2), n.p.

Dunn, L., 2009. The Gendered Dimensions of Environmental Justice: Caribbean Perspectives. *In:* F.C. Steady, ed., *Environmental Justice in the New Millennium.* New York: Palgrave Macmillan, 115–133.

EIGE, 2012. *Review of the Implementation in the EU of Area K of the Beijing Platform for Action: Women and the Environment.* Gender Equality and Climate Change. Report. Luxembourg: European Institute for Gender Equality.

Enarson, E., 2012. *Women Confronting Natural Disaster: From Vulnerability to Resilience.* Boulder: Lynne Reinner.

Fortier, C., 2017. *Unsettling the Commons: Social Movements Within, Against, and Beyond Settler Colonialism.* Winnipeg: ARP Books.

Gibson-Graham, J.K., 2006. *A Postcapitalist Politics*. Minneapolis/London: University of Minnesota Press.

Global Gender and Climate Alliance, 2016. *Gender and Climate Change: A Closer Look at Existing Evidence*. Washington, DC: IUCN Global Gender Office.

Godfrey, P. and Torres, D., eds., 2016. *Systemic Crises of Global Climate Change: Intersections of Race, Class and Gender*. New York: Routledge.

Goldsmith, R.E., Feygina, I., and Jost, J.T., 2013. The gender gap in environmental attitudes: A system justification perspective. *In*: M. Alston and K. Whittenbury, eds., *Research, Action, and Policy: Addressing the Gendered Impacts of Climate Change*. Dordrecht: Springer, 159–170.

Gorecki, J., 2014. 'No climate justice without gender justice': Women at the forefront of the People's Climate March. *Feminist Wire*, September 29. www.thefeministwire.com/2014/09/climate-justice-without-gender-justice-women-forefront-peoples-climate-march/ (accessed 31 January 2018).

Habtezion, S., 2013. *Overview of Linkages Between Gender and Climate Change: Gender and Climate Change Training Module 1*. New York: United Nations Development Programme.

Hemmati, M., 2008. *Gender Perspectives on Climate Change*. New York: United Nations Commission on the Status of Women, Emerging Issues Panel. www.un.org/womenwatch/daw/csw/csw52/panels/climatechangepanel/M.Hemmati%20Presentation%20Climate%20Change.pdf (accessed 31 January 2018).

Horn-Miller, K., 2017. Distortion and healing: Finding balance and a 'Good Mind' through the rearticulation of Sky Woman's journey. *In*: N. Kermoal and I. Altamirano-Jiménez, eds. *Living on the Land: Indigenous Women's Understanding of Place*. Edmonton: Athabasca University Press, 19–38.

IFRC, 2007. *World Disaster Report – Focus on Discrimination*. Geneva: International Federation of Red Cross and Red Crescent Societies.

ILO, 2008. *Green Jobs: Improving the climate for gender equality too!*Geneva: International Labour Organization.

ILO, 2016. *Gender, Labour and a Just Transition Towards Environmentally Sustainable Economies and Societies for All*. Geneva: International Labour Organization.

Isla, A., 2009. Who pays for the Kyoto Protocol? *In*: A. Salleh, ed. *Eco-Sufficiency and Global Justice: Women Write Political Ecology*. London: Pluto Press, 199–217.

Israel, A.L. and Sachs, C., 2013. A climate for feminist intervention: Feminist science studies and climate change. *In*: M. Alston and K. Whittenbury, eds. *Research, Action and Policy: Addressing the Gendered Impacts of Climate Change*. Dordrecht: Springer, 33–52.

Kaijser, A. and Kronsell, A., 2014. Climate change through the lens of intersectionality. *Environmental Politics*, 23 (3), 417–433.

Kaufman, C., 2012. *Getting Past Capitalism: History, Vision, Hope*. Lanham: Lexington Books.

Klein, N., 2014. *This Changes Everything: Capitalism vs. the Climate*. New York: Simon & Schuster.

Kronsell, A., 2017. The contribution of feminist perspectives to climate governance. *In*: S. Buckingham and V. Le Masson, eds. *Understanding Climate Change Through Gender Relations*. Oxon/New York: Routledge, 104–120.

Lambrou, Y. and Piana, G., 2006. *Gender: The Missing Component of the Response to Climate Change*. Rome: United Nations Food and Agriculture Organization.

Lindzon, J., 2016. There are now more Fortune 500 companies with all-male boards than in 2015. *Fortune*, March 28. http://fortune.com/2016/03/28/fortune-500-all-male-board-2016/ (accessed 31 January 2018).

Luft, R.E., 2009. Beyond disaster exceptionalism: Social movement developments in New Orleans after Hurricane Katrina. *American Quarterly* 61 (3), 501–509.

Macgregor, S., 2010. Gender and climate change: From impacts to discourses. *Journal of the Indian Ocean Region* 6 (2), 223–238.

Macgregor, S., 2017. Moving beyond impacts: More answers to the 'gender and climate change' question. *In*: S. Buckingham and V. Le Masson, eds. *Understanding Climate Change Through Gender Relations*. Oxon/New York: Routledge.

Mather, L., 2015. Dear white men: Five pieces of advice for 91 percent of Fortune 500 CEOs. *Huffpost*, August 4. www.huffingtonpost.com/laura-mather/dear-white-men-seven-piec_b_7899084.html

McNutt, K. and Hawryluk, S., 2009. Women and climate change policy: Integrating gender into the agenda. *In*: A.Z. Dobrowolsky, ed. *Women and Public Policy in Canada: Neoliberalism and After?* Don Mills: Oxford University Press, 107–124.

Mellor, M., 1992. *Breaking the Boundaries: Towards a Feminist Green Socialism*. London: Virago Press.

Mellor, M., 1997. *Feminism and Ecology*. London: Wiley.

Mies, M., 1986. *Patriarchy and Accumulation on a World Scale: Women in the International Division of Labour*. London: Zed Books.

Moosa, C.S. and Tuana, N., 2014. Mapping a research agenda concerning gender and climate change: A review of the literature. *Hypatia* 29 (3), 677–694.

Morrow, K., 2012. Climate change, major groups and the importance of a seat at the table: Women and the UNFCC negotiations. *In*: J. Penca and C. de Andrade, eds. *The Dominance of Climate Change in Environmental Law: Taking Stock for Rio +20*. Florence: European University Institute, 26–36.

Nagel, J., 2015. *Gender and Climate Change: Impacts, Science, and Policy*. London: Taylor and Francis.

Narine, S., 2015. Violence against aboriginal women not an aboriginal-only issue. *Windspeaker* 23 (1). www.ammsa.com/publications/alberta-sweetgrass/violence-against-aboriginal-women-not-aboriginal-only-issue (accessed 28 January 2018).

Nelson, J., 2012. *Is Dismissing the Precautionary Principle the Manly Thing To Do? Gender and the Economics of Climate Change*. Medford, MA: Tufts University Global Development and Environmenta Institute, Working Paper Number 12-04.

Neumayer, E. and Plümper, T., 2007. The gendered nature of natural disasters: The impact of catastrophic events on the gender gap in life expectancy, 1981–2002. *Annals of the Association of American Geographers* 97 (3), 551–566.

Nixon, L., 2015. Ecofeminist appropriations of Indigenous feminisms and environmental violence. *Feminist Wire*, April 30. www.thefeministwire.com/2015/04/eco-feminist-appropriations-of-indigenous-feminisms-and-environmental-violence/ (accessed 28 January 2018).

Osborne, N., 2015. Intersectionality and kyriarchy: A framework for approaching power and social justice in planning and climate change adaptation. *Planning Theory* 14 (2), 130–151.

Ostrom, E., 2014. A polycentric approach for coping with climate change. *Annals of Economics and Finance*, 15 (1), 97–134.

Perera, A., 2012. *Women Are the Foot Soldiers of Climate Change Adaptation – Expert*. Thomson Reuters Foundation, August 2. www.trust.org/item/?map=women-are-the-foot-soldiers-of-climate-change-adaptation-expert (accessed 31 January 2018).

Perkins, P.E., 2013. Environmental activism and gender. *In*: D.M. Figart and T.L. Warnecke, eds. *Handbook of Research on Gender and Economic Life*. Cheltenham/Northampton: Edward Elgar, 504–521.

Perkins, P.E., 2017a. Gender justice and climate justice, building women's economic and political agency through global partnerships. *In*: S. Buckingham and V. Le Masson, eds. *Understanding Climate Change Through Gender Relations*. Oxon/New York: Routledge, 45–63.

Perkins, P.E., 2017b. Canadian Indigenous female leadership and political agency on climate change. *In*: M.G. Cohen, ed. *Climate Change and Gender in Rich Countries: Work, Public Policy and Action*. London/New York: Routledge/Earthscan, 283–296.

Plumwood, V., 1994. *Feminism and the Mastery of Nature*. London/New York: Routledge.

Pyles, L. and Lewis, J.S., 2010. Women, intersectionality and resistance in the context of Hurricane Katrina. *In*: S. Dasgupta, I. Siriner, and P.S. De, eds. *Women's Encounter With Disaster*. London: Frontpage Publications, 77–86.

Rainham, D.G.C. and Smoyer-Tomic, K.E., 2003. The role of air pollution in the relationship between a heat stress index and human mortality in Toronto. *Environmental Research* 93 (1), 9–19.

Ravera, F., Martín-López, B., Pascual, U., and Drucker, A., 2016. The diversity of gendered adaptation strategies to climate change of Indian farmers: A feminist intersectional approach. *Ambio* 45 (Suppl. 3), S335–S351.

Roberts, M., 2009. War, climate change, and women. *Race, Poverty, and the Environment* 16 (2), 39–41.

Rodenberg, B., 2009. *Climate Change Adaptation From a Gender Perspective: A Cross-cutting Analysis of Development-policy Instruments*. Bonn: German Development Institute.

Rodriguez, M., 2015. Facing climate change through justice and intersectionality. *350.org*, September 3. https://350.org/facing-climate-change-through-justice-and-intersectionality/ (accessed 31 January 2018).

Röhr, U., Hemmati, M., and Lambrou, Y., 2010. Towards gender equality in climate change policy: Challenges and perspectives for the future. *In*: E. Enarson and P.G. Dhar Chakrabarti, eds. *Women, Gender and Disaster: Global Issues and Initiatives*. New Delhi: Sage Publications India, 289–304.

Röhr, U., Spitzner, M., Stiefel, E., and Winterfeld, U., 2008. *Gender Justice as the Basis for Sustainable Climate Policies*. Bonn: German NGO Forum on Environment and Development.

Salleh, A., ed., 2009. *Eco-sufficiency and Global Justice: Women Write Political Ecology*. New York: Pluto Press.

Schalatek, L., 2009. *Gender and Climate Finance: Double Mainstreaming for Sustainable Development*. Washington, DC: Heinrich Böll Foundation North America.

Skutsch, M., 2002. Protocols, treaties, and action: The 'climate change process' viewed through gender spectacles. *Gender and Development – Climate Change* 10 (2), 30–39.

Spencer, P., Erickson, J., and Perkins, P.E., 2018. Shoring up the base: Addressing the need for a strong voice on distribution and justice in Ecological Economics. *Ecological Economics*, 152, 191–198.

Terry, G., 2009. *Climate Change and Gender Justice*. Rugby: Practical Action Publishing in Association with Oxfam GB.

Toronto Public Health, 2009. *Climate Change Adaptation and Health Equity: Background Report*. Prepared by Clean Air Partnership.

Trosper, R.L., 2009. *Resilience, Reciprocity, and Ecological Economics*. London/New York: Routledge.

Tschakert, P. and Machado, M., 2012. Gender justice and rights in climate change adaptation: Opportunities and pitfalls. *Ethics and Social Welfare* 6 (3), 275–289.

Tuana, N., 2008. Viscous porosity: Witnessing Katrina. *In:* S. Alaimo and S. Hekman, eds. *Material Feminisms*. Bloomington: Indiana University Press, 188–213.

Tuana, N., 2013. Gendering climate knowledge for justice: Catalyzing a new research agenda. *In:* M. Alston and K. Whittenbury, eds. *Research, Action and Policy: Addressing the Gendered Impacts of Climate Change*. Dordrecht: Springer, 3–16.

UNDP, 2008. *Resource Guide on Gender and Climate Change*. New York: United Nations Development Programme.

Walsh, E., 2016. Why we need intersectionality to understand climate change. Center for World Indigenous Studies, *Intercontinental Cry*, June 8. https://intercontinentalcry.org/need-intersectionality-understand-climate-change/ (accessed 31 January 2018).

WEA & NYSHN, 2016. *Violence on the Land, Violence on Our Bodies: Building an Indigenous Response to Environmental Violence*. Berkeley/Toronto: Women's Earth Alliance and Native Youth Sexual Health Network.

WEI, 2015. *Women and Environments International Magazine*. Special issue on 'Women and Work in a Warming World,' (94–95).

Weiss, C., 2012. *Women and Environmental Justice: A Literature Review*. Thornbury: Women's Health in the North (WHIN).

White, K.P., 2014. Indigenous women, climate change impacts, and collective action. *Hypatia* 29 (3), 599–616.

WHO, 2012. *Mainstreaming Gender in Health Adaptation to Climate Change Programmes: User's Guide*. Geneva: World Health Organization.

WHO, 2014. *Gender, Climate Change and Health*. Geneva: World Health Organization.

Wilson, J., 2017. *Climate Change Politics in the UK: A Feminist Intersectional Analysis*. Oslo: European Consortium for Political Research General Conference.

WomenWatch, 2010. *Women, Gender Equality and Climate Change*. New York: Inter-Agency Network on Women and Gender Equality (IANWGE).

27

"No climate justice without gender justice"

Explorations of the intersections between gender and climate injustices in climate adaptation actions in the Philippines

Roa Petra Crease, Meg Parsons and Karen Toni Fisher

Introduction

Over the last decade, the slogan "no climate justice without gender justice" has become frequently used (Alvarez and Lovera, 2016; McKinney and Fulkerson, 2015; Rochette, 2016; Terry, 2009). While women's involvement in climate change science and policy-making at a global level remains circumscribed, women of the Global South often feature (alongside images of polar bears, people living on atolls, flooded and damaged settlements) as emblems of campaigns and debates about climate justice (Arora-Jonsson, 2011; Djoudi et al., 2016; Sultana, 2014; Vinyeta et al., 2016). Media, non-government organisations, politicians and scientists regularly depict women from the Global South as highly vulnerable victims of the negative impacts of climate change due to social norms that dictate their behaviours as well as their enhanced poverty due to reliance on the environment for subsistence (Arora-Jonsson, 2011; Denton, 2002). In this chapter, we examine the ways in which intersectionality thinking can help us to evaluate what constitutes sustainable and gender-equal climate adaptation policies and practices.

This chapter draws on critical climate adaptation, feminist political ecology and intersectionality approaches to examine efforts to address the intersections of climate and gender injustices in the Philippines. This research is based on a larger research project, led by the lead author, which explores how gender and climate change are conceptualised in policy and practice in the Philippines. Here, we examine one aspect of the research: how decision-makers take gender equality into account in climate change adaptation planning and projects. The ways in which vulnerability is conceptualised determines the types of adaptation responses undertaken. The majority of climate adaptation projects that have sought to address gender inequality framed it in terms of poverty reduction, with efforts to reduce women's vulnerability focused primarily on increasing women's participation in the market economy and the provision of technological solutions to moderate climate variability. We argue that market-based and techno-centric strategies hold the potential to exacerbate rather than reduce vulnerability to climate change, particularly for women in rural communities, as issues of power and privilege remain unaddressed.

We begin by providing a brief overview of some of the scholarship about climate justice, climate adaptation and gendered vulnerability. We then outline our case study of the Philippines focusing on the classification of women as highly vulnerable to climate change, as well as climate adaptation projects implemented in the Philippines to reduce vulnerability. Lastly, we discuss the ways in which the narrow focus on economic development is constraining efforts to address the specific climate injustices women in the Global South face.

Climate change adaptation and vulnerability

In international and domestic forums, scholars, activists, communities and other stakeholders employ diverse conceptualisations of climate justice to support their positions as equitable, as well as to advocate for the recognition of their interests and rights within climate policy (Comim, 2008; Fisher, 2015; Klinsky et al., 2012; Lander et al., 2009; Schlosberg and Collins, 2014; Smith and Rhiney, 2016). Broadly speaking, climate justice scholarship falls within two dominant categories: distributive justice and procedural justice (Fisher, 2015; Schlosberg and Collins, 2014). Theories of distributive justice relate to the distribution of the costs and benefits of climate change across and between societies. Procedural justice refers to "how and by whom decisions on adaptive responses are made" (Thomas and Twyman, 2005, p. 116). According to Schlosberg and Collins (2014), climate justice includes both distributive and procedural elements; not only the distribution of environmental goods and harms between nations, but also the distribution of the impacts of climate change at national and local levels, and the need for recognition and participation in decision-making.

In this chapter, we focus specifically on how decision-makers and local communities in the Philippines are planning for, and seeking to adapt to, the impacts of climate change, and the ways in which efforts to address gender and climate injustices are intertwined. Rather than seeking to define and articulate a universal concept of climate justice, we provide a contextualised understanding of different gendered vulnerabilities and capacities to adapt, and the justice implications of adaptation strategies. We draw on Fraser's (2008) definition of justice centring on parity of participation, which requires social, political and economic arrangements that permit all in society to participate on equitable terms. Thus, overcoming injustices involves the dismantling of institutionalised constraints that restrict some groups of people (in this instance, women) from participating as full partners in decision-making about development and climate change adaptation. Fraser (2008) identifies three key types of barriers to addressing injustices: (1) economic systems that inhibit the ability of individuals or groups to participate (a form of distributive injustice); (2) institutionalised arrangements of socio-cultural values that limit participation (such as gender and/or class inequalities); and (3) political structures that restrict the political representation of certain groups (such as misrepresentation) (Fraser, 2008). Our focus on efforts to address gender injustices in climate change adaptation in the Filipino context draws attention to how adaptation takes place and issues of fairness, equity and sustainability in adaptation decision-making.

Although there is still no one universally accepted definition for climate change adaptation, adaptation is increasingly described as a process, outcome and goal undertaken by individuals, households, communities and institutions in response to climatic and environmental extremes and changes (Adger et al., 2009; Brown and Siri, 2012; Dovers and Hezri, 2010; Pelling et al., 2015). Climate adaptation is increasingly linked to sustainable development, which is encapsulated in the concept of sustainable adaptation and explicitly referenced in the recently established Sustainable Development Goals (SDGs) of the United Nations (UN). Adaptation measures that do not address social justice issues are considered unsustainable (Brown and Siri, 2012). The capacity to respond and adapt to climate change is shaped by power relations influencing access knowledge, resources and the availability of choices. These factors are inextricably connected to social identities of people and groups. Gender is a key factor of these identities and social relations. A review of environmental policy and gender research demonstrates that, despite four decades of gender-focused development, gender inequity still persists (Agarwal, 1997; Arora-Jonsson, 2014; Bennett, 2005; Moser, 1993; Sultana, 2010). Thus, the critical question is how gender relations and gender inequalities intersect with the challenges posed by climate change.

The impacts of climate change are not evenly distributed across or between communities; rather, vulnerability to harm is differentially distributed. A large body of research has been directed towards understanding the degree to which nations in the Global South are vulnerable to the impacts of climate change, including climate-related hazards, and the ways in which vulnerability can be reduced (Adger, 1999; Eriksen et al., 2005; Leichenko and O'Brien, 2002). Although the term *vulnerability* is highly contested and there are multiple definitions, it is typically used by academics to refer to the degree to which a population is susceptible to, or unable to cope with, the adverse impacts of climate change (including climate variability and extreme weather events) (Adger, 1999; O'Brien et al., 2007). Many scholars argue that the Philippines is highly vulnerable to the impacts of climate change because the Filipino population is exposed to a wide range of hazards (such as typhoons, flooding, drought and inundation), who possess limited capacities to adapt (due to limited financial resources, lack of information and technologies, colonial legacies, uneven development, political corruption and instability) (Chandra et al., 2017; de Leon and Pittock, 2017; Gusyev et al., 2015; Landicho et al., 2015; Tolentino et al., 2016). Climate change exacerbates the frequencies and intensities of climate-related hazards and disasters, with existing social and gender injustices complicating climate adaptation strategies.

Vulnerability is not simply another word for poverty, despite the conflation of the two terms in development discourse (Sultana, 2018). Vulnerability is contextual and a result of the interactions among risks, capacities and susceptibilities to hazards (Leichenko and O'Brien, 2002; O'Brien et al., 2007; O'Brien and Wolf, 2010). In many places in the Global South, vulnerability and poverty are closely linked, and gender reinforces both the vulnerability and poverty individuals encounter in their day-to-day lives (Ahmed et al., 2016; Babatunde et al., 2007; Mason and Agan, 2015; Sultana, 2018, 2010). Vulnerabilities are connected to social, cultural, economic and biophysical factors, all situated within the deeper political ecologies of globalisation, neo-colonialism and development (Cameron, 2016; Chandra et al., 2017; Eriksen et al., 2005; Howitt et al., 2012; Veland et al., 2013). While there is greater focus on the diversity of gendered differences in vulnerabilities in specific places and groups of people, not all women are similarly vulnerable, even if their gender identity frequently contributes to them as a group being vulnerable to a multitude of systems and forces (Arora-Jonsson, 2011; Chandra et al., 2017; Djoudi and Brockhaus, 2011; Sultana, 2010).

Gender and vulnerability

Scholars and decision-makers are increasingly focusing their attention on the interactions between climate change and gender, particularly with regards to women's vulnerability to the impacts of climate change (Antwi-Agyei et al., 2017; Antwi-Agyei et al., 2013; Bhattarai et al., 2015; Cutter, 2017; Denton, 2002; Figueiredo and Perkins, 2013; Tall et al., 2014). The emergent body of scholarship, which draws primarily on disaster risk reduction (DRR) and development studies, highlights that women in the Global South are one of the most vulnerable groups to environmental crises, and the potential impacts of climate change are similarly likely to disproportionately affect women (Burton and Cutter, 2008; Cutter, 2017; Denton, 2002; Sultana, 2010). Gender influences access to and usage of climate-sensitive resources (including freshwater and food), risk perceptions, experiences and responses to disasters, and household climate adaptation strategies. Women and girls are often more likely than men and boys to be killed and injured during climate-related disasters (Cutter, 2017; Sultana, 2018; Waite, 2000). For instance, in rural communities in the Global South, women lack information about flood preparedness and evacuation procedures, are often unable to swim, are tasked with responsibility for care of children, elderly family members, and belongings, and stay home rather than going to disaster shelters (Sultana, 2018). Likewise, during disasters violence against women and girls frequently increases (Fisher, 2010; Sultana, 2010). Gendered violence, migration, and poverty, scholars argue, compound climate risks and increase vulnerabilities (Burton and Cutter, 2008; Chandra and McNamara, 2017; Cutter, 2017; Oliver-Smith, 2012).

Climate change, characterised as both gradual and sudden environmental crises, is occurring in socio-ecological locations that are saturated with gender and other power relations. Gender inequalities create distinctly gendered climate injustices. Difficulties of determining differential and complex overlapping vulnerabilities can contribute to the creation and implementation of ad hoc and inappropriate adaptation strategies, which can reinforce rather than alleviate social inequalities and heighten vulnerability to climate risks. Globally, women are generally less likely to be in positions of power in governments and organisations that are tasked with planning for and responding to climate risks (Beaumier et al., 2015; Nabikolo et al., 2012; Sultana, 2018).

Feminist scholars critique existing climate change research and policies for treating women as a homogenous group (Arora-Jonsson, 2011; Bee et al., 2015; Sultana, 2014). Women in the Global South are often presented as helpless victims of climate change or adaptation saviours tasked with ensuring their families are climate resilient (Arora-Jonsson, 2011; Djoudi et al., 2016; Figueiredo and Perkins, 2013; McNamara and Westoby, 2011; Onta and Resurreccion, 2011; Resurrección, 2013). Scholars highlight that a narrow focus on women as victims and/or caretakers, and which emphasises women's knowledge, responsibilities and roles, does not take power relations into account, and may contribute towards the feminisation of both vulnerability and responsibility for adaptation (Arora-Jonsson, 2011; Tschakert and Machado, 2012). This not only reinforces stereotypes of women but also fails to consider the diverse and unequal experiences within and between genders (women, men and gender diverse minorities) in research and decision-making (Djoudi et al., 2016; Gaillard et al., 2017). This lack of recognition of the intersection of identities and power relations means the underlying causes of differential vulnerability and adaptive capacities often remain unacknowledged and unaddressed. In some instances, lack of recognition can translate into policies and practices that serve to enhance rather than reduce gendered vulnerabilities (gendered climate injustices). Accordingly, it is critical that scholars, policymakers and climate adaptation practitioners consider ways to avoid reinforcing gender inequalities and creating future climate injustices in climate change adaptation research and actions.

Scholars adopting feminist political ecology and intersectionality approaches challenge the unsubstantiated depiction of women as a homogenous group by identifying multiple identities working together to construct differential experiences of power and powerlessness (Arora-Jonsson, 2011; Djoudi et al., 2016; Iniesta-Arandia et al., 2016; Nightingale and Ojha, 2013; Valentine, 2007). Furthermore, feminist social scientists question the legitimacy of the binary male-female perspective of gender (Bee et al., 2015; Fletcher, 2018; Osborne, 2015), and argue that people are subjected to multiple categories of social difference. As such, gender is always intersected by other subjectivities (class, race, ethnicity, caste, religion, physical abilities, sexual orientation, education and so forth) (Kaijser and Kronsell, 2014; Osborne, 2015; Yuval-Davis, 2016). An intersectional approach, therefore, recognises that social groups are dynamic and interact with one another to create distinct social locations, and that multiple forms of inequalities can operate at the same time. Thus, people can be simultaneously included and excluded from groups, and experience belonging and marginalisation. In the context of climate change, intersectionality thinking is helpful for challenging simplistic constructions of vulnerable groups as passive and innocent victims of climate change (Arora-Jonsson, 2011; Djoudi et al., 2016). An intersectional framing of climate change vulnerability, we argue, considers how power structures within particular social organisations shape individual and community experiences of climate variability and change. Power, as conceptualised by Bourdieu, is a social relationship rather than an external force, with power relations dictating access and entitlements to resources, including those to adapt to climate change (Bourdieu, 1991, p. 242). By adopting an intersectional approach in our study, we consider how women's experiences of environmental risks, climate-sensitive livelihoods and resources, and existing government and international development climate adaptation strategies are influenced by gender norms as well as other social categories.

Research methods and context

This research adopted a case study approach to investigate the gendered dimensions of climate change at a local level. The case study focuses on the City of San Fernando (CSF), located in the La Union Province of the Ilocos Region of the Philippines (see Figure 27.1). At the time of the 2015 census, 121,812 people lived in CSF. In addition to the city being the financial, political and industrial centre for the province, the city's coastal and mountainous location also supports significant primary industries (chiefly farming and fishing), with 80% of the city's total land area used for agricultural activities. There is also an uneven distribution of wealth and poverty between rural and urban areas, with farming and fisher-folk households experiencing higher rates of poverty compared to urban households. Rural poverty is associated with subsistence livelihoods not connected to the market economy and other factors (such as class, land tenure arrangements and education) (Bambalan, 2016; Posadas, 2016; Valdez, 2016).

The lead author conducted fieldwork for the case study over a two-month period in 2016. The empirical data comprises 25 semi-structured interviews (see Table 27.1), participant observation

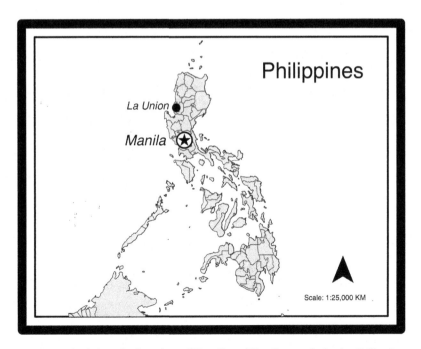

Figure 27.1 Map depicting the location of The City of San Fernando in the Philippines.

Table 27.1 List of interviewees.

Title	Name	Position	Organisation
Ma'am	Mary Jane Ortega	Former Mayor President	CSF Federated Asian-Pacific Association (FAWA)
Ma'am	Lilibeth D. Javilinar	Stall Owner Ambassador	Joe-Beth Papercrafts World Vision (Santa Maria Bulacan)
Sir	Eduardo S. Posadas	OIC	City Health Officer and Disaster Risk Reduction
Ma'am	Mickey Galang	Co-supervisor	LINK
	Wishes to not be identified	Employee 1	National Economic Development Agency (NEDA)
	Wishes to not be identified	Employee 1	NEDA
Ma'am	Almira B. Adrazado	Chapter Head (regional, provincial and municipal)	Red Cross
Ma'am	Julie Ann B. Hipina	Community-based organiser	Red Cross
Sir/ENG	Cezar Manuel Cabansag Jr.	Provincial planning officer	Provincial Planning and Management Division (PMD)
Ma'am	Mary Jane Alua	Provincial coordinator and GAD coordinator	Provincial Department of Agriculture (DA)
Ma'am	Katherine Iona Muller	Employee	City Environment and Natural Resources Office (CENRO)
Ma'am	Eduvijis T. Flores	City Agriculturist	Department of Agriculture (DA)
Ma'am	Florycel G. Obena	Employee	DA
Sir	Rudan S. Garin	Employee	CENRO (marine based fisheries projects)
Sir	Eduardo C. Apilado Jr	Employee	CENRO (Lingsat Marine Protected Area)
Sir	Ranilo C. Impac	Officer	Provincial Social Welfare and Development (SWD)
Sir	Bernando Casaga	Farmer (from Pao Norte) and Barangay appointed member	Head of Pao Norte Agricultural Committee
Ma'am	Rizalyn D. Medrano	OIC	Office of Strategy Management
Ma'am	Sally C. Matoza	OIC and GAD Coordinator	City Social Welfare and Development (SWD)
Prosecutor	Florence Marie A Gacad- Ulep	Associated Provincial Prosecutor	Office of the Provincial Prosecutor
Sir	Dexter A. Dumaguin	Employee Project coordinator	Department of Trade and Industry (DTI) The Great Women 2 Project
Sir	Valmar M. Valdez	OIC GAD coordinator	CENRO
Dr/Ma'am	Rizalina G. Cristobal	OIC and GAD coordinator	City Development Office
Ma'am	Gwendolyn Bambalan	OIC and GAD coordinator	Department of Natural Resources (DNR)
Ma'am	Gavina Tumbaga	OIC and GAD coordinator	City Fishing and Aquatic Resource Management Council

Table 27.2 Documents collected and analysed.

Title	Author/Publisher	Provided by
The Local Climate Change Action Plan of San Fernando (2016) (DRAFT)	The City of San Fernando Municipal Government	Katherine Iona Muller of CENRO
Harmonised Guidelines for Gender and Development (2014)	• The National Economic and Development Authority (NEDA) • The Philippine Commission on Women (PCW)	NEDA Employees
Gender and Development Annual Investment Budget (2016)	The City of San Fernando Municipal Government	Mary Ann Rodriguez Rivera on behalf of the Mayor of CSF
The GAD Income Generating Project: Rural women's livelihood project (2016)	• The City of San Fernando Municipal Government • The Department of Agricultural (City)	Florycel G. Obena of the City Department of Agriculture
Comprehensive Local Use Plan and City Development Plan	• The City of San Fernando Municipal Government	Katherine Iona Muller of CENRO
Asia Cities Adapt Project (2013)	Written by Javier, Deocariza, Aquitania, 2013 Funded by the Asian Development bank (ADb) and The Federal Ministry of Finance (BMF)	Katherine Iona Muller of CENRO
City Disaster Risk Reduction and Management Plan (2014–2019).	The National Disaster Risk Management Council	City Planning Office

and content analysis of key government policy documents (see Table 27.2). Interview participants included government and community leaders, as well as people whose livelihoods are considered climate-sensitive (farmers, and fisher-folks).

Climate variability chiefly associated with El Niño and La Niña events already negatively affects the livelihoods and wellbeing of people living in CSF. El Niño is associated with decreased rainfall and drought events, with water insecurity an ongoing problem for households both in urban and rural areas. La Niña events are characterised by higher rainfall, strong monsoon activity and the formation of more tropical cyclones; as a consequence, flooding, strong winds and landslides are common biophysical phenomena. CSF regularly experiences extreme weather events including tropical cyclones, flooding, strong winds, drought and coastal erosion, which are likely to become more frequent and/or more intense because of climate change.

Since 1979, the Philippines has been a signatory to a number of international agreements to address gender inequalities, and has introduced various legislation that recognises the rights of women (see Figure 27.2). The Philippines now ranks highly on the Global Gender Gap Index; however, statistics show more women are unemployed than men (World Economic Forum, 2016). Current statistics exclude women's unpaid roles in the informal sector, which are associated with particular gender roles and societal norms that vary between geographical location and socio-economic class. A 2006 United Nations report identified the need for more effective poverty-alleviation strategies to help poor women in both urban and rural areas, including those working in the informal sector, as they lack basic support systems such as social security and health insurance (United Nations, 2006). National legislation aims to ensure there are no gender

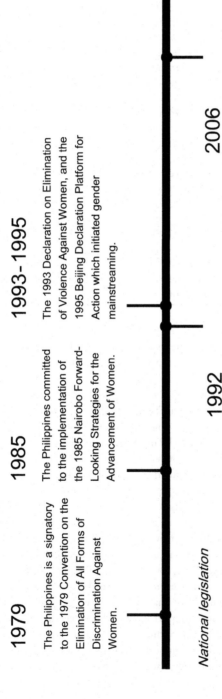

Figure 27.2 Timeline of key international agreements and Filipino national policies concerning gender equality.

biases within Filipino society, including in employment and in government. However, policy does not necessarily translate into practice, with gender biases especially difficult to regulate among fisher and farming communities who often reside in areas, or engage in practices, that fall within the informal economic sector.

There are various government and development organisations working to prepare farmers and fisher-folk to cope with the effects of climate-related hazards. Both men and women work on farms and in fisheries in the Philippines; however, access to resources, involvement in decision-making and government representation are often dominated by men because of unequal power relations and social norms. This results in the unequal distribution of resources and the under-representation of women in decision-making and government initiatives.

Gendered vulnerability: women as caretakers

Research participants conceptualised women's roles and responsibilities as being tied to caregiving duties (of taking care of the health and wellbeing of children, husbands and other family members), with women's role as caretakers lying at the centre of their vulnerability to the impacts of climate extremes and change. Ma'am Gwendolyn Bambolin explained that during climate-related disasters such as typhoons and flooding events, women in farming communities were more likely to die because they remained in their households. She put this down to social norms that dictated women's role as caretakers of their households, and their lack of education on DRR (Nabikolo et al., 2012; Sultana, 2014, 2018). Similarly, Ma'am Sally C. Matoza explained the implications for women based on gendered expectations about family. She argued that women's vulnerability was linked to familial and household expectations that they would provide additional help to prepare for climate-related risks and undertake DRR strategies because of socially ascribed gender roles positioning them as responsible for the family unit:

> I think women are more vulnerable during disasters because we are the ones that stay at home, we work inside the house: doing the household chores, taking care of our children, everything, so I think that the women, the female must be abreast whatever information they can receive.
>
> *(Matoza, 2016)*

This means, participants argued, women bear multiple responsibilities in their everyday lives as well as in times of environmental crises, which potentially increases their vulnerability to climate risks.

This point was echoed by Ma'am Mary Jane Alua, who said day-to-day caretaking responsibilities primarily fall to women in farming and fisher-folk communities, whereas men's roles are defined as protectors of home and livelihoods (Alua, 2016). During extreme weather events, these responsibilities are intensified:

> I think when there are disasters women are much more affected because they have to think of the children and everything; whereas, men are more concerned with the physical side of things like helping outside.
>
> *(Alua, 2016)*

Ma'am Rizalyn D. Medrano similarly observed how:

> During flood events women are most affected because in evacuation sites they look after the children, and the elderly; whereas, men are considered the protectors so they tend to the

houses and structures but, women prepare the food, the inside of the house, and prepare for disaster events such as making the candles or the lights.

(Medrano, 2016)

More broadly, participants provided examples of how climate change would affect women in the performance of their gendered roles in the future. Bambolin cited the example of procuring water, typically collected by women, and the difficulty in upland areas of CSF due to lack of infrastructure (Bambalan, 2016). Water scarcity is exacerbated by drought and flooding events (the frequency and intensity of which is increasing with climate change), which forces women to travel farther to collect water. These examples highlight how existing climate variability as well as future climatic changes place greater strain on women's gendered tasks.

Our research participants rearticulated the framing of women as mothers and caretakers, which aligns with narrow conceptualisations of women's vulnerability. This links to wider development and climate change scholarship and on-the-ground adaptation responses that frequently couples women together with children as a single category of discussion and analysis (Cutter, 2012, 1995; Masika, 2002; Sultana, 2010; Waite, 2000). This coupling is, however, problematic because it oftentimes (unwittingly) rearticulates traditional gender roles, whereby women are solely valued for their roles as mothers and caregivers. Indeed, other scholars criticise the simplistic classification of women as simultaneously victims and agents of change (Arora-Jonsson, 2011; Sultana, 2018). The climate adaptation policies and practices adopted in CSF were primarily centred on targeting women as agents of change, which conflated vulnerability with poverty and sought to alleviate rural poverty through the commodification of women's labour.

Poverty reduction as climate change adaptation

The Local Climate Change Action Plan (LCCAP) of San Fernando (2016) roots climate change within developmental concerns by asserting "Climate change is one of the strongest development agendas of the 21st century" (The City of San Fernando Municipal Government, 2016). The LCCAP states that CSF has already incurred significant financial loss and damage because of past climate-related disasters, and identifies the need to reclassify and convert marginally productive agricultural land for commercial purposes. The plan emphasises enhancing productivity and moving away from subsistence agriculture, which currently dominates rural livelihoods in CSF. Likewise, in 2008 the Philippine Commission on the Status of Women (CSW) acknowledged that climate change was not a "gender-neutral phenomenon" (Philippine Commission on Women, n.d.) and called for efforts to finance gender equality and women's financial empowerment through poverty-reduction measures.

Indeed, poverty remains a major issue in CSF and the Philippines more broadly, with the majority of our research participants citing poverty-reduction programs as the primary way to address women's vulnerability (Guido, 2018). Participants' conceptualisations of vulnerability were shaped by hegemonic development discourses that depict women in the Global South as vulnerable because they are poor. Our interviewees lamented about the Philippines being undeveloped: "we are a poor country," "we could do more if we had more funding," and so forth. Poverty reduction was the main approach suggested by research participants to reduce women's vulnerability to climate change. Ma'am Sally C. Matoza argued that people in the Philippines needed more resources to cope with environmental changes (Matoza, 2016). The CSF Social Welfare Development Department, Matoza reported, provides trainings to empower women especially on the financial side because families in the Philippines are not rich, therefore the wife should help her husband to provide additional income (Matoza, 2016). Programmes work in partnership with local schools. Activities targeting women include those emphasising domestic tasks (sewing, cooking and baking skills), whereas activities aimed towards men include welding and other male-dominated trades.

Other projects include those focusing on micro-financing women entrepreneurs, which includes providing financial training and support to assist women in poorer communities to "improve the competitiveness and sustainability of their enterprises" (Philippine Commission on Women, 2014). An example is the GREAT Women Project 2 (GW2), which is a joint project between the Philippine and Canadian governments that sells "sustainable handcrafted goods" made by coastal and rural women of CSF and the wider Ilocos region. An employee of the Department of Trade and Industry, who managed the GW2 stall in a shopping mall in CSF, explained how the governments of the Philippines and Canada were working together to "reduce the financial constraints that prevented women from realising their economic potential." He explained, "female resiliency was displayed in the ability of Philippine women's entrepreneurial skills." He elaborated that flooding and droughts associated with climate change could prevent farming activities in the future, hence, the diversification of women's livelihoods could provide rural families with a more reliable source of income. The GW2 project works with already established women entrepreneurs who are registered with local women's associations, and who are then required to enrol in training programs to improve and grow their businesses.

Participants identified Gender and Development Programs (GAD) as important for reducing women's vulnerability, with adaptation actions conceptualised as being tied to development efforts to reduce rural poverty. The CSF's Department of Agriculture collaborates with local Rural Improvement Clubs (RIC) to facilitate GAD income-generating activities in CSF rural *barangays* (communities or lowest administrative level in the Philippines). The barangays participating in the RIC are each provided with a water pump to alleviate water scarcity in rural areas due to remoteness. Since the collection of water is often delegated to women, the provision of water pumps is considered a GAD activity as it seeks to alleviate the burden of tasks often undertaken by women.

GAD RIC livelihood projects include small-scale *guluyan* (gardening) and backyard chicken- and goat-raising. Women predominantly undertake these activities; therefore, GAD RIC livelihood projects ostensibly address gender injustices. Although produce and livestock are grown and reared for home consumption, recipients are encouraged to sell their produce and livestock for additional household income. The highest-earning participants of the GAD RIC projects receive a cash reward to incentivise higher productivity yields. These entrepreneurial income-generating activities are promoted as vulnerability-reduction strategies as they "gradually strengthen and eventually help women raise their family income." Although the programs do not specifically mention climate change, the RIC are considered by both government officials and community members as being important for reducing vulnerability by providing women (and by extension, their families) with additional income needed to adapt to the impacts of climate change.

Government officials see the RIC as vital to poverty reduction and nation building, with gender injustices viewed through the lens of financial power. Rural women are charged with responsibility for augmenting "their present meagre income" (The GAD Income Generating Project: Rural women's livelihood project, 2016, p. 2) by entering the market economy. The "meagre income" of women implies that rural women are not participating enough in the productive (monetary) sector compared to men, who are considered the main income generator ('male breadwinner'). The economic activities of rural women, in particular, are undervalued because they are often situated within the informal economy (which includes subsistence, domestic labour, battering and other non-monetised activities). Development agendas privilege the formal economy over the informal economy. National Economic and Development Authority

(NEDA) employees further explained that government policy "emphasises that women should be equal partners of men in development aspects" so as to improve the family's socio-economic status and in turn contribute to "nation building." This discourse and associated policies and practices positions incorporation in the market economy as a key component of capacity building and livelihood diversification. This is problematic, we argue, because, within this discursive frame, women's capacities (to cope and adapt to both environmental and economic shocks and disruptions) are seen only in the interests of development goals rather than the promotion of "women's rights for their own sake" (Chant and Sweetman, 2012).

Research participants explained that, in addition to the Philippine government projects, international development agencies concentrated climate change adaptation activities in areas of economic development. There were numerous entrepreneurship programs, funded by government and international aid, in CSF specifically targeting women who worked as vendors in the marketplace and who assumed the marketing role within farming and fishing communities. A study about poverty alleviation strategies from Cebu in the Philippines (where child malnutrition is high) demonstrated that the more money women earned and controlled, the more households spent on food (Schmeer, 2005). Schmeer's (2005) study showed that, in the Philippines and throughout the Global South, the improvement of women's economic status can contribute towards greater spending on household goods that can materially benefit children. Similarly, our research participants drew links between women's enhanced involvement in the market economy, to changes in gender roles within the household and social expectations of women and men.

Development and climate change policies and projects are not gender-neutral, although scientific and policy discourses frequently portray them as such. How people understand the problems of climate change and poverty, and what solutions are chosen to be implemented, reflects existing socio-cultural relations of power and privilege, and of inclusion and marginalisation (Fletcher, 2018, p. 36). Gender – a set of social roles, relations and practices that vary over space and time – operates materially, ideologically and discursively. Gender shapes people's access to resources, decision-making roles, privileges and responsibilities, while also (re)creating specific "truths" that become naturalised in discourse and ideology. In the Philippines, women are concurrently represented as victims (of climate change, of poverty) and as agents of change (responsible for getting themselves and their families out of poverty and out of danger from climate risks). These stereotypes, we argue, do little to address the root causes of gender injustices, which manifest in interactions with the impacts of and responses to climate change, as specific gender-climate injustices.

Feminisation of poverty and gender injustices

Djoudi et al. (2016) and others argue that the feminisation of poverty within development literature is grafted onto climate change vulnerability assessments in a problematic manner, which we similarly observed in the context of CSF (Alston and Whittenbury, 2013; Arora-Jonsson, 2011; Djoudi et al., 2016). Government and NGOs rendered women simplistically as vulnerable due to their caregiving and lack of access to financial resources. The narrow focus on women as victims and caretakers emphasises women's knowledge, responsibilities and roles, which does not take into account power relations, and contributes towards the feminisation of both vulnerability and responsibility for adaptation (Arora-Jonsson, 2011; Tschakert and Machado, 2012).

Earlier research by Chant (2008) highlighted this trend towards the feminisation of responsibilities for poverty alleviation in the Philippines. Likewise, our study found participants similarly emphasised women's role as caretakers as key to poverty reduction. Women were, participants argued, more likely to be responsible with money (compared to men), and for ensuring the health and wellbeing of the family. Thus, women are simultaneously (and contradictorily) the most vulnerable to poverty (the victims) and the solutions to poverty (the saviours). This discourse of "smart economics" rests on the assumption of "female altruism" (Chant, 2008) and perpetuates notions that women are inherently more caring and sustainable than men. The development discourse of "smart economics" strives to use women (and girls) to solve the world's problems but, in doing so, neglects the role of structural inequalities and power imbalances that constrain the rights and choices of women and girls, and which contribute towards gendered vulnerability in the first instance. The appeal of these projects, as with other development programmes throughout the Global South, partly rests on the depiction that their "beneficiaries" (in this instance, rural Filipino women) merely require the provision of funds and/or training before becoming dynamos of agency and action. Women as business entrepreneurs are, thus, the supposed solutions to rural poverty as well as the risks of climate change. The danger with such projects, as Cornwall and Anyidoho (2010) observe, is that this places a high degree of responsibility for the success or failure of such projects (often part of government policies) on the shoulders of the women (and girls). Within this framing, women are represented as resourceful, strong and altruistic, and with the capacities to cope with and adapt to change not only for themselves but also for their families and their nations (Cornwall and Anyidoho, 2010).

The notion that investing in women and girls is smart economics is apparent in the prevalence of poverty-alleviating projects that aim to reduce vulnerability to climate change. The narrow preoccupation with economic empowerment can exacerbate gendered vulnerability rather than achieve goals of gender justice and in turn climate justice. However, as we said earlier, women's vulnerability is not just about poverty, and climate adaptation is not simply another term for poverty reduction. There is a wealth of information demonstrating that marginalised groups (which includes but is not limited to women in rural communities in the Global South) are more vulnerable to climate-related risks and the current and projected future impacts of climate change. Vulnerability and the socio-economic and political forces shaping individuals', households' and communities' vulnerabilities are multifaceted and dimensional. Although a disaster, for instance, may begin with a climate event (such as a flood or tropical cyclone), its impacts on a community are situated in the social system within which it occurs. Thus, the vulnerability of an individual is grounded in social, cultural and economic relations, which are determined by a multitude of factors, including gender, class, ethnicity, age and disability.

In the Anthropocene, attentiveness to the concept and substance of climate justice must consider the intersections between existing and predicted distributive impacts, social inequalities, and responsibilities and procedures for addressing interacting environmental and social injustices. Vulnerability is not simply a result of biophysical conditions (the impacts of climate change), nor the context in which particular hazards occur (such as a poor community located in a coastal location), but also the processes, assumptions and practices that inform problem definition, research and policy development, and climate adaptation plans and outcomes. The confluence of women as both victims of and solutions to climate change amounts to a form of procedural vulnerability wherein many researchers, policymakers, and development practitioners seek to rearticulate women's positions as subjects of hegemonic power relations, which emphasise existing models of globalising capitalism. This is evidence of misframing (Fraser, 2008), a form of injustice in a global world, wherein local solutions to women's increased vulnerability are only linked to the market-based economy and which fails to take into account the responsibilities of others (including Filipino men, development practitioners, and nations in the

Global North). The Philippines, along with other countries categorised as the Global South, is rife with poverty-alleviating projects that target women's vulnerability. This places economic development within the hands of the oppressed without necessarily establishing the ability for the oppressed to benefit from said economic development. Therefore, women can be seen as a conduit for economic development rather than as a recipient, thus bypassing gender justice in favour of economic development, with climate injustices similarly rendered as economic problems with economic solutions.

The misframing of women in the Philippines, as demonstrated by our case study, misrepresents and oversimplifies the position of women as simply a product of poverty (of the economic structures), thus contributing towards the dominance of market-based approaches to climate adaptation. Action to address gender injustices in the Philippines centres on the redistribution of means (economic remedies), with lesser attention given to recognition of the particular institutional arrangements and different socio-cultural identities (socio-cultural remedies), and political structures that restrict women's abilities to participate equally within political decision-making (political remedies).

The framing of climate change as fundamentally an economic problem requiring economic solutions connects with the ways in which gender equality issues are similarly rendered as matters of economic development. Women are deemed vulnerable to the impacts of climate change because they are poor, and by extension Filipino women's embrace of western development will enable them to escape poverty and reduce their vulnerability to climate change. Indeed, due to women's vulnerability, there are forceful arguments for the direction of domestic and international funding to projects to help poor women in the Global South. However, the gender inequalities that contribute towards women being more vulnerable to climate risks remain largely unaddressed. These go beyond economic development initiatives to encompass why individuals are exposed to hazards (such as women and girls travelling to collect water and wood fuel supplies for their households), and their capacities to adapt (such as access to information and essential services including healthcare and education). Consequently, when examining gender in climate change adaptation, it is critical that power relations between genders, a community's social and cultural norms, and how these shape perceptions of risks and adaptation preferences are taken into account. We advocate for scholars and practitioners to consider gender justice (comprised of recognition, participation and distribution) within climate change adaptation planning and projects through an intersectional lens to avoid rearticulating existing, and creating new vulnerabilities (see Figure 27.3).

Conclusion

The shortcomings of current approaches to climate adaptation in the Philippines highlight the need for the adoption of sustainable, equitable and just policies and practices that pay attention to contextual intersecting subjectivities (gender, race, class, education, abilities) that contribute towards differential vulnerabilities. It is therefore critical that scholars and decision-makers take into consideration gender relations and gendered vulnerabilities to ensure strategies to reduce the negative impacts of climate change are effective, efficient, equitable and sustainable. It is fundamental that women (and men and other genders) are not simply rationalised as neoliberal subjects who are actors in and further development agendas under the banner of poverty reduction as climate adaptation. Instead, we advocate for intersectional relational understandings of vulnerability to climate change that does not homogenise women (or other groups of people) and extract them from their social locations, but rather sees them as situated within specific

Distribution

Distribution of vulnerable to the impacts of climate change vary across communities, households and individuals. Gender norms, roles and responsibilities mean that women and girls are often more vulnerable to the impacts of climate-related hazards, and are less able to adapt to due power structures. The distribution of resources and the ability to command those resources and translate them into adaptation actions to current and future climate change lies at the heart of sustainable gender just climate adaptation measures.

Participation

The inclusion of women and gender minorities in climate change debates, and the development of gender-inclusive climate change policies and programmes. This requires participatory processes that address power imbalances, and socio-cultural norms. Such as women's-only climate adaptation planning workshops and capacity-building initiatives. Also the promotion of women's leadership and involvement in community and national climate change projects.

Gender Justice in climate adaptation

- Need to reconceptualise gender justice within climate change research, policy, and actions to beyond women's participation in climate change debates and development programmes.
- Requires recognition of gender inequalities (in access to and command of resources, education, information and skills, livelihood opportunities, tenure and governance regimes, reproductive rights).

  Inclusion of women in decision-making which moves beyond passive participation to active involvement in climate governance.

Recognition

Recognition of gender inequalities, which includes ability to access and command resources, and ability to participate in decision-making. It also includes recognition of gender bias in climate policies and projects. Acknowledgement and incorporation of gender-sensitive processes and measures are needed, designed to suit local contexts.

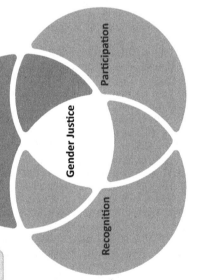

Figure 27.3   Gender justice in climate adaptation.

power relations and intersecting identities that are experienced in day-to-day life in the context of changing environmental conditions.

References

Adger, W.N., 1999. Social vulnerability to climate change and extremes in Coastal Vietnam – sciencedirect. *World Dev.* 27, 249–269.

Adger, W.N., Dessai, S., Goulden, M., Hulme, M., Lorenzoni, I., Nelson, D.R., Naess, L.O., Wolf, J., Wreford, A., 2009. Are there social limits to adaptation to climate change? *Clim. Change* 93, 335–354.

Agarwal, B., 1997. "Bargaining" and gender relations: Within and beyond the household. *Fem. Econ.* 3, 1–51.

Ahmed, A., Lawson, E.T., Mensah, A., Gordon, C., Padgham, J., 2016. Adaptation to climate change or non-climatic stressors in semi-arid regions? Evidence of gender differentiation in three agrarian districts of Ghana. *Environ. Dev.* 20, 45–58.

Alston, M., Whittenbury, K., 2013. Does climatic crisis in Australia's food bowl create a basis for change in agricultural gender relations? *Agric. Hum. Values* 30, 115–128.

Alua, M.J., 2016. *Interview with R. P. Crease.* 2 December, The City of San Fernando.

Alvarez, I., Lovera, S., 2016. New times for women and gender issues in biodiversity conservation and climate justice. *Development* 59, 263–265.

Antwi-Agyei, P., Dougill, A.J., Fraser, E.D.G., Stringer, L.C., 2013. Characterising the nature of household vulnerability to climate variability: Empirical evidence from two regions of Ghana. *Environ. Dev. Sustain.* 15, 903–926.

Antwi-Agyei, P., Quinn, C.H., Adiku, S.G.K., Codjoe, S.N.A., Dougill, A.J., Lamboll, R., Dovie, D.B.K., 2017. Perceived stressors of climate vulnerability across scales in the Savannah zone of Ghana: A participatory approach. *Reg. Environ. Change* 17, 213–227.

Arora-Jonsson, S., 2011. Virtue and vulnerability: Discourses on women, gender and climate change. *Glob. Environ. Change* 21, 744–751.

Arora-Jonsson, S., 2014. Forty years of gender research and environmental policy: Where do we stand? *Womens Stud. Int. Forum* 47, 295–308.

Babatunde, R.O., Owotoki, G.M., Heidhues, F., Buchenrieder, G., 2007. Vulnerability and food insecurity differentials among male and female-headed farming households in Nigeria. *Pak. J. Soc. Sci.* 4, 414–418.

Bambalan, G., 2016. *Interview with R. P. Crease.* 19 December, The City of San Fernando.

Beaumier, M.C., Ford, J.D., Tagalik, S., 2015. The food security of Inuit women in Arviat, Nunavut: The role of socio-economic factors and climate change. *Polar Rec.* 51, 550–559.

Bee, B.A., Rice, J., Trauger, A., 2015. A feminist approach to climate change governance: Everyday and intimate politics. *Geogr. Compass* 9, 339–350.

Bennett, E., 2005. Gender, fisheries and development. *Mar. Policy* 29, 451–459.

Bhattarai, B., Beilin, R., Ford, R., 2015. Gender, agrobiodiversity, and climate change: A study of adaptation practices in the Nepal Himalayas. *World Dev.* 70, 122–132.

Bourdieu, P., 1991. *Language and Symbolic Power.* Cambridge, MA: Harvard University Press.

Brown, K., Siri, E., 2012. *Sustainable Adaptation to Climate Change: Prioritising Social Equity and Environmental Integrity*, 1st ed. London: Routledge,.

Burton, C., Cutter, S.L., 2008. Levee failures and social vulnerability in the Sacramento-San Joaquin Delta Area, California. *Nat. Hazards Rev.* 9, 136–149.

Cameron, E., 2016. *Building Climate Justice: An Analysis of How the Nexus between Climate Change and Human Rights Shapes Public Policy Agendas and Alternatives.* Findland: Faculty of Social Sciences and Economics (FSE) of Åbo Akademi University.

Chandra, A., McNamara, K.E., 2017. In Philippines, climate change and conflict both conspire against rural women [WWW Document]. The Conversation. URL http://theconversation.com/in-philippines-climate-change-and-conflict-both-conspire-against-rural-women-77729 (accessed 8.21.18).

Chandra, A., McNamara, K.E., Dargusch, P., Caspe, A.M., Dalabajan, D., 2017. Gendered vulnerabilities of smallholder farmers to climate change in conflict-prone areas: A case study from Mindanao, Philippines. *J. Rural Stud.* 50, 45–59.

Chant, S., 2008. The 'Feminisation of Poverty' and the 'Feminisation' of Anti-Poverty Programmes: Room for Revision? *J. Dev. Stud.* 44, 165–197.

Chant, S., Sweetman, C., 2012. Fixing women or fixing the world? 'Smart economics', efficiency approaches, and gender equality in development. *Gend. Dev.* 20, 517–529. https://doi.org/10.1080/13552074.2012.731812

The City of San Fernando Municipal Government, 2016. *The Local Climate Change Action Plan of San Fernando (DRAFT)*.

Comim, F., 2008. Climate injustice and development: A capability perspective. *Development* 51, 344–349.

Cornwall, A., Anyidoho, N.A., 2010. Introduction: Women's empowerment: Contentions and contestations. *Development* 53, 144–149.

Cutter, S.L., 1995. The forgotten casualties: Women, children, and environmental change. *Glob. Environ. Change* 5, 181–194.

Cutter, S.L., 2006 *Hazards Vulnerability and Environmental Justice*. Earthscan, London and Sterling, VA: Routledge.

Cutter, S.L., 2017. The forgotten casualties redux: Women, children, and disaster risk. *Glob. Environ. Change* 42, 117–121.

de Leon, E.G., Pittock, J., 2017. Integrating climate change adaptation and climate-related disaster risk-reduction policy in developing countries: A case study in the Philippines. *Clim. Dev.* 9, 471–478.

Denton, F., 2002. Climate change vulnerability, impacts, and adaptation: Why does gender matter? *Gend. Dev.* 10, 10–20.

Djoudi, H., Locatelli, B., Vaast, C., Asher, K., Brockhaus, M., Basnett Sijapati, B., 2016. Beyond dichotomies: Gender and intersecting inequalities in climate change studies. *Ambio* 45, 248–262. https://doi.org/10.1007/s13280-016-0825-2

Djoudi, H., Brockhaus, M., 2011. Is adaptation to climate change gender neutral? Lessons from communities dependent on livestock and forests in northern Mali. *Int. For. Rev.* 13, 123–135.

Dovers, S.R., Hezri, A.A., 2010. Institutions and policy processes: The means to the ends of adaptation. *Wiley Interdisciplinary. Rev. Clim. Change* 1, 212–231.

Eriksen, S.H., Brown, K., Kelly, P.M., 2005. The dynamics of vulnerability: locating coping strategies in Kenya and Tanzania. *Geogr. J.* 171, 287–305.

Figueiredo, P., Perkins, P.E., 2013. Women and water management in times of climate change: Participatory and inclusive processes. *J. Clean. Prod.* 60, 188–194. https://doi.org/10.1016/j.jclepro.2012.02.025

Fisher, S., 2010. Violence against women and natural disasters: Findings from post-tsunami Sri Lanka. *Violence Women* 16, 902–918.

Fisher, S., 2015. The emerging geographies of climate justice. *Geogr. J.* 181, 73–82.

Fletcher, A.J., 2018. More than women and men: A framework for gender and intersectionality research on environmental crisis and conflict. In: *Water Security Across the Gender Divide, Water Security in a New World*. Cham: Springer, pp. 35–58. https://doi.org/10.1007/978-3-319-64046-4_3

Fraser, N., 2008. Abnormal Justice. *Crit. Inq.* 34, 393–422. https://doi.org/10.1086/589478

Gaillard, J.C., Sanz, K., Balgos, B.C., Dalisay, S.N.M., Gorman-Murray, A., Smith, F., Toelupe, V., 2017. Beyond men and women: A critical perspective on gender and disaster. *Disasters* 41, 429–447.

Guido, 2018. Poverty in the Philippines [WWW Document]. Asian Development Bank. URL https://www.adb.org/countries/philippines/poverty (accessed 4.8.18).

Gusyev, M.A., Hasegawa, A., Magome, J., Umino, H., Sawano, H., 2015. Drought assessment in the Pampanga River basin, the Philippines–Part 3: Evaluating climate change impacts on dam infrastructure with standardized indices. In: *Proceedings of the 21st International Congress on Modelling and Simulation (MODSIM 2015)*, November 29th–December 4th, Queensland, Australia.

Howitt, R., Havnen, O., Veland, S., 2012. Natural and unnatural disasters: Responding with respect for indigenous rights and knowledges. *Geogr. Res.* 50, 47–59.

Iniesta-Arandia, I., Ravera, F., Buechler, S., Díaz-Reviriego, I., Fernández-Giménez, M.E., Reed, M.G., Thompson-Hall, M., Wilmer, H., Aregu, L., Cohen, P., others, 2016. A synthesis of convergent reflections, tensions and silences in linking gender and global environmental change research. *Ambio* 45, 383–393.

Kaijser, A., Kronsell, A., 2014. Climate change through the lens of intersectionality. *Environ. Polit.* 23, 417–433.

Klinsky, S., Dowlatabadi, H., McDaniels, T., 2012. Comparing public rationales for justice trade-offs in mitigation and adaptation climate policy dilemmas. *Glob. Environ. Change* 22, 862–876.

Lander, E., Bello, W., Brand, U., Bullard, N., Mueller, T., 2009. *Contours of Climate Justice Ideas for Shaping New Climate and Energy Politics*. Uppsala: Dag Hammarskjöld Foundation.

Landicho, L.D., Visco, R.G., Paelmo, R.F., Cabahug, R.D., Baliton, R.S., Espaldon, M.L.O., Lasco, R.D., 2015. Field-level evidences of climate change and coping strategies of smallholder farmers in molawin-dampalit sub-watershed, makiling forest reserve, Philippines. *Asian J. Agric. Dev.* 12, 81–94.

Leichenko, R.M., O'Brien, K.L., 2002. The dynamics of rural vulnerability to global change: The case of Southern Africa. *Mitig. Adapt. Strateg. Glob. Change* 7, 1–18.

Masika, R., 2002. *Gender, Development, and Climate Change*. Oxford: Oxfam.

Mason, L.R., Agan, T.C., 2015. Weather variability in urban Philippines: A gender analysis of household impacts. *Clim. Change* 132, 589–599. https://doi.org/10.1007/s10584-015-1437-8

Matoza, S.C., 2016. *Interview with R. P. Crease*. 29 November, The City of San Fernando.

McKinney, L.A., Fulkerson, G.M., 2015. Gender equality and climate justice: A cross-national analysis. *Soc. Justice Res.* 28, 293–317. https://doi.org/10.1007/s11211-015-0241-y

McNamara, K.E., Westoby, R., 2011. Solastalgia and the gendered nature of climate change: An example from Erub Island, Torres Strait. *EcoHealth* 8, 233–236. https://doi.org/10.1007/s10393-011-0698-6

Medrano, R. D., 2016. *Interview with R. P. Crease*. 25 November, The City of San Fernando.

Moser, C., 1993. *Gender Planning and Development: Theory, Practice, and Training*. London: Routledge.

Nabikolo, D., Bashaasha, B., Mangheni, M.N., Majaliwa, J.G.M., 2012. Determinants of climate change adaptation among male and female headed farm households in eastern Uganda. *Afr. Crop Sci. J.* 20, 203–212.

Nightingale, A.J., Ojha, H.R., 2013. Rethinking power and authority: Symbolic violence and subjectivity in Nepal's Terai forests. *Dev. Change* 44, 29–51.

O'Brien, K., Eriksen, S., Nygaard, L.P., Schjolden, A., 2007. Why different interpretations of vulnerability matter in climate change discourses. *Clim. Policy* 7, 73–88.

O'Brien, K.L., Wolf, J., 2010. A values-based approach to vulnerability and adaptation to climate change. *Wiley Interdiscip. Rev. Clim. Change* 1, 232–242.

Oliver-Smith, A., 2012. Debating environmental migration: Society, nature and population displacement in climate change. *J. Int. Dev.* 24, 1058–1070.

Onta, N., Resurreccion, B.P., 2011. The role of gender and caste in climate adaptation strategies in Nepal: Emerging change and persistent inequalities in the far-western region. *Mt. Res. Dev.* 31, 351–356. https://doi.org/10.1659/MRD-JOURNAL-D-10-00085.1

Osborne, N., 2015. Intersectionality and kyriarchy: A framework for approaching power and social justice in planning and climate change adaptation. *Plan. Theory* 14, 130–151. https://doi.org/10.1177/1473095213516443

Philippine Commission on Women, 2014. The GREAT Women Project 2.

Philippine Commission on Women, n.d. Climate Change | Philippine Commission on Women [WWW Document]. URL http://www.pcw.gov.ph/focus-areas/environment/climate-change (accessed 4.15.18).

Pelling, M., O'Brien, K., Matyas, D., 2015. Adaptation and transformation. *Clim. Change* 133, 113–127.

Posadas, E.S., 2016. *Interview with R. P. Crease*. 13 December, The City of San Fernando.

Resurrección, B.P., 2013. Persistent women and environment linkages in climate change and sustainable development agendas. *Womens Stud. Int. Forum* 40, 33–43.

Rochette, A., 2016. Climate change is a social justice issue: The need for a gender-based analysis of mitigation and adaptation policies in Canada and Quebec. *J. Environ. Law Pract.* 29, 383–410.

Schlosberg, D., Collins, L.B., 2014. From environmental to climate justice: Climate change and the discourse of environmental justice. *Wiley Interdisciplinary. Rev. Clim. Change* 5, 359–374.

Schmeer, K.K., 2005. Married women's resource position and household food expenditures in Cebu, Philippines. *J. Marriage Fam.* 67, 399–409. https://doi.org/10.1111/j.0022-2445.2005.00124.x

Smith, R.-A.J., Rhiney, K., 2016. Climate (in) justice, vulnerability and livelihoods in the Caribbean: The case of the indigenous Caribs in northeastern St. Vincent. *Geoforum* 73, 22–31.

Sultana, F., 2010. Living in hazardous waterscapes: Gendered vulnerabilities and experiences of floods and disasters. *Environ. Hazards* 9, 43–53.

Sultana, F., 2014. Gendering climate change: Geographical insights. *Prof. Geogr.* 66, 372–381.

Sultana, F., 2018. Gender and water in a changing climate: Challenges and opportunities. In: *Water Security Across the Gender Divide*. Switzerland: Springer, pp. 17–33.

Tall, A., Kristjanson, P.M., Chaudhury, M., McKune, S., Zougmoré, R.B., 2014. Who gets the information? Gender, power and equity considerations in the design of climate services for farmers (Working Paper No. 89), CCAFS Working Paper.

Terry, G., 2009. No climate justice without gender justice: an overview of the issues. *Gender & Development* 17, 5–18. https://doi.org/10.1080/13552070802696839

Thomas, D.S., Twyman, C., 2005. Equity and justice in climate change adaptation amongst natural-resource-dependent societies. *Glob. Environ. Change* 15, 115–124.

Tolentino, P.L.M., Poortinga, A., Kanamaru, H., Keesstra, S., Maroulis, J., David, C.P.C., Ritsema, C.J., 2016. Projected impact of climate change on hydrological regimes in the Philippines. *PloS One* 11, e0163941.

Tschakert, P., Machado, M., 2012. Gender justice and rights in climate change adaptation: Opportunities and pitfalls. *Ethics Soc. Welf.* 6, 275–289.

United Nations, 2006. Women's anti-discrimination committee urges philippines to speed up legislation aimed at erasing stereotypes, combating violence against females | Meetings Coverage and Press Releases [WWW Document]. URL https://www.un.org/press/en/2006/wom1578.doc.htm (accessed 8.20.18).

Valdez, V.M., 2016. *Interview with R. P. Crease.* 6 December, The City of San Fernando.

Valentine, G., 2007. Theorizing and researching intersectionality: A challenge for feminist geography. *Prof. Geogr.* 59, 10–21.

Veland, S., Howitt, R., Dominey-Howes, D., Thomalla, F., Houston, D., 2013. Procedural vulnerability: Understanding environmental change in a remote indigenous community. *Glob. Environ. Change* 23, 314–326.

Vinyeta, K., Whyte, K., Lynn, K., 2016. Climate change through an intersectional lens: Gendered Vulnerability and Resilience in Indigenous Communities in the United States (SSRN Scholarly Paper No. ID 2770089). Rochester, NY: Social Science Research Network.

Waite, L., 2000. How is household vulnerability gendered? Female-headed households in the collectives of Suleimaniyah, Iraqi Kurdistan. *Disasters* 24, 153–172.

World Economic Forum, 2016. *The Global Gender Gap Report 2016.* Geneva: World Economic Forum.

Yuval-Davis, N., 2016. Power, intersectionality and the politics of belonging. In: *The Palgrave Handbook of Gender and Development: Critical Engagements in Feminist Theory and Practice.* London: Palgrave Macmillan, pp. 367–381.

28

A multiscale analysis of gender in climate change adaptation

Evidence from Malawi

Jane Maher

Introduction

Climate change is recognised as the greatest threat to societies across the world in coming decades. It has the potential to affect millions of people living in urban and rural regions alike, to varying degrees. Progress within climate change discourse has led to more in-depth discussions regarding the differentiated impacts on countries, societies, communities and individuals. Climate justice is concerned with addressing the disjunction between climate risk and responsibility across scales, places, spaces and temporalities. Recently, scholars have conducted empirical research of climate justice. There have been efforts to analyse climate justice within national discourse (Bailey, 2017); the agency of vulnerable groups in decision-making (Running, 2015), and climate change adaptation (CCA) and its corresponding finance have been viewed as proxy to measure climate justice (Barrett, 2014, 2013, 2012). CCA serves as a beneficial tool to measure the actualisation of climate justice because the finance for adaptation should, in theory, be assigned to the most climate-vulnerable communities, and within those communities, to those most affected by the impacts of climate change (Wong, 2016; Barrett, 2014).

CCA is defined by the IPCC (2014) as the process of adjustment to climate change impacts, actual and projected, and to moderate and avoid harm or exploit beneficial opportunities. Examples of adaptation include livelihoods diversification, climate-smart agriculture, water conservation projects and disaster risk management (DRM) (Barrett, 2013). Climate change and disasters are closely linked; as a result CCA and DRM are often interconnected. The realisation of the necessity for CCA and DRM has been acknowledged in recent years as the frequency and magnitude of climate-related events has increased (Eriksen et al., 2015; Jennings, 2011). Often, those who are most exposed to the impacts of climate change are the poor and marginalised living in low-income areas, who are generally under-represented at all levels of decision-making (Kaijser and Kronsell, 2014). Hence, access to CCA can result in profound change in livelihoods (Khan and Roberts, 2013).

Recent research has focused on the differentiated vulnerability of climate change amongst different groups in society. There is a growing body of research that focuses on gender and climate change (Jerneck, 2018; Wong, 2016; Gabrielsson, 2015; Arora-Jonsson, 2011; Nielsen and Reenberg, 2010). Often gender and climate change research focuses on women's vulnerability to climate change (Terry, 2009; Momsen, 2004; Dankelman, 2002; Denton, 2002; Dikito-Wachtmeister, 2000). Rural women in particular are reported to be at high risk of negative impacts from climate change (Jost et al., 2016). This is related to the roles and responsibilities women often assume as carers of family and in household maintenance and food production (Jost et al., 2016; Kakota et al., 2011). As a result, the need for gender mainstreaming, to leverage co-benefits of gender equality and climate action, has been increasingly recognised throughout policies, decisions and mandates made under the United Nations Framework Convention on Climate Change (UNFCCC) (UN Women, 2016; Burns and Patouris, 2014).

Gender mainstreaming became widely used after the Fourth Conference on Women held in Beijing in 1995. Gender mainstreaming was identified as the most important mechanism to reach the ambitious goals identified in the 12 critical areas established by the Beijing Platform for Action (BPfA) (Cornwall and Edwards, 2015). The BPfA aimed to be transformative. It called on governments and organisations to fully commit to gender equality and the empowerment of women, by addressing the issue through a whole organisation response across all activities, meaning for gender to be considered in all aspects of work. In 1997, the UN established that gender mainstreaming should be used in all policies and programmes in the UN system (Moser, 2005).

Despite the unprecedented uptake of gender mainstreaming within numerous sectors and arenas over the last 20 years, little substantive change has been witnessed, leading to gender mainstreaming facing weighty criticism from feminist scholars and activists. It is felt that gender mainstreaming lacks clarity, direction and an understanding of who is responsible for achieving equity (Payne, 2011; Moser, 2005). Feminist critiques have suggested that gender mainstreaming has been decoupled from the initial transformative potential to a routine bureaucratic process that does little to address the embedded social and cultural barriers women face (Meier and Celis, 2011; Prügl, 2010; Wittman, 2010). Finally, there is criticism that there is an absence of professional and political accountability to report back and measure gender mainstreaming (Mukhopadhyay, 2004).

Despite criticism, there is widespread reluctance to disregard gender mainstreaming and its transformative potential (Lessa and Rocha, 2011). Twenty years since after the BPfA was implemented (BPfA+20), the global commitment to gender mainstreaming was reaffirmed. Gender mainstreaming is still considered an imperative policy strategy for social change (UN Women, 2015). Moreover, the discourse of gender mainstreaming in the climate change space has increased over the last ten years. Alston (2014) suggests that key barriers of gender mainstreaming can be unmasked within the climate change and post-disaster space, and, additionally, that there can be a recommitment to the radical social justice and transformative nature intended. Alston (2014) suggests this is possible due to the unique interaction and greater inter-connection between local and global actors in working on climate change. Although criticisms persist, to date there has been limited analysis of gender mainstreaming in CCA across scales and on the impact current practices have on climate-vulnerable communities at local scale. This research sets out to better understand this process and present successes and shortfalls to date and to inform policy going forward.

Method

This study aims to review current gender mainstreaming practices taking place in the formation, implementation and impact of CCA and DRM in the Lower Shire Valley (LSV) in Malawi. To understand this, an international and national policy review tracking the advancement of gender mainstreaming over time was conducted, using coding and content analysis. The gender analysis

Table 28.1 Gender analysis ranking scheme.

Ranking	Meaning	Elaboration
1	Gender Blind	Document does not recognise distinction between sexes.
2	Gender included in text/ Women as "Vulnerable Group"	Refers to gender (often reports women as vulnerable). No reference to gender in action plan or implementation.
3	Gender Balance	Refers to gender. Makes some call for increased participation of women in project implementation.
4	Gender Sensitive	Document mandates the integration of gender norms, roles, and relations in the development of actions, policy, and implementation.
5	Intersectional	Document recognise gender inequality in addition to other forms of social discrimination.

Adapted from Burns and Patouris (2014).

of policies took place in two phases. In the first phase an assessment of the gender language used within the policy document was conducted. In the process of sorting policies, a ranking was assigned which determined the level of gender mainstreaming within the document. The ranking of gender considerations in policies is outlined in Table 28.1.

It is acknowledged that this ranking process only delivers surface-level analysis and does not provide an in-depth review of implementation strategies and actions of policies. Hence, the second phase of the gender analysis evaluated the processes, plans and actions outlined to achieve the stated gender considerations in policies. This evaluation used content analysis to examine the gender considerations made within the objectives, finance, implementation, capacity, and transparency sections of policies. A reflection on the implications of the inclusion and exclusion of gender considerations provides a greater insight into the broader implications of each policy reviewed. In total, six international policies and ten national policies were reviewed. A full list of policies reviewed can be found in Table 28.2, although not all reviews are presented in detail in this chapter.

Primary data was collected by means of interviews with national and subnational actors, focus group discussions (FGD) and surveys at local scale in Malawi over the period of September–October 2015 and April–July 2016. National and subnational stakeholders consisted of representatives from donor bodies, international non-governmental organisations (INGOs), non-governmental organisations (NGOs), civil society organisations (CSOs), national and subnational government, all working within the field of CCA and DRM in Malawi. In total, 12 national and 13 subnational scale interviews were conducted. Finally, 19 FGD were conducted and 350 surveys completed with communities in the LSV. These FGD were conducted with men (5), women (5), mixed, consisting of men and women (5), and youth (4) groups. The groups were made up of eight to twelve people. Coding and thematic analysis was conducted to analyse qualitative data collected, while survey analysis was conducted in Excel. In the following sections this chapter uses data collected to answer chapter objectives. Sections three and four outline the geographical, social and cultural relevance of the case study area; sections five and six presents the flow of gender mainstreaming from international to national policy formation and implementation drawing on policy analysis and interviews data; section seven presents insight into access to CCA among social groups in climate-vulnerable areas in Malawi, drawing on data from focus groups and household surveys.

Table 28.2 Outline of international and national policies reviewed.

International Policies	National Policies
1 Development Policies • The Millennium Declaration • The Millennium Development Goals (MDGs) • Agenda 2030 • The Sustainable Development Goals (SDGs)	1 Governing Strategies • Vision 2020 (1998) • Malawi Growth and Development Strategy II (MDGSII) (2011) • National Gender Policy (2015)
2 Climate Change Policies • The Kyoto Protocol • UNFCCC Decisions • The Paris Agreement	2 Climate Change Policies • Malawi's National Adaptation Programmes of Action (NAPA) (2006) • Malawi's [Intended] Nationally Determined Contributions ([I]NDC) (2015)
3 Disaster Risk Management (DRM) • The Sendai Framework for Disaster Risk Reduction (SFDRR) • The Hyogo Framework for Action (HFA)	Climate Change Policy (2012) • Climate Change Management policy (2016) 3 Disaster Risk Management (DRM) • Disaster Risk Management Policy (2015)

Case study overview: Malawi

Malawi was determined to be a suitable case study location to conduct this research, as with much of sub-Saharan Africa, it is highly vulnerable to the impacts of climate change. In addition, it is a largely rural country, with approximately 85% of the population relying on subsistence farming. Despite the potential for irrigation, over 90% of total land cultivated is dependent on rainfall alone, leaving a large proportion of the country highly vulnerable to climate change (Msowoya et al., 2016). In the past two decades, the climate in Malawi has become more variable, with the frequency of floods and drought rising. Most recently, severe flooding took place in 2014–15; this resulted in loss of life, livelihoods and displacement, and is described as the worst incidence of its kind on record. This was followed by low precipitation in 2015–16, resulting in drought in various regions. The culmination of two extreme weather events led to elevated levels of food insecurity (Government of Malawi, 2015)

As a result of these extreme weather events, CCA and DRM have been of significance to the Government of Malawi in recent years, and this is reflected in the development activities in the country. Malawi is highly dependent on Overseas Development Aid (ODA), with 40% of government expenditure being donor funded in 2015 (Arndt et al., 2015). Numerous scholars have examined climate aid, specifically CCA, within ODA flows to Malawi (Weaver et al., 2014; Barrett, 2014; Barrett, 2013; Baker et al., 2013; Peratskis et al., 2012). Barrett (2014) shows that Malawi receives higher levels of CCA finance compared to other African countries. Though Baker et al. (2013) indicates that only a relatively small amount of Malawi's total aid portfolio (up to 6%) explicitly targets CCA, their analysis indicates up to 20% of all ODA has the potential to reduce climate vulnerability and enhance people's adaptive capacity.

The LSV region in Southern Malawi, made up of two districts, Chikwawa and Nsanje, was chosen as a suitable location to focus this gender analysis of CCA as the region has a higher than national average of climate vulnerability. Malawi's National Adaptation Programme for Action (NAPA) (Government of Malawi, 2006) ranks the two districts as "severely climate vulnerable."

The LSV was badly affected by the consecutive extreme weather events of 2015 and 2016. In addition to being more likely to suffer the consequences of climate change, the region has higher than average levels of food insecurity, which has been further heightened since 2015 (Government of Malawi, 2016). Finally, Barrett's (2013) research reveals greater CCA finance flowing to both districts compared to other areas in Malawi.

Gender in Malawi

Traditional gender roles are at the core of how society functions in Malawi, especially in rural areas. Both matrilineal and patrilineal kinship systems exist, but society in Malawi is considered highly patriarchal (Molloy, 2016). Within this structure, descent and residence is patrilocal: when married, a wife leaves her home to reside on her husband's land, and the land is passed on to her sons. The LSV districts, Chikwawa and Nsanje, function largely under a patrilineal lineage system (Berge et al., 2014).

Women are often treated as secondary to men, and decisions are made mostly by men with little agency provided to women (White, 2007). In Malawi, women appear to be more disadvantaged, in almost all sectors, compared to their male counterparts. The country ranks 131 out of 187 in terms of gender equality, with a Gender Inequality Index − a measure of disparity based on three basic areas of human development: health, knowledge and standard of living − of 0.591 (Molloy, 2016; Government of Malawi, 2012). Women are more likely to be food insecure, with less control over land, less access to extension services and resources, and less agency in decision-making in households and communities.

However, women comprise 70% of the agricultural labour force and produce 80% of the household food supply (Government of Malawi, 2012). Their importance in the agricultural sector cannot be over-emphasised, yet women face persistent constraints inhibiting their agricultural production potential. It is estimated that 36.6% of individual agricultural landholders are female (Government of Malawi, 2017). The average landholding size is lower for female-headed households (FHH) at 0.803 hectares than it is for male-headed households (MHH) at 1.031 hectares (Government of Malawi, 2012). Restricted access to land rights results in limited agency for women to make agricultural-related decisions and limited access to extension services and inputs, which are often supplied based on land registers (Giovarelli et al., 2013; Kaarhus, 2010).

In addition to negative land rights affecting women's role as agricultural labourers, they face limited access to other economic activities. Women are burdened with household chores, agricultural activities and caring for family, which results in limited opportunities, compared to men, to engage in income-generating activities (Government of Malawi, 2012). A recent study found that 63% of women, compared to 81% of men, are employed (Government of Malawi, 2017), with women more likely to be employed in agriculture (44%) and unskilled labour (25%). Women have less access to markets, due to their productive and reproductive roles. In addition, men tend to dominate the latter stages of cash crop production, such as drying tobacco, organising for its sale and taking it to depots (Kaarhus, 2010). As a result, men have control over income generation. The long distances to markets further impede women's engagement in economic activities, particularly when considering their triple roles and cultural constraints, which can prevent them from travelling and accessing markets (Government of Malawi, 2012).

It is the closeness to natural resources in their role as household food producer and family carer, along with limited access to finance, inputs and resources that results in the narrative of women as vulnerable to climate change in literature and policy. Hence, it cannot be ignored that these issues create the absolute necessity for gender relations to be considered within CCA and DRM policies.

Gender analysis of policies

The year 2015 was considered a pivotal one in sustainable development, with new policies, agreements and agendas agreed on the world stage. The Paris Agreement, a global action plan to mitigate and adapt to climate change, was agreed at the 21st Conference of Parties (COP21), the Sustainable Development Goals (SDGs) of the 2030 Agenda were established, and the Sendai Framework for Disaster Risk Reduction (SFDRR) was adopted. Furthermore, 2015 marked 20 years since the Beijing Platform for Action (BPfA+20). The adoption of these policies, agreements and frameworks makes it a stimulating time to carry out gender analysis, reflecting on the progress over time in these policy areas. At the international level, there has been an increased trend of inclusion of gender considerations within the three core policy areas reviewed. This is in line with the view of gender mainstreaming undergoing a process of "global diffusion" post-BPfA, with CSOs and NGOs adopted gender mainstreaming terminology and practices (Alston, 2014; Moser, 2005; True and Mintrom, 2001).

The three 2015 policies are considered "intersectional" (ranked 5), from the ranking scheme presented in Table 28.1, for using progressive language within their objectives and throughout; gender is not only considered within the main objectives, and other social categories are identified as important as well. Within the three policy areas, there is a noted improvement against their predecessor policies: the Kyoto Protocol (ranked 1); the Millennium Development Goals (MDGs) (ranked 2); and the Hyogo Framework for Action (HFA) (ranked 3). However, upon detailed inspection of the gender considerations, it is clear these 2015 successor policies are not without their limitations.

Firstly, within the 29 Articles of the Paris Agreement, a call for gender-responsive activities only features in two: in Article 7 Adaptation and Article 11 Capacity-building. However, there is no indication on how these gender-responsive activities should be included within national strategies. Moreover, there is no call for gender to be included within country's [Intended] Nationally Determined Contribution ([I]NDC) (Article four). This is compounded by the gender-blind nature of Article 13 on transparency and Article 15 on implementation and compliance. By not creating tools or mechanisms to evaluate the gender-responsive nature of adaptation or capacity-building activities, the Agreement leaves little accountability of Parties that have not included gender within national plans.

Similarly, upon examining the SDGs, 53 of the 232 SDG indicators explicitly reference women, girls, gender or sex, including the 14 indicators from SDG 5, Achieve Gender Equality (UN, 2017). There are, however, key limitations to the transformative potential within the SDGs. For example, not all indicators are currently measureable. EUROSTAT (2017) reports that currently, data is widely available for approximately only one-third of the global indicators. Research conducted by Open Data Watch (2016) indicate that there are 20 "ready to measure" indicators with internationally agreed-upon definitions. Scholars have criticised the non-tangible or measurable outcomes of goals and targets (Fukuda-Parr, 2016; Koehler, 2016). Focusing on SDG 5, Koehler (2016) suggests the implementation of the Goal remains vague, with only a few targets and indicators equipped with policy recommendations. Koehler (2016) suggests the strongest gendered policy targets are those surrounding economic empowerment, and this ignores the role women play in non-economic circumstances.

A key area of criticism surrounds the potential to water down SDG targets and indicators to suit a national agenda. National monitoring is considered the most important level of monitoring (SDSN, 2015). As a result, countries can define the nature of indicators, specifications, timing, data collection methods and disaggregation to suit national needs and priorities (SDSN, 2015). This can be considered a positive, but some critics raise concerns that the most transformative goals and targets may be neglected through selectivity and national adaptation (Fukuda-Parr, 2016).

Finally, a detailed review of gender considerations in the SFDRR indicate that gendered actions within policy remain limited, despite its ranking as an intersectional document. The guiding principles of policy states that disaster risk reduction requires an "all-of-society" engagement and partnership, which requires a gender, age, disability and cultural perspective to be integrated in all policies and practices, and women and youth leadership should be promoted (UNISDR, 2015). Yet, within the four priorities for action, gender is only explicitly referenced once, in Priority Four: enhancing disaster preparedness for effective response to "Build Back Better" in recovery, rehabilitation and reconstruction. In this Priority, the Framework calls for capacity-building to empower women for preparedness and to secure alternate means of livelihoods, and to include persons with disabilities in the assessment of disaster risk, in design and implementation. However, there is no outline of how this capacity-building should take place, and there is no financial plan to support these action areas. Furthermore, there is a call for women and people with disabilities to lead and promote a gender-equitable and universally accessible disaster response. This maintains the view that gender relations are a women's issue and places the burden on creating a truly gender intersectional disaster response largely on women, ignoring the "all-of-society" objective the framework sets out.

The findings show that though there has been considerable improvement in the observation of differentiated experiences in CCA and DRM, with a marked increase in the gender language used in international policy. The responsive nature and actualisation potential of policies to achieve gender objectives remains limited.

Gender in policy formation and implementation in Malawi's CCA and DRM actions

At a national level in Malawi, much of the relevant policy evaluated was formed pre-2015. However, the analysis shows that over time, the national policies are fundamentally steered by international guiding documents, and the gender considerations featured are largely introduced from the top-down. This is especially seen within the Malawi Growth and Development Strategy II (MGDSII), where the acceleration towards the attainment of the Millennium Development Goals (MDGs) was noted as a key objective, along with poverty reduction (Goverment of Malawi, 2011, p. xiv). As such, the inclusion of gender in MGDSII is structured similarly to the MDGs: in isolation to other themes, and with a limited focus on social development, education, child poverty and maternal health. Figure 28.1 presents an overview of the gender analysis conducted of relevant policies within Malawi. It shows that half (five) of the policies reviewed mention gender or view women as a vulnerable group (ranked 2), making no calls for greater inclusion of women in policies, plans and actions.

There is noted progress since 2015, with all three policies published since then determined to be gender sensitive (ranked 4). These are: Malawi's [I]NDC (2015), the National Climate Change Management Plan (NCCMP) (2016) and the National Agricultural Policy (2016). A notable failing of national policy is seen within the National Disaster Risk Management Policy (NDRMP), launched in 2015, which remains gender blind (ranked 1). The document makes no reference to gender or to the vulnerabilities or capacities women have during disasters in Malawi. The MDGs and HFA are the two international guiding policies that influence the NDRMP, along with MGDSII, all of which refer to gender. The HFA explicitly outlined the need for gender to be integrated into all DRM policies, plans and decision-making processes. The failure to include gender considerations within the NDRMP highlights the key inadequacies within

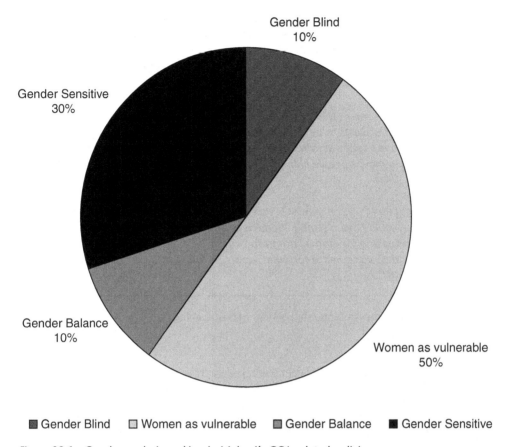

Figure 28.1 Gender analysis ranking in Malawi's CCA-related policies.

gender-responsive policy formation across the scales. Language may have improved to include intersections of social categories and experiences, but nationally influencing international policies continue to consistently exclude gender-responsive tools and mechanism for implementation, financing, monitoring and reporting. These findings affirm concerns of the potential to water down actions and indicators to suit a national agenda.

As stated, the language and gender considerations in Malawi's national policies are greatly influenced by international bodies and policies. Within the national structure, actors and stakeholders, along with culture and traditions, can still greatly influence policy formation and implementation. From interviews with national and subnational actors, numerous themes emerged that influence how gender is addressed within CCA and DRM in Malawi. Firstly, all actors across the two scales suggest there has been an increase in dialogue surrounding gender across all sectors. Despite this, it was felt that gender-responsive policy and actions in CCA and DRM activities were behind the national rate of progress. It was clear that within CCA and DRM, donors are unanimously considered the drivers of gender mainstreaming in Malawi; this is agreed upon by actors across scales (see quotes in Figure 28.2). This viewpoint is also supported by donors interviewed, who emphasised the requirement for gender considerations in project proposals to receive financial support.

> *"[Gender mainstreaming] is not all that vivid [in programmes and projects] … it is not a deliberate policy to say that so many women in this programme…but when you go out there because of the donor perspective we've ended up finding ourselves focusing on issues of gender"* (N/NGO_7)
>
> *"…at donor level, it seems there is an improvement because [gender mainstreaming] is very critical for projects to be funded. I will give an example of the programme we are doing we have specific activities on gender, so we see an improvement compared in the past when maybe people didn't care much about gender but just about results"* (L/NGO_2)
>
> *"[DONORS] put emphasis on gender in accordance with the gender equality act, so all programmes should have a strong component of gender for the inclusion of women and girls…[and] going forward all programmes will be look at through a gender lens, with beneficiaries' voice heard for what works for them and gender included in all programmes"* (N/Donor_1)

Figure 28.2 Actor quotes on donor-led gender mainstreaming.

The donor-led nature of gender mainstreaming in CCA and DRM actions is not unexpected, especially considering the top-down influence of gender language and considerations in national policy formation. However, as a result there is an apparent lack of ownership and responsibility by national and subnational actors implementing CCA and DRM projects to take ownership of gender mainstreaming. The findings further suggest that organisations may include gender considerations within project proposals without complete knowledge or capacity to implement them fully. As a result, it is common to see projects increasing women's participation to achieve gender balance, or parity, as the only gender consideration implemented. Finally, there is little emphasis on reporting and accountability of gendered targets. This lends itself to key concerns surrounding gender mainstreaming being a box-ticking exercise. It is likely that the emphasis on achieving gender balance within projects as the main means of gender mainstreaming is prominent because this is the easiest quantifiable box to tick.

A gendered lens on vulnerability to and coping with climate change in LSV

Another key theme that emerged from interviews with national and subnational actors was the view of women as more vulnerable to the impacts of climate change. Huyer (2016) suggests that international policy also maintains this view. Results from the local scale found that women do not self-identify as vulnerable to climate change. One female FGD strongly resisted the idea of female vulnerability to climate change, stating that able-bodied community members were not vulnerable. Large proportions of the community identified the elderly (23%), sick or disabled (grouped together in community dialogue) (3%) and children (5%) as vulnerable to climate change. In addition, a common suggestion of an "all-of-community" vulnerability to climate change (11%), especially after extreme weather events in 2015 and 2016.

Although vulnerability to climate change, if assigned at all, is largely attributed to those considered less able-bodied, there are clear differentiated experiences of climate change and resulting coping mechanisms noted within the LSV. There were various types of coping mechanisms recorded within communities. Firstly, members of the community accessed formal adaptation measures, which include any CCA mechanism supported by government, NGOs or donors. Formal adaptation recorded in the LSV was largely agricultural projects and inputs, such as new crop varieties and irrigation. Secondly, members of the community accessed humanitarian aid in the form of supported temporary relocation, relief items, food aid and social cash transfer. Both social cash transfers and food aid are designed to support the most vulnerable and ultra-poor households to alleviate food insecurity and poverty (Brugh et al., 2017). Thirdly, those living in the LSV utilised informal adaptation mechanisms not externally supported by government, NGOs or donors. This generally consisted of starting small-scale businesses such as selling fish, crops, baked goods, firewood, thatching or bamboo, or engaging in formal employment. "Ganyu," a traditional source of income through piece-work activities, was also noted as a coping mechanism within the communities. Finally, those living in Chikwawa and Nsanje adopted negative coping mechanisms, defined as anything deemed harmful to persons, communities or the environment. These practices were noted as deforestation, increased production of charcoal for sale, selling assets, eating non-traditional food sources, engaging in sex work, and engaging in illegal activities such as stealing from land and homes. The disaggregated distribution of coping mechanisms used is presented in Table 28.3 collated from survey data.

Table 28.3 shows that gender parity has been reached in the access to formal adaptation and humanitarian aid, with similar percentages of male and female participants reporting these activities as coping mechanisms. However, it should be noted that community sharing of food aid takes place, so it is likely that those who report receiving food aid do not maintain access to the whole package; rather, this is shared across the community with those not in direct receipt of food aid. This was viewed as a positive activity within community dialogue. The survey data further shows that women have a higher reliance on *ganyu* as a coping mechanism. Traditionally, ganyu is an activity conducted by all members of society, but it is a common practice for poorer households to create incomes or an extra food supply, regardless of gender (Fahy-Bryceson, 2006; Bezner-Kerr, 2005). The survey data does not show significant differences between men and women's employment of informal adaptation and negative coping mechanisms. However, FGD indicated that there are meaningful differences in the access and choice of men and women in the informal adaptation and negative coping mechanisms practices used. From community dialogue in FGD, it is clear that women have fewer income-generating opportunities, largely

Table 28.3 Disaggregated results of coping strategies employed by researched communities in LSV.

	Women		Men	
N (total)	*230*		*122*	
	n.	%	n.	%
Formal adaptation	70	31%	36	30%
Humanitarian aid	49	21%	24	20%
Informal adaptation	25	11%	15	12%
Ganyu.	193	84%	93	76%
Negative coping mech.	70	30%	40	32%

limited to selling crops or baked goods. There was a noted increase in male migration to sur-rounding districts to seek gainful employment, as cultural restrictions limit this as an option for women. One female FGD elaborated that women in their community were selling maize residue from the mill house, and their children were selling cups of water in order to obtain small amounts of income. One male FGD discussed the utilisation of environmental change for income-generating activities, through the operation of boat taxis to transport people across a river that changed course after the 2015 flooding. There was also a noted increase of women engaging in sex work, for food or income, as a coping mechanism to the heightened food inse-curity resulting from the extreme weather of 2015–2016. Traditionally in rural Malawi, women are responsible for ensuring adequate food within the household, hence during times of food shortage, with limited adaptive capacity, women can resort to high-risk activities to provide for families. This finding emerged, within male (3) and mixed (1) FGD, citing a key challenge of climate change was an increase of sexually transmitted diseases. The issue of increased sexually transmitted diseases and sex work as a key challenge were not raised by female FGD. Although unconfirmed, it is thought that this was not raised by women because discussions relating to sexual relations remains a taboo subject. A final gendered coping mechanism to note is that of increased engagement in early marriages, which despite recently being made illegal in Malawi, was cited by two youth FGD, along with other key actors, specifically a Senior Chief from Nsanje district (see quote in Figure 28.3).

The results from community dialogue show that there are key gendered coping strategies employed within communities in the LSV. Women's greater reliance on ganyu and negative coping mechanisms is acknowledged by numerous actors across national and subnational scales (Figure 28.3), yet there was no evidence of action to provide support or increase the adaptive capacity of women engaging in high-risk activities. Further to this, no policies across the scales refer to these critical gender relations or means to address them.

"Yeah [early marriages have] increased, why? Because soon after the flooding people were displaced, children – girls – lost their parents, so they had no one to look after them, so the only way out was to get married early. Even if [their] parents were there, they [have] lost everything they owned so it [is] like shedding off some of the children, so it [is] less responsibility. Yeah it has been a big problem" (L/TA_2)

"...the next thing, in the event that they don't have cash that means women may be able to offer their bodies to men who have got food...so that at the end of the day they are able to feed their children. This exposes the women to HIV and AIDS" (N/NGO_4)

"Even when we talk of sexual prostitution it is very high, women are just selling them-selves in order to get the food to feed the family" (L/NGO_3)

"So, I feel the lower shire [valley] has this culture thing that is affecting women, such as issues of early marriage, we [have] seen most girls dropping out of school, going into marriage, yeah so I think it has an impact" (N/NGO_7)

Figure 28.3   Key actor quotes on gendered negative coping mechanisms.

Conclusion: failures and shortfalls of gender mainstreaming

This chapter has aimed to present successes and shortfalls of gender mainstreaming in CCA and DRM activities to date by conducting a multiscale analysis. Amongst international, national and subnational scales, there has been a noted increase in the gender language used within policies, and this has impacted how organisations work, according to the national and subnational actors who participated in this research. The findings show, however, that policies have consistently failed to incorporate gender considerations within key aspects of policies such as implementation, guidelines for national strategies, follow-up, monitoring and evaluation. As a result, it seems critics are rightly concerned of the potential for national actors to water-down policies. Within Malawi, gender mainstreaming in CCA and DRM is donor-led, and organisations understand that when applying for funding it is a necessity to include gender considerations. As actors often do not have the knowledge or capacity to implement these fully, it is found that employing gender balance is often the only notable gendered activity conducted.

Women are consistently viewed as vulnerable to climate change within policies across scale and amongst actors interviewed at national and subnational scale. This view is rejected by women, and largely by communities at local scale in LSV, with only small numbers suggesting women are a vulnerable group. Communities largely identify elderly, sick, disabled and children, specifically orphan-headed households, as the most vulnerable to climate change. Within the body of international policies agreed in 2015, these social categories are identified as key groups. However, they are consistently grouped with gender considerations, and hence they are prone to and reflect the same key failings.

This research finds, most notably, that traditions and culture play a critical role within the gendered experience of climate change. Women are restricted in mobility, decision-making power and agency due to cultural practices. Yet, these issues are largely ignored within policy. In fact, it is found that national and subnational actors appear to disassociate from deep-rooted cultural and traditional practices and suggest this is only an issue at local scale. This may, along with top-down, non-specific gender considerations, shed light on why critical gender inequalities such as early marriage and sex work are acknowledged by actors, but not acted on. For gender mainstreaming to be effective, there is a need to challenge the cultural and traditional barriers, while not enforcing the Western feminist views to remove key activities such as community cooperation. Until the top-down nature of gender mainstreaming is challenged, it is likely that there will be limited meaningful change within gender roles, equity and adaptive capacities of women in rural climate vulnerable communities.

References

Alston, M., 2014. Gender Mainstreaming and Climate Change. *Women's Studies International Forum*, 47, pp. 287–294.

Arndt, C., Pauw, K. and Thurlow, J., 2015. The Economy-wide Impacts and Risks of Malawi's Farm Input Subsidy Program. *American Journal of Argicultural Economics*, 98(3), pp. 962–980.

Arora-Jonsson, S., 2011. Virtue and Vulnerabiltiy: Discourses on Women, Gender and Climate Change. *Global Environmental Change: Human and Policy Dimensions*, 21(2), pp. 1872–9495.

Bailey, I., 2017. Spatializing Climate Justice: Justice Claim Making and Carbon Pricing Controversies in Australia. *Annals of the America Association of Geographers*, 107(5), pp. 1128–1143.

Baker, J., McDuff, S. and Weaver, C., 2013. *Tracking Climate Aid in Africa: The Case of Malawi, Research Brief No. 18.* Austin: Robert S. Strauss Center for International Security and Law.

Barrett, S., 2012. The Necessity of a Multiscalar Analysis of Climate Justice. *Progress in Human Geography*, 37(2), pp. 215–233.

Barrett, S., 2013. Local Level Climate Justice? Adaptation Finance and Vulnerabilty Reduction. *Global Environmental Change*, 23, pp. 1819–1829.

Barrett, S., 2014. Subnational Climate Justice? Adaptation Finance Distribution and Climate Vulnerability. *World Development*, 58, pp. 130–142.

Berge, E., Kambewa, D., Munthali, A. and Wiig, H., 2014. Lineage and Land Reforms in Malawi: Do Matrilineal and Patrilineal Landholding Systems Represent a Problem for Land Reforms in Malawi? *Land Use*, 41, pp. 61–69.

Bezner-Kerr, R., 2005. Informal Labor and Social Relations in Northern Malawi: The Theoretical Challenges and Implications of Ganyu Labor for Food Security. *Rural Sociology*, 70(2), pp. 167–187.

Brugh, K. et al., 2017. Impacts of the Malawi Social Cash Transfer Program on Household Food and Nutrition Security. *Food Policy*, In Press.

Burns, B. and Patouris, J., 2014. *UNFCCC Decisions and Conclusions: Existing Mandates and Entry Points for Gender Equality, Technical Guide for COP20 Lima, Peru*. s.l.: WEDO.

Cornwall, A. and Edwards, J., 2015. Introduction: Beijing +20 – Where Now for Gender Equality? *IDS Bulletin*, July, 46(4).

Dankelman, I., 2002. Climate Change: Learning From Gender Analysis and Women's Experience of Organising for Sustainable Development. *Gender and Development*, 10(2), pp. 21–29.

Denton, F., 2002. Climate Change Vulnerability, Impacts, and Adaptation: Why Does Gender Matter? *Gender and Development*, 10(2), pp. 10–20.

Dikito-Wachtmeister, M., 2000. *Women's Participation in Decision-Making Processes in Rural Water Projects, Makoni District, Zimbabwe*. Bradford: University of Bradford.

Eriksen, S., Håkon Inderberg, T., O'Brien, K. and Sygna, L., 2015. Introduction. In: T. Håkon Inderberg, S. Eriksen, K. O'Brien and L. Sygna, eds. *Climate Change, Adaptation and Development: Transforming Paradigms and Practices*. London and New York: Routledge, pp. 1–18.

EUROSTAT, 2017. *EU SDG INDICATOR SET, Indicators for Monitoring the Sustainable Development Goals (SDGs) in an EU Context*. s.l.: European Commission, EUROSTAT.

Fahy-Bryceson, D., 2006. Ganyu Casual Labour, Famine and HIV/AIDS in Rural Malawi: Causality and Casualty. *The Journal of Modern African Studies*, 44(2), pp. 173–202.

Fukuda-Parr, S., 2016. From the Millennium Development Goals to the Sustainable Development Goals: Shifts in Purpose, Concept and Politics of Global Goal Setting for Development. *Gender & Development*, 24(1), pp. 43–52.

Gabrielsson, S., 2015. Gender Matters: Adaptive Capacities to Climate Variability and Change in the Lake Victoria Basin. In: T. Håkon Inderberg, S. Eriksen, K. O'Brien and L. Sygna, eds. *Climate Change, Adaptation and Development: Transforming Paradigms and Practices*. London and New York: Routledge, pp. 83–97.

Giovarelli, R., Wamalwa, B. and Hannay, L., 2013. *USAID Issue Brief, Land Tenure, Property Rights, and Gender. Challenges and Approaches for Strengthening Women's Land Tenure and Property Rights*[Online]. Available at: https://www.land-links.org/wp-content/uploads/2016/09/USAID_Land_Tenure_Gender_Brief_061214-1.pdf [Accessed 4 May 2018]

Government of Malawi, 2006. *Malawi's National Adaptation Programmes of Action (NAPA)*. Lilongwe: Environmental Affairs Department.

Government of Malawi, 2011. *Malawi Growth and Development Strategy II 2011–2012*. Lilongwe: Government of Malawi.

Government of Malawi, 2012. *Agriculture Sector, Gender, HIV and AIDS Strategy 2012–2017*. Lilongwe: Ministry of Agriculture and Food Security.

Government of Malawi, 2015. *Intended Nationally Determined Contribution*. Lilongwe: Government of Malawi.

Government of Malawi, 2016. *Malawi Vulnerability Assessment Committee (MVAC), National Food and Nutrition Security Forecast*, April 2016 to March 2017, Bulletin No. 12/16.

Government of Malawi, 2017. *Malawi Demographic and Health Survey 2015–2016*. Zomba: National Statistics Office.

Huyer, S., 2016. *Info Note: Gender and International Climate Policy, An Analysis of Progress in Gender Equality at COP21*. Montpellier: CGIAR, Research Program on Climate Change, Agriculture and Food Security.

IPCC, 2014. Summary for Policymakers. In: *Climate Change 2014: Impacts, Adaptation, and Vulnerability. Contribution of Working Group III to the Fifth Assessment Report of the Intergovernmental Panel on Climate Change*. Cambridge: Cambridge University Press.

Jennings, T., 2011. Transcending the Adaptation/Mitigation Climate Change Science Policy Debate: Unmasking Assumption About Adaptation and Resilience. *Weather, Climate and Society*, 3, pp. 238–248.

Jerneck, A., 2018. Taking Gender Seriously in Climate Change Adaptation and Sustainability Science Research: Views From Feminist Debates and Sub-Saharan Small-scall Agriculture. *Sustainability Science*, 13, pp. 403–416.

Jost, C. et al., 2016. Understanding Gender Dimensions of Agriculture and Climate Change in Smallholder Farming Communities. *Climate and Development*, 8(2), pp. 133–144.

Kaarhus, R., 2010. Women's Land Rights and Land Tenure Reforms in Malawi: What Difference Does Matriliny Make? *Forum for Development Studies*, 37(2), pp. 171–192.

Kaijser, A. and Kronsell, A., 2014. Climate Change Througgh the Lens of Intersectionality. *Environmental Politics*, 23(3), pp. 417–433.

Kakota, T., Nyariki, D., Mkwambisi, D. and Kogi-Makau, W., 2011. Gender Vulnerability to Climate Variability and Food Insecurity. *Climate and Development*, 3, pp. 298–309.

Khan, M. and Roberts, J., 2013. Adaptation and International Climate Policy. *Wiley Interdisciplinary Reviews: Climate Change*, 4(3), pp. 171–189.

Koehler, G., 2016. Tapping the Sustainable Development Goals for Progressive Gender Equity and Equality Policy? *Gender & Development*, 24(1), pp. 53–68.

Lessa, I. and Rocha, C., 2011. Food Security and Gender Mainstreaming: Possibilities for Social Transformation in Brazil. *International Social Work*, 55(3), pp. 337–352.

Meier, P. and Celis, K., 2011. Sowing the Seeds of Its Own Failure: Implementing the Concept of Gender Mainstreaming. *Social Politics*, 18(4), pp. 469–489.

Molloy, E., 2016. *Gender Analysis for MVAC Emergency Cash Transfer Programme.* s.l.: Concern Worldwide.

Momsen, J., 2004. *Gender and Development.* London: Routledge.

Moser, C., 2005. Has Gender Mainstreaming Failed? *International Feminist Journal of Politics*, 7(4), pp. 576–590.

Msowoya, K. et al., 2016. Climate Change Impacts on Maize Production in the Warm Heart of Africa. *Water Resource Managment*, 30, pp. 5299–5312.

Mukhopadhyay, M., 2004. Mainstreaming Gender or 'Streaming' Gender Away: Feminists Marooned in the Development Buiness. *IDS Bulletin*, October, 35(4), pp. 95–103.

Nielsen, J. and Reenberg, A., 2010. Cultural Barriers to Climate Change Adaptation: A Case Study From Northern Burkina Faso. *Global Environmental Change: Human and Policy Dimensions*, 1(SI), pp. 142–152.

Open Data Watch, 2016. *Ready to Measure: Twenty Indicators for Monitoring SDG Gender Targets* [Online]. Available at: https://opendatawatch.com/wp-content/uploads/2016/03/ready-to-measure.pdf [Accessed 4 May 2018].

Payne, S., 2011. Beijing Fifteen Years On: The Persistence of Barriers to Gender Mainstreaming in Health Policy. *Social Politics: Interanational Studies in Gender, State and Society*, Winter, 18(4), pp. 515–542.

Peratskis, C., Baker, J. and Weaver, C., 2012. *Tracking Climate Adaptation Aid: CCAPS Climate Codebook.* Austin: Robert S. Strauss Center for International Security and Law.

Prügl, E., 2010. Feminism and the Postmodern State: Gender Mainstreaming in European Rural Development. *Signs*, Winter, 35(2), pp. 447–475.

Running, K., 2015. Towards Climate Justice: How Do the Most Vulnerable Weigh Environment-Economy Trade-Offs? *Social Science Research*, 50, pp. 217–228.

SDSN, 2015. *Indicators and a Monitoring Framework for the Sustainable Development Goals, Launching a Data Revolution for the SDGs.* s.l.: Unite Nations.

Terry, G., 2009. No Climate Justice Without Gender Justice: An Overview of the Issues. *Gender and Development*, 17(1), pp. 5–18.

True, J. and Mintrom, M., 2001. Transnational Networks and Policy Diffusion: The Case of Gender Mainstreaming. *International Studies Quarterly*, 45, pp. 27–57.

UN, 2017. *HLPF Thematic Review of SDG 5: Achieving Gneder Equality and Empower All Women and Girls* [Online]. Available at: https://sustainabledevelopment.un.org/content/documents/14383SDG5format-revOD.pdf [Accessed 15 August 2017].

UNISDR, 2007. *Hyogo Framework for Action 2005–2015: Building Resilence of Nations and Communities to Disaster.* Kobe: United Nations Office for Disaster Risk Reduction.

UNISDR, 2015. *Sendai Framework for Disaster Risk Reduction 2015–2030.* Geneva: United Nations Office for Disaster Risk Reduction.

UN Women, 2015. *The Beijing Declaration and Platform for Action Turns 20, Summary Report.* New York: UN Women.

UN Women, 2016. *Leveraging Co-Benefits Between Gender Equality and Climate Action For Sustainable Development: Mainstreaming Gender Considerations in Climate Change Projects.* New York: UN Women.

Weaver, C. et al., 2014. *Malawi's Open Aid Map*. Washington: International Bank for Reconstruction and Development/The World Bank.

White, S., 2007. *Malawi: Country Gender Profile, Final Report*. Japan: Japan International Cooperation Agency (JICA).

Wittman, A., 2010. Looking Local, Finding Global: Paradoxes of Gender Mainstremaing in the Scottish Executive. *Review of International Studies*, January, 31(1), pp. 51–76.

Wong, S., 2016. Can Climate Finance Contribute to Gender Equity in Developing Countries. *Journal of International Development*, 28, pp. 428–444.

29

Participatory climate governance in Southeast Asia

Lessons learned from gender-responsive climate mitigation

So-Young Lee and Eric Zusman

Climate justice for women

Countries have long professed support for gender equality in international development policy. The most recent illustration of this pledged support is Sustainable Development Goal 5 (SDG 5) that aims to *achieve gender equality and empower all women and girls* by 2030. Although SDG 5 and similar efforts have the nominal backing of governments, current data shows there is a long way to go before that rhetoric becomes reality. In fact, many studies suggest the situation is becoming worse for women due to "deteriorating health, escalating violence, declining access to education, decent jobs, and civil rights, and rising poverty levels worldwide" (Di Chiro, 2008: 277). These inequalities are also apparent in employment data that show women have been marginalised in construction (9%), engineering (12%), in financial and business (15%), manufacturing (24%) and in positions in technical occupations (<6%) and top managements (<1%) (UN Women, 2012). Though countries have vowed to address these trends with foreign aid, a 2013–2014 study found only 2% of official development assistance (ODA) that went to economic and productive sectors targeted gender equality as a principal objective (OECD, 2017).

Environmental problems can unfortunately widen many of the inequities described here. To some extent, this is part of a larger problem where disadvantaged segments of society confront the most serious environmental risks. This larger problem can be seen in evidence of the strong correlation between environmental problems and social injustice – from toxic facilities, local waste management, wind farm development to broader postcolonial environmental justice – that have been found in more than 37 countries (Schlosberg, 2013). In recent years, more attention has focused on the interactions between climate change and the livelihoods of the underprivileged (O'Brien and Leichenko, 2000; Parks and Roberts, 2006; Roberts and Parks, 2007; Hejnowicz et al., 2015; Tagg and Jafry, 2018). This attention is a result of the realisation that those who produced no contributions to the increase of the climate change become subject to its concentrated adverse effects. That realisation is also helping an effort to see climate change as a general human rights issue that, if it remains unaddressed, can exacerbate race, gender, class and power relations (Bulkeley et al., 2013; Chatterton et al., 2013; Derman, 2014).

The impacts of climate change could be particularly serious for women. Not surprisingly, this situation tends to be worrisome in less-developed nations where there is a generally a larger dependence on local natural resources (Aguilar et al., 2010; Dankelman, 2010; UNESCO, 2013) and women rely more heavily on local natural resources for their livelihoods i.e., responsible for securing water, food and fuel for cooking that are affected by a changing climate (Demetriades and Esplen, 2008; UN WomenWatch, 2008, 2009; Terry, 2009; Figueiredo and Perkins, 2013; Alston, 2015). Women in this situation are at the forefront of maintaining their survival through protecting family lives and also the life of the planet (Merchant, 1992). To cite a specific example of these inequalities, poor women and their children suffer the most from household air pollution during the cooking and heating processes, as well as having to spend many hours collecting fuel (Bailis et al., 2015; WHO, 2014; Cameron et al., 2016; Ray, 2016). In many cases, climate change reinforces these long-running inequalities (UNDP, 2009); moreover, limiting access to information and political influence (Burkett, 2007; Gupta, 2015) makes women worse off. When McKinney and Fulkerson (2015) provide a preliminary empirical assessment of the relationship between women's status and climate justice across nations, they conclude that women and the environment are mutually reinforcing *dimensions of exploitation*.

For these reasons, the challenges women face *adapting* to climate change have tended to overshadow the contributions women make *mitigating* climate change (Hostettler et al., 2015; Leach et al., 2016). To some extent, the emphasis on adaptation has also fed false narratives of women as passive victims of climate change (UN WomenWatch, 2009; Alston, 2015). This chapter draws upon a series of applied case studies from Southeast Asia to demonstrate that women have frequently untapped potential to mitigate climate change. It argues that one of the keys to unlocking that potential is to take advantage of recent trends in international climate negotiations to make climate governance more participatory at multiple levels. On the ground level, pilot initiatives are needed to offer clear evidence of how women can mitigate climate change. One level up, policies are required to provide finance and other enabling reforms to help replicate gender-responsive mitigation pilot initiatives. At the highest institutional level, policymakers in gender and climate agencies need the skills and opportunities to work in mainstreaming gender into climate policies. This multi-level approach fits well with trends in global climate policy that encourage countries to move beyond projects to policies and institutional reforms.

Integrating gender into international climate change policy

To understand the potential for this multi-level approach, it is helpful to review where gender fits in the history of international climate change policy. This history got off to a slow start when the United Nations Framework Convention on Climate Change (UNFCCC) was negotiated at the United Nations Conference on the Environment and Development in Rio in 1992. Unlike the other major Rio agreements – the Convention on Biodiversity and the Convention to Combat Desertification – the UNFCCC lacked the active involvement of women; the language of the agreement reflected this limited engagement. The recognition of the links between climate change and gender equality began to gain ground at the Seventh Conference of the Parties (COP 7) to the UNFCCC in Marrakesh in 2001, but even then progress was slow (Gupta, 2015).

The clearest sign of the slow progress involved allocations of climate finance. The Clean Development Mechanism (CDM), for example, is a project-based offset mechanism created under the UNFCCC and its Kyoto Protocol – negotiated in 1997 and ratified in 2005 – to offer developed countries affordable mitigation opportunities and promote sustainable development. The support for sustainable development would suggest that some countries would aim to empower women; however, by 2012, only five of 3,864 projects listed gender issues on project documentation

(UNFCCC, 2012; Zusman, 2013). The Indian Bagepalli CDM Biogas Programme, one of the few successful gender-responsive cases, promoted the reduction of fuel-wood collection and health improvement as well as shared project revenues with 5,500 women participants (UNFCCC, 2005). The Bagepalli case was nonetheless the exception that illustrated the rule.

Fortunately, the situation has taken a turn for the better in recent years. Part of the reason for the improvement involves the advent of new climate finance mechanisms. The Green Climate Fund (GCF) was created in 2012 to allocate a portion of 100 billion U.S. dollars annually. Thanks to the dedicated effort of a coalition of non-governmental organisations (NGOs) and supportive countries, the GCF was mandated to take a gender-responsive approach to distributing resources for both mitigation and adaptation (GCF, 2015; Schalatek, 2015). Demonstrating this commitment, the GCF 9th Board Meeting in 2015 embraced a gender policy and action plan supported by a Civil Society Active Observer and a Private Sector Active Observer. At the same time the GCF Board acknowledged "the progress made in advancing a gender balance and gender equality within the context of climate change policies and in line with the individual country circumstances when applying said policy" (IISD, 2015: 13). The gender specialist at GCF (interviewed 16 September 2015) is expecting tangible examples of how gender can be meaningfully integrated at different levels of the decision-making process (i.e., from projects through policies into institutions). Making these multi-level connections will require more than just potential linkages; it will require people who have the knowledge and influence to pull the parts together. Though progress remains too slow for some observers (German Climate Finance, 2015), the potentially greater funding suggests that GCF opens opportunities for moving beyond simply projects to gender-sensitive policies and even wider institutional reforms.

Another possible area with growing support for not just projects but policy and institutional changes involves nationally determined contributions (NDCs). NDCs originated from an agreement at COP 19 in 2013, wherein countries would pledge broad roadmaps outlining how they would mitigate and adapt to climate change in the post-2020 period (UNFCCC, 2014). In many cases, the actions included in the NDCs accommodate both mitigation and adaptation elements as well as financial, technological and capacity-building needs (Boos et al., 2015). In addition to outlining varying needs, NDCs are supposed to consider other development concerns beyond greenhouse gas (GHG) reductions, such as human development and gender equality. In the years that followed, many countries are including the references to gender in their NDCs (UNFCCC, 2014, 2015). The inclusion of this language is also encouraging some countries to enable agencies or divisions focusing on gender to participate in decisions over climate policies. These trends, moreover, appear likely to continue with the Gender Action Plan (GAP) that was agreed at COP 23 in 2017 as the most recent example to increase climate-related finance for sets of actions that integrate gender priorities and reflect the needs of women and girls (UNFCCC, 2017).

Participatory climate governance

The question confronting many policymakers is how to take advantage of the trends described in the previous section. The easiest answer is to make climate governance more participatory. In many environmental policy areas, participatory forms of governance have been found to improve decisions because they incorporate wider-ranging values, accumulate richer information, and generate more equitable and effective outcomes (Fischer, 2000; Steele, 2001; Beierle, 2002; Pellizzoni, 2003; Richards et al., 2004; Koontz and Thomas, 2006; Newig, 2007). However, despite increasing efforts to make environmental governance more inclusive and participatory, especially climate policy, the complex interrelations between climate change and socio-economic development have been a barrier to moving forward (Meadowcroft, 2002; Young et al., 2006).

One way to overcome this barrier – and capitalise on the trends in international climate policy – is to harness the energies of the largest marginalised social group: women. Women have a strong body of knowledge and expertise that can help mitigate climate change as they often possess more knowledge about energy use and consumption in households and serve as stewards of natural resources (UN WomenWatch, 2008, 2009; Alston, 2015). In fact, since the early 1990s, there have been distinctive female-led social and environmental activities from the South, such as the Chipko in India and Kenya's National Council of Women, to protect their livelihood, to reverse ecological damage from mal-development and ultimately to practice harmonious and cooperative relationships among humans, and between humans and nature (Shiva, 1988; Merchant, 1992; Mies and Shiva, 1993; Mellor, 1997).

Heightened efforts to engage women may pay larger dividends for development. Lapniewska (2016: 131), for example, references Chant, who finds (2003) that in communities where women and men are more equal, "the poor climb out of poverty more quickly, economies tend to grow faster and the well-being of women, men, and children is enhanced." A similar yet stronger message is found in ecofeminist scholarship that pushes for greater efforts to legitimise the participation of women in political processes (Buckingham, 2010). Support for greater engagement from women could hence increase the status of women and make them powerful and effective agents of change (Aguilar et al., 2010; Dankelman, 2010; Resurrección, 2013; UNESCO, 2013; McKinney and Fulkerson, 2015.) Women have strong potential to become vital change agents to contribute to sustainable development and climate change mitigation, not only for climate justice but also for long-lasting success.

The challenge nonetheless remains of how to engage women in climate policy. A possible response to this challenge involves work on multi-level governance. One of the core insights of multi-level governance is that truly transformative change requires engagement at different levels of decision-making (Bache and Flinders, 2005; Papadopoulos, 2007). This can start at the local or community level where the inclusion of stakeholders delivers the implementation on the ground with locally appropriate solutions towards environmental issues (Macnaghten and Jacobs, 1997; Reed, 2008). It also extends upward to the institutions that shape policies and the language in the policies that influences the implementation and potential spread of local actions. This multi-level approach was employed in Southeast Asia through a technical assistance project described as follows.

Climate mitigation in Southeast Asia

In 2013, the Asian Development Bank (ADB) initiated a technical assistance project[1] entitled *Harnessing Climate Change Mitigation Initiatives to Benefit Women* that sought to make climate change mitigation more participatory in Cambodia, Lao PDR and Vietnam. Following international climate policy trends that encourage multi-level interventions to achieve transformative change, the activities focused on linking real projects with supportive changes to institutions and relevant policies. This multi-level approach was structured differently in the three countries. In Lao PDR, it worked at the national level with the top environmental agency; in Cambodia it worked at the national level within an agency focused on agriculture; and in Vietnam it worked with a city-level environmental agency. The remainder of the chapter describes[2] how this project operated in those three countries, starting with local projects and then moving up to policies and institutions.

Empowering women as agents of change in Lao PDR

In Lao PDR, the pilot initiative involved helping women work on the assembly and marketing of clean cook stoves. The decision to work in this area was based on the understanding that gender inclusion should recognise and acknowledge women not only as passive recipients of goods and services but as active contributors to a supply chain. The improved cook stove value chain offered such an opportunity in Lao PDR. The value chain originated with the Lao Disabled Women's Development Centre (LDWDC). This centre host 25 young women from disadvantaged families for nine-month internships. During this period, they received capacity building and training to develop income-generating skills and share experiences among each other. These experiences helped to build self-esteem and confidence in a mutually supportive environment (ACP, 2016a).

The process of creating this environment started with a long lead period during which the LDWDC visited nearby producers, and the possibilities of starting a stove production workshop were considered. After some consideration, the centre tested the market to ensure that production was financially viable. They did this by starting with door-to-door sales of stoves sourced from nearby producers while also dedicating a section of their on-campus shop for the stoves. They then established strategic partnerships with local authorities and the Lao Women's Union (LWU) to help them prime the market and get necessary support to enter into nearby villages. Through this preparatory work, they determined that the demand for the cook stove proved sufficiently high and stable to justify investments and related risks; the decision was then made to go ahead with the production centre.

Beyond this preparatory work, many additional adaptations were needed to make the production process operational for the women involved. The project team provided the necessary additional support to customise the fit of the centre as well as supplementary training, which led to the LDWDC achieving certification as an accredited production facility. This creation of a functioning cook stove production centre helped to establish a more entrepreneurial approach to production as a business rather than a more familiar charitable perspective. At the end of 2016, LDWDC had made more than 1,300 cook stoves for the market. Perhaps more importantly, it helped empower a segment of the population that is frequently left out of the employment market.

In addition to the local cook stove activities, the project worked with the Ministry of Natural Resources and Environment (MONRE), the principal government agency responsible for all climate change-related issues, as well as with the Lao Women's Union (LWU), the key women's organisation. The project deliberately aimed to enhance both agencies' understanding of gender mainstreaming, climate change and the importance of gender-responsive approaches to climate change mitigation. After three years of continued engagement on these issues, MONRE, the designated leader of the National Climate Change Technical Working Group, invited an LWU representative to join this inter-ministerial climate change coordinating group. The participation in the group was intended to increase women's involvement in climate change mitigation activities and clean energy technology supply chains. The National Climate Change Technical Working Group members including LWU are now working together to promote gender-responsive climate change mitigation.

One of the models that is looking to achieve that goal is the *National Climate Change Action Plan 2013–2020* (CCAP). A close examination of CCAP revealed that the gender dimension of climate change impacts and responses had not been considered in the policy; it was decided that review and revision of the CCAP should be carried out to integrate gender-responsiveness through a series of consultative workshops and meetings with key players. The draft CCAP now addresses gender issues in all sectors across all four focus areas – institutional strengthening, adaptation and education as well as mitigation. As a result of this intervention, MONRE can approach the formal review process for updating the CCAP as an example for other policies, and is now equipped with an understanding of how to ensure their next plan addresses the gender dimension of climate change mitigation.

Gender integration in Cambodia

In Cambodia, pilot activities focused on bringing women into the supply chain for advanced cook stoves. The distribution of renewable energy products has been dominated by men in Cambodia due to the perception that men are better equipped to handle technology. Men also have greater access to vehicles; since selling requires extensive travel to demonstrate and promote products, women are typically viewed as less active sales agents. To overcome these hurdles, the Cambodia pilot initiative was designed in close cooperation with a prominent advanced cook stove distributor in Phnom Penh. Through discussions with the distributor, it was possible to create opportunities to engage women as sales agents in an already established marketing network. Some 67 women were brought into this network to demonstrate and promote advanced clean cook stoves. In this role, they were not only making fuel-efficient, low-emission technology accessible to communities, but they were also generating livelihood benefits for their families. To date, 500 stoves have been sold by women agents, reducing 500 tonnes of CO_2 emissions annually or 1,500 tonnes over the expected three-year lifetime of the stove – each advanced cook stove contributes to reducing CO_2eq emissions by approximately 1 tonne per stove per year (ACP, 2016b).

In Cambodia, the main institutional partner was the Ministry of Agriculture, Forestry and Fisheries (MAFF). The decision to partner with MFAA reflected the significant participation of women in agricultural activities. Within MAFF, the project team decided to work closely with the then recently reconstituted Gender and Children's Working Group (GCWG). When consulting with the GCWG, it was revealed that one of MAFF's key policies, the *Gender Mainstreaming Policy and Strategic Framework* (GMPSF), was under review in 2015 and could benefit from references to climate change mitigation. Working with the GCWG, gender-responsive climate change mitigation strategies were integrated into the revised GMPSF scheduled to run from 2016 to 2020. The revised GMPSF now has a new section focusing on women's participation in climate change initiatives, gender-related climate change issues, climate change-related indicators and institutional capacity building.

The provisions on capacity building created a platform for key members of GCWG to demonstrate their knowledge of climate change and led to an invitation to the MAFF's Technical Working Group for Policy and Strategy to Respond to Climate Change. This step has helped to institutionalise GCWG participation in future climate policy decisions made at MAFF. It has also enabled the Provincial Gender Focal Points in all 25 provinces to promote clean energy technologies and encourage their clients to participate in clean energy supply chains.

Carving out a new role for women in Vietnam

The pilot initiative in Vietnam focused on engaging women in the biogas supply chain in the coastal city of Dong Hoi. For the Dong Hoi pilot initiative, women were equipped with the technical, construction, business and marketing skills needed to create a bio-digester supply business. The trainings were initiated in cooperation with the Dong Hoi Women's Union (DHWU). Through this cooperation, it was decided to update training materials and methods to make them more compatible with the needs of women trainees and enhance the capacity of male trainers to build capacities of women masons. The project also created an opportunity for the National Biogas Programme to bring in women producers and users of biogas technologies. Within the last decade, the Vietnam National Biogas Programme had trained over 1,700 masons, but less than 0.2% were female.

As a result of the pilot initiative, eight Biogas Mason Enterprises (BMEs) were established and seven of them were women-led; that is, they were enabled to run their own accredited BMEs.

Creating the women-led BMEs doubled the income of those women who moved from trainees to assistant ($10 US per day) to leadership roles ($17.5–20 US per day for the BME leaders). The formation of these companies also resulted in the construction of 300 new digesters in Dong Hoi and the avoidance of around 1,569 tonnes CO_2eq annually – each biogas digester reduced CO_2eq by around 5 tonnes per year. Furthermore, the utilisation of bio-slurry as a source of fertiliser avoided the production and use of chemical fertiliser that contributes to GHG emissions. Beyond the direct impacts of the pilot, around 400 people, including suppliers, end users and DHWU members (90% women), gained knowledge and skills in natural resource and energy management to support climate mitigation in Vietnam. Women increased their understanding of opportunities and rights, and they are actively involved in promoting sustainable development through addressing climate change, gender equality and poverty reduction (ACP, 2016c).

In Vietnam, the lead institution was the Dong Hoi Department of Natural Resource and Environment (DONRE). In consultation with the Dong Hoi People's Committee (DHPC), DONRE decided to work with the Dong Hoi Women's Union (DHWU) in reforming the *Dong Hoi City Action Plan for Climate Change Mitigation and Adaptation, Strengthening Resource Management and Environment Protection 2016–2020*. A review of this plan revealed that there was no discussion of climate change mitigation and that the gender dimension of climate change impacts and responses had not been adequately addressed. In consultation with DHPC and DONRE, it was agreed that the project would help introduce both climate change mitigation and gender elements into the city's main climate change plan.

Many of the revisions were made during a stakeholder consultation workshop that enabled city agencies and civil society organisations to contribute to the plan. The workshop also offered the DHWU in particular an opportunity to have a stronger voice in policymaking. National representatives from the Ministry of Labour, Invalids and Social Affairs and MONRE made further valuable contributions, bringing a broader national perspective to the discussion. After the consultation, further iterations resulted in a final version of the *Action Plan 2016–2020* being signed that specifically addressed gender concerns. Just as importantly, the DHWU was included in the city and commune-level implementation planning that followed the passage of the plan to ensure that both women's and men's priorities would be addressed.

Lessons from gender-responsive climate mitigation

This chapter began with the contention that women could play an important role in mitigating climate change. Allowing them to realise that potential would help break down misperceptions of women as passive victims of climate change. It would also help capitalise on reforms in the international climate regime that could provide more support for gender-responsive mitigation. At the same time, the chapter argued that the best way to take advantage of these reforms is to introduce reforms that encourage participation in pilot initiatives as well as policies and institutions. The chapter then described how this multi-level approach was adopted in three countries in Southeast Asia as part of an ADB project. In each of those countries, gender-responsive pilots involved women in concrete on-the-ground initiatives that built knowledge and skills to mitigate climate change while earning other livelihood benefits. Simultaneously, institutional capacity building and policy mainstreaming empowered women and women's groups to engage in decisions that could help achieve longer-lasting results beyond these pilots. The project concluded that these multi-levels of activities reinforced each other – institutions supported policies that encouraged pilot initiatives.

The project generated several lessons that could inform future efforts to mitigate climate change and mainstream gender. First, women's active engagement in clean energy supply chains proved effective. Women's entrepreneurship was supported in different enterprises in the three countries and, in each country, it was demonstrated that women could enjoy success as clean energy technology entrepreneurs, doing work that had previously been thought of as the domain of men. In relation to this finding, a second noteworthy point is that pilot initiatives demonstrated that gender-responsive climate change mitigation on the ground is an essential piece of the multi-level approach. Before the pilot initiatives were initiated, participating stakeholders found it difficult to envisage gender-responsive climate change mitigation. However, once implementation of the pilots began, interactions between institutional capacity building, policy mainstreaming and pilot initiatives could form and support each other. Third, the project demonstrated that women, armed with knowledge and confidence, could participate actively in efforts to strengthen climate institutions and policies. The Cambodia GCWG now has one-third of the seats in the MAFF climate policy working group; the LWU participates in national climate change working group deliberations; and the DHWU in Vietnam has a voice in determining priority climate change-related actions. Fourth, country-driven approaches are gaining more attention from funders, and this emerging focus is on supporting well-articulated national priorities for an integrated, multi-sector approach rather than single-sector project-based initiatives. Hence, groups seeking funding need to create alliances to promote their agenda in a broader framework. The multi-level approach was well aligned with these trends.

There are also some possible limitations of this work. Arguably, the most significant limitation involves a critical view on the effects of cook stove interventions. Some have argued that improved and advanced cook stoves actually generate small reductions in indoor air pollution, marginal health improvements (Grieshop et al., 2011; Ruiz-Mercado et al., 2011; Anenberg et al., 2013) and negligible effects on climate change mitigation (Venkataraman et al., 2010; Casillas and Kammen, 2012). This is partially because stove users continue to use conventional technologies alongside the improved models. Those involved in this project also noticed that users tended to keep the conventional stoves along with the cleaner stoves, making it difficult to quantify impacts, especially health benefits (WHO, 2014; Bruce et al., 2015; Sambandam et al., 2015). Nonetheless, while this project's findings suggested that there was some *leakage* due to the tendency to use older stoves, on balance those households that purchased the stoves experienced better air quality and produced fewer GHGs. This project, furthermore, emphasised not only the importance of quantifying the impacts on the climate but also the qualitative effects from women's knowledge of resource management, their willingness to take leadership positions and their potential to effect long-term change.

A second possible limitation involves the sustainability of this work. A legitimate question is whether these efforts will prove sustainable after the support ends. This remains an open question. To be truly transformational, the next critical step is transitioning from this grant-financed project to Southeast Asian governments investing in their own gender-responsive climate change programmes. Making this transition will help ensure that the vital role women play in climate change mitigation will continue to be recognised and institutionalised enough to be sustainable over space and time.

All stakeholders and project participants, from the cook stove producer at Lao Disabled Women's Development Centre to the governmental officers, gathered together for the regional closing workshop. They acknowledged that women steered communities down low-carbon development paths when opportunities were opened. They reiterated commitments to promoting gender-inclusive climate change responses while the need for ongoing support was also highlighted. They also hoped to seek further opportunities for strategic relationship-building with global climate finance partners. This closing workshop furthermore provided introductions to many key influencers in the global climate change space, especially those promoting women's greater participation in climate change actions. The workshop was a good depiction of Rahman's saying (1993) that women "can plant the seed for a brighter future, if they have the right tools" (Jafry, 2000: 2), leading to transitions that are at once environmentally sustainable and socially just.

Notes

1 The project was financed by the Nordic Development Fund (NDF), managed by the Asian Development Bank (ADB) and jointly implemented by the Institute for Global Environmental Strategies (IGES) and SNV Netherlands Development Organisation.
2 The findings are mainly based on the analysis of: (1) average one-hour in-depth interviews conducted with Ministry of Women's Affairs; Ministry of Environment; Ministry of Agriculture, Forestry and Fisheries on 19–21 January 2015 in Cambodia and also with Ministry of Natural Resources and Environment; Lao Women's Union; World Bank and UNDP on 22–23 January 2015 in Lao PDR; (2) workshops on 4–6 August 2015, 21–23 December 2015, 30–31 May 2016, 14 December 2016 in Cambodia; 18–19 August 2015, 2–3 June 2016, 16 December 2016 in Lao PDR; 24–25 December 2015, 19–20 December 2016 in Vietnam; and (3) three sets of leaflet for the pilot initiatives produced by the authors (i.e., ACP 2016a; b; and c), listed under references.

References

Asian Co-benefits Partnership (ACP) (2016a) 'Gender integration in the supply of improved cook stoves in Lao PDR', *ACP Good Practice Map*. ACP, Hayama. Available at www.cobenefit.org/good_practice/detail/pdf/ACP_lao-ics.livelihood.pdf

ACP. (2016b) 'Advanced Clean Cookstove supply chain in Cambodia', *ACP Good Practice Map*. ACP, Hayama. Available at www.cobenefit.org/good_practice/detail/pdf/ACP_cambodia-accs.livelihood%20.pdf

ACP. (2016c) 'New roles for women in the biogas supply chain in Vietnam'. *ACP Good Practice Map*. ACP, Hayama. Available at www.cobenefit.org/good_practice/detail/pdf/ACP_vietnam-bio.livelihood.pdf

Aguilar, L., Araujo, A., and Quesada-Aguilar, A. (2010) 'Gender and climate change', *Gender Fact Sheet*, IUCN. Available at http://cmsdata.iucn.org/downloads/gender_factsheet_climatechange.pdf

Alston, M. (2015) *Women and Climate Change in Bangladesh, ASAA Women in Asia Series*. Routledge, London

Anenberg, S.C., Balakrishnam, K., Jetter, J., Masera, O., Mehta, S., Moss, J., and Ramanathan, V. (2013) 'Cleaner cooking solutions to achieve health, climate, and economic cobenefits', *Environmental Science & Technology*, vol 47, pp 3944–3952

Bailis, R., Drigo, R., Ghilardi, A., and Marsera, O. (2015) 'The carbon footprint of traditional woodfuels', *Nature Climate Change*, vol 5, pp 266–-272

Bache, I. and Flinders, M. (2005) 'Multi-level governance: Conclusion and implications', in I. Bache and M. Flinders (eds) *Multi-level Governance*. Oxford University Press, Oxford

Beierle, T.C. (2002) 'The quality of stakeholder-based decisions', *Risk Analysis*, vol 22, pp 739–749

Boos, D., Broecker, H., Dorr, T., Luepke, H. von, and Sharma, S. (2015) *How are INDCs and NAMAs Linked?* Deutsche Gesellschaft für Internationale Zusammenarbeit (GIZ), Eschborn and UNEP DTU Partnership, Copenhagen

Bruce, N., Pope, D., Rehfuess, E., Balakrishnan, K., Adair-Rohani, H., and Dora, C. (2015) 'WHO indoor air quality guidelines on household fuel combustion: Strategy implications of new evidence on interventions and exposure-risk functions', *Atmospheric Environment*, vol 106, pp 451–457

Buckingham, S. (2010) 'Call in the women', *Nature*, vol 468, no 7323, p 502

Bulkeley, H., Carmin, J., Broto, V.C., Edwards, G.A.S., and Fuller, S. (2013) 'Climate justice and global cities: Mapping the emerging discourses', *Global Environmental Change*, vol 23, pp 914–925

Burkett, M. (2007) 'Just solutions to climate change: A climate justice proposal for a domestic clean development mechanism', *Buffalo Law Review*, vol 56, no 3, pp 169–243

Cameron, C., Pachauri, S., Rao, N.D., McCollum, D., Rogelj, J., and Riahi, K. (2016) 'Policy trade-offs between climate mitigation and clean cook-stove access in South Asia', *Nature Energy*, vol 1, January. International Institute for Applied Systems Analysis (IIASA), Laxenburg

Casillas, C.E. and Kammen, D.M. (2012) 'Quantifying the social equity of carbon mitigation strategies', *Climate Policy*. doi:10.1080/14693062.2012.669097

Chant, S. (2003) 'New contributions to the analysis of poverty: Methodological and conceptual challenges to understanding poverty from a gender perspective', *CEPAL – SERIE Mujer y desarrollo*, no 47. UN, Santiago

Chatterton, P., Featherstone, D., and Routledge, P. (2013) 'Articulating climate justice in Copenhagen: Antagonism, the commons, and solidarity', *Antipode*, vol 45, no 3, pp 602–620

Dankelman, I. (ed). (2010) *Gender and Climate Change: An Introduction.* Earthscan, London

Demetriades, J. and Esplen, E. (2008) 'The gender dimensions of poverty and climate change adaptation', *IDS Bulletin*, vol 39, no 4

Derman, B.B. (2014) 'Climate governance, justice, and transnational civil society', *Climate Policy*, vol 14, no 1, pp 23–41

Di Chiro, G. (2008) 'Living environmentalisms: Coalition politics, social reproduction, and environmental justice', *Environmental Politics*, vol 17, no 2, pp 276–298

Figueiredo, P. and Perkins, P.E. (2013) 'Women and water management in times of climate change: Participatory and inclusive processes', *Journal of Cleaner Production*, vol 60, pp 188–194

Fischer, F. (2000) *Citizens, Experts and the Environment: The Politics of Local Knowledge.* Duke University Press, London

German Climate Finance. (2015) *Green Climate Fund: The Ten-billion-dollar Question.* Available at www. germanclimatefinance.de/2015/04/21/green-climate-fund-ten-billion-dollar-question/

Green Climate Fund (GCF). (2015) *Gender Policy for the Green Climate Fund.* Available at www.greenclimate. fund/documents/20182/319135/1.8_-_Gender_Policy_and_Action_Plan.pdf/f47842bd-b044-4500-b7ef-099bcf9a6bbe

Grieshop, A.P., Marshall, J.D., and Kandlikar, M. (2011) 'Health and climate benefits of cook stove replacement options', *Energy Policy*, vol 39, pp 7530–7542

Gupta, H. (2015) 'Women and climate change: Linking ground perspectives to the global scenario', *Indian Journal of Gender Studies*, vol 22, no 3, pp 208–420

Hejnowicz, A.P., Kennedy, H., Rudd, M.A., and Huxham M.R. (2015) Harnessing the climate mitigation, conservation and poverty alleviation potential of seagrasses: Prospects for developing blue carbon initiatives and payment for ecosystem service programmes. *Frontiers in Marine Science*, vol 2, no 32, pp 1–22.

Hostettler, S., Gadgil, A., and Hazboun, E. (eds). (2015) *Sustainable Access to Energy in the Global South.* Springer, Switzerland

International Institute for Sustainable Development (IISD). (2015) *GCF Bulletin: A Summary Report of the Ninth Meeting of the Green Climate Fund Board*, vol 172, no 20. IISD

Jafry, T. (2000) 'Women, human capital and livelihoods: An ergonomics perspective', *Natural Resource Perspectives*, no 54 April. Department for International Development, London

Koontz, T.M. and Thomas, C.W. (2006) 'What do we know and need to know about the environmental outcomes of collaborative management?', *Public Administration Review*, vol 66, pp 111–121

Lapniewska, Z. (2016) 'Reading Elinor Ostrom through a gender perspective', *Feminist Economics*, vol 22, no 4, pp 129–151

Leach, M. (ed). (2016) *Gender Equality and Sustainable Development.* Routledge, London.

Macnaghten, P. and Jacobs, M. (1997) 'Public identification with sustainable development: Investigating cultural barriers to participation', *Global Environmental Change*, vol 7, no 1, pp 5–24

McKinney, L.A. and Fulkerson, G.M. (2015) 'Gender equality and climate justice: A cross-national analysis', *Social Justice Research*, vol 28, pp 293–317

Meadowcroft, J. (2002) 'Politics and scale: Some implications for environmental governance', *Landscape and Urban Planning*, vol 61, pp 169–179

Mellor, M. (1997) *Feminism and Ecology.* New York University Press, New York

Merchant, C. (1992) *Radical Ecology: The Search for a Livable World.* Routledge, London

Mies, M. and Shiva, V. (1993) *Ecofeminism.* Zed Books, London

Newig, J. (2007) 'Does public participation in environmental decision lead to improved environmental quality? Towards an analytical framework. Communication, cooperation, participation', *Research and Practice for a Sustainable Future*, vol 1, pp 51–71

O'Brien, K.L. and Leichenko, R.M. (2000) 'Double exposure: Assessing the impacts of climate change within the context of economic globalization', *Global Environmental Change, Part A: Human and Policy Dimensions*, vol 10, pp 221–232

Organisation for Economic Co-operation and Development (OECD). (2017) *The Pursuit of Gender Equality: An Uphill Battle.* OECD Publishing, Paris

Papadopoulos, Y. (2007). 'Problems of democratic accountability in network and multilevel governance', *European Law Journal*, vol 13, no 4, pp 469–486

Parks, B.C. and Roberts, J.T. (2006) 'Globalization, vulnerability to climate change, and perceived injustice', *Society and Natural Resources*, vol 19, no 4, pp 337–355

Pellizzoni, L. (2003). 'Uncertainty and participatory democracy', *Environmental Values*, vol 12, no 2, pp 195–224

Rahman, F.H. (1993) 'Not a burden but a force', *International Agricultural Development*, January/February, pp 11–12

Ray, I. (2016). 'Transformative investments for gender-equal sustainable development', in M. Leach (ed) *Gender Equality and Sustainable Development*. Routledge, London

Reed, M. (2008) 'Stakeholder participation for environmental management: A literature review', *Biological Conservation*, vol 141, pp 2417–2431

Resurrección, B.P. (2013) 'Persistent women and environment linkages in climate change and sustainable development agendas', *Women's Studies International Forum*, vol 40, pp 33–43

Richards, C., Blackstock, K.L., and Carter, C.E. (2004) 'Practical approaches to participation', *SERG Policy Brief*, no.1. Macauley Land Use Research Institute, Aberdeen

Roberts, J.T. and Parks, B.C. (2007) *A Climate of Injustice: Global Inequality, North-South Politics, and Climate Policy*. MIT Press, Cambridge, MA

Ruiz-Mercado, I., Masera, O., Zamora, H., and Smith, K.R. (2011) 'Adoption and sustainable use of improved cook stoves', *Energy Policy*, vol 39, pp 7557–7566

Sambandam, S., Balakrishnan, K., Ghosh, S., Sadasivam, A., Madhav, S., Ramasamy, R., Samanta, M., Mukhopadhay, K., Rehman, H., and Rammanthan, V. (2015) 'Can currently available advanced combustion biomass cook-stoves provide health relevant exposure reductions? Results from initial assessment of select commercial models in India', *Ecohealth*, vol 12, no 1, pp 25–41

Schalatek, L. (2015) *Moving Beyond "Business as Usual"*, Heinrich Böll Stiftung, DC

Schlosberg, D. (2013) 'Theorising environmental justice: The expanding sphere of a discourse', *Environmental Politics*, vol 22, no 1, pp 37–55

Shiva, V. (1988) *Staying Alive: Women, Ecology and Development*. Zed Books, London.

Steele, J. (2001) 'Participation and deliberation in environmental law: Exploring a problem-solving approach', *Oxford Journal of Legal Studies*, vol 21, no 3, pp 415–442

Tagg, N. and Jafry, T. (2018) 'Engaging young children with climate change and climate justice', *Research for All*, vol 2, no 1, pp 34–42

Terry, G. (2009) 'No climate justice without gender justice: An overview of the issue', *Gender and Development*, vol 17, no 1, pp 5–18

United Nations Development Programme (UNDP). (2009) *Resource Guide on Gender and Climate Change*. Available at www.uneca.org/acpc/about_acpc/docs/UNDP-GENDER-CLIMATE-CHANGE-RESOURCEGUIDE.pdf

United Nations Educational, Scientific and Cultural Organisation (UNESCO). (2013) *Tracking Key Trends in Biodiversity Science and Policy*. UNESCO. Available at http://unesdoc.unesco.org/images/0022/002205/220530E.pdf

United Nations Framework Convention on Climate Change (UNFCCC). (2005) *CDM Executive Board Project 0121: Bagepalli CDM Biogas Programme*. Available at http://cdm.unfccc.int/Projects/DB/DNV-CUK1131002343.1/viewUNFCCC. (2012) CDM Executive Board: Benefits of the Clean Development Mechanism. Available at http://cdm.unfccc.int/about/dev_ben/ABC_2012.pdf

UNFCCC. (2014) Further Advancing the Durban Platform, Decision 1/CP.19. Available at http://unfccc.int/resource/docs/2013/cop19/eng/10a01.pdf

UNFCCC. (2015) Submitted INDCs. Available at www4.unfccc.int/submissions/indc/Submission Pages/submissions.aspx

UNFCCC. (2017) *Establishment of a Gender Action Plan*. Available at http://unfccc.int/files/meetings/bonn_nov_2017/application/pdf/cp23_auv_gender.pdf

UN Women. (2012) *Fact-forwarding Women's Leadership in the Green Economy*. Available at www.unwomen.org/en/news/stories/2012/6/fast-forwarding-women-s-leadership-in-the-green-economy

UN WomenWatch. (2008) 'Gender perspectives on climate change', *52nd Session of the Commission on the Status of Women*. Available at www.un.org/womenwatch/daw/csw/csw52/issuespapers/Gender%20and%20climate%20change%20paper%20final.pdf

UN WomenWatch. (2009) 'Women, gender equality and climate change', *Fact Sheet, The UN Internet Gateway on Gender Equality and Empowerment of Women*. Available at www.un.org/womenwatch/feature/climate_change/downloads/Women_and_Climate_Change_Factsheet.pdf

Venkataraman, C., Sagar, A.D., Habib, G., Lam, N., and Smith, K.R. (2010) 'The Indian national initiative for advanced biomass cookstoves: The benefits of clean combustion', *Energy for Sustainable Development*, vol 14, pp 63–72

World Health Organization (WHO). (2014) *WHO Indoor Air Quality Guidelines: Household Fuel Combustion*. WHO. Available at www.who.int/indoorair/publications/household-fuel-combustion/en/

Young, O.R., Berkhout, F., Gallopin, G.C., Janssen, M.A., Ostrom, E., and van der Leeuw, S. (2006) 'The globalization of socio-ecological systems: An agenda for scientific research', *Global Environmental Change*, vol 16, pp 304–316

Zusman, E. (2013) *IGES Issue Briefs on Gender and Climate*. IGES, Hayama

Part VII
Climate justice movements and struggles

30

"Climate change is about us"

Fence-line communities, the NAACP and the grounding of climate justice

Brandon Derman

Introduction

Founded in 1909, the National Association for the Advancement of Colored People (NAACP) is the most long-lived organisational actor associated with the movement for racial justice in the U.S. (Berg, 2007; Sullivan, 2009). Though best known for its role in realising the judicial and legislative civil rights milestones of the 1950s and '60s, the group's voter registration and mobilisation efforts have remained influential (Berg, 2007; Goluboff, 2007). Recent reporting places its membership at approximately 500,000, across more than 2,000 chapters (Shipp, 2018). Since 2009, "climate justice" has emerged and risen in prominence among its areas of advocacy, amidst changes in the organisation's priorities as it responds to evolving social justice concerns and political conditions (NAACP, 2018a).

The NAACP's Environmental and Climate Justice Program (ECJP) pursues a politics of climate justice that differs importantly from those more prominent in UNFCCC negotiations and civil society summits. A participant in those settings, ECJP also leverages the NAACP's extensive organisational infrastructure and membership to mobilise political and legal resources across local, state and national scales within the U.S. on behalf of poor and minority communities disproportionately affected by climate change. ECJP extends the NAACP's work against discrimination by exposing and mobilising around the many connections that link racial, gender and economic inequality with the production, impacts and regulation of climate change. ECJP's analysis of climate injustice contextualises local experiences of harm and resistance through systemic analyses of fossil energy extraction-to-use cycles and racial injustice. Correspondingly, its local strategies vary with conditions and capacities in communities, even as local knowledge and activism inform broader efforts pursued through the NAACP's policy and legal advocacy, and its network in civil society. This chapter draws on interview data, transcripts and field notes from participant observation at meetings, and the ECJP's organisational and external communications to analyse the development and roll-out of its work for climate justice.

The need to ground a politics of climate justice

ECJP's work suggests empirical models of mobilisation and advocacy that respond to the "grass-rooting" imperatives sensed by a variety of analysts and participants in climate justice and other global movements against social and ecological marginalisation (see, e.g., Featherstone, 2008;

407

Routledge and Cumbers, 2009; Routledge, 2011; Bond, 2012; Mueller, 2012). Routledge and Cumbers (2009) argue, for example, that, "though global events and networks are important, arguably more time and resources should be spent on networking locally and nationally" (215). Routledge (2011) extends this point in application to the climate justice movement particularly, tying a similar call with the aim of "constructing more effective *grounded* resistance to injustice and responses to climate change" (394, emphasis in original).

Arguably, however, the efforts examined in this chapter – and the necessity of grounding a politics of climate justice more generally – escape the frame of many analysts' preoccupation with *transnational* resistance *per se*. Whereas Routledge and Cumbers (2009) note, for instance, that "the significance of [Global Justice Networks] and their potential . . . is in strengthening local struggles" (216),[1] the disappointments of recent transnational mobilisation around COPs and the general recalcitrance of global climate governance to the influence of people's movements has inspired some insiders to assert the priority of local and national initiatives in preparing the ground for, legitimating, or even obviating transnational ones (see, e.g., Bond, 2012; Mueller, 2012; Ecosocialist Horizons, 2011). ECJP represents one such autonomously developed effort.

The operative mechanism in the ECJP's efforts is the linking of global socio-ecological processes associated with climate change to the situated histories, priorities and resources of identity- and place-based constituencies. This linking results from politicising analyses of the more-than-human which differ in emphasis from those that underpin many transnational solidarities. Whereas the latter consist of highlighting the global ties of responsibility that link emitters and affected people, and constructing similarly extensive solidarities among dispersed and diverse affected groups, work like that of the ECJP gives equal or greater emphasis to historically, socially and geographically specific conditions. As discussed in this chapter, these include precarious life in poor, Black neighbourhoods adjacent to ageing coal-fired power plants, refining centres and/or rising and warming seas.

And yet these efforts also differ from the politically and spatially exclusive movements for place-based social and environmental protection warned against by Williams and Harvey (Harvey, 1996, cf. Featherstone, 2008). True, ECJP's efforts centre on particular injustices and protective measures proper to Black neighbourhoods. At the same time, however, extensive patterns and solidaristic ties are constitutive within its advocacy and activism. The full spatial and temporal extents of global warming's industrial ecology are logically necessary for ECJP's analysis of climate change as an issue of civil rights as understood in the U.S. context, and of the shared fate of coastal and continental communities of colour.

The ECJP: grounding climate justice in political community, accessing infrastructure for advocacy

> When folks think about climate change, what often comes to mind are melting ice caps and suffering polar bears. Historically, American society has failed to make the connection in terms of the direct impact of environmental injustices, including climate change, on our own lives, families, and communities. . . . Climate Change and other environmental injustices are about US.
>
> *(NAACP, 2018a)*

The work of the NAACP's ECJP resolves some of the challenges of constituency building and giving voice faced by transnational mobilisation efforts, through what are fundamentally connective analyses and strategies. First are analyses of climate injustice in the context of political community, linking the social dimensions of climate change with the core concerns of the NAACP's comparatively well-defined and established constituency. Second, those situating analyses support the ECJP in leveraging existing channels of advocacy: mobilising the equally well-established organisational and political infrastructure through which the larger organisation has long represented Americans of colour in legal and policy debate.

Grounding in the context of political community requires an analysis linking the core thematic commitments of the larger organisation, which are not commonly defined in environmental or ecological terms, with the differential impacts experienced by people of colour from the production, impacts and regulation of climate change. In the ECJP's research reports and campaigns, places, bodies and biographies join spatial and demographic patterns as the elements through which the socio-ecological ties and socio-spatial disparities of anthropogenic climate change are demonstrated and framed as issues of civil rights, health and economic injustice.

By tying the continued social marginality of Black Americans with the industrial and ecological processes of the fossil fuel economy, ECJP socialises, historicises and politicises those processes. Its connective analyses thereby provide the basis for climate justice advocacy in the American civil rights tradition, and for solidarity-building beyond the historical geographic purview of that movement, with people of colour facing differential climate impacts worldwide. In the domestic context specifically, framing climate change-related impacts on Black Americans in terms of their disproportionate health, education and economic effects renders those impacts as issues for local, state and national policy intervention, and thereby as topics for advocacy and comment utilising the NAACP's considerable public profile and expertise. Drawing on those resources, the ECJP can challenge the political disenfranchisement that underpins the continuation of racialised local concentrations of socio-ecological injustice: highlighting, for instance, energy companies' decisions about plant location, fuel and technology, which disproportionately affect communities of colour (see, e.g., NAACP et al., 2012).

In the following sections, I examine the ECJP's connective analyses and practices, with particular attention to its engagement with the wider NAACP mandate, involvement with constituents and partner organisations and policy work. This analysis of the ECJP's efforts also draws upon an in-depth interview with one of its leaders, and observations at open forums in Durban during COP 17, where members of the group were organisers as well as participants.

Fossil fuels and fence-line communities: making climate connections

The ECJP demonstrates the socially consequential ties linking fossil fuel production and resulting climate change impacts to the lives and life chances of Black Americans – for NAACP members as well as decision-makers and broader audiences. This demands deeply connective forms of analysis. An ECJP organiser described beginning the process with trainings among the organisation's regional assemblies.

> We have regional meetings, and do training on our civil rights agenda. So, when I did the "Climate Justice 101" training . . . [participants] said "Oh, I thought this was going to be about climate and workplace discrimination." And . . . "I thought this was going to be about a climate of justice in the world." It made me really see how far people were coming even with the term. But on the other end of that statement was, "wow, we really get how this connects to everything," because it was very story-based.

One example of ECJP's story-based technique is the *Women of Color for Climate Justice Road Tour*, which resulted in a series of short online videos (NAACP, n.d.) profiling individual women who "are experiencing differential impact, are involved in local self-reliance campaigns and are undertaking efforts to resist negative environmental developments" (Patterson, 2009a). Many videos document individual women's experiences of living with and fighting coal-fired power plants in or near their neighbourhoods and workplaces. Some speak from the experience of weathering Hurricanes Katrina and Rita and later BP's Gulf oil spill. Showing the women themselves, often in their homes or outside the plants they oppose, the videos foreground the embodied, place-based realities underlying wider patterns of disproportionate industrial location and disaster risk in poor neighbourhoods and communities of colour, with particular attention to the gendering of health impacts and resistance efforts.

Video sets juxtaposing the local consequences of fossil fuel energy production with the "downstream" impacts of rising tides and intensifying storms in coastal communities exemplify a more general analytical strategy of the ECJP. This consists of highlighting the demographically patterned, differential social impacts associated with multiple stages in the industrial-ecological production of anthropogenic climate change. These stages include the mining, refining, combustion and waste disposal steps in the fossil energy production process, in addition to its climatic consequences in sea-level rise and severe weather (see, e.g., NAACP, 2013; NAACP et al., 2012).[2] The processes of human development, agricultural industrialisation and incarceration, too, thicken and ground ECJP's analyses of climate-related injustice. The organiser continued:

> [Using narrative] was really how I was able to illustrate the connections between everything from the drivers of climate change, to coal power plants, to these other greenhouse-gas emitting facilities, to talking about how this affects us on the other side with Hurricane Katrina. . . . [T]he whole picture around not only climate change itself, but the corporate entities that are driving climate change and are also driving those markets that affect us in all these different ways.
>
> And even talking about criminal justice . . . one of [the NAACP's] foundational issues . . . is that we have a school-to-prison pipeline. . . . [W]hen half our kids have asthma and half have ADHD, both of which are affected by toxins in the air, how 70% of us live in communities and counties in violation of air pollution standards, and then we wonder why so many of us are incarcerated. Because the rates show that if you're not reading at grade level by grade 3, you're more likely to be involved in the criminal justice system.
>
> So these are things that people see every day, but they don't necessarily make those ties.

ECJP's narrative approach is also complemented by the more conventional quantitative and spatial analytic work of its research reports. *Coal Blooded: Putting Profits Before People*, for instance, analysed the dominance of coal-fired energy in the U.S. and demonstrated its disproportionate impacts on poor communities and people of colour at local, national and global scales through air pollution and climate change (NAACP et al., 2012). *Coal Blooded* ranks the "Environmental Justice Performance" of 378 U.S. coal plants, combining individual plant scores with demographic analysis to demonstrate just how unequally the health impacts of coal energy production are socialised, reproducing the marginalisation of Americans of colour.[3] The report also assigns a ranking to the 59 energy companies operating coal plants in the U.S., and calls for the closure of 75 "failing plants" (NAACP et al., 2012).

Importantly, ECJP's work is also sensitive to the economic drivers of fossil fuel energy production and the potential consequences of mitigation and renewable alternatives on poor communities. Thus, its critiques of coal have been tightly tied to proposals for increasing economic justice and opportunity based in an emergent clean energy economy (e.g., NAACP, 2010a; NAACP et al., 2012).[4] This emphasis also links the ECJP's work with the current programmatic priorities of the larger organisation, which include economic justice (NAACP, 2010a, 2010b). Its analytical consideration of economy-ecology connections has led the ECJP to expand its focus on energy policy, as in the 2013 report *Just Energy Policies: Reducing Pollution and Creating Jobs*, which argues, "[p]owering our nation, protecting the environment and empowering communities of color are not mutually exclusive concepts. In fact they are essential and interrelated calls to action" (NAACP, 2013, 535). Thus, as the report states, in addition to addressing the environmental injustices of a fossil-fuelled economy chronicled in *Coal Blooded* and elsewhere, "energy policy can create real public benefits, including millions of good green-collar jobs and building an inclusive green economy strong enough to lift people out of poverty" (5). That is, if energy production is the core socio-ecological process that reproduces the marginalisation of people of colour, as recorded in the bodies, places, biographies and spatial statistics presented, it is also a potentially potent lever with which to redress that marginalisation.

One broad constituency, many local strategies

The NAACP's core mandate suggests a perspective highlighting the climate-related fate of people of colour in aggregate, connecting the dots of local impact in communities dispersed across the country, and indeed the globe. Linking issues in different places and highlighting racial identity as a component of understanding the uneven impact of climate change raises awareness and builds solidarity. Further, the organisation's structure and partnerships facilitate education and collective action in response to these racialised patterns of differential, albeit diverse, impacts. The point here is that analysing climate-related consequences upon the demographic aggregate "people of color," and working within the geographically extensive network of the NAACP's U.S. organisational structure as well as its national and transnational partners plays an important part in constructing its constituency-based, solidaristic and resolutely humanistic politics of climate justice. Moreover, these ties are co-constitutive with the organisation's particular analysis, which emphasises racialised as well as gendered and classed forms of climate injustice over regionally or culturally specific ones. At the same time, however, the initiative's interventions (e.g., in addressing the worst-ranked coal-fired power plants identified in *Coal Blooded*) are attuned to the role of *local* social relations in individual communities' place-based struggles. The campaigns and reports already introduced, and further efforts of the ECJP, provide examples of these locally rooted and crosscutting strategies.

The racialised pattern linking storm impacts in the coastal U.S. South with the toxic shadow of coal production in the Midwest, for instance, is central to the group's internal education practice as well as its policy advocacy (see, e.g., Patterson, 2011; NAACP et al., 2012, 30). The ECJP's online splash page (NAACP, 2018a), excerpted earlier, continues:

> Environmental injustice is about people in Detroit, Ohio, Chicago, Memphis, Kansas City, and elsewhere who have died and others who are chronically ill due to exposure to toxins from coal fired power plants and other toxic facilities.
>
> Climate change is about the increase in the severity of storms which means that storms like Sandy and Isaac, which devastated communities from Boston to Biloxi, will become more of the norm. Our sisters and brothers in the Bahamas, as well as Inuit communities in Kivalina, Alaska, and communities in Thibodaux, Louisiana and beyond, who will be losing their homes to rising sea levels in the coming few years.
>
> Climate change and environmental injustice are about sisters and brothers from West Virginia to Tennessee who are breathing toxic ash from blasting for mountain top removal.

Assembling videos that document such diverse impacts on widely dispersed individuals and communities of colour, and sharing them both online and at trainings and teach-ins around the country is part of motivating state-level involvement in the NAACP's climate justice campaigns. Further, collecting local and state-level analyses in the videos and reports constructs solidarity across sites and geographic constituencies, as well as providing opportunities for sharing models and stories of success. *Just Energy Policy*, for instance, includes a table presenting promising policy approaches by state, while *Coal Blooded* features summaries of successful plant closure and retro-fitting campaigns; both reports and the ECJP *Climate Justice Toolkit* include model letters and statements that local and state activists can adopt as templates (NAACP, 2010a, 2013; NAACP et al., 2012).

Complementing these efforts toward broad awareness and action, the site-specific response work undertaken by the initiative exemplifies its attention to differences in the dynamics of power and opportunity among local places. The interviewee quoted earlier spoke to the strategic logic behind this careful attention to context, motivated in part by communities' economic necessities:

> We have all these tools in our tool box . . . for example in [community A, the power plant] has no revenue for the community, they don't bring any jobs to the community. . . . So [community leaders] have developed two strategies. One is that they developed a local ordinance that they're trying to get passed through city council. . . . On the other hand, they're really pushing hard with a big PR campaign making sure that people know how bad this is, how the company isn't doing anything: basically calling out the company.
>
> In a place like [community B], if you're not directly employed [at the plant] then your business depends on the fact that everyone [else] is employed there. So that's a place where the best we can hope for is pollution control. . . . So what we end up doing and how we end up doing it is very much dependent on where.

These examples suggest how the ECJP employs both geographically extensive collective action and contextually sensitive site-specific tactics.

ECJP also partners with other national and community-based environmental and climate justice groups, and leverages the institutional relationships of the larger NAACP organisation. In the first instance, ECJP partnerships with the broader environmental justice/climate justice community support the development of solidarity among affected constituencies, and facilitate projects that benefit from the capacities and publicity apparatuses of multiple groups. The comprehensive analysis presented in *Coal Blooded*, for instance, was authored collaboratively with the Indigenous Environmental Network, Chicago-based Little Village Environmental Justice Organization and the Rainforest Action Network. Several individuals involved in climate justice analysis and mobilisation are also thanked for their contributions (NAACP et al., 2012, 1). Similarly, the *Women of Color for Climate Justice Road Tour* and the video library it launched began in partnership with Women of Color United, Women's Environment and Development Organization and the Environmental Justice and Climate Change Initiative (Patterson, 2009a). ECJP's website also includes a page linking to national, state-level, youth and campus-based "resource organisations" (NAACP, 2018b). In the second instance, the NAACP's well-established institutional connections further amplify its climate justice work, and link it with additional intellectual resources and political actors. For instance, in 2010 ECJP staff convened a forum of representatives from Historically Black Colleges and Universities (HBCUs) and U.S. governmental agencies "to discuss the engagement of HBCUs in planning and executing a research agenda on the oil drilling disaster, as well as ongoing sustainability in the Gulf region" (Patterson, 2010b).

The initiative has also reached further to develop and strengthen transnational alliances, reporting on and organising both "inside" and "outside" activities during UN climate change negotiations (e.g., Patterson, 2009b). ECJP leadership coordinated several events with the Pan African Climate Justice Alliance before and during COP17, for instance (Patterson and Njamnshi, 2011).[5] These efforts expand the NAACP's global orientation even as they ground the transnational discourse of climate justice, through solidaristic analyses of common drivers and issues affecting people of colour in the U.S. and abroad.

Climate change as a civil rights issue

ECJP's connective ecological and social analyses underpin its position that climate change poses civil as well as human rights issues: the production and impact of climate change affect different communities in different ways, but examined in aggregate each of its moments differentially harm people of colour across the U.S. and the globe (NAACP, 2010a, 2018a).[6] In an early summary statement for *The Root*, ECJP director Jacqueline Patterson (2010a) linked the diverse modalities of climate change impact with existing vulnerabilities in Black communities, and formulated political responses based in the civil rights guarantees of U.S. citizenship and membership in the larger human community:

> Whether it is sea-level rise causing dislocation; severe storms taking homes, lives and communities; black children and families starving or sick from respiratory illnesses or exposure to carcinogenic toxins; children missing school or performing poorly due to resulting illness; or heat exposure resulting in illness or death; African-American communities are often starting from a place of substandard school systems, compromised access to quality health care, as well as job, housing or other vulnerability which makes facing these challenges even more impactful than they would be on a person or community with more resources and access to quality services. . . .
>
> From those we have elected to office as decision makers and duty bearers, we must demand real reductions in emissions; representation in policy and program design, planning, implementation and evaluation processes; and reparations for what has been taken from us through the excesses of the many, through provision of resources; and preservation and upholding of our civil rights as constituents and our human rights as people.

Framing climate change as an issue of human rights links ECJP's work with a major thread of transnational advocacy for climate justice. Understanding it as an issue for domestic civil rights in turn supports the mobilisation of the NAACP's considerable organisational capacities for giving voice to the concerns of communities of colour in advocacy for legal protection and policy change.

Mobilising existing organisational resources in climate justice advocacy

Policy work is a major focus for ECJP, which both complements and benefits from its other central mission of education. Examining its policy focus makes plain that the NAACP's established organisational infrastructure helps ECJP address the challenges of political disenfranchisement, which tend to isolate groups most affected by climate change and critical civil society actors from representative politics and consequential decision-making processes. The group's policy work, which is facilitated by the connective analyses and practices described earlier, mobilises both the

413

broad constituency and the institutional capacities of the larger organisation. Accordingly, its repertoire for advocacy efforts includes detailed policy analysis and recommendations, mobilising voters and branch organisations, occasional direct access to agency officials, legal mobilisation and public comment across a variety of platforms.

The Program's *Just Energy Policy* report, and to a somewhat lesser extent *Coal Blooded* and the *Climate Justice Toolkit*, present detailed rights- and economic justice-based analyses of existing government policy and corporate practice regarding energy, health, environment and minority opportunities. Each document offers comprehensive recommendations for policy change, grounded in existing provisions within model state-level provisions where those exist (e.g., NAACP, 2013). Further, the initiative's connective analyses shape more targeted and time-sensitive policy statements and campaigns, articulated in press releases, action alerts, and organisation-wide resolutions (e.g., NAACP, 2011, 2018c).

Action alerts, press releases, resolutions and "toolkits" associated with the initiative's reports (e.g., NAACP, 2012) also facilitate independent actions by individual NAACP members and chapters. Toolkits and action alerts typically include templates for letters that constituents can send to their elected representatives and ideas for local campaigns and educational programs. Voter education and mobilisation also takes place through action alerts, blog posts and the NAACP's yearly national and state-level "Legislative report cards," which track representatives' performance on matters of concern to the organisation (e.g., Patterson, 2010c; NAACP, 2018c, 2018d). With these tools, then, the ECJP can work to mobilise the broader NAACP constituency and empower units across its organisational structure. Importantly, it also strives to ground its advocacy in constituents' experiences and amplify constituents' voices through advocacy. The organiser quoted previously described one of the forms this linking takes, which also illustrates the close tie between ECJP's education and policy work as these involve NAACP members and units:

> [We've] been doing teach-ins around the country [on the EPA's Mercury Air Toxics Standards rulemaking process]. At the end of the teach-in, we all sit and do testimony . . . and then the state conference president might write a letter to the editor or the policy maker, and will include the quotes from their constituents that say "this is why we need strong policy."

Through processes like this one, the organisation's membership provides resources for advocacy, while shaping it in ways that ensure and reinforce legitimacy.

In addition to mobilising the NAACP's large member base, the ECJP leverages its well-established political and legal advocacy arms. These sometimes allow ECJP leaders direct contact with agency officials around climate change impacts affecting Americans of colour. Examples include an inter-agency briefing and a gathering of agencies and educational institutions focused, respectively, on response planning and research needs following BP's Gulf oil spill (Shannon, 2010; Patterson, 2010b). Legal mobilisation, a historically important NAACP strategy, also forms an aspect of ECJP's work, as in a 2014 appeals court battle for which it partnered with other environmental justice and environmental organisations to successfully defend EPA Mercury Air Toxics Standards (Earthjustice, 2014).

Finally, ECJP and NAACP leaders contribute public comment on climate justice-relevant policy issues as authors and sources across a variety of progressive, environmental, Black and mainstream media outlets (see, e.g., Jealous, 2010, 2013; Anft, 2013; Fontaine, 2014; Mock and Patterson, 2014; Tincher, 2014). In each of these ways, ECJP leverages the NAACP's organisational capacities to give voice to analyses of climate injustices affecting people of colour, and pursue just responses through institutional channels.

Conclusion

The ECJP's work exemplifies a politics based in connection, that grounds "climate justice" in relation to existing community and capacity. By linking constituents' core concerns for racial, economic and gender justice with the disproportionate impacts at multiple moments in the process of climate change, ECJP socialises, historicises and politicises that process as a whole. This grounding enables the group to leverage the energy of NAACP constituents as well as its organisational resources, to pursue change through institutional and wider political channels.

Whereas transnational initiatives have struggled to mobilise local and regional constituencies, and to make the voices of marginalised affected communities heard in consequential governance fora, grounded ones, articulated with the concerns of existing political communities and established advocacy infrastructures, can help to fulfil those aims. At the same time, as the ECJP's work suggests, they can also help to amplify and legitimate the efforts of likeminded transnational coalitions as well as less well-resourced community groups.

Together with a growing number of such community, national and transnational partners, ECJP is beginning to fill important lacunae in U.S. awareness and political action, around the social inequalities of climate change. In this sense, ECJP's connective analyses and practices are strategically central in its own contributions and toward a broader national awakening to the imperatives of climate justice. As critical scholars and activists well know, however, the articulation of emerging needs or transformative demands with any pre-existing discursive or institutional frame is likely to be slow, difficult and subject to limits. In assessing the broader implications of ECJP's work for other movements and organisations concerned with climate justice, it is worth briefly considering those aspects most and least likely to provide synergies and models, as well as possible limiting factors on ECJP's own efforts.

The local focus ECJP brings to the legibility of climate injustice and suitability of responses is both essential to its own strategy and widely shared by groups coalescing out of or joining in movements for climate justice (see, e.g., Stephenson, 2015; Our Power Campaign, 2016). Recognising this, the ECJP leader quoted previously highlighted the importance, and some of the insights, of community-based groups. The Project's mission statement has evolved to explicitly prioritise supporting such groups (NAACP, 2018a).

ECJP's focus on educating and mobilising potential constituencies for climate justice is also shared by civil society groups that are active across a range of sites and scales. To some extent, its considerable membership and name recognition offer assets in education and mobilisation. Yet the NAACP as a whole is better known for institutional strategies than broad-based ones, prompting criticism from observers who characterise the latter as particularly urgent (Berg, 2007; Harris-Perry, 2017).

While environmental and climate organisations have often framed the stakes of their work in wider geographic terms, local chapters and locally relevant concerns remain cornerstones of most broad-based mobilisation strategies across issue areas. I have argued, therefore, that the analytical work of climate justice organisers is crucially important, in rendering the globally extensive, socio-ecologically complex relations and mechanisms of climatic injustice legibly connected with the everyday realities and pre-existing concerns of differentially affected groups (Derman, 2013, 2015). This form of articulation can support both mobilisation and advocacy, to the extent channels for the latter exist. Arguably, the projects ECJP has been associated with accomplish such analytical connections with unusual clarity and comprehensiveness, using epistemologies and methods diverse enough to resonate with multiple audiences. As noted in this chapter, these are in many cases collaborative endeavours, which draw upon the participation of other groups and identify disproportionate impacts across a range of communities.

Some of the analytical strategies ECJP uses resonate, for instance, with those developed or deployed by groups focused on indigenous people's rights, energy sovereignty and economic justice (e.g., Our Power Campaign, 2016; Indigenous Environmental Network, 2018; Poor People's Campaign, 2018). It may be, however, that the popular understanding, legal and policy framing of civil rights already established by the NAACP and other groups present unusual opportunities, at least in the U.S. context, for articulation with the social inequalities that climate change and fossil energy use tend to re-inscribe. Economic justice, for instance, has lacked comparable institution-alisation and, until recently, comparable salience in the U.S. (Scheingold, 1974; Chomsky, 2013; Booker, 2018).[7] Class-based mobilisation for climate justice may therefore present even greater challenges than efforts cantered around civil rights and racial justice in the same context. At the organisational level, ECJP's own effective pivot from analysis to advocacy depends not only on the cultural, legal and policy infrastructure surrounding civil rights, but to some degree also on the NAACP's unique membership, resources, institutional ties and expertise.

Finally, like any other organisation, ECJP faces limits to the realisation of its goals, which are also particular to its own history and the wider socio-political context in which it operates. The paucity of direct legal avenues for environmental justice in the U.S., for instance (Herbert et al., 2013), dictates that despite the NAACP's recognised capacity for effective litigation, much of ECJP's work must proceed by other means: adding motivation, perhaps, to the extra-legal analytical and alliance building efforts discussed above.

On the one hand, then, ECJP's work represents a case study in the practice, potential and conditionality of articulation. On the other hand, it suggests the broad outlines of potentially myriad strategies and tactics of analysis, mobilisation, alliance and advocacy for climate justice linked with exiting concerns, communities, capacities and opportunities. It is precisely through the analytical and practical labour of articulation in such diverse contexts that constituencies, decision-makers and observers will come to know what climate justice means, and what principles and resources can be brought to bear to further it.

Notes

1 See the similar argument in Routledge's discussion of "translocal climate justice solidarities" in Routledge (2011).
2 For instance, their 2013 *Just Energy Policies* report (discussed later) states:

> Not only do low-income neighborhoods and communities of color suffer more of the direct health, educational, and economic consequences of these facilities, but also devastating natural disasters such as Hurricanes Katrina and Sandy, along with rising food prices and water shortages, harm low-income people and people of color disproportionately partly due to pre-existing vulnerabilities.
>
> (NAACP 2013, 5)

In the report *Coal Blooded: Putting Profits Before People* the group discusses these as the intersection of environmental and climate justice. NAACP et al. (2012).

3 The report calculates that:

> Approximately two million Americans live within three miles of one of [the] 12 [worst] plants and the average per capita income of these nearby residents is $14,626 (compared with the U.S. average of $21,587). Approximately 76% of these nearby residents are people of color.
>
> (NAACP et al. 2012, 29)

A 2002 report determined that 68% of African Americans live within the toxic release zone (designated by a 30-mile buffer) of a coal-fired power plant. See Black Leadership Forum et al. (2002).

4 *Coal Blooded* argues that closing the 75 most environmentally unjust coal-fired energy plants would cut energy supply by a mere 8%, which could be recuperated through increased energy conservation and renewable energy production. NAACP et al. (2012, 58).

5 I attended a jointly organised panel discussion in Durban, in which members of the two groups discussed struggles and means of resistance, including advocacy and legal levers, in the U.S. and in various African country settings. The initiative also added to its online video collection during the COP, posting testimonials from African women facing climate impacts. NAACP (n.d.).

6 This claim runs throughout ECJP's statements and frames its mandate, articulated on its splash page:

> Environmental injustice, including the proliferation of climate change, has a disproportionate impact on communities of color and low income communities in the United States and around the world. The NAACP Environmental and Climate Justice Program was created to support community leadership in addressing this human and civil rights issue.
>
> (NAACP 2018a)

Its *Climate Justice Toolkit*, an early comprehensive statement prepared for NAACP constituents' use toward these ends, enumerates implications for rights:

HUMAN RIGHTS VIOLATIONS
Climate change negatively impacts the following human rights:

- Right to Self Determination
- Right to Safe and Healthy Work Conditions
- Right to Highest Standard of Physical and Mental Health
- Right to Food
- Right to a Decent Living Condition
- Equal Rights Between Men and Women
- Right of Youth and Children to be Free From Exploitation

CIVIL RIGHTS VIOLATIONS
Climate change negatively impacts the following [civil] rights

- Ensuring peoples' physical integrity and safety
- Protection from discrimination on grounds such as gender, religion, race, sexual orientation, national origin, age, immigrant status, etc.
- Equal access to health care, education, culture, etc.

See NAACP (2010a, 4).

The two categories of rights are also linked, in that international human rights doctrine mandates the elimination of racial discrimination, a principle ECJP leadership has mobilised in the context of consultation with U.S. federal agencies.

7 The neglect of economic justice as a social value in the U.S. may be changing, however, as indicated by the staying power of the idea of the "1%" associated with the Occupy movement, the attribution of recent surprises in electoral politics to "economic fears," and the recent reemergence of a poor people's movement connected with the late work of Dr. Martin Luther King Jr.

References

Anft, M. (2013), "Benjamin Jealous Leaves the NAACP a Far Stronger Place", *The Chronicle of Philanthropy*, 8 September, available at: http://philanthropy.com/article/Benjamin-Jealous-Leaves-a/154431/.

Berg, M. (2007), *The Ticket to Freedom: The NAACP and the Struggle for Black Political Integration*, Gainesville: University Press of Florida.

Black Leadership Forum, The Southern Organizing Committee for Economic and Social Justice, The Georgia Coalition for the Peoples' Agenda and Clear the Air. (2002), *Air of Injustice: African Americans & Power Plant Pollution*, October, available at: www.energyjustice.net/files/coal/Air_of_Injustice.pdf.

Bond, P. (2012), "Durban's Conference of Polluters, Market Failure and Critic Failure", *Ephemera*, vol. 12, p. 42.

Booker, B. (2018), "The Poor People's Campaign Seeks to Complete Martin Luther King's Final Dream", *All Things Considered*, National Public Radio, 14 May, available at: www.npr.org/2018/05/14/610836891/the-poor-peoples-campaign-seeks-to-complete-martin-luther-king-s-final-dream

Chomsky, N. (2013), *Occupy: Reflections on Class War, Rebellion and Solidarity*, Second edition, Westfield, NJ: Zuccotti Park Press.

Derman, B.B. (2013), "Contesting Climate Injustice During COP17", *South African Journal on Human Rights*, vol. 29 (1), p. 170.

Derman, B.B. (2015), *Making Climate Justice: Social Natures and Political Spaces of the Anthropocene*, Unpublished Doctoral Thesis, University of Washington, Seattle.

Earthjustice. (2014), "Court Upholds Air Safeguard that Would Prevent Thousands of Deaths", *Earthjustice*, 15 April, available at: https://earthjustice.org/news/press/2014/court-upholds-air-safeguard-that-would-prevent-thousands-of-deaths.

Ecosocialist Horizons. (2011), *Ecosocialist Horizons – Ecosocialism or Barbarism*, available at: http://ecosocialisthorizons.com/.

Featherstone, D. (2008), *Resistance, Space and Political Identities: The Making of Counter-Global Networks*, Hoboken: Wiley-Blackwell.

Fontaine, T. (2014), "Sides Present Health Concerns, Job Loss Worries at EPA Hearings", *TribLIVE.Com*, 1 August, available at: http://triblive.com/news/adminpage/6532254-74/hearings-building-federal.

Goluboff, R.L. (2007), *The Lost Promise of Civil Rights*, Cambridge, MA: Harvard University Press.

Harris-Perry, M. (2017), "How to Save the N.A.A.C.P. From Irrelevance", *The New York Times*, 30 May, available at: www.nytimes.com/2017/05/30/opinion/melissa-harris-perry-naacp.html.

Harvey, D. (1996), *Justice, Nature and the Geography of Difference*, Hoboken: Wiley-Blackwell.

Herbert, S., Derman, B., and Grobelski, T. (2013), "The Regulation of Environmental Space", *Annual Review of Law and Social Science*, vol. 9 (1), p. 227.

Indigenous Environmental Network, (2018), *Indigenous Environmental Network*, available at: www.ienearth.org/

Jealous, B. (2010), "Crisis in Cancún", *The Huffington Post*, 9 December, available at: www.huffingtonpost.com/benjamin-todd-jealous/crisis-in-cancun_b_794688.html.

Jealous, B. (2013), "This Is the Moment for Action on Climate Change", *Post News Group*, 17 July, available at: www.oaklandpost.org/2013/07/17/oped-this-is-the-moment-for-action-on-climate-change/.

Mock, B. and Patterson, J. (2014), "Want to Support Clean Energy? Fight for Voting Rights", *Grist*, 25 July, available at: http://grist.org/politics/want-to-support-clean-energy-fight-for-voting-rights/.

Mueller, T. (2012), "The People's Climate Summit in Cochabamba: A Tragedy in Three Acts", *Ephemera*, vol. 12, p. 70.

NAACP (National Association for the Advancement of Colored People). (2010a), *Climate Justice Initiative Toolkit*, available at: http://naacp.3cdn.net/112a13293ef36d1c41_o6m6bktqq.pdf.

NAACP (National Association for the Advancement of Colored People). (2010b), *Handbook for Advocacy/ Programs*, available at: http://action.naacp.org/page/-/toolkits/Handbook_FINAL.pdf.

NAACP (National Association for the Advancement of Colored People). (2011), *NAACP Passes Resolution Supporting Strong Clean Air Act*, 4 August, available at: https://web.archive.org/web/20140808054436/www.naacp.org/press/entry/naacp-passes-resolution-supporting-strong-clean-air-act.

NAACP (National Association for the Advancement of Colored People). (2012), *Coal Blooded Action Toolkit*, available at: http://action.naacp.org/page/-/Climate/Coal_Blooded_Action_Toolkit_FINAL_FINAL.pdf.

NAACP (National Association for the Advancement of Colored People). (2013), *Just Energy Policies: Reducing Pollution and Creating Jobs*, available at: http://naacp.3cdn.net/8654c676dbfc968f8f_dk7m6j5v0.pdf.

NAACP (National Association for the Advancement of Colored People). (2018a), *Climate Justice Initiative*, available at: www.naacp.org/programs/entry/climate-justice.

NAACP (National Association for the Advancement of Colored People). (2018b), *Resource Organizations*, available at: www.naacp.org/climate-justice-resources/resource-organizations/.

NAACP (National Association for the Advancement of Colored People). (2018c), *The Latest*, available at: www.naacp.org/latest/?cat=0&topic=47.

NAACP (National Association for the Advancement of Colored People). (2018d), *Civil Rights Legislative Report Cards*, available at: www.naacp.org/report-cards/.

NAACP (National Association for the Advancement of Colored People). (n.d.). *NAACP ECJP – YouTube*, available at: www.youtube.com/user/Katrina2Copenhagen.

NAACP (National Association for the Advancement of Colored People), Indigenous Environmental Network, and Little Village Environmental Justice Organization. (2012), *Coal Blooded: Profits Before People*, available at: www.naacp.org/wp-content/uploads/2016/04/CoalBlooded.pdf.

Our Power Campaign. (2016), *Our Power Campaign*, available at: www.ourpowercampaign.org/campaign/.

Patterson, J. (2009a), "Natural Disasters, Climate Change Uproot Women of Color (2)", *Truthout*, 17 November, available at: http://truth-out.org/archive/component/k2/item/86799:natural-disasters-climate-change-uproot-women-of-color.

Patterson, J. (2009b), "The NAACP Offers 10 Lessons From Copenhagen Climate Change Conference", *The Root*, 21 December, available at: www.theroot.com/10-lessons-from-copenhagen-1790873906.

Patterson, J. (2010a), "Your Take: Climate Change Is a Civil Rights Issue", *The Root*, available at: www.theroot.com/your-take-climate-change-is-a-civil-rights-issue-1790879295.

Patterson, J. (2010b), *NAACP Convenes HBCUs in the Gulf Region to Discuss Sustainability Research Agenda*, 29 September, available at: www.naacp.org/latest/hbcu-covening-the-research-agenda-on-the-oil-disaster-and-and-sustaina/.

Patterson, J. (2010c), *Vote as If Your Life Depends on It: Especially for US, It Does!*, 1 November, available at: https://climatejusticeinitiative.wordpress.com/page/4/.

Patterson, J. (2011), *Nature's Fury – Chronicling the Devastating Effects of Climate Change in the US South*, 8 May, available at: https://climatejusticeinitiative.wordpress.com/2011/05/08/nature%E2%80%99s-fury%E2%80%94chronicling-the-devastating-effects-of-climate-change-in-the-us-south/.

Patterson, J. and Njamnshi, A. (2011), *From the Bronx to Botswana: Making a Climate Change Connection*, 30 July, available at: https://thegrio.com/2011/07/30/from-baltimore-to-botswana-making-the-climate-change-connection/.

Poor People's Campaign. (2018), *Demands*, available at: www.poorpeoplescampaign.org/demands/.

Routledge, P. (2011), "Translocal Climate Justice Solidarities", in Dryzek, J.S., Norgaard, R.B. and Schlosberg, D. (Eds.), *The Oxford Handbook of Climate Change and Society*, Oxford: Oxford University Press, pp. 384–398.

Routledge, P. and Cumbers, A. (2009), *Global Justice Networks: Geographies of Transnational Solidarity*, Manchester: Manchester University Press.

Scheingold, S.A. (1974), *The Politics of Rights*, New Haven: Yale University Press.

Shannon, M.J. (2010), *NAACP Hosted an Interagency Briefing on July 29 in New Orleans*, 17 August, available at: www.naacp.org/latest/interagency-briefing/.

Shipp, E.R. (2018), "NAACP Poised to Lead Once Again", *The Baltimore Sun*, 7 April, available at: www.baltimoresun.com/news/opinion/oped/bs-ed-op-0418-shipp-naacp-leadership-20180417-story.html.

Stephenson, W. (2015), *What We're Fighting for Now Is Each Other: Dispatches From the Front Lines of Climate Justice*, Boston: Beacon Press.

Sullivan, P. (2009), *Lift Every Voice: The NAACP and the Making of the Civil Rights Movement*, New York: New Press.

Tincher, S. (2014), "WV Shows Dim Efforts in Energy Efficiency", *The (West Virginia) State Journal*, 24 July.

31

Mother Earth and climate justice

Indigenous peoples' perspectives of an alternative development paradigm

Alan Jarandilla Nuñez

Introduction

Indigenous peoples' fights and struggles are historical. Neither colonisation nor the existing coloniality of power (Quijano, 1992, 1997, 2014) and knowledge (Castro-Gómez, 2000) has stopped the claim of indigenous peoples for respect of their territories, ways of life and political organising, culture, knowledge and natural resources. Some Eurocentric development theories assumed that as a result of development, indigenous cultures would extinguish (Hettne, 2007); however, contrary to that perception, indigenous peoples are emerging as key actors in the national and international arenas. While there have been some recent victories at the international level, with the adoption of the Declaration on the Rights of Indigenous Peoples within the United Nations (UN), indigenous peoples continue to call for justice. The demand for justice of indigenous peoples includes, among others, climate justice.

Climate justice is not a concept originated within indigenous peoples' communities or knowledge. Also, there is no agreed-upon academic concept for climate justice. It is said that Edith Brown Weiss (1991) first used the term *climate justice* (Mary Robinson Foundation, 2013) and, gradually, the term became popular in the political discourse around climate change. Climate justice could be understood in terms of ensuring that societies and individuals have the ability to deal with the preparation, response and recovery from the adverse impacts of climate change, taking into account the differences between the level of vulnerability, the availability of resources and differences in capacities (Preston et al., 2014). Also, it could be understood in terms of equity (Huntjens and Zhang, 2016). Developed countries have a historical responsibility with regards to climate change: their level of development is a result of the rapid increase of their emissions of greenhouse gases (GHGs) since the Industrial Revolution (Adams and Luchsinger, 2009). On the other hand, the least responsible will suffer the greatest adverse effects of climate change. This equity approach takes into account the perspective that some developing countries will need to continue emitting GHGs (or even increase their emissions) to meet their development needs; thus, the responsibility of cutting down emissions drastically relies on developed countries, who additionally need to cooperate with financial resources and technology transfer to help with mitigation and adaptation strategies. Other perspectives around climate justice add the importance of participation of the most vulnerable in decision-making processes related to climate change and excluding the so-called *false solutions* in the policy responses to climate change (Tokar, 2013).

Certainly, one common aspect of the most-used concepts of climate justice is what some authors define as a human-centred approach, where development and human rights are linked (Huntjens and Zhang, 2016). However, we prefer to define them as anthropocentric concepts of climate justice, acknowledging the philosophical paradigm that underpins those concepts. This paradigm, Eurocentric, considers human beings as the centre of climate justice efforts and demands. This paradigm also dominates the conceptions around sustainable development that are included in international instruments (United Nations, 1992).[1] Although the origin and anthropocentric conception of climate justice is Eurocentric, indigenous peoples have deconstructed, resignified and appropriated it with new connotations to raise their voices and visions for climate change action. As the effects of climate change are already being felt by many indigenous communities around the world (Henriksen, 2007), indigenous peoples have joined the climate justice movement and are contributing with their views, cosmovision and knowledge.

This chapter aims to describe the indigenous peoples' perspectives on climate justice. In its first part, the chapter presents a background of indigenous peoples and climate change, the vulnerability of indigenous peoples, how indigenous peoples are emerging as important actors in climate change policy and how coloniality of knowledge is trying to subalternise indigenous peoples' knowledge. The second part provides an in-depth analysis of the cosmocentric concept of climate justice that indigenous peoples propose and promote at different levels, the demands of indigenous peoples around climate justice and climate change, and some victories of indigenous peoples of Bolivia and Ecuador. The last part aims to explain one of the most important contributions of indigenous peoples to the climate justice movement, the proposal of an alternative development paradigm for the world based on their knowledge, cosmovision and values.

Indigenous peoples are a diverse and heterogeneous group. Although many of them share some sort of values and concepts, it is not possible to talk about indigenous peoples as a whole. It would mean having the reductionist approach we aim to avoid. In this sense, to clarify, the concepts and analysis provided in this chapter are referring to indigenous peoples from the Andean region of South America, specifically, the Quechuas and Aymaras from Bolivia and Ecuador.

Climate change and indigenous peoples

To have a brief and initial approach of the context of indigenous peoples with regards to climate change, it is important to consider three aspects: (1) the impact of climate change they are already experiencing, (2) the fact that indigenous peoples are being systematically marginalised in international climate change negotiations and (3) how the implementation of climate action initiatives are not including their voices and knowledge.

Indigenous peoples are already suffering the effects of climate change (Kronik and Verner, 2010). In the Amazon basin, climate change has caused a variation in flooding since 1999, which has important consequences to the reproduction of fish, affecting the main livelihoods of indigenous communities that live near the Amazon River (Kronik and Verner, 2010). In Asia, the typhoon Soudelor hit Taiwan in 2015 and nearly caused the disappearance of the Wulai Tribe (Carling et al., 2015). In the Arctic region, the Inuit are facing climate change impacts as the snow cover is declining, food insecurity is rising and permafrost is melting rapidly, among other impacts; this situation has been brought to the attention of the Inter-American Commission on Human Rights (IACHR) (Atapattu, 2013) and filed as a petition before the IACHR against the U.S. government (Wagner and Goldberg, 2004). These are only a few examples of some climate change effects being felt by indigenous communities around the world.

If developing countries have little responsibility for climate change, then indigenous peoples have the least (Müller and Walk, 2013). However, they are systematically excluded from decision-making processes of climate policy at the international and national levels and in the implementation of mitigation and adaptation strategies in their countries and territories. In the United Nations Framework Convention on Climate Change (UNFCCC) processes, some indigenous representatives are able to attend the negotiations, but their participation is not meaningful and their contributions and proposals are hardly ever included in outcome documents. Proofs of that are the different criticisms from indigenous peoples about the Paris Agreement (Leaness, 2017). Also, the number of indigenous peoples' representatives in the UNFCCC negotiations cannot be compared with the large delegations of non-governmental organisations (NGOs), other civil society organisations (CSOs) and the private sector (United Nations Framework Convention on Climate Change, 2017).

To counter this systematic exclusion, indigenous peoples have organised some conferences and gatherings to share proposals and develop common positions around the UNFCCC processes. Some examples include the Indigenous Peoples' Global Summit on Climate Change, a global gathering of indigenous representatives where The Anchorage Declaration was adopted in April 2009. It recognised that Mother Earth is facing a period of climate crisis and the "vital role of indigenous peoples in defending and healing Mother Earth" (Indigenous Peoples' Global Summit on Climate Change, 2009). A few months later, in September 2009, the International Indigenous People's Forum on Climate Change was held in Bangkok, and a Policy Paper on Climate Change was developed. Both documents compile a series of demands from indigenous peoples, such as the respect for their lands, territories, natural resources and environment, the recognition and respect of the right to self-determination, among others.

Moreover, the government of the Plurinational State of Bolivia organised the World People's Conference on Climate Change and the Rights of Mother Earth with broad participation of indigenous peoples' representatives. The People's Agreement recalled that "Mother Earth is wounded and the future of humanity is in danger" (Bolivia, Plurinational State of, 2010b). This Agreement also recognises that the civilising model, based on patriarchy and the destruction of Mother Earth, is facing a terminal crisis. As part of the outcome documents of the conference, a proposal for Universal Declaration of the Rights of the Mother Earth was adopted (Bolivia, Plurinational State of, 2010b). This is an important declaration that translates part of the indigenous peoples' perspectives on climate justice and provides a concrete proposal based on indigenous peoples' cosmovision. There are other declarations of indigenous peoples that were drafted in regional summits. To mention a few, the Iximche Declaration (2007), the La María Declaration (2013), the Mama Quta Titikaka Declaration (2009) and the Temuko Declaration (2009) are some declarations of indigenous peoples' summits of the Latin American region.

Indigenous peoples are key stakeholders in climate change action. Their ways of life, their holistic cosmovision and their relationship to the different systems of life and Mother Earth provide them with a unique knowledge that is currently misunderstood and undervalued. In recent years, the incorporation of indigenous peoples' knowledge into adaptation strategies has been neglected (Müller and Walk, 2013), and many opportunities have been lost. In this sense, indigenous peoples continuously oppose some strategies that do not take into account their knowledge on their lands and territories, such as initiatives under the mechanism of Reducing Emissions from Deforestation and Forest Degradation (REDD+) (Kill, 2015).

It is important to acknowledge that some initiatives that make efforts to recognise and include indigenous knowledge have started (Fabiyi and Oloukoi, 2013), but a robust coloniality of knowledge still exists in the sphere of climate solutions. Unfortunately, the common coloniality of knowledge – where power relations and the Eurocentric epistemology defines what is considered science, and where rationalism is the unique lens of knowledge generation (Lander, 2000) – is reinforced with a misunderstanding of an element of climate justice. Apparently, the historical responsibility of developed countries is not only understood in terms of their responsibility for cutting down their GHG emissions in an accelerated way, but also in terms of their exclusive responsibility for "finding the solutions" to climate change; hence, developed countries assume they are the only ones that will develop that knowledge. In this sense, the power relations between the centre and the periphery of the world system (Wallerstein, 1989) explains the idea of the developed world as the generator of the solutions and the developing world as the receptor (Ulloa, 2012). All of these perspectives consolidate a vision in which the "expert knowledge" of developed countries' universities will draw a course of action on climate policy (Ulloa, 2012). In this scenario, indigenous peoples' voices are silenced, and their knowledge is not considered as important as "science" coming from developed countries' experts.

Providing meaningful participation mechanisms for indigenous peoples should be considered as an important opportunity for establishing a horizontal dialogue of multiple rationalisms and different systems of knowledge. Further, in the academic arena it is important to promote and spread indigenous peoples' knowledge, not considering it less important, but equal to the knowledge developed with what is currently considered as "scientific methodology." This Eurocentrism and coloniality of knowledge not only affects the rights of indigenous peoples but also establishes a systematic exclusion where humanity loses opportunities of solving the climate crisis with a broad range of different perspectives and rationalities. The current context of climate change for indigenous peoples is a context in which they have limited opportunities of influencing international climate change policies, and participation difficulties and barriers in local climate action.

Indigenous peoples and climate justice

As mentioned before, climate justice is not a concept that has an origin in indigenous peoples' language or knowledge. Nevertheless, indigenous peoples have deconstructed, resignified and appropriated it; they have included their perspectives, knowledge and cosmovision in the climate justice concept and, in this regard, have joined the climate justice movement as important stakeholders. To comprehend indigenous peoples' conception of climate justice, it is important to mention and describe the key elements that they added to the most-used concepts of climate justice. Similarly, it is important to have a clear understanding of the demands made by indigenous peoples in the search for climate justice.

As opposed to the anthropocentric concept of climate justice, indigenous peoples propose a "cosmocentric" concept of climate justice, based on their cosmocentric conception of life (Pacheco Balanza, 2013). The anthropocentric concept of climate justice is human-centred, places all reasoning behind climate justice in the impact of climate change to the most vulnerable populations that have the least responsibility for causing climate change. In opposition, the rationality of the cosmocentric conception of climate justice of indigenous peoples goes far beyond. The cosmocentric conception of climate justice is rooted in the protection of life, not only human life but all systems of life that coexist and are interrelated in our world.

According to indigenous peoples' rationality, we, as human beings, are part of Mother Earth and coexist with different living beings. The interrelationship among beings is strong, and everything has an impact on the whole system. On the contrary, the modern rationality leads us to conceive of humans and nature as two different things: on the one side, nature as a source of resources for humanity – food, water, minerals, air, etc. – and on the other side, human beings as rational, with the capacity to transform and use those resources, with the idea of them being unlimited. For indigenous peoples, there is no such division. Both humans and Mother Earth are beings that have the right to life. In this sense, humans should not consider themselves as superior to other living beings in the world, who also have different ways of organising and contributing to the systems of life on earth.

For indigenous peoples, the demands around climate justice need to include the claim for recognition of the rights of Mother Earth. Therefore, indigenous peoples have actively contributed to the draft of the Universal Declaration of the Rights of Mother Earth adopted in the World People's Conference on Climate Change and the Rights of Mother Earth (Bolivia, Plurinational State of, 2010b). This Declaration demonstrates the understanding of indigenous peoples of Mother Earth as a living being, and as such, with rights that need to be guaranteed. That is one of the most important aspects of the resignified concept of climate justice, that it transforms the concept from an anthropocentric vision to a cosmocentric one. This does not mean that other aspects of the concept of climate justice as developed initially are not taken into account by indigenous peoples. Indigenous peoples recognise the common but differentiated responsibilities and respective capabilities principle as a basis of climate justice (emphasising the historical responsibility of developed countries), and they also endorse the demand for inclusion of voices of the most vulnerable to the effects of climate change in international climate policy-making, and the need of financial cooperation for adaptation and mitigation strategies.

When demanding climate justice, indigenous peoples also oppose market-based approaches and other approaches that aim to establish a commodification system of the functions of Mother Earth (Pacheco Balanza, 2013), such as payments for ecosystem services. In addition, indigenous peoples oppose the REDD+ initiative – a payment for ecosystem services scheme – as it only considers the carbon capture function of forests. For indigenous peoples that live in forestry lands, forests are not only their primary source of livelihoods, but they are an integral part of the system of life that permits the reproduction of their way of living, their communities and the different species that coexist in that ecosystem; forests also have a spiritual value. Further, indigenous peoples are critical to the false solutions related to technology that are trying to be implemented. Carbon capture technologies, geoengineering, synthetic biology, genetically modified organisms, among others, are some technologies that represent a high risk not only for humanity but for Mother Earth as a whole. Those "innovations" are presented by companies and scientists as promising solutions for climate change and some of its effects. However, they do not address the root causes of climate change, the unsustainable consumption and production patterns of society and the hegemonic civilising model and development paradigm.

In addition to the demands described earlier, indigenous peoples have specific demands related to their way of living, lands, territories and the respect of their rights. In many countries, indigenous peoples have problems in their lands and territories as governments are not willing to recognise their collective ownership. Issues also arise when governments give licenses and permissions to transnational companies to extract natural resources located in indigenous territories without prior, free and informed consent as a right recognised in the Covenant 169 of the International Labour Organisation (ILO) and the Declaration on the Rights of Indigenous Peoples. Continuously, indigenous peoples demand the end of extractives not only because of the occupation of part of their territory, but most important because they also pollute rivers, lands and cause severe environmental impacts that affect the ecosystem, water and livelihoods of indigenous peoples, putting in danger their communities and Mother Earth.

According to the indigenous peoples' conception of climate justice, it cannot be achieved unless there is a change in the current developed paradigm. The current development paradigm, based on capitalism as the economic system, is Eurocentric, anthropocentric, hegemonic and destructive, and perpetuates and reproduces inequalities and social exclusion, establishes unsustainable consumption and production patterns, considers nature as a resource and commodity and upholds the idea of the unlimited economic growth, among other characteristics. Capitalism imposes new forms of coloniality and constitutes a domination system for the entire world and Mother Earth. For the sake of generating unlimited income, capitalism does not consider planetary boundaries and the regeneration capacities of Mother Earth. In this sense, the demand for recognition of the rights of Mother Earth and the construction of a new development paradigm are at the core of the indigenous climate justice concept.

The indigenous peoples' call for climate justice is present at all levels. At the national level, indigenous peoples from Bolivia and Ecuador have also demanded the recognition of their rights and the rights of Mother Earth. In the case of Bolivia, the Political Constitution approved in 2009 expressly recognises the rights of indigenous peoples to self-determination and territoriality, to cultural identity, to the collective ownership of land, to the protection of their sacred places, and to the practice of their political, juridical and economic systems according to their worldview (Bolivia, Plurinational State of, 2009). Further, the law on the rights of Mother Earth was approved in 2010 and recognises Mother Earth as a subject of rights (Bolivia, Plurinational State of, 2010a); the Framework Law of Mother Earth and Holistic Development for Living-Well, which aims to establish the vision and the basics of the holistic development in balance and harmony with Mother Earth, is a special governmental effort to incorporate a new framework for development that respects the regeneration capacities of the components and systems of life of Mother Earth (Bolivia, Plurinational State of, 2012). Those are some of the victories of indigenous people's demands for climate justice that have been incorporated into concrete legal texts in Bolivia.

In Ecuador, the recognition of the rights of Mother Earth starts in its Constitution. Ecuador approved a new Constitution in September 2008, and both the Bolivian and Ecuadorian processes of developing the constitutional texts happened almost at the same time. Although the constitutional text mentions Mother Earth or "Pacha Mama" only twice, Chapter 7 of Title II recognises a range of rights to nature. Ecuador recognises that nature has the right to integral respect for its existence and for the maintenance and regeneration of its life cycles, its structure, its functions and its evolutionary processes (Ecuador, 2008). The constitutional text enables every person to call upon public authorities to enforce the rights of Mother Earth. Rights of nature recognised in Ecuador are related to restoration, the prevention of extinction of species, and the mitigation of environmental impacts related to the extraction of non-renewable natural resources, among others.

As we can see, in the search for climate justice, indigenous peoples are making important progress at the national level. It is important to note that both in Bolivia and Ecuador this process is full of contradictions and shortfalls – the Yasuni initiative in Ecuador and the TIPNIS case in Bolivia are just two examples – but, as in every process, these contradictions need to be addressed with participative dialogue. These are just initial steps towards the broad recognition of the rights of Mother Earth worldwide.

An alternative development paradigm

Our world is facing multiple crises (Dierckxsens, 2011), and the climate crisis is just one of them. To overcome this situation and achieve climate justice, indigenous peoples propose an alternative development paradigm. The reasons behind the need for an alternative development paradigm are diverse. The current economic system has caused climate change and, at the same time, it produced, reproduced and exacerbated economic, social and cultural inequalities both among and within countries. Capitalism has imposed new forms of coloniality that reinforce the domination system at the global level and has established a Eurocentric worldview and civilising model as a unique, non-questionable and hegemonic horizon for humanity. Also, the false solutions that were developed within this logic do not provide real answers on how to deal with the climate crisis.

According to the anthropocentric rationalism, human beings are the centre of everything, and Mother Earth is just a source of merchandises to be traded with the rules of the free market (with some regulations in a few cases). In this sense, the current development paradigm conceives economic growth as having no limits and as an end unto itself – economic growth is supposed to produce a number of benefits such as poverty alleviation, even though data demonstrates that the growth of the world's economy has increased inequalities (Alvaredo et al., 2018) – so it privileges economic growth against social and cultural inclusion, environmental protection, biodiversity conservation, ecosystem restoration and holistic approaches that take into account all dimensions of the systems of life.

Nevertheless, rethinking development is not an easy process. Eurocentrism has already imposed an epistemology that does not allow us to make sense and provide meaning to alternative world-views and development paradigms and the basis that support them (Artaraz and Calestani, 2013). It is a common limitation that requires to be acknowledged. In response to that, the development of an "epistemology of the South" (De Sousa Santos, 2010) is necessary. This epistemology of the South would allow us not only to understand different worldviews but also to contribute to the development of those alternatives we need to consolidate.

In this context, indigenous peoples have resisted coloniality and maintained their worldview and values, which provide the basis of their proposed alternative of development. The Andean cosmovision has already been studied by some researchers. Yet, their limitations to understand the worldview of indigenous peoples from the Andean region are those explained here. These limitations tend to cause some misunderstandings and misconceptions of their values and cosmovision. For example, according to Elmar Schmidt, the indigenous peoples' concept of "buen vivir" or living-well[2] is an appropriation of some environmental imaginations managed and proposed at the global level. Consistent with that theory, the concepts of the good life of Aristotle and other well-known Eurocentric philosophies are transformed and adapted by indigenous peoples. (Schmidt, 2016). We firmly disagree with that hypothesis. It is a reductionist approach that aims to subalternise indigenous knowledge and cosmovision and reproduces the coloniality of knowledge established in the academia. Nevertheless, we acknowledge that some concepts developed in other regions – including Europe – like "eudaimonia" from Aristotle share some values and ideas with indigenous concepts, but different paradigms, worldviews, and historical processes led to the development of each of them.

There is a broad range of concepts of the Andean cosmovision and philosophy that need to be understood because they are key elements of the proposed alternative development paradigm. It is important to notice the presence of language barriers to fully describe the indigenous cosmovision. "Pacha Mama," "Pachamama" or Mother Earth[3] is a complex con-cept, and it cannot be understood only in terms of "nature." *Pacha* is a form of life that participates in the "multiverse" (Huanacuni, 2010) with the consciousness of space-time of here and now; thus, Mother Earth means more than both words; it expresses life as a broad concept, the nature of life (Estermann, 1998). We, as human beings, are part of Mother Earth and its systems of life. All elements of Mother Earth are complementary and interrelated. The strong relation with Mother Earth of indigenous peoples influences their culture, knowledge and ways of organising. That relation is not instrumental; it is a relation between mother and sons (Bautista, 2013). Mother Earth has cycles, and everything has cycles according to the Andean cosmovision.

"Suma Qamaña," "Sumak Kawsay," "Sumakawsay" or living-well[4] is the alternative development paradigm in itself. It is not a unique concept, but rather a concept with multiple but similar meanings (Calestani, 2009). Living-well is a civilising horizon that differs from the "common good" concept. The common good is only referred to the wellbeing of human beings, while living-well refers to everything that exists, the Mother Earth and the different systems of life, promoting the balance and harmony among all of them (Huanacuni, 2010). Living-well is life in fullness, in harmony, balance and respect with everything that exists, with the cosmos and Mother Earth. It is a process of reconstructing the sense of life and being critical to the current development model. It is a concept that comes from within indigenous peoples' cosmovision and values. It is not about returning to the past, but it is about recovering the rationality of a community of life (Bautista, 2013), proving a new sense and meaning to the present and drawing new perspectives for the future of the world, where Mother Earth and all beings that coexist live in balance and harmony. Living-well opposes the notion of living better. Living better (Huanacuni, 2010) is a notion that underpins the capitalist ideology, where economic growth has no limits and where the objectives of humans are related to an infinite accumulation of goods. Living better stimulates consumerism and the depredation of the systems of life (Huanacuni, 2013). Living-well promotes the balance of life and harmony of all systems of life.

Harmony should not be understood in terms of everything being perfect. The Andean cosmovision acknowledges that harmony has lots of contradictions but, from an indigenous perspective, contradictions are complementary. That's the Principle of Complementarity of Opposites, which states that if two things are opposite, one does not exclude the other, but each one complements the other (Medina, 2011). This idea, already present in the indigenous paradigm, has been explained in the theory of the wave-particle duality and recent developments of quantum physics. The western concept of the Law of the Excluded Middle states that one idea can be true or false, nothing else; however, the complementarity of opposites does not categorise in true or false, but instead, it focuses on the interrelations and the complementarity of the contraries, not excluding any of them and finding a balance between them.

Living in harmony with Mother Earth and walking towards living-well implies not excluding the different contradictions that exist in the world, even the contradictions between civilisations, paradigms and worldviews; it implies acknowledging the complementarity of them, their value for the systems of life and developing a horizontal interaction between them. Living-well is not about returning to the past, with no technology; it is about changing the way we conceive life. According to living-well, technology should serve life and not put it at risk; it should serve Mother Earth and everything that exists, not only humans and capitalism.

Living-well means transforming the dominant anthropocentric worldview and walking towards a cosmocentric one. It is important to rethink and transform our current relations with Mother Earth and recognise that human beings and Mother Earth are equal (Pacheco Balanza, 2013). Living-well is based on reciprocity, where the interdependence, interrelations and balance are considered. Reciprocity is present in all spheres of life, in all forms of relations, not only in the relations among humans but with all living beings of the systems of life. Being aware of the strong relationships that coexist in the different systems of life makes us take care of all forms of life. Living-well is based on living in community, where Mother Earth, the different species and elements of life are integral and important parts of the community, together with humans.

Living-well is a holistic concept and a systemic alternative. It considers human beings, Mother Earth, the systems of life, the importance of all the elements of the cosmos, its relations, contradictions, its complementarity and its interdependence. It embraces contradictions to find balance, complementarity and reciprocity for life. It promotes balance and harmony for all. However, there is not a recipe to achieve living-well, for it is an ongoing reconstruction process. It is not a proposal that is totally finished (Ibáñez Izquierdo, 2013, 2014), and it is receptive to other concepts and approaches. There are some concepts that are being critical to the current development paradigm that could start a knowledge dialogue with the civilising horizon of living-well, such as degrowth, ecofeminism, decolonialism and others. The knowledge dialogue should not aim to subsume one concept into the other, but on the contrary, should acknowledge their contradictions and emphasise the complementarity and interrelations between them.

With the current situation of the world, walking towards living-well is not an easy process, but it is a need for humanity and Mother Earth. Even in countries like Bolivia and Ecuador, where living-well is recognised within their legal frameworks, the implementation of an alternative development paradigm is demonstrating difficulties (Artaraz and Calestani, 2013) and is the subject of a range of criticisms. There is a need for more awareness and a better understanding of living-well at all levels.

Indigenous peoples propose a new and alternative development paradigm to be integrated into the search for climate justice worldwide. Together with this, indigenous peoples propose to transform the rooted anthropocentrism in the climate justice concept and to build a cosmocentric conception of climate justice, integrating the respect of Mother Earth, recognising the rights of Mother Earth and ceasing considering humans as the centre of all efforts around climate justice. Implementing the living-well civilising horizon will be a complex process, but it should be considered a unique opportunity for humanity to recognise the mistakes from the past and reconstruct a future based on values of a community of life.

Notes

1 The Rio Declaration on Environment and Development, adopted in 1992, in its Article 1 states that "Human beings are at the centre of concerns for sustainable development."
2 In this chapter, when referring to "buen vivir" or "vivir bien" we will use the translation of living-well.
3 When referring to Mother Earth, we aim to translate the indigenous words of "Pacha Mama" or "Pachamama."
4 Suma Qamaña is the Aymara equivalent to "vivir bien" in Spanish and living-well in English, Sumak Kawsay or Sumakawsay is the Quechua equivalent. These indigenous concepts don't have a direct translation, so we aim to describe them acknowledging that limitation. When using living-well, we refer to these concepts indistinctively.

References

Adams, B. and Luchsinger, G., 2009. *Climate Justice for a Changing Planet: A Primer for Policy Makers and NGOs.* New York: UN-NGLS, United Nations Non-Governmental Liaison Service.

Alvaredo, F. et al., 2018. *World Inequality Report 2018.* Paris: World Inequality Lab.

Artaraz, K. and Calestani, M., 2013. Vivir Bien, entre Utopía y Realidad. *Tabula Rasa*, 18, pp. 105–123.

Atapattu, S., 2013. Climate Change, Indigenous Peoples and the Arctic: The Changing Horizon of International Law. *Michigan State International Law Review*, 22(1), pp. 377–408.

Bautista, S. R., 2013. El nuevo horizonte civilizatorio del "Vivir Bien". In: I. Farah and V. Tejerina, eds. *Vivir Bien: Infancia, Género y Economía. Entre la teoría y la práctica.* La Paz: CIDES-UMSA, pp. 11–34.

Bolivia, Plurinational State of, 2009. *Constitución Política del Estado Plurinacional de Bolivia.* La Paz: Gaceta Oficial del Estado.

Bolivia, Plurinational State of, 2010a. *Ley 071 de Derechos de la Madre Tierra.* La Paz: Gaceta Oficial del Esatdo.

Bolivia, Plurinational State of, 2010b. *Peoples' Voices on Favor of the Defense of Life and the Mother Earth: Conclusions and Action Plans of the First World People's Conference on Climate Change and the Rights of Mother Earth.* La Paz: Ministry of Foreign Affairs.

Bolivia, Plurinational State of, 2012. *Ley 300 Marco de la Madre Tierra y Desarrollo Integral para Vivir Bien.* La Paz: Gaceta Oficial del Estado.

Brown Weiss, E., 1991. In Fairness to Future Generations: International Law, Common Patrimony, and Intergenerational Equity. *Yearbook of International Environmental Law*, 1(1), pp. 392–397.

Calestani, M., 2009. *An Anthropology of Wellbeing: Local Perspectives and Cultural Constructions in the Bolivian Plateau, Doctoral Thesis*. London: Goldsmiths College, University of London.

Carling, J., Carino, J. and Sherpa, I. N., 2015. *Asia Report on Climate Change and Indigenous Peoples*. Chiang Mai: Asia Indigenous Peoples Pact.

Castro-Gómez, S., 2000. Ciencias sociales, violencia epistémica y el problema de la "invención del otro". In: E. Lander, ed. *La colonialidad del saber: eurocentrismo y ciencias sociales. Perspectivas latinoamericanas*. Buenos Aires: CLACSO, Consejo Latinoamericano de Ciencias Sociales, pp. 88–98.

De Sousa Santos, B., 2010. *Refundación del Estado en América Latina: Perspectivas desde una epistemología del Sur*. La Paz: Plural.

Dierckxsens, W., 2011. *Siglo XXI: Crisis de una civilización. ¿Fin de la historia o el comienzo de una nueva historia?*. La Paz: Grito del Sujeto.

Ecuador, República del, 2008. *Constitución Política del Estado*. Quito: Registro Oficial del Ecuador.

Estermann, J., 1998. *Filosofía Andina, estudio intercultural de la sabiduría autóctona andina*. Quito: Abya-Yala.

Fabiyi, O. O. and Oloukoi, J., 2013. Indigenous Knowledge System and Local Adaptation Strategies to Flooding in Coastal Rural Communities of Nigeria. *Journal of Indigenous Social Development*, 3(1), pp. 1–19.

Henriksen, J. B., 2007. *Report on Indigenous and Local Communities Highly Vulnerable to Climate Change Inter Alia of the Arctic, Smaill Island States and High Altitudes, With a Focus on Causes and Solutions [UNEP/CBD/WG8J/5/INF/]*. Montreal: Convention on Biological Diversity.

Hettne, B., 2007. Ethnicity and Development – An Elusive Relationship. *Contemporary South Asia*, 2(2), pp. 123–149.

Huanacuni, F., 2010. *Vivir Bien/Buen Vivir. Filosofía, políticas, estrategias y experiencias regionales*. La Paz: CAOI.

Huanacuni, F., 2013. Cosmovisión Andina y Vivir Bien. In: I. Farah and V. Tejerina, eds. *Vivir Bien: Infancia, Género y Economía. Entre la teoría y la práctica*. La Paz: CIDES-UMSA, pp. 35–54.

Huntjens, P. and Zhang, T., 2016. *Climate Justice: Equitable and Inclusive Governance of Climate Action Working Paper 16*. The Hague: The Hague Institute for Global Justice.

Ibáñez Izquierdo, A., 2013. El buen vivir: Una utopía en proceso de construcción. *Contextualizaciones Latinoamericanas*, 9.

Ibáñez Izquierdo, A., 2014. El buen vivir como un proyecto civilizatorio intercultural. *Contextualizaciones Latinoamericanas*, 11.

III Cumbre de Continental de Pueblos y Nacionalidades Indígenas del Abya Yala, 2007. *Declaración de Iximche. Soñamos nuestro pasado y recordamos nuestro futuro*. Iximulew: s.n.

Indigenous Peoples' Global Summit on Climate Change, 2009. *The Anchorage Declaration*. Anchorage: s.n.

IV Cumbre de Continental de Pueblos y Nacionalidades Indígenas del Abya Yala, 2009. *Declaración de Mama Quta Titikaka*. Puno: s.n.

Kill, J., 2015. *REDD: A Collection of Conflicts, Contradictions and Lies*. Montevideo: World Rainforest Movement.

Kronik, K. and Verner, D., 2010. *Indigenous Peoples and Climate Change in Latin America and the Caribbean*. Washington, DC: The World Bank.

Lander, E., ed., 2000. *La colonialidad del saber: eurocentrismo y ciencias sociales. Perspectivas latinoamericanas*. Buenos Aires: CLACSO, Consejo Latinoamericano de Ciencias Sociales.

Leaness, J., 2017. Vulnerability and the Voice of Indigenous Peoples Through the Lens of Climate Change Policy. In: K. Peterman, G. Foy and M. Cordes, eds. *Climate Change Literacy and Education Social Justice, Energy, Economics, and the Paris Agreement*. Washington, DC: American Chemical Society, pp. 1–11.

Mary Robinson Foundation, 2013. *Climate Justice Baseline Report*. s.l.: Mary Robinson Foundation.

Medina, J., 2011. Acerca del Suma Qamaña. In: I. Farah and L. Vasapollo, eds. *Vivir bien: ¿Paradigma no capitalista?*. La Paz: Plural, pp. 39–64.

Müller, M. and Walk, H., 2013. Democratizing the Climate Negotiations System Through Improved Opportunities for Participation. In: M. Dietz and H. Garrelts, eds. *Routledge Handbook of the Climate Change Movement*. New York: Routledge, pp. 31–49.

Pacheco Balanza, D., 2013. *Vivir Bien en Armonía y Equilibrio con la Madre Tierra: una propuesta para el cambio de las relaciones globales entre los seres humanos y la naturaleza*. La Paz: Universidad de la Cordillera/Fundación de la Cordillera.

Pre Cumbre Indígena de Temuki, 2009. *Declaración de Temuko*. Temuko: s.n.

Preston, I. et al., 2014. *Climate Change and Social Justice: An Evidence Review*. s.l.: Joseph Rowntree Foundation.

Quijano, A., 1992. Colonialidad y modernidad/racionalidad. *Parú Indígena*, 13(29), pp. 11–20.

Quijano, A., 1997. *The Colonial Nature of Power and Latin America's Cultural Experience*. Colonia Tovar: International Sociological Association.

Quijano, A., 2014. Colonialidad del poder, eurocentrismo y América Latina. In: D. Assis Clímaco, ed. *Cuestiones y horizontes: de la dependencia histórico-estructural a la colonialidad/descolonialidad del poder*. Buenos Aires: CLACSO, pp. 777–832.

Schmidt, E., 2016. Latin American Environmental Discourses, Indigenoues Ecological Consciousness and the Problem of 'Authentic' Native Identities. In: H. Zapf, ed. *Handbook of Ecocriticism and Cultural Ecology*. Berlin: De Gruyter, pp. 413–437.

Tokar, B., 2013. Movements for Climate Justice in the US and Worldwide. In: M. Dietz and H. Garrelts, eds. *Routledge Handbook of the Climate Change Movement*. New York: Routledge, pp. 131–146.

Ulloa, A., 2012. *Producción de conocimientos en torno al clima. Procesos históricos de exclusión/apropiación de saberes y territorios de mujeres y pueblos indígenas. DesiguALdades.net Working Paper Series No. 21*. Berlin: desiguALdades. net Research Network on Interdependent Inequalities in Latin America.

United Nations, 1992. *Rio Declaration on Environment and Development*. New York: United Nations.

United Nations Framework Convention on Climate Change, 2017. *Conference of the Parties Twenty-third Session List of Participants [FCCC/CP/2017/INF.4]*. Bonn: United Nations Framework Convention on Climate Change.

V Cumbre de Continental de Pueblos y Nacionalidades Indígenas del Abya Yala, 2013. *Declaración de La María. ¡La vida es sagrada, la vida es armonía! El Buen Vivir es vda y armonía. ¡Para el Buen Vivir y la Vida Plena, la paz es ineludible!*. La María: s.n.

Wagner, M. and Goldberg, D. M., 2004. *An Inuit Petition to the Inter-American Commission on Human Rights of Climate Change for Dangerous Impacts of Climate Change*. Buenos Aires: Earthjustice, Center for International Environmental Law.

Wallerstein, I., 1989. *The Modern World-System*. New York: Academic Press.

32

Negotiating climate justice at the subnational scale

Challenges and collaborations between indigenous peoples and subnational governments

*Colleen M. Scanlan Lyons, Maria DiGiano,
Jason Gray, Javier Kinney, Magaly Medeiros,
and Francisca Oliveira de Lima Costa[1]*

On a chilly morning in late August, governmental and indigenous leaders from Peru, Brazil, Indonesia, Panama and the United States convened at San Francisco International Airport. For eight hours, two large white vans travelled slowly in tandem northward out of the city, through wine country, through small towns and golden hued hills covered in dry chaparral. Late at night, the van lights shone on massive redwood trees lining a winding, desolate, two-lane highway. Fog hung in the air. Near midnight, a group of people from different regions of in the world, with diverse histories, identities, and languages finally convened at a lodge amidst the redwood forest of Northern California. The purpose of this coming together? To determine what they held in common as subnational governments, indigenous peoples, and local-level community leaders trying to work better – together – to conserve forests, promote sustainable development, and preserve forest-based communities' rights and ways of life. How this would work in practice, however, no one knew.

Forests are some of the most critical natural environments for addressing the realities of climate change in our world today. Forests play a fundamental role in climate regulation by absorbing nearly one-third of annual global anthropogenic CO_2 emissions over the last two decades (Pan et al., 2011). But forest loss has contributed an estimated 12% of global greenhouse gas emissions over the last decade (Quéré et al., 2018). Furthermore, forests are much more than carbon repositories (Gupta et al., 2012). Forests are central to people's livelihoods, connect the physical with the spiritual (Scanlan Lyons, 2012; Tucker, 2012), and are critical for culture and wellbeing (Seymour and Busch, 2016). Debates on how to manage climate change equitably and effectively arise from this tension between forests as a global commons that is critical for mitigating climate change and the multiple (and often locally specific) environmental, economic and cultural values of forests (Marion Suiseeya, 2017; Martin et al., 2016; Vucetich et al., 2018). These debates raise important and urgent questions: Who claims rights and authority over forests? How can policies for mitigating climate change through forest conservation also engage and address the historical marginalisation and specific vulnerabilities of the people who live in and depend upon forests (Adger, 2006; Marino and Ribot, 2012)? Can international frameworks, like Reducing Emissions from Deforestation and Forest Degradation (REDD+),[2] respect indigenous peoples' and local communities' values and improve their forest-based livelihoods (Agrawal et al., 2011; Chhatre et al., 2012; Godden and Tehan, 2016; Marion Suiseeya, 2017; Mustalahti et al., 2012)?

Climate justice – which strives to protect human rights and the right to self-determine development, to share the benefits as well as the burdens of climate change equitably across populations, and to promote equitable, participatory decision-making around climate change issues and challenges[3] – is central to these questions. And climate justice is shaped by the reality that the effects of climate change transcend geopolitical boundaries, such as between tribal, national, state and private lands (Maldonado et al., 2013). Though indigenous peoples and their territories have been historically invisible and marginalised within decision-making processes around land and forest conservation strategies (Brugnach et al., 2014; DiGiano et al., 2016; Maldonado et al., 2016), indigenous and local populations are increasingly recognised as important actors and spaces for climate change mitigation (Nepstad et al., 2006; Ricketts et al., 2010; Vergara-Asenjo and Potvin, 2014; Walker et al., 2014). Relatively little attention, however, has been paid to emerging governance regimes and the negotiations among state and non-state actors, such as indigenous peoples and local communities, in response to climate change (Fisher, 2015).

This chapter explores how climate change mitigation strategies for forest conservation have reconfigured partnerships between indigenous peoples and subnational governments. We explore three cases written from the perspective of tribal leaders, state-level bureaucrats, academics and practitioners. First, we investigate how a carbon offset program in California renegotiated the relationship between tribal and state authorities and served as an instrument to further the Tribe's agendas of land re-acquisition and cultural repatriation. Next, we examine how a state government in the Brazilian Amazon partnered with indigenous communities and organisations to co-design and implement state-wide policies and benefit-sharing mechanisms connected to REDD+, which led to new forms of recognition and political participation. Lastly, we explore the process of translating diverse efforts into collective action by looking at how a dynamic, international network of subnational governments and indigenous and community leaders established a community of practice for forest conservation and rights recognition.

These cases cross a diverse body of literature that is helpful for thinking through how subnational actors and actions are important (and often overlooked) scales and spaces for negotiating new arrangements of power and practice at the core of climate justice debates. To understand emerging partnerships between the state and indigenous peoples, we use the theoretical concepts of *capabilities*, *recognitional justice* and *communities of practice*. These perspectives challenge us to think about intersections between theory and practice, as well as to look across different sets of actors and scales as we strive for climate justice in an era of climate change.

Climate justice through the lenses of capabilities, recognitional justice and communities of practice

A *capabilities* approach focuses on humans' ability and freedom to function and flourish in a self-determined way as the underlying conditions for justice (Sen, 1999). Capabilities, also stated as "freedoms necessary for realizing a healthy and meaningful life" (Vucetich et al., 2018), include environmental or ecological conditions,[4] political participation and cultural and social recognition. New work has advanced the idea of "community" capabilities, as opposed to individual freedoms and capabilities, which is particularly relevant to understanding how climate justice concerns are articulated by indigenous communities and tribes (Schlosberg and Carruthers,

2010). The cases explored here demonstrate how partnerships between indigenous peoples and subnational governments have led to multiple outcomes and fostered community capabilities, such as political participation and cultural recognition, which advance both climate justice and forest conservation.

Building on this, recognition – political, social and cultural – is considered an important aspect or "capability" within the multidimensional capabilities approach to climate justice (Martin et al., 2016). *Recognitional justice* seeks to understand how dominant cultural practices, political institutions and economies render some peoples invisible or "mis-recognized" (Schlosberg, 2012). This framing is especially relevant for indigenous peoples, not only in terms of understanding how historical, structural and procedural inequities have often rendered these communities mis-recognized, or invisible, but also in understanding how indigenous peoples' relationships between the environment, their cultural practices and their identity is often overlooked or overshadowed in climate change discourse (Schlosberg, 2012). However, as Schlosberg notes, "[r]ecognition . . . can only go so far; justice also requires converting that recognition into practices of political participation" (2012, p. 452). In the following cases, we explore how indigenous peoples are working for cultural, social and political recognition in their partnerships with subnational governments, and how these partnerships are establishing new practices of political participation that unite forest conservation with climate justice.

Capabilities and recognition also align with the "communities of practice" framework, which asserts that as diverse actors come together around common interests and objectives, this very process of coming together creates new ways of thinking and, in turn, new practices for collaboration (Amin and Roberts, 2008; Wenger, 1998; Wenger, 2000). Participants in communities of practice often grow through this experience, and new expertise can be the outcome of these interactive processes (Lave and Wenger, 1991). As the cases in this chapter show, the coming together of subnational governments, Tribal governments, and indigenous communities is creating new communities of practice, communities that are far from perfect, but are arguably proponents of new forms of climate justice.

A Native American Tribe and a State: Territorial History Meets Contemporary Climate Policy

> *We have lost most of our old trees because of historical logging practices performed by others on our land, and our native fish and wildlife species are struggling because of it; these forest carbon projects enable the Tribe to help transition thousands of acres back into a Tribally managed, old-growth forest ecosystem, where wildlife and cultural resources such as elk, tanoak acorns and medicinal plants will thrive.*
>
> – Thomas P. O'Rourke, Sr., Chairman, Yurok Tribe

California is known not only in the United States, but throughout the world, as a leader on global climate change (Anderton and Setzer, 2017; Lutsey and Sperling, 2008). Over the past several decades, the State of California has implemented some of the most progressive environmental regulations to reduce harmful greenhouse gas (GHG) emissions. In 2006, California passed the landmark Global Solutions Warming Act, requiring by law a 15% reduction in GHG emissions by 2020 and setting into motion a long-term plan for climate change mitigation. A key strategy from within the suite of policies introduced by the Global Warming Solutions Act was the establishment of an economy-wide carbon market, called the California Cap-and-Trade Program, implemented by the state's regulatory air pollution control and climate agency, the California Air Resources Board (CARB) (California Air Resources Board, 2017). The Cap-and-Trade Program (hereafter referred to as the Program) establishes limits, or "caps," for state-wide

GHG emissions and requires large, stationary sources of GHG emissions, electricity importers and suppliers of transportation fuels and natural gas to report their annual emissions and to acquire and surrender what are called "compliance instruments" (allowances and a limited number of offset credits) that are issued by CARB to meet the state's emissions caps (California Code of Regulations, 2017a). California's Program also provides for the issuance of offset credits. These offsets are issued to projects that align with specific CARB-approved quantification methodologies (called Compliance Offset Protocols) for GHG emissions reductions and sequestration activities that come from sources outside of the previously mentioned capped sectors. These Protocols include methodologies for U.S. Forest projects, the destruction of ozone-depleting substances, urban forests, dairy digesters and, more recently, the capture and destruction of methane from rice cultivation and mining operations. Altogether, these Compliance Offset Protocols offer the opportunity for robust emissions-reducing projects to generate climate financing if they meet the Protocol requirements.

However, when CARB first began its regulation development process in 2010, it "didn't get it right" with respect to engagement with Tribes.[5] Since California state law does not normally apply to air pollution sources on Tribal lands, CARB did not include mechanisms for some of the state's most important conservationists – Native American Tribes and Tribal entities – to benefit from its innovative Program.[6] As CARB's regulatory development process began to take shape, a Native American Tribe based in Northern California, the Yurok Tribe, came to CARB with questions and a firm insistence and advocacy on being included in the process. The Yurok Tribe posed questions such as: Why was California not including Tribes in this process? How could Tribes benefit? What was the process to participate in the design of the program? When would Tribes be included?

The Yurok Tribe is the largest federally recognised Tribe in California, with over 6,200 Tribal citizens. The Yurok ancestral territory spans over 500,000 acres along the Klamath-Trinity Rivers in Northern California, encompassing over 86 miles of California coastal lands (The Yurok Tribe, 1993). The Yurok Tribe's history has been marked by struggles for cultural survival, self-determination and sovereignty. As the United States expanded westward in the 1800s, the Yurok were forcibly displaced by violence and government policies, their population decimated and their cultural practices suppressed (DeLeon Kandel, 2018; Johnston-Dodds and Burton, 2002). It was not until the 1980s, following a series of legal actions, that the Yurok Tribe was recognised by state and federal authorities as a sovereign entity (DeLeon Kandel, 2018). In 1993 the Yurok Tribe ratified its Constitution. The natural resources of the Klamath-Trinity Basin are an integral component of the Yurok way of life for subsistence, economic, legal, political and ceremonial purposes, and the Yurok Tribe view themselves as stewards of these resources (Ben Blom and Jason Teraoka, 2014; Frederickson, 1984; The Yurok Tribe, 2007).

For the Tribe, asserting its inherent rights and authority of Yurok Ancestral Lands is critical to the Tribe's nation-building objectives of self-governance, self-determination and sovereignty. Therefore, the Tribe's long-term vision for the management of Yurok lands is strategically fundamental to its broader nation-building objectives. This vision is deeply rooted in Yurok traditions, governance and culture and is guided by modern, science-based adaptive management (Sloan and Hostler, 2011). The Tribal government's natural resource management strategies include monitoring its fish stocks from year-to-year and regulating its timber harvesting and assessing varying resource-based economic ventures to ensure that they correlate with traditional values and objectives. As managers of their ancestral lands, the Yurok believe that both short- and long-term sustainable resource management, including ongoing, conservation-based forest management, will provide sustainable economic opportunities for the Tribe while preserving and enhancing natural and cultural resources for future generations of Yurok People (The Yurok Tribe, 2007).

This integrated vision of land management was at the forefront of the Yurok's negotiations with the State of California in the context of the Program. Specifically, the Yurok were interested in participating in California's Program by developing forest management projects which could be eligible to receive offset credits. These credits, once issued by CARB, could be sold to compliance entities to meet up to 8% of their emissions obligations. The Yurok had specific legal, political, environmental, climate, cultural and economic goals in mind that could be served by incorporating offset credit financing into the Tribal governance strategy, including increasing its land base, restoring salmon fisheries and improving water quality through forest restoration (Barboza, 2014). This includes key objectives of combating climate change and addressing the direct impacts these actions have on Tribal natural resources. The Tribe's engagement in the Program was seen as one strategy within the Tribe's diverse portfolio of strategies for natural resource management and climate change mitigation.

Operationalising Cap-and-Trade with a Tribal government

Once the Yurok brought the agency's oversight to its attention, CARB (from its most senior decision-makers to staff) sought to correct its initial failure to engage with Tribes. CARB first worked through the Tribal Advisory Committee of the California Environmental Protection Agency (CalEPA) to inform the Yurok and other tribes on the regulatory development process and timeline and how to most effectively participate. Next, CARB began holding consultations directly with the Yurok and other interested Tribes pursuant to a Tribal Consultation Policy developed by CalEPA to ensure effective state agency coordination on matters impacting Tribes (California Environmental Protection Agency, 2018; Governor of California, 2011).

To the Yurok, as a sovereign Nation with recognised Ancestral Lands within the State of California, consultation, decision-making and full inclusion in the design process of the offsets provisions of the Program was key. These consultations focused on developing a mutual understanding of historical challenges and wrongs that have existed between Tribes and state government, as well as an emerging effective government-to-government relationship in which Tribal interests, CARB mandates and opportunities for partnership became clearer. Ultimately, the consultations sought to develop specific regulatory language that would allow Tribal projects to participate on an equal footing with all other projects, while recognising the unique sovereign nature of Tribes and Tribal lands as well as satisfying the State of California's legal obligation to be able to oversee and enforce against any offset project if the need arose. In addition to the consultations described above, representatives of the Yurok Tribe and other Tribal entities participated in public meetings at CARB, in which CARB shared outcomes of its rulemaking process with California constituents to ensure that these consultations and Tribal interests were reflected in CARB's ultimate decision-making process (see, for example, Corbett, 2011). This process was successful from the Yurok's perspective; public comments submitted by Tribal attorney John Corbett (2011) note, the "Yurok Tribe appreciates [CARB's] efforts in including tribes in this rulemaking process."

What resulted from this consultation were carefully negotiated regulatory provisions that establish principles of partnership and ensure the ongoing ability of Tribes to participate in California's strategy for climate change mitigation (Regulations, 2017, California Code of Regulations, 2017b, 2017c). Out of this process, the Yurok Tribe became the first Tribe (and the first project) to receive CARB-issued offset credits under California's Cap-and-Trade Regulation and the Compliance Offset Protocol for U.S. Forest Projects, creating its own Carbon Sequestration Program.

As anticipated by the Yurok Tribe, the revenue from its participation in California's Cap-and-Trade Program provided a set of landmark opportunities for the Tribe: it allowed the Yurok Tribe to re-acquire Ancestral Lands, promote sustainable conservation-based resource management, leverage funding to increase economic opportunities for disadvantaged Tribal communities, promote self-determination and progress towards co-management, and protect and preserve important cultural resources of the Yurok Tribe (The Yurok Tribe, 2017; DeLeon Kandel, 2018). This carbon financing helped bolster ongoing land re-acquisiton efforts and set the stage for future efforts. In an historic opportunity, in 2010 the Western Rivers Conservancy, a non-profit conservation organisation, joined with the Yurok Tribe to acquire nearly 47,000 acres from a timber company to establish the Blue Creek Sanctuary and Yurok Community Forest on lands along the Wild and Scenic Klamath River. The Blue Creek Watershed is a vital cold-water refugium located in the Lower Klamath tributary along California's Northern Coast that is a lifeline for migrating salmonids. This stretch of river is essential to the survival of anadromous fish running throughout the Klamath Basin, and the Yurok's practical and cultural identity are closely connected to salmon. The Yurok Tribal government is allocated a percentage of the annual fish stock, and Tribal cultural, commercial, subsistence and ceremonial livelihoods supports its identity as people dependent upon fishing and water. The Yurok had been using this particular stretch of river for fisheries and cultural practices since time immemorial; however, over time, the Yurok lands on the Lower Klamath River were vastly diminished.

Returning part of this culturally, economically and politically significant land back to the Yurok Tribe started a process of transforming the landscape along the Klamath-Trinity Rivers from an industrial tree farm to a diverse fish and wildlife preserve and sustainable forest that could, once again, be managed by the land's original stewards, the Yurok. Today these lands, once managed solely for commercial timber purposes, are now being managed for multiple uses, including carbon sequestration, old-growth forest restoration, watershed restoration and sediment reduction, anadromous fisheries restoration, cultural purposes and endangered species protection. And each of these activities has, in turn, generated jobs for the Yurok people that are connected to forest, water, environmental and fisheries management as well as tourism. Additional income from the Tribe's Carbon Sequestration Program will be used to fund further land acquisition, ongoing natural resources management bridging traditional and adaptive management practices, and additional "resource-based" (forest- and water-based) Tribal employment opportunities, or "green jobs."

The Yurok's participation in the Cap-and-Trade Program also advanced their mission of cultural preservation. The re-acquisition of ancestral lands and expansion of the Tribe's land base also signified that lands were now accessible to Yurok Tribal citizens for cultural uses, including gathering traditional medicines, foods and basket-making materials. In addition, revenues from the sale of offset credits provided much-needed funds for repatriating important cultural heritage objects, such as a large and historic basket collection (that was previously obtained by a private collector), which serves as an important symbol for the Yurok people and is considered critical for the Tribe's cultural preservation (The Yurok Tribe, 2017).

While the partnership and collaboration between the Yurok Tribe and the State of California set a new tone of reconciliation in Tribal affairs, there were many challenges. This relatively new form of engagement between Tribal governments and state governments required substantial education on both sides on legal instruments and policies that could be better adapted to meet the needs of both the State and the Tribe. Furthermore, this process was not quick; it evolved over a number of years, and today the current principles of partnership reflect the State of California and the Yurok Tribe's interests as a result of these interactions.

Today, the Yurok are implementing new approaches at the local, state, federal and international levels to promote conservation finance and Tribal development that go above and beyond California's Cap-and-Trade Program and aim to show that wise, tribally driven conservation-based land management can improve the long-term food security, health and wellbeing of Yurok Tribal members now and for generations to come (Sloan and Hostler, 2014). The Yurok are also working to build public awareness and solidarity with other indigenous communities that are also working to advocate for their specific objectives of asserting their rights and privileges.[7] They assert that partnerships and collaboration must establish and support initiatives that promote climate justice through Tribal and indigenous self-governance and self-determination of their natural resource management.

Looking ahead

By serving as an example for other Native American Tribal governments and indigenous peoples through its successful interactions with California and through its integration of forest management and carbon sequestration,[8] the Yurok are showing that Native American Tribes and indigenous peoples have a right to be decisions-makers in governmental actions that directly and indirectly impact Tribal resources. From the Yurok's perspective, partnerships between Tribal, federal, state, international, public and private interests are vital for developing innovative solutions that can address the complex problem of anthropogenic climate change and critical to mitigating impacts and increasing the resiliency of natural and socio-economic systems. These partnerships and collaborations reflect the diversified approach and natural resources management portfolio that Tribal and State governments can take together.

Based on the principles of partnership that resulted from the Yurok's intervention, CARB is now partnering with seven Tribes from six states across the United States (California Air Resources Board, 2015b). As of April 2018, CARB has issued more than 41 million offset credits to these Tribal projects and to an Alaska Native Corporation (Sealaska) project (California Air Resources Board, 2018). These offsets, which represent greater than 50% of all forest offset credits issued to date (California Air Resources Board, 2018), have a climate finance value of approximately $432 million.[9]

This case study highlights one instance in which a Native American Tribal government affirmatively sought to redress how the State of California would engage with and include Tribes in the development of one of California's signature climate programs. In essence, by insisting on full and effective engagement in the decision-making process and leveraging the structures in which CARB operates – the regulatory design and Tribal consultation processes – the Yurok Tribe created a strong partnership with CARB. As a result of this partnership, the Yurok were able to advance multiple goals, including the re-acquisition of ancestral lands, cultural preservation, forest restoration and food security. But beyond these direct benefits, the Program also provided an opportunity for the Yurok to promote the acknowledgement of the Tribe's inherent rights to manage its natural resources and to press for greater equity in decision-making around natural resources. In negotiating and co-designing the principles of the partnership, a community of practice was created. The Yurok achieved important political recognition as partners – a state government and a Tribal government. As demonstrated in other co-management arrangements in California (Diver, 2016), this case highlights how a policy mechanism, such as cap-and-trade, may be used as an instrument for self-determination, political recognition and climate justice.

Indigenous peoples, REDD + and Acre, Brazil as a leader in tropical forest conservation

> *We don't want the government to come and do things for us, we want to do them together.*
> *– Francisca Oliveira de Lima Costa, Shawadawa Tribe, Acre Brazil[10]*

While the partnership between California and the Yurok Tribe outlines one mechanism for promoting climate justice, the case of Acre, Brazil, also highlights an innovative partnership with indigenous peoples and a subnational government around the design and implementation of a state-wide climate change mitigation program. The process and structure of this partnership bear insights on the interrelated themes of climate justice and forest conservation.

Acre is located in Brazil's far Western Amazon. This remote location, relatively far from Brazil's expanding agricultural frontier, has, in part, shaped a development trajectory that is distinct from other parts of the Brazilian Amazon,[11] and today 87% of Acre's land is forest. Since 1998, Acre's government has enacted a series of progressive environmental policies that have created the conditions for the development of a socially inclusive, low-carbon model of sustainable economic development (Schmink et al., 2014), which includes extractive reserves, indigenous lands, state forests and sustainable development reserves. Together, these protected lands account for 48% of Acre's territory (Schmink et al., 2014). As a result of these integrated initiatives, Acre's average annual deforestation (2015–2017) decreased by 51% from the baseline (average deforestation rate for 1996–2005) (Earth Innovation Institute and Government of Acre, 2017).

Acre's progressive policies may also be attributed to the people-centred approach to conservation that was championed by rubber tapper Chico Mendes, who brought the plight of Brazil's rubber tappers and their fight against deforestation to the world's attention (Allegretti, 1990; Vadjunec et al., 2011). The social movement catalysed by Chico Mendes in the 1980s, and carried forth after his murder in 1988, focused on securing forest rights for forest-dependent communities and established extractive reserves as a unique sustainable-use land tenure regime. Importantly, key leaders from Acre's social movement transitioned from their civil society advocates to civil servants, filling key positions in municipal, state and federal governments and incorporating core values and demands into public policy (Schmink et al., 2014).

In 2010 Acre's forest government enacted a state law creating a state-wide Environmental Services Incentive System (SISA) (Assembleia Legislativa do Estado do Acre, 2010), thus beginning a new chapter in their recent history of progressive environmental policies. The state developed a jurisdictional REDD+ program to establish a financial mechanism to attract funding for its climate change mitigation initiatives based on performance-based payments for state-wide reductions in emissions (Greenleaf, 2018; Instituto de Mudanças Climáticas e Regulação, n.d.). The construction of Acre's REDD + Jurisdictional Program under the SISA law was the result of an intense participatory process, involving diverse actors and potential beneficiaries, including environmental service providers, governmental and non-governmental institutions and research and development institutions. This participation also included input from local, national and even international leaders (Instituto de Mudanças Climáticas e Regulação de Serviços Ambientais-IMC, 2012).

This participatory process also attracted the attention of key international forest and climate donors. When the Government of Germany developed the Global Redd Early Movers (REM)[12] Program in 2011 to support actors taking risks and pioneering REDD+ initiatives, it found that Acre had the ideal conditions for implementing the REM pilot. Acre was the first pilot jurisdiction for Germany's REM program, which is now operating in two additional jurisdictions, Ecuador and Colombia. Specifically, Germany's REM program provides performance-based financing to jurisdictions on the basis of documented and verified reductions in emissions from deforestation. Finance is contingent, however, on a portion of REM funds being distributed to indigenous peoples and local communities.

The participation of indigenous peoples and the results of dialogue processes

Acre has 36 Indigenous Lands with 15 different ethnic tribes (AMAAIAC, 2018). Deforestation rates are low within indigenous territories, contributing just 3% to state-wide emissions from land-use land cover change (DiGiano et al., 2016). While Acre's state-led program had a widespread participatory process, indigenous leaders were some of the key protagonists in the process of building the state's REDD+ Jurisdictional Program (Greenleaf, 2018). Indigenous engagement influenced a number of elements of the state REDD program, including an interinstitutional "Indigenous Working Group," a Charter of Principles and guidelines for the design and implementation of the indigenous subprogramme[13] under the REDD+ Jurisdictional Program. The Indigenous Working Group,[14] established in 2012, serves as a forum for dialogue between government actors and agencies engaged in the implementation of SISA, indigenous communities and civil society. This Working Group emerged from the understanding of the importance of indigenous peoples in forest conservation and natural resource management. The Charter of Principles also serves as an instrument to guide Indigenous Peoples' action in the SISA REDD+ Jurisdictional Program. This Charter outlines implementation of incentives for environmental services within indigenous lands in Acre, addresses rights in federal processes and procedures and international legislation, and works to guarantee the collective wellbeing of indigenous peoples. Acre, for example, was a leader in developing and applying a state-wide safeguards framework that was consistent with the international REDD+ Social and Environmental Standards (KfW Development Bank, 2017).

Indigenous Agroforestry Agents as key actors within Acre's SISA REDD+ jurisdictional program

Acre's REDD+ program seeks to maximise the state's potential for generating environmental and social co-benefits through conserving forests and biodiversity, expanding ecosystem services, and revitalising the cultural and spiritual identity of indigenous peoples. And one of the most significant aspects of this approach has been the government's investment in resources from REDD+ to create a program to train and deploy Indigenous Agroforestry Agents (*Agentes Agroflorestais Indigenas*, or AAFIs), who serve as key actors for not only forest conservation, but also for promoting the rights and interests of forest-based people, namely Acre's indigenous population.

While AAFIs have multiple purposes, their main objective is to develop and implement Territorial and Environmental Management plans (known by their abbreviation in Portuguese, PGTAs) to harmonise environmental goals established by SISA while improving livelihoods and valuing traditional ecological knowledge. In order to act as local leaders in the implementation of these plans, AAFIs route their activities in specific diagnostic and planning instruments, using participatory methodology for "ethnozoning" as well as the aforementioned PGTAs.[15] AAFIs are also connected to other key state-level actors. For example, a civil society organisation called the *Comissão Pro-Indio* (Pro-Indian Commission) works closely with AAFIs on training (among other activities), and today, 36 AAFIs have completed their technical secondary education and another 156 AAFIs are currently taking courses toward this certificate. AAFIs work on 31 of the 36 different indigenous lands and represent 14 of the 15 different ethnic tribes in 11 municipalities.

To strengthen and defend the interest of the AAFIs, the Acre Agroforestry Agents Association of Acre (AMAAIAC) was created in 2002. When AMAAIAC was formed, REDD+ was seen not as an end, or a goal to be achieved, but as a means of valuing the forest as part of a comprehensive, state-wide process that includes forest conservation and sustainable development, including on indigenous lands. One of the most important aspects of AMAAIAC is its contribution to Acre's state-wide REDD+ Program. The state passes REDD+ resources to AMAAIAC which, in turn, works to ensure the effective participation and participation of indigenous peoples and their organisations and to establish a fair distribution of benefits among communities that historically manage and conserve forests (AMAAIAC, 2018). Toward this end, AMAAIC works with indigenous leaders across Acre, monitors and evaluates the results and advances achieved by AAFIs, and coordinates with the government, indigenous organisations, associations and other partners. Today, AMAAIAC has become a reference and strong interlocutor in national and international spaces for how states can construct policies for environmental services that respect, and further, indigenous rights.

The case of Acre highlights two key points related to climate justice. First, Acre has created a suite of progressive environmental policies that explicitly address and engage climate justice issues. The Agroforestry Agent program, for example, demonstrates that climate change mitigation initiatives can, and should, pay equal attention to the generation of co-benefits such as improved livelihoods and resilience and (re)valorisation of traditional ecological knowledge. Public consultation and the creation of institutional mechanisms such as the Indigenous Working Group and AMAAIAC advance the political participation of indigenous peoples in the design and implementation of locally relevant, but universally recognised, safeguards that promote capabilities fundamental to climate justice. With parallels to the Yurok Tribe, Acre's REDD+ program is a policy instrument for achieving cultural recognition, along with a broader array of political and economic benefits that improve the capabilities of indigenous peoples in Acre for attaining climate justice. The history of Acre's forest government (Allegretti, 1990; Vadjunec et al., 2011), with its origin in a social justice movement, signals that the political will of civil servants may be key in ensuring that social justice issues remain on the forefront of climate change mitigation initiatives. Further, insight into the translation of social movement demands into policy, however, may illuminate how climate justice can be better understood and advocated for by bureaucrats in other jurisdictions (Harrison, 2016; Harrison, 2017).

The Governors' Climate and Forest Task Force and Emerging Spaces for Articulation between Governments and Indigenous Peoples

The opportunity for representation by indigenous peoples in the [GCF Indigenous Peoples and Local Communities] Working Group is an opportunity to influence climate change policies. The Working Group initiative is one that recognizes rights, recognizes participation, builds capacities and promotes joint actions – not just between indigenous peoples and subnational governments but also with the rest of society.

– Cándido Mezua, a member of the Embera tribe in Panama and representative of the Mesoamerican Alliance of People and Forest

While the case of the Yurok-California and Acre's indigenous leadership around REDD+ indicate subnational approaches to climate justice around forest conservation and community-defined development, can climate justice be promoted *across* jurisdictions and, if so, how? To address this question, we examine the challenges – as well as the potential – for using a unique, subnational governmental coalition, called the Governors' Climate and Forests Task Force (GCF Task Force), to encourage new forms of political participation and collaboration among state and provincial governments and indigenous and local communities. While there has been some inquiry into how transnational alliances of indigenous organisations can advance claims around territorial and human rights (Kauffman and Martin, 2014; Whyte, 2016), there is less documentation about how governments, especially at the subnational level, can come together with indigenous and local communities organisations. We explore the GCF Task Force as a dynamic community of practice that is attempting to serve as a platform for enabling and strengthening partnerships among indigenous peoples, local communities and subnational governments. This case analyses the factors joining these actors as a community of practice, as well as the challenges faced communicating across different historical, linguistic, cultural and geographic contexts in an attempt to transform political commitments into concrete processes.

The GCF Task Force was established in 2008 on the premise that subnational governments, states and provinces are important innovators in climate change mitigation policy and would benefit from a global network for collective action and knowledge exchange. Founding members of the GCF Task Force included the subnational governments of California (USA) and Acre (Brazil), among eight others from the United States, the Brazilian Amazon and Indonesia. Over the past ten years, the network has more than tripled in size to be the world's largest subnational governmental network dedicated to promoting tropical forest conservation and low emissions development. While more than one-third of the world's tropical forest jurisdictions are GCF Task Force states and provinces, the GCF also includes more than 200 distinct indigenous people's tribes and countless local community groups representing rubber tappers, river-dwelling communities, family farmers and others.

In 2014 the GCF Task Force network drafted and endorsed the Rio Branco Declaration (RBD),[16] which commits GCF Task Force members to substantially reducing tropical deforestation in their states and provinces *while partnering with and sharing the benefits of these actions with indigenous peoples and traditional communities.* With this formal recognition of the importance of subnational governmental and indigenous or traditional community relationships, indigenous groups began more formally approaching the GCF Task Force network. At the Annual Meeting in Barcelona in 2015, the GCF Task Force received two requests from indigenous organisations to more formally engage with the GCF Task Force,[17] and indigenous leaders increasingly made it clear that they wanted deeper engagement with the subnational governmental leaders of the GCF Task Force. Though the GCF Task Force membership consists of subnational (not Tribal) governments, the Task Force members recognised the need to enhance the possibilities for partnership between governments and indigenous peoples and local communities. Building from the RBD and the 2015 GCF Task Force Annual Meeting requests, over the course of the following years, GCF Task Force members launched a series of efforts to try to put meaningful processes in place.

From political commitments to concrete processes: efforts to come together across regions, cultures and histories

While the RBD created an important political platform, translating this commitment of GCF members into practice has taken place (and still is very much a work in process) over a series of events and important "moments." First, at the 2016 GCF Task Force Annual Meeting, GCF Task Force members, indigenous and community leaders and civil society representatives decided to form a global-level GCF-Indigenous Peoples and Local Communities Working Group (GCF IP/LC WG) to develop specific strategies for better collaboration and inclusion of indigenous peoples and local communities into subnational governmental efforts to reduce deforestation and promote low emissions development. Leveraging the network of the GCF Task Force and its diverse laboratory of policy experiments, the working group aims to share lessons learned and replicate the government-community partnerships that have been pioneered in the case studies, with the States of California and Acre.

Brazilian GCF member states as a whole, led by Acre, have also been an early mover in this process and have had two important convening moments. The first moment took place in Brasilia in 2016, when Acre united other GCF Task Force delegates with civil servants from other state-level agencies as well as with representatives of federal government agencies involved in indigenous peoples' issues. The purpose of this gathering was to discuss the challenges and opportunities of designing state-level programs for climate change mitigation which brought benefits to indigenous peoples. Over a year later, GCF delegates met with indigenous leaders to learn about Acre's model of an indigenous peoples-focused climate change mitigation program, and to develop recommendations to policymakers across the Brazilian Amazon for advancing commitments laid out in the Rio Branco Declaration.

On a global scale, in August 2017, the GCF IP/LC WG held an inaugural meeting to bringing together some 34 different leaders, including GCF Task Force representatives, indigenous and community leaders and civil society representatives from Central and South America, Indonesia and California on Yurok Tribal Lands. This meeting was a watershed moment in the GCF Task Force IP/LC evolution; participants shared their experiences and drafted a preliminary strategy for collective action that incorporated efforts for forest conservation and climate change mitigation with rights recognition for indigenous peoples and forest communities, greater participation in decision-making processes and a fair share of climate change finance to recognise their role as "forest guardians" as some indigenous leaders emphasized. To guide these actions, the group drafted "Guiding Principles for Collaboration and Partnership between Subnational Governments, Indigenous Peoples and Local Communities" (Principles for Collaboration and Partnership).[18]

The inherent friction in complex processes of governmental–indigenous–local community collaborations

The inaugural meeting of the GCF IP/LC WG, and the advent of the idea of creating universal Principles for Collaboration and Partnership, were critical moments in the broader strategy for establishing communication and trust among governments, indigenous peoples and local communities. Moments such as this, however, have also been important, and sometimes difficult, spaces of negotiation and friction as distinct visions, demands and power are negotiated. These challenging dynamics were apparent in the drafting and review process of the Principles for Collaboration and Partnership. Representatives of subnational governments rejected any principles perceived to be overreaching their powers as subnational entities subject to federal legal frameworks (for example, in Brazil, subnational governments cannot recognise indigenous territories, as these fall under the mandate of the federal government). There was also an inherent tension between universal relevancy, respect for limits of powers of subnational entities, and the urgent demands of indigenous organisations seeking to recognise carbon rights, decriminalise forest defenders and attain greater respect for indigenous cosmo-visions.[19] The words and verbs themselves were studied and negotiated; in one series of negotiations, a change of verb in Spanish from "we commit" to "we aim" was contested by a community leader who pointed out that "there is definitely a great distance between the words 'aim' and 'commit'."[20] In sum, the diverse Tribal, "indigenous leaders," state-level and even regional concerns and contexts made developing a common foundational document a complex and challenging process.

Beyond the drafting process, socialising these principles within each stakeholder group and subnational government also presented its own set of challenges. A month after the inaugural meeting in California, GCF member states gathered in Indonesia at the 2017 GCF Task Force Annual Meeting, where indigenous representatives and GCF Task Force governors and delegates met to discuss the advances of the GCF IP/LC WG and to present the Principles for Collaboration and Partnership to high-level decision-makers for their endorsement. While all entered the meeting with high expectations, it soon became apparent that further socialisation of these key Principles for Collaboration and Partnership needed to happen among subnational governments, and the anticipated adoption of this guiding document fell to pieces as the fragmented process of communication and information dissemination came to light. Nevertheless, as one indigenous leader present noted when it seemed the meeting was a failure, "this wasn't a failure at all – for the first time we sat, face to face, at the same table with governors. This was big!" All parties left the meeting still asserting that the Principles for Collaboration and Partnership were critical for establishing a foundation for stronger partnerships between subnational governments and indigenous and local communities and vowed to continue the review and socialisation process. In fact, the Principles for Collaboration and Partnership will be brought to the GCF delegates by members of the GCF IP/LC WG for an official vote at the 2018 GCF Task Force annual meeting.

Today, the GCF IP/LC WG continues to work to advance complex political commitments across equally complex historical, cultural and geographical contexts by defining a workable and effective structure at the global level through addressing issues such as governance and management issues, membership,[21] representation, language and obtaining a sustainable support base. Each of the primary GCF Task Force regions is also working to build similar, multi-stakeholder Regional Working Groups.[22] This process of coalescing GCF IP/LC WGs across scales and scopes is giving rise to new communities of practice. For example, the process of developing the Principles for Collaboration and Partnership has brought governmental and indigenous leaders together around a common goal. New leaders have also emerged in this process, learning from more seasoned governmental leaders that, in turn, are generating new forms of collaborative, inclusive, forest governance and management.[23]

Conclusion

Back in Northern California in late August 2017, in the course of three days the participants of the GCF Task Force IP/LC WG had met for endless hours both together and separately, across regional groups. They had mapped out issues and goals. They had taken a boat trip up the Klamath River in Yurok Territory, and had taken off their shoes to bathe their feet in the frigid water – the "best way to feel the spirit of this place and ensure a return," according to the Yurok guides. Some of the group had even seen a good omen – a baby bear appeared on the side of the river.

And as the group stood under a vast redwood forest holding hands, many had tears in their eyes at the powerful force that was developing in the effort to break down longstanding barriers and build meaningful partnerships among governmental leaders, indigenous peoples and civil society partners for better forest conservation and climate justice. The group had come together. At the closing moment, Rukka Somboliggni, Secretary General of the Indigenous Peoples' Alliance of the Archipelago (AMAN), reflected, "This work is not just for indigenous peoples, but for all of us. Our goal is to reach the point where we will leave the world for the next generation in a better way. I see this group starting to reach that point – where indigenous peoples, local communities and governments work together, because that is the real work. I hope that we have lit a candle, that we inspire others . . . that we rely on each other, that we work together, hand in hand, like the roots of the redwood tree."

One of the compelling questions of our time is if, and how, efforts to address climate change by conserving forests can also safeguard the culture, livelihoods and right to self-determination of forest-based communities. For forest-based communities, climate justice claims are part of even broader struggles for self-determination, visibility in decision-making spaces, territorial rights and livelihoods (Schlosberg and Carruthers, 2010; Doolittle, 2010).

As these cases reveal, partnerships among subnational governments, indigenous peoples and local communities are complex, dynamic and imperfect works in progress. However, these partnerships represent new processes and spaces for exploring climate justice in practice. California's Cap-and-Trade Program afforded new opportunities for the Yurok Tribe's self-determination, and Tribal conceptions of capabilities led in these negotiations. This process created a new community of practice that, through this interaction, pushed California and the Yurok to co-determine better processes for inclusion of Tribal interests in the Cap-and-Trade Program. Today the Yurok view the Program not as an end in and of itself, but as a means to enable the Tribe's capabilities for self-determination and for protecting land that was integral to their cultural practices and identity, or, in other words, as a form of recognitional justice.

Acre's state-level leadership, combined with a strong indigenous presence across the jurisdiction, also pushed both a state government and diverse indigenous tribes to co-develop, through an innovative, active community of practice, several different processes that align with tenets of climate justice such as participatory development, self-representation and benefit-sharing in forest conservation activities. Acre's SISA program points to created opportunities for recognitional justice by generating the institutional mechanisms for new forms of indigenous peoples' participation in state-wide governmental policy-making. As with California and the Yurok, this process, too, created new communities of practice, both between the Acre state government and indigenous peoples across the state, in general, as well as within indigenous organisations (the Indigenous Working Group, the AAFIs and AMAAIAC).

Finally, the GCF Task Force's efforts to come together within regions (like Brazil), across regions (such as the Amazon) and also transcending even broader borders (the global GCF Task Force network as a whole) indicate the complexities, and the possibilities, for forming communities of practice in a way that aligns subnational jurisdictional conceptions of forest conservation and natural resource management and, at the same time, promotes indigenous and local communities' cultural resilience, right to self-determination, visions of livelihood development and participation in decision-making processes around forest management.

These attempts and acts of coming together lead us to key issues at the core of climate justice concerns – redefining power relationships among governments, indigenous peoples and communities; promoting leadership of subnational governments and indigenous and local level community leaders; and looking carefully at how political commitments are negotiated, and ultimately enacted, across complex social, political and ecological landscapes. While challenging, these partnerships are not only possible, they are essential for addressing the multiple values of forests and, in turn, for addressing existential threats like climate change.

Notes

1 This chapter was written in the authors' personal capacities and does not necessarily represent the views of their respective organisations or governments.
2 Reducing Emissions from Deforestation and forest Degradation (REDD+) is a mechanism developed by the United Nationals Framework Convention on Climate Change (UNFCCC). REDD+ is designed to offer financial incentives to developing countries for reducing emissions, enhancing carbon stocks and investing in low-emissions development (www.unredd.net, accessed May 20, 2018).
3 Excerpted from "The Principles of Climate Justice" (www.mrfcj.org/principles-of-climate-justice/, accessed May 18, 2018).
4 Holland (2012) argues that these are in fact a "meta-capability" which enables other capabilities, such as health and food security.
5 Statement made by California official at 2017 GCF Annual Meeting, Balikpapan, East Kalimantan, Indonesia.
6 CARB did include provisions indicating that Tribes are not subject to State law, specifically with respect to electricity purchasing and selling entities, www.arb.ca.gov/regact/2010/capandtrade10/capv1appa.pdf at A-15, with definition of "Tribal Nations" on p. A-36. These provisions were modified following discussions with the Yurok Tribe to allow for the participation of projects on Tribal Lands. See, for example, CARB, Proposed 15-day modifications (July 25, 2011) at pp. A-171 and A-176 to A-177, www.arb. ca.gov/regact/2010/capandtrade10/candtmodreg.pdf and Proposed 15-day modifications (September 12, 2011) at p. A-205 (www.arb.ca.gov/regact/2010/capandtrade10/2ndmodreg.pdf).
7 This should not include incidences of violence, adverse tactics or governmental actions that seek to usurp Tribal and indigenous nation-building development.
8 Yurok Tribal Resolution 12–24, "Yurok Tribe Support for the United Nations Declaration on the Rights of Indigenous Peoples," February 24, 2012.
9 This value accounts for the removal of credits to the Forest Buffer Account pursuant to the Compliance Offset Protocol for U.S. Forest Projects (see section 3.5.3 of the Compliance Offset Protocol for U.S. Forest Projects California Air Resources Board 2015) and uses a rough estimate of today's offset credit

price (approximately \$12.35 per offset credit based on an estimated 15% discount from current allowance prices of \$14.53). This 15% value is derived from a past weighted average price of offset credit transfers, available here: www.arb.ca.gov/cc/capandtrade/2016transferssummary%20final.xlsx.

10 Quoted in "The Power of Partnerships," Video Produced by Earth Innovation Institute (https://earth innovation.org/resources/browse/the-power-of-partnerships/, accessed May 2, 2018).

11 The Legal Amazon is an area that corresponds to 59% of the Brazilian territory, totalling 5.0 million km² and including nine states, where 56% of the Brazilian indigenous population lives. Its main purpose is to plan the economic development of the region of the political-administrative units in function of their climatic characteristics INSTITUTO DE PESQUISA ECONÔMICA APLICADA (www.ipea.gov.br/ challenges/, accessed May 21, 2018).

12 The REDD Early Movers Program is funded by the German Federal Government's Energy and Climate Fund and is managed by the German Development Bank KFW.

13 The SISA subprograms are planning tools and guidelines for fair benefit-sharing to SISA beneficiaries.

14 The Indigenous Working Group, created in 2012, is made up of representatives of indigenous organisations, indigenist institutions, and state and federal government agencies (Resolution No. 001, of August 20, 2012).

15 Ethnozoning was based on a participatory methodology to conduct diagnostics and scenario planning combined with indigenous thematic maps on a georeferenced cartographic base, in the scale of 1:80,000. This methodology was inspired by ethnomapping carried out by the Comissão Pro-Indio (CPI, Pro-Indigenous Commission) and complements the development of the Management Plans for indigenous lands by the AAFIs. Currently, 29 PGTAs have been prepared (AMAAIAC 2018; contribution of the Acre Agroforestry Agents of Acre to the climate balance).

16 https://gcftf.org/news/2017/5/11/rio-branco-declaration, accessed May 20, 2018.

17 These requests came from AIDESEP (Asociación Interétnica de Desarrollo de la Selva Peruana, Inter-ethnic Association for the Development of the Peruvian Rainforest) and COICA (*Coordinadora de las Organizaciones Indígenas de la Cuenca Amazónica*, Coordinator of Indigenous Organizations of the Amazon River Basin).

18 At the time of publishing, The Principles for Collaboration and Partnership were planned to be presented at 2018 GCF Task Force Annual meeting and voted on in the full GCF Task Force Assembly in September 2018. The principles include core elements of climate justice partnership, including respect and recognition of rights and recognition of international agreements that safeguard indigenous rights, cultures and self-determination (such as the Paris Accord, United Nations Declaration on the Rights of Indigenous Peoples (UNDRIP) and the Cancun Safeguards).

19 A word used by indigenous leaders in the GCF IP/LC WG to denote a way of understanding the world, constructed by values, knowledge systems and identities.

20 Translated from Spanish, email communications among working group members, September 2017.

21 One key challenge is defining membership in the working group. While GCF Task Force membership is clearly defined, thus facilitating the process of defining GCF Task Force representatives to participate in the working group, determining who should represent indigenous peoples and local communities within regional working groups is complex, especially as most GCF member jurisdictions lack state-level representative organisations of indigenous peoples or traditional communities.

22 Regional working groups would comprise both governmental and indigenous peoples and local communities' representatives, with participation from other stakeholders, such as national governments and civil society organisations, as determined by each working group.

23 For example, at the August 2018 meeting, a representative from a national donor organisation noted she was there "to learn" from the participants as she thought about her funding priorities and how to be instrumental in climate justice and forest conservation strategies. Communities of practice can be important mechanisms for developing social capital (Lesser and Storck, 2001).

References

Adger, W. N. (2006). Vulnerability. *Global Environmental Change*, 16, 268–281.

Agrawal, A., et al. (2011). Reducing emissions from deforestation and forest degradation. *Annual Review of Environment and Resources*, 36, 373–396.

Allegretti, M. H. 1990. *Extractive Reserves: An Alternative for Reconciling Development and Environmental Conservation in Amazonia. Alternatives to Deforestation: Steps Towards Sustainable Use of the Amazon Rain Forest.* New York: Columbia University Press.

Colleen M. Scanlan Lyons et al.

AMAAIC. 2018. Relatório Final do Convênio 001/2014 AMAAIC/SEMA-FEF: TOMO I- Contribuição dos Agentes Agroflorestais Indígena do Acre para o Equilibrio do Clima. Rio Branco: Acre.

Amin, A. and Roberts, J. 2008. Knowing in action: Beyond communities of practice. *Research Policy*, 37, 353–369.

Anderton, K. and Setzer, J. 2017. Subnational climate entrepreneurship: Innovative climate action in California and São Paulo. *Regional Environmental Change*, 18, 1273–1284.

Assembleia Legislative do Estado do Acre. 2010. Lei N. 2.308. Available: http://www.al.ac.leg.br/leis/wp-content/uploads/2014/09/Lei2308.pdf

Barboza, T. 2014. *Yurok tribe hopes California's cap-and-trade can save a way of life.* LA Times, December 16.

Brugnach, M., et al. (2014). Including indigenous peoples in climate change mitigation: Addressing issues of scale, knowledge and power. *Climatic Change*, 140, 19–32.

California Air Resources Board. 2011. *Meeting: State of California Air Resources Board. California Air Resources Board.* Available: https://www.arb.ca.gov/board/mt/2011/mt102011.pdf

California Air Resources Board. 2015a. *Compliance Offset Protocol U.S. Forest Projects.* Available: https://www.arb.ca.gov/cc/capandtrade/protocols/usforest/usforestprojects_2014.htm

California Air Resources Board. 2015b. *Offset Project Listing Requirements for Native American Tribes.* Available: https://www.arb.ca.gov/cc/capandtrade/offsets/offset-tribes.htm

California Air Resources Board. 2017c. *California's 2017 Climate Change Scoping Plan: The Strategy for Achieving California's 2030 Greenhouse Gas Target.* Available: https://www.arb.ca.gov/cc/scopingplan/scoping_plan_2017.pdf

California Air Resources Board. 2018. *ARB Offset Credits Issued.* Available: https://www.arb.ca.gov/cc/capandtrade/offsets/issuance/arb_offset_credit_issuance_table.pdf

California Code of Regulations. 2017a. *California Cap on Greenhouse Gas Emissions and Market-Based Compliance Mechanisms, 17.* Available: http://oal.ca.gov/publications/ccr/

California Code of Regulations. 2017b. Listing of Offset Projects Using ARB Compliance Offset Protocols, 17. https://govt.westlaw.com/calregs/Document/I5459EF9B1F5D43E097DD2F850F8E3764?viewType=FullText&originationContext=documenttoc&transitionType=CategoryPageItem&contextData=(sc.Default)

California Code of Regulations. 2017. Requirements for offset projects using ARB compliance offset protocols, 17. https://govt.westlaw.com/calregs/Document/I85738619E75B4E34AD177B5B14070412?viewType=FullText&originationContext=documenttoc&transitionType=CategoryPageItem&contextData=(sc.Default)&bhcp=1

California Environmental Protection Agency. 2018. *California Native American Tribal Relations* [Online]. Available: https://calepa.ca.gov/tribal/ [Accessed May 8, 2018].

Chhatre, A., et al. (2012). "Social safeguards and co-benefits in REDD+: A review of the adjacent possible." *Current Opinion in Environmental Sustainability* 4(6): 654–660.

Corbett, J. 2011. *Public Comment Letter Submitted on Behalf of the Yurok Tribe.* California Air Resource Board.

Deleon Kandel, B. 2018. *The Yurok and California's Carbon Market: A Case Study on the Yurok Tribe in Contemporary California.* B.A. University of California Berkeley.

DiGiano, M. L., Stickler, C., Nepstad, D., Ardila, J., Becerra, M., Benavides, M., Bernadinus, S., Bezerra, T., Castro, E., Cendales, M., Chan, C., Davis, A., Kandel, S., Mendoza, E., Montero, J., Osorio, M. and Setiawan, J. 2016. *Increasing REDD+ Benefits to Indigenous Peoples and Traditional Communities Through a Jurisdictional Approach.* Earth Innovation Institute.

Diver, S. 2016. Co-management as a catalyst: Pathways to post-colonial forestry in the Klamath Basin, California. *Human Ecology: An Interdisciplinary Journal*, 44, 533–546.

Doolittle, A. 2010. The politics of indigeneity: Indigenous strategies for inclusion in climate change negotiations. *Conservation and Society*, 8, 256.

Earth Innovation Institute and Government of Acre. 2017. Acre produce, protect and include platform [Online]. Available: http://acreppp.org [Accessed May 23, 2018].

Fisher, S. 2015. The emerging geographies of climate justice. *The Geographical Journal*, 181, 73–82.

Frederickson, D. A. 1984. *The North Coast Region: MJ Moratto, California Archaeology.* Orlando: Academic Press, 471–527.

Godden, L. andTehan, M. (2016). "REDD+: Climate justice and indigenous and local community rights in an era of climate disruption." *Journal of Energy & Natural Resources Law*, 34(1), 95–108.

Governor of California 2011. *California Executive Order B-10-11.* Available: https://www.gov.ca.gov/2011/09/19/news17223/

Greenleaf, M. 2018. Using carbon rights to curb deforestation and empower forest communities. *The NYU Environmental Law Journal*, 18, 507.

Gupta, A., et al. (2012). In pursuit of carbon accountability: The politics of REDD+ measuring, reporting and verification systems. *Current Opinion in Environmental Sustainability* 4(6), 726–731.

Harrison, J. L. 2016. Bureaucrats' tacit understandings and social movement policy implementation: Unpacking the deviation of agency environmental justice programs from EJ movement priorities. *Social Problems*, 63, 534–553.

Harrison, J. L. 2017. 'We do ecology, not sociology': Interactions among bureaucrats and the undermining of regulatory agencies' environmental justice efforts. *Environmental Sociology*, 3, 197–212.

Holland, B. (2012). Environment as meta-capability: Why a dignified human life requires a stable climate system. *Ethical adaptation to climate change: human virtues of the future*, 145–164.

Instituto De Mudanças Climáticas E Regulação De Serviços Ambientais-Imc. 2012. *Construção Participativa da Lei do Sistema de Incentivos a Serviços Ambientais – SISA do Estado do Acre*. Rio Branco: Acre.

Instituto De Mudanças Climáticas E Regulação. n.d. Programa para pioneiros em REDD+ (REM) [http://imc.ac.gov.br/programa-para-pioneiros-em-redd-rem/]. [Accessed May 21, 2018].

Instituto De Pesquisa Econômica Aplicada. Available: www.ipea.gov.br/challenges/ [Accessed May 21, 2018].

Johnston-Dodds, K. and Burton, J. L. 2002. *Early California Laws and Policies Related to California Indians*. Sacramento, CA: California State Library, California Research Bureau.

Kauffman, C. M. and Martin, P. L. 2014. Scaling up Buen Vivir: Globalizing local environmental governance from Ecuador. *Global Environmental Politics*, 14, 40–58.

KFW Development Bank. 2017. *REDD+ in the State of Acre, Brazil: Rewarding a Pioneer in Forest Protection and Sustainable Livelihood Development*. Frankfurt, Germany: Federal Ministry for Economic Cooperation and Development (BMZ).

Koopman, M., DellaSala, D, van Mantgem, P., Blom, B., Teraoka, J., Shearer, R., LaFever, D. and Seney, J. 2014. Managing an ancient ecosystem for the modern world: Coast redwoods and climate change. Available: https://climatewise.org/images/projects/coast-redwoods-report-manuscript.pdf

Lave, J. and Wenger, E. 1991. *Situated Learning: Legitimate Peripheral Participation*. Cambridge: Cambridge University Press.

Lesser, E. L. and Storck, J. 2001. Communities of practice and organizational performance. *IBM Systems Journal*, 40, 4831–4841.

Lutsey, N. and Sperling, D. 2008. America's bottom-up climate change mitigation policy. *Energy Policy*, 36, 673–685.

Maldonado, J. K., et al. (2013). The impact of climate change on tribal communities in the US: Displacement, relocation, and human rights. *Climatic Change*, 120, 601–614.

Maldonado, J., et al. (2016). Engagement with indigenous peoples and honoring traditional knowledge systems. *Climatic Change,* 135, 111–126.

Marino, E. and Ribot, J. (2012). Special issue introduction: Adding insult to injury: Climate change and the inequities of climate intervention. *Global Environmental Change,* 22, 323–328.

Marion Suiseeya, K. (2017). Contesting justice in global forest governance: The promises and pitfalls of REDD+. *Conservation and Society*, 15, 189.

Martin, A., Coolsaet, B., Corbera, E., Dawson, N. M., Fraser, J. A., Lehmann, I. and Rodriguez, I. 2016. Justice and conservation: The need to incorporate recognition. *Biological Conservation*, 197, 254–261.

Mustalahti, I., et al. (2012). Can REDD+ reconcile local priorities and needs with global mitigation benefits? Lessons from Angai Forest, Tanzania. *Ecology and Society* 17.

Nepstad, D., Schwartzman, S., Bamberger, B., Santilli, M., Ray, D., Schlesinger, P., Lefebvre, P., Alencar, A., Prinz, E., Fiske, G. and Rolla, A. 2006. Inhibition of Amazon deforestation and fire by parks and indigenous lands. *Conservation Biology*, 20, 65–73.

Pan, Y., et al. (2011). A large and persistent carbon sink in the world's forests. *Science*, 333, 988–993.

Quéré, C. L., et al. (2018). Global carbon budget 2017. *Earth System Science Data*, 10, 405–448.

Ricketts, T. H., Soares-Filho, B., Da Fonseca, G. A., Nepstad, D., Pfaff, A., Petsonk, A., Anderson, A., Boucher, D., Cattaneo, A., Conte, M., Creighton, K., Linden, L., Maretti, C., Moutinho, P., Ullman, R. and Victurine, R. 2010. Indigenous lands, protected areas, and slowing climate change. *PLoS Biology*, 8, e1000331.

Scanlan Lyons, C. (2012). *Suffering, Service, and Justice: Matters of Faith and How Faith Matters to the Environmental Movement in Brazil's Atlantic Forest. Nature, Science, and Religion: Intersections Shaping Society and the Environment*. Santa Fe, NM: School of Advanced Research.

Schlosberg, D. and Carruthers, D. (2010). Indigenous struggles, environmental justice, and community capabilities. *Global Environmental Politics*, 10, 12–35.

Schlosberg, D. (2012). Climate justice and capabilities: A framework for adaptation policy. *Ethics & International Affairs*, 26, 445–461.

Schmink, M., et al. (2014). 'Forest Citizenship in Acre, Brazil. No. IUFRO World Series no. 32. Available: https://www.cifor.org/library/5093/forest-citizenship-in-acre-brazil/ [Accessed September 25, 2018].

Sen, A. (1999). *Development as Freedom*. New York, Anchor.

Seymour, F. and Busch, J. (2016). *Why Forests? Why Now?: The Science, Economics, and Politics of Tropical Forests And Climate Change*. Washington, DC: Centre for Global Development.

Sloan, K. and Hostler, J. (2014). *Utilizing Yurok Traditional Ecological Knowledge to Inform Climate Change Priorities, The North Pacific Landscape Conservation Cooperative, US Fish and Wildlife Service: 12*. Available: https://nplcc.blob.core.windows.net/media/Default/2012_Documents/Utilizing_Yurok_traditional/Yurok%20Final%20Report%20TEK%20and%20CC%20to%20NPLCC%20%20w%20NWCSC.pdf

The Yurok Tribe (2007). Yurok Tribe History.

The Yurok Tribe (2017). The Yurok Tribe 2017 Annual Report.

Yurok Tribal Constitution. 1993. Available: http://yuroktribe.org/government/councilsupport/documents/Constitution.pdf

Tucker, C. M., Ed. (2012). *Nature, Science, and Religion: Intersections Shaping Society and the Environment*. Santa Fe, NM: School of Advanced Research.

Walker, W., et al. (2014). Forest carbon in Amazonia: The unrecognized contribution of indigenous territories and protected natural areas. *Carbon Management*, 5, 479–485.

Wenger, E. (1998). *Communities of practice: Learning, meaning, and identity*. New York: Cambridge university press.

Wenger, E. (2000). Communities of practice and social learning systems. *Organization*, 7, 225–246.

Whyte, K. P. (2016). *Indigenous Environmental Movements and the Function of Governance Institutions. In:* T. Gabrielson, C. Hall, J. Meyer & D. Schlosberg, Eds. The Oxford Handbook of Environmental Political Theory. United Kingdom: Oxford University Press.

Vadjunec, J. M., et al. (2011). Rubber tapper citizens: Emerging places, policies, and shifting rural-urban identities in Acre, Brazil. *Journal of Cultural Geography*, 28, 73–98.

Vergara-Asenjo, G. and Potvin, C. (2014). Forest protection and tenure status: The key role of indigenous peoples and protected areas in Panama. *Global Environmental Change*, 28, 205–215.

Vucetich, J. A., et al. (2018). Just conservation: What is it and should we pursue it? *Biological Conservation*, 221, 23–33.

33

Understanding the crises, uncovering root causes and envisioning the world(s) we want

Conversations with the anti-pipeline movements in Canada

Jen Gobby and Kristian Gareau

Introduction

As we write this chapter, controversy is continuing to erupt in Canada over the construction of Kinder Morgan's Trans Mountain pipeline, which would transport non-conventional oil from the Alberta tar sands through the province of British Columbia (BC) to the Pacific Coast. In what is being called a "constitutional crisis" (Ljunggren, 2018), the Federal government and the province of Alberta continue to pledge that this pipeline will be built while fierce opposition mounts in BC. Prime Minister Justin Trudeau has repeatedly stated that the pipeline is in the "national interest" and that Canada must balance the needs of "the environment and the economy" (Judd, 2018). Despite such justifications, Kinder Morgan operations on the ground became increasingly difficult in the face of political and activist resistance, and these tensions culminated in a surprising announcement in spring 2018 that the company wanted out of the Trans Mountain pipeline project and, in response, the Trudeau government would buy it (Harris, 2018). All in all, the escalating conflict continues to exacerbate already fraught relationships between the federal government and First Nations regarding treaty and rights violations, while also sparking widespread public concern about serious risks to water, land and climate.

The Kinder Morgan controversy is part of a larger fight against pipelines and the expansion of the Alberta tar sands over the last decade, around which has coalesced a movement of movements that includes Indigenous communities, local citizens, social justice groups and environmental non-governmental organisations (ENGOs) across Canada. As social ecologist Brian Tokar (2015, p. 6) writes, "The emergence of new communities of resistance to tar sands oil, fracking for oil and gas and the construction of extensive new pipeline networks may be the most persistent contribution of the evolving climate justice movement." In Canada, the pipeline conflict has helped raise awareness and mobilise diverse groups of people around two urgent and overlapping crises: an ongoing violation of Indigenous rights that has led to staggering inequality between Indigenous and non-Indigenous people, and a climate crisis that increases threats and harms to land, ecosystems and people.

Both authors have been involved with the anti-pipeline movements in Canada from the dual position of researcher and activist. This chapter brings together findings from our respective graduate research projects wherein we both interviewed movement actors. On the whole, the chapter takes the form of a conversation with anti-pipeline movements, shedding light on how people in these movements are understanding the crises and envisioning the world they want. Section two provides an overview of the inequality and climate crises, arguing that political and mainstream ENGO responses have been inadequate to address the systemic nature of the crises and to produce adequate solutions. From there, we describe the social resistance against pipelines across Canada.

In section three, we ground our work in various relevant academic literatures and explain the methods used in our respective research projects. We then dedicate section four to presenting the conversations we had with people in the movements. Section five moves into a discussion of what has been learned through bringing our research findings together. We conclude that this movement of movements is blazing the trail to theories, stories and worldviews that are more apt to deal with the twin crises of inequality and environmental change. As part of the global climate justice movement, these activists are broadening conceptions of "environment" to include the wellbeing of both people and planet, thereby rejecting narrow, false solutions and calling for radical transformation of the political, economic and thought systems driving the climate crises.

Crises and responses

Canada's inequality crisis: pushing people to the margins for more power and land

In his recently published book, "*Reconciliation Manifesto*," the late Arthur Manuel, Secwepemc leader and respected Indigenous thinker, makes clear the deep inequality between Indigenous and non-Indigenous people in Canada. Manuel (2017, p. 78) writes:

> If you want to measure the effects of Canada's racist and colonial policies towards Indigenous peoples you only have to look at the fact that while Canada was recently number one in the international quality of life indicator, Indigenous people within its borders languished at number seventy-eight.

The findings of the Truth and Reconciliation Commission of Canada (2015, pp. 146–147) corroborate the systemic inequality:

> The income gap is pervasive: non-Aboriginal Canadians earn more than Aboriginal workers. . . . The proportion of Aboriginal adults below the poverty line, regardless of age and gender, is much higher than that of non-Aboriginal adults. . . . The depth of poverty is also much greater, with Aboriginal people having an average income that falls further below the poverty line on average than that of non-Aboriginal adults.

Systemic poverty crises in First Nations communities are exacerbated as they continue to lose their land base and face infringement by resource companies, property developers and pipeline builders. Indigenous scholars Alfred and Corntassel (2005, p. 612) call this Canada's long tradition of "colonial dispossession." Similarly, Barker and Lowman (2015) remark that both the Canadian nation-state and economy are dependent on the land that was taken from Indigenous nations; lands that those nations continue to contest. In response to these colonial projects, in September 2017 the United Nations Committee on the Elimination of Racial Discrimination "urged the [Canadian] government to remedy what it found were persistent violations of the rights of Indigenous peoples" (Human Rights Watch, 2018, n.p.).

Canada's climate crisis: pushing the planet to the brink for more oil

The resource extraction economy that has driven colonial dispossession and ongoing violation of Indigenous rights is also driving climate change. Whereas the unprecedented transformation of planet Earth in the modern era would have been impossible without the vast amounts of energy unleashed by fossil fuels (Mitchell, 2011), the negative impacts of carbon fuels on the Earth's climate have multiplied at an alarming rate in recent years (e.g., Steffen et al., 2015; Crutzen, 2006). Sixteen of the seventeen warmest years on record were in the 21st century as the average global surface temperature has increased by 1.1 degrees Celsius since the 1800s (NASA, 2018). The effects of these changes on ecosystems, weather patterns and ocean circulation, as well as on food systems, land use and more are tremendous.

Despite knowledge about the catastrophic effects of fossil-fuelled climate change, and government promises to "provide national leadership" to "put a price on carbon and reduce emissions" (Government of Canada, 2015), the production of polluting, unconventional fuels like tar sands and shale oil has increased sharply, leading to Canada becoming the fourth largest global oil producer in 2017 (Energy Information Administration, n.d.). With much of Canadian oil and gas reserves in the landlocked province of Alberta, fossil fuel companies require pipeline infrastructure to expand tar sands oil production and meet market demand, further complicating public policy attempts toward decarbonisation.

Failure of political and mainstream environmental responses

It becomes apparent that Canada and the entire world are facing two interrelated crises of climate change and inequality. Both crises call for massive social transformations, but current top-down governance is failing to bring about the required changes at many scales. Despite symbolic gestures such as the Truth and Reconciliations Commission, and grand statements about signing the United Nations Declaration on the Rights of Indigenous Peoples (UNDRIP) and the Paris Climate Accord, the Canadian government pursues the extractive economy status quo, profoundly aggravating the climate crisis while systemically violating the rights and wellbeing of Indigenous people. Whether due to subsidies, industry lobbying, lack of public or political will, or a combination of all these factors, a fair and equitable energy transition to cleaner renewables is thoroughly stalled in Canada, even if it is both urgently needed (Jacobson, 2011) and affordable (CCPA, 2015).

In times of socio-ecological emergencies and political impasses, people's movements working from the bottom up hold much promise for advancing social transformation (Bond, 2012). With a need for such action to counter inertia from government, mainstream environmental NGO efforts to catalyse a shift in Canada's energy economy – despite some victories – have come up short. Moreover, their narrow framing of "the environment" may inadvertently reinforce the Trudeau Liberal narrative of balancing the oil-based economy with the environment (Judd, 2018). Geographer Erik Swyngedouw (2011, p. 265) argues that a trend in NGO discourse and strategy that frames environmental and climate change mostly in terms of carbon and greenhouse gas emissions can work against social movements' work for deeper systemic transformation. Quantification of impacts is certainly one important step in climate mitigation. However, an insufficiently deep engagement with the cultural dimensions and lived experiences of climate change may be blocking progress toward justice and sustainability and, at worst, institutionalising false solutions that exacerbate the problems.

The anti-pipeline movement(s) in Quebec and across Canada

As government and mainstream organisational efforts to act on Canada's climate and inequality crises sputter, a vibrant, diverse and committed grassroots "movement of movements" has coalesced around pipelines to stop the expansion of the tar sands (Black et al., 2014). This opposition consists of at least four distinct but overlapping convergences of people, including (1) Indigenous communities defending their lands and waters and rights as part of the wider Indigenous resistance that has been going on since European contact, (2) environment/climate justice movements mobilising in solidarity with Indigenous people and espousing both environmental and social justice goals, (3) mainstream ENGOs espousing primarily environmental goals, and (4) communities and citizens along pipeline routes mobilising to protect local ecosystems and their private property. These groups have joined forces in various ways and in different places to oppose pipeline development proposed to go west, south and east from the Alberta Tar Sands.

Tactics and strategies used by these movements range from education, divestment campaigns and lobbying to lawsuits, protests and direct action. But arguably, the most powerful leverage in these movements comes from the inherent, treaty, constitutional and international rights of Indigenous people (Ditchburn, 2018). In Quebec, actions were focused on policy concertation, lobbying and publishing reports, and pressure tactics to shame government and corporations for environmentally irresponsible actions, as well as a month-long march (*La marche des peuples pour la Terre Mère*, or the People's Walk for Mother Earth) along a proposed pipeline route. In British Columbia (BC), tactics have centred around Indigenous re-occupations on traditional territories to block pipeline construction. Building resistance communities and permanent structures at key sites along pipeline routes became a way to assert Indigenous sovereignty over threatened lands and waters. In both BC and Quebec, as well as Ontario, there have also been acts of civil disobedience, including manually shutting off existing pipelines. This has led to multiple and serious criminal charges against anti-pipeline activists and Indigenous land defenders.

A pivotal example of a campaign linking together resistance efforts across the country was led by Kanien'kehá:ka/Mohawk Grand Chief Serge Simon. The "Treaty Alliance Against Tar Sands Expansion" (2016) mobilised more than 100 Indigenous Nations across North America to oppose "the increased destruction and poisoning of the lands, waters and air of the Indigenous Peoples directly on the frontlines and downstream of the Tar Sands." As of the writing of this chapter, anti-pipeline opposition has managed to contribute to the cancellation of several pipelines in Canada, including the Northern Gateway and Energy East projects, and is currently fiercely resisting the Kinder Morgan pipeline.

Grounding our work in academic literature and presenting methodologies

This section explains the analytical and theoretical frameworks and research methods used in the respective authors' research projects. The two projects are based on different but complementary theoretical and methodological frameworks involving in-depth interviews with activists and organisers in anti-pipeline movements in Canada. Interviewees include people from communities directly threatened by the pipeline development (via potential spills and/or through the violation of Indigenous rights), as well as people acting in solidarity with directly impacted communities. All interviewees can be considered to be threatened indirectly, over the longer term, by pipeline contributions to climate change. The findings from the two qualitative research projects have been brought together in this chapter so that their overlaps and divergences may shed more light on how the people in these movements are understanding the crises and envisioning the future.

PROJECT 1

The analytical and theoretical frameworks for Project 1 draw primarily on environmental sociology and political ecology, providing important intellectual tools to unpack the forces and counterforces at play in Canada's energy and economic systems. Sociologists Murphy and Murphy (2012) argue that a century of fossil fuel dependence has resulted in major legislative, infrastructural and cultural barriers to scaling back hydrocarbon fuel extraction and consumption in Canada. In turn, environmental sociologists bring in important critiques of how capitalist regimes organise social and economic relations in ways that are often at odds with the Earth's biophysical limits (Foster et al., 2011). Political ecology scholars also examine how dominant political-economic regimes of neoliberalism play a chief role in shaping policy and economic responses to fossil-fuelled environmental change (Castree, 2008; Heynen et al., 2007) while also warning against reducing complex social relations to overarching political-economic structures (Labban, 2014; Huber, 2013). Finally, in response to political-economic and infrastructural "carbon lock-in" (Unruh, 2000), other scholars demonstrate a global trend of social resistance to resource extraction (Veltmeyer and Bowles, 2014; Willow, 2014; Horowitz, 2012). Amidst the sticky intricacies of pipeline politics, such fine-tuned critiques were well-appreciated.

As part of a Master's research project, "Pipeline Politics: Capitalism, Extractivism, and Resistance in Canada," at Concordia University, Kristian conducted a series of in-depth, semi-structured interviews with activists, organisers and community members involved in the anti-pipeline movement in the province of Quebec. Between November 2014 and February 2015, interviews were conducted with 17 different people through snowball sampling based on contacts made through involvement in climate justice movements in Canada. The composition of respondents is elaborated in Table 33.1 in Section 6.

As the overwhelming scientific consensus about climate change's severity contrasts with meagre attempts at international and domestic policy action to address the crisis, listening to and analysing diverse perspectives of resistance against tar sands pipelines helped bring to the surface grievances regarding a lack of fit between pipeline expansion projects and Canadian government climate policy promises. Within this context, the central question of the research project was: "What is the basis of the anti-Energy East pipeline argument in Quebec, and how is that argument articulated, enacted and legitimised by civil society and social movement actors?" The project's hypothesis was that resistance to pipelines has become a major proxy for a deeper debate about how governance of natural resource extraction and pipeline construction has become dominated by capitalist economic calculations, thereby eclipsing crucial social and ecological considerations. While the project did not map out the entire public debate on pipelines, it focused on how discourses of disagreement with pipeline projects attempted to challenge the normativity of fossil fuel extraction. Within this context, critical discourse analysis (Blommaer and Bulcaen, 2000; Dryzek, 2013) was used for analysing the interview data as a means of bringing breadth and depth to dissenting voices.

PROJECT 2

Project 2 is grounded in Social Movements Studies, Transformations Studies and Indigenous Scholarship, all of which shed light on the ways that social movements work to bring about social change (Carrol, 2016; Solnit, 2016; Scheidel et al., 2017; Kothari et al., 2014; Temper and Del Bene, 2016). Movement actors' framings of problems, solutions and visions of a better world help guide their strategies for catalysing social transformation (Moore et al., 2014; Snow and Benford, 1988; Davis, 2012). As Kelley (2002, quoted in Choudry, 2015, p. 39) writes: "Revolutionary dreams erupt out of political engagement; collective social movements are incubators of new knowledge." Through engaging in social change, activists develop, store and offer insight into society's most pressing problems.

The vital intellectual work of social movements involves what various scholars refer to as framing, sense-making and storytelling. Social Movement scholars are attentive to "*collective action frames*," which movement actors formulate to express their "grievances, strategies and reasons for action" (Davis, 2012, p. 7). Social-ecological systems transformation scholars Moore et al. (2014) identify "*sense-making*" as a way that activists strive to make sense of their current situation by analysing which facets most need changing (Moore et al., 2014). Related to this process is the work of *envisioning*, which helps foster the idea that a different order of things is possible through conceiving alternative pathways (Moore et al., 2014).

Such social movement processes help create a *common story* to help motivate action (Buechler, 2011; Moore et al., 2014). Stories are indispensable to social change. As Reinsborough and Canning (2010, p. 45) put it, "Every social change effort is inherently a conflict between the status quo and the change agents to control the framing on an issue. This is the battle of the story." Stories and storytelling is central to many Indigenous cultures and approaches to change and are directly relevant to addressing the crises of inequality and climate in Canada. As Pottawatomi and Ojibwe scholar Hayden King affirms, "[T]he understanding and interpreting of Indigenous stories may be a principled way of beginning to reimagine healthy relationships among Indigenous peoples, and perhaps if they are willing to listen, with non-Indigenous people" (paraphrased by Coburn, 2015, p. 37). Though social movement theorising and analyses do not necessarily follow standards of academic inquiry, movement actors are experts, in their own right, about the processes of social change (Choudry, 2015). Their expertise is derived from practice and lived experience. Movement theories are crucially meaningful for being grounded in and arising organically out of engagement in the hard work of social change. These voices are underheard in academia. But, as Choudry (2015) emphasises, the intellectual work that takes place within and between movements provides vital contributions to identifying and implementing better, more all-encompassing solutions and designing transformative policies and projects.

As part of a PhD research project at McGill University, entitled "Systems Change in the Anthropocene: Towards Decolonizing and Decarbonizing Canada," 36 in-depth, semi-structured interviews were conducted with people active in Indigenous land defence and environmental/climate justice movements across Canada between May and October 2017. For this project, the research question was "How do people in these movements understand the problems and their causes and how do they envision the world they want?" Selection of interviewees was conducted through snowball sampling methods, with initial interviewees being identified through intensive participant observation in the movements. The make-up of this sample is detailed in Table 33.2. The data analysis process involved multiple stages of coding using QDA Miner software and was guided by Grounded Theory, which allows the research findings to constitute original theory that emerges directly from the voices and viewpoints of the people interviewed, rather than the interview data being used to confirm or refute existing academic theory.

The conversations

All of the people who were interviewed in these two research projects share the common cause of stopping pipelines. Interestingly, none of them framed pipelines as the crux of the problem, instead naming larger concerns about resource extraction, the violation of Indigenous rights, climate change, inequality, water pollution and other issues. Furthermore, respondents presented these issues as being symptoms of and driven by deeper forces and structures, including capitalism, colonialism, systems of domination and a fundamental disconnection from land and from each other. They shared their visions of a more just and ecologically viable world they are actively working to bring about in their own respective ways. To date, much of Canada's energy future conversation has occurred in government or corporate public consultation forums and in mainstream media that are usually constrained by "narrow techno-economic considerations" (Hiemstra, 2013, p. 1). In the following pages, we aim to show that these movements are serving to correct that systemic bias. We represent respondents' analyses and visioning by relying heavily on their own words, weaving them together into a conversation we feel to be more productive of just and sustainable alternatives. *N.B.: Activists are not named to conform with the requirements of the respective research ethics protocols in protecting respondents' identities.*

Understanding the problems and their causes

As people got involved with resisting pipelines, they further broadened their understanding of associated environmental and social problems and their causes. One ENGO campaigner framed resistance against pipelines as an opportunity to "get through to people about the risks related to a fossil fuel-based economy" (K16). Similarly, another campaigner from a Montreal-based ENGO said that the pipeline "was a great educational vector. Getting people from a year ago [who] would be just:'Oh, I don't want this in my backyard!' to actually start talking about climate change, and how we need to be moving away from fossil fuels" (K04).

Key social actors blocking a wide-ranging transition from fossil fuels were, according to one citizen who campaigned against tar sands oil refineries in Montreal, "oil companies . . . [who] don't care about the environment, who don't care about people's health, who don't care about the rivers" (K08). This touches upon the complex issue of responsibility. As one climate justice organiser from Quebec said, "When it comes to climate change, we know who's responsible for the worst of emissions and also who's profiting from those emissions . . . climate change is about power and who has the power in society" (J36). One Quebec resident of a town threatened by a pipeline project and member of a province-wide anti-pipeline network specified that the fight was not strictly against oil, pipelines and fossil fuel companies. Naming tar sands pipelines as mere aspects of a broader system of exploitation that benefits a few "foreign companies" to the "detriment of the local population," she said that

> [t]he conclusion we come to is that we are all facing a wall . . . that we'll hit very soon. We see that it's not working anymore, that there is something that just doesn't work in our society. In fact, it's capitalism that is put into question in a very global way.
>
> *(K10)*

Similarly, a social justice organiser from southern Ontario also pinned the current crises on "capitalism. I mean, we're never going to have, in my opinion, climate justice or any sort of sustainable energy system under capitalism" (J17). An Anishinabe qwe activist and scholar from Northern Ontario pointed out that "it goes back to . . . overconsumption, right? It's just a great big vicious circle we are living in, and the government is promoting it" (J09).

The accumulation of capital and the unhindered production of oil in a finite, living system like the planet Earth is clearly problematic, and respondents raised questions regarding the unfair, uneven impacts of that system. As a young woman student organiser in Quebec put it: "Development of fossil fuel projects [impacts] communities that are already more marginalised because of the way that society is set up" (J10). Regarding such deep-seated environmental injustices in society, one social justice organiser in Vancouver said: "I talk about environmental racism. . . . It's about how violence is enacted on communities and land. . . . Line 9 pipeline is a good example. The pipeline goes thru Jane and Finch which is a highly racialised neighbourhood and then goes through Indigenous territories" (J29). A Kanien'kehá:ka activist said, "It's easy to say environmental racism, right. There is classism attached to it also" (J05).

Beyond capitalism, both Indigenous and non-Indigenous people in the anti-pipeline movement named systemic colonialism as a root cause of both the climate and inequality crises in Canada. One interviewee stated that "the colonization and disregard for Indigenous rights is what has allowed for all the fossil fuel extraction project in Canada" (J23). Another put it like this: "What we have seen over centuries is the forced displacement of people from their original lands, [followed by] the wholesale destruction of those lands . . . [and] their way[s] of life" (J08). An Anishinabe/Ojibway scholar reminds us that "we're still living in the midst of colonialism. Though some Canadians may not see this, it is because these unequal, unjust systems are so ingrained and foundational to Canadian culture and economy it can remain invisible to people" (J31).

Indigenous people not only suffer from unjust, colonial systems; they are often blamed for the damage those systems cause. As one Mi'kmaw warrior and thinker asserted, "The government and industry has never given up a single inch of indigenous soil back to us. They've never given us our freedoms back. . . . [Yet they see it as] somehow our fault. Poverty is our fault. Social dysfunction is our fault" (J36). Furthermore, a Kanien'kehá:ka/Mohawk activist explained that "They condescend to us. . . . [They] make us think we're stupid, that we don't know the science about the extractive projects. . . . [T]hey say it's for the economy. It's part of the system, to break you down. . . . to keep Indigenous people off the land [and] to open the land to exploitation and occupation" (J05).

It becomes clear that inequality, climate change, colonialism and capitalism are not separate forces and structures, but linked in deep-seated, complex ways. In several interviews, people explained how they understand these links. A Montreal-based activist blamed "an ongoing process of empire that requires constant growth of resources, expansion of territories and constant growth. It has different faces, [including] misogyny . . . [and] racism. All of those things are true, but empire and capitalism are the flip side of one another" (J08).

Dominion and domination came up in several interviews. One Montreal activist associated the concept of domination with white supremacy, the idea that "people want to be on top of other people" (J18). West-coast anti-logging veteran activist expressed it like this: "Capitalism is the problem, and patriarchy, and that whole mind set. We can clearly see that it is designed to subjugate not only the natural world but also people" (J11). A Kanien'kehá:ka/Mohawk activist named "dominionism" as a mind set, explaining that "these companies . . . [t]hey've trained the public to think about the natural world as a resource. . . . Everything that exists becomes commodity. Things to be bought and sold." He goes on to explain the links between dominion, colonisation and superiority: "This idea of colonization, this idea that we can be above other peoples. You see that again and again, the notion of dominionism. . . . God made the earth and gave Man dominion over earth. It's all here for you to exploit" (J05). He went on to describe how "dominionism" is driving the oppression of and violence against women, but that this mindset is fundamentally at odds with Indigenous worldviews.

Here, we begin to see how respondents framed the links between climate change, colonialism and the oppression of women. In a recent webinar hosted by Indigenous Climate Action (ICA), Eriel Tchekwie Deranger, the executive director of ICA and member of the Athabasca Chipewyan First Nation, emphasised that "climate justice is gender justice" and that "violence against land is violence against women." She said that women are "disproportionately impacted by climate and the drivers of climate change" in many ways, including through the increase in sexual violence that accompanies the "man camps" that house transient workers in the oil and gas industry. Also on the webinar, Melina Laboucan-Massimo, member of the Lubicon Cree First Nation and leader in community-led solar energy projects, said:

> We are fighting resource extraction, we are fighting violence against the land, and we're fighting for justice for our women. Our families are constantly fighting on many spheres. It's not just climate justice, it's [also] justice for the women, for the four-legged ones, the two-winged ones, that are all integral to our being on mother earth.

Envisioning the world(s) we want

Though most of the people we talked to are directly involved in opposing pipelines, in all cases stopping pipelines is not their end goal. They evoked visions of equality and justice and of healing relationships, of decentralised, autonomous communities powered by clean energy. Almost all of author Jen Gobby's respondents talked about decolonising Canada with the self-determination and rebuilding of diverse Indigenous Nations. They talked about lives of deeper connection with the land and with each other.

Several people specifically voiced their visions for an energy transition away from fossil fuels. A campaigner whose day job was with an ENGO and who volunteered on her own time for an anti-pipeline citizen group said, "Not everyone is on the same page, but everyone shares a vision of a more egalitarian society: more just[ice], greener, more for the citizens and not for big corporations . . . [and] definitely toward more green energies" (K09). A community organiser in Northern BC who works closely with First Nations discussed how the

> industry can come in here and . . . say whatever they want and we're like, "Actually, that's not our story." . . . [The] vision is we want jobs and we want a solid economy. . . . [W]e want fish and clean air and rich, alive, functioning cultures that are respected.
>
> *(J34)*

For her, a post-carbon economy can create good jobs while protecting the environment and people's rights. A Prairie-based activist and journalist also discussed links between energy transition and respecting Indigenous rights: "Respect . . . for treaties [and] Indigenous rights . . . goes hand in hand with a very rapid transition, all the way from fossil fuel extraction towards other forms of social order, community living, [and] energy use" (J23). A Dene writer and organiser said that in her work, her goal is "to better the lives of Indigenous people. . . . I feel like I need to care for and nurture Indigenous culture, and hopefully, Canada will be on this side of the story as well" (J22). As if in response, a Mi'kmaw warrior and thinker spoke about how "decolonization . . . [is] the displacement of western nation state sovereignty over Indigenous lands" (J36). For him,

> this becomes a bigger solution. . . . The rebuilding of Indigenous nations becomes the answer to how do we deal with climate change. It isn't just another issue of political justice off to the side, completely segmented and away from the issue of climate change and pipelines. It's one and the same. It is a bigger solution to these problems.
>
> *(J36)*

To him, addressing the environmental and inequality crises in Canada means Indigenous self-determination and "eradicating the coloniser." In this, he is seeking to dismantle "the political economic social structures that support colonialism" (J36).

In their varying visions of decolonisation, most respondents evoked the need for a radical transformation in the distribution of power and land. Such a move would pose a monumental challenge to the status quo in Canada and, in so doing, offer profound solutions to the climate and inequality crises. Though decolonial theorising is being led by Indigenous peoples in Canada and in these movements, many non-Indigenous people also echoed these visions of a decolonial Canada. One anarchist activist remarked upon

> a slogan that says a lot: . . . for a life unmediated by the state, we must defend the land. . . . I don't see decolonization as returning to the past . . . [T]hat's impossible. But as a way forward . . . the goal is the creation of autonomous zones that are able to meet own needs without the fossil fuel economy and the state.
>
> *(J06)*

These visions of autonomy connect with a Vancouver-based social justice organiser's "dream of decentralised, self-determined communities" (J29). She expressed this vision as a radical alternative to the "hetero-patriarchal colonial capitalism system [that] is so predatorial. It just doesn't allow anything else to exist" (J29). She feels that the "idea of having this mosaic of beautiful ecosystems of communities actually self-determining. [This] is very decolonising in my imagination. . . . I truly believe that there's a world out there that is so much better" (J29).

The flourishing, decentralised communities resonated with other interviewees' visions of building community, of reconnecting to land, and of healing relationships. A young, Montreal-based Jewish woman spoke about love as central to the world she wants. "The boiled-down essence of what I believe in is that it's about love. Cornel West said it best when he said . . . 'Justice is love in public.' I think that justice work is, so much of it is about this is how we interact with each other" (J07). Correspondingly, amidst a colonial and capitalist society, social relations of care and love require activism and shared struggle. As one Montreal-based film-maker and climate justice organiser said about her work,

> It's like Alice Walker's famous quote of [how] activism is the rent I pay for living on this planet. . . . It goes back to the Indigenous worldview. . . . If people are taught that they are all stewards of the land, then it becomes a natural way to respond to the crisis. If we're taught from an early age that your job is to be kind and support people, you figure out ways to do good.
>
> *(J08)*

In the end, the story that rings through most poignantly from bringing these conversations together is that *capitalism and colonialism have separated us from one another and from the land and that to create a more justice and viable world, we need to reconnect with each other and reconnect with the land.* Eriel Deranger concluded in her aforementioned webinar that "connection with the land will be the answer to climate change." To do that, decolonisation is necessary and to do so "doesn't have to be complicated. It is the return to and connection with the land. . . . Return it to the rightful owners and we all return to it and develop the connection, then the solutions come more naturally."

Discussion and conclusion

Through our process of listening, weaving together and retelling the analyses, theories and visions shared with us by people in anti-pipeline movements, we see stories emerge that offer much-needed counter-narratives to the mainstream discourse in Canada about the climate and inequality crises. These are not the stories we hear in the media, government policy briefs or corporate publicity. They offer a fundamentally different story of what is wrong in Canada and what needs to be done about it that is rooted in the lived experiences of people most impacted by the crises. These deeply grounded understandings, stories and visions of the problems and solutions are crucial to bringing about the kinds of transformations necessary. As Eriel Deranger (2018, n.p.) said, "We are at a moment, we either change the narrative, change the story, bring in the people who have been marginalised, or we go ahead with business as usual." As follows, Canadian scientist, activist and broadcaster David Suzuki described the clash between pro-oil and anti-oil positions within the pipeline debate as a:

> battle of mind sets [against] the dominant worldview that sees this [land] not as sacred territory but as opportunity. And that's our problem! If we continue to look at the world and the land around us just in terms of dollars and cents, we're going to destroy the very things that make that land so precious, the very things that keep us alive and healthy.
>
> *(cited in Vancouver Observer, 2014)*

For some respondents, these are not new stories. Rather, they are based in longstanding Indigenous worldviews that understand the fundamental link between people and lands and waters. For others, through beginning to feel the impacts of the fossil fuel economy and/or through engagement in pipeline resistance with Indigenous and social justice and decolonial movements, they are deepening their understandings of the problems and beginning to envision radically different futures.

In bringing together our separate research projects and these separate sets of interviews, we see much overlap in the understandings and visions present, but there are also important differences that we do not wish to gloss over. Indeed, as an Anishinaabe scholar pointed out, "I have a couple of mantras that have been on my mind recently. One is *'nuance is sacred'* and another is Nigerian writer Chimamanda Ngozi Adichie's line *'Beware the dangers of a single story'*." As committed activists and scholars, we too understand the benefit of nuanced critique while also doing justice to the multiplicities of understandings and visions that were shared with us.

One key difference is that while the predominantly white activists with whom author Kristian Gareau spoke in Quebec went as far as naming capitalism as driving the climate crisis, most of author Jen Gobby's respondents from across Canada went deeper in bringing a decolonial analysis to their understandings of the problems and visions of the world they want. Many of the latter respondents identified colonial land dispossession as an inherent tool of capitalist accumulation, and that the related forces of capitalism and colonialism are key drivers of both the climate crisis and the inequality crisis in Canada. The variation between the analyses offered by the two sets of interviews likely reflects our different research projects' timelines, objectives and research questions, as well as who we interviewed. This divergence also potentially reflects regional variations in the composition of anti-pipeline movements, with movements in BC being led by Indigenous peoples and involving more social justice groups, whereas in Quebec the movement has been predominantly composed of white environmental groups and citizens. In turn, anti-pipeline movement participation likely reflects important differences between culture and colonial history in Quebec and other parts of Canada. The country and these movements are anything but homogeneous.

Despite these very important divergences in how environmental and other social movements are taking up decolonial principles and praxis (explored much further elsewhere, e.g., Fortier, 2017 and Walia, 2012), there is much overlap in the stories emerging from these interviews. They are all challenging the common story of Canada as a peaceful, nature-loving and human-rights-abiding country whilst exposing deep-seated contradictions and injustices at the heart of the nation. In short, these movements offer important analysis showing that a large part of Canada's economy – guided predominantly by the logics of capitalist accumulation and settler colonialism – is based on the destruction of natural systems and the theft of Indigenous land and the violation of Indigenous rights.

Another commonality to the stories we heard was an uncovering and exposing of *root causes* of the crises faced. To varying degrees of depth, we heard people articulate, in their own words, root-cause analyses of the forces driving pipeline development. We see in this a broad taking up of intersectional analysis. Coined by black feminist Kimberle Crenshaw, an *intersectional analysis* explores how different injustices that may seem separate, such as racism, sexism or classism, interact and are linked through a complex of social forces and structures that often share root causes (cited in Collins and Bilge, 2016). Seeing these connections between environmental and social struggles opens the possibility of bringing together previously disparate social movements, which together can exert more influence to bring about change than they can alone. Indeed, Canadian thought-leader Naomi Klein has pointed out that there is a long legacy in Canada of movements working in silos on "separate issues" and failing to see the crucial overlap in their visions. She argues that moving past this siloed approach and creating a "movement of movements" is necessary for creating a strong enough force to shift the trajectory of Canadian energy and economic systems (Klein, 2017).

The anti-pipeline fight in Canada has brought together such a movement of movements, and this chapter has sought to present a brief overview of the deepening analysis that this convergence has been forging. Overall, these analyses make clear that pipelines are the dominion of a few large companies and misguided economics driven by capitalist colonial logic. In an age of multiple, overlapping social and environmental emergencies, very often pipelines exist to the detriment of local people and the land and waters. And, with the intended purchase of the Trans Mountain pipeline project in British Columbia, the government of Canada has demonstrated its preference to align itself with capitalist accumulation and tar sands expansion instead of climate action, social justice, and reconciliation with Indigenous peoples. Nonetheless, the pipeline has not been built yet and resistance continues. Therein, this and other anti-pipeline struggles continue to serve as crucial vectors for collective learning about the social and environmental risks of capitalism, as well as fostering broader understanding of, and making visible, Canada's ongoing systemic colonialism.

While navigating divergent worldviews, sometimes competing interests, and fraught relationships, this convergence of activists, organisers, land defenders and water protectors are working together and apart, to forge pathways forward – ones that work simultaneously toward decarbonising and decolonising Canada, one pipeline at a time.

Appendix

Tables with data about interviewees

Table 33.1 Overview of interviewees for Project 1.

Code	Date	Involvement	Gender	Ethnicity (Indi: Indigenous, Non-Indi: non-Indigenous)	Capacity (Ind: Speaking as Individual Rep: Representing organisation)
K01	Nov. 24, 2014	ENGO	M	Non-Indi	Ind
K02	Nov. 27, 2014	Grassroots	F	Non-Indi	Ind
K03	Nov. 27, 2014	ENGO	F	Non-Indi	Rep
K04	Nov. 28, 2014	ENGO/ Community	F	Non-Indi	Ind/Rep
K05	Dec. 4, 2014	ENGO	M	Non-Indi	Rep
K06	Dec. 4, 2014	Grassroots	Mixed focus group (4 men, 6 women)	Non-Indi	Ind
K07	Dec. 4, 2014	Grassroots	F	Non-Indi	Ind
K08	Dec. 5, 2014	Grassroots	M	Non-Indi	Ind
K09	Dec. 12, 2014	ENGO	F	Non-Indi	Ind
K10	Dec. 12, 2014	Grassroots	F	Non-Indi	Ind
K11	Dec. 15, 2014	Grassroots	M	Non-Indi	Ind
K12	Jan. 6, 2015	Grassroots	M	Non-Indi	Ind
K13	Jan. 9, 2015	ENGO	F	Non-Indi	Ind
K14	Jan. 9, 2015	ENGO	M	Non-Indi	Ind
K15	Jan. 17, 2015	ENGO	M	Non-Indi	Ind
K16	Jan. 20, 2015	ENGO	M	Non-Indi	Ind/Rep
K17	Jan. 28, 2015	Grassroots	M	Non-Indi	Ind

Table 33.2 Overview of interviewees for Project 2.

Code	Date	Involvement	Gender	Ethnicity (Indi: Indigenous Non-Indi: non-indigenous)	Capacity (Ind: Speaking as Individual Rep: Representing organisation)
J01	May 19, 2017	Grassroots	M	Non-Indi	Ind
J02	May 23, 2017	Grassroots	M	Non-Indi	Ind
J03	May 26, 2017	Organisation	M	Non-Indi	Rep
J04	May 29, 2017	Community/Grassroots	M	Indi	Ind
J05	June 1, 2017	Grassroots	M	Non-Indi	Ind
J06	June 2, 2017	Community	M	Indi	Ind
J07	June 5, 2017	Grassroots	M	Indi	Ind
J08	June 6, 2017	Grassroots	F	Non-Indi	Ind
J09	June 7, 2017	Community	F	Indi	Ind
J10	June 7, 2017	Grassroots	F	Non-Indi	Ind
J11	June 7, 2017	Grassroots	F	Non-Indi	Ind
J12	June 9, 2017	Organisation	F	Non-Indi	Org
J13	June 12, 2017	Grassroots	M	Non-Indi	Ind
J14	June 12, 2017	Grassroots	F	Non-Indi	Ind
J15	June 12, 2017	Grassroots	F	Non-Indi	Ind
J16	June 12, 2017	Organisation/Grassroots	M	Non-Indi	Ind
J17	June 13, 2017	Grassroots	F	Indi	Ind
J18	June 15, 2017	Grassroots	M	Non-Indi	Ind
J19	June 20, 2017	Community	F	Indi	Rep
J20	June 22, 2017	Grassroots	M	Non-Indi	Ind
J21	June 22, 2017	Grassroots	M	Non-Indi	Ind
J22	June 23, 2017	Grassroots/Community	F	Indi	Ind
J23	June 26, 2017	Grassroots	M	Non-Indi	Ind
J24	June 26, 2017	Grassroots/Organisation	F	Non-Indi	Ind
J25	June 28, 2017	Grassroots	F	Non-Indi	Ind
J26	June 28, 2017	Organisation	M	Non-Indi	Ind
J27	July 6, 2017	Grassroots	M	Non-Indi	Ind
J28	July 10, 2017	Organisation	F	Non-Indi	Rep
J29	July 11, 2017	Grassroots	F	Non-Indi	Ind
J30	July 13, 2017	Organisation	F	Non-Indi	Ind
J31	July 17, 2017	Community/Scholar	M	Indi	Ind
J32	Aug 7, 2017	Organisation	M	Non-Indi	Rep
J33	Aug. 10, 2017	Grassroots/Scholar	F	Non-Indi	Ind
J34	Aug. 11, 2017	Organisation	F	Non-Indi	Rep
J35	Aug 28, 2017	Grassroots/Community	M	Indi	Ind
J36	Oct. 3, 2017	Organisation	F	Non-Indi	Ind

References

Alfred, T. and Corntassel, J. (2005) 'Being Indigenous: Resurgences Against Contemporary Colonialism'. *Government and Opposition*, vol 40, no 4, pp 597–614

Barker, A.J. and Battell Lowman, E. (2015) *Settler: Identity and Colonialism in 21st Century Canada*. Fernwood Publishing, Halifax, Canada

Black, T., D'Arcy, S., and Weis, T. (eds.). (2014) *A Line in the Tar Sands: Struggles for Environmental Justice*. PM Press, Oakland

Blommaert, J. and Bulcaen, C. (2000) 'Critical Discourse Analysis'. *Annual Review of Anthropology*, vol 29, no 1, pp 447–466

Bond, P. (2012) *Politics of Climate Justice: Paralysis Above, Movement Below*. University of Kwa Zulu Natal Press, Cape Town

Buechler, S.M. (2011) *Understanding Social Movements: Theories From the Classical Era to the Present*. Routledge, London

Carroll, W.K. and Sarker, K. (2016) *A World to Win: Contemporary Social Movements and Counter-hegemony*. ARP Books, Winnipeg, Canada

Castree, N. (2008) 'Neoliberalising nature: the logics of deregulation and reregulation'. *Environment and planning A*, vol 40, no 1, pp 131–152

CCPA – Canadian Center for Policy Alternatives. (2015) *The Alternative Federal Budget 2015: Delivering the Good*. www.policyalternatives.ca/publications/reports/alternative-federal-budget-2015

Choudry, A. (2015) *Learning Activism: The Intellectual Life of Contemporary Social Movements*. University of Toronto Press, Toronto

Coburn, E. (ed.). (2015) *More Will Sing Their Way to Freedom: Indigenous Resistance and Resurgence*. Fernwood Publishing, Winnipeg, Canada

Collins, P.H. and Bilge, S. (2016) *Intersectionality*. Polity Press. Cambridge

Crutzen, P.J. 2006. 'The "anthropocene"'. In *Earth System Science in the Anthropocene* (pp. 13–18). Springer, Berlin, Heidelberg

Davis, J.E. (ed.). (2012) *Stories of Change: Narrative and Social Movements*. SUNY Press, Albany

Deranger, E. (2018) Violence Against the Land Is Violence Against Women Webinar. *Indigenous Climate Action*. www.indigenousclimateaction.com/single-post/2018/03/19/Violence-Against-the-Land-is-Violence-Against-Women

Ditchburn, J. (2018) 'Indigenous Rights Aren't a Subplot of Pipeline Debate'. *Policy Options*, April 11, n.p.

Dryzek, J.S. (2013) *The Politics of the Earth: Environmental Discourses*. Oxford University Press, Oxford

Energy Information Administration. (n.d.) *World Oil Production*. www.eia.gov/beta/international/index.cfm?view=production

Fortier, C. (2017) *Unsettling the Commons: Social Movements Within, Against, and Beyond Settler Colonialism*. ARP Books, Winnipeg

Foster, J.B., Clark, B., and York, R. (2011) *The Ecological Rift: Capitalism's War on the Earth*. NYU Press, New York

Gareau, K. (2016) *Pipeline Politics: Capitalism, Extractivism, and Resistance in Canada*. MA thesis, Concordia University, Montreal, Canada

Government of Canada. (2015) *Minister McKenna Congratulates British Columbia on Its Commitment to Climate Action*. www.canada.ca/en/environment-climate-change/news/2015/12/minister-mckenna-congratulates-british-columbia-on-its-commitment-to-climate-action.html

Heynen, N., McCarthy, J., Prudham, S., and Robbins, P. (2007) *Neoliberal Environments: False Promises and Unnatural Consequences*. Routledge, London

Hiemstra, J. (2013) 'The Northern Gateway Pipeline Panel and the Public Interest: The Shaping Influence of Canada's "Plausibility Structure" and "Symbolic Universe"'. *Paper Delivered at Canadian Political Science Association Annual Conference, June 4–6, 2013*. University of Victoria, Victoria, British Columbia

Horowitz, L.S. (2012) 'Power, Profit, Protest: Grassroots Resistance to Industry in the Global North'. *Capitalism Nature Socialism*, vol 23, no 3, pp 20–34

Huber, M.T. (2013) *Lifeblood: Oil, Freedom, and the Forces of Capital*. University of Minnesota Press, Minneapolis

Human Rights Watch. (2018) *World Report 2018*. www.hrw.org/world-report/2018/country-chapters/canada

Jacobson, M.Z. and Delucchi, M.A. (2011) 'Providing All Global Energy With Wind, Water, and Solar Power, Part I: Technologies, Energy Resources, Quantities and Areas of Infrastructure, and Materials'. *Energy Policy*, vol 39, no 3, pp 1154–1169

Judd, A. (2018) 'We're Standing Up for the National Interest: Trudeau Weighs in on Alberta, B.C. Dispute'. *Global News*, February 7, globalnews.ca/news/4011102/standing-up-for-national-interest-trudeau-weighs-in-alberta-b-c-dispute/

Kelley, R. D. (2002) *Freedom dreams: The black radical imagination.* Beacon Press, Boston

Klein, N. (2017) *No Is Not Enough: Resisting the New Shock Politics and Winning the World We Need.* Knopf Canada, Chicago

Kothari, A. (2014) 'Radical Ecological Democracy: A Path Forward for India and Beyond'. *Development*, vol 57, no 1, pp 36–45

Labban, M. (2014) 'Against Value: Accumulation in the Oil Industry and the Biopolitics of Labour Under Finance'. *Antipode*, vol 46, no 2, pp 477–496

Ljunggren, D. (2018) 'Canada's Trudeau to Meet Premiers on Pipeline Strife'. *Reuters*, April 12, www.reuters.com/article/us-kinder-morgan-cn-pipeline-canada/canadas-trudeau-to-meet-premiers-on-pipeline-strife-idUSKBN1HJ2P7

Manuel, A. and Derrickson, R. (2017) *Reconciliation Manifesto: Recovering the Land, Rebuilding the Economy.* James Lorimer & Company, Ontario, Canada

Mitchell, T. (2011) *Carbon Democracy: Political Power in the Age of Oil.* Verso Books, London

Moore, M.L., Tjornbo, O., Enfors, E., Knapp, C., Hodbod, J., Baggio, J., . . . and Biggs, D. (2014) 'Studying the Complexity of Change: Toward an Analytical Framework for Understanding Deliberate Social-ecological Transformations'. *Ecology and Society*, vol 19, no 4, article 54

Murphy, R. and Murphy, M. (2012) 'The Tragedy of the Atmospheric Commons: Discounting Future Costs and Risks in Pursuit of Immediate Fossil-Fuel Benefits'. *Canadian Review of Sociology/Revue canadienne de sociologie*, vol 49, no 3, pp 247–270

NASA. (2018) *Global Climate Change: Vital Signs of the Planet, Evidence.* climate.nasa.gov/evidence

Reinsborough, P. and Canning, D. (2010) *Re: Imagining Change: How to Use Story-based Strategy to Win Campaigns, Build Movements, and Change the World.* PM Press, Oakland

Solnit, R. (2016) *Hope in the Dark: Untold Histories, Wild Possibilities.* Haymarket Books, Chicago

Scheidel, A., Temper, L., Demaria, F., and Martínez-Alier, J. (2017) 'Ecological Distribution Conflicts as Forces for Sustainability: An Overview and Conceptual Framework'. *Sustainability Science*, pp 1–14

Snow, D.A. and Benford, R.D. (1988) 'Ideology, Frame Resonance, and Participant Mobilization'. *International Social Movement Research*, vol 1, no 1, pp 197–217

Steffen, W., Richardson, K., Rockström, J., Cornell, S.E., Fetzer, I., Bennett, E.M., Biggs, R., Carpenter, S.R., De Vries, W., de Wit, C.A., and Folke, C. (2015) 'Planetary Boundaries: Guiding Human Development on a Changing Planet'. *Science*, vol 347, no 6223, p 1259855

Swyngedouw, E. (2011) 'Depoliticized Environments: The End of Nature, Climate Change and the Post-political Condition'. *Royal Institute of Philosophy Supplement*, vol 69, pp 253–274

Temper, L. and Del Bene, D. (2016) 'Transforming Knowledge Creation for Environmental and Epistemic Justice'. *Current Opinion in Environmental Sustainability*, vol 20, pp 41–49

Tokar, B. (2015) 'Democracy, Localism, and the Future of the Climate Movement'. *World Futures*, vol 71, nos 3–4, pp 65–75

Treaty Alliance Against Tar Sands Expansion. (2016) *Treaty Alliance Against Tar Sands Expansion.* www.treatyalliance.org/wp-content/uploads/2016/12/TreatyandAdditionalInformation-20161216-OL.pdf

Truth and Reconciliation Commission of Canada. (2015) *Final Report of the Truth and Reconciliation Commission of Canada: Honouring the Truth, Reconciling for the Future.* www.trc.ca/websites/trcinstitution/File/2015/Findings/Exec_Summary_2015_05_31_web_o.pdf

Unruh, G.C. (2000) 'Understanding Carbon Lock-in'. *Energy Policy*, vol 28, no 12, pp 817–830

Vancouver Observer. (2014) *David Suzuki Gives Fiery Speech at Kinder Morgan Protest.* www.vancouverobserver.com/news/david-suzuki-burnaby-mountain-support-kinder-morgan-protest

Veltmeyer, H. and Bowles, P. (2014) 'Extractivist resistance: the case of the Enbridge oil pipeline project in Northern British Columbia.' *The Extractive Industries and Society*, vol 1, no 1, pp 59–68

Walia, H. (2012) Decolonizing Together. *Organize! Building From the Local for Global Justice*, pp 240–253

Willow, A.J. (2014) 'The New Politics of Environmental Degradation: Un/expected Landscapes of Disempowerment and Vulnerability'. *Journal of Political Ecology*, vol 21, no 1, pp 237–257

Part VIII

Emerging areas in climate justice

34

Beyond the academy

Reflecting on public scholarship about climate justice

Sonja Klinsky

It is widely acknowledged that climate justice has steadily grown as a field of academic engagement and is now an identifiable strand of enquiry within a number of academic traditions and arenas (Barrett 2013; Gardiner et al. 2010; Okereke and Coventry 2016; Klinsky, Roberts, et al. 2017). While this development is a common part of the academic narrative around climate justice, there has been less interrogation of public scholarship in the climate justice arena.

Public outreach, public scholarship and academic activism are all terms widely used to refer to a range of activities focused on the participation of academics – *as academics* – outside the boundaries of the academy (hooks 1994; Blomley 2008; Burgess 2005; Maxey 2005; Pain 2006; Derickson and Routledge 2015; Burawoy 2004; MacKinnon 2009). The diversity of the terms reflects the reality that engagement takes many forms depending on the aspirations of both the academics and those with whom they are interacting, the political context and the capacities of all those involved. Public scholarship and forms of academic activism feature in many scholarly traditions, and there are undoubtedly overlaps in the experiences of those working in the climate justice context with those in other fields. This being said, considering the speed with which "climate justice" has become a focus of scholarship and the relative silence about this practice within this literature, this chapter is offered as a reflection of some particular features of and decision points about trying to do public scholarship in the climate justice context.

My own efforts to build a practice of public scholarship in the climate justice context have unfolded over almost a decade and have included: sharing research results with members of the public and particular stakeholders directly or through the media; conducting transdisciplinary research with non-academic collaborators; and co-designing and implementing public engagement activities with non-profit organisations. Much, although not all, of this activity has been focused on climate mitigation.[1] Specifically, I will discuss the challenges and opportunities presented by the breadth and multidimensionality of the issue, the complexity of solidarity in this multifaceted and multiscalar context, and the moral weight of climate injustice. Before exploring each of these areas I reflect on the motivations for academics to step beyond the normal bounds of the academy and argue that some degree of public scholarship should be considered an essential metric for evaluating the merit of academic work on climate justice.

Why might public engagement matter to climate justice research?

I suggest that there are two primary motivations for conducting research on the intersections of justice and climate change (Klinsky, Roberts et al. 2017), both of which have implications for framing public scholarship as an important part of academic work on climate justice.

The first reason why scholars might focus on justice and climate change is that researchers are fundamentally called upon to investigate how things work. Moreover, especially for those of us working in public institutions, this research ought to be tailored to benefit society broadly. To the extent that climate change is a central human challenge of our current era, then we need research that identifies and describes the core political dynamics of human interactions with climate change. As David Victor has argued in a call for greater participation of social and political scientists in the climate change context, "the insights that matter are out in the darkness, far from the places that the natural sciences alone can illuminate" (Victor 2015).

Interrogating the justice aspects of climate change is essential because political action is sensitive to people's perceptions of justice. The human sense of fairness is acute and is connected to many behavioural decisions (van den Bos and Lind 2002; Skitka and Mullen 2002; Greene and Haidt 2002). Perceptions about fairness and related justice issues can also be purposefully utilised in the political arena. If we accept the notion that perception of (in)justice can shape political action, then as scholars we need to understand something about how actors themselves perceive (in)justice issues in the climate context, as these are very likely to be contributing to political activity. For example, without understanding companies' concerns about fairness in relation to competitors facing differential economic regulations, it would be impossible to understand the political challenges that have underpinned the design and implementation of greenhouse gas policies in a range of jurisdictions (Grubb and Neuhoff 2006; Convery, Dunne, and Joyce 2013; Meckling 2011).

In addition, because of the depth of inequalities across a wide range of dimensions (including but extending beyond income), we cannot assume that all people will be affected equally by climate change or climate policies. Individuals and groups of individuals will experience the same action (or inaction) differently depending on a range of pre-existing statuses and resources (Olsson et al. 2014). Without acknowledging systemic components that shape different people's choices and vulnerabilities, we cannot accurately understand the true costs, benefits and trade-offs of any policy action.

In both of these situations, accessing "good data" about the perceptions and motivations driving political action, or about the actual lived costs and benefits of climate policy actions (or inactions) necessarily requires understanding the perspectives of the actors involved. How are scholars to develop such understanding without some level of public engagement? From this perspective, *some element of public engagement is a prerequisite to accessing or generating high-quality data* about motivations and perceptions in a context in which these motivations may be very politically relevant. Listening to and learning from are core components of public scholarship.

The second reason for researchers to focus on the justice dimensions of climate change builds on but is distinct from the first. In addition to merely "understanding" a situation, for some academics the presence of justice dimensions triggers an additional reason to work in this area:

to try to address these injustices. The ubiquitous justice tensions across all dimensions of the climate context raise pointed questions about the ethics of academic work in which researchers personally or professionally benefit from studying situations of injustice if their work is not intended to address them or to facilitate others to do so. Is it morally acceptable for academics to reap benefits directly from their knowledge of injustice and not to orient their work towards addressing these injustices directly or indirectly? Personally I think it is not, particularly in light of all of the other privileges that I as a white, middle-class, well-educated woman in North America already benefit from.

Arguments about the need for scholarship to address societal concerns are increasingly communicated (at least on the surface) by academic institutions facing pressure to renegotiate their social contract by more explicitly explaining how research activities can benefit society. For instance, the Research Excellence Framework system in the UK explicitly acknowledges impact (although aggregated by department); Australia has been experimenting with an Engagement and Impact Assessment framework; and the U.S.-based National Science Foundation requests evidence of "broader impacts" for its large grants. Even if work is not designed to immediately contribute to a remedy, it is increasingly accepted that it should contribute to society directly, or create new ways of seeing the situation that could enable different pathways of action indirectly. Any attempt to "make research useful" is dependent on establishing some forms of public engagement, even if this is only to share knowledge with non-academics in ways that enable them to use it.

From these entwined perspectives, incorporating public engagement within academic work on climate justice is essential both because this engagement allows us to deepen our analyses of the lived experiences and political challenges of climate change, and because it allows us to move towards satisfying broader obligations to contribute positively to remedying – directly or indirectly – injustices.

Challenges and opportunities for public engagement with climate justice

Applied or publicly engaged scholarship has routinely presented individual academics with a number of well-documented challenges and opportunities (Burgess 2005; Pain 2006; McIntyre 2007; MacKinnon 2009). For instance, building the relationships necessary for this type of work takes substantial time – time that is not spent producing publications. In my own case, efforts to get to know and build trust with actors working to shape the international climate regime took several years and thousands of dollars' worth of travel, and were dependent on initial introductions from key gatekeepers. During those years I had few publications emerging directly out of this substantial time, money and energy investment, and these efforts are ongoing.

In addition, the types of products such engagement produces are not always seen as legitimate forms of scholarship within the academy, and if co-created are not under complete control of the academic. Unclear ownership, limited control over research processes and outputs, and large time-to-publication ratios all work against quantified publication metrics that are widely used within academia to assess adequate productivity. It is not surprising that the common wisdom is for junior and non-tenure track faculty to avoid substantial public engagement, as they are more vulnerable to these metrics.

Another common challenge is that value in the academy has often been predicated on notions of objectivity and the ability of the scholar to separate themselves from the political context of their research. Efforts to do more engaged research routinely trigger concerns that such scholarship will be biased or will erode the status of science as a rigorous, disinterested enterprise. This critique has been widely dismissed by those already committed to public scholarship. As Michael Burawoy has argued, because of the scope of political contestation in society, "the pure science position that research must be completely insulated from politics is untenable since antipolitics is no less political than public engagement" (Burawoy 2004, p. 1605). Coming from a slightly different perspective, Dan Sarewitz has argued that even the most "objective" form of research becomes politicised as soon as it is brought as evidence into a political venue (Sarewitz 2004). From this perspective a truly neutral stance is impossible within a politically contested arena, and moreover our choices about what we work on and how we do it is an expression of our core values anyway.

I argue that some form of public engagement is necessary in the climate justice context if we are to fully understand the justice-related concerns and experiences of diverse stakeholders, or to even be able to characterise the true trade-offs that policy decisions may entail. To the extent that academics want their work to benefit a broader community beyond themselves, some form of public scholarship is also essential and unavoidable. The general professional challenges of public scholarship are discussed elsewhere (e.g., MacKinnon 2009; Burgess 2005), so in this essay I want to focus on three aspects of the climate justice context that I think are particularly important to consider for public scholarship: the breadth and multidimensionality of the issue, the complexity of solidarity in this multifaceted and multiscalar context, and the moral weight of climate injustice.

First, because of its breadth and complexity, public engagement around climate justice **necessarily forces academics into a position in which they cannot be "the expert"** or in which they are constantly working at the edges of their expertise. This provides both challenges and opportunities to scholars in this arena.

The climate justice context is too broad, dynamic and multifaceted for one person to ever grasp all its dimensions. Depending on the context in which one is working, you could end up engaging with a wide range of both academics and non-academics. Each sub-community frames the issue in its own way and brings with it particular concerns and forms of expertise. In a journal entry I wrote during the Durban (COP 17) climate negotiations in 2011, I recorded speaking about climate change and justice issues with people using the following frames during just one single day:

- A black American environmental justice activist mobilising around the linkages between race, class, local pollution and climate change
- A white South African union representative concerned about the need for just transitions to "green" jobs
- A South African journalist exploring the intersection of AIDS, community capacity, vulnerability and climate change
- A government official from Sri Lanka concerned that the country would be prevented from building any additional coal power plants to meet domestic electricity demand, despite having only recently completed their first one
- Two European academics working on human development and its connections with adaptation
- A former chief negotiator for a large developed country concerned that sufficient mitigation achievements are becoming impossible due to the political tensions around justice within the UNFCCC
- A Maasai herder representing his community's concerns that drought combined with changing land tenure could impede their ability to successfully depend on herding as a form of livelihood and way of life

- A group of economists and policy advisors from both the Global South and Global North trying to find a way to fund "nationally appropriate mitigation actions" (NAMAs) in developing[2] countries in order to support country sovereignty and facilitate mitigation

Each of these entrances into the climate justice conversation leverages different components of the issue, forms of expertise and types of evidence. Engaging with any (or all) of these people requires acknowledging and pushing the boundaries of one's own expertise and being willing to learn from others. Being open to these alternate framings helps us understand why and how people are using or resisting certain kinds of justice claims. The multiplicity of entry points can be seen to present an opportunity because they can open up new lines of enquiry and help us reflect on the limitations of our own assumptions about the boundaries and meanings of climate justice.

In addition, this diversity of entry points and the potential for them to coexist and overlap also challenges the theoretical or conceptual resources commonly relied upon to make the Gordian climate justice knot tractable within academia. These challenges can either be resisted or embraced as a point of reflection.

For example, starting with my early work on public understandings of climate justice (Klinsky, Dowlatabadi, and McDaniels 2012), it became immediately apparent that lay participants understood the climate justice issue in a much more holistic way than is typically done within the academic context. People regularly linked many different issues – race, non-GHG forms of pollution, gender, human rights, daily constraints to action – together in ways that fell outside the lines of more formal analyses conducted within philosophy or policy analysis. Over time the grassroots climate justice movement has also articulated a multiplicity of considerations that they see as interconnected (CJN! 2007; PWCCC 2010), even though this runs directly into conflict with dominant frameworks for conceptualising climate policy, including those using the identification and measurement of discrete harms or benefits to evaluate equity within climate policy (Stern 2006; Tol 2001).

As academics we have a choice. We can capture what we can using policy analysis tools that separate climate issues from each other and other aspects of people's lives and use these to communicate the justice or equity issues as best as we can. The benefit of taking this path is that bounding justice issues so that they fall in line with dominant academic discourse and analytical traditions can have greater currency with stakeholders who are accustomed to working within this framework. These stakeholders can include policymakers, other academics or other powerful groups who we may feel have strong responsibility or capacity to act upon research insights.

Alternately, we can follow the lead of those stressing the integrated nature of life (including our non-human relations) or other framings excluded by dominant discourses, and find or create ways of including these concerns in our work. From this perspective the argument is that only by articulating alternative visions of the possible world can we hope to move to a more just future. If we take this path, our work may resonate more with those outside rather than inside privileged circles of policy decision-makers, academics or others comfortable within mainstream policy contexts.

Choosing our entry point into climate justice is possibly one of the most important – and strategic – decisions a scholar in this field has to make. This choice will largely determine who s/he engages with, in what capacity this engagement occurs and what the goals of this engagement are. From a personal perspective the challenges of navigating the diversity of climate justice frameworks was highlighted when working through a transdisciplinary project that centred around a series of international workshops that convened stakeholders involved in climate policy across multiple scales and settings, and transitional justice scholars and practitioners. The purpose of these workshops (coordinated in conjunction with a science–policy interface organisation) was to identify theoretically desirable and politically feasible ways of using transitional justice examples to inform climate policy justice disputes (Klinsky and Brankovic 2018). Throughout this project a core tension was between being so "idealist" or "radical" that the project would alienate more dominant and possibly more powerful stakeholders, and being so "realist" and "reformist" that it would lose intellectual and moral credibility, particularly from those facing climate injustice on the ground or who see climate injustice as embedded within other systemic forms of oppression.

The complexity of the climate justice issue necessarily means that our work will be partial and able to engage with only some components of the problem. The diversity of this arena provides an immense opportunity for academics to self-reflect on the assumptions they have made about how they conceptualise the central dynamics of climate injustice, what they miss through their conceptualisations, and to use this to open new areas of work and collaboration. The challenge of this multiplicity of entry points is also that each one is likely to privilege some actors and forms of evidence over others. Deciding how to frame the issue is a highly political decision that can result in professional and personal tensions. The incompleteness of work in this arena also warrants paying attention to another central issue – that of solidarity.

The depth of power imbalances within all scales of the climate justice context and the range of avenues for entering into discussion means that **solidarity is a particularly salient issue** for those doing publicly engaged work on climate justice. For those working closely with civil society organisations or participating in social movements directly themselves, the difficulty of forging solidarity is well-established. The challenges of what solidarity requires for public scholarship has been less clearly articulated, although several people have written about this in the non-climate context (Mathers and Novelli 2007; Derickson and Routledge 2015), and I know of many academics in the climate justice arena who do work within a solidarity lens.

The importance of reflecting on solidarity was highlighted for me while working on a transdisciplinary project in collaboration with the World Resources Institute. The goal of this project was to explore ways of better integrating concerns about climate justice into the UNFCCC process in the lead-up to the Paris Agreement. This project was rooted in concern about the depth of the stalemate in policy action at the global level and the limited extent to which human development inequalities were, or could, be integrated into climate policy at all scales. In recognition of the political sensitivity of this topic, the report was guided by a group of international advisors and underwent multiple levels of internal and external review and stakeholder consultation.

As the project lead for this transdisciplinary effort, I was responsible for shaping the intellectual frame of the contribution and for finding a coherent and constructive way to integrate stakeholder contributions within the specific political context of the UNFCCC. Following the ideas of Amartya Sen (1999, 2005), I have largely based my climate justice work on a recognition of the multiple ways in which the creation and impacts of climate change intersect with pre-existing social, economic and ecological forces and shape people's individual capabilities to live in ways that they would choose. If we think of individual people as the ultimate "subjects" of a concern for justice, then it is essential to root our work in the acknowledgement of the unequal opportunities and constraints experienced by individuals and groups of individuals. Moreover, I see inequality as an issue around which there could be significant solidarity across country borders as it is a widely experienced characteristic of climate justice challenges. In my early drafts for this project, domestic inequality was highlighted as an important part of the climate justice story.

However, during the drafting process, representatives from several countries in the Global South objected to my inclusion of domestic inequality in this framing of climate justice. One of the core tensions within the global climate regime revolves around the potential for UN-based climate agreements to perform a neo-colonial role in regulating developing countries' domestic arrangements. While all of the stakeholders I was working with have in their own spheres demonstrated significant dedication to addressing domestic inequalities and have prioritised access to human development, it was considered inappropriate for a globally oriented report, especially one written in collaboration with a northern-based institution and headed by a northern researcher, to focus on these issues. In this context, focusing on domestic inequality could be seen to provide a pathway for undermining the sovereignty of countries continuing to deal with colonial legacies, and would also undermine, not nurture, solidarity. Accordingly, neither the policy-oriented outcome (Klinsky et al. 2014) nor the subsequent academic paper that emerged from this process (Klinsky, Waskow, et al. 2017) feature a substantive discussion of domestic inequality, although the notion of capabilities itself continues to bring this forward.[3]

This example illustrates the importance of sensitivity to the multiscalar nature of the climate justice challenge and to the ways that multiple forms of privilege and experience shape this. Politics and power dynamics at different nodes within this system vary, and efforts that would build solidarity and be seen as constructive within one node can undermine trust or be counterproductive in another. How we deal with solidarity can change not only how we do public engagement but also the results of scholarly work.

Notably, I have chosen to work primarily around the mitigation dimensions of climate justice. I have focused on transdisciplinary efforts to create ways of better addressing justice within the global climate regime, and on enabling deeper engagement with the concept of climate justice in North American communities who may feel removed from climate change generally. Working in solidarity in the context of other faces of climate justice would look different. For instance, if working with frontline communities, such as indigenous communities facing threats either from climate change or fossil fuel extraction directly, solidarity would entail following their lead in terms of the type of engagement or product production would be considered useful. Instead, I have chosen the path I have in the hopes that it can create space for other forms of climate justice work, including that emerging in collaboration with such communities. The scope of the challenge and the inevitable limitations of our work means that thinking about solidarity is important in two ways: not only does it shape how we work with a particular community, but also how we conceptualise these efforts in the context of the myriad efforts being undertaken by other communities engaging with different facets of climate injustice.

Finally, dealing with **the moral weight of climate injustice** is a distinctive characteristic of public engagement with climate justice, particularly when working with people who have benefitted from the processes underpinning climate injustices. As mentioned, part of my work has been centred in North American communities who are not frontline communities but whose consumption, political and cultural decisions profoundly shape climate (in)action. I suggest that greater attention to moral weight could be productive not only to public engagement efforts, but also for shaping scholarship in this field broadly.

Part of my public engagement practice has been a commitment to provide information about climate change, including climate justice, to any group that invites me. I have spoken in community centres, church basements, government offices and to service clubs, NGOs, political representatives and community organisers. The moral weight of climate injustice was highlighted during a workshop held by an NGO I often collaborate with. The facilitator asked everyone how they felt about climate justice issues. Words like "shame," "guilt," "despair" and "overwhelmed" came to the surface. People simultaneously discussed being "unsure what I can do" and feeling that the main issues were "outside my control." I have had people get up and walk out of the room when I have shown graphs of cumulative emissions and the role that the United States has played in this. Quite often after a presentation on climate justice, people declare their support for science, but then ask whether or not it is possible that any number of unlikely non-anthropogenic scenarios could be the ultimate driver of climate change. It would feel far less onerous if climate change was not caused by the very actions that daily life in the United States[4] is built on, as this would dissolve key responsibilities and injustices its anthropogenic nature brings to the fore.

Other people directly address the moral challenge of mitigation. They have often said things like, "for other presentations you might not want to bring in this inequality stuff; I'm okay with it but other folks won't be," or "we're good people, we just don't know what to do." Simultaneously, even in one-on-one conversations the most climate justice–sympathetic negotiators from the Global North steadfastly refuse claims of historical responsibility, and in our project on transitional justice in the climate context we routinely were advised to avoid any discussion of reparations for climate harms. As Maxine Burkett (2015, p. 95) says, reparations have become "a third rail" capable of killing discussion. These observations at both local and global scales resonate with the work of others. In her ethnographic work in Norway, Kari Norgaard (2006) identifies many subtle ways that people avoided taking responsibility for climate change, despite acknowledging its existence and expressing concern about it.

With more practice I have come to understand the North American mitigation challenge embedded within any framing of climate justice more fully. Literature on public understanding of risk and of justice issues highlights the extent to which our moral perceptions are filtered through emotions (Damasio 1994) and through our sense of identity (Skitka 2003; Wenzel 2004). When faced with justice dilemmas, people often selectively engage in order to maintain their understandings of how the world works, including the extent to which it is seen as "just" and their own positive identity within this (Lerner 2002). For those of us working on climate justice issues within the North America mitigation context, these human responses to injustice are highly salient. Currently, per capita emissions in Canada and the United States are amongst the highest in the world, and this is built upon a substantial accumulation of wealth and infrastructure generated through the production of emissions spread over several hundred years. Looking at mitigation and the causation of climate change from a justice lens necessarily means engaging with this accumulation of privilege. In her work on climate communication in the adaptation context, Susi Moser has noted that the "communication challenge is not merely, and maybe not even primarily one of conveying science and information about adaptation options, but about respecting, holding, and dealing with perceived threats to the self" (Moser 2010). I would suggest that the mitigation context – a key aspect of public engagement with climate justice in the Global North – adds a level of intensity to these concerns about identity and threats to the self.

As a white woman in the United States, I am well aware of how difficult confronting one's own privilege can be. Recognising how often I have failed to see my privilege, or failed to take actions to dismantle it, has helped me to better understand how difficult it is to absorb and act on information that calls into question our moral worthiness and problematises habitual, systemic patterns of our lives. What we are asking the North American public to do when we discuss climate injustice is very hard. Initial work suggests that in a context of political polarisation, communication that focuses on climate victims could have a boomerang effect and deepen pola-rised positions about climate change (Hart and Nisbet 2012). In addition, with some American populations, stressing injustice could be counter-productive because it contradicts people's belief in a just world and their perceived identity within this (Feinberg and Willer 2011). Recognising how conversations about climate injustice can challenge central aspects of people's identities as "good people" can help us think about how to discuss productive ways forward. For instance, what can we learn about the strategies others have used to make privilege visible? Are there pathways of opening these discussions that do not feed into denial, retaliation or hardening of protective binary positions?

Work more specifically examining privilege in communications research in the U.S. around systemic racism suggests that there are subtle but important differences between experiences of "white guilt" and "white shame" and the likelihood that those experiencing these feelings will engage in efforts to address white privilege (Harvey and Oswald 2000). Similar work has explored differences between guilt and shame in people's support for reparations in the Chilean context (Brown et al. 2008). Further explorations of the dynamics of effective engagement on facets of climate justice that challenge identity and privilege would be a productive avenue to help guide practice and research in this arena.

Concluding thoughts

Perhaps the unspoken thread running through all three of these discussions about academic engagement in climate justice is that this is a highly political – and politicised – context. Because climate change and climate policy intersect with so many aspects of life and have the potential to affect so many groups of individuals differently, there is no neutral approach to climate justice. Moreover, in order to do in-depth analysis of the dynamics of these debates, and to avoid benefit-ting from situations of deep injustice, I have argued that scholars in this arena have an obligation to undertake some elements of public scholarship. Considering the professional pressures against public scholarship by junior or non-tenure track faculty juxtaposed against the enormous inter-est and moral concern for this issue that I have observed especially amongst younger scholars, I think we need to have a deeper discussion about the challenge, opportunities and obligations of attempting to build public scholarship into academic practice.

In the spirit of contributing to broader discussions about what public scholarship could or should look like in the climate justice context, I have reflected on some of the opportunities and challenges that I have personally encountered in my attempts to work beyond the bounds of the academy in this context. This is clearly an idiosyncratic account based on the limited amount of work I have been able to do within a relatively short career. Many other aspects could also be explored and would certainly yield other important insights – for instance, I have not discussed collaboration with frontline communities, which is a key aspect of climate justice work. However, I think these challenges of managing an inherently multifaceted topic, figuring out how to work in solidarity, and being aware of the challenges inherent to questioning people's core identities and feelings of moral worthiness are likely to be central points for all scholars trying to express a call for public scholarship in the climate justice context.

If nothing else, I would challenge all of us to pause while planning our next research project. In light of the systemic inequalities that shape how climate change has been and will continue to be created, how it is and will affect people along with our non-human relations, and how the benefits and burdens of attempts to address it are experienced, climate change brings with it a multitude of justice issues. For each project we have to make decisions: Which groups should I engage with, and why? Where can I use my capacities most effectively within this system? What do I hope to achieve with any collaboration? What do my collaborators hope to achieve? And who will benefit – or be harmed – by my actions? One of the benefits of explicitly considering the notion of public scholarship in the climate justice context is that it forces us to be reflexive about our decisions, our assumptions and our obligations as scholars and as humans.

Notes

1 I have also been involved in a range of more confrontational political actions such as protests. In my case this participation in explicitly political protest has been motivated by personal concern and a desire to be part of particular social movements. In my case this political participation has not been conducted explicitly within or to inform my formal academic research, so I have not included these activities in this essay.

2 In the context of NAMAs, I use the term "developing countries" because this is the legal term on which their existence is predicated and is the term used within the global context to discuss them.

3 Multiple researchers from the Global South have since expressed their mistrust of the capabilities approach we developed, and to some extent of me personally, because the report's emphasis on capabilities at the international level could be seen as either promoting a "prioritising multi-dimensional human development" perspective, which is what we had intended, or an "avoiding responsibility by building capabilities" perspective, which we had not. This experience was a needed reminder for me to be more sensitive to, and think more critically about, the intersections of oppression across scale in the climate justice context.

4 Obviously the residents of the United States are not the only ones who have benefited from the use of fossil energy or who have contributed to climate change, and emissions are not uniform within this country, nor are the benefits and burdens of fossil energy use. However, as those I am working with quite commonly refer to themselves as "Americans" and talk about an "American position" on climate change, this is the frame of reference I am using in this particular chapter.

References

Barrett, Sam. 2013. "The Necessity of a Multiscalar Analysis of Climate Justice." *Progress in Human Geography* 37 (2): 215–233.

Blomley, Nicholas. 2008. "Activism and the Academy." In *Critical Geographies: A Collection of Readings*, 28–32. Kelowna, Canada: Praxis ePress.

Brown, Rupert, Roberto González, Hanna Zagefka, Jorge Manzi, and Sabina Čehajić. 2008. "Nuestra Culpa: Collective Guilt and Shame as Predictors of Reparation for Historical Wrongdoing." *Journal of Personality and Social Psychology* 94 (1): 75–90.

Burawoy, Michael. 2004. "Public Sociologies: Contradictions, Dilemmas, and Possibilities." *Social Forces* 82 (4): 1603–1618.

Burgess, Jacquelin. 2005. "Follow the Argument Where It Leads: Some Personal Reflections on 'Policy-Relevant' Research." *Transactions of the Institute of British Geographers* 30 (3): 273–281.

Burkett, Maxine. 2015. "Rehabilitation: A Proposal for a Climate Compensation Mechanism for Small Island States." *Santa Clara Journal of International Law* 13: 81.

CJN! 2007. "Climate Justice Now! Principles." https://lists.riseup.net/www/info/cjn.

Convery, Frank, Louise Dunne, and Dierdre Joyce. 2013. "Ireland's Carbon Tax and the Fiscal Crisis: Issues in Fiscal Adjustment, Environmental Effectiveness, Competitiveness, Leakage, and Equity Implications. OECD Working Papers No. 59." OECD.

Damasio, Antonio R. 1994. *Descartes' Error: Emotion, Reason, and the Human Brain*. New York: G.P. Putnam.

Derickson, Kate Driscoll, and Paul Routledge. 2015. "Resourcing Scholar-Activism: Collaboration, Transformation, and the Production of Knowledge." *The Professional Geographer* 67 (1): 1–7.

Feinberg, Matthew, and Robb Willer. 2011. "Apocalypse Soon?: Dire Messages Reduce Belief in Global Warming by Contradicting Just-World Beliefs." *Psychological Science* 22 (1): 34–38.

Gardiner, Stephen, Simon Caney, Dale Jamieson, and Henry Shue, eds. 2010. *Climate Ethics: Essential Readings*. Oxford: Oxford University Press.

Greene, Joshua., and Jonathan. Haidt. 2002. "How (and Where) Does Moral Judgment Work?" *Trends in Cognitive Sciences* 6 (12): 517–523.

Grubb, Michael, and Karsten Neuhoff. 2006. "Allocation and Competitiveness in the EU Emissions Trading Scheme: Policy Overview." *Climate Policy* 6 (1): 7–30.

Hart, P. Sol, and Erik C. Nisbet. 2012. "Boomerang Effects in Science Communication: How Motivated Reasoning and Identity Cues Amplify Opinion Polarization About Climate Mitigation Policies." *Communication Research* 39 (6): 701–723.

Harvey, Richard D., and Debra L. Oswald. 2000. "Collective Guilt and Shame as Motivation for White Support of Black Programs1." *Journal of Applied Social Psychology* 30 (9): 1790–1811.

hooks, bell. 1994. *Teaching to Transgress: Education as the Practice of Freedom.* New York: Routledge.

Klinsky, Sonja, and Jasmina Brankovic. 2018. *The Global Climate Regime and Transitional Justice.* 1 edition. Abingdon, Oxon and New York: Routledge.

Klinsky, Sonja, Hadi Dowlatabadi, and Timothy McDaniels. 2012. "Comparing Public Rationales for Justice Trade-Offs in Mitigation and Adaptation Climate Policy Dilemmas." *Global Environmental Change* 22 (4): 862–876.

Klinsky, Sonja, Timmons Roberts, Saleemul Huq, Chukwumerije Okereke, Peter Newell, Peter Dauvergne, Karen O'Brien, et al. 2017. "Why Equity Is Fundamental in Climate Change Policy Research." *Global Environmental Change* 44 (May): 170–173.

Klinsky, Sonja, David Waskow, Wendy Bevins, Eliza Northrop, Robert Kutter, Laura Weatherer, and P. Joffe. 2014. "Building Climate Equity." World Resources Institute.

Klinsky, Sonja, David Waskow, Eliza Northrop, and Wendi Bevins. 2017. "Operationalizing Equity and Supporting Ambition: Identifying a More Robust Approach to 'Respective Capabilities.'" *Climate and Development* 9 (4): 287–297.

Lerner, Melvin. 2002. "Pursuing the Justice Motive." In *The Justice Motive in Everyday Life,* edited by Michael Ross and Dale Miller. Cambridge: Cambridge University Press.

MacKinnon, Shauna T. 2009. "Social Work Intellectuals in the Twenty-First Century: Critical Social Theory, Critical Social Work and Public Engagement." *Social Work Education* 28 (5): 512–527. https://doi.org/10.1080/02615470802406494.

Mathers, Andrew, and Mario Novelli. 2007. "Researching Resistance to Neoliberal Globalization: Engaged Ethnography as Solidarity and Praxis." *Globalizations* 4 (2): 229–249.

Maxey, Ian. 2005. "Beyond Boundaries? Activism, Academia, Reflexivity and Research." *Area* 31 (3): 199–208.

McIntyre, Alice. 2007. *Participatory Action Research.* Thousand Oaks: California. SAGE Publications.

Meckling, Jonas. 2011. *Carbon Coalitions Business, Climate Politics, and the Rise of Emissions Trading.* Cambridge: MIT Press.

Moser, Susanne C. 2010. "Communicating Climate Change: History, Challenges, Process and Future Directions." *Wiley Interdisciplinary Reviews: Climate Change* 1 (1): 31–53.

Norgaard, Kari 2006. "'We Don't Really Want to Know' – Environmental Justice and Socially Organized Denial of Global Warming in Norway." *Organization & Environment* 19 (3): 347–370.

Okereke, Chukwumerije, and Philip Coventry. 2016. "Climate Justice and the International Regime: Before, During, and After Paris." *Wiley Interdisciplinary Reviews: Climate Change* 7 (6): 834–851.

Olsson, Lennart, Maggie Opondo, Petra Tschakert, Arun Agrawal, Siri Eriksen, Shiming Ma, Leisa Perch, et al. 2014. "Livelihoods and Poverty." In *Climate Change 2014: Impacts, Adaptation, and Vulnerability. Part A: Global and Sectoral Aspects. Contribution of Working Group II to the Fifth Assessment Report of the Intergovernmental Panel on Climate Change,* edited by Field, Christopher., Vincente R. Barros, David Jon Dokken, Katharine J. Mach, Michael D. Mastrandrea, T. Eren Bilir, Monalisa Chatterjee, Kristie L. Ebi, Yuka Otsuki Estrada, Robert Genova, Betelhem Girma, Eric S. Kissel, Andrew N. Levy, Sandy MacCracken, Patricia R, Mastrandrea, Leslie, L. White. IPCC Working Group II. Cambridge, UK: Cambridge University Press.

Pain, Rachel. 2006. "Social Geography: Seven Deadly Myths in Policy Research." *Progress in Human Geography* 30 (2): 250–259.

PWCCC. 2010. "People's Agreement on Climate Change and the Rights of Mother Earth: Final Declaration of the World People's Conference on Climate Change and the Rights of Mother Earth." World People's Conference on Climate Change and the Rights of Mother Earth. Cochabamba, Bolivia. https://pwccc.wordpress.com/support/.

Sarewitz, Daniel. 2004. "How Science Makes Environmental Controversies Worse." *Environmental Science & Policy, Science, Policy, and Politics: Learning From Controversy Over the Skeptical Environmentalist* 7 (5): 385–403.

Sen, Amartya. 1999. *Development as Freedom.* Oxford: Oxford University Press.

———. 2005. "Human Rights and Capabilities." *Journal of Human Development* 6 (2): 151–166.

Skitka, Linda 2003. "Of Different Minds: An Accessible Identity Model of Justice Reasoning." *Personality and Social Psychology Review* 7 (4): 286–297.

Skitka, Linda, and Elizabeth Mullen. 2002. "Understanding Judgments of Fairness in a Real-World Political Context: A Test of the Value Protection Model of Justice Reasoning." *Personality and Social Psychology Bulletin* 28 (10): 1419–1429.

Stern, Nicholas. 2006. "Stern Review on the Economics of Climate Change." http://apo.org.au/?q=node/4420.

Tol, Richard. 2001. "Equitable Cost-Benefit Analysis of Climate Change Policies." *Ecological Economics* 36 (1): 71–85.

van den Bos, Kees., and E. Allan. Lind. 2002. "Uncertainty Management by Means of Fairness Judgments." *Advances in Experimental Social Psychology* 34: 1–60.

Victor, David. 2015. "Embed the Social Sciences in Climate Policy." *Nature* 520: 27–29.

Wenzel, Michael. 2004. "Social Identification As a Determinant of Concerns About Individual-, Group-, and Inclusive-Level Justice." *Social Psychology Quarterly* 67 (1): 70–87.

35

Climate migration

The emerging need for a human-centred approach

Sennan Mattar and Enyinnaya Mbakwem

Introduction

Migration due to the impacts of climate change has attracted the interest of researchers and policymakers over the last two decades. Both climatic and environmental factors influence migration flows, as people have historically left places with harsh or deteriorating conditions (IOM 2016). However, the impact of anthropogenic climate change on migration is an emerging area of research as the loss of arable land, increased severity and intensity of climate-related disasters is expected to exacerbate existing vulnerabilities. The Internal Displacement Monitoring Centre (IDMC) GRIP report shows that about 227.6 million people have been displaced globally by extreme weather events between 2008 and 2016 (IDMC 2016). Based on current trends, there are predictions that climate change will cause further increases in the scale of human displacement and migration (Oliver-Smith 2009; McMichael et al. 2012).

Within literatures, there is the debate on the linearity or complexity of the link between climate change and migration (Perch-Nielsen et al. 2008). Further still, "migration" and "displacement" are not synonymous terms, with a migrant simply being an individual who has left their residence to settle elsewhere whilst a displaced person is an individual "forced" to leave their residence at least temporarily (IOM 2017). As a result, a range of highly contested terms has emerged to describe people involved in climatic-induced environmental change such as environmental refugees, environmental migrants, climate refugees and climate migrants, among others (Boano et al. 2008). However, in reference to climate-related natural disasters, the United Nations Refugee Agency often categorises these people as "displaced persons" rather than as "refugees" because the displacement has occurred within national borders (UNHCR 2017).

The 1951 Geneva Convention Relating to the Status of Refugees limits the use of the term "refugee" to trans-boundary flight from political persecution, which excludes (a) internal migration, (b) economic and social persecution and (c) victims of climate-related natural disasters (Biermann and Boas 2012). The implication of the inconsistency of an appropriate and agreed-upon "label" to describe people moving due to climatic-induced environmental change as well as the lack of a concise practice definition undermine so-called climate/environmental refugees' recognition and avenues for potential assistance (Fatima et al. 2014, p. 3).

As Wilkinson et al. (2016, p. 2) note, most narratives of climate-induced migration and displacement adopt a "risk-centric" approach, where the dominant focus is on mitigation of conditions that trigger the movement as a function of risks associated with climate change (Pelling 2011; Bassett and Fogelman 2013; Ribot 2014). The shortcoming of this approach is that it fails to take into consideration an actualised movement of people due to the primary focus on prevention of such an eventuality and lacks the long-term objective of restoring lost human rights after that eventuality becomes reality.

Generally, protecting the rights of people moving in response to the impacts of climate change is concerned with safety, security, dignity, reducing vulnerability, as well as safeguarding political, civil, social, economic and cultural rights including freedom of movement (Zetter and Morrissey 2014). In this context, the acknowledgement of the material needs of people displaced by climate and environmental change focuses on the physical assistance to overcome the immediate impacts of displacement – this would be referenced as a "materialist-centric" approach. But this materialist approach again fails to address the structural challenge of affording political and social rights that guarantee quality life for affected peoples in the long term.

While the risk and materialist-centric approaches emphasise preventing a displacement from occurring and providing reactionary material assistance when displacement does take place, they lack considerations for long-term consequences of displacement on affected peoples' human rights beyond the confines of their current residence and situation.

It is apparent that the debate on climate-induced migration is deeply entangled with ethical implications such as societal injustices and effects on human rights. Therefore, to comprehensively address and respond to climate-induced migration and displacement requires a multifaceted and human-centred approach capable of bridging the social gap associated with climate-induced migration. In this regard, a framework that links climate change, development and human rights, such as the climate justice approach, provides a way forward (Mary Robinson Foundation 2016a). Climate justice advocates the safeguarding of rights of the most vulnerable by recognising the inherent injustice owing to the asymmetrical impacts of climate change. The climate justice approach requires that responses to climate change are participatory, transparent and accountable and pay particular attention to the specific needs for protection of people who are disproportionately impacted by climate change (Mary Robinson Foundation 2016a).

Therefore, this chapter seeks to bring to the fore the need for a shift in approach by drawing on examples of climate-induced migration from this emerging field in climate research. The chapter seeks to address the need for a paradigm shift from the current material and risk-centred approaches in dealing with climate-induced migration and displacement to a more human-centred approach that focuses on the needs and rights of the most vulnerable, taking into account the pitfalls of the existing approaches. The chapter will first analyse the consequences and policy implications associated with climate-induced migration with a view to highlight any injustices associated with this migration paradigm. Using cases from Nigeria and Zambia to represent a rural and urban context, the chapter makes a case for a climate justice approach as a foundation for the development of socially inclusive climate migration policies.

Consequences of climate-induced migration

The potential for climate-induced migration is widely recognised, albeit the estimated number of displaced persons varies among projections. A widely cited report by Stern (2007) projects 200 million people may be displaced as a result of climatic change by 2050. Another report by Strauss et al. (2015) suggests between 470 and 760 million people could be displaced by sea-level rise in the event of 4 degrees Celsius warming of global temperatures. At the larger end of projections found in literature, one billion people could be displaced by the end of 2050 (Christian Aid 2007).

The variety of figures for "displaced persons" caused by climate change stems from the complexities behind determining what is "climate-induced" and not simply migration for other reasons (Perch-Nielsen et al. 2008). Further compounding the issue of projections for climate migration is the diverse range of warming scenarios and potential impacts of climate change (IPCC 2014). However, despite the range in projections, the adverse impact of climate change on individuals who are forced to move is a common theme throughout this area of emerging research.

The human consequences of climate-induced migration are more pronounced in cases of forced migration as displaced people are compelled to move for safety and survival purposes. The reality for the affected population is the potential loss of livelihood sources, homes, family ties, cultural heritage and the possible loss of community cohesion as people may disperse to different destinations (William 2008). A typical example is the movement of people displaced by flood events. A precise outcome of such displacement is the loss of property and other physical assets capable of pushing affected households into poverty or limiting their opportunity to escape from poverty (Shepherd et al. 2013; Wilkinson and Peters 2015).

There are also consequences of insecurity due to lack of protection, deprivation of socio-economic rights, territorial dispossession, loss of cultural identity, violation and abuse of basic human rights and psychological challenges owing to inhumane living conditions (Heyward 2015; Bettini 2012). As Zetter (2008) notes, there are concerns that people forced to move as a specific group of migrants are significantly at risk to face a host of material, social, cultural, economic and psychological challenges resulting from their movement. Echoing these concerns, William (2008) argues that climate-induced migration creates enormous injustice and inequality as migrants are faced with uncertain futures as they are largely unaided both by their national governments and the international community – even though in most cases, they did not contribute to these impacts at all.

As already mentioned, socio-cultural implications are another significant consequence of climate-induced migration (Leckie et al. 2012; Burson 2010; McAdam 2011). The potential loss of cultural identities and community cohesion in the course of movement is one example. Bhugra (1994) describes religion, language, rites of passage, dietary habits and some leisure activities as components of cultural identity synonymous with rural settlements. Culture plays an important role in providing "frameworks of meanings" through which people understand themselves as a key component of identity (Heyward 2015); the loss of this identity as a result of migration due to climate change impacts raises the case of injustice.

In this context, Eisenbruch (1990) notes that the loss of cultural identity can cause grief as individuals, households and sometimes communities are compelled to abandon their homes and traditional lands. The implication is that the moving population tends to lose the familiar language (colloquial and dialect), traditional practices, social structures and support networks, their status as members of a self-governing community with control over its own affairs and their distinctive ways of life, as well as sites of religious or cultural significance (Nickel 1994; Eisenbruch 1991). Bhugra and Becker (2005) refer to these losses as "cultural bereavement."

Therefore, a situation in which individuals, households or even whole communities are displaced from their traditional homes as a result of climatic events that they have contributed least to should be interpreted as an injustice. In the words of Mary Robinson (2015, p. 6), a UN Special Rapporteur on Human Rights and Environment, who delivered a speech to the London School of Economics, "human mobility in the context of climate change is an issue of climate justice." The strength in her claim is the linkage between climate change, sustainable development and human rights – where the impacts of climate change undermines the sustainable development of the less-developed countries by exacerbating existing vulnerabilities when their capacity to adapt is stagnant or diminished. Roberts and Parks (2007) describe climate injustice as the current inequalities between the developed and the less-developed countries with regards to their climate responsibility, vulnerability, adaptation and mitigation. Climate injustice encapsulates the unequal and unfair contribution to or unequal experiences of the effects of climate, including displacement and migration due to its impacts.

As various reports and studies show, climate-induced migration has been predicted to occur predominantly in less-developed countries (Bardsley and Hugo 2010; Carballo et al. 2008). Individuals, households and communities in these states who live in precarious conditions owing to existing vulnerabilities of poverty, deprivation, social exclusion, poor healthcare and low adaptation capacity will find their situation exacerbated by the impacts of climate change (McMichael et al. 2012); being forced to abandon their homes and move due to loss of habitable land, deteriorating livelihoods, resource shortages and extreme health risks.

The abandonment of rural communities due to climatic change is consistent with evidence showing that climatic conditions can influence rural-urban migration patterns in sub-Saharan Africa, notably an increase in the rate of urbanisation during times of environmental stress (Barrios et al. 2006; Heath et al. 2012). Subsequently, many rural migrants find themselves living in informal settlements (commonly called "slums") due to lack of affordable and safe housing (UN-Habitat 2015). These settlements, often illegally constructed and subject to demolition by governmental authorities, are poorly regulated spaces with high levels of unemployment, prostitution, child labour, crumbling houses, yearly floods and disease outbreaks (Huchzermeyer 2009; Ngugi et al. 2012; Hove et al. 2013; Onyango and Tostensen 2015). Owing to a lack of infrastructure and proper urban planning, these settlements are also highly vulnerable to the impacts of climate change (UN-Habitat 2015).

In both the departure and final destination, basic human rights of access to water, adequate food, shelter, quality of life, freedom and right to self- determination are compromised through displacement (CPRD2015). Throughout this ordeal, as is often the case, vulnerable groups such as young women and children are exploited and abused because of their unprotected status as internal migrants (Adepoju 2005; Akpalu 2005; Mosberg and Eriksen 2015). The relevance of climate justice is evident in the cases of climate-induced migration and displacement, not only for the actualised displacement or loss of home, but also for the double injustice of the series of hardships and abuses faced by those seeking a new home.

Policy frameworks and implications

The debate on climate change and migration is attracting a strong following both in the media and in the academic sphere, thus making the topic gain serious attention in the international debate on migration and displacement. Of the varied consequences associated with climate-induced migration, the most debated is the human rights implications which have resulted in questions related to safeguarding the rights of migrants (Klepp 2017; Wilkinson et al. 2016). The quest for a comprehensive understanding of the protection needs of those forced to move by slow or sudden-onset events has intensified over the last few years, although attempts to strategically address the issue at the international level have remained limited in scope and participation.

Moreover, the ambiguous nature of international frameworks poses significant challenges for their implementation, particularly at the national level as national governments struggle to incorporate the provisions of the international frameworks into their own developmental objectives (Wilkinson et al. 2016). Regardless of the widespread knowledge of the consequences that climate change has on displacement and migration, a formal recognition of climate-induced migration has long been lacking in international climate change agreements. For instance, climate-induced migration and displacement was first mentioned in the United Nations Framework Convention on Climate Change (UNFCCC) Assembly document in 2008 at the 14th Conference of Parties (COP 14) in Poznan, but was not mentioned in the outcomes of that COP.

Subsequently, climate-induced migration appeared next in the 2010 UNFCCC agenda of the 16th Conference of Parties (COP 16) in Cancun, known as the Cancun Adaptation Framework (CAF). As Warner (2012) notes, the CAF was the first COP text to formally recognise climate-induced migration as a "technical cooperation issue." In paragraph 14 (f) of CAF, the COP of the UNFCCC agreed:

> To enhance on adaptation under the Cancun Adaptation Framework . . . by undertaking inter alia, the following . . . measures to enhance understanding, coordination and cooperation with regard to climate change induced displacement, migration and planned relocation where appropriate, at national, regional and international levels.
>
> *(UNFCCC 2011)*

In 2011, the General Assembly report from the Special Rapporteur on the rights of internally displaced persons stated that "effective responses to the human rights challenges related to climate change-induced internal displacement will require the international community to move beyond the traditional humanitarian assistance and reactive governance models" (UN General Assembly 2011). This recognition gave rise to the Nansen initiative, which is a state-led, bottom-up consultative process aimed at identifying effective practices and building consensus on key principles for the protection of people displaced in the context of climate change (Mary Robinson Foundation 2016a).

More recently, in December 2015, the lead-up to COP 21 in Paris saw a renewed interest in climate-induced migration and displacement. Records show that the first draft of the Paris Agreement included texts on the creation of a "climate change displacement coordination facility" aimed at helping with emergency relief for displaced people and planned relocations (UNFCCC 2015a: Articles 5. Option II, Paragraph 3). Surprisingly, this reference was removed in the second revision of the text. The implication is that it negates any clear commitment by the signatories of the COP 21 to addressing the needs of climate-induced migrants.

However, in the final text of the Paris Agreement, migration and displacement were mentioned twice. It did so first in the preamble of the text with regards to the vulnerability of migrants (UNFCCC 2015b). It was further mentioned in the text under the Loss and Damage mechanism (paragraph 50) with a request to establish a taskforce to "develop recommendations for integrated approaches to avert, minimise and address displacement related to the adverse impacts of climate change." This request is aimed at strengthening the recommendations of the CAF (Mary Robinson Foundation 2016b).

As empirical studies on climate-induced migration show, people moving in response to climate change will predominantly be within the same country or region, thereby making them "internally displaced persons" (IDPs) (UNHCR 2015, p. 8). Perhaps in theory, they should be protected by national laws under the UN's Guiding Principles on Internal Displacement and the international human rights laws. The principle contains recommendations regarding the protection, dignity and security of IDPs. However, it is a guiding principle that is not binding on any of the UN member states (Kolawole 2013). On a regional level, the African Union in 2006 developed a legal framework for IDPs and in 2009 adopted a regionally binding legal norm on all member states (Kolawole 2013).

The 2009 African Union Convention for the Protection and Assistance of Internally Displaced Persons in Africa, held in Uganda and popularly known as "The Kampala Convention," outlines the basic obligations of states to IDPs. This convention, formulated under the auspices of the United Nations Guiding Principles on Internal Displacement, addressed the rights and guarantees for persons or groups of persons who have been forced to flee their homes, communities or cities due to incidences of conflict, climate change-induced weather events, natural disasters or a generalised state of violence, but are trapped or displaced within the boundaries of their countries.

The roles and responsibilities for national authorities, their duties at each phase of displacement ranging from prevention to the humanitarian response, and durable solutions were all clearly outlined in the 2009 Kampala Convention. More so, upon ratification of this convention, member states are expected to develop and integrate their provisions into domestic laws and/or national policies and strategies for internal displacements. However, there is an important legal gap with regard to those who are displaced across borders, as they are not covered under the 1951 Geneva Refugee Convention and do not fit the definition of a refugee as described by the convention (Nansen Initiative 2015).

As mentioned earlier in this chapter, the acknowledgement by national governments of the material needs of people displaced by climate and environmental change focuses on the physical assistance to overcome the immediate impacts of displacement, thus subverting the structural challenge of affording political rights such as the full participation of the affected population in decision-making as well as meeting long-term needs that guarantee quality of life.

Going a step further, there is the political denial of migration and displacement in the context of climate change as a social challenge. This denial is evident in the political stalemate owing to the lack of enthusiasm to develop systematic and structural responses for the protection of rights. In the example of rural migrants seeking refuge in cities, city authorities often blame the migrants for the squalid conditions they find themselves living in and bringing their poverty to the city (STWR 2010; Awumbila et al. 2014). Hence, prospects for human rights-based protection of those displaced by climatic and environmental changes remain poor and fragmented.

In summary, the international community's efforts at developing policy frameworks to delegate responsibility for internal displacement have expanded beyond the limitations of the Geneva Convention, but important gaps remain. There is still a lack of a comprehensive international policy framework and national policy instruments tailored to address the needs of people displaced by climate change. The fundamental challenge in addressing this protection gap lies in the difficulty to appropriately conceptualise the nature of climate-induced migration. The conceptualisation relates to the voluntary or forced nature of movements, whether the movement is temporary or permanent, and the different protection needs between internal and international displacements (Zetter 2011). More so, the ability to attribute migration to climate change with certainty presents another challenge.

As Saul (2008, p. 3) asks, is climate-induced migration to be viewed as a "refugee issue, a migration issue, a human rights issue, an environmental issue, a security issue or a humanitarian issue?" Viewing climate-induced migration from a human rights standpoint will assist us to understand the process from the perspective of the most vulnerable. Moreover, there is now the increased need to amplify the voices of the most affected people. Recognising their stories and analysing their experiences would enhance the development of better responses and outcomes for future displacements and movements. The next section will discuss such stories and experiences by rural and urban communities that have to live with the consequences of climate change.

Climate injustice: The rural communities of Nigeria

Studies have shown that internal migration is the dominant pattern of migration in Nigeria, commonly characterised by rural-urban movements of people (NPC 2010). An Internal Migration Survey conducted in 2010 recorded that 23% of the sampled population had changed residence within the last 10 years (NPC 2010). The survey also showed that a staggering 60% of the Nigerian population live in the urban areas and projected an annual urban growth rate of 3.2% between 2012 and 2030 (NPC 2010; NBS 2012). The statistics from the survey strengthens Nwokocha's (2007) claim of high rural-urban dichotomy in Nigeria, which he attributes to factors such as governmental neglect, endemic poverty in rural areas, social exclusion and marginalisation of rural communities in Nigeria.

As a result of these factors, there has been a significant increase in the number of rural inhabitants moving to urban areas with hopes of overcoming the status of powerlessness associated with rural living (Abbass 2012). The evidence of this increase was highlighted in a report by the Federal Ministry of Environment (2015), which showed an increase in the urbanisation rate from 15% in 1950 to 55.9% in 2015. However, in the context of what drives migration in Nigeria, the involuntary or forced movement of people as a result of climatically induced environmental changes, civil strife and terrorists' insurgencies (Boko Haram, most notably) currently pose major concerns (Onyia 2015).

As of 2014, Nigeria had the highest number of IDPs in sub-Saharan Africa, with an official figure of 3.3 million people, thus representing 2% of the total population (IDMC 2014). A report by the Scalabrini Institute for Human Mobility in Africa (SHIMA) showed that the largest mass displacement events in the country are flood-induced disasters and conflicts (SHIMA 2014). A typical incidence was the devastating floods of 2012 occasioned by excessive rainfall between the months of July and October ranked as the largest disaster-induced displacement event worldwide (IDMC 2013).

According to reports of the National Emergency Management Agency (NEMA), a total of 3,870 rural (and predominantly coastal) communities in 256 local government areas were affected, and more than 6 million people were displaced nationwide (NEMA 2014). Outcome of the disaster included the loss of homes, arable lands, livelihoods, personal assets as well as damage to infrastructures. The Post Disaster Need Assessment (PDNA) report on the 2012 nationwide flooding revealed the total damage to be in excess of $16.9 billion, representing 1.4% of GDP in that year (FGN 2015). In terms of the human cost, many of the displaced persons were compelled to move to other parts of the country, particularly to the urban centres (SHIMA 2004).

There are psychological, socio-cultural and human rights implications associated with forced migration. Article 15(2) of the International Covenant of Economic, Social and Cultural Rights (ICESCR) requires Parties to conserve the cultural heritage of people within their jurisdiction. This implies that the conservation of cultural rights is a recognised fundamental human right. However, this right is threatened by the potential loss of community cohesion, cultural heritage and identity when people are displaced and are compelled to leave their cultural lands – "the bones of their ancestors" (Mary Robinson Foundation 2016c).

This became evident during interviews with individuals who were forced to move from their coastal communities in southwestern Nigeria to the urban centres in the southeast due to frequent floods and sea-water incursion. A man from one of these communities, in response to a question on the challenges of being a forced migrant, highlighted the impact of his situation on cultural rights:

> It's sad that I cannot speak my native language here. I cannot cook my native food as often as I would want to. I grew up in my traditional home, participated in cultural festivals,

experienced the proper way of life of an Ilaje (his tribe) man. But all that is in the past now. What hurts most is that my children will not get the chance to have the same experiences because there's no ancestral home anymore. Water has destroyed it all. Being told stories of your culture and experiencing your culture are two different things.

Man, 43, Ebietomiye Compound, Umuahia, Nigeria

An implication of being compelled to move results in the inability of the affected people to realise their human rights through their traditional way of life (Mary Robinson 2015). However, considering the already discussed gaps in policies and legal frameworks in addressing climate-induced migration, their human rights are violated as migrants occupy a legal void where no policy comprehensively addresses their needs. As most cases of climate-induced displacement will occur in less-developed countries such as Nigeria, and will be predominantly internal, the responsibility of protection technically lies with national governments (Brown 2008). However, with climate change being a global issue that requires a global response, the question of responsibility and assistance by the developed countries – that are most responsible for the climate problem – to help with the displaced population in the less-developed countries arises.

Therefore, it is suggested here that holistically addressing climate-induced migration could be achieved by adopting a human rights perspective. In this frame, there is a need for a rights-based approach that seeks to protect the full range of human rights of people displaced or compelled to move due to the impacts of climate change. A human rights-based approach to climate justice would advocate that the needs of the moving population should be at the centre of decision-making and policies. Climate justice recognises humanity's responsibility for the poorest and most vulnerable people in society in the context of climate change, protecting their human rights included. Therefore, it provides the impetus to confront the human implications of climate change such as displacement and migration.

Climate injustice: The urban communities of Zambia

Urbanisation in Zambia has seen the country's demography change sharply since independence from Great Britain in 1964 and the lifting of colonial restrictions on the movement of rural farming communities (Ogura 1991). The percentage of those living in urban areas increased from 22% in 1964 to 39.8% by 1980 (World Bank 2017). There was a period of "de-urbanisation" during the 1990s when economic recession and falling copper prices saw an uptake of agricultural work before urbanisation rates picked up again from the 2000s (Potts 1995; Ammassari 2005). The United Nation's (2014) World Urbanization Prospects 2014 for Zambia projects that the majority of the population will live in urban areas by 2030, and the urban population will continue to rise.

The concentrating of population in urban centres due to high fertility and rural-urban migration is often described as a significant contributing factor behind the dominance of informal settlements in Zambia's cities (UN-Habitat 2010; CSO 2013). In Zambia's capital, Lusaka, the informal settlements are peri-urban areas on the city's outskirts, or along the corners of industrial areas, that have developed without regulation or outside the purview of urban planners. These areas are characterised by overcrowding, dense housing, no obvious layout of houses or roads and lack of statutory tenure (sometimes referred to as "squatting"). The "informality" of the areas also hinders legal connections to water and sewerage networks. The results are poor access to improved water sources and even worse access to sanitation, the latter issue further exacerbated by failing waste management and obvious dumping. Further, due to densely packed housing and lack of drainage infrastructure, the areas are vulnerable to yearly floods. The annual high rains also bring the high probability of destruction of poorly built housing stock. The people living in the "compounds" survive by informal employment. A common example is "pieceworks," where an individual will carry charcoal from depot to shop, or break up wood for cooking.

In 2014, the percentage of Zambia's urban population who lived in informal settlements was estimated to be 54% (World Bank 2017). This translated into 2.9 million "informal dwellers" living in 187 informal settlements across the country (Taylor et al. 2015). In Lusaka alone, the most popular final destination for rural migrants since the 1960s, approximately 60–70% of the 2.3 million residents live across 45 informal settlements (World Bank 2002; CSO 2013; Taylor et al. 2015; World Bank 2017).

The explicit link between rural-urban migration and the growth of informal settlements in Zambia, and much of sub-Saharan Africa, is a social phenomenon which has often been implied by researchers (Barrios et al. 2006; Tacoli et al. 2015), but rarely observed or recorded in any comprehensive manner. Rather, the movement of rural peoples to informal settlements is projected due to the bolstered urban growth rates, limited affordable housing stock and the poor socio-economic circumstances faced by migrating rural communities (Barrios et al. 2006; Ooi and Phua 2007; Girardet 2008; Tacoli et al. 2015; Awumbila 2015). However, the exact scale of that projected movement into informal settlements is an approximation.

The projected migration trends in Zambia mirrors the difficulty of determining the scale of climate-induced displacement discussed earlier in this chapter. However, Zambia's Vulnerability Assessment Committee (ZVAC 2016) conducted a survey of 5,948 rural households and found that 16% of households would consider migration if prolonged dry spells persisted. The survey, which followed the El Niño event in 2015–2016, also found that 36.6% of households moved long distances in search of pasture for their cattle.

Although only a small percentage might consider migration, the report by ZVAC (2016) estimated as many as 975,738 people would require food and cash support owing to dry conditions (including emergency support to 13,699 farming households unable to procure food through markets). This is to say, regardless of whether rural communities may voluntarily migrate owing to climatic conditions, the potential for forced migration is evident in the vulnerability of rural communities demonstrated by the scale of aid required.

However, once the migration to cities does occur, rural migrants are known to have problems with financially sustaining themselves as there is a mismatch between the skills obtained in rural areas and those demanded of an urban workforce (Englund 2002; Bryceson and Potts 2006). Hence, it is a common observation to find migrants making up a disproportionate share of urban poor (Tacoli et al. 2015).

Under these circumstances, informal settlements are attractive destinations to recent arrivals because short-term accommodation is available at a low cost (Awumbila et al. 2014). This pattern is observed among sub-Saharan Africa's seasonal or temporary migrants, who have traditionally moved between farm and city for work (Barrios et al. 2006; Tacoli et al. 2015). These types of migrants do not permanently settle in urban areas, but they require a house for a short period to conduct their business.

As a seasonal migrant to Lusaka's Misisi Compound explained when describing his migration patterns between farm and city:

> When you build a house, you put it on rent to the tenant. The money buys you a bag of mealie-meal [grounded maize] then you do other things. You go to the village and grow crops during rainy season, but you stay there, while there is your house in town.
>
> *Man, 58, Misisi Compound, Lusaka, Zambia*

However, for many rural migrants and seasonal workers, living in these areas is not a choice but an economic necessity. Even many landlords in informal settlements are as poor as their tenants (Kumar 2010). But, ironically, the poor conditions found in informal settlement are what makes the housing affordable. As a man from Lusaka's George Compound explains why he chose his current residence and not a planned area:

> Here, there is cheap accommodation. You will find a household for 100 kwacha [per month] of which you can't find in Chunga or Lilanda.* But here you can afford the household for 100 kwacha. Due to the kind of business or employment you are in, [you] can't afford to go out there. . . . You choose where you can manage, you can manage to buy food, you can manage to buy clothes.
>
> *Man, 27, George Compound, Lusaka, Zambia*
> ★ = *reference to formal, planned areas*

There is a clear need to address the socio-economic and environmental burdens faced by rural migrants and established residents in informal settlements. Yet, an element that is rarely acknowledged within risk and materialist-centric approaches is that there is a lack of guarantees by governments and international community to respect the informal dwellers' right to development, and subsequently, the failure to provide basic human rights in terms of safe drinking water and adequate sanitation, as well as the right to health and education.

In Zambia, the informal dwellers are caught in a legal limbo; Zambia's Urban and Regional Planning Act (2015, p. 30) describes their communities as "groups of people living on land they have no legal claim to," and therefore their communities do not qualify for infrastructure investment. This theme of purposeful exclusion of informal settlements from infrastructure investment needed for securing basic human rights is observed in other developing countries as well (Satterthwaite 2007). Under this situation, informal dwellers (and new arrivals) are treated as the cause of urban planning failures and penalised by further retreat of urban planners.

Thus, a cycle of injustice is seen to have developed; rural communities face the prospect of losing their "home" and livelihoods due to increasingly frequent extreme weather events and changing seasons. Yet, despite being forced to migrate with little prospect of returning to their farms, they are marginalised and carry the burden of poorly planned, environmentally hazardous conditions of informal settlements without assistance from their government or the international community. This double injustice is embodied by a woman from a farming community but settled in Lusaka, when asked what prevents her from returning to her parents and grandparents' rural home. She put it bluntly;

> I cannot go home, because I don't have any money to buy a cow or plough. That's how we live in Western Province. If you don't have a cow and plough, how can you live there? Even the children, how are they going to live there? If I can take them home, how can I go feed them there? So, I had no choice to go home.
>
> *Female, 46, Chawama Compound, Lusaka, Zambia*

Conclusion

The deterioration of livelihoods in rural areas due to climate change has the potential to displace and provoke migration to the cities. However, these injustices do not stop at the city's gate. The subsequent challenges faced by the migrants, and the settled residents affected by the influx of migrants, is a continuation of the original climate injustice. Here, the men, women and children forced to abandon their rural communities and to live in the informal settlements of sub-Saharan Africa face the double injustice of losing their home and the challenge of finding another one in an unwelcoming city.

Despite the pressing need for redress, current international treaties are predominantly focused on risk and materialist-centric approaches to climate-induced displacement that fail to guarantee basic human rights of displaced individuals beyond the confines of their immediate situation and surrounding. For this reason, climate justice is uniquely positioned in the migration debate as it recognises that the plight of individuals forced to migrate due to climatic change, beyond having obvious negative effects on those individuals, involves broader societal consequences as well. As such, a climate justice perspective offers a more nuanced and comprehensive approach towards achieving a (climate) just society.

When analysed from a climate justice perceptive, climate-induced displacement or migration is recognised as a loss of human rights in a person's home region and the continued deterioration of rights of a migrant in their ultimate destination (Mary Robinson Foundation 2016b). In this context, an approach that recognises and seeks to redress this injustice would include measures to restore and then protect the human rights of individuals affected by climatic events. By virtue of being concerned with the individuals and not a specific locality, it would not only follow migrants to their new residence but also equally apply to their home and receiving communities' broad situation to transform the society to address the root causes of the climate injustice. This long-term commitment to effect societal change, prevent injustices and protect human rights is simply overlooked by the risk or materialistic approaches concerned with the immediate needs or minimising the risk of existing vulnerabilities in a specific location.

Therefore, there is now an urgent need to incorporate the justice aspects of climate change in the entire process of decision-making, developing response mechanisms and frameworks, and fostering cooperation between the developed and the developing countries as it relates to climate change. As an emerging field of research, climate justice, which encompasses the fundamental facets of the climate change problem, recognises that any deterioration of migrants' rights and focuses on the wellbeing of the most vulnerable can be a cohesive basis for policy development aimed at addressing climate-induced migration. More so, with the burdens, benefits and responsibility for climate change unevenly distributed between the developed and the developing countries, climate justice is capable of bridging the gap between climate change science and social justice as it addresses the challenge from a "people" and "social" dimension (Jafry and Platje 2016).

References

Abbass, I.M., 2012. Trends of Rural-urban Migration in Nigeria. *European Scientific Journal*, 8(3), 1857–7881.

Adepoju, A., 2005. Review of Research and Data on Human Trafficking in Sub-Saharan Africa. *International Migration*, 43(1–2), 75–95.

African Union, 2009. *Kampala Declaration on Refugees, Returnees and Internally Displaced Persons in Africa*, 23 October 2009, Ext/Assembly/AU/PA/Draft/Decl.(1).

Akpalu, D.A., 2005. *Response Scenarios of Households to Drought-driven Food Shortage in a Semi-arid Area in South Africa*. Thesis (MA), University of the Witwatersrand.

Ammassari, S., 2005. *Migration and Development: New Strategic Outlooks and Practical Ways Forward* [online]. Available from www.iom.int/sites/default/files/our_work/ICP/IDM/MRS21.pdf [Accessed 4 August 2017].

Awumbila, M., 2015. Linkages Between Urbanization, Rural-Urban Migration and Poverty Outcomes in Africa. *International Organization for Migration*, Background Paper, University of Ghana, Ghana.

Awumbila, M., Owusu, G., Teye, J.K., 2014. Can Rural-Urban Migration Into Slums Reduce Poverty? Evidence From Ghana. *Migrating Out of Poverty*, Working Paper 13, April 2014.

Bardsley, D.K., Hugo, G., 2010. Migration and Climate Change: Examining Thresholds of Change to Guide Effective Adaptation Decision-making. *Journal of Population and Environment*, 32(2–3), 238–262.

Barrios, S., Bertinelli, L., Strobl, E., 2006. Climatic Change and Rural-urban Migration: The Case of Sub-Saharan Africa. *Journal of Urban Environment*, 60, 357–371.

Bassett, T.J., Fogelman, C., 2013. Déjà vu or Something New? The Adaptation Concept in the Climate Change Literature. *Geoforum*, 48(1), 42–53.

Bettini, G., 2012. Climate Migration as an Adaption Strategy: De-securitizing Climate Induced Migration or Making the Unruly Governable? *14 Critical Studies on Security*, 2(2), 180–195.

Bhugra, D., 1994. Depression Across Cultures. *Primary Care Psychiatry*, 2, 155–165.

Bhugra, D., Becker, M.A., 2005. Migration, Cultural Bereavement and Cultural Identity. *World Psychiatry*, 4(1), 18–24.

Biermann, F., Boas, I., 2012. Climate Change and Human Migration: Towards a Global Governance System to Protect Climate Refugees. In: Scheffran, J., Brzoska, M., Brauch, H., Link, P., Schilling, J. (eds). *Climate Change, Human Security and Violent Conflict, Hexagon Series on Human and Environmental Security and Peace*, 8, 291–300, Springer, Berlin, Heidelberg.

Boano, C., Zetter, R., Morris, T., 2008. Environmentally Displaced People: Understanding the Linkages Between Environmental Change, Livelihoods and Forced Migration. *Forced Migration Policy Briefing 1*, Refugee Study Centre, Department of International Development, University of Oxford, Oxford.

Brown, O., 2008. Migration and Climate Change. *International Organisation on Migration (IOM)*, Geneva, Switzerland.

Bryceson, D.H., Potts, D., 2006. *African Urban Economies: Viability, Vitality or Vitiation?* [online]. Available from www.palgraveconnect.com/pc/doifinder/view/10.1057/9780230523012 [Accessed 31 August 2017].

Burson, B., 2010. *Climate Change and Migration South Pacific Perspectives*. Wellington: Victoria University of Wellington.

Carballo, M., Smith, C., Pettersson, K., 2008. Climate Change and Displacement: Health Challenges. *Forced Migration Review*, 31, 32–33.

Center for Participatory Research and Development (CPRD). 2015. *Climate-Induced Displacement and Migration: Policy Gaps and Policy Alternative* [online]. Available from https://unfccc.int/files/adaptation/groups_committees/loss_and_damage_executive_committee/application/pdf/briefing_paper_climate_induced_displacement_and_migration.pdf [Accessed 4 August 2017].

Central Statistical Office (CSO), 2013. 2010 Census of Population and Housing – Migration and Urbanisation Analytical Report. *Central Statistical Office*, Lusaka, Zambia.

Christian Aid, 2007. *Human Tide: The Real Migration Crisis* [online]. Available from www.christianaid.org.uk/resources/about-us/human-tide-real-migration-crisis-2007 [Accessed 4 August 2017].

Convention Relating to the Status of Refugees, Geneva, 28 July 1951. *United Nations*, Treaty Series, vol. 189, p. 137. Available from https://treaties.un.org/Pages/src-TREATY-mtdsg_no-V~2-chapter-5-lang-_en-PageView.aspx [Accessed 4 August 2017].

Eisenbruch, M., 1990. The Cultural Bereavement Interview: A New Clinical Research Approach for Refugees. *Psychiatric Clinics North America*, 13, 715–735.

Eisenbruch, M., 1991. From Post-traumatic Stress Disorder to Cultural Bereavement: Diagnosis of Southeast Asian Refugees. *Social Science & Medicine*, 33, 673–680.

Englund, H., 2002. The Village in the City, the City in the Village: Migrants in Lilongwe. *Journal of Southern African Studies*, 28(1), 137–154.

Fatima, R., Wadud, A.J., Coelha, S., 2014. *Human Rights, Climate Change, Environmental Degradation and Migration: A New Paradigm*, Bangkok and Washington, DC. International Organization on Migration and Migration Policy Institute, March 2014.

Federal Government of Nigeria (FGN), 2015. Nigeria's Intended Nationally Determined Contribution. *Federal Ministry of Environment*, Abuja, Nigeria.

Federal Ministry of Environment, 2015. Nigeria's Intended Nationally Determined Contribution. *Federal Ministry of Environment*, Abuja, Nigeria.

Girardet, H., 2008. *Cities, People, Planet*. 2nd ed., John Wiley & Sons Ltd, Chichester.

Heath, T.T., Parker, A.H., Weatherhead, E.K., 2012. Testing a Rapid Climate Change Adaptation for Water and Sanitation Providers in Informal Settlements in 3 Cities in Sub-Saharan Africa. *Environment and Urbanization*, 24(2), 619–637.

Heyward, C., 2015. New Waves on Climate Justice: Climate Change as Cultural Injustice. In: Thom B. (eds). *New Waves in Global Justice*, Palgrave Macmillan, Basingstoke.

Hove, M., Ngwerume, E., Muchemwa, C., 2013. The Urban Crisis in Sub-Saharan Africa: A Threat to Human Security and Sustainable Development. *Stability, International Journal of Security and Development*, 2(1), 7.

Huchzermeyer, M., 2009. The Struggle for in Situ Upgrading of Informal Settlements: A Reflection on Cases in Gauteng. *Development Southern Africa*, 26(1), 59–73.

Intergovernmental Panel on Climate Change (IPCC), 2014. *Climate Change 2014: Impacts, Adaptation, and Vulnerability.* Cambridge University Press, Cambridge.

Internal Displacement Monitoring Centre (IDMC). 2013. *Global Estimates 2012 People Displaced by Disasters* [online]. Available from http://www.internal-displacement.org/sites/default/files/publications/documents/2012-global-estimates-corporate-en.pdf [Accessed 8 August 2017].

Internal Displacement Monitoring Centre (IDMC), 2014. *A Record 33.3 Million Displaced By Conflict and Violence Worldwide, With Nigeria in the Top 5 Countries Most Affected* [online]. Available from https://tinyurl.com/ycyw94uf [Accessed 8 August 2017].

Internal Displacement Monitoring Centre (IDMC), 2016. Global Report on Internal Displacement (GRID) 2016. *Internal Displacement Monitoring Centre*, Geneva, Switzerland.

International Organization for Migration (IOM), 2016. *Migration and Climate Change* [online]. Available from www.iom.int/migration-and-climate-change [Accessed 3 August 2017].

International Organization for Migration (IOM), 2017. *Key Migration Terms* [online]. Available from www.iom.int/key-migration-terms [Accessed 28 December 2017].

Jafry, T., Platje, J.J., 2016. Climate Justice- a New Narrative Informing Development and Climate Policy. *International Journal of Climate Change Strategies and Management*, 8(4), 474–476.

Kelpp, S., 2017. *Climate Change and Migration, Oxford Research Encyclopedia of Climate Science.* Oxford University Press, New York.

Kolawole, A.A., 2013. Towards the Evolution of Legal and Institutional Framework for the Protection of Internally Displaced Persons (IDPs) in Nigeria. *OIDA International Journal of Sustainable Development*, 6(5), 141–154.

Kumar, S., 2010. Gender, Livelihoods and Rental Housing in the Global South: The Urban Poor as Landlords and Tenants. In: Chant, S. (ed). *The International Handbook of Gender and Poverty: Concepts, Research and Policy*, 367–372, Edward Elgar Publishing, Cheltenham, UK.

Leckie, S., Simperingham, E., Bakker, J., 2012. *Climate Change and Displacement Reader.* Earthscan, Abingdon.

Mary Robinson, 2015. Climate Change and Migration to Europe – Mary Robinson Initial Remarks. *Mary Robinson Foundation for Climate Justice*, London School of Economics, November 2015.

Mary Robinson Foundation, 2016a. Human Rights, Migration and Displacement Related to the Adverse Impacts of Climate Change. *The Office of the High Commissioner on Human Rights (OHCIR)*, Discussion Paper, September, 2016.

Mary Robinson Foundation, 2016b. Protecting the Rights of Climate Displaced People. *Mary Robinson Foundation for Climate Justice*, Trinity College, Dublin, Ireland.

Mary Robinson Foundation, 2016c. The Future of Humanitarian Action: Delivering Justice in the Face of Climate Change. *Mary Foundation for Climate Justice*, Keynote Address, Hilton Humanitarian Symposium, New York.

McAdam, J., 2011. Climate Change Displacement and International Law: Complementary Protection Standards. *Legal and Protection Policy Research Series*, United Nations High Commissioner for Refugees, Geneva, Switzerland.

McMichael, C., Barnett, J., McMichael, A.J., 2012. An Ill Wind? Climate Change, Migration and Health. *Journal of Environmental Health Perspectives*, 120(5), 646–654.

Mosberg, M., Eriksen, S.H., 2015. Responding to Climate Variability and Change in Dryland Kenya: The Role of Illicit Coping Strategies in the Politics of Adaptation. *Global Environmental Change*, 35, 545–557.

Nansen Initiative, 2015. *Agenda for the Protection of Cross-border Displaced Persons in the Context of Disasters and Climate Change Volume 1* [online]. Available from www.nanseninitiative.org/wp-content/uploads/2015/02/Protection-agenda/volume-1.pdf [Accessed 3 August 2017].

National Bureau of Statistics (NBS), 2012. *Annual Abstract of Statistics 2012.* Federal Republic of Nigeria, Abuja, Nigeria.

National Emergency Management Agency (NEMA), 2014. Statistics on 2012 Floods. *The Federal Government of Nigeria*, Abuja, Nigeria.

National Population Commission (NPC), 2010. *Internal Migration Survey in Nigeria, 2010.* National Population Commission, Abuja, Nigeria.

Ngugi, E., et al., 2012. Partners and Clients of Female Sex Workers in an Informal Urban Settlement in Nairobi, Kenya. *Culture, Health & Sexuality*, 14(1), 1–16.

Nickel, J., 1994. The Value of Cultural Belonging. Expanding Kymlicka's Theory. *Dialogue*, 33, 635–643.

Nwokocha, E.E., 2007. Gender Inequality and Development in Nigeria: A Review on Antithesis. *South-South Journal of Culture and Development*, 1, 11–18.

Ogura, M., 1991. Rural-urban Migration in Zambia and Migrant Ties to Home Villages. *The Developing Economies*, 29(2), 145–165.

Oliver-Smith, A., 2009. Sea Level Rise and the Vulnerability of Coastal People: Responding to the Local Challenges of Global Climate Change in the 21st Century. *Intersections No. 7*. United Nations University Institute for Environment and Human Security, Bonn, Germany.

Onyango, P., Tostensen, A., 2015. *The Situation of Youth and Children in Kibera*. Chr Michelsen Institute, Bedriftssenteret, Norway.

Onyia, C., 2015. Climate Change and Conflict in Nigeria: The Boko Haram Challenge. *American International Journal of Social Science*, 4(2), 181–190.

Ooi, G.L., Phua, K.H., 2007. Urbanization and Slum Formation. *Journal of Urban Health*, 84(1), 27–34.

Parliament of Zambia, 2015. *The Urban and Regional Planning Act 2015*, No. 3 of 2015, 23.

Pelling, M., 2011. *Adaptation to Climate Change – From Resilience to Transformation*. Routledge, Oxon.

Perch-Nielsen, S., Battig, M., Imboden, D., 2008. Exploring the Link Between Climate Change and Migration. *Climate Change*, 9(3–4), 375–393.

Potts, D., 1995. Shall We Go Home? Increasing Urban Poverty in African Cities and Migration Processes. *The Geographical Journal*, 161(3), 245–264.

Ribot, J., 2014. Cause and Response: Vulnerability and Climate in the Anthropocene. *The Journal of Peasant Studies*, 41(5), 667–705.

Roberts, J.T., Parks, B., 2007. A Climate of Injustice: Global Inequality, North-South Politics and Climate Policy. *Ethics & International Affairs*, 22, 229–230.

Satterthwaite, D., 2007. *The Transition to a Predominantly Urban World and Its Underpinnings*. Human Settlements Discussion Paper Series, 4.

Saul, B., 2008. An Insecure Climate for Human Security? Climate-Induced Displacement and International Law. *Human Security and Non-Citizens, A. Edwards and C. Ferstman, eds., Cambridge University Press, 2009, Sydney Centre for International Law Working Paper No. 4. Sydney Law School Research Paper No. 08/131.*

Saul, B., McAdam, J., 2009. *An Insecure Climate for Human Security? Climate-Induced Displacement and International Law, Human Security & NON-CITIZENS*. Cambridge University Press, Cambridge.

Scalabrini Institute for Human Mobility in Africa (SHIMA), 2014. Migration Profile of Nigeria. *Scalabrini Institute for Human Mobility in Africa*, Cape Town, South Africa.

Share the World's Resources (STWR), 2010. *The Seven Myths of 'Slums': Challenging Popular Prejudices About the World's Urban Poor* [online]. Available from www.stwr.org/sevenmyths [Accessed 20 August 2017].

Shephard, A., Mitchell, T., Lewis, K., Lenhardt, A., Jones, L., Scott, L., Muir-Wood, R., 2013. *The Geography of Poverty, Disasters and Climate Extremes in 2030* [online]. Available from https://www.odi.org/sites/odi.org.uk/files/odi-assets/publications-opinion-files/8633.pdf [Accessed 4 August 2017].

Stern, N., 2007. *The Economics of Climate Change: The Stern Review*, Cambridge University Press, Cambridge.

Strauss, B. H., Kulp, S., Levermann, A., 2015. Mapping Choices: Carbon, Climate, and Rising Seas, Our Global Legacy. *Climate Central Research Report*, 1–38, Princeton.

Tacoli, C., McGranahan, G., Satterthwaite, D., 2015. *Urbanization, Rural-urban Migration and Urban Poverty*. International Institute for Environment and Development, London.

Taylor, T.K., Banda-Thole, C., Mwanangombe, S., 2015. Characteristics of House Ownership and Tenancy Status in Informal Settlements in the City of Kitwe in Zambia. *American Journal of Sociological Research*, 5(2), 30–44.

UNFCCC, 2015a. *Draft text 1 of 9 on COP 21 agenda item 4(b): Draft Paris Outcome. Proposal by the President.* Available from http://unfccc.int/resource/docs/2015/cop21/eng/da01.pdf [Accessed 24 August, 2017].

UNFCCC, 2015b. *Draft decision CP.21 on Agenda item 4(b): Adoption of the Paris Agreement. Proposal by the President.* Available from https://unfccc.int/resource/docs/2015/cop21/eng/l09r01.pdf [Accessed 24 August, 2017].

UNFCCC., 2011. *Report of the Conference of the Parties: The Cancun Agreements, Outcome of the work of the Ad Hoc Working Group on the Long-term Cooperative Action under the Convention FCCC/CP/2010/7/Add.1, Part Two: Action taken by the Conference of the Parties at its sixteenth session.* Available from http://unfccc.int/resource/docs/2010/cop16/ eng/07a01.pdf. [Accessed 23 August 2017]

UN-Habitat, 2010. *State of the World's Cities 2010/2011* [online]. Available from http://tinyurl.com/jxnaekv [Accessed 9 July 2017].

UN-Habitat, 2015. *22 – Informal Settlements, Habitat III Issue Papers* [online]. Available from unhabitat.org/wp-content/uploads/2015/04/Habitat-III-Issue-Paper-22_Informal-Settlements-2.0.pdf [Accessed 4 August 2017].

United Nations, 2014. *World Urbanization Prospects 2014* [online]. Available from https://esa.un.org/unpd/wup/ [Accessed 1 August 2017].

United Nations General Assembly, 2011. *Report of the Special Rapporteur on Human Rights of Internally Displaced Persons, Chaloka Beyani*. Human Rights Council, 19th session, Agenda 3, A/HRC/19/54. Available from www.ohchr.org/Documents/HRBodies/HRCouncil/RegularSession/Session19/A-HRC-19-54_en.pdf [Accessed 17 September 2017].

United Nations High Commission on Refugees (UNHCR), 2015. *Global Trends: Forced Displacement in 2015, 20 June 2016*. Available from www.unhcr.org/576408cd7.pdf [Accessed 19 August 2017].

United Nations High Commissioner for Refugees (UNHCR), 2017. *Internally Displaced People* [online]. Available from www.unhcr.org/uk/internally-displaced-people.html [Accessed 1 August 2017].

Warner, K., 2012. Human Migration and Displacement in the Context of Adaptation to Climate Change: The Cancun Adaptation Framework and Potential for Future Action. *Environment and Planning C: Government and Policy*, 30(6), 1061–1077.

Wilkinson, E., et al., 2016. *Climate Induced Migration and Displacement: Closing the Policy Gap*. Overseas Development Institute, London.

Wilkinson, E., Peters, K., 2015. *Climate Extremes and Resilient Poverty Reduction: Development Designed With Uncertainty in Mind* (eds). Overseas Development Institute, London.

William, A., 2008. Turning the Tide: Recognizing Climate Change Refugees in International Law. *Law and Policy*, 30(4), 503–529.

World Bank, 2002. *Upgrading low income settlements – Country Assessment Report Zambia* [online]. Available from http://tinyurl.com/pz2pzmb [Accessed 31 August 2017].

World Bank, 2017. *World Bank Data* [online]. Available from http://data.worldbank.org/ [Accessed 4 August 2017].

Zambia Vulnerability Assessment Committee (ZVAC), 2016. In-depth Vulnerability and Needs Assessment Report. *Zambia Vulnerability Assessment Committee*, Lusaka, Zambia.

Zetter, R., 2008. Protecting Environmentally Displaced People: Developing the Capacity of Legal and Normative Frameworks. Research Report. *Refugee Studies Centre*, University of Oxford, Oxford.

Zetter, R., 2011. Protecting Environmentally Displaced People. Developing the Capacity of Legal and Normative Frameworks. Research Report. *Refugee Studies Centre*, University of Oxford, Oxford.

Zetter, R., Morrissey, J., 2014. Environmental Stress, Displacement and the Challenge of Rights Protection. In: Martin, S., Weerasinghe, S., Taylor, A. (eds). *Humanitarian Crises and Migration: Causes, Consequences and Responses*. Ch.9, Routledge, London.

36

Climate justice education

From social movement learning to schooling

*Callum McGregor, Eurig Scandrett,
Beth Christie and Jim Crowther*

Introduction

The overarching aim of this chapter is to offer a theoretical analysis of the challenges and opportunities for a climate justice education (CJE), which both recognises the distinctive educative and epistemological contributions of social movements and positions itself critically both "in and against" the Scottish educational policy contexts of the Curriculum for Excellence (CfE) and Learning for Sustainability (LfS). As authors located across a constellation of educational spaces – from the informal (e.g., social movements, communities) to the formal (e.g., Scottish schools and universities) – we position this chapter as a moment in ongoing praxis, which draws on insights from our collective experience and considers the challenges and opportunities of working across such spaces whilst paying attention to matters of cognitive justice.

In order to achieve this task, we conceptualise processes of CJE as *hegemonic encounters*: since the logic of hegemony performs various conceptual functions, we begin by adumbrating this concept and its importance in relation to CJE. This lays the foundations for the remainder of the chapter, which theorises CJE through a consideration of the relationship between social movement learning and formal schooling. As regards the former, we focus on the educational contributions of climate justice movements. Moving on, we consider how the educative potential of social movements might be harnessed as a pedagogical resource in schools, grounding our discussion in a critical reading of the challenges and opportunities for working within the Scottish policy context.

Hegemony as a key concept for climate justice education

> [C]limate change is too urgent and important to suffer "death by formal curriculum."
>
> *(Kagawa & Selby, 2010, p. 242)*

By now, it is widely recognised by climate change educators and communicators that we are all capable of disavowing knowledge which, when confronted, generates feelings of existential discomfort. Without wishing to be overly reductive, this issue ought to be recognised as being fundamentally *ideological*, since the actions necessary to tackle climate change are literally unthinkable within any educational space circumscribed by the ideational limits of extractivist neoliberal capitalism (Klein, 2014). In other words, public concern over climate change consistently comes second to propping up what David Harvey (2010) calls the state-corporate nexus, whose health is hypostasised as the health of the entire body politic. The best available empirical evidence unequivocally tells us that increasing scientific certainty has not led to increased public concern (Ratter and von Storch, 2012, p. 374). In fact, in a landmark study, Scruggs and Benegal (2012), drawing on aggregate public opinion trends from all EU countries and the U.S., found that decreased concern about, and *belief in*, climate change from 2008 was most strongly determined by worsening economic conditions. The authors hypothesised that citizens disavow climate change knowledge when they see economic growth and recovery as being at odds with taking action on climate. In this context, climate justice (and the associated concept of "just transition" away from fossil fuels) represents an attempt to provide a politically credible narrative whereby action on climate isn't perceived by ordinary struggling people to further compound their material difficulties.

An understanding of hegemony must therefore be front and centre in any process of CJE, because it furnishes us with a vocabulary which allows us to understand that the problem of climate change "has a lot less to do with the mechanics of solar power than the politics of human power" (Klein, 2014, pp. 23–25). The challenge, therefore, is to analyse the roots of these dynamics, which are always partly educational. Gramsci (1971) viewed the institutions of civil society, including schools, as arenas of intellectual work and political learning, through which political alliances are formed. He understood hegemony as a "war of position," meaning a slow cultural process through which elites attempt to fabricate consent through linking their particular interests with the fragmentary "common sense" of different, often disparate, groups. Such ideological settlements, frequently fragile and always unfinished, are often necessarily protected by the coercive armour of political society, including legal institutions, the police and the military.

Nevertheless, the process of establishing connections of equivalence between particular communities and their interests (who come to see these interests collectively reflected in the particular interests of elites) is a precarious one, requiring both cognitive and affective investment. Social movements can, and do, disrupt and rearrange these links through social mobilisations that highlight and target both cognitive and affective weaknesses in the bonds between groups that hold a particular ideological edifice together. Public intellectual Naomi Klein (2014, p. 8) has recently argued that a discourse of climate justice holds the potential to dislocate the fatally compromised vision of climate action under neoliberalism and realign particular interests under a shared vision of the future, whereby tackling climate change delivers positive social change and galvanises community building:

> [T]hrough conversations with others in the growing climate justice movement, I began to see all kinds of ways that climate change could become a catalysing force for positive change – how it could be the best argument progressives have ever had to demand the rebuilding and reviving of local economies; to reclaim our democracies from corrosive corporate influence; to block harmful new free trade deals and re-write old ones; to invest in starving public infrastructure like mass transit and affordable housing; to take back ownership of essential services like energy and water; to remake our sick agricultural system into something much healthier; to open borders to migrants whose displacement is linked to climate impacts; to finally respect Indigenous land rights – all of which would help to end grotesque levels of inequality within our nations and between them. And I started to see signs – new coalitions and fresh arguments – hinting at how, if these various connections were more widely understood, the urgency of the climate crisis could form the basis of a powerful mass movement, one that would weave all these seemingly disparate issues into a coherent narrative.

If this is seen as an educational task, then we claim that the ideological impact of such a movement needs to extend far beyond social movement constituencies and into schools (as well as further, higher and community-based educational institutions) through a recursive engagement with state power. In the following section, we go on to elaborate on how schools are key sites of hegemonic struggle in this sense.

Creating a "reservoir of sentiments" for mobilisation: CJE and the state

Knowledge claims about climate justice can partly be attributed to a heterogeneous movement of movements for global justice (Jamison, 2010). Following Klein's optimistic reading, the frame of climate justice could potentially act as a galvanising force, a nodal point, around which a movement of movements might articulate a counter-hegemonic position. However, as environmental sociologist Jamison argued in 2010, the heterogeneous nature of the "movement of movements," alongside its anti-statist intellectual influences, have led to only modest success in this regard. We are tempted to say that not much momentum has been gathered in the intervening period. Jamison (ibid., p. 817) suggested that the self-identifying climate justice movement has inherited organisational knowledge favouring horizontalism, which has, in turn, been influenced by Hardt and Negri's (2004) political philosophy of the "Multitude." Whereas the theory of hegemony sees the construction of "the people" (through the educational work of "translating" equivalences between particular struggles) as the central task of radical politics (Laclau, 2010), the "Multitude" describes an "internally different, multiple social subject," whose actions are only related through their objective subjection to capitalist norms of (re)production (Hadrt and Negri, 2004, p. 100). As such it offers a political philosophy of immanence, which posits a globally networked, technologically mediated "Multitude." Sovereignty shifts towards biopolitical (re)production, thus rendering irrelevant the state and its various institutions (including, presumably, schools) since, "under the new post-fordist forms of production characterised by the centrality of immaterial labour, capitalists . . . have become parasites who simply appropriate the general intellect, without playing any positive role" (Mouffe, 2013, p. 71).

The upshot of this position is, we argue, a problematic favouring of cultural authenticity over efficacy, with respect to the learning and knowledge generated by climate justice movements. Hegemony, on the other hand, favours an approach of "radical negativity," which recognises that an insurgent discourse of climate justice and its ensemble of demands can always be "appropriated by the existing system so as to satisfy them in a way that neutralizes their subversive potential" (ibid., p. 73). Arguably, we already see hints of this dynamic in the different interpretations of climate justice by activists in the Global North and South, as well as the way in which climate justice has been incorporated into carbon markets and international development discourses (Lohmann, 2008). From a position of hegemonic politics, this implies a recursive strategic "engagement with" rather than "withdrawal from" the state (ibid.). If we understand social movements both cognitively and affectively as types of what Zald (2000, p. 3) calls "ideologically structured action" (that is, action "shaped by ideological concerns – belief systems defending and attacking current social relations and the social system"), then we can extend the study of the ideational and educational impact of climate justice movements into the classroom. As Zald (ibid., p. 9) explains:

> The schools teach hegemonic ideologies. Movements of any duration breach the curriculum as adherents who are educators reshape the curriculum. The parts of movement ideologies that achieve high consensus in the population are especially likely to become part of the explicit curriculum, and even more conflictual versions of the ideology are more likely to

enter the curriculum in schools catering to the part of the population that is especially drawn to the ideology. . . . The school curriculum, in conjunction with family, community and media, contributes to the spread of a movement ideology far beyond the initial group of cadre and activists. Put another way, changes in the curriculum are an outcome of social movements; in turn, socialization in school helps to create the reservoir of sentiments that are mobilizable at later stages of a movement.

In the most general sense, understanding CJE as hegemonic encounter therefore implies an epistemological commitment to the mutual co-imbrication of education and politics, such that one is irreducible to the other. Specifically, if a normative dimension is necessary (but not sufficient) to distinguish education from mere learning, then we must concede that educational institutions work to secure cognitive and affective investment in particular worldviews. We might call this the *objectively hegemonic* function of education, and it arguably operates in all contexts, including LfS and climate change education. However, we are interested in making LfS an *explicitly hegemonic* affair. That is to say, we are interested in the ways in which educators and learners can collectively render visible the material interests, social relations and structures of feeling, which often tacitly shape "common sense" representations of climate change-related issues within mainstream educational spaces. Since, at its most straightforward, climate justice is about unjust distributions of the burdens and benefits resulting from a hydrocarbon economy, CJE is a useful starting point.

Yet, the very discourse of climate justice must be recognised as being the contested stake of hegemonic encounters among different social actors such as grassroots activists, policymakers, governments, NGOs, business lobbies, workers' unions and the UN (Lohmann, 2008; Jamison, 2010; Scandrett et al., 2012; Scandrett, 2016). The discourse of climate justice cannot be considered to be "post-political" in the sense that the mainstream discourse of "sustainable development" can be (Sklair, 2001) – specifically the construction of undifferentiated responsibility and the erasure of any contradiction between the imperatives of capital accumulation and climate action. However, like any discourse, its dominant meaning at a given moment, in a given social formation, is contingent upon the ways in which particular groups seek to elevate their *particular* articulations of climate justice as *universal* (Butler, 2000; Laclau, 2000).

At a general level, grasping this relationship between the particular and the universal is essential to understanding how hegemonic processes work: universal categories are the product of political struggle, whereby the particular values, norms, claims and interests embodied and performed by particular social actors appear to transcend their own standpoints. Education functions in such contexts to provide not only cognitive frameworks but also affective commitments to such frameworks, that provide vocabularies of motive for why the interests of one group are in the best interests of everyone, as well as the expulsion of those "others" whose interests and identities are not easily subsumed. Although this dynamic can be described as discursive, the success of particular groups in contingently universalising a political category, such as action on climate change, cannot be adequately understood as the outcome of language games – as the simple metonymic and relativistic sliding of meaning (Howarth, 2000). Instead, we must grasp that even the dominant meaning of *climate justice* as an educational construct or policy discourse is, to a large extent, the product of the ways in which power dynamics of gender, racialisation and class intersect to: (1) define categories/scales of analysis and political frontiers between actors and (2) shape the terms of participation by both constructing certain groups and populations as passive objects, rather than active shapers, of "just" climate policy, and policing the boundaries of legitimate and illegitimate expressions of citizen action.

In relation to the first point, Scandrett (2016, p. 479) has recently illustrated how in Scotland the discourse of climate justice is politically framed "in terms of the relationship between North and South and the histories of colonialism of and solidarity with the people of the South." More specifically:

> The Scottish Government's Climate Justice Fund provides seed funds for development projects in the South (primarily in Malawi, with which Scotland has a strong historical relationship), using public funds to leverage private capital investments into development projects that promote adaptation and resilience to climate change. At the launch of the Fund, the Scottish Government came under criticism from some who were otherwise supporting the initiative, for failing to meet its own ambitious targets for carbon dioxide emission reductions and continuing to support the fossil fuel industry at home.
>
> *(ibid.)*

We might then argue that this "North-South" framing obfuscates corporate-state collusion, whereby the Scottish state continues to rely on the transnational capital investment in the hydrocarbon industry in order to secure economic growth. Simply put, this international development framing, whilst redistributive, doesn't do much to challenge the class project of neoliberalism and its entanglement with racialised regimes of resource expropriation (Fraser, 2016). On the other hand, protest movements such as the Camp for Climate Action (CCA) have, over the past decade or so, sought to render such dynamics visible to the public through assembling autonomous camps at power stations, airports and financial institutions such as the Royal Bank of Scotland (RBS). This has applied brief moments of pressure to parts of the system that are least coherent to highlight "the wider web of communities of interest directly involved in maintaining and profiting from capitalism's destruction of ecosystems, landscapes, homes and livelihoods" (CCA, 2010, p. 8). Such actions are counter-hegemonic insofar as they are able to disrupt dominant meanings of "climate action" and their assumptions about the passive limits of citizen agency (e.g., paying tax, "behaving" in green ways, etc.). They are also educative to the wider public insofar as they highlight policy contradictions (between climate policy and economic, energy, transport, food policy, etc.), which, in turn, disrupt "neoliberal public pedagogy" that fosters and secures cognitive and affective investment in a narrative that equates the particular interests of the transnational capitalist class (corporate profit) and the "national interest" (Graham & Luke, 2011, p. 117). But climate-oriented movements are also educative by simultaneously rendering visible a number of other issues, not least the social organisation of power that is deployed in such moments to police the boundaries of what is legitimate citizen action (McGregor & Crowther, 2018). As Lohmann (2008) argues, the direct contribution of grassroots movements to the reduction of carbon emissions is rendered invisible by regimes of calculation that are designed to make greenhouse gas emissions fungible.

To reiterate, such actions cannot be said to be counter-hegemonic unless ephemeral and horizontal outbursts of action engage with, rather than withdrawing from, state policies and institutions (Mouffe, 2013). Although formal curriculum can *learn from* social movements, we ought to recognise that social movement constituencies have much to learn from interventions which test the cultural (that is, cognitive *and* affective) purchase of their ideational work in formal educational spaces. In other words, we are interested in the challenges and opportunities that exist when we push what can tentatively be called the "dialectic" between social movement learning and schooling. This is also a sociologically valuable goal to the extent that the literature on social movement learning has paid very little attention to the efficacy of grassroots knowledge-producing practices in educational spaces.

Cognitive justice, affective justice and translation

Jamison (2010, p. 820) has argued that the efficacy of climate justice knowledge claims will rest on their ability to foster what he calls a "hybrid imagination," whereby "movement intellectuals" are successful in creating spaces where "scientists, engineers, and citizens can come together to learn from each other and bring their different kinds of knowledge into fruitful combinations." However, we argue that this epistemological "hybridity" cannot be merely disciplinary, but must address the "coloniality of knowledge and power" by "learning from the South" (de Sousa Santos et al., 2007, p. xiv).

This suggests that, as educators, we ought to recognise that there can be no climate justice without "cognitive justice" (de Sousa Santos et al., 2007). Cognitive justice involves moving from the "monoculture" of Eurocentric epistemology to a non-relativistic "ecology" of knowledge-producing practices. A key concept in such educational work is "translation," meaning the conversion of "incommensurability into difference, a difference enabling mutual intelligibility among the different projects of social emancipation" (ibid., p. xi). Writing on the need to re-politicise sustainability education, Sund and Öhman (2014, p. 646) helpfully relate this back to the relationship between the particular and the universal – a key dynamic in the theory of hegemony: drawing on the work of Butler (2000), they argue that "[i]n the act of translation, the one who has been excluded from the universal concept will haunt the concept until it changes." Concretely, this means that CJE ought not to abandon universal claims, but recognise that they are always contingent, stained by particularity, and "haunted" by the exclusions that constitute the closure of any discourse.

We might then draw a comparison between the movement from "incommensurability" to "mutual intelligibility," and what Mouffe (2005, p. 102) terms the movement from "antagonism" to "agonism," where "[a]ntagonism is a struggle between enemies, while agonism is a struggle between adversaries." In drawing this comparison, we are, in fact, moving towards the reiteration of a crucial point for CJE: the educational act of translation (between different communities of struggle or between movements and schools) is as much to do with what we might clumsily term "affective justice" as it is about "cognitive justice." An "agonistic" curriculum would have to recognise the affective repertoires of "adversaries" as legitimate, and this involves establishing "affect as a site and resource of political learning and struggle" (Amsler, 2011, p. 58). The implications of this are not easy to draw out, but we have already hinted at what this might entail, for example, the analysis of how, in any educational space, desire, hope, happiness, anger, frustration, disgust, embarrassment and so on are keyed to ideological commitments. In the context of climate change, it involves recognition that "conformism, anger and the desire for positive emotions are therefore within the range of possible responses to critique" (Amsler, 2011, p. 52), especially where attributions of privilege and responsibility are brought to the fore. It involves finding space to address the ways in which educational spaces work to silence those thought of as being "too willful" (Ahmed, 2014), and how wilfulness and desire are harnessed and channelled in particular directions. In the next section, we move on to develop this line of thought, focusing specifically on climate justice movements.

The climate justice movement as an educational phenomenon

Climate justice and social movements

As various authors in this volume have described, climate justice is a varied and disputed concept, often deriving from policy discourses (e.g., Mary Robinson Foundation) or liberal contractarian philosophy (e.g., Schlosberg 2008, 2013) somewhat distant from the climate justice movements that have a vested interest in validating such definitions. What is understood to be the climate justice movement (CJM) is subject to dispute, including the extent to which we can include diverse movements, organisations and individuals which either claim to be part of the CJM or else such claim has been made on their behalf. Candidates include the self-named CJM, which developed the declarations of Cochabamba and Margarita, and the people's movements, social movement organisations and more radical NGOs which constitute this CJM (e.g., La Via Campesina, Focus on the Global South, Global Justice Now, Friends of the Earth International). However, many more mainstream NGOs, policy think tanks, academic institutions and state enterprises which advocate climate justice (e.g., see Christian Aid, Mary Robinson Foundation, Glasgow Caledonian University Centre for Climate Justice and Scottish Government Climate Justice Fund) have been included under the umbrella of CJM. The term is also claimed by autonomous and direct action groups such as the Camp for Climate Action (CCA). Some authors have included action groups and environmental justice campaigns focused against locally unwanted land uses which happen to be part of the hydrocarbon industry (e.g., coal mines, oil pipelines, fracking developments and petrochemical factories) irrespective of whether the groups welcome such a label (Bond & Dorsey 2010; Scandrett 2016). Still others have included an even broader category including climate refugees, communities mobilising around mitigation and adaptation efforts, social groups disproportionately affected by climate-damaging or emission reduction policies, and governments in most affected countries and crucially for work with young people in schools, future generations.

We previously defined social movements as forms of ideologically structured action, in order to guard against their reification. We would, moreover, agree with Cox and Nilsen (2014) that social movements should be understood as fundamental animating forces in the process of struggle between social groups seeking to defend or enhance, redistribute, or prevent redistribution of access to limited resources, whether material and symbolic. Therefore, the underlying social processes make possible, generate, constrain and are changed by social movements, both from below, amongst those making claims to justice by collectively challenging injustice, and from above, amongst groups seeking to perpetuate or enhance privilege and obfuscate the injustices on which this privilege is based. The social-ecological process of climate change generates and constricts movements from above which protect – as well as from below which challenge – the interests of capital and social privilege. The resulting "war of position" leads to periodic conflicts orientated around "truce lines" between these movements, and such conflicts become essential sources of curriculum which can help make the hegemonic encounter explicit.

Theorising social movement learning (SML)

Social movements have been identified as a rich source of learning beyond the formal organisation of education such as schools. Biesta (2011) makes the point that what is central to learning is change and the capacity to influence how it is valued and perceived. However, not all change is valued as learning. This is pertinent to social movement learning and action, which involves contesting what is valued by creating new frames of meaning, at the micro level of the individual and their interactions, as well as the macro level of society and beyond (see Scandrett et al., 2010). Unlike schooling, social movement learning has no fixed disciplinary curriculum categories; instead, their educative potential needs to be understood broadly in relation to context and purpose, relations of power and social action.

The educative nature of social movements is, for Eyerman and Jamison (1991), their defining characteristic: a process of what they call "cognitive praxis," emerging from "dynamic interaction between different groups and organisations." However, "cognitive praxis" remains an educational misnomer for this process to the extent that it imagines political learning to be a process of rational public deliberation, whereby passions are consigned to the private sphere. It is important to highlight that movements often arise because of feelings of injustice, anger at how things are, fear that things cannot go on as they are, hope and passion for living differently to the dominant hegemonic frames of meaning and valuation. Therefore, social movements are vehicles for "educating desire" (Crowther and Shaw, 1997). Utopian thinking, as E.P. Thompson (1976, p. 97) states, is "to teach desire to desire, to desire better, to desire more, and above all to desire in a different way."

Movements are inescapably normative projects in that some seek to bolster dominant values, harbour residual values of the past or profess emergent values (Williams, 1977). Emergent movements can, in some cases, be incorporated and lose their radical potential in order to circumvent their threat to the dominant hegemony (e.g., carbon trading is used as a means of commodifying pollution in response to climate change movements), or else they may remain outside, alternative and ultimately irrelevant to hegemonic struggle (arguably, the fate of many rejectionist, self-sufficient communities or anarchist direct action movements). However, emergent movements may also retain their oppositional challenge too, as they engage in hegemonic encounter with movements from above. These tensions between incorporation by, exodus from, and opposition to, the social, economic and political interests supporting hydrocarbon neoliberalism can be educationally generative for climate justice activists, and the wider public.

Learning in social movements can occur by merely involving the type of instrumental skill set any organisation needs to possess. However, to survive and prosper, social movements need to foster "learning loops" (systematic processes of learning through reflection) to further their organisational capacity and the goals of the movement. And to function at another level, movement learning needs to address the ontological challenge of what it means to be human. Learning for action might involve learning how to relate the movement's aims to everyday life and how to interpret or communicate values and beliefs textually, or artistically, using a full range of media, to different audiences which the movement seeks to influence. These are particular challenges for CJMs, since this ontological challenge must be capable of spanning the felt experience of personal, or local, injustices not just to larger social structures, but to the so-called Anthropocene.

In summary, learning for social movement occurs at multiple layers of analytical complexity, including transitions between stages of a "social movement process" (Cox & Nilsen, 2014). For example, the experience of failing to stop a fracking development through mobilising around a planning inquiry can result in a deeper knowledge of the role such administrative processes play in reflecting the interests of powerful groups through a rhetorical veneer of democratic participation and objective fairness. Movements can, through such learning processes, develop an awareness of their own "historicity" (Touraine, 1977), meaning their role in the self-transformation of society. However, it should always be emphasised that this is a task of hegemonic articulation. For example, localised anti-fracking struggles may be driven by a variety of motivations, and a discourse of climate justice may remain too spatially, temporally and conceptually abstract to have any affective resonance for those involved without space for sustained educational work. As such, a key task of the public pedagogy of climate change-related movements is to generate narratives establishing relations of equivalence with other social movements, both contemporaneously and historically (McGregor, 2015).

What is distinctive about movements, from other voluntary bodies which provide learning experiences, is that they involve social action which is also educative and can be characterised as a form of messy learning. By messy learning we mean "the unordered, fragmented, often unfinished, incidental and episodic learning" constituting the "rich but invariably partial mosaic of social movement learning (Crowther & Martin, 2010, no pagination)." This is a form of learning through which activists take into account the complexities of "real-life" circumstances to put theory into practice, respond to unexpected reactions and take into account a range of context-specific considerations that authentic circumstances generate. What they learn is, of course, often unpredictable. They may learn more about the aims of the movement, its strategy and values, but they may also learn about the ways of power, or about themselves as activists. Participation in social movements is a relational experience, and this is central to it as a generator of messy learning.

Learning *from* social movements refers to the wider public learning and education that movements generate. As a movement becomes more powerful, its repertoire of cultural artefacts can be assimilated into the wider cultural field, to contribute towards a new structure of feeling. Movements can be responsible for generating a whole range of public pedagogies through books, journalism, television, film, photography, art, poetry, social media and so on. The public pedagogy of nascent movements can be more difficult to identify, as transforming public discourse may require more time to become visible. However, it is in making visible new ways of thinking and feeling – creating an alternative hegemonic frame of meaning that has wide public appeal – that makes social movement learning, and in particular learning in, for and from CJM, an important resource for professional educators in a variety of settings and educational institutions.

Opportunities for developing curriculum from and with social movements

Returning to the context of climate justice movements, a mass rejection of COP 15 (15th Conference of Parties to the United Nations Framework Convention on Climate Change – UNFCCC) in Copenhagen in 2009 marked a crucial turning point, whereupon a variety of different activist practices sought to disrupt its hegemonic frame and produce alternative knowledge claims based on analyses of ecological debt and social injustice. This included confrontational and creative direct action (of groups such as "Climate Justice Action," "Reclaim the Power" and "Shut It Down"), as well as parallel civil society summits such as Klimaforum09, which could be conceived as an informal adult learning space consisting of workshops, exhibitions, performances and so on (Harrebye, 2011). Taken as a whole, COP15 could provide valuable case study material for secondary school teachers on the relationship between climate change and learning through social action, focusing on the different tactics and approaches employed to question the hegemonic framing of "climate action."

Notably, a collection of protest groups convened at Cochabamba in Venezuela to address the crisis (Bond and Dorsey, 2010). The declaration they produced (and its sequel produced in 2014 in Margarita, also Venezuela), along with the context in which they were generated, provide invaluable curricular materials. The Cochabamba Declaration constitutes a 4,000-word "People's Agreement" on Climate Change and the Rights of Mother Earth, accompanied by a global plan of action aimed at the 2010 COP16 in Cancun, and many other associated documents. The Agreement clearly connects the climate crisis with capitalism and its associated structures (commodification, limitless growth, patriarchy, militarism etc.) and confronts the UNFCCC process for treating "climate change as a problem limited to the rise in temperature without questioning the cause, which is the capitalist system." The Agreement posits a stark choice: "Humanity confronts a great dilemma: to continue on the path of capitalism, depredation, and death, or to choose the path of harmony with nature and respect for life." Counterpoised to capitalist climate change is an alternative system of economic and social organisation based on the "Rights of Mother Earth." The slogan adopted by many parts of the movement encapsulates this approach to climate justice as "System Change not Climate Change."

Although in a less accessible form, further important curricular content can be developed from examples of local conflicts related to the fossil fuel industry. Whilst many of these local action groups do not identify themselves with a climate justice movement, there are valuable lessons to learn from including within the CJM all such local responses in opposition to the cradle-to-grave process of hydrocarbon industry development, from investment and extraction, through distribution and manufacturing, to consumption and the waste stream, which is directly contributing to the enhanced greenhouse effect. A source of curriculum can be derived from this conflict between local action and hydrocarbon capitalism. Direct engagement with such local action groups, campaigns or, where available, climate camps or direct action protests are a significant potential source of curriculum. It is through such engagement, direct or indirect (via the many protest materials, websites, videos, blogs, etc.), where acts of translation occur: the challenge of making connections between narratives of local resistance in order to construct a discourse of resistance to hydrocarbon capitalism in the form of the CJM is an important source of curricular development.

Other, more tangential, parts of the CJM provide challenging opportunities for curricular engagement, especially aspects which highlight social contradictions of tackling climate change without addressing the structural causes of injustice. This is particularly significant in issues related to poverty. For example, campaigns on fuel poverty might expose how distributing domestic energy (largely gas or electricity) through market mechanisms systematically generates inequality. Infrastructure designed on the basis of cheap fossil fuels means that those with the least economic leverage are most dependent on this infrastructure and therefore most exposed as the market price increases. Market mechanisms, such as carbon trading or state interventions in fuel prices, without addressing the infrastructure of cheap oil capitalism, will increase fuel poverty, and campaigners risk being left lobbying for cheaper fossil fuel. Thus, fuel poverty campaigners who focus on infrastructure (such as improved standards for public housing stock) rather than fuel prices because of an awareness of climate change, also constitute a CJM source of the curriculum.

Many more such examples might be developed, if space permitted. However, the key point is that the weakness of much discourse on climate justice often arises from attempts to reify the concept as a fixed definition or policy objective, rather than as a dynamic process where movements expose conflicts in deeper socio-economic and socio-ecological systems. An analysis of the CJM which neglects these wider systemic processes can reinforce that reification.

By way of summary, we claim that CJ movements (both those which emerged from the failure of the UNFCCC in Copenhagen and the broader CJM generated from contradictions throughout the cradle-to-grave of hydrocarbon capitalist industrial process) provide a rich source of curricular resources which challenge this reification that often prevents education on climate, and LfS more generally, from breaking out of the presumption that neoliberal capitalism is here to stay. In this context, to say that there is no climate justice without cognitive and affective justice is to claim that it is only a useful counter-hegemonic concept to the extent that it recognises the praxis of diverse communities of struggle, and, further, that is capacious enough to be recognised *by* these communities, who draw equivalences between their particular struggles under this name (Laclau, 2000). As argued here, this "war of position" is fundamentally educational, involving acts of democratic learning, whereby solidarity is developed through acts of "translation" (de Sousa Santos et al., 2007). Furthermore, to make CJE *explicitly* hegemonic is to recognise that this war of position is vertical, as much as it is horizontal, insofar as we must find ways to translate these insights in formal educational spaces. Following we consider the challenges and opportunities for this, by way of exploring the politics of policy in Scotland, particularly LfS.

Learning for sustainability: the current educational policy context in Scotland

LfS became part of Scottish educational policy and discourse following the publication of the One Planet Schools Ministerial Advisory Group report (titled "Learning for Sustainability") in December 2012 (Scottish Government, 2012).[1] This report introduced a model of LfS as an organising concept for three areas – Sustainable Development, Global Citizenship Education and Outdoor Learning – with a singular overarching aim to develop:

> a whole school approach that enables the school and its wider community to build the values, attitudes, knowledge, skills and confidence needed to develop practices and take decisions which are compatible with a sustainable and more equitable future.
>
> *(Scottish Government, 2012, p. xx)*

This internationally significant development – which recognises the need to develop curricular links between schools and their wider communities – "builds on a number of factors such as: a greater awareness of the scale of our impacts and significance of 'sustainability';... developments by the General Teaching Council for Scotland (GTCS), the "third sector" and academia; a range of UN and other international initiatives; and changes in government policy focus' (Higgins & Christie, 2018). In short, the term LfS can be understood as offering an ostensibly holistic pedagogical approach that seeks to build the values, skills and knowledge necessary to develop practices within schools, communities and within teacher education, that accord with the collective aim of taking action for a sustainable future. It is woven into the warp and weft of educational policy in a number of ways, for example, professional standards and self-evaluation frameworks.

On the face of it then, Scottish schools sit within an internationally recognised policy context, offering learning opportunities to address the various dimensions of climate (in)justice generated through "messy" democratic learning taking place in the wider community. However, we know that the teachers who implement new approaches "may not construct the same philosophical understanding of the reform philosophy as the creators of the model" (Wallace & Priestley, 2011, p. 361). This is particularly the case with "sustainability," an object of hegemonic struggle *par excellence*, in that it "floats" between a commitment to social justice and neoliberal commitments to "sustainable" economic growth and post-welfare forms of entrepreneurial citizen agency, in which local community action steps in to replace a hollowed-out public sector. In this sense, sustainability can be thought of as a "vehicular idea," that is, "an idea which can reabsorb opposition, evolve with the times, and move across sites" (McKenzie et al., 2015, p. 320). Although this presents certain challenges for professional practice, such tensions made explicit are a rich form of curriculum and offer opportunities to legitimise climate justice knowledge claims. However, as argued in this chapter, this can only happen if teachers are prepared, and able, to engage with social mobilisations that make these tensions concrete (for example, by highlighting concrete manifestations of policy contradiction between climate policy and transport, labour rights, food and agriculture, energy, etc.).

In the long term, one practical consequence for "upstream" teacher education, in relation to LfS, is to mainstream an understanding of "policy as discourse" (Bacchi, 2000, p. 48), the premise of which is that "it is inappropriate to see governments as responding to 'problems' that exist 'out there' in the community. Rather 'problems' are 'created' or 'given shape' in the very policy proposals that are offered as 'responses'."

Far from implying a retreat to negative critique, such critical faculties are urgently required in order to create the conditions for acknowledging "the enormity of the challenge, the uncertainties it brings, and discover[ing] and develop[ing] appropriate strategies and disciplines for living, now" (Marshall et al., 2011, p. 4). We need to consider how educational policy frames the "sustainability" agenda in formal education, how young people are invited to respond, how political and open-ended those responses can be, and consider how comfortable teachers and school leaders are with inviting diverse affective responses, which encourage the exploration of antagonisms as educationally generative, and create space for political and active citizenship, which engage directly or indirectly, with social movements and diverse communities of struggle.

The challenge offered by LfS is internationally significant as the policy does urge us to deeply question and imagine new ways of being, doing and thinking. Griffiths and Murray (2017, p. 45), in reference to LfS policy, recognise this potential and suggest that if "students are to learn to engage enough with the world to develop informed, critical heartfelt judgements, a pedagogy is required that inspires, persuades and encourages them to pay attention and to re-think their outlook on the world." Developing a pedagogical approach that not only creates space for this inquiry but also encourages the messiness and open-ended thinking required when faced with "the chance of understanding something new, something unforeseen by us" (Arendt, 1961, p. 196) is demanding, uncomfortable and, in some cases, troubling. Yet, as we have outlined, it is precisely this "messiness" that marks social movement learning. Thus, the praxis of CJMs offers an opportunity to model the challenges involved in LfS, through providing authentic exemplars of collective democratic learning, which necessitate risk, dissent and awkwardness. Of course, the aim of this cannot be to merely indoctrinate students into social movement ideologies, and this means finding space and time to explore emotionally ambivalent reactions through what Spivak calls "uncoercive rearrangements of desire," whilst nonetheless recognising that "there can be no education if there is no shoving and pushing" (2014, p. 80).

Towards a conclusion: considerations for CJE in schools

Without claiming to provide any straightforward roadmap, we conclude by clarifying the main considerations that we believe are necessary to shape the development of CJE within and through LfS policy in Scottish schools.

Arguably, although Scottish educational policy emphasises the importance of experiential learning through active citizenship in communities, "community" has arguably been constructed as a site of consensus rather than plurality and difference (Biesta, 2008). Framed within this context, climate justice is interesting because it is positioned against facile constructions of citizenship, through which individuals act locally, as part of a wider global community of undifferentiated responsibility. Climate justice claims are historically and geographically contingent (Jamison, 2010, p. 818), and the disputes they create are generally disputes over appropriate geographical, political, economic and generational boundaries and relations (Walker, 2012). CJE must challenge teacher educators, teachers and students to understand how these boundaries of legitimate citizenship are constituted, negotiated and challenged, thus placing citizenship learning, as an aspect of LfS, in a more overtly political context.

Current LfS policy offers an opportunity to develop "open-ended pedagogy" – educational spaces that create and foster alternatives to the mono-cultured, mainstreamed thinking that invite everyone to be involved but only require us (teachers and learners) to take note without provoking us to pay focused critical attention, nor to become who we are not yet (Griffiths & Murray, 2017). Developing a similar line of analysis, Sund and Öhman (2014, p. 649) argue that "sustainability education" can become an explicitly hegemonic affair to the extent that it offers strategies and opportunities for students to reframe antagonisms as agonism – developing the affective, as well as cognitive, capacity for "conflictual consensus" (Mouffe, 2005). This is not an easy task, nor a comfortable space to operate within. In fact, it challenges many of the assumptions tacitly shaping what "responsible citizenship" – a central tenet of Scottish CfE – is imagined to be. As education theorist Biesta (2011) argues, our vision of CJE poses a fundamental *challenge to* the "socialisation conception of democratic learning and education," since the (re)making of political subjectivities is constitutive of democratic politics, not an *a priori* condition for participation in it. Perhaps counter-intuitively, such pedagogical approaches must see universal claim-making as the very condition of democratic politics. However, as Laclau (2000) and Butler (2000) convincingly argue, universal claims (including those aspiring to climate justice) represent the contingent outcome of acts of translation between actual political struggles, not transcendental knowledge claims imposed by above.

Undoubtedly, LfS provides exciting opportunities for CJE, but there is a danger that such curricula might become incorporated if untethered from the knowledge claims made and produced through collective action. Within this constellation of knowledge claims, the social organisation of power may be described as *collateral* curriculum, but this does not make it *incidental* curriculum – precisely the opposite. It offers educators the opportunity to explore a fundamental insight about the relationship between the generation of knowledge and action for social change. Likewise, "working in and against" the limitations of policy and practice in schools might provide a valuable resource to systematise the "messy learning" generated within and between different communities of struggle, by clarifying the ways in which young people experience, negotiate, endorse or dismiss the knowledge claims of CJMs.

Note

1 See Higgins and Christie (2018) for a more detailed historical perspective on this policy development.

References

Ahmed, S., 2014. *Willful subjects*. Durham: North Carolina Press.
Amsler, S.S., 2011. From 'therapeutic' to political education: The centrality of affective sensibility in critical pedagogy. *Critical Studies in Education*, 52(1), 47–63.
Arendt, H., 1961. *Between past and future: Six exercises in political thought*. New York: Viking.
Bacchi, C., 2000. Policy as discourse: What does it mean? Where does it get us? *Discourse: Studies in the Cultural Politics of Education*, 21(1), 45–74.
Biesta, G., 2008. What kind of citizen? What kind of democracy? Citizenship education and the Scottish Curriculum for Excellence. *Scottish Educational Review*, 40(2), 38–52.
Biesta, G., 2011. *Learning democracy in school and society: Education, lifelong learning and the politics of citizenship*. Rotterdam: Sense Publishers.
Bond, P. & Dorsey, K., 2010. Anatomies of environmental knowledge & resistance: Diverse climate justice movements and waning eco-neoliberalism. *The Journal of Australian Political Economy*, 36(66), 286–316.
Butler, J., 2000. Competing universalisms. *In:* J. Butler, E. Laclau, & S. Zizek, eds. *Contingency, hegemony and universality: Contemporary dialogues on the left*. London: Verso, 136–181.
Camp for Climate Action, 2010. *Never mind the bankers*. [online] Available from: www.climatecamp.org.uk/actions/edinburgh-2010/never-mind-the-bankers [Accessed 1 September 2010].
Clover, D.E. & Hall, B.L., 2010. Critique, create and act: Environmental adult and social movement learning in an era of climate change. *In:* F. Kagawa & D. Selby, eds. *Education and climate change: Living and learning in interesting times*. London: Routledge, 161–174.
Cox, L. & Nilsen, A., 2014. *We make our own history: Marxism and social movements in the twilight of neoliberalism*. London: Pluto Press.
Crowther, J. & Martin, I., 2010. Messy learning? Legitimate peripheral participation in a community campaign. *40th Annual SCUTREA Conference*, 6–8 July 2010, University of Warwick, Coventry. Available from: www.leeds.ac.uk/educol/documents/191529.pdf [Accessed 14 November 2017].
Crowther, J. and Shaw, M., 1997. Social movements and the education of desire. *Community Development Journal*, 32(3), 266–279.

de Sousa Santos, B., Nunes, J.A., & Meneses, M.P., 2007. Introduction: Opening up the cannon of knowledge and recognition of difference. *In:* B. de Sousa Santos, ed. *Another knowledge is possible: Beyond Northern epistemologies.* London: Verso, xxix–lxii

Eyerman, R. & Jamison, A., 1991. *Social movements: A cognitive approach.* Cambridge: Polity Press.

Fraser, N., 2016. Expropriation and exploitation in racialized capitalism: A reply to Michael Dawson. *Critical Historical Studies*, 3(1), 163–178.

Graham, P. & Luke, A., 2011. Critical discourse analysis and the political economy of communication: Understanding the new corporate order. *Cultural Politics*, 7(1), 103–132.

Gramsci, A., 1971. *Selections from the prison notebooks of Antonio Gramsci.* London: Lawrence & Wishart.

Griffiths, M. & Murray, R., 2017. Love and social justice in learning for sustainability. *Ethics and Education*, 12(1), 39–50.

Harrebye, S., 2011. Global civil society and international summits: New labels for different types of activism at the COP15. *Journal of Civil Society*, 7(4), 407–426.

Hardt, M. & Negri, A., 2004. *Multitude: War and Democracy in the Age of Empire.* London: Penguin.

Harvey, D., 2010. *The enigma of capital.* London: Verso.

Higgins, P. & Christie, B., 2018. Learning for Sustainability. *In:* T.G.K. Bryce, W.M. Humes, D. Gillies, & A. Kennedy, eds. *Scottish education.* 5th ed. Edinburgh: University of Edinburgh Press, 554–564.

Howarth, D., 2000. *Discourse.* Milton Keynes: Open University Press.

Jamison, A., 2010. Climate change knowledge and social movement theory. *Wiley Interdisciplinary Reviews*, 1, 811–823.

Kagawa, F. & Selby, D., 2010. Climate change education: A critical agenda for interesting times. *In:* F. Kagawa & D. Selby, eds. *Education and climate change: Living and learning in interesting times.* New York: Routledge, 241–243

Klein, N., 2014. *This changes everything: Capitalism vs the climate.* London: Allen Lane.

Laclau, E., 2000. Identity and hegemony: The role of universality in the constitution of political logics. *In:* J. Butler, E. Laclau, & S. Zizek, eds. *Contingency, hegemony and universality: Contemporary dialogues on the left.* London: Verso, 44–89.

Laclau, E., 2006. Why constructing a people is the main task of radical politics. *Critical Inquiry*, 32(4), 646–680.

Lohmann, L., 2008. Carbon trading, climate justice and the production of ignorance: Ten examples. *Development*, 51, 359–365.

Marshall, J., Coleman, G., & Reason, P., 2011. *Leadership for sustainability: An action research approach.* Sheffield: Greenleaf Publishing.

McGregor, C., 2015. Direct climate action as public pedagogy: The cultural politics of the Camp for Climate Action. *Environmental Politics*, 24(3), 343–364.

McGregor, C. & Crowther, J., 2018. The transition movement as politics and pedagogy in communities. *Community Development Journal*, 53(1), 8–24.

McKenzie, M., Bieler, A., & McNeil, R., 2015. Education policy mobility: Reimagining sustainability in neoliberal times. *Environmental Education Research*, 21(3), 319–337.

Mouffe, C., 2005. *On the political.* New York: Routledge.

Mouffe, C., 2013. *Agonistics: Thinking the world politically.* London: Verso.

Ratter, B.M.W., Philipp, K.H., & von Storch, H., 2012. Between hype and decline: Recent trends in public perception of climate change. *Environmental Science & Policy*, 18, 3–8.

Scandrett, E., Crowther, J., Hemmi, A., Mukherjee, S., Dharmesh, S., and Tarunima, S. (2010). Theorising education and learning in social movements: Environmental justice campaigns in Scotland and India. *Studies in the Eduction of Adults*, 42(2), 124–140.

Scandrett, E., 2016., Climate justice: Contested discourse and social transformation. *International Journal of Climate Change Strategies and Management*, 8(4), 477–487.

Scandrett, E., Crowther, J., & McGregor, C., 2012. Poverty, protest and popular education: Discourses of climate change. *In:* A. Carvalho & T.R. Peterson, eds. *Climate change politics: Communication and public engagement.* New York: Cambria, 277–306.

Schlosberg, D., 2008. *Defining environmental justice: Theories, movements and nature.* New York: Oxford University Press

Schlosberg, D., 2013. Theorising environmental justice: The expanding sphere of a discourse. *Environmental Politics*, 22(1), 37–55.

Scottish Government, 2012. *Learning for sustainability report.* Available from: www.scotland.gov.uk/Topics/Education/Schools/curriculum/ACE/OnePlanetSchools/LearningforSustainabilitreport [Accessed 30 August 2017].

Scruggs, L. & Benegal, S., 2012. Declining public concern about climate change: Can we blame the great recession? *Global Environmental Change*, 22(2), 505–515.

Sklair, L., 2001. *The transnational capitalist class.* Oxford: Blackwell.

Spivak, G., 2014. *Readings.* London: Seagull.

Sund, L. & Öhman, J., 2014. On the need to repoliticise environmental and sustainability education: Rethinking the postpolitical consensus, *Environmental Education Research*, 20(5), 639–659.

Thompson, E.P., 1976. Romanticism, moralism and utopianism: The case of William Morris. *New Left Review*, I(99), September–October, 83–111.

Touraine, A., 1977. *The self-production of society.* Chicago: The University of Chicago Press.

Walker, G., 2012. *Environmental justice: Concepts, evidence and politics.* London: Routledge.

Wallace, C. & Priestley, M., 2011. Teacher beliefs and the mediation of curriculum innovation in Scotland: A socio-cultural perspective on professional development and change. *Journal of Curriculum Studies*, 43(3), 357–381.

Williams, R., 1977. Base and superstructure in Marxist cultural theory. *New Left Review*, I(82), November–December, 3–16.

Zald, M.N., 2000. Ideologically structured action: An enlarged agenda for social movement research. *Mobilization: An International Journal*, 5(1), 1–16.

37

Transformative approaches to address climate change and achieve climate justice

Dunja Krause[1]

Introduction: why we need transformative approaches

Transformation has become the new buzzword in debates around climate change and development. The need for "transforming our world" is recognised not only by academics but also in the commitment of national governments to the 2030 Agenda for Sustainable Development. While there seems to be far-reaching agreement on the need for transformation for addressing the paramount challenges of climate change and sustainable development, there is less clarity and agreement on what transformation means, what it entails in practice and how it can be realised in order to both tackle climate change and achieve climate justice.

It has been recognised that transformation is needed to overcome current economic and governance systems that tend to reproduce inequalities and injustices, in particular related to environmental and climate change. Climate change is fraught with a potential triple injustice where people who are least responsible for climate change are most exposed to its impacts and, in addition, further disadvantaged by approaches to address climate change which reproduce or exacerbate existing inequalities (UNRISD 2016). The climate crisis is thus prone to produce a crisis of social justice (Steger et al. 2013) in which the poorest people pay the highest price and are least able to influence policy-making to address climate change (Meikle et al. 2016; Preston et al. 2014).

Despite these injustices, policymakers and practitioners alike have increasingly focused on promoting climate change resilience and the idea of self-reliance and community responsibility in withstanding disasters. While the concept of resilience thinking has a lot to offer in addressing climate change as social-ecological problem (see, for example, Folke et al. 2010; Walker et al. 2004), it was criticised for ignoring power relations and politics that make up the root causes of climate change vulnerability and the injustices associated with it (Evans and Reid 2014; MacKinnon and Derickson 2013). While the concept's richness would allow for differentiated analyses, a growing policy uptake of resilience has led to a dominant use and interpretation of the term in a narrow sense of robustness to withstand external shocks. This has in turn resulted in policy responses that often tackle symptoms rather than root causes.

The new focus on "transformation" can thus be seen as a shift away from the focus on robustness (and safeguarding the status quo) and towards the recognition that fundamentally different economies and societies are needed to effectively tackle the root causes of climate change and to achieve climate justice. This recognition acknowledges that we must go beyond "quick fixes" which promise short-term solutions but can erode resilience in the long run (Adger et al. 2011; Sterner et al. 2006). The increasing use of "transformation" in both policy documents and scholarly literature faces the same problem as resilience, however: without a clear definition and debate of the meaning and implications of the concept, it runs the risk of being reduced to a mere buzzword that goes unchallenged and has little power to make a real difference.

This chapter thus seeks to first unpack notions of transformation and transformative change to contribute to a better understanding of its justice implications before discussing specific approaches to address climate change. It will first outline a key distinction between analytical and normative interpretations and framings of transformation and transformative change and then focus on two key aspects of addressing climate change: first, it will introduce the debates on broader socio-economic transformation for sustainable development which is intrinsically linked to climate change mitigation and addressing the causes of climate change. Second, the chapter will introduce the debates on transformative adaptation to climate change and illustrate approaches that aim to tackle the impacts of climate change. The chapter will close by bringing together the common threads from the different transformative approaches to address climate change which can inform rights-based decision- and policy-making for climate justice.

Distinguishing normative and analytical concepts of transformation

Common definitions of transformations evolve around qualitative change implying a positive change to something preferable, but there are no clear definitions that would allow an easy distinction between transformation and other types of change (Mustelin and Handmer 2013). In the context of sustainable development and climate change resilience, much of the scholarship on transformation defines it in terms of the magnitude and nature of change it implies. Based on social-ecological systems theory, transformation is seen, for example, as a systemic shift from one system configuration to another. In this systems approach, transformation can occur forcefully, resulting from large-scale impacts on the system at hand or deliberately, resulting from changes in social systems in order to navigate change towards a desirable outcome (Folke et al. 2010). In the case of climate change, it is generally recognised that large-scale transformations in social and economic systems are required in order to respect planetary boundaries and prevent catastrophic shifts in the climate system (Clarke et al. 2014; Kates et al. 2012). These definitions of transformation contain implicit normative assumptions, such as the desirability of the current climate system over alternatives. There is little to no discussions on the specificity of these normative assumptions in part of the literature, however, so that a key distinction can be made between more analytical, system-theoretical approaches to transformation and those that are explicitly normative with regard to its social implications.

System-theoretical approaches to transformation aim to analyse whether or not a given system has transformed or has the capacity to deliberately transform to remain within planetary boundaries but do not prescribe what such transformation should look like within the broader framework of sustainability. Instead, literature in this school of thought focuses on distinguishing transformation from less radical and less fundamental types of change in response to climate change and environmental hazards. There are several strands of literature within the broader community of scholars studying social-ecological system transformation. One main strand sees changes in governance arrangements and management regimes as key to navigating transformation within social-ecological systems (Berkes et al. 2003; see Patterson et al. 2015). In this view, transformation is seen as more of a management challenge that needs to overcome lacking environmental governance and the "command-and-control" approach to nature (see Olsson and Galaz 2012). Another strand of literature focuses on the role of social innovation and agency in transformations towards sustainability, emphasising the need for changing values, beliefs and behaviours that shape governance and management systems (Westley et al. 2011; Westley et al. 2013). Here, the direction of transformation addressed is usually one from unsustainable practices towards ecosystem stewardship and large-scale resilience, for example, shifting cultivation patterns towards sustainable resource management or shifting from fossil fuels to renewable energy systems. While social justice is often mentioned, the political dimensions of transforming to sustainability remain underemphasised (see Patterson et al. 2015; Schulz and Siriwardane 2015).

There are, however, scholars who are more specific about the explicit normative nature of transformation and highlight, for example, the necessary shifts in power and representation of interests that distinguishes transformation from other types of change (Pelling 2011). These build on political economy approaches and use vulnerability as a starting point of their analysis rather than a result of climate change (O'Brien et al. 2004; Oliver-Smith 2004; Wisner et al. 2004). Transformation is then a way to address vulnerability and overcome development failures. Using a rights-based approach is promoted as a pathway that has both intrinsic and instrumental value in the pursuit of multiple, environmental and social, goals (Ziervogel et al. 2017).

Transformation as fundamental change raises questions of who gets to decide on it and whom it is for (Fazey et al. 2017), as well as how deliberate transformation can be brought about in an ethical and fair manner (Cook et al. 2012; O'Brien and Sygna 2013). Mustelin and Handmer (2013) point out that not all transformation is desirable and call for a better understanding of underlying drivers that shape transformative outcomes. There is little guidance, however, on assessing and evaluating the transformation of power structures and governance systems that currently reproduce inequalities and put the most vulnerable people at greatest risk of climate change.

In its 2016 flagship report, *Policy Innovations for Transformative Change*, the United Nations Research Institute for Social Development (UNRISD) has put forward a definition of transformative change that can outline normative cornerstones for desirable transformations to sustainability and equity: transformative change tackles the root causes of poverty, inequality and environmental destruction. It can be driven by innovative policies that are grounded in normative values of social justice and environmental sustainability and forged through inclusive political processes, equitable forms of partnership, governance reforms and increased state capacity. Transformative change requires changes in social structures and relations, addressing the growing economic and political power of elites, and patterns of stratification related to class, gender, ethnicity, religion or location that can lock people into disadvantage (UNRISD 2016).

Based on this explicit normative definition of transformative change, it can be made out that approaches conducive to transformations to sustainability and equity are those that "are grounded in universal and rights-based policy approaches; reverse normative hierarchies within integrated policy frameworks; re-embed economic policies and activities in social and environmental norms; and foster truly participatory decision-making approaches" (UNRISD 2016:222). In order to effectively address climate change and achieve climate justice, it is necessary to adopt an approach for significant change towards something qualitatively better that is rooted in normative values of social justice and equity. Empowerment and participation in decision-making processes are central to the achievement of fair solutions because transformation is inherently social and political and thus fraught with divergent views of what is desirable and necessary (see Krause 2017; UNRISD 2016). The subsequent sections will discuss transformative approaches first in the context of climate change mitigation and second in the context of adaptation to climate change.

Dunja Krause

Transformative approaches to mitigating climate change

The question of justice and fairness in climate change mitigation has historically been a source of disagreement and stalemate in international climate negotiations. From the beginning of the UN Framework Convention on Climate Change, there has been a divide between developing and developed countries. Based on their historically negligible greenhouse gas emissions, developing countries argued for their right to international support in tackling climate change and for their right to further emit in order to speed up their economic development. Developed countries were reluctant to accept full responsibility for climate change and rejected the call for paying up on their ecological debt (see Martínez-Alier 2012). One of the key challenges of effectively tackling climate change can thus be seen in the domain of justice and finding fair approaches for burden-sharing while ensuring that developing countries do not view "climate justice as the justice of following the North down the fossil-fuel path" (Baer and Athanasiou 2002).

The adoption of the Paris Agreement on climate change in December 2015 marked an important milestone in overcoming some of the barriers to effective climate policy, and it should be commended that there finally is an international climate agreement that is universal in nature and captures the majority of global climate change emissions.[2] Overall, a growing tendency for voluntary commitments has entered most domains of environmental and climate governance, also reflected in the Paris Agreement and its nationally determined contributions with which each party to the agreement communicates its own mitigation intention and goal. While the approach might have been necessary to facilitate consensus and reach an agreement in the first place, it shows that debates on justice dimensions and fair shares of climate change mitigation have been side-lined. Rose et al. (2017) show, for example, that the emission reduction pledges expressed by countries at COP21[3] are not in line with equity principles (such as ability to pay and egalitarian equity). Other scholars have critiqued the process for its neglect of regional variations in climate change impacts and the reflection of global power asymmetries in the decision of what constitutes "safe" levels of global warming. Many lower and middle-income countries, in particular small island developing states, object to the 2 degrees Celsius goal with regard to their high levels of exposure (see Tschakert 2015). This is underlined by the inclusion of the aspirational target of 1.5 degrees Celsius in the Paris Agreement. It is to some extent accounted for in the agreement's article on adaptation, which acknowledges the needs of vulnerable developing countries, and reflected in the decision to expand the financial support to developing countries per the set goal of mobilising US$100 billion per year by 2025 (UNFCCC 2015). Special funds to support climate action in developing countries can be seen as a redistributive mechanism and progress in climate justice (Roberts and Parks 2007), but their transformative potential remains limited as long as root causes of injustice are not addressed.

Transformations in the area of climate change mitigation are discussed mostly in terms of changing socio-economic systems for more sustainable production and consumption patterns, for example, through decoupling of ecological impacts and economic activities (Jackson 2009). There are several pathways for tackling global crises, including the climate crisis. Utting (2013) distinguishes market liberalism, embedded liberalism that entails a stronger regulatory framework and alter-globalisation that entails changing state-society-market relations. The most prominent approaches in climate change mitigation range from relatively conservative approaches such as green growth and greening the economy to more progressive "eco-social" and alter-globalisation approaches. These pathways have different justice implications.

Greening the economy seeks to decouple emissions from economic growth and achieve higher environmental sustainability of economic activities. It also aims to improve human well-being and social equity while addressing environmental sustainability (UNEP 2011), but seeks to do so without questioning the larger political economy at play. Green economy initiatives are rooted in market liberalism or embedded liberalism depending on the level of regulation and state intervention at play. Green economy does not tackle issues of reversing normative hierarchies that subordinate social and environmental goals to economic profitability and does not discuss ways for ensuring true participation in decision-making processes. While it is embedded in clear environmental norms, it is thus less explicit about how social equity and wellbeing can be addressed. As a result, green economy approaches have had unintended social impacts, particularly on already disadvantaged groups and have, for example, hampered the rights of indigenous peoples (Banerjee and Sood 2012; Cook et al. 2012). Biofuel production is a prominent example for conflicts between customary and legal property rights (Bastos Lima 2012), but there are further examples from payment for ecosystem services schemes that have reproduced power relations to the disadvantage of poor and marginalised people (McAfee 2012). In many of the examples, lacking participation can be seen as a source of unintended consequences, as assumptions made in projects were not met in reality: in India, for example, non-food crops for biofuel production were only pursued on marginal lands in order to ensure food security, but it was overlooked that these marginal lands were often used by rural poor people who perceived the land use changes as massive land grabbing (Bastos Lima 2012). In South Africa, a project for the promotion of solar home systems to improve electricity access and women's employment struggled to deliver on its gender equality objectives because the work that was created was perceived as inappropriate for women (Musyoki 2012). Active participation of local communities in the project design phases could have addressed these issues from the beginning.

At the more radical and progressive end of the spectrum of transformative approaches, alter-globalisation opposes neoliberal globalisation and seeks to promote participation and empowerment to support local development and collective action (UNRISD 2016; Utting 2013). Alter-globalisation aims to tackle power relations and structural inequalities that underpin unsustainable practices and that are rooted in neoliberal capitalism. Examples for alter-globalisation include movements for degrowth and voluntary simplicity (see, for example, Asara et al. 2015; Martínez-Alier 2012). Another increasingly relevant example of progressive transformation that is rooted in sustainability and justice is social and solidarity economy (SSE). SSE is an umbrella term used to describe approaches to the economy that prioritise social and often environmental objectives over growth orientation and profit-making and that operate based on principles of solidarity, cooperation and democratic self-management (see UNRISD 2016; Utting 2015). SSE comprises a wide range of initiatives and organisations such as fair trade networks, cooperatives, social enterprises, women's self-help groups and mutual associations. Based on this wide range and the differences between SSE initiatives and organisations, their impact on social justice varies from expanding people-centred approaches in the social economy to pushing for redistributive justice and alternatives to capitalism in the solidarity economy (Utting 2015). While SSE is still seen as a "fringe economy," it is rapidly growing and scaling up and "provides ample space for connecting more conventional notions of enterprise, entrepreneurship and social protection with more transformative concepts of rights, equality, active citizenship, ethics, solidarity, emancipation and (social, environmental and distributive) justice" (Utting 2015:36).

While SSE faces a number of challenges in terms of resource availability and upscaling without undermining its principles, it does hold transformative potential. This potential lies in its adherence to the criteria for transformative change as outlined earlier: it adopts a rights-based and eco-social approach that reflects a significant change in perspective; it sees economic activities as a means to reach equity and environmental sustainability and thus conditions economic activities and choices on fair social outcomes and environmental sustainability (Cook and Dugarova 2014; UNRISD 2016). This can be seen as a reversal of normative hierarchies. With its principles of solidarity, reciprocity and cooperation, it promotes true participation and re-embeds economic activities in social and often environmental norms.

Transformative adaptation to climate change

The official recognition that mitigation will in itself not suffice to prevent disastrous climate change was made relatively late for political reasons. It was feared that acknowledging the urgent need for adaptation would shift away the focus from emissions reduction and therefore hinder effective mitigation. With the growing number of climate-related disasters and an increasing understanding of social vulnerability as a central element of risk, the promotion of adaptive or "climate-proof," disaster risk reduction (ADB 2005; Birkmann et al. 2011; GIZ 2011) and innovative and transformative adaptation to the unavoidable impacts of climate change grew in importance (IPCC 2012; IPCC 2014).

Adaptation is usually described as either incremental, for example, when it seeks to maintain a status quo and protect communities against climate change impacts, or as transformative, which refers to larger or more radical change. Transformative adaptation can be defined in terms of its scale, novelty or change of places (Kates et al. 2012) or in terms of a regime change to overcome inequalities and root causes of vulnerability (Pelling 2011). Whereas the former definition is more in line with an analytical approach to transformation and applies to large-scale technical solutions as well as changing management and governance systems, the latter takes a more political approach and addresses questions of power and justice. In rights-based approaches to climate change responses, entitlement failures resulting largely from the institutional context are seen as root causes of disaster vulnerability that need to be addressed and overcome (Ziervogel et al. 2017). In this line of thinking, it is recognised that resilience is not always desirable and may need to be overcome in order to promote transformative change towards more equitable and sustainable systems.

Adger et al. (2009) argue that adaptation is limited by social factors rather than environmental thresholds and that those factors are determined by ethics, knowledge, risk perception and cultural values. Similarly, Eriksen et al. (2011) identify normative principles of adaptation to ensure that adaptation contributes to social justice and environmental integrity. They highlight the role of vulnerability context, differing values, local knowledge and feedbacks across scales. This line of argumentation undermines the universal character of adaptation, which is often promoted as being equally beneficial across scales and for all. To achieve sustainable development and reduce risk in the long term, adaptation should be evaluated based on normative principles (Eriksen et al. 2011) and criteria of equity, efficiency, legitimacy and effectiveness (Adger et al. 2005). Such an approach requires inclusive negotiation and decision-making processes on adaptation as well as mechanisms that support vulnerable people in building adaptive capacities.

Compared to mitigation, adaptation to climate change lends itself more easily to a discussion of transformative change as it is closely linked to debates on resilience and development. Many adaptation policies and approaches focus on local impacts of climate change and seek to result in overall social development benefits that can be linked to questions of rights, vulnerabilities and justice. Adaptation is often linked to discussions of "no-regret" solutions that bring about additional, hazard-independent benefits for human wellbeing and social development. Such solutions include, for example, adaptive social protection systems or community-based disaster risk reduction and climate change adaptation interventions that entail capacity-building and livelihood diversification strategies. There are still relatively few case studies and examples of transformative adaptation, the majority of which are coined transformative in terms of novelty or scale of change, rather than radical social change. It has been pointed out that as transformation, adaptation can be either forced or deliberate. It can occur, for example, as distress migration in response to a disaster or as planned resettlement in anticipation of changing hazard exposure (Pelling et al. 2015). Other examples of deliberate transformation include the integration of ecological objectives in urban planning in order to address past underlying development failures (Roberts 2010).

Integrated policy approaches that address development, adaptation and environmental issues, for example, in land use planning that provides safe (and affordable) housing while accounting for climate risks, tend to be more conducive to transformative change (Revi et al. 2014). Social policy has also been emphasised as an important policy field for intervention that can address both poverty alleviation and climate vulnerability and bring about social development benefits, in particular meeting the needs of poor and vulnerable people, independent of climate change impacts (Heltberg et al. 2010). In a similar vein, Brooks et al. argue that "[s]uccessful adaptation keeps inclusive development on track" (Brooks et al. 2011:10). Based on these intrinsic links of adaptation and development, it has also been argued that "a minimum level of adaptive capacity everywhere is central to efficient, effective and equitable adaptation, and yields immediate benefits irrespective of future climate regimes" (Fankhauser and Burton 2011).

Contributing to more equitable development thus seems a key characteristic of transformative adaptation. Many examples that illustrate how social protection – for example, in the form of social funds, safety nets, livelihoods programmes, or microfinance instrument – can support development goals stay within a rather narrow definition of social policy that is explicitly targeted at poor or disaster-affected people only (see Heltberg et al. 2009). In view of transformative change, empowerment and equitable development, a universal approach to social policy may be more promising in addressing social relations and underlying root causes of vulnerability (IDS 2012; UNRISD 2006).

Transformative change to achieve climate justice

Similar to transformative climate change mitigation, transformative adaptation takes many forms and is subject to divergent views and framings of the problem at hand. With the wide range of different pathways to tackle climate change, it becomes clear that transformative change is essentially a bargaining process that needs to ensure true participation and empowerment in order to tackle climate injustice and support inclusive development.

This bargaining needs to address inequalities at different scales to produce fairer outcomes, for example, in terms of responding to the triple injustice of climate change, which requires the international discussion not only of mitigation commitments, but also necessitates a "principle-based and transparent process for determining national burden-sharing contributions to international adaptation funding" (Klein 2010). One of the key justice issues in international climate policy is the discrepancy between an arrangement-focused conception of justice and social realisations of it. Emphasis is put, for example, on constructing complex institutions for fair climate response, whereas compliance mechanisms that could ensure appropriate implementation are neglected (Ciplet et al. 2013, based on Sen 2010).

Discussions also need to take place within nation-states to identify not only the key risks associated with climate change but also winners and losers of mitigation and adaptation policies. There is increasing recognition of the potentially adverse social and distributional consequences of climate policies, which in some areas leads to "second-order adaptation" when vulnerable populations need to adapt not just to hazards and global warming but also to the policy interventions that seek to address them (Birkmann 2011). These challenges point to the importance of focusing not only on procedural and distributive aspects of justice but also on its political dimension, which establishes decision rules for contestation and claims-making and thereby shapes who is included and excluded (Fraser 2005). Focusing on the political dimension and facilitating collective bargaining processes can also advance debates on framing and identifying which kind of transformative change is positive and desirable from a justice point of view.

Climate change has very direct implications on justice that require normative approaches in addressing it, but there has so far been comparatively little policy guidance with respect to specific norms and principles of transformation in the academic literature. New coalitions of social movements, climate activists and scholars contribute to increasing debates on such principles and criteria for equity and fairness in climate change response. Voices that call for a redistribution of rights and responsibilities and shifts in power and representation of interests and values are growing louder (Mustelin and Handmer 2013; Pelling 2011). In order to foster transformative change towards sustainability and equity, change processes need to be navigated through inclusive and participatory mechanisms rooted in recognition and procedural justice (see Paavola and Adger 2006). Given the global nature of climate change and its distinct impacts on different regions and places, it has been argued that a multi-level framework for procedural justice is required to account for all affected parties across different spatial scales and constituencies (Bulkeley et al. 2013; Paavola and Adger 2006). Equally important, however, is a renewed focus on the realities of distribution and ensuring progress in actual outcomes. In terms of international climate negotiations, participation can, for example, be hindered by budgetary constraints that prevent lower-income countries from sending large delegations and legal teams to ensure that their views are sufficiently represented in the negotiations. Taking a justice perspective on climate change mitigation and adaptation reveals serious issues of inequality that hinder sustainable development. The uneven distribution of both responsibilities for and repercussions of climate change call for a shift in the normative hierarchy for decision-making. Establishing an "eco-social" rationale, it is argued, can support the integration of the different dimensions of sustainability and equity and minimise trade-offs among different approaches.

Conclusion: bringing about transformation

While transformation seems to be the latest buzzword in international development, truly transformative approaches to address climate change are currently limited to niches and fringes of socio-economic development. While the concept of transformation is often found in conceptual and theoretical discussions around climate change resilience and sustainability, it holds a lot of potential for merging debates on climate change, development and justice. Both in its analytical and normative use of the concept, it allows questioning of the status quo and looking at ways of reducing resilience in systems that are locked-in to undesirable states (Olsson and Galaz 2012). Based on the study of ecological systems, it has been argued that both crises and actor coalitions that utilise windows of opportunity can lead to the unlocking of a system for transformative change (Gunderson 2009). Research in disaster vulnerability and climate change adaptation has also argued that radical change and transformation is most likely to occur in times of crisis or in the aftermaths of disasters (Birkmann et al. 2010; Pelling 2011).

In the spirit of social and climate justice, change must be brought about by new coalitions of actors rather than through increasingly severe crises and disasters. From the study of climate change responses, there is relatively little knowledge on how desirable transformation can be brought about. Broader studies of policy innovations for sustainable development have identified ingredients for transformative change that are rooted in justice, participation and re-embedding markets (UNRISD 2016). Activists and social movements hold an important role in pushing for this transformation, in particular with regard to fostering bargaining processes and participation that are inclusive and rights-based. New actor coalitions are already forming to demand transformation – both in the economic sphere as well as around climate change response. They have kick-started change around the world to transition out of fossil fuels, to promote solidarity and collaboration and to protect the rights of all people. While unsustainable practices still dominate economics, undeniable progress has been made. Eventually progressive approaches at the fringes need to take over if we are to tackle climate change and achieve climate justice.

Notes

1 The views expressed in this chapter are those of the author and do not necessarily reflect the views of the United Nations Research Institute for Social Development.
2 The share of emissions captured by the agreement might be reduced should the U.S. administration go through with its intention to withdraw from the agreement.
3 COP21 was the twenty-first session of the Conference of the Parties to the United Nations Framework Convention on Climate Change, held in Paris in 2015.

References

Adger WN, Arnell NW, Tompkins EL. 2005. Successful adaptation to climate change across scales. *Global Environmental Change* 15(2):77–86.

Adger WN, Brown K, Nelson DR, Berkes F, Eakin H, Folke C, Galvin K, Gunderson L, Goulden M, O'Brien K, Ruitenbeek J, Tompkins EL. 2011. Resilience implications of policy responses to climate change. *WIREs Clim Change* 2(5):757–766.

Adger WN, Dessai S, Goulden M, Hulme M, Lorenzoni I, Nelson DR, Naess LO, Wolf J, Wreford A. 2009. Are there social limits to adaptation to climate change? *Climatic Change* 93(3):335–354.

Asara V, Otero I, Demaria F, Corbera E. 2015. Socially sustainable degrowth as a social – ecological transformation: Repoliticizing sustainability. *Sustainability Science* 10(3):375–384.

Asian Development Bank (ADB). 2005. Climate Proofing: A Risk-based Approach to Adaptation. Available from: www.adb.org/sites/default/files/publication/28796/climate-proofing.pdf.

Baer P, Athanasiou T. 2002. *Dead Heat: Global Justice and Global Warming*. New York: Seven Stories Press.

Banerjee P, Sood A. 2012. The Political Economy of Green Growth in India. *Social Dimensions of Green Economy and Sustainable Development Occasional Paper* 5. Geneva: UNRISD. Available from: www.unrisd.org/publications/op-banerjee-sood.

Bastos Lima MG. 2012. An Institutional Analysis of Biofuel Policies and their Social Implications: Lessons From Brazil, India and Indonesia. *Social Dimensions of Green Economy and Sustainable Development Occasional Paper* 9. Geneva: UNRISD. Available from: www.unrisd.org/publications/bastos-lima.

Berkes F, Colding J, Folke C (eds.). 2003. *Navigating Social-Ecological Systems: Building Resilience for Complexity and Change*. Cambridge: Cambridge University Press.

Birkmann J. 2011. First- and second-order adaptation to natural hazards and extreme events in the context of climate change. *Natural Hazards* 58(2):811–840.

Birkmann J, Buckle P, Jaeger J, Pelling M, Setiadi N, Garschagen M, Fernando N, Kropp J. 2010. Extreme events and disasters: A window of opportunity for change? Analysis of organizational, institutional and political changes, formal and informal responses after mega-disasters. *Natural Hazards* 55(3):637–655.

Birkmann J, Chang Seng D, Suarez D. 2011. *Adaptive Disaster Risk Reduction: Enhancing Methods and Tools of Disaster Risk Reduction in the Light of Climate Change*. DKKV Publication Series 43. Bonn: DKKV.

Brooks N, Anderson S, Ayers J, Burton I, Teilam I. 2011. Tracking Adaptation and Measuring Development. *Climate Change Working Paper* 1. London: IIED.

Bulkeley H, Carmin J, Castán Broto V, Edwards GA, Fuller S. 2013. Climate justice and global cities: Mapping the emerging discourses. *Global Environmental Change* 23(5):914–925.

Ciplet D, Roberts JT, Khan M. 2013. The politics of international climate adaptation funding: Justice and divisions in the greenhouse. *Global Environmental Politics* 13(1):49–68.

Clarke L, Jiang K, Akimoto K, Babiker M, Blanford G, Fisher-Vanden K, Hourcade J-C, Krey V, Kriegler E, Löschel A, McCollum D, Paltsev S, Rose S, Shukla PR, Tavoni M, van der Zwaan BCC, van Vuuren DP. 2014. Assessing Transformation Pathways. In: Edenhofer O, Pichs-Madruga R, Sokona Y, Farahani E, Kadner S, Seyboth K et al., editors. *Climate Change 2014: Mitigation of Climate Change. Contribution* of *Working Group III to the Fifth Assessment Report of the Intergovernmental Panel on Climate Change*. Cambridge: Cambridge University Press. pp. 413–510.

Cook S, Dugarova E. 2014. Rethinking social development for a post-2015 World. *Development* 57(1):30–35.

Cook S, Smith K, Utting P. 2012. Green Economy or Green Society? Contestation and Policies for a Fair Transition. *Social Dimensions of Green Economy and Sustainable Development Occasional Paper* 10. Geneva: UNRISD. Available from: www.unrisd.org/publications/op-cook-et-al.

Deutsche Gesellschaft für Internationale Zusammenarbeit (GIZ). 2011. Climate Proofing for Development. *Adapting to Climate Change, Reducing Risk*. Eschborn. Available from: www.preventionweb.net/files/globalplatform/entry_bg_paper~giz2011climateproofing.pdf.

Eriksen S, Aldunce P, Bahinipati CS, D'Almeida Martins R, Molefe JI, Nhemachena C, O'Brien K, Olorunfemi F, Park J, Sygna L, Ulsrud K. 2011. When not every response to climate change is a good one: Identifying principles for sustainable adaptation. *Climate and Development* 3:7–20.

Evans B, Reid J. 2014. *Resilient Life: The Art of Living Dangerously*. Cambridge: Polity.

Fankhauser S, Burton I. 2011. Spending adaptation money wisely. *Climate Policy* 11(3):1037–1049.

Fazey I, Moug P, Allen S, Beckmann K, Blackwood D, Bonaventura M, Burnett K, Danson M, Falconer R, Gagnon AS, Harkness R, Hodgson A, Holm L, Irvine KN, Low R, Lyon C, Moss A, Moran C, Naylor L, O'Brien K, Russell S, Skerratt S, Rao-Williams J, Wolstenholme R. 2017. Transformation in a changing climate: A research agenda. *Climate and Development*. Available from https://doi.org/10.1080/17565529.2017.1301864.

Folke C, Carpenter SR, Walker B, Scheffer M, Chapin T, Rockström J. 2010. Resilience thinking: Integrating resilience, adaptability and transformability. *Ecology and Society* 15(4):20.

Fraser N. 2005. Reframing justice in a globalizing world. *New Left Review* 36:1–19.

Gunderson LH. 2009. *Foundations of Ecological Resilience*. Washington: Island Press.

Heltberg R, Siegel PB, Jorgensen SL. 2009. Addressing human vulnerability to climate change: Toward a "no-regrets" approach. *Global Environmental Change* 19(1):89–99.

Heltberg R, Siegel PB, Jorgensen SL. 2010. Social Policies for Adaptation to Climate Change. In: Mearns R, Norton A, editors. *Social Dimensions of Climate Change: Equity and Vulnerability in a Warming World*. Washington. pp. 259–276.

Institute of Development Studies (IDS). 2012. Adaptive Social Protection: Making Concepts a Reality. *Guidance Notes for Practitioners*. Available from: www.ids.ac.uk/files/dmfile/ASPGuidanceNotes_FINAL.pdf.

Intergovernmental Panel on Climate Change (IPCC). 2012. Managing the Risks of Extreme Events and Disasters to Advance Climate Change Adaptation: A Special Report of Working Groups I and II of the Intergovernmental Panel on Climate Change. Cambridge and New York: Cambridge University Press.

Intergovernmental Panel on Climate Change (IPCC). 2014. Climate Change 2014: Impacts, Adaptation, and Vulnerability. Part A: Global and Sectoral Aspects: Contribution of Working Group II to the Fifth Assessment Report of the Intergovernmental Panel on Climate Change. Cambridge and New York.

Jackson T. 2009. *Prosperity Without Growth: Economics for a Finite Planet*. London: Earthscan.

Kates RW, Travis WR, Wilbanks TJ. 2012. Transformational adaptation when incremental adaptations to climate change are insufficient. *Proceedings of the National Academy of Sciences of the United States of America* 109(19):7156–7161.

Klein RJT. 2010. Mainstreaming Climate Adaptation Into Development: A Policy Dilemma. In: Ansohn A, Pleskovic B, editors. *Climate Governance and Development*. Washington: World Bank. pp. 35–52.

Krause D. 2017. Linking Resilience Thinking and Transformative Change: Taking Development Debates to a New Level. *UNRISD Blogs and Think Pieces*, 16 August. Available from: www.unrisd.org/resilience-krause.

MacKinnon D, Derickson KD. 2013. From resilience to resourcefulness. A critique of resilience policy and activism. *Progress in Human Geography* 37(2): 253–270.

Martínez-Alier J. 2012. Environmental justice and economic degrowth: An alliance between two movements. *Capitalism Nature Socialism* 23(1):51–73.

McAfee K. 2012. Nature in the market-world: Ecosystem services and inequality. *Development: Greening the Economy* 55(1):96–103.

Meikle M, Wilson J, Jafry T. 2016. Climate justice: Between mammon and mother earth. *International Journal of Climate Change Strategies and Management* 8(4):488–504.

Mustelin J, Handmer J. 2013. Triggering Transformation: Managing Resilience or Invoking Real Change? Proceedings of Transformation in a Changing Climate. pp. 24–32; 19–21 June; Oslo, Norway.

Musyoki A. 2012. Emerging Policy for a Green Economy and Social Development in Limpopo, South Africa. *Social Dimensions of Green Economy and Sustainable Development Occasional Paper* 8. Geneva: UNRISD. Available from: www.unrisd.org/publications/op-musyoki.

O'Brien KL, Eriksen S, Schjolden A, Nygaard L. 2004. What's in a Word? Conflicting Interpretations of Vulnerability in Climate Change Research. *CICERO Working Paper* 2004:4. Oslo: CICERO.

O'Brien KL, Sygna L. 2013. Responding to Climate Change: The Three Spheres of Transformation. Proceedings of Transformation in a Changing Climate. pp. 16–23; 19–21 June; Oslo, Norway.

Oliver-Smith A. 2004. Theorizing Vulnerability in a Globalized World: A Political Ecological Perspective. In: Bankoff G, Frerks G, Hilhorst T, editors. *Mapping Vulnerability: Disasters, Development, and People*. London, Sterling: Earthscan. pp. 10–24.

Olsson P, Galaz V. 2012. Social-Ecological Innovation and Transformation. In: Nicholls A, Murdock A, editors. *Social Innovation: Blurring Boundaries to Reconfigure Markets*. London: Palgrave Macmillan. pp. 223–247.

Paavola J, Adger WN. 2006. Fair adaptation to climate change. *Ecological Economics* 56(4):594–609.

Patterson J, Schulz K, Vervoort J, Adler C, Hurlbert M, van der Hel, Sandra, Schmidt A, Barau A, Obani P, Sethi M, Hissen N, Tebboth M, Anderton K, Börner S, Widerberg O. 2015. Transformations Towards Sustainability: Emerging Approaches, Critical Reflections, and a Research Agenda. *Earth System Governance Working Paper* 34. Lund and Amsterdam.

Pelling M. 2011. *Adaptation to Climate Change: From Resilience to Transformation*. Abingdon and New York: Routledge.

Pelling M, O'Brien K, Matyas D. 2015. Adaptation and transformation. *Climatic Change* 133(1):113–127.

Preston I, Banks N, Hargreaves K, Kazmierczak A, Lucas K, Mayne R, Downing C, Street R. 2014. *Climate Change and Social Justice: An Evidence Review*. York. Available from: www.jrf.org.uk/sites/default/files/jrf/migrated/files/climate-change-social-justice-full.pdf.

Revi A, Satterthwaite D, Aragón-Durand F, Corfee-Morlot J, Kiunsi RBR, Pelling M, Roberts D, Solecki W, Gajjar SP, Sverdlik A. 2014. Towards transformative adaptation in cities: The IPCC's Fifth Assessment. *Environment and Urbanization* 26(1):11–28.

Roberts D. 2010. Prioritizing climate change adaptation and local level resilience in Durban, South Africa. *Environment and Urbanization* 22(2):397–413.

Roberts JT, Parks BC. 2007. *A Climate of Injustice: Global Inequality, North-South Politics, and Climate Policy*. Cambridge, London: MIT Press.

Rose A, Wei D, Miller N, Vandyck T. 2017. Equity, emissions allowance trading and the Paris agreement on climate change. *Economics of Disasters and Climate Change* 1(3):203–232.

Schulz K, Siriwardane R. 2015. Depoliticized and Technocratic? Normativity and the Politics of Transformative Adaptation. *Earth System Governance Working Paper* 33. Lund, Amsterdam.

Sen A. 2010. *The Idea of Justice*. London: Penguin Books.

Steger MB, Wilson EK, Goodman J. 2013. *Justice Globalism: Ideology, Crises, Policy*. Los Angeles: Sage.

Sterner T, Troell M, Vincent J, Aniyar S, Barrett S, Brock W, Carpenter S, Chopra K, Ehrlich P, Hoel M, Levin S, Mäler K-G, Norberg J, Pihl L, Söderqvist T, Wilen J, Xepapadeas A. 2006. Quick fixes for the environment: Part of the solution or part of the problem? *Environment: Science and Policy for Sustainable Development* 48(10):20–27.

Tschakert P. 2015. 1.5°C or 2°C: A conduit's view from the science-policy interface at COP20 in Lima, Peru. *Climate Change Responses* 2(1):3.

United Nations Environment Programme (UNEP). 2011. Towards a Green Economy. Pathways to Sustainable Development and Poverty Eradication: A Synthesis for Policy-Makers. UNEP. Available from: https://sustainabledevelopment.un.org/content/documents/126GER_synthesis_en.pdf.

United Nations Framework Convention on Climate Change (UNFCCC). 2015. Adoption of the Paris Agreement: FCCC/CP/2015/10/Add.1. 12 December.

United Nations Research Institute for Social Development (UNRISD). 2006. Transformative Social Policy: Lessons From UNRISD Research. *UNRISD Research and Policy Brief 5*. Geneva: UNRISD. Available from: www.unrisd.org/rpb5.

United Nations Research Institute for Social Development (UNRISD). 2016. Policy Innovations for Transformative Change: Implementing the 2030 Agenda for Sustainable Development. Geneva: UNRISD. Available from: www.unrisd.org/flagship2016-fullreport.

Utting P. 2013. Pathways to Sustainability in a Crisis-Ridden World. In: Genevey R, Pachauri RK, Tubiana L, editors. *Reducing Inequalities: A Sustainable Development Challenge*. Delhi: TERI. pp. 175–190.

Utting P. 2015. Introduction: The Challenge of Scaling up Social and Solidarity Economy. In: Utting P, editor. *Social and Solidarity Economy: Beyond the Fringe*. London: Zed Books, UNRISD. pp. 1–37.

Walker B, Holling CS, Carpenter SR, Kinzig A. 2004. Resilience, adaptability and transformability in social-ecological systems. *Ecology and Society* 9(2):5.

Westley FR, Olsson P, Folke C, Homer-Dixon T, Vredenburg H, Loorbach D, Thompson J, Nilsson M, Lambin E, Sendzimir J, Banerjee B, Galaz V, van der Leeuw S. 2011. Tipping toward sustainability: Emerging pathways of transformation. *AMBIO* 40(7):762.

Westley FR, Tjornbo O, Schultz L, Olsson P, Folke C, Crona B, Bodin Ö. 2013. A theory of transformative agency in linked social-ecological systems. *Ecology and Society* 18(3).

Wisner B, Blaikie P, Cannon T, Davies I. 2004. *At Risk: Natural Hazards, People's Vulnerability and Disasters.* 2nd ed. London and New York: Routledge.

Ziervogel G, Pelling M, Cartwright A, Chu E, Deshpande T, Harris L, Hyams K, Kaunda J, Klaus B, Michael K, Pasquini L, Pharoah R, Rodina L, Scott D, Zweig P. 2017. Inserting rights and justice into urban resilience: A focus on everyday risk. *Environment and Urbanization* 29(1):123–138.

38

Conclusion

Tahseen Jafry

Overview

The diversity and range of chapters presented in this Handbook is a tribute to the vast scope that climate justice has to offer. From the outset, we set about not only highlighting complexities of the concept and exploring the range of definitions, philosophies and images associated with it, but also discussing how we can work towards climate justice. The different sections presented in the Handbook clearly exemplify this goal. Despite the chapters espousing different perspectives – covering theory, practice and policy – all have one thing in common: the need to foreground the views, circumstances and needs of those who have contributed least to climate change while being most affected by it, whether they reside in rural or urban areas in the Global North or South. Climate change is an issue facing all of humanity, and it is our responsibility to address the root causes of climate inequality and prioritise those who are the most vulnerable. To do this, we need a strong political will and an effective and enabling policy environment that will help us to transition to a low-carbon future. Arguably, this can only be achieved by working in partnerships and engaging in processes of governance that aim to transform the lives of those who are on the receiving end of climate change–related impacts. Getting commitment from political leaders at all levels (international, national, regional and local) to champion the cause and steer the way forward is critical. We have to some extent come a long way with the signing of the Paris Agreement and, moving on from that, the United Nations Sustainable Development Goals (SDGs) provide the global community with a sense of direction and platform for action. Goal 13, on Climate Action, sets out a lofty set of targets to combat climate change and its impacts. To what extent some of the targets are coming to fruition remains unclear, though the results of the in-depth review at the High Level Political Forum in 2019 may provide some insights into this (United Nations Sustainable Development Knowledge Platform, 2018). Perhaps what is required is for that in-depth review of progress to be conducted through a climate justice framework? Herein lies a challenge for researchers and scholars: in addition to being considered at theoretical and conceptual levels, climate justice also needs to be operationalised and to become a touchstone of climate action. To do this will require new research on the development of methodologies or tools that can be used to appraise climate injustice or justice. We need research that will lead to the development and testing of targets and indicators of climate justice. Indeed, how do we – and can we – measure climate justice? Without being able to do this, there is a danger that climate justice will remain merely aspirational.

Despite the lack of explicit methodologies for climate justice, the case studies presented in this Handbook indicate that in some domains change is happening. Individuals and communities are making up their own minds about adaptive strategies and taking ownership of their futures.

Critical issues, insights and reflections on climate justice

Presented as follows are some key critical issues, insights and reflections that have emerged from each of the sections in this Handbook, demonstrating the complex nature of climate justice and the formidable challenge of achieving it.

Theories of climate justice

While it is simply impossible to provide a comprehensive overview of the theoretical body of work that underpins climate justice, the four chapters featured in this part of the Handbook have two things in common. First, they reflect the reliance of climate justice scholarship on moral theory to bring out what is seen as essential unfairness in how climate change has come to be and how its impacts will be distributed (for example, see: Roser and Seidel, 2017). This is made clear by Idil Boran, who notes the use of moral theory to articulate duties of justice and their corresponding rights. Jörg Tremmel uses the normative concern for the wellbeing of future generations to exemplify how thought experiments – if conducted successfully – can lead to a moral justification for combating the notorious short-termism of global climate policy. It is perhaps this unashamedly forward, non-negotiable and some may say radical normative focus on the lives and livelihoods of the most vulnerable people on our planet that sets climate justice apart from other fields concerned with the social dimensions of climate change.

Second, these contributions make it clear that climate justice should be seen as spatially and temporally embedded. For instance, climate justice research and activism interacts with various kinds of social justice discourses and other "kindred justice movements," as suggested by Brian Tokar. As such, climate justice shapes and is shaped by other global issues, discourses and events, of which the global climate negotiations are an example. The temporal aspect of this embeddedness, in particular, is made all but transparent by Nejma Tamoudi and Michael Reder, who argue for narrative rather than static and rationalistic accounts of climate justice. They suggest that switching to narrativity helps to root climate justice claims in cultural practice, making them more relevant and potentially more operationalisable. These insights are certainly of high importance for a field that has historically struggled to find relevance among policymakers and development practitioners.

Climate justice, governance, policy and litigation

At the core of the discussions that run through the chapters presented in Part 2 is the following message: the need to embrace equity and inclusivity. For instance, Susan Murphy focuses on raising the voices of the most vulnerable, whereas Katharine Knox considers the circumstances of the marginalised whether in a developed or developing country. Tom Sparks shines a spotlight on those who may become displaced due to "loss of state." Encouragingly, there is emerging evidence from South Asia that the most vulnerable can be protected, as exemplified by the engagement and the creativity of South Asian judges in advancing climate justice. This has been achieved through the development of environmental constitutionalism, the expansion of access to justice in courts in South Asia and the development of innovative judicial remedies, as discussed by Emeline Pluchon. Ritwika Basu and Amir Bazaz urge for re-imagining "justice" and the imperatives of improving procedural and distributive justice. While the failures of distributive justice manifest in the practice and politics of social protection and welfare, the absence of explicit mention of (climate) justice as a stand-alone frame often obscures agency and representation, and oversimplifies the diverse terrain of climate injustice at scale. At the same time, there are emerging concepts of benefit-sharing informed by biodiversity and human rights law that can provide a strong normative understanding of what climate justice means and how it can be used to prioritise those in need. This positivity, presented by Annalisa Savaresi and Kim Bouwer, is a refreshing outlook leading us to think that changes in terms of climate litigation is possible and can be effective in prioritising the most marginalised and vulnerable.

Climate justice finance and business

The collection of chapters on climate justice, finance and business is a reflection on how climate finance needs to be (re-)defined and how it should be utilised. Emilie Prattico states that climate finance needs to move beyond sharing the burden of climate change to building resilience against its impacts, which requires investment at scale. Public climate finance must therefore be complemented to include all of the available levers that move money around the globe, including private investment and procurement from both the public and private sector. This is consolidated further where Tessa Sheridan and Tahseen Jafry consider that above all climate finance must be guided by principles of fairness, promoting equality and inclusiveness. This view is supported by Alexandre Gajevic Sayegh, who observes that climate justice finance should be constituted of "new and additional" funds, which moreover must not contradict the objectives of climate justice. The principles of historical responsibility and capacity should be applied to define and quantify the contribution of national governments. He goes on to indicate that carbon pricing should be used to seek the contribution of subnational agents who can thus complement the national effort following the polluter pays principle, with national governments remaining the site of application of the two central principles of climate justice: historical responsibility and capacity. In this way, this normative framework offers a structured and morally justified way for the annual replenishing of climate funds. Edward Cameron highlights that almost 40 countries and more than 20 cities, states and provinces already use carbon pricing mechanisms or are planning to implement them. In addition, close to 1,400 companies are disclosing their plans or current practice of putting a price on carbon emissions. With that in mind, he recommends a set of design elements for carbon pricing informed by climate justice, with the goal of ensuring effective, efficient and equitable greenhouse gas emissions reductions in a Paris-compliant world.

Just transition

The chapters in Part 4 point to critical issues associated with transitioning away from a carbon-intensive economy. Marco Grasso points to recent evidence that two-thirds of the global industrial greenhouse gas (GHG) emissions over the past two centuries can be traced to the activities of 100 companies, hailing prevalently from the oil and gas industry. He argues that "Big Oil" has played a critical role in causing climate change by creating a dependence of the global economic system on fossil fuels, thus gaining from unsustainable growth and development. Therefore, it is of critical importance to understand the inequalities arising from energy production and consumption on various political and social levels as major sources of social injustice. To achieve this goal, a more comprehensive understanding of climate justice as entailing "energy justice" is necessary, as proposed by Anna Fünfgeld.

A just energy transition, or transitioning away from these carbon-intensive sources of energy, is urgently needed in order to tackle social injustice but requires long-term planning, resource dedication and multi-stakeholder processes to ensure that countries reliant upon carbon-intensive industries can diversify their economies and transition workers and communities into a low-carbon future. Mijin Cha highlights the Ruhr region in Germany as a good example of how this transition can be achieved. On the other hand, Anna Fünfgeld considers the need to go beyond an exclusively large-scale, technological transition to renewables to furthering small-scale, community-based energy systems, as described in her case study of the Indonesian coal sector. Another way for reducing global emissions – or more accurately offsetting them – are REDD+ projects, which are not free from controversy. David Brown in his chapter points to findings that indicate REDD+ funders are primarily driven by a motivation to cost-effectively reduce global GHG emissions, which is likely to conflict with the rights, needs and interests of forest-dependent communities. He observes that the livelihood or poverty alleviation aspects of REDD+ tend to become de-valued and rendered secondary in the policy discourse. The current framing of REDD+ in this context appears to be configured primarily in the interest of the industrialised nations such as Norway by "politically offsetting" their responsibility to scale back their expansive petroleum industries. Despite the evolution in REDD+ policy and the integration of safeguards and non-carbon benefits into the REDD+ framework, analysis of the policy discourse suggests that significant and undue burdens are to be placed upon tropical-forested nations and forested communities in Ethiopia, who have little responsibility for climate change and have limited capacity to deal with its impacts.

Urban climate justice

The chapters in this section discuss the emerging nature of climate inequalities in urban spaces. Wendy Steele et al. stipulate that climate change is creating and exacerbating existing inequities in cities. The built environment and the social structure of cities are increasing the vulnerability of socially disadvantaged residents through, for instance, the "urban heat island effect," whereby rising temperatures intensify urban heat in specific locations and increase the frequency of heatwaves. People living at the economic and social margins are least capable of mitigating the effects of a changing temperature baseline and subsequently face the greatest adverse impacts, as explained by Bruce Mitchell and Jayajit Chakraborty. Sara Fuller states that we need an approach that is centred on the principles of common but differentiated responsibilities for carbon production and consumption to enable a more nuanced configuration of climate justice in the city. She goes on to say that a more critical understanding of responsibility is paramount for developing socially and politically just responses to climate change. Any configuration of climate responsibility needs to capture the specificity of people and place while invoking a moral and political obligation to act. But, based on work conducted in India, Eric Chu and Kavya Michael indicate that spatially and temporally "static" definitions of climate justice fail to account for the mobility of people and the transfer of vulnerabilities across space. Anne Maree Kreller and Sonia Graham posit that local governments avoid difficult conversations with residents about how to adapt to climate change. Whilst this might avoid angst and conflict in the short term, it may be creating conditions that undermine fairness and trust for long-term adaptation. Equal participation in climate adaptation planning requires all interests to be actively included and for power to be shared among actors. New methods of engaging residents in adaptation planning and implementation are needed that enable fairness concerns to be explicitly incorporated into transformational adaptation. Perhaps crucial here is to be able to frame "the climate-just city" as the key to transformative urban practice and change, as proposed by Wendy Steele et al.

Climate justice and gender

Gender emerges as a fundamental analytical dimension in climate justice. Patricia Perkins provides a gendered analysis of distributive, procedural, intersectional and intergenerational justice. She calls, in the first instance, for disaggregation of data so that gendered impacts can be better understood. This is supported by Roa Crease et al., who highlight that complexities and diversities need to be recognised: "women" are not a homogenous group but represent a great diversity of cultural, ethnic, societal, sexual, economic and political constructs. Moreover, "women" experience climate change in a multitude of ways. The authors consider it vital that governments and aid organisations understand the multifaceted and dimensional factors that contribute towards vulnerability. This is taken further by Patricia Perkins, who indicates that the richness in lived experience, explored through an intersectional lens, holds enormous power to inform policy and suggests that an intersectional perspective can bring about social, economic, political and environmental change.

Considerable efforts have been made at various levels to ensure policies are gender sensitive. Jane Maher notes that there is an upward trend of gender considerations in international governance, which has had a positive impact on Malawi's national policies. However, when analysed in more depth, she indicates that the current top-down approach of gender-responsive policy ignores societal and cultural structures and enforces blanket, non-specific gender considerations. On paper, this parity in access to resources appears positive, but in practice women are often left with limited adaptive capacity and remain less resilient compared to men. Therefore, whilst efforts to empower women to fully participate in social structures and institutions in which the climate change response is shaped are welcome, there is an ongoing need to question the gendered nature of these very structures.

So-Young Lee and Eric Zusman also note that international climate policy is creating incentives for countries to integrate gender into not only projects that mitigate climate change but also wider policies and institutions, evaluating how in Southeast Asia, gender has been integrated into projects, policies and institutions designed to mitigate climate change.

Finally, it is important to also question the representations of women as "vulnerable." Instead of merely hearing their accounts of the plurality of their lived experiences, celebrating their views and perspectives, their strengths, their voices, their active roles in society, their relationships, and their visions for change must also form part of "gender mainstreaming" if policies and practice are to be considered climate-just.

Climate justice movements and struggles

The chapters in this section explore the linkages between climate justice and other, much older struggles for emancipation. The chapters focus on contextualising the need for climate justice in a long history of injustices that have resulted from fossil fuel dependence, the capitalist economy and colonial history.

Grounding climate justice in social movements not only provides it with narratives, thus illustrating the diversity of lived experience, but also amplifies the theoretical analyses from within those movements. Brandon Derman emphasises the need to ground a politics of climate justice by linking climate justice to the American civil rights movement. Whilst justice for people, and specifically for the historically oppressed people of colour in the U.S. and around the globe, is central to the vision of the civil rights and racial justice organisations, Alan Jarandilla Nuñez explores how indigenous people offer an alternative conceptualisation of climate justice. This alternative considers the interrelations, interdependence, complementarity and reciprocity of everything that exists, including Mother Earth, human beings and all forms of life. People are part of this interconnected, holistic vision, but not necessarily central to it. It is interesting then that Jen Gobby and Kristian Gareau describe how the anti-pipeline movement in Canada is providing a critical counter-narrative to the mainstream response to environmental and climate injustices by identifying colonialism and capitalism as underlying causes of injustice. On the other hand, Colleen Scanlan Lyons et al. describe how indigenous people have been able to participate in the process of governing climate at the subnational level by co-informing climate mitigation policies in California and Acre, Brazil, and how these policies have generated revenues that have enabled them to re-acquire important historical and cultural assets.

Emerging areas in climate justice

It is evident that the academic field of climate justice is very dynamic and, like most disciplines, responds both to the exigencies of its critics and to the social, economic and political processes that shape the everyday across scales. This results in new directions and themes in climate justice research, and so the diversity of chapters in this part of the Handbook should come as no surprise. Perhaps one of the most significant among the recent global developments is the increasing incidence of climate-induced migration – the subject of Sennan Mattar and Enyinnaya Mbakwem's chapter. The international regime on governing this relatively new kind of migration is only forming, and has not kept up with the current and anticipated flows of climate-affected people within and across countries. Hence the authors' call for a human-centred approach to managing this issue, which they see as necessarily rooted in the principles of universal human rights.

As mentioned in the Introduction, the practical application of climate justice has been seen as one of the field's weaknesses. Indeed, to what extent can we say that global and national responses to climate change have been guided by the principles of justice, however defined? Sonja Klinsky reflects on this challenge in the context of public engagement, recognising both the necessity for academics to undertake some elements of public scholarship and the difficulties associated with this daunting task. This is further underlined by Callum McGregor et al., who delve into the slowly emerging field of climate justice education. Like Sonja Klinsky, they recognise the highly political and politicised nature of climate justice, and note that school environments are not free from political manipulations of the term by the elites who seek to render it harmless to a neoliberally governed society. Thus, they argue for cognitive justice to become part of climate justice, since only then will we be capable of noticing and acting on what they describe as a disempowering hegemonic social structure.

Finally, there is a growing trend – not just in climate justice but in critical climate change research in general – of theorising what transforming our society to make it more socially, economically and politically equitable should actually entail. As Dunja Krause notes in her chapter, visions for societal transformation differ greatly, but most are rooted in political emancipation and inclusiveness in crucial processes of governing. As such, these critical scholars reject what are seen as insufficiently bold approaches to addressing climate change rooted in "coping," "resilience," "risk management" or "business-as-usual" conceptions of development and economic growth. The discourse of transformation seems to fit well within the climate justice agenda, though more research is required to establish conceptual and practical links between the two fields.

Final comments – climate justice leaders of the future

The Handbook authors have provided valuable insights into a range of climate justice themes. The evidence presented in their chapters delivers a clear message: we need to find new ways forward to address climate inequality and the associated deep poverty and social, economic and political marginalisation that may ensue for many. As Jay Naidoo (2013) posits, "poverty is driven by inequality and overcoming poverty is an act of justice." This requires an emphasis on and real commitments to tackling the injustices caused by a changing climate, embracing issues such as inclusivity, voice and empowerment, political equality, gender sensitivity, human rights and dignity, compassion and justice.

To make this happen will require new research, critical thinking, dialogue and conversation to converge the knowledge of indigenous and local communities and activists with scientists, practitioners, industry leaders, policy and decision makers to co-design and develop "solutions" to handle the social impacts and human costs of climate change. Catalysing this process will require climate justice champions and leaders of the future. Mary Robinson (2017) highlights that education for climate stewardship, when delivered in an effective and multidisciplinary manner, can increase consciousness of climate change and sustainable development and produce new insights not only at the scientific but also at the sociological and political levels. Kanbur (2015) argues that education can and will play a key role in addressing climate justice. As this Handbook draws to a close, it also opens the gateway to a new challenge and a fundamental research question: to what extent can the transformative power of education generate in people a critical awareness of their rights in relation to climate change, which would allow them to tangibly influence the status quo and bring about societal change? Finding ways to establish transformative and sustainable empowerment processes amongst all members of society regardless of age, wealth, ethnicity, or any other status should be considered as a cornerstone for tackling climate inequality and achieving climate justice.

References

Kanbur, R. (2015) Education for Climate Justice, Working Paper, Charles H. Dyson School of Applied Economics and Management, Cornell University, Ithaca, New York 14853-7801 USA.

Naidoo, J. (2016) Learning Circle 2 Exploring Responsive Policy Making in Dealing With Hunger, Nutrition and Climate Justice Challenge, Hunger, Nutrition and Climate Justice, A New Dialogue: Putting People at the Heart of Global Development, 15–16th April 2013, Dublin Ireland.

Robinson, M. (2017) Climate Justice: Preserving Dignity in the Face of Adversity, 15 February 2017 Lecture, Mary Robinson Foundation for Climate Justice.

Roser, D., Seidel, C. (2017) *Climate Justice: An Introduction*. Routledge, Taylor & Francis Group, London and New York.

United Nations Sustainable Development Knowledge Platform (2018) Sustainable Development Goal 13, Take Urgent Action to Combat Climate Change and Its Impacts, Accessed on 11 June 2018. https://sustainabledevelopment.un.org/sdg13.

Index

Printed in the United States
by Baker & Taylor Publisher Services